Michael Rockwell
Jonathan J. Moons
Pierre Boutquin
Bill Brown
Robert Crouch

SAMS Teach Yourself

Microsoft®
Windows® DNA Programming
in 21 Days

SAMS

A Division of Macmillan USA
201 West 103rd Street, Indianapolis, Indiana 46290

Sams Teach Yourself Microsoft® Windows® DNA Programming in 21 Days

Copyright © 2000 by Sams Publishing

International Standard Book Number: 0-672-31897-0

Library of Congress Catalog Card Number: 99-068488

Printed in the United States of America

First Printing: August 2000

02   01   00   4   3   2   1

Trademarks

Warning and Disclaimer

PUBLISHER
Bradley L. Jones

ACQUISITIONS EDITOR
Chris Webb

DEVELOPMENT EDITOR
Steve Rowe

MANAGING EDITOR
Charlotte Clapp

PROJECT EDITOR
Paul Schneider

COPY EDITOR
Mary Ellen Stephenson

INDEXER
Chris Barrick

PROOFREADER
Katherin Bidwell

TECHNICAL EDITOR
Arthur English

TEAM COORDINATOR
Meggo Barthlow

MEDIA DEVELOPER
Maggie Molloy

INTERIOR DESIGNER
Gary Adair

COVER DESIGNER
Aren Howell

COPYWRITER
Eric Borgert

Contents at a Glance

Contents

Foreword

With the advent of new tools such as Visual Basic, ActiveX and PowerBuilder, building basic, data-driven applications has become increasingly easier. It has become a matter of dropping controls onto a pallet, adding some code, and testing.

However, building robust, secure, scalable, bulletproof applications that can stand the test of high-volume Internet traffic, and that contain components that can be leveraged is another story. Building host-based *systems* that leverage distributed computing and the availability of high-bandwidth networks that can service tens or hundreds of thousand people is a real challenge.

Building Internet applications used to be a matter of writing some HTML and CGI scripts that might interface with a flat disk file or, perhaps, a relational database. However, Web sites built upon this technology are not adequate for today's demands.

Most useful Web sites offer transactional functions, such as purchasing products, viewing your stocks, or booking travel plans. These types of systems combine rich user interfaces, complex business logic, and high-performance database infrastructures that must scale and offer transactional integrity. All of this goes well beyond the capabilities of standard application or Web platforms. Truly robust online systems require

- Vertical and horizontal scalability—Being able to scale with more servers as well as "larger" servers
- Rich Inter-Process Communications (IPC) infrastructure to allow application components to communicate with each other
- Management tools to facilitate the assurance of maximum uptime
- Resource sharing and management facilities to make cost-effective use of precious resources such as communications and database connections
- Transactional integrity management to assure proper commitment of successful transactions or reversal of failed transactions
- Security infrastructure to meet the demands of the Internet economy

As you might imagine, laying all of this "plumbing" is a lot of work and very expensive. Many organizations have attempted to "roll their own" distributed infrastructure, based on primitive IPC, such as TCP/IP sockets. Most have found that this is not cost effective, and impossible to maintain.

Enter Microsoft .NET platform which builds upon Internet technologies like HTTP, XML, and SOAP. The .NET servers still utilize the Component Object Model (COM and

COM+) to offer all the rich services needed to design, construct, deploy, and manage a complete distributed system. Continuous improvements in Microsoft technologies have brought the Windows NT operating system, and subsequently the Windows 2000 OS, into the realm of large system performance and dependability. Combining powerfully rich, world-class development tools (probably the best in the business) with all the system services that you could want in a high-demand package enables developers to focus on the business problems that need to be solved, rather than the technical ones.

This reader will most likely know what it is as they come to the book. They will be a bit more advanced from true beginners.

Understanding distributed, component systems such as Windows DNA is vital to any modern computing career. It is *not* enough to understand HTML, or Perl scripting, or PHP, or any of a number of Web development languages. In order to be of real value in the Internet age, it is vital to understand how to architect and develop bulletproof component systems. Barnesandnoble.com is not built upon a set of pirated and thrown together scripts on a Linux machine. The lead developers responsible for that site created one of the largest online stores based upon Microsoft DNA technology.

Sams Teach Yourself Windows DNA in 21 Days takes you step-by-step through all of the concepts, tools, and technologies that make up Windows DNA. It is a complete guide and learning instrument that not only introduces you to the subject, but also takes you through some real life examples and prepares you to actually work within the environment. By reading this book, studying the examples, and taking the quizzes, you will begin your journey onto a new plateau of application development. Soon, you will truly understand what systems development is all about.

Happy coding!

Ira Klein
Director/Practice Manager
e-business Applications
CoreTech Consulting Group Inc.

About the Authors

MICHAEL ROCKWELL is a global architect for Lante Corporation with a specialization in Microsoft technologies. He has been working with information technology for the past 20 years. He holds the following Microsoft certifications: MCP+Internet, MCP+Site Building, MCSE+Internet, MCSD (Premier Member), MCDBA, and MCT. He enjoys envisioning, architecting, and ultimately developing Internet applications, which he has done for several large and small organizations. This book, his first, is the result of a course that he developed to train IT professionals to be Internet developers. Michael's concept of using case-based examples allowed students to put all the pieces into context.

JONATHAN J. MOONS (jonathanmoons@hotmail.com) has more than four years' experience designing, developing, and administrating dynamic Web sites involving all parts of the Windows DNA platform. This includes Active Server Pages with VBScript and client-side JavaScript, Visual Basic components, XML, and SQL Server. Jonathan has also used Microsoft Site Server 3.0, Commerce Edition, and the Commerce Server Pipeline to create business-to-consumer and business-to-business Web sites. He has instructed on various Web technologies, both in the classroom as an MCT and as a corporate instructor and also as a peer to fellow consultants and clients. Jonathan is an MCT and currently has an MCP+Site Building certification. He also hosts a Web site that provides resources for Windows DNA, www.windowsdnaworld.com.

About the Contributors

PIERRE BOUTQUIN has more than a decade of experience implementing PC-based computer systems with in-depth knowledge of object-oriented analysis and design, data warehousing, C++, Visual Basic, and SQL. He has written extensively, mainly about Visual Basic and SQL. You can reach him at boutquin@techie.com.

BILL BROWN is the founder of Knowledge Wave International, LLC., a technical and business consulting firm focused on customer-centric Internet solutions. He is now managing the implementation of a distributed Internet application for one of the top 10 health information sites for consumers. Bill can be reached at bill.brown@knowledge-wave.com.

ROBERT CROUCH is the author of *Sams Teach Yourself Database Programming with Visual InterDev 6 in 21 Days*. He has more than 15 years in the information systems industry and is a Microsoft MCT, MCSD, MCSE, and PMI Certified Project Management Professional. He can be reached at robert@crouch.org.

About the Technical Editor

ARTHUR ENGLISH, an award-winning software developer, book author, and columnist, is a Systems Architect for Unisys Corporation. He specializes in system architecture and application construction for Windows 2000 Server Enterprise systems. Mr. English has been a Windows software developer since 1988; he is a Microsoft Certified Solution Developer and the MSDN Regional Director for Pennsylvania.

Dedication

To Amy, Emmanuel, and Amelia, who endured my nights and weekends away from them in my home office writing this book.—Michael Rockwell

To my parents, Tom and Ethel, for making me who I am and inspiring me to keep on reaching higher. To Kristine, my girlfriend and now my fiancée, for being so patient and so supportive during those months of writing. Thank you.—Jonathan Moons

Acknowledgments

My thanks to all the hundreds of authors who, over the years, have written the books that have provided the knowledge and insight that helped me along the way. I hope by writing this book I can, in some way, give back and continue the education process.

I want to thank the staff at Macmillan/Sams Publishing for giving me the opportunity to develop this book. To Chris Webb, acquisitions editor, who went to bat with the publisher to get this book developed, who put up with the schedule slippage when family members got ill, and when my employer changed, and when a co-author dropped off the book. Chris found the next person I would like to thank, Jonathan Moons, who contributed seven plus chapters to the book and worked with the other contributing authors to ensure that their contributions matched our goal of providing you with the best information and insight possible. I want to thank Steve Rowe and the other editorial staff who reviewed this book, providing extensive editing and feedback to ensure everything was covered and that the chapters were consistent with each other.

My wife and family stood by while I fulfilled this dream of writing a book. To my wife, Amy, who had her hands full with two small children—Emmanuel, 4 years, and Amelia, 5 months—as well as a number of unexpected crises, I cannot thank you enough.

—Michael Rockwell

I would like to thank everyone who helped pull this book together.

To all the staff at Macmillan who participated including Chris Webb and Steve Rowe for initially getting me going. Thanks for keeping me on task and on track and for all the helpful feedback. Thanks to Michael Rockwell for spearheading this title and getting it under way. Thank you also to the rest of the editors, who took this book from a raw form to a finished product.

Thanks to my wonderful friends and family who didn't forget about me while this book was in progress. I couldn't have done it without your encouragement and prayers. The life events that occurred while I was writing this book were incredible. I thank God for taking me through it all and teaching me along the way.

—Jonathan Moons

Tell Us What You Think!

As the reader of this book, *you* are our most important critic and commentator. We value your opinion and want to know what we're doing right, what we could do better, what areas you'd like to see us publish in, and any other words of wisdom you're willing to pass our way.

As a Publisher for Sams, I welcome your comments. You can fax, email, or write me directly to let me know what you did or didn't like about this book—as well as what we can do to make our books stronger.

Please note that I cannot help you with technical problems related to the topic of this book, and that due to the high volume of mail I receive, I might not be able to reply to every message.

When you write, please be sure to include this book's title and authors as well as your name and phone or fax number. I will carefully review your comments and share them with the author and editors who worked on the book.

Fax: 317-581-4770

Email: adv_prog@mcp.com

Mail: Bradley L. Jones
          Associate Publisher
          Sams Publishing
          201 West 103rd Street
          Indianapolis, IN 46290 USA

Introduction

Welcome to an exciting 21-day lesson in developing Microsoft Windows Distributed interNet Applications (DNA). The book is structured around a fictitious project to develop a web application for a bank. By taking a single project from start to finish you will be better able to see how the pieces of Windows DNA work together.

Overview

This book is designed to teach you the best practices in developing Windows DNA applications. We have avoided making this book a primer on every technology associated with Windows DNA. If we had followed this course, this would be an encyclopedia set. Everyone has their favorite authors and books on the various technical subject areas. The market is full of books to teach you the basics, the how, this book tries to be different in that we pull out the important points to teach you about the why. If you need training in a particular technology covered in this book, Sams has a number of 24-hour and 21-day books that cover a wide range of topics.

Straight off it should be understood that you most likely will not be working in all aspects of Windows DNA, rather you will tend to choose an area where you feel comfortable and then become a deep expert in that area. Nevertheless, you will want to know about the other areas so that you have a better understanding of how you can best work with the other members of your team. This book will give you a comprehensive view of the entire Windows DNA landscape.

Windows DNA is an evolving model for how to build applications that utilize Internet technologies. Since the emergence of Windows DNA in 1997, it has evolved greatly and continues to do so as the Internet industry evolves. Even during the time it took to write this book, the model was changing to support emergent technologies like BizTalk and SOAP. It will become very clear that transactions, messages, XML, and HTTP play a major role in the model.

We hope that this book meets your needs and expectations. We have tried to add a great deal of value to the book by teaching best practices so that you can reach maximum productivity quickly. You may feel tempted to jump around the book, and that is OK, keep in mind though that this book is building a single project so subsequent chapters build upon previous chapters. All chapters that utilize code have a directory on the CD with the chapter beginning state and ending state so that you can jump in at any point.

Who Should Read This Book?

This book is intended for anyone from beginners to seasoned Internet programmers who want to take their skills to the next level and learn about the exciting world of Windows DNA software development. The Windows DNA strategy can be applied to any software project, but its strength really shines in Internet applications using Microsoft Visual Studio, Office 2000, and Windows NT. If you are interested in creating professional, reliable, and high-performance Internet, extranet, or intranet applications in the fastest way possible, then this book is for you.

What You Will Learn

This book will teach you how to design and implement Windows DNA solutions using Microsoft tools in conjunction with the latest component technologies like ActiveX Components, COM, COM+, and Transactions. We will also cover Windows NT server-side products such as SQL Server 7, IIS, and Microsoft Transaction Server. Internet specific technologies like XML, ASP, HTML, and DHTML. Our goal is to educate the reader on the various aspects of advanced distributed Internet applications and allow you to write your own commercial-grade scalable Internet solutions using Microsoft products after 21 days of instruction.

What We Won't Cover

Windows DNA and all of the products and technologies it encompasses are huge. Although we have made every effort to make this book as thorough as possible, we have also chosen to "fast path" you through Windows DNA. We will take you through the development of a three-tier Windows DNA Web application. All the steps are explained and are scripted out in the book and/or on the CD. We will not be able to cover all the capabilities of the tools and technologies used in this project. Fortunately, many books that specifically address particular tools are available, as well as on-line resources. Microsoft Developers Network `http://msdn.microsoft.com` is a particularly useful site for specific product and development information.

Site Server and Site Server Commerce Edition, for example, are powerful Web administration and e-commerce development tools that are beyond the scope of this book's goal, due to their complexities. Windows Load Balancing Services (WLBS), Component Load Balancing (CLB), and Microsoft Clustering Services (MSCS) are also essential ingredients to the most scalable and reliable Web sites. Then there are SNA Server, Host Integration Server, and COM TI, for mainframe and legacy system integration. Covering these products in a pragmatic way would require a lot more than 21 days! This book will, however, make note of these and other products wherever their application would be appropriate. It will also indicate where to go for more information.

We want to stress to our readers that many of the products we are leaving out are reserved for only the super-scalable and fault-tolerant systems that process millions of transactions a day with multi-platform constraints. The applications you will learn to develop here, although highly scalable, are designed for significantly less activity.

What Is the Difference Between Windows DNA and .NET Platform?

It is important to make the distinction between Windows DNA and .NET Platform. Microsoft has been constantly evolving the Windows DNA model since 1997. .NET Platform is a major shift in focus from the earlier model and thus needs some explanation.

Windows DNA was introduced in 1997 as an architectural model to help developers make the move from a client/server architecture to a three-tier development model. This early DNA model is very tuned to the developer's perspective. The Windows DNA architecture evolved to add capabilities to handle the complexities of developing scalable robust systems. As the architecture developed, it became clear that many of the capabilities being developed could be handled by the operating system and other services. As the Windows DNA architecture developed, so did the supporting systems and services. Microsoft Transaction Server was the first service developed that caused a change in thinking about what needed to be developed and what could be handled by the operating system. It became clear that the supporting systems could take over more of the plumbing and services required by a robust scalable architecture. As a result, Microsoft decided to recast Windows DNA as a services platform, rather than as a development model.

Windows 2000 is a major architectural upgrade to the NT operating system and offers the best opportunity to integrate this new vision of the operating system and support services as the enablers for their new Windows DNA platform. All of the Microsoft business server products are being updated to work with the many new capabilities enabled by Windows 2000. The new name for these capabilities is .NET Platform. Microsoft does not call this latest version an *architecture*; instead, it refers to .NET Platform as a *services platform*. Does this mean that the Windows DNA architecture is outdated? No, as a developer, Windows DNA architecture is a very good thing to know and will allow you to develop applications that are robust and scalable. Applications that are built to the Windows DNA architectural standard will work best with the .NET Platform services platform. Applications that are built to be standalone or that utilize a client/server model will have their lives extended by .NET Platform, but will still have architectural limitations.

Another major evolution in Windows DNA is the realization that the Web applications of the future will interact more and more between systems and have less user involvement. This shift in usage patterns has a profound impact on the view one has of the entire system. The capabilities that need to be in place for systems to communicate are very different from the requirements to interact with users. Scalability needs to occur in both a horizontal and vertical direction. To scale horizontally, a system must be able to add new computers and devices into the environment as they are connected, thus distributing the work load across the entire system. Windows Load Balancing Services enables horizontal scaling. To scale vertically, a system must be able to take advantage of the addition of more resources such as memory, processors, interface cards, and storage as they are added to the system. Windows Clustering Services enables vertical scaling as well as fault tolerance. Component Load Balancing Services is a new capability to perform both horizontal and vertical scaling by allowing components to be spread across systems. By allowing the system to figure out where is the best place to run components at any particular time, both additional systems as well as additional resources are factored into the scalability. To manage the scaling of systems, Microsoft is introducing Application Center 2000, a centralized management server for the entire system. All of the Microsoft 2000 business products are being designed to work with Application Center 2000.

The shift in focus for Windows DNA from an architecture to a services platform can be seen in the recasting of the three DNA tiers. The original tiers were presentation, business logic, and data. The new .NET Platform tiers are Web farm, application servers, and data stores. Clearly this change is targeted to deal with the operational issues within an organization. It is clear that Windows DNA will change to address the evolving needs of organization using the "Business Internet." .NET Platform is clearly aimed at dealing with the management of the ever expanding operational needs caused by the rapid expansion of the Internet. As the model evolves, the artifacts of the previous model are not rendered useless. Rather, the model is simply moving on to tackle new issues. This book explores the development architecture addressed by Windows DNA.

Requirements

As you will read about on Day 1, Windows DNA is an abstraction and does not dictate any specific Microsoft products. However, all Microsoft business and development products available today have been designed with Windows DNA in mind. Due to their availability and low cost, it makes perfect sense to use Microsoft tools when building a DNA solution. It is for this reason that we have adopted Microsoft's Visual Studio 6.0 (with its latest service pack) and Office 2000 as our development environments. The Enterprise edition of Visual Studio is recommended since it has a greater collection of database and modeling tools. Windows NT (with the latest service pack) running IIS is strongly recommended, however, Windows 95/98 with Personal Web Services could also be used. All of the component code we present will work on NT4 and Windows 2000. To take advantage of COM+ features presented in the advanced topic will require Windows 2000.

All three tiers of services can be run on a single computer or across multiple computers. The architecture is a logical not physical design. The ability to add hardware and to distribute the tiers across multiple computers is what gives Windows DNA a great deal of scalability.

We also assume that your system(s) meet all the respective hardware requirements for the various software and that you have the latest service packs installed.

Tip

Getting the installation order correct for the various products can be difficult. This is supposed to be fixed with Windows 2000. In the meantime, you can check the Microsoft web site for installation order. The Site Server installation script at: `http://support.microsoft.com/support/siteserver/install_ss3.asp` is the best one that I have found. Even if you are not installing Site Server, it has the correct order for all the products and service packs so that you can avoid DLL hell by getting older versions mixed with newer versions.

Browsers

For viewing the application, we recommend Internet Explorer 5. As you will see, there are many standards across browsers when it comes to client-side scripting. We will stick to the basics and have made an effort to minimize any incompatibilities as much as possible, but some advanced examples (like client-side XML scripting), may not work on non-IE browsers. In Week 3, when we cover the presentation layer, we will actually build several versions to accommodate a full range of interfaces. We will also talk about using server-side ISAPI filters to convert XML and XSL to standard HTML for legacy browsers.

Skills You Need

The reader is assumed to have beginner knowledge of Visual Basic and some exposure to HTML and scripting technologies (like JavaScript or VBScript). All the examples are scripted out in the book as well as made available on the CD so you will be able to work in the various tools. We will not work with Visual C++ or ATL directly, but when appropriate we will mention its strengths and values to Windows DNA.

For the database examples, we will use the Microsoft Data Engine (MSDE), which is freely available from Microsoft. MSDE is a scaled down version of SQL Server 7 and from a programming perspective, they are indistinguishable. You may use SQL Server 7 if you wish; the code we will show works for both.

The CD

A word about the CD, we have added more code on the CD than is shown in the book. We trust that you can glean information from reading code. In the book we highlight code snippets that are important to the subject area and need further explanation. The CD also contains a number of tools, utilities, SDKs, and documentation that supplement the materials in the book.

Chapter Layout

We have structured the book like a mini Windows DNA project. In Week 1, we present a high-level overview of Windows DNA Architecture. We present a business problem and then architect it into a Windows DNA solution. We also cover the first layer of Windows DNA, the data tier.

In Week 2, we cover the business logic tier. You will learn to develop the server-side business components. You will learn how to build and test our business components. We will cover the creation of data-enabled components and connect these components to the data tier developed in Week 1. Throughout the week, we will look at how the development tools make it easy to work with data.

Finally in Week 3, we will cover the presentation tier. In this week we will cover many different types of presentation tiers, from a rich 32-bit Windows executable all the way down to a generic HTML interface. The advantages and disadvantages of each will be discussed. We will also discuss using Office 2000 to present your application. Finally, it will all be drawn together into a digital dashboard.

Feedback

We have worked hard to make this book a valuable addition to your library. If you see things you would like covered more or less extensively or have suggestions for making the book better, let Macmillan know. We will try to get it into the next revision or create another book that delves deeper into that particular subject.

Conventions Used in This Book

This book uses the following typeface conventions:

- Menu names are separated from menu options by a comma. For example, File, Open means "select the Open option from the File menu."

- New terms are set off by the icon **NEW TERM** and appear in *italic*.

- Many code-related terms within the text also appear in monospace.

- Placeholders in code appear in *italic monospace*.

- When a line of code is too long to fit on one line of this book, it is broken at a convenient place and continued to the next line. A code continuation character (➡) precedes the continuation of a line of code. (You should type a line of code that has this character as one long line without breaking it.)

- Paragraphs that begin with the analysis icon **ANALYSIS** explain the preceding code example.

- The syntax icon identifies syntax statements.

SYNTAX

Special design features enhance the text material.

Note
Notes explain interesting or important points that can help you understand Windows DNA concepts and techniques.

Tip
Tips are little pieces of information that will help you in real-world situations. Tips often offer shortcuts to make a task easier or faster.

> **Caution**
>
> Cautions provide information about detrimental performance issues or dangerous errors. Pay careful attention to Cautions.

 New terms are words or phrases that may not be familiar to you. New terms are explained so that everyone has the same understanding of the meaning and usage of each term.

WEEK 1

At a Glance

During this week you will cover three things:

- Learning about the Windows DNA Model (Days 1 and 2)
- Architecting a Windows DNA Solution (Day 3)
- Developing the Data Tier (Days 4 through 7)

This is an important foundational week. Days 1 and 2 will give you a good overall understanding of the Windows DNA model and provide the basic knowledge of how the model fits together and what you will find in each of the three tiers.

Day 3 takes you through the analysis and design of a fictitious Windows DNA solution for Smalltown Bank. The remainder of the book will develop this solution highlighting the various solution tiers and the technologies used at each of these tiers.

Days 4 through 7 are focused on the development of the data tier. In Day 4, you will build the actual database tables using SQL DDL scripts. In Day 5, you will add business logic in the data tier using defaults, triggers, rules, constraints, and stored procedures. We will discuss when you will want to have business logic in the DBMS and when to contain it in COM components. In Day 6, you will learn about Active Data Objects (ADO) and the importance it plays in building a robust data interface. In Day 7, you will learn about the importance of transactions in the data tier and the mechanisms available for working transactionally.

This week is foundational to your understanding of Windows DNA and for the establishment of the example project and data tier.

You may be wondering why we chose to start with the data tier rather than the presentation tier, where most books start. The reason is that we are developing a Web application, not just Web pages. In reality you would be working from both ends towards the middle. You would develop data structures because most applications are centered around working with data. You would be developing the presentation tier as a way to model for the users what they expect in terms of functionality. The two tiers would then come together and integrate at the business logic tier.

DAY 1

Understanding Windows DNA

On our first day I will try to answer all your questions about DNA in the context of application development. We will cover the various development models available and how they have evolved. We will cover the Windows DNA platform model and associated technologies and terminologies. So, today you will learn

- Windows DNA fundamentals
- Different architectures for developing applications
- Windows DNA design principals
- Component architectures, especially COM
- Object-oriented terminology and concepts
- Development in a team environment

Defining Windows DNA

Windows DNA is not a product but a collection of products and technologies all designed to work together to help you develop robust, scalable, extensible applications. Here is how Microsoft defines Windows DNA: "Microsoft Windows Distributed interNet Applications Platform is the application development model for the Windows platform." Windows DNA is an evolving platform that changes to support the evolving needs of Windows applications developers. Think of Windows DNA as a platform on which to build applications. Microsoft has built its example applications and has designed it operating systems, development tools, and other services to support this way of development.

Evolution in Application Design

To fully understand how Microsoft arrived at this development model, we need to look at how Windows application development has evolved over time.

Classic Monolithic

In the beginning when the personal computer was truly a personal computer, applications were developed to be run solely on a single computer by a single user. Referred to as classic, monolithic, or standalone applications, these programs basically own and have access to all the computer's resources. They are the easiest to develop because you do not have to worry about sharing resources with other applications. DOS applications are good examples of this single-person, single-program type of application.

As computers got more powerful and processors and operating systems evolved to support multiprocessing, they still needed to support monolithic applications. The solution was to create virtual machines (several logical computers within a single physical computer) to run these applications. The Windows operating system oversees all these virtual machines. Windows divides the processing into time slices, enabling each virtual machine to run in turn for a set time period; this time-sharing allows multitasking.

NEW TERM   *Multitasking* is the process by which multiple processes or threads are allowed to run within a system. Actually, only one task is allowed to run at any given time. It just appears that they are running simultaneously. Unless of course you have multiple processors (CPU) in your system.

1

Windows multitasking has evolved over time. In Windows 3.x, all Windows applications ran in a single virtual machine. Windows 3.x used what is termed *cooperative multitasking*, which requires that the running Windows 3.x application yield the processor before another application can run. One poorly behaved application can affect the whole system adversely by not letting other applications run.

With Windows 9x and NT came *preemptive multitasking*. With preemptive multitasking the operating system is in total control of the processor and thus can completely manage processor time-slice allocation. This fixed the problem somewhat; however, a poorly written application could still waste a great deal of processor time. Good programming practices are still required so one will not waste finite system resources. These best practices are found throughout the book.

Windows 9x and NT provided a number of features that enabled the programmer to use system resources easily and more effectively. By building a great deal of the complexity of performing these tasks into the operating system, tools, and technology of Windows applications, Microsoft eased the development of multithreaded, multitasking applications. You will see that reducing the development complexity of managing resources is a theme very central to Windows DNA. Even though Windows is assuming more of the complexity, it is still a good idea to know what Windows is doing so you can better work with the embedded services and technologies.

Client/Server Model

The client/server development model came out of the fact that organizations were networking their computers together and wanted a way to distribute work between computers. Clients are the consumers of services provided by a server. And servers are the providers of services to requesting clients. Applications can act as both clients and servers and any number of clients can request services from a server. Windows DNA has its roots in client/server development. Even though the client/server concept can describe a network of cooperating computers, the term has become synonymous with cooperation between only two computers, a client and a server. The issue then is how to divide the work between the client computer and the server computer. Figure 1.1 illustrates the variations and evolution of this process. You can see that the various programming architectures revolve around where to put the process boundaries.

The pros and cons of where to physically place processes in both the client and server are shown in the following list. We will discuss logical placement of processes later.

FIGURE **1.1**

*Application evolution,
from classical, single
program applications
to multitier ones.*

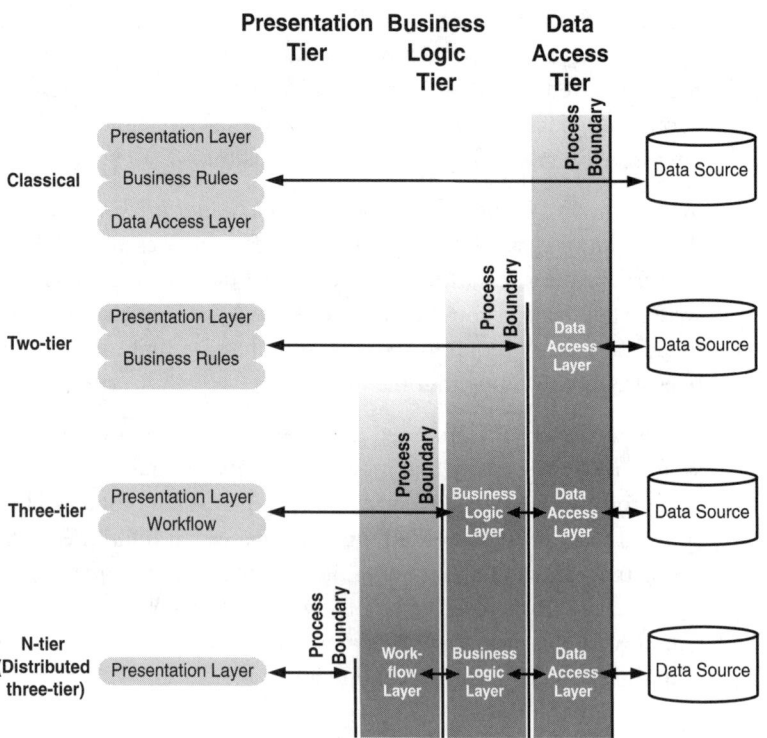

For the Client

Pros   **Better performance**   Performance improves because the client
is a dedicated processor, or at least can provide more dedicated
processing time than the server processor might. As new clients
access the system they bring more processing power to the system, thus enabling the application to scale better to handle
increased loads.

NEW TERM   *Scalability* is a term used in the development of enterprise class applications that
refers to the ability of the application to handle increasing work loads. If an
application can easily handle increasing loads it is said to be highly scalable.

Cons   **Version compatibility**   The application needs to make sure that
the client computer is running the correct version of the client
software. The server needs to determine if the correct version of
the client software is running and if not have some way to send
the correct version to the client computer. This can be an administrative nightmare if the client software frequently changes.

Network latency   This might also affect performance if a great deal of data needs to be exchanged between the client and server. Since network speeds are much slower than the internal speed at which computers can exchange data, dividing a process across a network can severely affect performance if a great deal of data needs to be exchanged.

Security   You might be passing sensitive data across the network into the client's computer where it can be intercepted.

Multi-user management   When multiple users need to work with the same data, it can cause problems if the data is already checked out to another user.

For the Server(s)

Pros	**Better security** Because the data never leaves the server's control, it is less likely to end up in the wrong hands.
	Better resource management When the server owns the resources, it can better manage the use of those resources.
	Better control of software components Because the server is a single point of update, it is much easier to have the correct and most current software in place.
Cons	**Limited resource** Because many users are sharing the server's resources, performance degrades as more users access the server concurrently.

You can see that there are advantages to having parts of the application physically run on the server and other parts run on the client.

So many factors play into the equation that it is almost impossible for a human to hand-tune an application. You need to consider network traffic against system load and capabilities. As more servers are added to the system, the problem grows; you now need to have better resource management and balancing capabilities. Fortunately, computer-assisted tuning is not far off. At a conference in 1998, I saw Microsoft Advance Research Labs demonstrate a technology that watched the interactions among all the components of an application and then tuned the application by moving components to the optimal place on the network for them to run. Microsoft is not promising when or if we will see this technology. However, if we do see it, it will most likely turn up under Windows DNA. In the meantime it will be up to you, as the developer, to consider these process placement issues while developing your application.

| Tip | If you are in doubt where to place a process then place it server-side. You can be assured that it will have the lowest risk on the server. Then if scalability and client richness becomes an issue then you can start moving some of the processing to the client. This will all become clearer as you learn more about the Windows DNA platform. |

Exploring a Classic Three-Tier Architecture

Windows DNA is nothing new; it is a classic three-tier architecture (see Figures 1.1 and 1.2). The tiers are data, business logic, and presentation. These are logical, not physical, tiers—that is, they all can run on a single computer or be distributed across hundreds of computers. The goal is to categorize by functionality the components that will live in each tier. Each week of this book is dedicated to covering one of these tiers. As you complete this book you will know the purpose of each tier and what functionality they contain.

The components that live in the presentation tier are responsible for formatting and presenting an interface with the user. This tier will validate entered data to ensure that it meets the requirements to be further processed by the business tier components. The business tier components accept data from the presentation tier and then work with the data tier and system services to enforce business rules. The business tier acts as a gatekeeper between the data and presentation tiers. The data tier is responsible for abstracting the data store from the business tier. The data tier also acts to ensure that transactional integrity is maintained.

Note that nothing in the Windows development environment keeps you from having the presentation tier interact with the data tier. In fact, this is precisely what the monolithic applications did. However, this is not the best design for a robust, scalable application. The Microsoft development tools support all types of applications, they will not prevent you from developing monolithic or client/server applications which will introduce limitations into your solution. It is up to you to use the correct practices to ensure that your applications can take advantage of Windows DNA capabilities. This book is designed to teach you the correct way to develop three-tier, Windows DNA applications.

You will notice in Figure 1.2 two additional elements of the Windows DNA platform, system services and tools. The system services provide the foundation on top of which the logical tiers (presentation, business logic, and data) are built upon. The tools element is the development languages and the tools that support the development process.

FIGURE 1.2

A Windows DNA model.

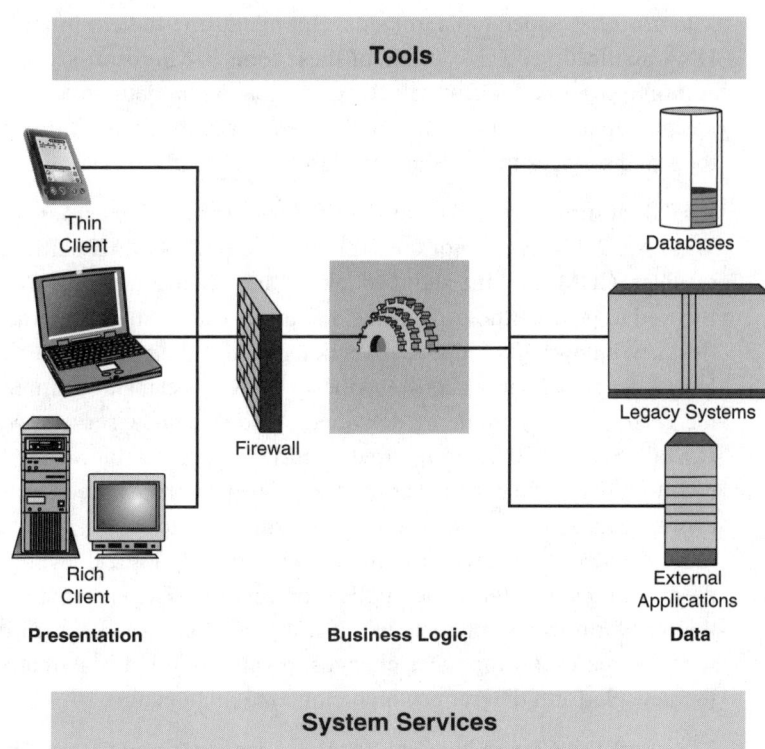

The Microsoft Commitment

Microsoft has committed to the Windows DNA architecture and has positioned its tools and technologies to work at all the DNA tiers. Microsoft has written many of its applications using the Windows DNA model. As we will see in Day 3, "Architecting a DNA Solution," a number of tools and techniques exist to help you design and build Windows DNA applications.

Microsoft has committed to the Windows DNA platform as a way to help developers, both internally and externally, move toward a new enterprise class development process. As we saw in the evolution process Microsoft came from a desktop, personal use past and is now evolving to provide enterprise class operating systems, services, and applications. Windows DNA helps them move to this new level of service.

Since Windows DNA was introduced in 1997, Microsoft has been busy making its development and system services products fit this model.

Microsoft has added tools to its development suite to help in the creation of Windows DNA applications. An example of these tools is Microsoft's Visual Modeler, a limited edition of Rational Software's Rose application modeling software, which helps you design applications that conform to three-tier architecture. Microsoft continues to add tools and services to the Windows DNA platform.

.NET Platform is an update of the platform that revolves around the core services of Windows 2000. The major core services are COM+, XML, IIS, data access, and security services. COM+, XML, and data access are all covered in this book. .NET Platform is focused to provide the capabilities to build "The Business Internet." Beyond the capabilities of Windows 2000, updated versions of SQL Server 2000, Exchange Server 2000, Host Integration Server 2000 (formerly SNA server), and Commerce Server 2000 (formerly Site Server) are being delivered. And three new servers, Application Center 2000, BizTalk Server 2000, and Internet Security and Acceleration Server 2000 are being delivered to provide the needed services to deliver Internet based applications. The platform is evolving around this model so don't be surprised to see that the business tier become more detailed in the area of these services. From a logical level the business tier will be divided into a web farm and application servers. The presentation tier will interact with the web farm which interacts with the application servers which interact with the data tier. The reason I bring these changes to your attention is so that you are not confused by the new platform diagrams which cloud the architecture.

Microsoft Developers Network (http://msdn.microsoft.com) is an entire Web site devoted to the development of Windows application. At the site, you will find white papers, code examples, discussion groups, and reference materials, all designed to help you succeed in the development of Windows applications. You will want to frequent MSDN to see the latest information on Windows development.

Finally, Microsoft keeps improving and evolving its tools, technologies, and operating system services to better support the Windows DNA architecture. Much of this enhancement is the result of incorporating complex resource management into the operating system services. By doing this Microsoft frees you the developer from having to make resource management part of your code. This is good because you can now spend your efforts on solving business problems rather than building infrastructure.

Focusing on Solutions, Not Infrastructure

The bottom-line goal of using Windows DNA is to enable you to focus on solutions, rather than infrastructure. When your application is built using Windows DNA, the various components will be able to scale up to meet user demands. Microsoft has built much

1

of the complexity of scaling into the system services and operating system. By doing this Microsoft lets you focus on the solution, rather than on the complexities, of building transactional scalable systems. Taking advantage of the system services is one of the great benefits of using the Windows DNA architecture.

Caution

One word of caution up front: Because of backward compatibility in development tools, it is possible to develop applications that will not benefit from or actually are hurt by these services.

The goal of this book is to show you how to design and develop applications that take full advantage of the services provided. Keep two things in mind when designing and building your application: state management and encapsulation. What do we mean by this?

State Management

State management refers to information that the program keeps to remember where you are in a process. You might hear or read about *stateless programming*. This is a bit misleading—applications must maintain state in order to function. The question of maintaining state is actually a matter of where the state is persisted. If the state is persisted in server memory, that memory resource is committed to maintaining that state and, therefore, the server's capability to manage that resource has been limited. Maintaining state in memory on the web server limits the system from dynamically balancing the workload across several computers, thus affecting the systems ability to scale effectively. On the other hand, if the state is persisted in a database or on the client computer, then the server can reclaim the memory resource and more effectively use all the resources within the system. COM components should not be expected to keep state between method calls because you should not expect to always connect to the same system every time. You should pass to the method everything that it needs and it should return everything that is expected to you. By following this design the system can now reclaim resources and balance the workload across all the computers in the system. This is one of the basic rules of Windows DNA: Enable the system to effectively manage its resources. Do not limit it with poor programming practice.

Encapsulation

Encapsulation refers to making each component self-contained. Each component should be thought of as a black box with clearly defined public interfaces. These components can call other components but should not be dependent upon the caller having set the state of another component unless the latter component is a parameter for the method being called. For example, an ADO recordset object requires that a connection object be passed to it with an established connection to a database. This is OK because it is a parameter of the method called. You cannot assume that an object will have knowledge of any other object in the system.

By encapsulating objects the system can manage the objects' activation and cleanup more efficiently. For example, the overhead to create an object is quite expensive from a processing standpoint. The system might decide to keep an object alive in memory so that it can more efficiently dispense the object when a program calls for it. When I cover Microsoft Transaction Server later in the book, you will see how it manages resources to make systems work more efficiently.

 Tip

When passing parameters to objects you should always pass them by value, rather than by reference. This is because when you pass a reference you are actually passing a pointer to a memory location within the calling process. This makes it very difficult for the operating system to effectively manage resources because it has to deal with a reference to memory that spans between two objects. This gets to be a real problem when the components are running on two separate computers. Not that the system cannot handle it, rather it takes a great deal of overhead to marshal the resources between the components. This also defeats the notion of encapsulation.

Investigating the Windows DNA Building Blocks

The building blocks for Windows DNA are component objects (COM), scripts, and services. Throughout this book these topics will be covered in detail. Components are the program objects that expose interfaces to methods that can be called to perform units of work. Scripts, typically Visual Basic Script, are the interpreted code that is used to orchestrate the interactions between the components. And the services are the system level programs that provide things like the script interpretation, resource allocations, and the transaction management.

Introduction to the Three-Tiered Windows DNA Model

As you recall, Windows DNA follows the classic three-tier architecture by breaking the services into three tiers: presentation, business logic, and data. These tiers are logical, not physical, tiers. This mean that all the tiers might run on one physical machine or a tier might be spread across several machines. This is the beauty of the model; it allows you more flexibility in your deployment and thus greater scalability. Within a tier you might also see sub-tiers. For example, within the business logic tier you might see it divided into a web farm tier and an application server tier. Or you might divide the interactions between services into sub-tiers. For example, Commerce Server interacting with BizTalk Server. The point is that you will see various architectures represented in different ways, however, they all can be distilled into the three classic tiers.

Another benefit of developing in these three tiers is that you can change components in any of the tiers without having to change the other tiers. The types of changes that occur in most environments can be categorized as presentation, business logic, and data changes. These are precisely the activities of the Windows DNA tiers. Because Windows DNA clearly distinguishes the boundaries between these tiers the interfaces between the tiers are well defined and thus it is easier to change the internals of each tier.

The Presentation Tier

The interface to the end user, the presentation tier presents information to the user as well as accepts information from the end user. It very often validates data before sending it to the business tier.

Figure 1.3 illustrates the wide range of presentation options available. You can choose a rich Windows client, which would run exactly like a client/server executable. This is a good option when you are converting a client/server application to the Windows DNA architecture. The next level down is components, ActiveX controls which must be hosted by another application. We will see in Week 3 how to develop ActiveX components and how to host them in Microsoft Office. The final three presentation options are related to Web presentation. The selection in the range of options depends upon the capabilities of your browser.

You can expect this tier to add other ways of representing information. For example, wireless devices like cell phones and PDA's are being delivered with Internet access capabilities. These devices have very unique presentation requirements. The latest thinking in this area is to use XML to represent the information internally and then have different device specific transformations to represent the data.

FIGURE **1.3**

The presentation tier.

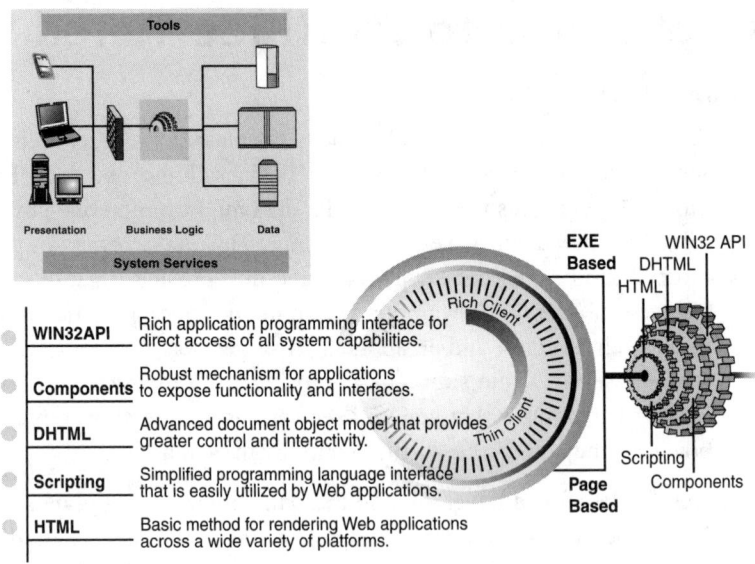

WIN32API — Rich application programming interface for direct access of all system capabilities.

Components — Robust mechanism for applications to expose functionality and interfaces.

DHTML — Advanced document object model that provides greater control and interactivity.

Scripting — Simplified programming language interface that is easily utilized by Web applications.

HTML — Basic method for rendering Web applications across a wide variety of platforms.

The Business Tier

The business tier is where you keep all the logic about how to perform the various usage scenarios. You will see in Figure 1.4 how you use Component Object Model+ (COM+), Microsoft Message Queue (MSMQ), and Internet Information Server (IIS) to provide services to your business components. COM is everything in the Windows environment. You will develop all your business logic as either COM components or as scripts. Week 2, "Business Logic," will cover COM and Microsoft Transaction Server, which have been combined to form COM+ in Windows 2000, and the new capabilities of COM+.

The other technology mentioned in this tier is Microsoft Message Queue (MSMQ), a system service that enables objects to communicate asynchronously through the use of messages. By using messages, the system can manage resources better. MSMQ is also covered in more detail in Week 2.

NEW TERM *Asynchronously* means that the requesting process does not wait for a result to be returned from the called operation. The calling program expects that the work will get done or be notified later of a problem. An example is when you call to order a pizza, you do not stay on the phone until the pizza arrives, you trust that it will be delivered.

Internet Information Server (IIS) is the final service mentioned in the business layer. IIS actually operates in two tiers, the presentation tier and business tier. Think of IIS as the interface between the two tiers. Its primary job is to receive information from the business tier and to then format it for presentation by a Web browser. IIS uses a technology called Active Server Pages (ASP) to script the interaction between the business components and the end-user presentations. Active Server Pages are covered in Week 3.

FIGURE 1.4

The business tier.

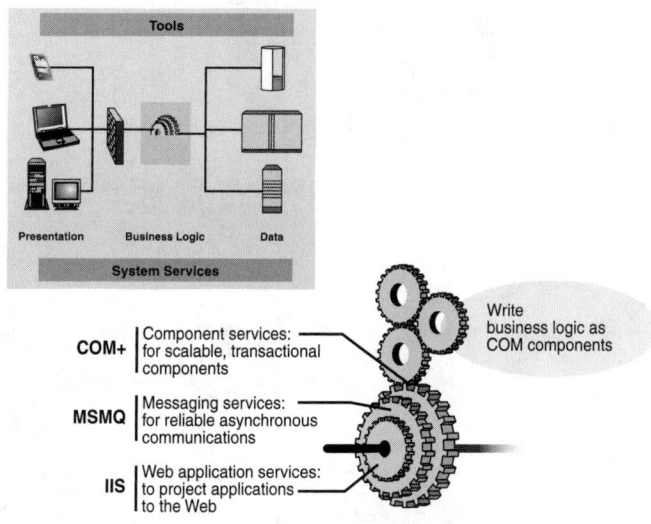

> **Tip**
>
> Try to minimize the amount of code in an Active Server Page. All the code in the page needs to be interpreted by the server, which can slow down processing. Try to encapsulate most of the logic in your business components. Use the ASP to orchestrate the interaction between the various components.

> **Tip**
>
> If you will be taking certification tests from Microsoft, it is good to remember that Microsoft considers IIS to be in the presentation tier, not the business tier.

Looking forward XML is becoming a very important enabler within the business tier and thus you can expect to see it being used in many places in the future. A good example of this is in SOAP and BizTalk Server which are covered in Day 14, "Best Practices and Other Services."

The Data Tier

The data tier contains Active Data Objects (ADO), OLE DB, and XML as interfaces into a number of varied data sources (see Figure 1.5).

FIGURE 1.5

The data tier.

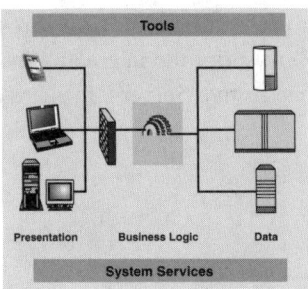

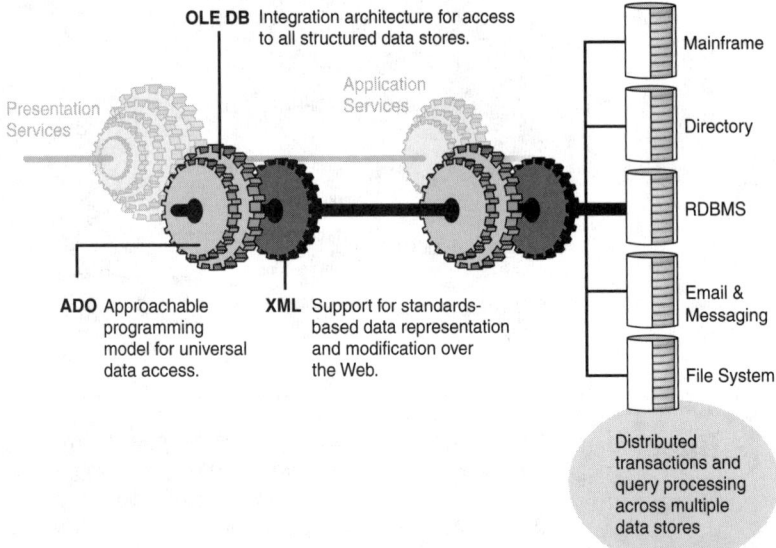

Active Data Object (ADO) is the current standard for universal access to data sources. ADO is a very flexible data access component that enables anything to be a data provider. Example of data providers are relational databases (SQL Server for example), Flat databases (Access for example), Directory services (Active Directory for example), Messages systems (Exchange for example), and file systems to name a few. Practically anything can act as a data store. You can also programmatically create your own data stores using ADO.

OLE DB is a new, low-level data provider that offers a faster interaction with underlying data stores. OLE DB was developed to get around the limitations of ODBC. OLE DB is written as a low-level COM component that allows for more efficient access to data stores. Over time more OLE DB providers will become available, and perhaps eventually replace ODBC. Currently there is an ODBC bridge that allows ODBC drivers to gain the benefits of OLE DB. Currently, however, there are only a limited number of OLE DB providers available. Naturally, they are available for Microsoft products like SQL Server and Access. Whenever possible be sure to use the OLE DB provider rather than the ODBC provider.

Extensible Markup Language (XML) is a self-defining, standard way to define data as text and send it to other systems. Because XML is text data (rather than binary), it can flow freely across the Internet. Because XML self-defines its data structure, any system can understand the data relationships. XML is VERY important to .NET Platform. XML is becoming the standard way that data and parameters flow between systems. I've dedicated a whole day in Week 2 to this important subject. In Day 14 we will also cover a couple of XML related subjects—BizTalk, a new XML based document interchange format, and SOAP, a way to use XML to pass parameters between objects across the Internet.

Note

> If you have been programming for Windows for a while, you will have noticed that Microsoft has changed its data access technology about every two years. Because of backward compatibility in the development tools, DAO and RDO are both still supported. You however, should use ADO because it is the best data access mechanism currently for Windows DNA solutions. When configuring a Data Source Name (DSN), you can select between ODBC and OLE DB providers. Again, if available, select OLE DB. We'll look at databases in detail later in this week.

You can see from Figure 1.5 that data sources can be mainframes (databases and transaction systems), directories, relational databases (RDBMs), messaging and email systems, the file system, or anything else you can develop. Through the use of OLE DB providers and ADO as the data access component, all these data sources look the same to the program. This abstraction of the data store allows great flexibility in how you provide data. For example, you can start with a low-end relational database and, as your transaction processing needs grow, you can move the data to a mid-range database or mainframe. From a programmatic standpoint you will need to change little, if any, code.

Multitiered Design Principles

Multitiered applications (Windows DNA) are the most complex applications to develop because of all the things you need to know and standards to which you must conform. Windows DNA is a double-edged sword, in that it can make your applications extremely robust and flexible if you are willing to learn and conform to its standards. If you do not conform to the Windows DNA way of doing development then you can develop applications that are not robust, do not scale up well, and are difficult to maintain. This section introduces you to Windows DNA at a high-level so that you can understand how everything fits together, and then we get deep into the details in Day 2, "Building a Windows DNA Application."

Exploring Components: The New Promise of Software Reusability

DNA components are essential to gain the flexibility and modularity of Windows. Components are the self-contained units of code that you orchestrate to deliver the capabilities of your application. Components are available from three sources: the operating system, third-party developers, and your own development efforts.

Examples of operating system components are Active Data Objects (ADO), Collaborative Data Objects (CDO), and all the components that come bundled with the operating system and development tools. Generally, system components can be freely redistributed. That is you can include them with your application without further approval from the component creator. Typically, when you choose to build an installation package, the build program looks at the dependencies of all the components and includes all the components necessary to run your application into the package.

Third-party components are ones you have purchased to provide a specific capability. Thousands are available on the market. Third-party components come with specific licensing agreements which note what you are allowed to freely redistribute. Many of the Microsoft components should be considered third-party, as they are part of applications that require a license to use. We will be using some of these components in Day 20, "Office 2000 and Web Components," and Day 21, "Implementing Digital Dashboards in Windows DNA Applications."

Finally, the components you have developed are yours to do with as you please. However, keep in mind that if you call system or third-party components, you must understand redistribution rules and the dependencies of your components. Microsoft provides a tool in Visual Studio that displays a component's dependencies. To see how this works, run Start, Program Files, Microsoft Visual Studio 6, Microsoft Visual Studio 6 Tools, Depends. This will launch the Dependency Walker. Now open up any .exe, .dll, .sys, .drv, .ocx, .cpl, .scr, or .com file to see how this looks. Figure 1.6 shows msado15.dll's dependencies. You can see that this DLL requires many other components for it to work. And the components it uses also have their own dependencies, thus you see a tree of dependencies.

FIGURE 1.6

Visual Studio's Dependency Walker.

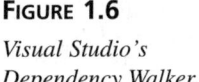

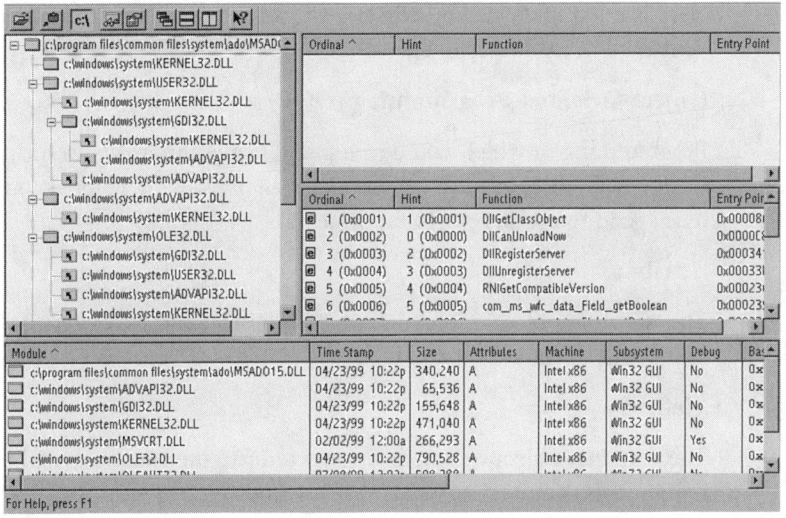

You can see that a large number of additional components are associated with any component. Many of the associated components are from the operating system, which can be both good and bad. The good part is that the operating system provides functionality you can use out of the box. The bad part is that, if something is wrong with any of these components, you can be affected. You might have heard the term "DLL Hell." This is what happens during an installation process when an application replaces one of these DLLs, either with an older or newer version that consequentially affects your application's components. This can require countless hours of debugging and troubleshooting to unravel. One of the major goals of Windows 2000 is to deal with this problem by not letting this happen. Windows 2000 uses several ways to keep the DLL from getting accidentally changed. First, only Microsoft can update DLL's in the system directory. All other DLLs are either kept in the applications directory or are versioned and tracked by operating system services. The new Microsoft installer does a better job of tracking all the changes made to the system as well as actively working with the system to fix corrupted applications. For example, let's say that a needed DLL from your application gets deleted. The system will call the Microsoft Installer which will repair the problem by reinstalling that missing component. This is a quick introduction of the solutions available for these issues.

Understanding Object Speak

Components bring with them a new set of terminology that you must understand in order to communicate about them. Many of the terms used come from object-oriented programming.

Here is a list of terms you will need to know and understand as a foundation for Windows DNA development.

Object-Oriented Programming (OOP)

Programming in which you develop and use components to form applications. Component/object–based development enables the developer to reuse components and thus speed future development projects.

Attributes

The way that object-oriented systems refer to data. In objects data exists only to represent some attribute of the object.

Method

The way that object-oriented systems refer to the functions and procedures the object implements. You may also see that methods are referred to as behaviors of the object.

Object

An independent software component that contains the data (attributes) and behaviors (methods) that represent something within the problem/solution domain. Objects are reusable components.

Class

A pattern for an object. The class defines all the attributes and methods that make up an instance of an object. A class is only the blueprint for a type of object, an abstraction of an actual object. For example, if you have a class called *person*, you can then create instances of that class as *Bob*, *Mary*, *Paul*, and so on.

Abstract Data Type

A user defined data type that represents and categorizes the problem domain. As an abstract data type, a class can contain real or other abstract data types. For example, a class of *pet* would be an abstract data type for *dog* and *cat*.

Inheritance

The process by which children objects inherit all the attributes and behaviors of their parents. The child can use attributes or methods as is; it can augment them; or it can override them with its own definitions. You will generally see two types of inheritance in the world whole/part and specialized/generalized. For example, whole/part describes the relationship of an *automobile*, which is the whole, to its parts *tires*, *chassis*, *engine*, and so on. An example of generalized/specialized inheritance is *fruit* as a general object and *banana* as a specialized *fruit*.

Instance

When you create an object, you are creating an instance of a class. As with variables, instances are declared within a program, they have a user-defined name, and they are abstract data types. You can create as many instances of a class as you want. Each instance will have a different variable name and hold attributes unique to that object. The methods will always behave the same for every instance of a particular class. To clarify, classes are like cookie cutters and objects are the cookies. Once a cookie is cut you can change its attributes by using different colored frosting and decorations.

Instantiate

To create an instance of a class. An example would be to cut out cookies (objects) using a cookie cutter (class).

Member

A variable or routine that is part of a class. Both attributes and behaviors are considered to be members of a class.

Multiple Inheritance

A feature of some object-oriented programming languages that enables a new class to be derived from several existing classes. Multiple inheritance both extends and combines existing types. This is what happens in whole/part inheritance.

Polymorphism

The capability to redefine a routine in a derived class (a class that inherited its data structures and routines from another class). Polymorphism enables the programmer to define a base class that includes routines, which perform standard operations on groups of related objects, without regard to the exact type of each object. The programmer then redefines the routines in the derived class for each type, taking into account the characteristics of the object.

Encapsulate

To treat a collection of structured information as a whole without affecting, or taking notice of, its internal structure. The implementation details of a class are encapsulated in a separate file, whose contents do not need to be known by a programmer using that class.

These are the terms you will most likely hear or read when discussing components. The key thing to remember about components is that they are self-contained units of logic containing functions and procedures—called *methods* in object-oriented terminology—and data—called *attributes* in object speak. The four main characteristics of an object-oriented system are abstraction, encapsulation, inheritance, and polymorphism.

Microsoft's Definition of Objects (COM)

Microsoft has the largest install base of object-oriented components, because of all the components distributed with Windows 95, 98, NT and 2000, along with all the recent component-based applications. The objects that run in the Windows environment are designed according to Microsoft's Component Object Model (COM). COM defines standard interfaces and calling conventions that must be included in all components to enable them to work together and for the system to know about them. The good news is that most development tools comply with the COM standards.

Some of the key features of COM are

- *Iunknown Interface*   All interfaces objects must have an Iunknown interface with a `QueryInterface` method so that a calling program can make a call to `QueryInterface` and receive a list of all the interfaces that the object supports. Iunknown has two other methods, `AddRef` and `Release`, which track how many programs are actively using the object. By keeping track of the number of instances of the object in use, the operating system knows which objects can be safely cleaned out of memory.

- *Idispatch Interface*   This interface is not called directly but rather used as an automation interface for controllers that do not use COM interfaces directly. An executable file or DLL that uses Idispatch is known as an Automation server. Idispatch has a number of methods that allow the automation server to discover the method and attribute names as well as the type and parameter information for a COM components interface. Basically, Idispatch enables an object to tell you what parameters it needs for its methods. When Intelisenses is invoked in the development environment, it gets this information from the Idispatch interface. The COM component maintains a list of all the interfaces with the binding information in a virtual table. If the object is early bound, the call is made directly to the interface in the virtual table. If the object is late bound, the call goes to Idispatch, which then passes it to the correct entry in the virtual table.

NEW TERM   *Early* and *late binding* refers to when a program knows the component that it will be instantiating. If the program knows which component it will be calling at compile time, then the program is called *early bound*. It can do tighter type-checking and make calls directly to the object interfaces. If the program decides at runtime which components it will call, then it is referred to as *late bound*. To late bind a program, call into the Iunknown and Idispatch interfaces to discover the entry points and data types for the object. Late bound programs are more flexible but incur a greater overhead and looser type checking as a result.

- *Language independence*   Components can be written in any language, as long as the required interfaces are provided.

- *Global Unique Identifiers (GUIDs)*   Each component and all its interfaces have a global unique identifier. These GUIDs are stored in the registry along with other relevant information about the object, such as file location. GUIDs ensure that COM components do not accidentally connect with the wrong component, interface, or method.

Windows DNA and the Team Environment

Because of the way it is tiered, Windows DNA is very conducive to dividing the work so that different teams can build the various layers. In fact, Microsoft provides many tools to help teams work together. The tools include

- *Source Safe*   A source code management system that tracks all revisions made to the source code between check-in and check-out.

- *Repository*   An online library where you can share components, programs, documents, and so on. with the rest of your development team or organization.

- *Visual Modeler*   An application modeling tool that enables the team to share a common application model. Visual Modeler can reverse-engineer the object interfaces so that team members do not need the source code of components in the application in order to put them into the model.

Partitioning the Work

One of the best ways for a team to work together is to have a multistage application development environment. This model, shown in Figure 1.7, enables components to pass through various stages of testing before making it to the final production environment.

FIGURE 1.7

Application develop-
ment staged
environments.

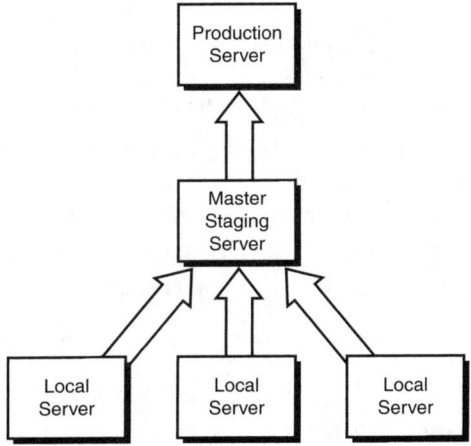

Development Environment

In Figure 1.7, you will see that at the top of the model you have production environment, under which you have an integration stage environment, and under that you have local unit environments. Each of these environments is a working copy of the production environment, plus the development, debugging, and testing tools at the integration and local unit levels.

On a day-to-day development project, you will be working at the integration and local levels. In Visual Studio they are called master mode and local mode, respectively.

Master and Local Modes

Microsoft's Web development tools use a concept of local mode and master mode. This model requires that each developer have a complete working copy of the production services running on his local machine. With this model the developer can run all the code in local mode on his own development workstation. The developer has complete control of the environment as well as complete isolation from other team members so other developers will not experience system and code problems during component development.

When a developer feels that a component is stable and ready for other developers to use and test, he returns it to the master server, which in this model is the integration server. The developer will typically notify the other developers that the new component is available; the other developers will then receive the new component into their local environments when they do a refresh.

Source Control Using Source Safe

The process of source control serves two purposes: It enables versions of code to be tracked and it provides a history of changes to the application code.

The source control system can actually manage any sort of text-based data such as documents and source listings. It is a good way to track the revision of documentation. Microsoft provides a source control system called Source Safe which is included in the Enterprise Version of Visual Studio. Source Safe is a nice package to use if you are using the Microsoft development suite because it integrates well. To use Source Safe a Source Safe database is set up on a server that is accessible by all the developers. When they install Source Safe, the developers will specify to use the common database for source control. From that point forward, file access and changes will be controlled and tracked in this central database.

The Repository

The Repository is a library for sharing finished components. Unlike source control, the Repository is where you share things that have been finished. The Repository keeps metadata about the things you store in it, so it's easier for users to search and find what they are looking for.

The Repository is a fairly new tool for Microsoft. It has been around for a while but has been buried in the menu structure. Often times people will use Source Safe as a repository for project collateral. Nothing prevents you from using Source Safe in this way. However, the Repository is a better place to share things, especially, finished work because you can have a great deal of metadata about the items you are sharing.

NEW TERM   *Metadata* is data about the data. Metadata is typically information that allows for better searching and classification of the information. It can be thought of as being similar to the card catalog at a library.

To clarify when to use Source Safe and when to use Repository, use Source Safe when you have work in progress that you need to control access and track changes. Use the Repository to make available finished work that you want to make easily accessible.

Summary

Today, we started looking at the Windows DNA architecture. We looked at how software development has evolved from a monolithic model to client/server and now to the multitiered Windows DNA model. We looked at the importance of components to a scalable application architecture and we looked at how Microsoft implements components as objects.

You learned about the three tiers of the Windows Distributed interNet Application (DNA) platform. The data tier is responsible for all activities that have to do with managing and accessing data. The business logic tier is where the components exist that implement your applications specific business logic. The presentation tier is responsible for the interface to the user. You learned that the Windows DNA is an evolving platform. In Day 2, we will dive deeper into working with Windows DNA.

Today you also learned about object-oriented terminology and how Component Object Model (COM) is implemented. You recall that the four attributes of an object-oriented system are abstraction, encapsulation, inheritance, and polymorphism.

Finally, you learned about the tools that Microsoft provides to help you work as a team. The Source Safe is a source control management system that controls access to project source files and track changes. The repository is a place to put finished work that you want to make available to others. Because of the Repository's metadata capabilities, it makes it very easy to provide information that users can search to find the things in the repository they are looking for.

Q&A

Q **Most books have only three attributes (encapsulation, inheritance, and polymorphism) of an object-oriented system, why do you include abstraction as a fourth?**

A The whole object-oriented concept is based upon abstraction. Real world things are represented as units of data and behaviors combined together in what are called objects. Abstraction is the single fundamental tenant of object-oriented development. Objects are abstract representations of the things in a problem domain.

Q **Why has Microsoft changed the meaning of what the Windows DNA acronym means?**

A Yes, Microsoft originally defined it as Windows Distributed interNet Application Architecture and has recently changed it to mean Windows Distributed interNet Application Platform. This is a sign that Windows DNA is an evolving specification that Microsoft is using to be inclusive of new technology as it arrives. .NET Platform is a services oriented platform that is focused on delivering Internet based applications. .NET Platform builds upon the architectural concept of Windows DNA that is presented throughout this book.

Q **You mentioned several data access methods DAO, RDO, and ADO, what are they and which should I use for a Windows DNA solution?**

A Data Access Objects (DAO) go back to the day when most applications were either standalone or client/server on a fast network. DAO only has a client-side cursor so all data must go to the client to be processed. This can put quite a load on a network. Remote Data Objects (RDO) was developed to solve this problem by allowing for a server-side cursor. With a server-side cursor, the data is processed on the server and only the requested records travel across the network reducing the network load. Active Data Objects (ADO) add to the RDO capabilities by abstracting the data source so that practically anything can act as a data store and yet the ADO interface stays the same. ADO is the data access method that should be used in a Windows DNA solution.

Q **Are all DLLs considered COM components?**

A No, some DLL's are simply static libraries that are loaded into a program. To be considered a COM component it must implement a query interface. The Iunknown interface needs to be supported. It has three required methods QueryInterface, AddRef, and Release. These methods allow the object to return its public interfaces to the caller and to track references to the object. The Idispatch interface must be supported if you will be calling the COM object from Visual Basic or a scripted environment like an Active Server Page. Objects with a dispatch interface are often called "Dual Interfaced." The dispatch interface allows these environments to access the Iunknown methods. So to be a COM component, at minimum, the Iunknown interface needs to be implemented.

Workshop

The workshop provides quiz questions to help solidify your understanding of the material covered, as well as exercises to provide you with experience in using what you have learned. Try to answer the quiz and exercise questions before checking the answers in Appendix A.

Quiz

1. What is the component model that Microsoft uses in Windows-based systems?
2. What are the benefits of using COM?
3. What are the advantages and disadvantages of using a monolithic application?
4. What are the advantages and disadvantages of using a client/server application?
5. Define an object.

DAY 2

Building a Windows DNA Application

Today, we revisit the Windows DNA three-tiered model, but this time you will learn

- The implementation details of each tier
- The tools and skills you will need to build successful Windows DNA systems
- The responsibilities of each tier
- The tools used at each tier
- What you might expect when working in a team environment
- Other system-administration issues like security and scalability
- Typical system configurations for Windows DNA systems

The Three Tiers Revisited

The three tiers of a Windows DNA application are presentation, business logic, and data. All these tiers are supported by system services and are developed against a backdrop of development tools. In Day 1, "Understanding Windows DNA," we covered the tiers from a usage perspective. Today, we will cover them from a development and services perspective.

Presentation Tier

The presentation tier is the part of the system that the user sees. This tier often is developed first in conjunction with the users so that they can see what the system will look like. It is often easier for users to relate to working with the visual interface in making functionality and usage decisions. As developers, we know that the real heavy work will occur in the business logic and data tiers. However, the visual presentation is very important to the users because they will need to view and interact with it in order to use the applications.

The Internet has changed the way we construct and maintain the interface. In native Windows applications, screens are developed by creating forms and dialog boxes by dragging controls and other elements from a toolbar onto these forms. The native Windows graphics engine then renders these native Windows interfaces. These types of applications are great when all the users are running Microsoft Windows. However, your target audience might also be using Macintosh, UNIX, and other systems that have no knowledge of how to run Windows applications.

The Internet changed this by delivering its content as a text stream that contained markup instructions. A Web browser is an application that can read the text stream and render the content based upon the markup instructions. The markup language is called *Hypertext Markup Language* (HTML). This approach to delivering content has the benefit that it can be rendered on any system with a browser able to understand and display the form as the markup instructions indicate. The downside of HTML is that the developer has little control of how the browser will interpret and display the instructions sent. For this reason HTML has evolved, adding more markup instructions as well as the ability to specify attributes for the markup instructions. This helped control the way that the browser displays the form.

The next challenge to Web-based content is the interactivity and presentation level validation logic. Native Windows applications have a very rich set of events that allow for a great deal of control by the developer over the user's interactions. To provide this capability to Web pages, Dynamic Hypertext Markup Language (DHTML), scripting, and components were added to newer versions of the HTML specifications. Developers can now deliver Web-based content that comes very close to the capabilities of a rich Windows native client. The only problem with using these capabilities is that the user needs to have a browser capable of understanding these instructions. Applications that use the new capabilities lose their capability to also reach the widest audience possible. When you look at the range of client delivery possibilities, you will hear this issue described as thin (browser only) versus thick (native Windows application) clients or reach (uses only straight HTML) versus rich (uses more features that all clients might not have) clients. See Figure 2.1 for a graphic display of the presentation tier spectrum of options. These dimensions represent a spectrum of capabilities that you will need to evaluate and pick where best to place your application. We cover these issues later in this chapter. In Week 3 the presentation option will be covered in great detail.

FIGURE 2.1

Presentation Tier Spectrum.

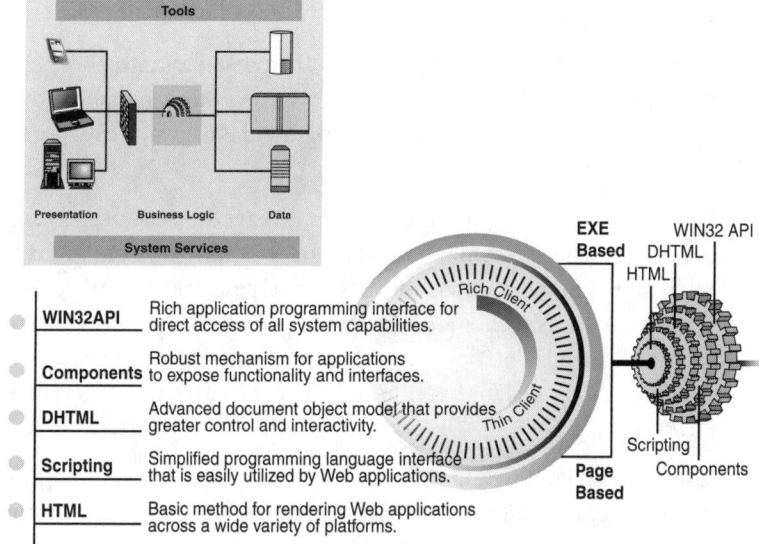

It is very important that you determine the target audience for your application up front so that you know how to target your presentation layer. Users commonly ask for a reach client, based upon the assumption that the application will be accessible by the widest audience. This reach capability comes at the expense of user functionality and higher development cost. Yes, you read that right—the simpler interface is often the most expensive to build. The simpler interface has added workflow logic and HTML screens needed to address all the logical conditions within an application. The richer clients are less expensive to build because all the logic and functionality is contained within a few screens. With this in mind, it is always best to push the presentation tier to the highest level of richness that your users can support. If you need to extend the application's reach, it is always possible later to degrade presentation functionality based upon the users' browser capabilities. You may also choose to offer a number of presentation clients to meet a wide range of client needs, this is what we have done in Day 3, "Architecting a DNA Solution."

Remember that you can develop several different versions of your client presentation tier to service different audiences. Because the business logic and data tiers are separate from the presentation tier, all the various presentation spaces can use the business logic and data capabilities.

With these thoughts in mind, let's look at the presentation layer in more detail.

Navigation, Layout, and Scripting

The three aspects of the presentation layer are navigation, layout, and scripting.

Navigation is the workflow aspect of the presentation space. Navigation can occur within the same page or it can lead to other pages within an application. When dealing with Web sites the navigation will refer to how the user moves from page to page within the Web site.

Layout refers to how the elements are arranged on the user's screen. Depending upon the richness of your presentation layer, you will have a range of layout capabilities. Richness refers to the number of capabilities available on the client's presentation tier. For example, a Visual Basic client is considered to be very rich because you can control every aspect of the presentation and validation. Pure HTML would be considered to be a reach client (not rich) because you have little control over the presentation and validation of the information.

Logic is executed within the client's presentation space through *scripting*. The two predominant client-side scripting languages are JavaScript and VBScript. Scripting is the only way that you execute programming logic in many of the Windows DNA scenarios. Scripting has an advantage in that scripted logic does not require a compile, link process before it can execute. In fact, you can add the Visual Basic Scripting Engine to your Windows DNA solutions to allow greater component flexibility. This is an advanced topic and will not be covered in this book. We mention it so that you are aware that this capability exists in the event that you may need it.

Client-Side Presentation

Client-side presentation can occur through a wide range of presentation technologies like HTML, Scripting, DHTML, Component, Executables, and new formats being developed for other devices. Each level of capability requires that the client have the software necessary to use these capabilities. The client-side footprint required for the technology to be supported is commonly referred to as its level of *thickness*. If you require that the entire Visual Basic runtime and all of your application specific components be installed—for example, if you have a Visual Basic client—then you have a thick client. On the other hand, if you simply require a basic Web browser, then you have a thin client because you are not asking for anything particularly special in terms of client capabilities. Another way that Microsoft puts this is *richness* versus *reach*. We will look at the client presentation technologies and what they require in order to be used.

HTML

Hypertext Markup Language (HTML) is the most basic of the presentation development technologies. HTML is a text stream with defined markup tags embedded in it. The tags can be interpreted by the user's Web browser and then be displayed as instructed. The markup tags look like `<tag>your content</ tag>`. The tag name is contained within angle brackets followed by the content to which the tag will be applied. Finally the tag is closed with an angle bracket, slash, tab, angle bracket to close the statement. Attributes assigned to tags can provide additional functionality. An attribute is represented as `tag attrib1="value1", attrib2="value2"`, and so on. The attributes are name value pairs within the opening tag of a tag pair. HTML will be covered in more detail in Week 3. The point to remember with HTML is that it is a simple text stream; it must have a browser that understands the markup and can render the page.

HTML has a few sets of different tag types. The first set defines how the page is laid out, delineating certain sections of the text stream to be sent to the browser. The entire page is contained in a set of <HTML> tags. Within the page you have two sections—a <HEAD>, or *header*, and <BODY>. The header contains scripts and other information that is applied page-wide. The body section is where we find the actual data and formatting tags.

Other sets of HTML tags define how the page actually looks when it is displayed. The bulleted list below will demonstrate some of these tags:

- *How text is displayed and formatted*   These tags define how text is displayed and formatted. These tags assign attributes such as bold and italic fonts, bulleted or sequenced lists, and paragraph formatting.
- *Multimedia elements, rules, and images*   They allow things like pictures, animation, and sounds to be included in a Web page.
- *Input forms*   Input fields like radio buttons, check boxes, and pick lists send information to the server.

- *Hyperlinks* Basic to Web content is the capability to hyperlink between elements on a page and between pages, so a set of tags exists for this purpose.
- *Tables* These tags allow the developer to insert data in table form. These can help consolidate larger amounts of data or improve the aesthetics of the page.
- *Frames* Frames divide a page into several sections, which each contain other Web pages. One page defines the frames, and the other pages provide the content. So to have a page with three frames, you will need four pages—one to define how the page is to be divided into frames (the *parent* frame) and the others to define the content of each frame. All the frames are independent of each other yet they are able to communicate with each other via the parent frame.

HTML is an evolving standard. This raises some compatibility issues depending upon how many browser versions back you want to support. It is generally safe to assume that most people will be using browsers that support HTML versions 3.2 and later, which have the previously mentioned tags. The standardized capabilities are defined by the World Wide Web Consortium (`http://www.w3c.org`) . If you want to know the definitive specification for any approved standard this is the place to get it. Browser developers also add their own extras to their browsers that implement capabilities they are working on that will be presented to the W3C in the future, or are still in the review process by W3C. Vendors may also implement capabilities to support their specific architectures; such is the case for Microsoft Internet Explorers support for ActiveX controls. In Week 3, we will discuss way that you can determine at the server what capabilities exist at the client and then adjust your presentation capabilities to take advantage of browser specific features.

Other Types of Markup

HTML is not the only form of markup language that is in use, several variations are emerging to support new Internet enabled devices. The new devices have varying presentation capabilities and thus the information needs to be presented in different ways. You could either have different pages for each device, at last count there were 47 varying presentation formats, or you could have programmatic logic to alter the presentation. The current trend is to separate the information from the presentation and then have a transformation and styling layer to handle the requirements of the different client devices. XML is the defacto standard that is evolving to represent information and XSL and XSLT are the styling and transformation standards for presentation. This is a fast evolving area and should slow down in a year or two. XML technologies will be discussed on Day 12, "The Power of XML."

Client-Side Scripting

Client-side scripting gives you a level of control over what happens on the client's browser. The two most commonly used scripting languages are JavaScript and VBScript. JavaScript is the most widely supported. VBScript is available to all the Microsoft browsers.

All scripts are based upon client-side events. Examples of an event are when the user clicks the mouse or the mouse passes over a screen element. Events usually occur as a result of user activity, however, they can also occur because of a system event like a timer going off. Scripts can be associated with an event. An event must occur for the script to be executed. So, for example, if I want a script to run when the mouse passes over MyElement, I might have a function called MyElement_onMouseOver. When the mouse goes over MyElement, the script is run. Several different ways exist to associate a script with an event, this is just an example of one way. Event handling scripts can be implemented in several ways. They can be embedded within the actual HTML tag so that they are specific to that tag only. They can be placed in the header section (like our example), where they are accessible to the entire page. Or they can be placed in an include file, where they can be included in several pages.

The event models for Netscape and Internet Explorer browsers differ greatly in implementation. Netscape uses a top-down approach, in which the event triggers at the top level and then is passed down to the child elements. Internet Explorer uses a bubble-up approach: The event starts at the child element level and then bubbles up to the parent. The event handling order will not affect simple scripting but, for more sophisticated tasks, you should be aware of how events are processed.

 Note Because we are talking about Window application development, it should be noted that both JavaScript and VBScript are implemented outside of the browser as part of the operating system. They can be used by the Windows Scripting Host and any application that wants to use either scripting engine.

JavaScript

Netscape developed JavaScript as a scripting language for its browser. The language has no relationship to the Java programming language except for its syntax, which is similar to that of C. JavaScript is supported in both the Netscape and Internet Explorer languages.

VBScript

Microsoft conceived Visual Basic Script as a scripting language for its browser. It is a subset of the popular Visual Basic language and has the same syntax as Visual Basic. VBScript is used everywhere within Microsoft products. In fact, VBScript is the preferred language for use in Microsoft Internet Information server. So server-side VBScript is the preferred language.

Only Microsoft's Internet Explorer supports VBScript natively. A plug-in is available to add VBScript to the Netscape browser; however, because of the different event handling models between Netscape and Internet Explorer, this is not always the best solution. I advise using JavaScript for the client and VBScript for the server, unless you know that you will be supporting only Internet Explorer. Then, you can use VBScript on both sides.

DHTML

Dynamic HTML is an evolved version of HTML, which adds different capabilities depending upon the browser used. Both Netscape and Microsoft have created their own versions of DHTML. Of the two implementations, Microsoft's is the closest to the W3C standard. One of the most exciting enhancements is the capability to change the client presentation display without having to round-trip the page to the server. For example, you can show or hide screen elements simply by running scripts at the client. The Document Object Model (DOM) has been updated, allowing you to access every element on a page. DHTML works very closely with the DOM to provide functionality. The DOM provides the namespace which allows the DHTML scripts to access and manipulate page elements. Not only can you manipulate the presentation with DHTML but you can also access the screen values and have logic run based upon the values entered. With DHTML, the browser-based presentation comes close to having the same programmatic control as native Windows applications.

Components

Components are objects hosted within the browser presentation space. Components allow developers to provide capabilities that are impossible with HTML. The two types of components available are ActiveX and Java. Components add capabilities that are not available with HTML, DHTML, or scripts. ActiveX controls are binary components that are hosted within the browser's presentation space. ActiveX controls have full access to the components and operating system functions on the user's computer. As such, they can perform any of the functions that a Windows native application can perform.

Microsoft's ActiveX COM components are downloaded from a location designated in the control definition, the first time called. They are saved on the client's computer typically into the Windows/Downloaded Program Files directory and instantiated by the client browser. The component will continue to live on the client's computer until a newer version is detected; then a replacement component is downloaded. ActiveX components are much faster than Java components because they are only downloaded once and because they are written in Windows binary code, so they are already optimized for best performance. ActiveX controls have some benefits over COM components in that not only can they have a presentation space but they also tie into the event model of the hosting container so that they receive the same events that the container receives as well as are able to produce events that the container can choose to respond. We will be creating ActiveX controls on Day 16, "Using ActiveX Controls to Move Business Logic from the Server to the Client." We will be looking at a number of the Microsoft Office 2000 Web Component ActiveX controls on Day 20, "Office 2000 and Web Components."

Java components are either downloaded as binary or as source code which is compiled just-in-time by the browser. Java code needs to be sent down the first time it is called during a session. This need to download the Java code every time it needs to be used during a session can account for load-time delays. Java is portable to many platforms, whereas ActiveX technology is exclusive to Microsoft Windows. Most java code is compiled into a binary format called byte code. This byte code then runs in what is termed a Java Virtual Machine (JVM). JVM's exist for a number of platforms allowing Java to be portable across several platforms.

ActiveX

ActiveX has taken on several meanings as a marketing term for Microsoft. For our purposes ActiveX components are COM components evolved out of Object Linking and Embedding (OLE). ActiveX controls, on the other hand, have a presentation space and ties into the hosting containers event chain. For clarity sake we will always call ActiveX components COM components and ActiveX Controls ActiveX controls. Microsoft's goal was to develop a slimmed-down component model that could be used in Internet applications. ActiveX controls can be developed within most every development environment. ActiveX *controls* typically have presentation elements associated with them. As mentioned, ActiveX controls have additional interfaces that must exist to handle the event notifications between the container and the control. Fortunately, wizards are provided in the development tools that make easy work of implementing these interfaces.

On Day 16, you will build an ActiveX control for use in a Windows DNA application. Then the details of ActiveX will be covered.

Java Applets

Sun Microsystems developed and licenses the Java language. Java is intended to be machine independent; to achieve this, a program runs on the client computer called a *virtual machine*. This virtual machine knows how to interpret and run the Java code. Java is unique in that it can send either binary pseudocode or source code to the virtual machine, which will then be run—or compiled and then run—by that virtual machine. Most current Java applets are in the form of compiled binary code. In the early days, Java interpreters existed that downloaded and did just-in-time compilation of the code. For performance reason this way of distributing Java applets has all but gone away.

Java runs much slower than ActiveX controls because of the overhead of the virtual machine. However, if portability to non-Microsoft systems or non-Microsoft browsers is important, then Java is your best bet.

Java can be run on the client computer or at the server. Microsoft provides support for Java but do not expect to see them going out of their way to support the latest greatest features of Java in their platforms. Microsoft feels that you can get better performance and compatibility by using ActiveX and COM components.

Windows Native Clients

The most rich client architecture is a full Windows native client application. You have developed the same type of applications for standalone desktop and client/server solutions. Native Windows applications are not often mentioned when discussing Internet applications because they are considered old-fashioned. In reality, native Windows applications provide the best user experience at the least cost. As we saw in Day 1, deployment and portability can pose problems with these applications. However, if these issues are not high on your consideration list, then a native Windows application can yield great benefits.

Server-Side Scripting

Not all scripting is reserved for the client side. Scripting can occur on the server side as well. Client-side scripting is primarily used to validate user input, coordinate the interaction between client components, and to dynamically change the presentation. Server-side scripting is used to coordinate the interaction between business components and to dynamically generate the presentation elements to be sent to the client's browser. There are exceptions to this. For example, Microsoft has a capability called *remote scripting,* which allows clients to run scripts on the server. You will want to run scripts on the server if you need to keep their implementation details private. However, remote scripting is slower because of the network latency. The reason for this being an issue is because the user can view client-side scripts by simply viewing the HTML source code. Microsoft has addressed this in recent versions of the scripting engines, allowing scripts to be hashed so that they are unreadable by the casual browser. However, the user must be using the latest scripting engine, which adds to the reach problem.

The speed of client-side scripting can also become an issue. Because scripts need to be interpreted by the clients scripting engine in order to run, they are slower than binary code such as ActiveX. With casual scripting this tends to not be a problem. However, if you say want to have a scrolling banner in which you perhaps move the text every 10th of a second by having a timer run a script, you will see a substantial performance degradation on slower computers. We all like to have the latest fastest computers, and we need them, however, we should keep a slow computer around so that we can test our application performance on a slow system. Application performance is always more important than wiz bang flash stuff.

Active Server Pages (ASPs), Internet Server Application Programming Interface (ISAPI), and Common Gateway Interface (CGI) are all ways to enable server-side scripting. Each of these technologies has specific benefits and limitations when it comes to providing server-side logic.

Common Gateway Interface (CGI)

The oldest of the server-side scripting techniques, CGI defines the standard by which form data is sent across the Internet. The standard specifies that data is sent in name/value pairs. This format for sending data is the standard for the Internet.

The name value pair format is very commonly used on the Internet and you definitely will be working with it so let's explain it a bit more. The HTTP protocol used to communicate on the Internet has two major commands GET and POST. The GET command sends requests to a server in a single stream called a header message (not to be confused with the <HEAD> tag. This message looks like

```
GET /mypage.htm?parm1=one&parm2=two HTTP/1.1
Host: 123.123.1.2
Content-Type: text/html
...
```

The values are passed as <name>:<value> in the header. You cannot affect these from the Web page. You will also notice that in the URL the parameters are appended to the page request. They are in the format ?<name>=<value>&<name>=<value>&.... This is the format you can use from your Web page. You start the parameter string with a question mark and then pass name value pairs separated by ampersands.

The other format is a POST. A POST message has both a header and a body, again not to be confused with the <BODY> tag. This type of message looks like:

```
POST /mypage.htm HTTP/1.1
Host: 123.123.1.2
Content-Type: text/plain
Content-Length: 123

Parm1 = one
Parm2 = two
...
```

This type of message is similar to the GET. However, it has a new section called the body, which is denoted by a Content-Length, and it being set off from the header by a blank line. The parameters will not appear in the URL window, the server will read the specified number of characters following the blank line.

In Day 3, you will learn how Microsoft Internet Information Server takes these parameters and makes them available to you in a collection. Other techniques like CGI and ISAPI need to parse these parameters themselves.

The data is sent to a program or script running on the server. The program is specified in the action attribute of a form or in a hyperlink. The program or script is executed and the results are returned to the user.

CGI programs are fairly easy to write but do not scale well in a Windows DNA solution. It is hard to manage their resource usage because they run outside of the Web server process.

Internet Server Application Programming Interface (ISAPI)

ISAPI is the next logical evolution in server scripting. ISAPI filters are DLLs that are loaded into the Web service processing space. As such they can take advantage of Web server capabilities and gain the efficiency of running in a single process space. Usually, only one instance of the ISAPI filter is loaded and then requests are multithreaded through the filter. Of course, the ISAPI DLL must be tread-safe, so that multiple-client request can be handled simultaneously. This is a very efficient way to mange resources. Although more efficient than CGI, ISAPI filters are difficult to develop and can currently only be developed in C, not VB, because of the required threading model and static interface requirements. VB developers, if this sounds too technical, don't worry. The C++ developers will understand this explanation.

Very few developers have experience in developing these filters. ISAPI needs to be bug free because, if the filter crashes, it takes the whole Web service down as well. To make any sort of change, the entire DLL needs to be recompiled and loaded into the server by restarting the Web service. To solve this problem, Microsoft developed Active Server Pages (ASPs).

Active Server Pages (ASPs)

Active Server Pages (ASPs) are enabled by the use of server-side scripts. ASPs use scripts to orchestrate the interaction of COM components and to enable the pages to respond to a user's request. ASPs were introduced with Microsoft Internet Information Server (IIS) 3.0, and were greatly enhanced in the 4.0 and 5.0 releases.

An Active Server Page is a collection of server-side scripts and HTML tags in files that reside on the server. When the server sees that a user calls a file with an ASP extension, it passes the file to an Internet Server Application Programming Interface (ISAPI) filter, called *asp.dll*. The filter interprets the script and emits the results back to the client. This is the best of all worlds; it provides the most flexibility while using a very efficient process to interpret the scripts.

Any scripting language can be used with ASPs as long as an ActiveX Scripting Engine is available. The standard scripting engines that ship with NT and IIS are VBScript and JavaScript. PerlScript, REXX, and Python require a third-party ActiveX Scripting Engine.

Tip

Many people who are new to ASPs often put a great deal of business logic into their pages. This is a mistake because the code needs to be interpreted every time the page is run. The better solution is to implement your business logic as COM components and then call these components from your ASP script. Try to minimize the size of your ASP scripts. Extensive ASP processing can greatly slow down a Web server.

Another pitfall is to use ASPs when the same thing can be done with straight HTML. Use HTML where possible because it is cached by the server and can be served up very quickly because they do not need to pass through the asp.dll before being returned. If you are using ASPs to insert data that rarely changes, you might want to use the following trick. Modify your ASP to write the HTML results to an HTML file on the server. Have the user link to the HTML file instead of the ASP. When the data changes, simply run the ASP file to create an updated HTML file. If the data is updated on a frequent schedule, you can take this technique to the next step by using the NT scheduler to run the ASP file at a regularly scheduled time.

ASP development is covered further in Week 3.

Business Logic Tier

The business logic tier is made up of services and components that run on the server to implement the specific logic required for a business solution. In the Windows DNA platform, COM components are the basic building blocks. Other systems may use Java applets or Java Beans to provide component functionality. The components are either developed in-house or are purchased to provide a specific type of service like processing file uploads or sending SMTP mail messages.

The services found at this tier are Windows NT services that your application can call upon to add functionality to your application. Services such as Microsoft Transaction

Server, Microsoft Message Queue, Directory Service, and Web Services are just a few of the many services available to your application.

You develop your business logic using standard development languages like C++, Visual Basic, and ASP. You could also use Cobol and other languages as long as you have a compiler that can produce COM compliant components. We have already discussed scripting options.

The business tier is the most complex tiers because it contains all of the business logic and system services. You may often see this tier sub-divided into sub-tiers which are divided either on server type boundaries and/or service type boundaries. For example the tier could be divided into a web server farm and an application server farm. The application server farm could be divided into Commerce Server, Host Integration Server, and BizTalk Servers. The point is that within the tier you have a number of way to divide and configure your system to provide logical organization as well as management and scalability options. I will go into more detail on Day 3 when we cover solution architecture.

Component Technology

Components are the building blocks used to build Windows DNA applications. These components are created according to the Windows Component Object Model (COM) specifications. Two types of components exist—those with a graphical user interface and those without. Components with a user interface, often called ActiveX controls usually have an .ocx extension. The other type of component, a COM component, has no connection to the screen or keyboard. These components need to be hosted by another application. They usually have a .dll extension. DLL COM components run in the process and memory of the program that loaded it. It is possible to create a COM component that is an executable. In this case the component has an .exe extension and acts as an automation server, which runs in its own process and manages its own resources. Processes own memory and all the threads that run in that memory. If the component fails, it will not take down the calling process. This process safety comes at the cost of extra overhead to marshal requests and return data across process boundaries.

COM is a mature object model and interface that is well integrated in the Windows operating system. Windows developers are comfortable working with COM components. So it make senses to put COM wrappers around non-COM business processes so as to make them easily accessible for Windows application developers. Companies like BAAN and SAP provide COM interfaces in their proprietary databases and interfaces. Many other companies are doing the same so they can use Windows NT and COM as integration points between their disparate systems.

Visual Basic

Visual Basic is the number one programming language. Because of its ease of use combined with its powerful capabilities, Visual Basic offers great efficiency in application development. With Visual Basic you can develop a whole range of Windows objects:

- *Standard executables*   A traditional desktop application.

- *ActiveX EXE*   A COM application server. It has its own process that it uses to instantiate components.

- *ActiveX DLL*   A COM component that loads into the process of the calling program.

- *ActiveX control*   A COM component that has a graphical interface. These controls are hosted within a client application's presentation space.

- *ActiveX document EXE*   Hybrid standard EXEs, which can be hosted within a Web browser. This concept has not caught on, partially because it can run only in certain ActiveX document containers. The currently available container applications are Office Binders, Visual Basic Tools Windows, and Internet Explorer 3.0 or later.

- *ActiveX document DLL*   The same as the ActiveX Document EXE, except that they run in the calling program's process.

- *IIS application*   A very easy way to write business components to be run on Microsoft Internet Information Server. Often referred to as *Web Classes,* these components combine compiled Visual Basic code and HTML. All of the code runs on the server dynamically, sending code to the client and then processing requests as they are returned from that code. The VB code and HTML is very tightly coupled. This type of project produces code that is optimized for IIS and browser independence.

- *DHTML application*   Very similar to ActiveX documents in terms of functionality and client requirements, DHTML applications only run in Internet Explorer 4.0 or later. They provide functionality that lets the client Web pages take on heightened levels of interactivity.

As you can see, Visual Basic provides functionality in a number of ways. With so many options, how does one choose the best option? In this book we will cover creating a standard EXE with calls into the business logic tier across the Internet, ActiveX controls hosted in DHTML pages, and ActiveX DLLs for building business and data objects.

2

Visual Basic Versus C++

I often hear developers debating the merits of using VB versus C++. I used to develop in C++ and now the majority of my time is spent developing in Visual Basic. I can tell you that Visual Basic is a very quick, high-level language that comes close to—and in some instances—beats C++ in performance. This is because both Version 6 of Visual C++ and Visual Basic share the same compiler. I find that I can develop components four times faster with Visual Basic, and, when the name of the game is "time-to-market," this is a winning strategy. If bottlenecks do occur, Visual Studio has a number of tools to profile an application and determine which components are executing slowly. After a careful review of the slow components, I might rewrite them in C++ if I can find a benefit in doing so. Another reason to write in C++ is to perform operations that are close to the hardware or operating system. Often C++ is used to write the high-level COM components favored by application developers. Also C++ is the only language that you can currently develop free threading components. However, on Day 14, "Best Practices and Other Services," you will learn about how the new capabilities of Visual Basic 7 will eliminate these differences.

Server-Side Scriptlets

Server-side scriptlets allow you to run scripts on the server by making calls from the client. This has the benefit of hiding the script logic and reduces the network overhead required to ship the script code to the client for processing. The downside is that the client needs to have the ability to call scriptlets, which is a capability found only in Internet Explorer 4.0 or later. Network latency can also slow down responsiveness.

NEW TERM *Network latency* is the accumulated delays caused by the network routing equipment as a message travels between computers. In this case if the network is running slow, then the delays can add unacceptable wait times to the processing because a trip needs to be made to the server and back in order to run a scriptlet.

CORBA and ORBs

There is one other component architecture used by non-Microsoft platforms, called Common Object Request Broker Architecture (CORBA). CORBA has not gained the popularity of COM, yet it is an important interface to support if you need to interact with non-Microsoft systems. The easiest way to achieve this interactivity is to use a COM-CORBA bridge. Several bridges are available that allow objects built with these two component architectures to communicate. These bridges are often referred to as Object Request Brokers (ORBs).

On Day 14, you will read about SOAP, which is a new protocol that is positioned to replace Distributed COM (DCOM) and CORBA as a way to run objects on distributed systems.

Data Tier

The data tier encompasses a large number of data sources. These sources can be relational databases, directory services, messaging systems, legacy systems, or user-defined data providers. The data tier is actually the COM interfaces to these data stores. The components in this tier ensure data integrity and provide a consistent interface.

Transactions

2

When we talk about transactions we are referring to several individual tasks grouped together as a single unit of work where all tasks successfully complete or all fail. The classic example is when you transfer money from one account to another. This includes two tasks, taking money out of one account and putting it into another. If the first task worked and the second did not this would not be fair. So in this case the money would be returned to the first account. A transaction coordinator oversees all tasks that are considered to be running as a transaction. The transaction coordinator uses what is known as a two phase commit. In the first phase all the tasks are run and report success or failure to the transaction coordinator. If they all succeed, then in phase two, the transaction coordinator instructs the data stores to commit the changes to the database. If any of the tasks fail, then in phase two, the transaction coordinator instructs the data store to roll back the data store to the previous state before the task.

Transactions are critical to any system because they provide the mechanisms to ensure that units of work complete as expected in order to ensure system integrity. Transactional systems use the "ACID" test to define the general characteristics of a transactional system:

- A for *Atomic*   This is the all-or-nothing characteristic of a transaction. Either all the steps in the transaction complete successfully or else the system is returned to its previous state before the transaction began.

- C for *Consistent*   A transaction is consistent if it resolves the data state in the same way every time and always leaves the data integrity preserved.

- I for *Isolated*   This is the capability to hide the work of the transaction from other transactions. Isolation must be enforced at both the database and component levels. The work of the transaction needs to be hidden so that other transactions do not act upon data that has not yet been committed by the transaction.

- D for *Durable*   It is critical that, after the transaction is committed, the results of the transaction are permanent modifications to the database.

Transaction coordination is critical when a unit of work spans a variety of data stores.

XML: Use It in All Tiers to Handle Data

Extensible Markup Language (XML) has become a very hot technology because it allows data to move across the Internet as text. Along with the data goes the field names and hierarchical relationships of the fields to each other. This structure that flows with the XML data is called the schema. It is like sending a letter to someone in another country and including a dictionary that defines each word in the letter. XML uses the same syntax as HTML, except that the tag names are defined by the user, and the syntax is much stricter. We will spend all of Day 12, "The Power of XML," discussing XML and its supporting technology.

By using a combination of HTML and XML, you can create a dynamic Web site. You do this by representing the changeable data on the Web page as XML. You represent the format and layout of the page in HTML. You then merge the two files to produce a very flexible set of Web pages. We will see how this is done in Day 12.

Many databases can return data that is already marked up in XML format. ADO 2.1 and later can convert its recordset to and from XML, enabling data in any data store to be represented as XML. Throughout this book you will see how XML can be used effectively at every level within the Windows DNA architecture.

On Day 14 you will see how XML is being used in many ways to make the Windows DNA more robust. For example you learn about BizTalk Server that can take data in many different formats and transform it into XML. BizTalk Server uses XML as the native format for internal use as well as a way to interact with other Microsoft servers. You will also see how XML is being used to remotely invoke services on other systems using a standard called SOAP.

Begin with Scalability in Mind

Scalability is the name of the game when it comes to Internet application development. Scalability refers to the applications ability to easily grow with an increasing work load without having to rewrite the application. In the past you had a sense of the limits within which your application must scale. For example, if your company has 1,000 employees, you could plan for a worst case scenario on 1,000 users maximum. Move that application to the Internet—now what is your upper limit? Millions of users. How do you even start planning for such a massive number of users? The answer is to build your application in such a way that you can simply add more hardware and the application will scale up automatically to the new capacity. The Windows DNA architecture is designed to do just this type of scaling. The best part is that scaling is virtually automatic when you follow the Windows DNA architecture. The system services that support your application in conjunction with the NT operating system can automatically adapt.

Scalability Is Expensive

Even though scalability has been made easy for you by Microsoft's inclusion of scalability within the NT operating system and supporting services, it does not mean that a price isn't paid. To achieve scalability you need to do thorough analysis and design. Day 3 covers this very important area. Taking the time to ensure the analysis and design are correct can pay off big down the road by having much less rework to do.

After you know what you want to develop, you need to develop your application using efficient, effective code. The development chapters of this book give insights into the best practices for writing good code. You can write very straightforward code after you understand how to use the objects and services provided by Microsoft.

Fast Servers

Hardware speed is one of the determining factors of application scalability. Obtaining suitable hardware often is the answer to scalability issues. Some people will argue that rewriting the code in C++ or assembler can improve performance, and they are correct. However, a cost-benefit analysis would clearly show that it is far more economical to throw hardware at the problem before trying to rewrite code. You will also find that the number of lines of code you actually write will be small when you use the components and technology provided by the NT operating system and supporting services. The best pieces of code are ones you do not need to write. Therefore, a best practice is to use the objects provided by Microsoft; they are the ones that are best integrated and tested with Microsoft's operating systems and services.

Fast Code

I do not want to imply that code execution speed is not important. An application with performance problems isn't considered very usable. Performance strongly affects how users perceive the application. Companies turn to developers to locate and repair performance problems, which can be difficult to pinpoint. It can be hard to identify exactly which part of the code is causing the problem. The growing complexity of applications is making it even more difficult to track down performance bottlenecks. Developers can end up spending valuable time tuning performance in the wrong areas of an application.

A number of tools are available to help identify performance bottlenecks. Microsoft provides a number of tools that monitor the execution speed of code so that users can identify and perhaps eliminate bottlenecks.

Application Performance Explorer

Application Performance Explorer (APE) is a tool found in the Enterprise Edition of Visual Studio 6. APE allows you to run various what-if scenarios against your system to test the resource consumption.

Application Performance Explorer (APE) models your application design and tests the expected performance and interactions of a distributed architecture. With APE, you can understand the consequences of certain design choices and test design alternatives as you tune your application's performance. You can automate the tests, scheduling them for certain times of day to experience peak network traffic or other throughput parameters. Additionally, you can modify APE's source code for customized performance testing.

Many developers are unfamiliar with the system loads and requirements of the various implementation options with distributed applications. APE allows you to try the various options and observe what the effect is upon the system.

Visual Studio Analyzer

Another tool available in the Enterprise version of Visual Studio 6 in the Visual Studio Analyzer. Understanding what a distributed application is doing means understanding the application's structure and flow. Visual Studio Analyzer can show you all the components and communications in your application, plot them in a diagram, and annotate the diagram with detailed information. You or your development team can use Visual Studio Analyzer to help new team members understand the application you are building.

As a debugging tool, Visual Studio Analyzer helps you locate which component is causing problems. Visual Studio Analyzer provides a complete view, at a central location, of all the components and communications in your application. You can watch your application execute in real-time, or you can record a session of your application and play it back. At any point you can request detailed information on a specific component. Visual Studio Analyzer makes it easier for you to identify a problem component, and to use your debugging resources in the most cost-effective way.

You can use the Visual Studio Analyzer views at two different points in the application life cycle:

- In real-time, as the application executes.
- After the application finishes, for postmortem analysis, provided you have collected data while the application executed.

Isolating faults typically involves both real-time and postmortem (after the application crashes and dies) analysis. You run the application, browse through the Visual Studio Analyzer views to understand what happened, and set breakpoints on individual lines of code with a traditional debugging tool. When your application reaches a breakpoint, it suspends execution. You then switch to Visual Studio Analyzer and play back what has happened so far. When you locate a possible problem within a single component, you switch to your traditional debugging tool to identify the problem.

Performance analysis almost always happens after an application has finished running. Several Visual Studio Analyzer views analyze how much time each piece of an application required to execute. Visual Studio Analyzer shows in which pieces of code time was spent using a line chart, Gantt chart, and timeline view.

Although knowing where in the code time was spent is useful, you might be interested in other information as well. For example, did a particular SQL query take a long time because it was complex and time-consuming, or because the machine that runs it was very busy handling many requests? To address these types of questions, you can collect information from Windows NT Performance Monitor counters while your application is executing. You can, for example, collect the current load on the database machine every few seconds. By looking at the Performance Monitor information at the time the application was executing, you can get additional information about performance bottlenecks.

NuMega TrueTime

Another non-Microsoft tool I use is NuMega TrueTime. TrueTime adds instrumentation to code so that you know the exact true execution time of your code. TrueTime allows you to measure execution times down to the line level. TrueTime is a good tool to use after you have identified slow-running components with Visual Studio Analyzer.

Load Balancing

Microsoft provides three types of load balancing capabilities that allow you to scale your system up by adding more computers to the system. The three types of load balancing capabilities are; Windows Load Balancing Services (WLBS), Cluster Services, and Component Load Balancing Services (CLBS).

Windows Load Balancing Services

Windows Load Balancing Services (WLBS) allows request to the web server to be balanced between up to 32 web servers. WLBS is included with Windows NT 4.0 Advance Server and Windows 2000 Server. It is a software load balancing service that balances traffic by using a round-robin approach. For this reason you do not want to keep state on the web server because you can not be assured that you will get the same server between requests. The WLBS that comes with Windows 2000 does have the ability to set an affinity that allows you to configure it so that the same IP address or entire class C address goes to the same server every time in the event that you want to maintain server state. However, the use of affinity has many limitations, for example if you are behind a firewall the client IP address is abstracted that is the reason for the class C capability. The class C affinity has limitations because it limits the number of concurrent sessions to 255, which is not enough for many sites. The best solution is not to maintain state on the web server.

Cluster Services

Clustering services is the capability to have two to four computers acting as one unit. The purpose of a cluster is to provide fail-over support between the computers in the cluster. The clustered computers have identical software configurations and keep each other updated as to their status. If a computer fails to report then the other computers remove it from the cluster and assume the handling of all the traffic. Two types of clustering exist, active – active and active – passive. With active – active clustering both computers share the workload in normal operations. With active – passive only one computer does the work and the other runs in stand-by mode waiting for the other to fail. Most services run as active – active, however, a few, like SQL Server need to run as active – passive.

Component Load Balancing Services

Component Load Balancing Services (CLBS) is a feature that was in Windows 2000 through beta 3 and then was pulled out to become a feature of Application Center 2000. What is nice about CLB is that it works at the component level to distribute processing across several computers. The way that it works is that components are configured to work with CLBS. What that means is that COM+ will collect performance information on the component. The next step is to register the component on all of the computers that you intend to include in the CLBS. Now that the components are in place you need to configure the Application Center Load Balancing Router WLBR). One computer in the system takes on the responsibility as the load balancing router. On the WLBR you provide a list of all the servers within the system that you wish to run components remotely. The term for this grouping of servers is an Application Center Cluster. The Application Center cluster should not be confused with clustering services. The CLBR then communicates with these computers collecting performance information about the components on that system. When a request for component services arrives at the CLBR it dispatches the request to the least busy computer. By doing this it ensures that the system delivers the best performance.

The obvious advantage of all of these load balancing capabilities is that you can almost linearly increase the capacity of your system by adding more computers to the system.

Typical DNA Configurations

Although you can run a Windows DNA application on a single computer, this is not always the best configuration for testing. You should have a test environment which is representative of your final configurations so that you will be able to see the true network and system service impacts of your application.

The ideal configuration would consist of the following group of computers:

- *Client PCs configured to represent your target users*   If you will have multiple target configurations, you might want to have a system for each. You will need several client machines when you start running stress tests. Make sure you test various speeds and software configurations.

- *A business server for each of the BackOffice products you will be using*   For example, if you use SQL Server and Exchange, you will need a minimum of three computers, one running NT and IIS, one running NT and SQL Server, and one running NT and Exchange. You'll want to separate the services out onto their own machines so that each has its own resource and configuration requirements. When multiple services are installed on a single computer, the services often fight for resources. By having the services isolated on their own computers, you can get true measurements on the actual system performance and resource requirements.

    If you will be running load balancing services then you will need additional computers to configure and test the load balancing capabilities of the system.

- *A performance monitoring computer*   Again, you can run the performance monitor on each server. However, you will also incur the additional overhead of the performance monitoring processing, which can skew your results. By having a single computer doing the monitoring, you will also keep a unified timeline so that you can see how the interactions between the systems affect each other.

Development, Staging, and Production Servers

As mentioned in Day 1, the three levels of deployment are development, stage, and production. Development happens on your workstation, which is running all the services within the system on a single computer. This allows you to develop components isolated from the rest of the team. You would also employ a development central server, a storage and exchange point for all the developers. You could copy components that other developers have promoted to the central server to your local development machine so that you can keep up to date with the latest changes. When you complete a component, you would deploy it to the central development server so that it could be tested interactively with other components.

When the development effort is complete and the development team members feel that the code is relatively bug free, they will deploy the code to a staging server. This server is a copy of the production system which includes all the applications in addition to yours. The staging server is the place to do final testing and resource monitoring before the application rolls into production.

After it has been determined that the application is a good citizen on the staging server and that it is performing as expected, it is rolled out to production for the world to have at it.

The Future of DNA

Windows DNA is a platform, not a single technology or architecture. The Windows DNA platform evolves as IT needs and technologies evolve. For example, in 1998 when Windows DNA was introduced, it was very focused on aligning Microsoft's various tools and technologies into a single solution architecture. Early implementation efforts to develop Windows DNA applications uncovered many issues such as "DLL Hell," solution development complexity, and scalability problems with the NT 4 operating system. I understand that these problems got raised to the highest levels at Microsoft and they were resolved in Windows 2000.

To make development easier and scalability better, COM+ now offers Transaction Server (MTS), Message Queue (MSMQ), and some new capabilities. This enhancement is really great news because it automatically makes your components enterprise strength. Components that are built with COM+ automatically receive attributes that you would have previously had to enable by hand. With COM+, you can spend less time building the foundation of the component and more time on its higher-level purpose.

The rise of the Internet has also affected the focus and shape of .NET Platform. Every service and BackOffice product has been changed to support the requirements of Windows 2000 and the Internet. For example, every product supports Internet formats such as XML. New protocols like Simple Object Access Protocol (SOAP) and servers like BizTalk are being developed and adopted to support this new Internet based foundation. .NET Platform has taken on a services oriented direction; however, it does not replace the Windows DNA development architecture that is detailed in this book.

Windows 2000

Windows 2000 is a major upgrade of Microsoft Windows. At first glance it might appear to be a minor upgrade of NT 4 with some added new services. In actuality much of the internal plumbing has either been updated or ripped out and millions of lines of new code have been added to address the limitations of the previous versions. Enhancements have been made to virtually every component of the operating system—extending the performance, reliability, security, and management features and incorporating major usability features, new hardware support, and new media capabilities.

The major areas that have been changed include the following:

- The registry has been replaced with an Active Directory. The Active Directory, unlike the registry, is fast, expansive, compliant to LDAP standards, and accessible. LDAP stands for Lightweight Directory Access Protocol, and it is a standard for sharing directory information. By consolidating the configuration and user information from all the system applications, the Active Directory enables better interoperability between applications and better management of user and configuration information.

- The system now tracks and manages multiple versions of components and ensures that the correct version is used with an application.

- Hardware management details have been improved and a stricter standard for hardware vendors has been established in terms of driver design and development. The results are better operational stability. For example, the number of reboots required has been minimized.

COM+

COM+ is the other enabler for the future of Windows DNA. By beefing up COM and the system services that support COM to add extensibility and self-management to the system, Microsoft gives developers new possibilities. COM+ can intercept and redirect functionality to call various services at runtime, rather than being bound to a single service. Interceptors can receive and process events related to instance creation, calls and returns, errors, and instance deletion. Interceptors provide the means to implement transaction and system monitoring. Interception allows the system to better manage itself. COM+ will be covered in detail in Week 2.

Application Center 2000

Application Center 2000 is a new service that allows the system to be centrally monitored, managed, and supported. For Windows 2000 to be enterprise class, it must have automated management, scalability, and recovery capabilities. Additionally the applications running on the system must be included in the system's fail-over and recovery activities. Application Center 2000 is the coordination point for application load balancing and fail-over.

Summary

Today, we took a closer look at the Windows DNA tiers and the tools, technologies, and services that support this architecture. You learned that you have a wide range of user interface options depending upon the target audience's abilities. You learned about the trade-offs between the richness and reach of the presentation tier. You learned how COM objects are the building blocks for the business tier and how scripts are the glue that holds these blocks together. Regarding the data tier, you learned that you have a wide range of data store options and that OLE DB and ADO give you universal access to these data stores through a consistent interface.

You learned more about the supporting system services in Windows NT and how they work, how to monitor and profile them, and how they will be improved in Windows 2000. You learned about the development tools and some of the fundamental Windows DNA development philosophies such as using the services provided by the system instead of developing your own. You learned about tools to monitor and tune your application.

Q&A

Q Can components in the business tier be transactional?

A Actually yes they can through the use of transaction server. Typically, the transaction will eventually involve some data tier components. To use transaction server you register your COM components with Transaction Server. Using Transaction Server will be covered later in this book.

Q Why is a rich client presentation less expensive to develop than a reach client?

A Although simpler in their presentation, reach clients require a much greater number of supporting Web pages and thus extensive workflow logic that takes more time and effort than rich clients do. In contrast, a rich client is self-contained in a single client application.

Q Compare and contrast client-side versus server-side scripting.

A Client-side scripting validates input from the user and dynamically modifies the presentation. Server-side scripting coordinates the interaction between components.

Q What are the benefits of ASPs over ISAPI and CGI?

A ASPs are implemented as a flexible ISAPI filter that processes scripted logic. As a multithreaded ISAPI filter, ASPs benefit by running in the same processing space as the Web service. Because an ASP is a script engine, it does not need to be recompiled to add new functionality. ASPs excel over CGI in that they are standardized and managed by the system services allowing them to work more efficiently than a one-time CGI program.

Q Why is transactional support essential to a Windows DNA system?

A Transactional support provides the mechanism to ensure that the system's integrity stays intact. Transactions ensure reliable, consistent results every time.

Q Why is XML so special?

A XML enables any data to be represented and transported across the Internet. XML is self-defining; each end needs have minimal knowledge of the other system in order to work with the data. XML improves the opportunities for application and business-to-business interoperability. XML is a foundational technology for all future Microsoft technologies and services.

Workshop

The Workshop provides quiz questions to help you solidify your understanding of the material covered and exercises to provide you with experience in using what you've learned. Try to understand the quiz and exercise answers before continuing to the next lesson. Answers are provided in Appendix A.

Quiz

1. What are the presentation options available to a Windows DNA application?
2. What are the scripting languages available in Windows DNA?
3. What are the two types of components supported by Internet Explorer?
4. What is the difference between ActiveX components and ActiveX controls?
5. What are the two performance tools provided in Visual Studio 6 Enterprise Edition?

Exercises

1. Run the Application Performance Explorer and try various application design scenarios. What kind of results did you get?
2. Launch Visual Basic and notice all the different types of applications the wizard can create for you. Try creating a standard EXE, an ActiveX DLL and an IIS application. How do they differ?

DAY 3

Architecting a Windows DNA Solution

Today's lesson will teach you some analysis and design techniques that are useful in architecting your solution. You will practice these techniques by working through a sample Windows DNA application process. You will continue to develop this application throughout the book. This chapter is very important because it teaches the tools and techniques necessary to develop the blueprint that you and the development team will use to build the solution.

Before you actually begin to build your application, make sure that you fully understand what the application needs to do and how you will achieve this functionality. Today, you are going to gather user requirements, analyze them, and then map those requirements into a Windows DNA solution. The first part of the process is commonly referred to as *analysis*, and the second part is known as *design*. Solution options are numerous, and it is critical that you can select the right one. You want to ensure that the solution you develop is reliable, available, scalable, and interoperable with other systems. Therefore, today you will learn the following in order to develop these solutions:

- Developing a business case
- Analyzing the problem
- Defining the business process
- Defining object/data requirements
- Defining use cases and sequence diagrams
- Mapping the solution to the Windows DNA architecture

Performing Analysis

Analysis is the most important part of the application building process. Yet, in many applications, it is often skipped or done hastily. There is a common joke that if you put programmers on a job without specifications, you would still get code (a program). I have to admit I have, in the past, raced through the analysis phase so I could get to the "real tangible work," only to find that I must revisit the code repeatedly to fix omissions. In the end, it would have taken far less time and effort if I had done thorough analysis upfront.

Of course, there is another extreme known as "paralysis by analysis." This occurs when the analysis takes so long that the problem domain keeps changing. In such a case, you might need to reduce the scope to a manageable effort. A typical rule of thumb is to use three-by-three time boxing. You divide the work so three people can achieve the result in three months.

If enterprise applications are very complex, you might ask, "How can I be expected to do a reasonably good job with a limited effort?" The answer is to use the object-oriented tools, methods, and techniques presented today to derive reasonable specifications for application designers. In this book, you will wear all the hats. In the real world, the role of analyst can be a full-time job. Certainly, after reading this chapter, if you are interested in analysis (or any other aspect of the work described here), you can read more about its particular tools and techniques.

Business Case

The first task in the analysis process is to develop a business case. A business case answers these questions:

What business need are we trying to meet?

What customer need are we trying to provide for?

What will be the required investment?

What is the expected return on this investment?

What are the risks and benefits?

These are the kinds of questions that company executives ask, and the ones you must be prepared to answer to their satisfaction in order to get your project funded. This is not a time to talk technology, at least not in depth. A business case presents to management the problem that needs to be solved along with the best solution to this problem. You might want to discuss the advantages and disadvantages of other solutions so that management can see that you have thoroughly considered all the options. This is especially important if you know that management is considering or favoring other solutions. Your proposed solution should be backed up by thoughtful cost/benefit analysis, as well as a risk analysis.

Risks are of two types: business and technical. Business risks are categorized as financial cost, revenue, corporate image, and customer service. Technical risks are categorized as technological change, technological immaturity, skilled labor shortage, and obsolescence.

Business Risks

The following list explores some of the business risks that might be encountered while creating a business case. These are some items you must take into account as you generate a plan that will be acceptable to you and the business's management team.

- *Financial cost* refers to the money that must be invested to develop the solution. It represents a risk because money is being committed to develop the solution. The cost of the project comes directly off the organization's bottom-line profits. You need to have good, sound financial justification in order to get your project approved. If the organization falls on hard times, it might need to reclaim the budgeted funds, in essence, halting the project without realizing the expected returns. Funding can be withdrawn for other reasons as well, such as the problem going away or it being solved through another solution.

- *Revenue* refers to the fact that if the solution does not solve the problem, then revenue could be affected. Revenue is lost when customers are lost or new customers are not coming to the organization or customers spend less with your organization. Generally revenue loss is a low risk; on the other hand, revenue growth is a benefit.

- *Corporate image* refers to how the organization is perceived by others. This is very important for publicly held companies because the perception of the organization affects the stock price. For example, getting the organization on the Internet can cost a great deal and produce no revenue and yet be a good thing because it might cause the stock price to rise. This would increase the value of the corporation to stakeholders.

- *Customer service* refers to how the project affects the organization's capability to serve its customers. This is a very important issue because it affects many of the other risk areas. For example, your solution could improve customer service efficiency, thus reducing customer service head count and cost. Good customer service can increase revenue and improve corporate image.

Technical Risks

Technical risks are the biggest problems most projects face. In fact, many solution development projects are never completed or are killed because of technical risks. The following list highlights some of the more common technical risks you might encounter.

- *Technological change* refers to the rate at which the technology is evolving. For example, the Internet has been evolving at such a fast pace that solutions need constant updating to stay current. Windows DNA is, as we have seen, a way to keep pace with the change.

  The way to mitigate this risk is to hire consultants who are experienced with the technology to review and validate the solution design.

- *Technological immaturity* refers to a technology's capability to deliver on its intended benefits. It is a well-known fact that most Microsoft technologies don't really stabilize until around version three. If the solution uses new technology, be prepared for the possibility that it might not deliver the intended results. Your solution might also fall into the technologically immature category if this is the first time you are developing this type of solution.

  To mitigate immaturity risks, hire consultants to assess the technology and work with the testing organizations to identify possible problem areas and propose corrections and contingency plans.

- *Skilled labor shortage* refers to the ability to find people with the required skills to build and maintain a solution. For all the previous technical risks, it is difficult to find skilled resources in new technologies. Often, a technology is so new that no time has elapsed for a consulting base to develop. In this case, if a vendor has a consulting organization, it may be your only option.

  You have two options to mitigate this risk. You can have developers train in the new technology, or you could contract already trained, usually vendor-provided developers for the development phase.

- *Obsolescence* refers to the possibility of the solution architecture becoming obsolete. I can think of two recent examples of this happening. In the first, a national network of real estate brokers was in year three of a four-year, $15 million client/server development effort when the Internet took off. To the brokers' credit, at $12 million into the project, they realized that the Internet made their solution obsolete. They quickly redesigned for the Internet, and one year and $2 million later, they had a new solution. In the second case a higher education institution was rebuilding a new system in Smalltalk when Java came out and overnight killed Smalltalk. The project was dropped and an off-the-shelf package was selected. In both of these cases, you can see how neither of these situations could have been anticipated.

In your business case you want to make sure that you have considered the various risks. By doing this you will be prepared to answer any concerns that the project sponsors might raise.

3

A Business Scenario

First, you will create your business scenario. A business scenario states the facts about the background and reason for the problem. You develop a business scenario by interviewing key people to get a good perspective on the problem and the various issues being faced in different areas within the organization. Typically you will want to conduct one-on-one interviews with the stakeholders so that you can uncover issues that might not come out in a group meeting. Later in the process you might want to start conducting *Joint Application Development* (JAD) sessions, to which you invite subject matter specialists to provide specific information.

NEW TERM *Joint Application Development* (JAD) session is a technique developed by IBM Canada in the 1970s to quickly gather requirements for applications. The technique is used often and sometimes goes under a variation on the name, like *Joint Applications Requirements* (JAR) session or *Facilitated Sessions*. The key players in a JAD are the facilitator, participants, and scribe. The job of the facilitator is to provide non-biased direction to the participants and to ensure that a consensus is reached. The scribe is responsible for documenting the activities of the session to provide a transcript of what was said and done for later reference.

The people you will be interviewing for the business scenario will be the sponsors of the JAD but are unlikely to be attendees. A sponsor very often will kick off the JAD with a speech to inform the participants of the objective and the importance of what they are being empowered to develop. When you have questions or concerns about the business case, consult with your sponsors; they are the one group that ultimately needs to be satisfied with the case presented.

Caution   Make sure that you get explicit consensus on everything from all participants in a facilitated session. Take a vote or have them verbally agree. Don't
assume consensus from a nod or anything else that can be disputed as
agreement. Some participants will be making concessions and you want it
noted that they explicitly agreed to those concessions. By securing these
agreements, you avoid problems later.

Typical Business Case Scenario Questions

The business case scenario seeks to answer a number of questions that the business sponsors might have. Some general questions are

   What is the problem to be solved?

   What are the business requirements?

   What are the customer quality requirements?

   What will be the impacts of adding new technology?

   Who is the audience?

   Are there any organizational constraints?

   Are there any political issues?

   How quickly does the solution need to be implemented?

   What are the security requirements?

   Are there any government or regulatory constraints?

This is a good list of questions to get you started thinking about the issues of developing
a solution. Not all the questions will apply to your situation, nor have all situations been
addressed in this list. Work with your sponsor(s) to ensure you understand their issues
and be prepared to address their concerns. Also, anticipate questions and be prepared to
answer them.

The easiest way to understand a business case scenario is to see one, so here is the business case scenario for the application developed in this book.

Smalltown Bank Is Expanding

Smalltown, USA is experiencing tremendous growth because of a recent influx of high-
tech firms. Smalltown's city planners have done a great job of giving Smalltown a high-
technology infrastructure, ensuring that all households have low-cost, high-speed

Asynchronous Digital Subscription Lines (ADSL) access to the Internet. The new high-tech workers are very comfortable conducting their business online.

Smalltown Bank (STB) wants to retain and expand its customer base by making all its services available via the Internet. STB currently has an open licensing agreement with Microsoft and is very happy using Microsoft products in its business. You have been hired to design, build, and implement a solution based upon Microsoft technology. You decide that Windows DNA will be the best architecture for this solution.

You start by defining the business requirements. You conduct interviews with the CEO, CIO, MIS director, and a customer focus group. They tell you the following:

- *CEO.*   We have always been a small town bank, serving the local farm community. However, with the recent influx of high-technology businesses, our customers want to be able to work with the bank via the Internet. We added an ATM a few years back, and that was a great improvement for our customers. However, we see more of our customers switching to Bigtown Bank because it offers online banking. Bigtown does not even have a branch here in Smalltown; this does not seem to bother the customers. We feel we need to get online fast with basic banking services and then grow the online service offering over time.

   I am also concerned with security; we need to protect our customers and the bank from computer hackers and other malicious attacks.

   The solution you create must insulate the user from our back-end computers. You need to put in place rules that limit the amount and types of transactions users conduct over the Internet and that alert our MIS department to any deviations from these rules.

- *CIO.*   We are a small town bank, but we have very talented IT professionals. They are loyal and hard working. Our main systems currently run on a DEC VAX. We have a 100MB Ethernet network, and we use Cisco routers for the entire network. The database is Oracle 7, and all the applications are developed in-house. We also have a number of adjunct systems running Windows NT. These NT systems act as file servers for all the bank's computers. All the bank's workstations run Windows NT workstations, with Office 2000 installed. We have an Exchange server that handles all email within the bank, as well as provides us access to customers via the Internet. The Internet connection is through a Microsoft Proxy Server connection and a Cisco router.

   We currently have a Web site that is hosted by a local ISP. The IT staff really likes working with Windows NT. Several of them have formed a study group, have become Microsoft Certified System Engineers, and are working on becoming Microsoft Certified Solution Developers. The application development environment we use for NT is Visual Studio. Most of the applications are written in Visual Basic.

3

I understand the CEO's concern about getting our business online, but I want to make sure that our systems are protected from attack from the outside world. The FDIC requires that all banking transactions that use the Internet must be encrypted.

I would prefer that the new system does not directly transact with the DEC VAX. I would like to have a shadow database that has a snapshot of the online users' account data. This should synchronize with the DEC through a daily process. I also want detailed transaction logs so that we have a record to fall back on if any disputes arise.

We are not sure how much our customers will use this new system. I want you to build it in a way that will accommodate scaling and fault tolerance, and is maintainable by our MIS staff. The banking industry is very highly regulated. Because of this, rules change—often with short time frames to delivery. The new system should be built in a way that enables us to make changes easily to the system without having to overhaul the other pieces.

We also need to have multiple interface programs. For example, the bank staff will want a full 32-bit client application that's very efficient to use. Our customers have a wide range of browsers, so I would like the customer interface to use the full power of the browser and degrade gracefully for less-powerful browsers. Did I mention that everyone in the bank has Office 2000? The CEO really likes viewing things in Outlook 2000. Do you think we can give him access via Outlook?

Finally we need to keep the costs in line. Yes, we are a bank but all this money is not ours. We have to invest wisely. Ideally, I want this to start out small in a very short time frame and then expand and enhance the system as more and more users access the system.

- *MIS Director.* My staff and I are very excited about developing this new system with you; we have been developing small productivity applications with Visual Basic, but we have not, to date, developed anything as large as this new application. We have a diverse set of talents in the department. Some of our people are very data oriented; others are more focused on the business logic; others have a flare for presentation and usability. We feel comfortable using Microsoft Visual Studio and Microsoft BackOffice.

- *Customer focus group members.* Our companies provide us with the best technologies at home so that we can telecommute to work. We are comfortable with conducting business on the Internet, as long as the company takes precautions to ensure that the network is secure and that there are good authentication policies.

    Just because a company offers Web access does not mean that we will use the service. The service must be easy and quick to use. Efficiency is very important to us.

Analyzing the Problem

Now that you understand the business case, you must propose a solution. In order to propose a solution, you must understand the business processes, as well as the way that a user will interact with the system. Again, you want to try to answer questions similar to the following:

What is the current technology platform?

What will be the impacts of adding new technology?

How willing is the organization to accept technology?

What are the training needs?

How quickly does the solution need to be implemented?

Are there any dependencies for the solution to work? What are they?

What are the security requirements?

What are the maintenance requirements?

Are there any government or regulatory constraints?

How cost effective is the solution?

You will notice many of the questions are repeated from the discussion of the business case perspective. Now they are being considered from a solution perspective. For example, the question of government regulatory constraints in the business case scenario mentioned that federal regulations require all banking transactions on the Internet to be secure. In the problem analysis phase, you discover that strong encryption is required and thus put it into the specifications.

The process of analysis requires that you understand the desired future state and the current state so that you can then develop a plan for the transition between these two states.

The goal here is to understand the current systems by looking at the business process, systems, and activities. You then determine how closely they meet the desired future state. You can use your understanding of the current system to design the changes needed to implement the new solution. If you fail to understand the current systems and processes, you risk incompatibility, and you might waste time and effort building something that already exists, or create political problems for your solution. Political problems that could occur include that your solution might go against the agenda of someone high up within the organization. If you do not have your facts straight, superiors could use that weakness to shut down your project. Another common political problem is that you might not get complete buy-in from the top. Subsequently, when you go to deploy, and technical difficulties cause the solution to have some rough spots, no one is willing to stand behind you through the difficulties, and the project is scrapped.

When looking to solve a problem you should always look to see whether a packaged solution exists before deciding to build one in-house. Packaged solutions generally cost less, have more dedicated resources working on the solution, can be implemented quicker, and reduce your risk. Of course, in this book we are going to build a solution to show you the tools and processes for doing so. Having an understanding of how robust solutions are built can help you when selecting a package because you will be able to ask more insightful questions about the packages.

Defining Business Processes

When you define business processes, you want to document the future desired business processes. You also want to document the current business processes. Once you understand both the future state and the current state you can develop the transition plan. The transition plan can range anywhere from simple system upgrades to a complete process re-engineering. It should be noted that Internet commerce has really caused radical changes in business process. So don't be surprised if you are starting with fresh business processes.

The way that you define an existing business process is to first determine if documented processes exist. If so, you can start with them. The next step is to interview the subject matter experts to validate the process. If the processes are not documented, then this is the time to document them. Now you know the current processes.

Next you need to determine the future state. If you are new to the problem domain, the first thing you need to do is become knowledgeable about the solution space. For example, if you are asked to develop an online banking capability, you may want to visit other banks' online systems to see how they operate. If packages already exist to provide this capability, you can visit the other banks' Web sites or request literature to learn how they solved the problem. Often times, businesses have white papers and other backgrounders that can teach you a great deal about the particular problem domain. Armed with this knowledge you can start crafting the information gathered from the requirements gathering sessions and current process information into a solution. Often times, you can use JAD as a way to involve subject matter experts and stakeholders in the process.

Gathering Smalltown Bank's Business Requirements

Now that you have been introduced to business processes, let's look at the requirements and information needed for the Smalltown bank project. The following material in this section is the information you gathered about Smalltown Bank's business.

The bank is very batch oriented. Every night, processes are run on the DEC to verify the daily activity and to post cleared checks, deposits, and transfers to customer accounts. The process is fairly straightforward. The bank receives a feed from the central bank with all the activity that has taken place against customer accounts at other financial institutions. The bank runs the central bank transactions against the bank accounts and prepares a response file for the central bank—accepting or declining the transaction requests. This process is fairly well established on the VAX, and nothing in the new application seems to require a change in this process. However, whatever is done with the new system needs to coordinate with the VAX. This will ensure that all activity is in the VAX before the central bank reconciliation process. After reconciliation, the online system must reflect the changes.

The new system introduces a new complexity to the bank, that of offering 24-hour banking. The ATM system is similar, except that the ATM vendor provides a turnkey solution that integrates well with Smalltown Bank's current system. During the batch process, the ATM does inquiries against the system. This ensures that the user has sufficient funds, but it also creates a transaction log. The log is run against the system after the nightly updates, effectively posting the ATM activity to the next day. It would be best if the online system did something similar.

The bank employees must perform the same tasks as the customers, as well as some special processing. Because the online system will be a subset of the main system, for now, the main system consoles will be sufficient for the special tasks. To provide support for investigation of disputes, the employees should also have the ability to view the detailed audit logs for any customer.

Defining Object/Data Requirements

The identification of the objects in your system is very important because they determine the entities you will be working with when defining the new process. Objects are system representations of the entities that will be interacting. Identifying the right objects can be difficult; one trick that I use is to look at the nouns used when talking about the business. The objective is to anthropomorphize the system so that you can talk about every object as if it were alive. For example, you would say that the customer [object] asks the transaction object to transfer money between accounts. As you are gathering the requirements, the subject matter experts are going to tell you what objects exist in the system by the nouns they use—for example, customer, transaction, teller, account, and federal clearing house. Use these nouns as a starting point for the objects in your system.

You will most likely find that many of the objects you identify have relationships to each other. These relationships can be classified in two ways: whole/part or general/specific. For example, a car is the whole of wheels, engine, seats, body, and so on. Car is the general of Neon, Mustang, Camry, and so on. Both of these types of relationships will be

seen in your objects. You want to understand them because the way that they are implemented differs. General/specific objects have an inheritance wherein the children inherit
all the attributes and methods from a parent. General/specific is a *vertical relationship*.
Whole/part is a *horizontal relationship*. Whole objects are made from a collection of
unrelated objects. These classifications are not mutually exclusive; objects have both
general/specific and whole/part relationships.

The next issue you will face is how granular you want to make the objects. That is, how
much do you want to decompose your objects into component parts. One common mistake is to get obsessed with making fine-grained objects so that you can recombine them
later into other things. Rarely does this happen, and it adds excess complexity and overhead to the architecture. Just define the objects you need and will be using.

Many times the objects map directly to a normalized database table. If you have an information engineering background, this is the way that you were taught to build systems. In
information engineering, you first identify the data and then build all the processes
around that data.

Again the best way to learn this is by seeing it done for our case study.

You first identify the objects in the bank's environment that you want to represent in the
system. The objects you identify in this environment are Customer, Account, Transaction,
and Spouse. You then want to identify the relationship between these objects. The relationship between these entities can be described. There is a one-to-many relationship
between a customer and an account. An account has a many-to-many relationship with
transactions. A customer has a one-to-one (in most states) relationship with a spouse.
The object/data diagram looks like Figure 3.1.

FIGURE 3.1

Smalltown's data model.

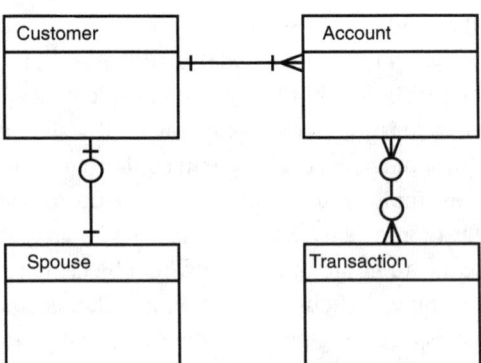

In reality, you would have many more tables than these in your database. These have been chosen to represent the different types of relationships that exist in a data structure. It so happens that these objects map directly to a database schema.

You now want to determine the attributes for each object. We start with the Customer object and identify the following attributes: first, last, and middle names; address, city, state, ZIP code; phone number; Social Security number; email address; and branch number.

For the Account object, you identify the following attributes: account number, account type, customer number, and balance.

For the Transaction object, you identify the following attributes: account number, date/time, transaction type, and amount.

For the Spouse object, you identify the following attributes: customer number; first, middle, and last names; Social Security number.

Again this is a very simple data structure. In reality, you might have many more attributes for each object and many more objects in the system. In order to have referential integrity, you need to provide primary–foreign key links between objects. The links between these objects are seen Table 3.1.

TABLE 3.1   Links Between the Bank's Objects

Primary Key	Foreign Key
Customer: social_security_number	Account: customer_number
Account: account_number	Transaction: account_number
Spouse: customer number	Customer: social security number

In Day 4, "Exploring Database Fundamentals," you will create the actual physical tables.

Executants and Emissaries

One of the basic requirements of a scalable, robust Windows DNA application is never to allow clients to have direct access to critical resources. Instead, the client issues a request to a component that performs the business or data operation the system is designed to automate. This type of component is known as an *executant*. An example of an executant would be the lookup of a customer's account information or the transfer of funds between accounts. By limiting the client's access to system resources, you can maintain complete control of the resources. Because of this design *you* must pay close attention to

3

how you use and manage system resources. By understanding this requirement, you will have a better understanding of why you are designing and building the various components. You will also learn in Week 2, how system services such as NT, MTS, and MSMQ make the job of interacting with resources easier.

Before an executant performs any operation for a client, it first must authenticate that the user is allowed to perform the operation. The executant then check the parameters passed to it to ensure that they are what the method expects. If the user does not authenticate or the parameters are out of compliance, the method stops all further operations. It is also good practice to raise an error event so that the client can react to the error if it so chooses. With such a degree of validation it is reasonable to expect that numerous requests will be denied, which is why your application should provide *executant emissaries*, or *emissaries* for short.

Emissaries are components designed to help clients issue perfect requests to executants. One way that they do this is to provide the user with a limited set of valid choices that the user can pick from. These parameter sets are usually the same ones used by the executants to do their validation. Another way that emissaries help is by validating the parameters at the presentation tier before transmitting them across the network; this helps reduce network traffic. When transmitting requests to the executant, the client can use any means at his disposal (for example, DCOM, MSMQ, WinSock, and so on).

Figure 3.2 shows executants and emissaries in action.

Emissaries can support both interactive and non-interactive user interfaces. Interactive presentation services are capable of providing feedback on a form-by-form or field-by-field basis. For example, a native Visual Basic application or a DHTML client could immediately display an error message in response to the data entered into a form.

Non-interactive presentation services can only provide feedback to the client on a form-by-form basis. For example, HTML 3.2 user interfaces require the form be submitted to the server before any validation processing can be done.

If you need your application to support a wide range of clients in the presentation tier, you will need to design both interactive and non-interactive emissaries into your solution. To do this you must design both property-level validation and object-level validation into solutions. Property-level validation ensures that the individual property contains a valid value. Object-level validation ensures that all the properties of an object are valid. An object-level validation routine might simply call all the property-level validation routines.

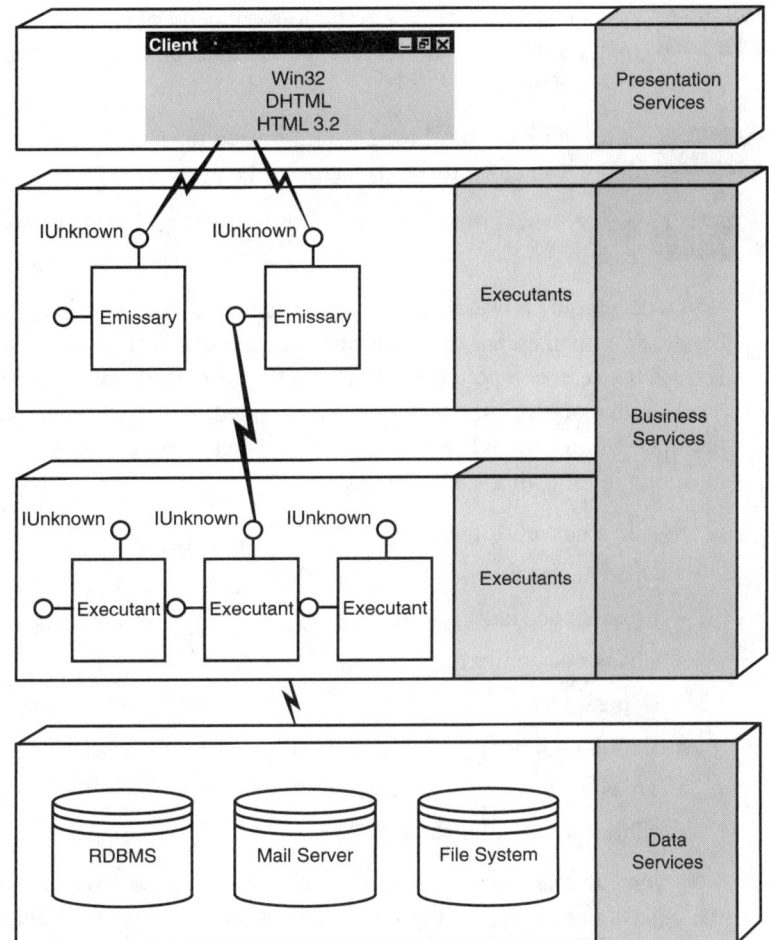

FIGURE 3.2

Executants and emissaries.

Client — Win32 DHTML HTML 3.2

Presentation Services

IUnknown — Emissary   IUnknown — Emissary

Executants

Business Services

IUnknown — Executant   IUnknown — Executant   IUnknown — Executant

Executants

RDBMS   Mail Server   File System

Data Services

3

Exploring Use Case and Sequence Diagrams

Use cases are what the name implies—mapped out usage scenarios. A *use case* documents the ways that various users will interact with the system. A *sequence diagram* documents the flow of interactions between objects for a selected use case. These diagrams do not directly relate to the tiers of the Windows DNA architecture. The diagrams will help determine that the business scenarios are well-thought-out before you actually develop your business objects. The use case is the blueprint that the developers and testers use to ensure that the system is performing as expected.

NEW TERM   An *actor*, as a user of a system, is typically in some sort of role such as a customer, teller, account representative, and so forth. An actor can be a real person or an automated agent.

NEW TERM   A *use case* defines how a user, referred to as an *actor*, will use the system. You define use cases for every actor in the system.

NEW TERM   *Sequence diagram* is the flow of transactions between objects for a particular use case.

When developing a use case, you first discover all the scenarios you want your system to handle. You then assign the scenarios to actors and then map out the details of the interactions between components to perform the case. Let's map out a use case for Smalltown Bank so that you can see how one is developed. For this system, you will limit the number of scenarios. In reality, you would have many more scenarios. For this book, you will develop the following scenarios:

- Add a new customer
- Open an account
- Close an account
- Change customer data
- Deposit money
- Withdraw money
- Transfer funds between accounts
- Check account balance

Now you can map each of these scenarios to the transactions that are required between the objects in the system. Figure 3.3 shows the use case and sequence diagram for checking an account balance.

FIGURE 3.3

Account balance lookup use case and sequence diagram.

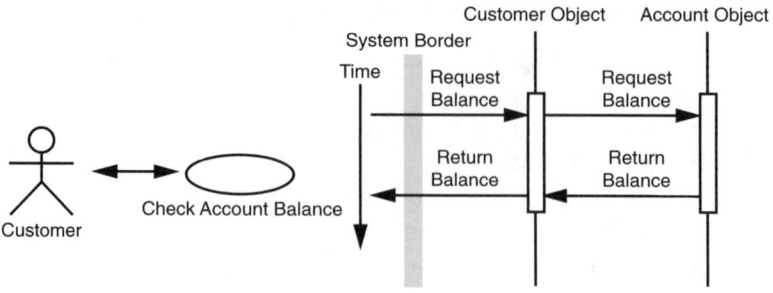

You will notice that I have added a Customer to the left side of the diagram to denote the interactive user. This user can be a person sitting at a computer, or it can be an automated business process. You will create a diagram for each of the scenarios. Again for teaching purposes, I will keep the scenarios simple.

You should also create a narrative for each of the cases describing the various transactions. The arrows denote an interaction between objects; the direction of the arrows denotes who is requesting the interaction (where arrow starts) and who is fulfilling the request (where arrow ends). Braces around the conditional blocks of transactions denote conditional logic about how a transaction will flow.

Mapping the Solution to the DNA Architecture

You'll now begin the process of taking the information you collected about the requirements of the system and mapping that information into the design for the final solution. In this design phase, you are developing the blueprint that the developers will use to develop the actual solution.

You will learn how to use Microsoft Visual Modeler to design your solution. Visual Modeler will be used throughout this book to document design. As you will see in the development chapters, Visual Modeler works well with the Microsoft development tools. You will learn how Visual Modeler works with the development tools to create your system components. The work that you do in the development tools will also be reverse-engineered back into the modeling tool so that the two stay in sync.

Universal Modeling Language

Universal Modeling Language (UML) is the consolidation of three popular object modeling languages by Grady Booch, Ivar Jacobson, and Jim Rumbaugh. UML has become an industry standard for modeling, constructing, and documenting object-oriented applications. Rational's Rose software and Microsoft's Visual Modeler, among others, implement UML.

UML enables you to define components that are the building blocks of all Windows DNA applications. You then define the interactions between these components. You'll want to learn UML and take the extra effort to model your components before jumping into the code, because at some point you will need to communicate with users and other developers regarding how your solution operates. UML provides this documentation in a standard form that can be understood by a wide range of audiences. In fact, UML is used, in the form of Microsoft Visual Modeler models, throughout this book to document and deliver the example code to you.

For more information on UML, I would like to direct you to
http://www.rational.com/uml/. Here you will find the latest specifications for the language. Several very good books exist on the subject and are readily available.

I am using Visual Modeler as a way to document the system objects. The UML specification has a number of other types of diagrams and artifacts that can be created for a project. However, the additional artifacts often times are not needed and those in use do not
provide all the detail that is needed to completely represent a system.

Using Visual Modeler

Now that you have your business case and objects identified, you can start developing
the logical model of your system. You will use Microsoft Visual Modeler to design the
objects that will live at each of the DNA tiers. Visual Modeler complies with the
Universal Modeling Language (UML) standard. The models you create in Visual
Modeler can also be used in other tools, like Rational Rose, that conform to the UML
standard.

You might not have used Visual Modeler in the past, and are now asking yourself, "Why
should I learn to use it?" It is true that Visual Modeler is not required for developing
applications. However, when you are developing in a team situation, you will need to
communicate the design of the system to others and to keep this design up to date with
all the team members' changes. Visual Modeler is a round-trip tool for doing this. From
Visual Modeler you can generate the code shell for your application and work on the
application in your standard development environment. Then, through Visual Modeler or
the development tool, you will reverse-engineer your code and changes back into the
model.

The reverse-engineering capability is very nice because it can also model any COM-
compliant component, that is, any DLL or executable you are using in the system, not
just the ones you are developing. So, if you are making calls into COM components, they
can be represented in the model. You will see this capability later in the chapter. This
ability to extract the model from classes without the source code is very cool.

When should you use Visual Modeler? Every time you develop any code. It is a good
habit to always model your components, and is a behavior found in professional development efforts. After you get through the initial learning curve, you will find it very natural
to work with the models and easy to switch back and forth between the development
environment and model.

I cannot emphasize it enough: Information technology solutions have become so complex and sophisticated that we must use high-level tools such as Visual Modeler in order
to build, document, and maintain solutions. Microsoft realized this, and thus paid a great

deal of money in order to include Visual Modeler in the Professional version of Visual Studio.

Visual Modeler is a subset of the full capability of the Rational suite of modeling tools. You might want to explore the capabilities of the full-featured version of Rational tools. Please visit their Web site at `http://www.rational.com`. The Rational tools enable you to develop class, component, deployment, and activity diagrams. They also let you use cases diagrams, sequence diagrams, collaboration diagrams, and state diagrams. For more information on these added features visit the Rational Web site.

To launch Microsoft Visual Modeler, select Start, Programs, Microsoft Visual Studio 6.0, Microsoft Visual Studio 6.0 Enterprise Tools, Microsoft Visual Modeler. You will see the screen in Figure 3.4.

FIGURE 3.4

Visual Modeler default screen.

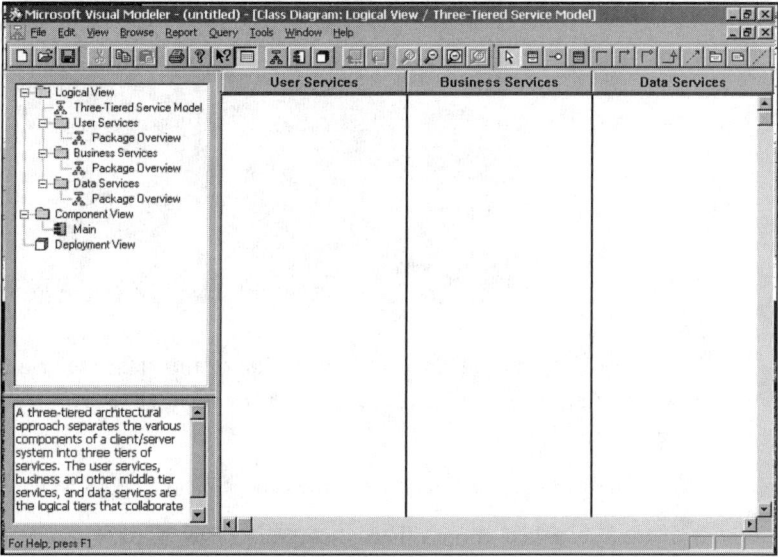

When you open Visual Modeler, you see a tree view on the left with Logical, Component, and Deployment views. On the right, you see a three-panel, three-tier Service Model view with panels for User Services, Business Services, and Data Services. These areas, along with the menus and toolbars, are what you will use to build your application model.

The first class you will create is for data services. You build the Customer data class. You can use the Class Wizard to make this class. As with most options, you have several ways to invoke the wizard. For this example, use the context-sensitive menu. Right-click with the mouse anywhere in the three services panel and select Class Wizard.

NEW TERM *Class* is an object-oriented term that describes a template for a software object. A class defines the attributes (data) and methods (functions and procedures) that will work together to form an object. When the system implements an object, it specifies the class from which the object will be created. Think of a class as the factory and the object as the product produced. Multiple instances of objects created from the same class can exist, all representing different objects.

You will be prompted for the class name (see Figure 3.5). Enter `Customer`, and then select Next.

FIGURE 3.5

Class Wizard asks you to name the new class.

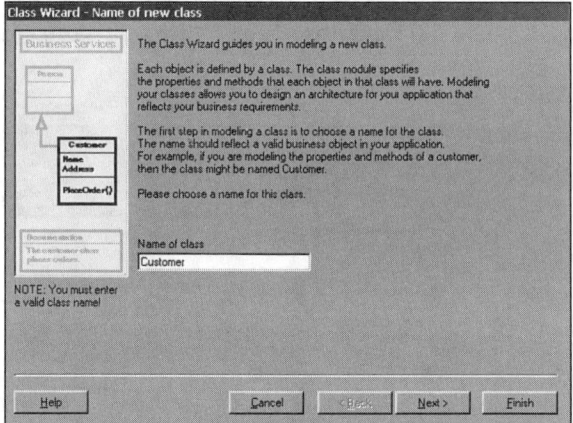

You are now asked to provide a description of the class (see Figure 3.6). Enter a behavioral description such as **This class is responsible for managing the customer data**. Then select Next.

Now you are asked to select a service type. Select Data Service, Next.

You are now asked about inheritance. Select No, Next.

NEW TERM *Inheritance*, in Visual Basic, is the capability to take a skeleton class description and apply it to a class. The *skeleton class* is a pattern that defines standard interfaces that you want to make consistent across various classes. Suppose you are developing a skeleton class for entertainment appliances (televisions, radios, VCRs). You might want to have the following standard interfaces: volume, channel, and power. Typically, you might name the classes in the form `IentertainmentApplicanceControls`. The `I` stands for Implements and the name describes what it implements. Then, when you define your Television, Radio, and VCR classes, you specify the `Implements` class for inheritance. By doing this, you ensure that the class is required to implement the defined control methods.

FIGURE 3.6

*Class Wizard asks you
to document the
Customer class's
responsibilities.*

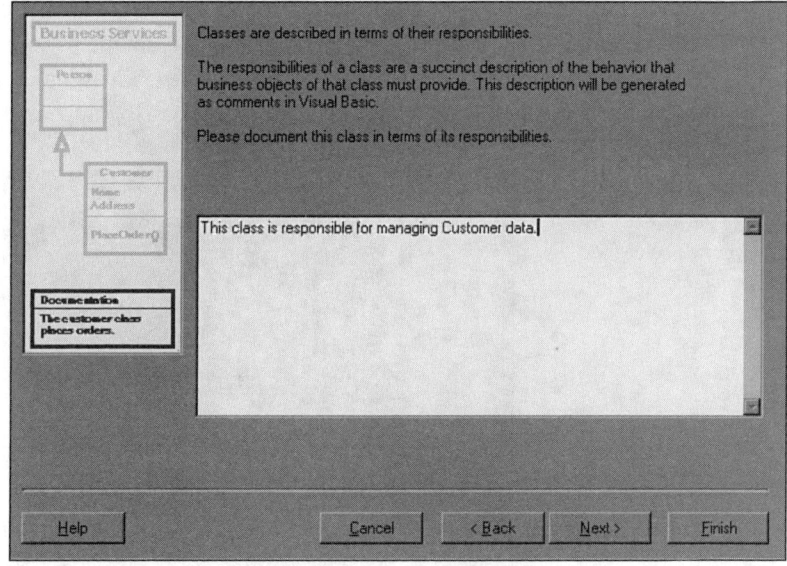

You are now presented with a dialog box in which you can define the methods for your
class (see Figure 3.7). If you had selected an inheritance class, you would see the methods that are already defined in the Implements class. You are given a drop-down box
listing fundamental type languages. Select Visual Basic for your project.

FIGURE 3.7

*Class Wizard asks you
to define the methods
of the Customer class.*

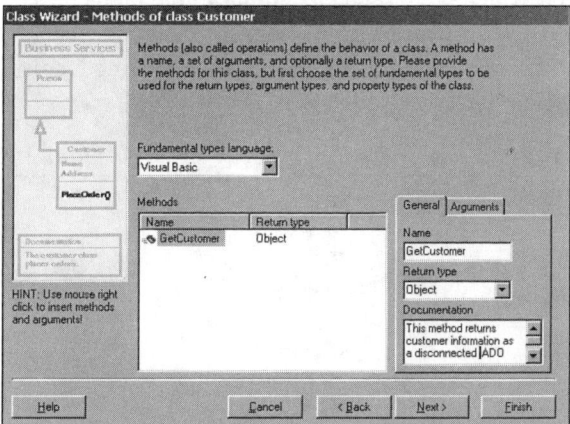

To add a method, right-click the Methods list box and select Insert. You will see a New
Method appear, and the General Tab on the right will display NewMethod as the default.

Change the method Name and Return Type to GetCustomer and Object, respectively. Also add a brief description of the method in the Document Comments box. You now need to specify your arguments if any. You will have an argument, so select the Arguments tab. The Properties of class Customer dialog appears (see Figure 3.8) .

FIGURE 3.8

Class Wizard Properties of class Customer dialog.

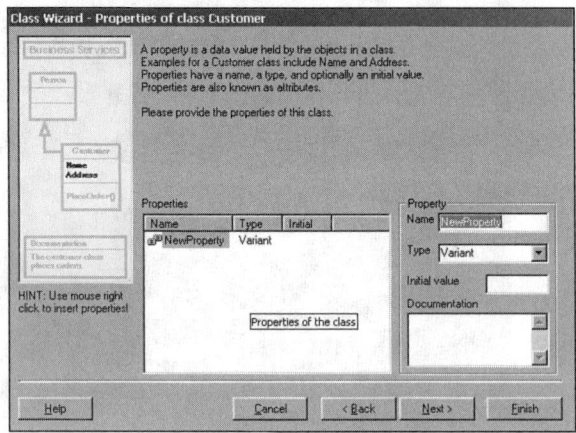

Right-click Insert. The name in the Name and Type input boxes changes to NewArgument and Variant, respectively. Change these to CustomerID and String, respectively. Continue adding methods to your class. When finished, press Next.

You are now presented with a screen, similar to the methods screen, that enables you to enter the properties for your class. As with the method screen, right-click in the Properties list box and select Insert. Fill in the following Name, Type, Initial Value, and related documentation.

Name	Type	Initial Value
CustomerID	String	""
FirstName	String	""
MiddleName	String	""
LastName	String	""
...	String	""

Select Next, and you are presented with a summary screen. When you have finished reviewing the summary, select Finish. You now see your class defined in standard UML notation.

Choose File, Save to save your work. Right-click with the mouse on the class and notice all the operations you can perform.

Reverse-Engineer and Document Existing Programs and DLLs with Visual Modeler

Not only does Visual Modeler enable you to create your own class models, but it can also reverse-engineer and document existing programs and DLLs. To demonstrate this, pick a DLL such as the `windna21.dll` on the CD-ROM that comes with this book; drag and drop it onto the Visual Modeler class diagram. Visual Modeler will go to work representing the DLL. When it is done, you will have several different views of the WinDna21 model. Explore and see how various types of components are represented. You might want to drag the elements around so that you have a better view.

Exploring Other Visual Modeler Characteristics

By now, you are probably getting interested in all the Visual Modeler capabilities. At this point, select Help, Visual Modeler Help Topics. You are presented with the help file for Visual Modeler. Read through the Visual Modeler and Quick Start with Visual Modeler Help topics. They will give you a good sense of what this tool is capable of doing. I have included a full working model on the CD-ROM. You will use these models to generate your code shells in later chapters.

3

Development Frameworks

As you saw in Day 2, "Building a Windows DNA Application," basing your solution on Windows DNA is a good way to reduce risk. Another way to manage risk is to use a development framework. Development frameworks are organizations tools and techniques for managing and delivering complex solutions. Many development frameworks exist, however, the ones that are best for a Windows DNA solution use iterative development cycles. Here are two frameworks that work well for delivering Windows DNA solutions; Microsoft Solution Framework and Extreme Programming.

Both of these frameworks emphasize the need to use an iterative process for delivering functionality. The cycle of design, develop, test, and implement and continue repeating this pattern is key to the ability for these frameworks to allow you to deliver complex solutions. Some people misinterpret this iterative approach to mean that you jump past design and start coding the solution. This is not the case, in fact it is quite the reverse, you need a very solid infrastructure and high-level design to be able to follow these frameworks. Having the infrastructure and high-level design worked out you can then develop and implement use cases in parallel. This is where you get the extreme results because you are able to cycle through more development and test cycles in a shorter period of time.

Using Microsoft Solution Framework to Generate Business Solutions

Microsoft Solution Framework (MSF) is the process that Microsoft uses internally to analyze and develop its applications. In brief, the Microsoft Solutions Framework is a collection of models, principles, and practices that helps organizations be more effective in their creation and use of technology to solve their business problems. MSF does this by providing rigorous guidance that is flexible enough to be adapted to meet the needs of a project and an organization.

Microsoft describes the six core building blocks for this MSF-based guidance as follows:

- *The Enterprise Architecture Model* provides a consistent set of guidelines for rapidly building enterprise architecture through versioned releases. The model aligns information technology with business requirements through four perspectives: business, application, information, and technology. Using this model will help shorten your enterprise architecture planning cycle.

- *The Team Model* provides a flexible structure for organizing teams on projects. It emphasizes clear roles, responsibilities, and goals for team success. It increases team member accountability through its structure—a team of peers. Its flexibility means that it can be adapted to the scope of the project, the size of the team, and the skills of the team members. Using this model and the principles and practices that underlie it will help you have more engaged, effective, resilient, and successful teams.

- *The Process Model* provides project structure and guidance through a project life cycle that is milestone based, iterative, and flexible. It describes the phases, milestones, activities, and deliverables of a project and their relationships to the Team Model. Using this model will help you improve project control, minimize risk, improve quality, and shorten delivery time.

- *The Risk Management Model* provides a structured and proactive way to manage risk on projects. It sets forth a discipline and environment of proactive decisions and actions to assess continuously what can go wrong, determine what risks are important to deal with, and implement strategies to deal with those risks. Using this model and the principles and practices that underlie it will help teams focus on what is most important, make the right decisions, and be better prepared for when the unknown future becomes known.

- *The Design Process Model* provides a three-phase, user-centric continuum that enables a parallel and iterative approach to design for the greatest efficiency and flexibility. The conceptual, logical, and physical design phases provide three different perspectives for three different audiences—the user, the team, and the developers. Moving through conceptual design to physical design will show the translation of user-based scenarios to services-based components so that application features can be traced back to end-user requirements. Using this model will help ensure that your applications are created, not just for the sake of technology, but to meet your business and user needs.

- *The Application Model* provides a logical three-tier, services-based approach to designing and developing software applications. The use of user services, business services, and data services enable parallel development, better use of technology, easier maintenance and support, and the greatest flexibility in distribution. The services that make up the application can reside anywhere from a single desktop to servers and clients around the world.

For more information about Microsoft Solutions Framework, please visit the Web site at http://www.microsoft.com/msf. Here you can read about MSF resources, courses available on MSF, and other related information.

Extreme Programming

Kent Beck, the developer of the extreme programming approach has the following to say about it:

"Extreme Programming (XP) was conceived and developed to address the specific needs of software development conducted by small teams in the face of vague and changing requirements. This new lightweight methodology challenges many conventional tenets, including the long-held assumption that the cost of changing a piece of software necessarily rises dramatically over the course of time. XP recognizes that projects have to work to achieve this reduction in cost and exploit the savings once they have been earned."

Fundamentals of XP include:

- Distinguishing between the decisions to be made by business interests and those to be made by project stakeholders.
- Writing unit tests before programming and keeping all of the tests running at all times.
- Integrating and testing the whole system—several times a day.
- Producing all software in pairs, two programmers at one screen.

- Starting projects with a simple design that constantly evolves to add needed flexibility and remove unneeded complexity.
- Putting a minimal system into production quickly and growing it in whatever directions prove most valuable.

Why is XP so controversial? Some sacred cows don't make the cut in XP:

- Don't force team members to specialize and become analysts, architects, programmers, testers, and integrators—every XP programmer participates in all of these critical activities every day.
- Don't conduct complete up-front analysis and design—an XP project starts with a quick analysis of the entire system, and XP programmers continue to make analysis and design decisions throughout development.
- Develop infrastructure and frameworks as you develop your application, not up-front—delivering business value is the heartbeat that drives XP projects.
- Don't write and maintain implementation documentation—communication in XP projects occurs face-to-face, or through efficient tests and carefully written code.

Summary

Today's lessons demonstrated the importance of doing a good job analyzing the business and user requirements before designing and building the application. You learned how to develop a good business case by looking at the current scenario, identifying problems/opportunities, doing a risk benefit analysis, and becoming fully prepared to defend your proposal. The chapter suggested some general questions to ask in order to gather requirements, as well as some tools and techniques for gathering and documenting requirements. You learned about developing use cases and sequence diagrams for each operation your system will perform for the users. Moving into the design phase of the project, you saw how to use Microsoft Visual Modeler to create a three-tier UML model of your application by designing COM components with the tool. Existing code and COM objects can be included in a model by simply dragging and dropping them into Visual Modeler.

The rest of this book will use the Smalltown Bank solution to demonstrate how to build the various tiers of a Windows DNA application.

Q&A

Q Why is it important to create a good business case?

A Without a good business case, it is unlikely that you will be able to convince management to fund your project. A good business case assesses the risks, benefits, and alternatives, which helps ensure that you have selected the correct solution.

Q Why do you need to spend time doing a reasonable analysis of your requirements?

A By doing a reasonable analysis of your solution, you define the parameters of your project. Defined parameters can help you set metrics for tracking progress.

Q Do I have to use a modeling tool?

A No, many applications are developed without being modeled. But, as solutions become more complex and involve teams of developers, modeling tools help in communications by defining and documenting the solution in a standard way.

Q How should classes, methods, and attributes be named?

A Many different standards exist for naming elements of your solution. Microsoft uses Hungarian notation, which uses a prefix to tell what type of data the attribute contains or method returns. I feel that this is okay for internal attributes and methods but that Hungarian notation should not be used for all public interfaces. The object browser and Intellisense will tell the caller what the parameters require.

3

Workshop

The Workshop provides quiz questions to help you solidify your understanding of the material covered and exercises to provide you with experience in using what you've learned. Try to understand the quiz and exercise answers before continuing to the next lesson. Answers are provided in Appendix A.

Quiz

1. What are some of the tools and techniques you can use to gather and document requirements?

2. What tool does Microsoft provide to model your application?

3. What are some of the benefits of using Microsoft Visual Modeler?

4. What are the different relationships that can exist between data elements?

Exercises

1. The new high-tech businesses are asking their trading partners to all have Internet-based trading capabilities. They require the banks they deal with—Smalltown is one—to have the capability to process electronic funds transfers. Smalltown Bank has been given one year to enable these capabilities or lose the business. Put together a business case for this problem.

2. Open the model with Visual Modeler and add objects in the data tier for Account, Transaction, and Spouse.

DAY 4

Exploring Database Fundamentals

Databases have been around for decades, and despite all the new applications for databases, like streaming media, data warehousing, and analytical reporting, the fundamental algorithms of databases have not changed. Today you will cover the fundamentals of database design, and you will build the database for the bank. Today, you learn the following:

- The architecture of a database
- The basics of Structured Query Language (SQL)
- Use of VB's Data View Window as a visual designer

The Basics of Database Architecture

Before you learn about the architecture of databases, you need to be clear on the two ways the word *database* is commonly used. It is used to describe both the information being managed and the program managing the information. Let us use an analogy to clarify the database vocabulary. You are probably familiar with at least one word processing program, such as Microsoft Word. You use such a program to manage information stored in a document. There are other word processing programs, such as Corel WordPerfect. Each word processor program stores a document in a proprietary format. The same story applies to database management programs. There are several database management programs, such as Microsoft Access, Microsoft SQL Server, and Oracle.

Note

> Database programs come in different categories. These categories vary by the size of information you can store and how many concurrent users can access this information. Microsoft Access, for example, is not in the same league as SQL Server and Oracle. Microsoft Access is designed to be a workgroup database, whereas SQL Server and Oracle are enterprise-class databases.

All database management programs manipulate data stored in a database. Each database software package uses a proprietary format to store the data.

NEW TERM   A *database* is an integrated collection of data, a repository of information.

Database Tables: The Backbone of Databases

Now, when you have to type a letter, you know this can be done using a word processor. When do you use a database? You use a database to store and maintain structured information and generate reports. Structured information is any type of data that is kept in an organized fashion. You can use a database to store contact information, recipes, maintain a membership list, keep track of your investments, and so on. Your favorite online bookstore uses a database to keep track of which books are in stock, who its customers are, and what they order. This is a vast amount of information, but you can equally use a word processor to write a large book or a short memo.

Just as a document can be broken down into pages containing paragraphs and sentences, a database can be broken down into tables and columns.

NEW TERM   An *entity* is a person, thing, place, or event of interest about which data is collected.

NEW TERM   A *table* is the fundamental building block for database applications and contains information about an entity.

So the information about books, customers, and orders in an online bookstore is kept into three distinct tables. (Of course, an actual online bookstore actually requires more than three tables, as there is more information that needs to be kept, such as authors, publishers, shipping and billing addresses, and so on.) These tables contain related information (an order consists of one or more books and is placed by a customer). Later in this chapter, you will learn more about table relationships and what they mean to the organization of a database.

NEW TERM A table consists of one or more *columns*. A column contains a characteristic or attribute of an entity. If the entity is a person, then the attributes may be first name, last name, marital status, and so on.

So, a book may be an object of interest or an entity stored in a table. Qualities defining the book, such as tpdpice, are contained in columns. An author table might contain columns storing first name, last name, and so on.

Note

> You typically want to break down information in as many columns as possible. This is because the database software is optimized to easily retrieve the entire content of a column. Retrieving a subsection of a column is much slower and also requires a bigger programming effort. For example, if you put the whole address in one column, you will have difficulty retrieving information by city, or by postal code. It is more flexible to divide the address information into individual columns for street, number, apartment number, city, state/province, postal code, and so on. You want to create non-decomposable columns (columns that cannot be divided into smaller, usable columns). An address offers a great example. You can divide an address into the street, suite, city, state, and ZIP Code. But if you divide the street address into the numeric part and street name, you've gone too far. So "240 Presley Avenue" is okay, but "240" and "Presley Avenue" separated may not be as useful.

4

NEW TERM A table consists of one or more *rows*. A row describes a single entity. Storing information about three different books requires three rows in the Book table.

Each author for whom you store information takes up a row in the Authors table. A row consists of a concrete value for each column of the table. The row containing the information about William Shakespeare will contain "William" in the first name column, "Shakespeare" in the last name column, and so on. Of course, after you put this information in a tabular form, as in Figure 4.1, these database names become obvious.

Note

> Synonyms exist for row and column. Instead of row, you can also use the term *record*. Instead of column, you can also use the term *field*. In this book, we will mostly stick to row and column.

FIGURE **4.1**

*A table consists of
rows and columns.*

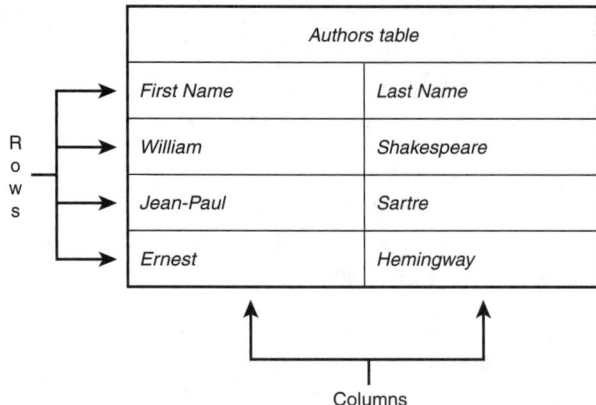

The speed with which you can easily retrieve information stored in a table increases with the judicious use of indexes.

Retrieving Database Information with Indexes

An *index* is a way to speed up the retrieval of information stored in a table at the expense of slightly slowing down insertion, deletion, and updating of the information.

You can think of an index as the tabs on your Rolodex. Thanks to these tabs, you can more easily find information about a certain person. However, each time you add a name to the Rolodex, you need to spend time to put it where it belongs. The database software maintains the sorting information stored in the indexes for you, but it still has more work to do when inserting, deleting, or updating rows in the presence of indexes. And more work translates into slower operations. An index comprises one or more columns. Searches using these columns will benefit from the index. For example, you can define an index on the Last Name and First Name column of the Authors table. A search for last name = "Christie" and first name = "Agatha" will then be faster than if you did not create this index.

Primary Keys

A *primary key* is a special type of index that serves to uniquely identify a single row. Because each row in a table represents a unique occurrence of an entity, you must ensure that your application can identify each occurrence with the data stored in a row. You do this by defining a primary key for the table. Just like an index, a primary key consists of one or more columns. Some tables have a natural choice for a primary key (the ISBN for the books table, for example). For other tables, you must add an artificial primary key. In the SQL DDL section later in the chapter, you will see that SQL Server offers two ways (an identity column and RowGUID) to create artificial primary keys.

Assigning Data Types

From the preceding examples, you might have noticed that a column always contains similar types of information. In some way this is similar to the way a variable is used in a programming language, such as Visual Basic. Just as with a variable, you assign a data type to a column. This data type is typically either textual or numeric. For a textual data type, you need to assign the maximum string length. For numerical data, you need to choose between integral or real values. Table 4.1 shows the data types available in SQL Server.

TABLE 4.1 SQL Server Data Types

Data Type	Description
BINARY	Fixed-length binary data with a maximum length of 8,000 bytes
BIT	Integer data with either a 1 or 0 value
CHAR	Fixed-length non-Unicode character data with a maximum length of 8,000 characters
DATETIME	Date and time data from January 1, 1753, to December 31, 9999, with an accuracy of three-hundredths of a second, or 3.33 milliseconds
DECIMAL or NUMERIC	Fixed precision and scale numeric data from $-10^{38} -1$ through $10^{38} -1$
FLOAT	Floating precision number data from $-1.79E + 308$ through $1.79E + 308$
IMAGE	Variable-length binary data with a maximum length of $2^{31} - 1$ (2,147,483,647) bytes
INT	Integer (whole number) data from -2^{31} (-2,147,483,648) through $2^{31} - 1$ (2,147,483,647)
MONEY	Monetary data values from -2^{63} (-922,337,203,685,477.5808) through $2^{63} - 1$ (+922,337,203,685,477.5807), with accuracy to a ten-thousandth of a monetary unit
NCHAR	Fixed-length Unicode data with a maximum length of 4,000 characters
NTEXT	Variable-length Unicode data with a maximum length of $2^{30} - 1$ (1,073,741,823) characters
NVARCHAR	Variable-length Unicode data with a maximum length of 4,000 characters
REAL	Floating precision number data from $-3.40E + 38$ through $3.40E + 38$

4

continues

TABLE 4.1   continued

Data Type	Description
SMALLDATETIME	Date and time data from January 1, 1900, through June 6, 2079, with an accuracy of one minute
SMALLINT	Integer data from 2^{15} (-32,768) through $2^{15} - 1$ (32,767)
SMALLMONEY	Monetary data values from -214,748.3648 through +214,748.3647, with accuracy to a ten-thousandth of a monetary unit
TEXT	Variable-length non-Unicode data with a maximum length of $2^{31} - 1$ (2,147,483,647) characters
TIMESTAMP	A database-wide unique number
TINYINT	Integer data from 0 through 255
UNIQUEIDENTIFIER	A globally unique identifier (GUID)
VARCHAR	Variable-length non-Unicode data with a maximum of 8,000 characters
VARBINARY	Variable-length binary data with a maximum length of 8,000 bytes

Most of these data types are familiar choices for a programmer used to create variables. In fact, when you create tables, you can even use a programming language to make these choices! This programming language is called Structured Query Language, or SQL for short.

Database Development Language (SQL)

Structured Query Language, or *SQL*, is the standard programming language used to create tables and manipulate data stored in tables.

In the next section, you will learn the basics of SQL.

Managing Data Input

Finally, just as you would validate any user input stored in a variable, you will validate input stored in columns. The database will help you to enforce the rules you define for each column. You may require that each book have a valid ISBN number and a title. You will see how to specify these rules. These validation rules include whether a column requires input but are flexible enough to handle any requirements your specific data might have. For example, you can easily specify a validation rule specifying that an order date must be larger or equal to today's date.

Exploring SQL Basics

You learned that SQL is the standard language for database manipulation. Unlike Visual Basic, which is controlled by Microsoft, SQL is governed by official standard organizations. SQL is used in the vast majority of database management programs. As with any standard, vendors choose to which degree they follow the standard in their implementation. Each vendor also typically adds non-standard extensions to their implementation. In SQL Server, the SQL implementation is called Transact-SQL. Entire books can (and have been) written about either Transact-SQL or standard SQL, so you will merely scratch the surface of SQL's capabilities in this chapter.

The SQL language is not case sensitive. Its keywords can be written in uppercase, lowercase, or mixed case. In this lesson and in the next one, we use uppercase for all SQL keywords so you can easily identify what is a keyword and what isn't. SQL identifiers, such as table names, column names, and so on, might or might not be case sensitive depending on the database program used. In SQL Server, they typically are not case sensitive. SQL statements can be spread over more than one line. You indicate the end of a SQL statement and the start of a new one by using a semicolon. (No semicolon is needed if there is only one SQL statement. A semicolon is not your only option; the word GO may also be used.)

> **Note** For more information on the SQL language, check out *Sams Teach Yourself SQL in 21 Days*, Third Edition.

SQL is divided into two subsets, the SQL Data Definition Language (DDL) and the SQL Data Manipulation Language (DML). The *SQL Data Definition Language* (DDL) consists of the SQL statements used to create the data stores (tables, indexes, and so on). The *SQL Data Manipulation Language* (DML) consists of the SQL statements used to manage the data stored in the database. DML allows you to perform four basic operations: add, retrieve, change, and delete.

Creating Tables with Visual Studio's Table Designer

SQL DDL mainly consists of CREATE TABLE, CREATE INDEX statements. However, Visual Basic 6 (or indeed all the members of the Visual Studio family) provides a graphical, intuitive way to create tables, so you do not need to learn the intricacies of SQL DDL to create a table.

This environment is available when you select View, Data Window inside of Visual Basic.

In the Data Window, each *Data Link* represents a connection to specific database.

Behind the scenes, Visual Basic uses ActiveX Data Objects (covered on Day 6) to process the SQL DDL statements created as a result of your choices in the GUI. Figure 4.2 shows the table designer.

FIGURE 4.2

The table designer in Visual Basic makes creating a table straightforward.

Column Name	Datatype	Length	Precision	Scale	Allow Nulls	Default Value	Identity	Identity Seed	Identity Increment	Is RowGuid
CustomerKey	int	4	10	0			✓	1	1	
FirstName	char	50	0	0						
MiddleName	char	50	0	0	✓					
LastName	char	50	0	0						
SuffixName	char	5	0	0	✓					
SocialSecurityNumber	char	9	0	0						
Address1	char	50	0	0						
Address2	char	50	0	0	✓					
City	char	50	0	0						
State	char	2	0	0						
PostalCode	char	10	0	0						
PhoneNumber	char	20	0	0	✓					
EMailAddress	char	50	0	0	✓					
UserID	char	20	0	0						
SpouseID	int	4	10	0	✓					

The purpose of many of the elements in this designer is obvious. In the first two columns you put the column name and select the column's data type from a drop-down list. Length for a character string is the number of characters. Length for a numeric data type is the number of bytes used to store the number. Precision is the number of digits in a number. Scale is the number of digits to the right of the decimal point in a number. For example, the number 12345.678 has a precision of 8 and a scale of 3. (Note that the decimal point is not counted in the precision.) The length is predetermined for integral data types. For real numbers, you typically set the precision and scale and accept the resulting length.

When Allow Nulls is checked off, you must not necessarily provide a value for this column when inserting a row in the table. Conversely, if Allow Nulls is not checked, this means that you MUST provide a value for this column for the database to accept a row for this table.

NULL is a special value that means "missing value." NULL values are not equal to each other or to any other non-NULL value.

In the Default Value column, you can provide a value that will be used when no value is provided for the column. You can, for example, have a Country column defaulting to the country you live in. Then, if you insert a row and do not provide a value (or provide a NULL value) for this column, the database will put the default value in the Country column.

Creating Artificial Row Identifiers

Sometimes there is no natural way to uniquely identify rows in a table. This is the case, for example, with people. Using their Social Security number may run into privacy issues. The first name and last name are insufficient to distinguish people with common names (John Smith to single one out). For these cases, you can create artificial row identifiers in a couple of ways.

NEW TERM An *identity column* is a way to automatically create sequential numbers in a table. An identity column starts with the seed (for the first row you add). Each subsequent row gets an identity equal to the last identity plus the increment. For example, a seed of 1000 and an increment of 100 would generate identity values of 1000, 1100, 1200, and so on.

NEW TERM A *RowGUID* column creates a non-numerical row identifier. A table can only have one RowGUID column. A RowGUID also creates a value that uniquely identifies a row, but the value is not numeric (instead it uses strange-looking values such as 6A418F47-DAAB-4266-84E2-640BB16F1303).

In the Design Table screen, you can set the primary key for the table by selecting the columns you want to be part of the key, right-clicking, and selecting Add to Primary Key. Note that you can only put non-NULL columns in the primary key.

Just in case, you want to know what the DDL SQL statement looks like, Listing 4.1 shows you how to create the Customer table.

LISTING 4.1   An Example of Data Definition Language

```
 1: CREATE TABLE Customer
 2: (
 3:     CustomerKey INT IDENTITY (1, 1) NOT NULL,
 4:     FirstName CHAR(50) NOT NULL,
 5:     MiddleName CHAR(50) NULL,
 6:     LastName CHAR(50) NOT NULL,
 7:     SuffixName CHAR(5) NULL,
 8:     SocialSecurityNumber CHAR(9) NOT NULL,
 9:     Address1 CHAR(50) NOT NULL,
10:     Address2 CHAR(50) NULL,
11:     City CHAR(50) NOT NULL,
12:     State CHAR(2) NOT NULL,
13:     PostalCode CHAR(10) NOT NULL,
14:     PhoneNumber CHAR(20) NULL,
15:     EMailAddress CHAR(50) NULL,
16:     UserID CHAR(20) NOT NULL,
17:     SpouseIDINT NULL
18: )
```

4

ANALYSIS The meat of the table creation code is the column definition taking place on lines 3 to 17. Line 3 shows how to define an identity column. The first number is the seed; the second one is the increment. All subsequent lines contain column name, data type, and whether a value is required.

SQL DML

SQL DML mainly consists of four statements, one for each of the basic data manipulation activities: inserting, updating, selecting, and deleting.

INSERT Statement

```
INSERT [INTO] table_name [(column_list)]
VALUES (value1 [,value2] ...)
```

Here is an example of an INSERT statement:

```
INSERT INTO TransactionType( TransactionTypeKey, Description)
VALUES( 1, 'Deposit')
```

The INSERT statement inserts rows into an existing table. If you do not supply a list of columns, then you must supply values for each of the columns of the table, in the same order as the columns were created. An error occurs if the data types do not match between the columns and the values you are trying to insert. When an error occurs, no data is inserted for the row. You can insert NULL into a nullable column by specifying NULL as the value to be inserted. If you supply a list of columns, then you must supply a matching number of values. Each value must have a valid data type for its respective column. A NULL is inserted into the columns that are not mentioned in the column lists, unless a default was defined for such columns. If a non-null column does not have a default, then omitting this column from the list will result in an error and no data will be inserted.

Normally, you do not insert values for identity columns, because the database program automatically enters these values for you. Sometimes you might want to add a set of values with specific identity values. In SQL Server, you can turn off the feature where identity columns are automatically maintained. You might do this for only one table at the same time. You do this with the SET IDENTITY_INSERT table_name [ON | OFF] statement. When you use the ON switch, you are allowed to enter data in the identity column. When you are done entering data in the table, be sure to turn IDENTITY_INSERT OFF; otherwise, SQL Server will not let you turn it ON for another table. Listing 4.2 shows you how this is used to enter data in the AccountType table.

LISTING 4.2   Inserting Data in an Identity Column Requires Special Handling

```
1:
2: /* AccountType */
3: SET IDENTITY_INSERT AccountType ON;
4: INSERT INTO AccountType(AccountTypeKey, Description)
5: VALUES (1, 'Checking')
6:
7: INSERT INTO AccountType(AccountTypeKey, Description)
8: VALUES (2, 'Savings')
9: SET IDENTITY_INSERT AccountType OFF;
```

An attempt to enter duplicate values for a table's primary key will also result in an error (and no data being entered).

ANALYSIS   In Listing 4.2, you specify a value for the `AccountTypeKey` column in the `INSERT` statements. Because this column is an identity column, you need to preface the `INSERT` statements with a `SET IDENTITY INSERT` statement (lines 3 and 9). After you have inserted all rows in the table, it is a good idea to turn `IDENTITY INSERT OFF`, so you can turn it `ON` when inserting into another table.

UPDATE Statement

SYNTAX

UPDATE table_name SET column_name1 = expr1 [, column_name2 = expr2] ... [WHERE where_expr]

Here is an example of an `UPDATE` statement:

```
UPDATE AccountType
SET Description = 'Chequing'
WHERE AccountTypeKey = 1
```

If the `UPDATE` statement has no `WHERE` clause, then all rows of the table are updated. In the following statement, for example, every employee is given a 10% raise:

```
UPDATE Salaries
SET Salary = Salary * 1.1
```

The values assigned to columns in an `UPDATE` statement must obey the nullable settings of each column or an error will occur. As always, no values are updated if there is even a single error within the `UPDATE` statement. You can combine conditions within the `WHERE` clause by using `AND` and `OR`. You can also use parenthesis to specify the order in which the conditions of the `WHERE` clause are evaluated.

```
UPDATE Salaries
SET Salary = Salary * 1.2
WHERE Employee_Type = 'Manager'
```

4

SELECT Statement

▼ SYNTAX

```
SELECT column_list FROM table_name [[INNER JOIN table_name2 ON join_condition1]
➥ [INNER JOIN table_name3 ON join_condition2] ...] [WHERE where_expr]
```

Here is an example of a simple SELECT statement:

```
SELECT Description
FROM AccountType
WHERE AccountTypeKey = 1
```

▲

If the SELECT statement has no WHERE clause, then all rows of the table are retrieved. If you want to retrieve all columns of a table, then you can use an asterisk (*) instead of the column list. If there is more than one table mentioned in the SELECT statement, then you can prefix the asterisk with the table name and a dot, for example, AccountType.* to specify you want all the columns from the AccountType table.

The syntax only shows one of the five join types. They are

- CROSS JOIN: Specifies that all rows from the first table should be combined with all rows from the second table.

- INNER JOIN: Specifies that only matching columns be returned.

- LEFT JOIN: Specifies that all rows from the first table (the table on the left side of the join operator) should be returned, even if there is no match in the second table.

- RIGHT JOIN: Specifies that all rows from the second table (the table on the right side of the join operator) should be returned, even if there is no match in the first table.

- FULL JOIN: Combines the effect of a LEFT and RIGHT JOIN. If matching columns are missing from either table, they will show up as NULL in the result set.

Of these, the INNER JOIN is by far the most often used. An example of a SELECT statement using an INNER JOIN is seen in Listing 4.3.

LISTING 4.3   An Inner Join Used to Retrieve Related Information from Two Tables

```
1:    SELECT AccountKey,
2:        AccountNumber,
3:        AccountTypeID,
4:        CustomerID,
5:        Balance,
6:        Description
7:    FROM Account INNER JOIN AccountType ON AccountTypeID = AccountTypeKey
8:    WHERE
9:        CustomerID = 1
```

In this statement, you expect to find exactly one record in the AccountType table that matches the row in the Account table and uses an INNER JOIN. The INNER JOIN is the only type of join needed to build the SmallTownBank application.

DELETE Statement

```
DELETE [FROM] table_name [WHERE where_expr]
```

Here is an example of a DELETE statement:

```
DELETE    FROM AccountType
WHERE AccountTypeKey = 1
```

Be careful: If the DELETE statement has no WHERE clause, then all rows of the table are deleted.

> **Tip**
>
> Because there is no easy way to undo a deletion, I recommend first issuing a SELECT query to see which rows will be deleted. If you are satisfied that these rows need to be deleted, you can then change the SELECT * to DELETE without fear of making a mistake, for example:
>
> ```
> SELECT * FROM AccountType
>     WHERE AccountTypeKey = 1
>
>     DELETE    FROM AccountType
>     WHERE AccountTypeKey = 1
> ```

4

If you attempt to delete a row whose primary key is used in a foreign relationship, then an error occurs and the row is not deleted. For example, an attempt to delete the Savings row from the AccountType table will fail if you have created a savings account in the Account table.

Developing Table Relationships

You typically put repeating information in its own table. For example, the SmallTownBank application needs to identify account types (Checking and Savings). Instead of storing these descriptions in the Account table, it is better to store them in a separate AccountType table. This reduces the space needed for a row in the Account table (making it faster to retrieve). It also makes it easier to change the description of account types, should this need ever occur. Figure 4.3 shows the design of these two tables.

FIGURE 4.3

*The account descrip-
tion is best stored in a
separate table.*

Column Name	Datatype	Length	Precision	Scale	Allow Nulls	Default Value	Identity	Identity Seed	Identity Increment	Is RowGuid
AccountKey	int	4	10	0			✓	1	1	
AccountNumber	char	20	0	0						
AccountTypeID	int	4	10	0						
CustomerID	int	4	10	0						
Balance	money	8	19	4						

Design Table:AccountType

Column Name	Datatype	Length	Precision	Scale	Allow Nulls	Default Value	Identity	Identity Seed	Identity Increment	Is RowGuid
AccountTypeKey	int	4	10	0			✓	1	1	
Description	char	50	0	0						

Splitting the data in two tables is justified. The database program can ensure that you
cannot enter AccountTypeIDs that do not exist in the AccountType table into the Account
table. You tell the database program that you want these checks enforced by creating a
foreign key relationship.

A *foreign key relationship* is a relationship between two tables whereby the primary key
of one table is used in a second table.

Just as with table creation, the most convenient way to create foreign key relationships is
to use the Data View Window in Visual Basic. You do this in a Database Diagram. After
you have created a Database Diagram, you can drag and drop tables from the Tables
folder into the diagram. Then, you can create a relationship between two tables by dragging the primary key of the first table onto the corresponding field of the second table.
When you do this, you will get a foreign key creation dialog, as shown in Figure 4.4.

FIGURE 4.4

*You can easily create
foreign key relation-
ships using drag-and-
drop in a Database
Diagram.*

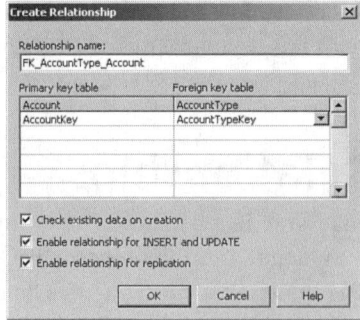

Summary

Today's lesson introduced you to the database vocabulary. After discussing the components of a database, you learned the basics of SQL, the programming language used to
manipulate database objects. You saw how to use the Data View Window in Visual Basic

to easily create tables. Then, you saw how to use diagrams to establish relationships between tables. Finally, you saw how to use SQL to insert, update, select, and delete rows.

Day 5, "Putting Business Logic in the Data Tier," will look at the SQL equivalent of subroutines in Visual Basic stored procedures.

Q&A

Q What happens if two tables that contain a similarly named column are used in a SELECT statement?

A This leads to ambiguity. In order to resolve this ambiguity, you need to preface these column names with the table name separated by a dot, for example Book.Title.

Q I generated a script from a SQL Server database. I see lots of square brackets in the SQL statement. Why are these used?

A SQL Server uses square brackets around keywords and identifiers. This enables you to use spaces in identifiers. Because few database designers use spaces in table or column names, you will rarely see these brackets in hand-written SQL code. SQL code generated by SQL Server often has these brackets, though.

Q Are RowGUIDs sequential?

A No. RowGUIDs are globally unique, meaning that each one is guaranteed to be different, even if multiple users simultaneously create a RowGUID, each on his own PC. However, RowGUIDs cannot be used for any sorting purposes.

4

Workshop

The Workshop provides quiz questions to help you solidify your understanding of the material covered and exercises to provide you with experience in using what you've learned. Try to understand the quiz and exercise answers before continuing to the next lesson. Answers are provided in Appendix A.

Quiz

1. What is the relationship between table and entity?
2. What is NULL?
3. What are other names for record and field?
4. True/False. A primary key can only contain one column.

5. What's a foreign key?

6. What's the difference between DDL and DML?

7. What SQL statement do you use to retrieve data from a table?

8. What is an INNER JOIN?

9. What is an identity column, and what is it used for?

10. What happens when an INSERT statement does not specify the names of the columns?

Exercises

1. Create an empty database for the SmallTownBank application. In the next exercise, you will populate this database with tables. In SQL Server, you use Enterprise Manager to manage databases. By default, you will find the shortcut in Programs, Microsoft SQL Server 7.

   Start the SQL Server 7 Enterprise Manager. Under Console Root, expand Microsoft SQL Server, SQL Server Group until you see the name of your server. Expand your server until you see the Databases, Data Transformation, Management, Security and Support Services folders.

   Right-click Databases and select New Database. Enter **SmallTownBank** as the database name. You can keep the default settings for the File growth properties and the Transaction log settings. Click OK. SQL Server only takes a short while to create the database. You can see the newly created database in the databases folder.

2. Populate the database created in exercise 1 with the tables used by the SmallTownBank application. You will also add sample data to these tables so you can test the application as you build it. Use the VB Data View Window to create the following tables:

```
CREATE TABLE Customer
(
    CustomerKey INT IDENTITY (1, 1) NOT NULL ,
    FirstName CHAR(50) NOT NULL ,
    MiddleName CHAR(50) NULL ,
    LastName CHAR(50) NOT NULL ,
    SuffixName CHAR(5) NULL ,
    SocialSecurityNumber CHAR(9) NOT NULL ,
    Address1 CHAR(50) NOT NULL ,
    Address2 CHAR(50) NULL ,
    City CHAR(50) NOT NULL ,
    State CHAR(2) NOT NULL ,
```

```
    PostalCode CHAR(10) NOT NULL ,
    PhoneNumber CHAR(20) NULL ,
    EMailAddress CHAR(50) NULL ,
    UserID CHAR(20) NOT NULL ,
    SpouseID INT NULL
);

CREATE TABLE TransactionType
(
    TransactionTypeKey INT IDENTITY (1, 1) NOT NULL ,
    Description CHAR(50) NOT NULL
);

CREATE TABLE Account
(
    AccountKey INT IDENTITY (1, 1) NOT NULL ,
    AccountNumber CHAR(20) NOT NULL ,
    AccountTypeID INT NOT NULL ,
    CustomerID INT NOT NULL ,
    Balance MONEY NOT NULL
);

CREATE TABLE Spouse
(
    SpouseKey INT IDENTITY (1, 1) NOT NULL ,
    FirstName CHAR(50) NOT NULL ,
    MiddleName CHAR(50) NULL ,
    LastName CHAR(50) NULL ,
    SocialSecurityNumber CHAR(9) NULL
);

CREATE TABLE AccountTransaction
(
    TransactionKey INT IDENTITY (1, 1) NOT NULL ,
    AccountID INT NOT NULL ,
    CustomerID INT NOT NULL ,
    TransactionTypeID INT NOT NULL ,
    Amount MONEY NULL ,
    Description VARCHAR(50) NULL ,
    CheckNumber CHAR(10) NULL ,
    Payee CHAR(50) NULL ,
    DateEntered DATETIME NOT NULL
);
```

3. Create the relationships between the tables used by the SmallTownBank application. You will also add sample data to these tables so you can test the application as you build it. Use the VB Data View Window to create the relationships in Figure 4.5.

FIGURE 4.5

The relationships in the `SmallTownBank` *application.*

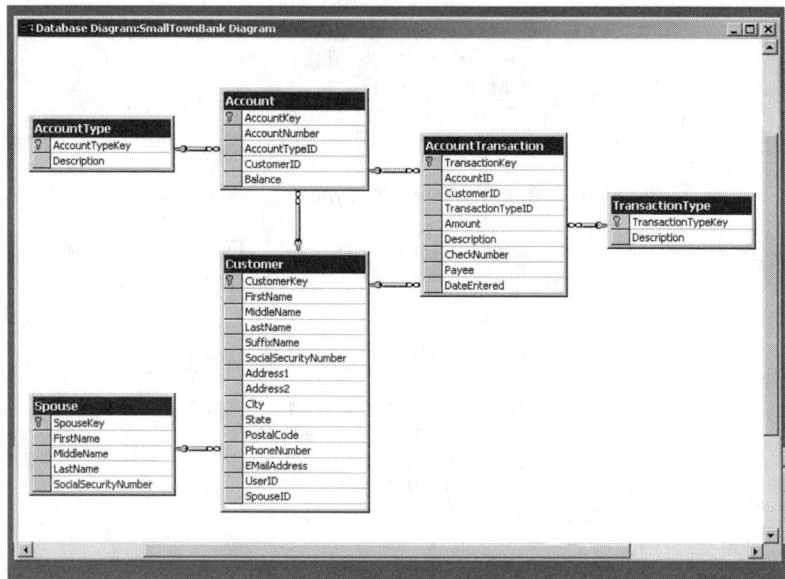

Then, you can add data to the tables. To avoid typing all the SQL statements, you can run a script found on the CD-ROM accompanying this book. You can use the SQL Query Analyzer (Programs, Microsoft SQL Server 7.0, Query Analyzer) to run the SQL statements. Make sure that the database selected in the DB combo box is the `SmallTownBank` database. Then select File, Open and locate the `InitialData.sql` file on the CD-ROM. Run this script. You can then run a few `SELECT` statements to verify that the data was entered in the tables.

DAY 5

Putting Business Logic in the Data Tier

Modern day relational database management systems (RDBMS) can do a great number of things, including applying business rules to your data. The ability to apply business rules at the DBMS level adds a great deal of efficiency and ensures that your data is consistent. However, as with anything, it is possible to do too much in the RDBMS and thus affect scalability, portability, and maintainability. Although there are no hard and fast rules, we will look at the factors that go into deciding where to place data validation rules. Business rules are the practices and policies that define a company's behavior. Examples of business rules are return policies, credit rules, and so on. SQL Server and most other databases provide you with a plethora of ways to enforce these rules in the data tier. Today, you will learn about

- Defaults and constraints
- Stored procedures and when you use them
- Triggers
- Tools that can help you create stored procedures
- When to use a stored procedure versus a business component

Ensuring Data Integrity

You probably have heard the popular dictum "Garbage in, garbage out." It means that you cannot get good results based on shaky input. So, it is no small wonder that data integrity is crucial to the success of a database application.

NEW TERM   *Data integrity* guarantees the consistency of data stored in the database.

You will see how you can have SQL Server enforce data integrity for you by specifying the rules that need to be followed. There are three types of data integrity:

- Entity integrity
- Domain integrity
- Referential integrity

Entity Integrity

Entity integrity, sometimes also called *table integrity*, requires that all rows in a table have a unique identifier. You can have SQL Server (or any other commercial database system for that matter) enforce entity integrity by defining a primary key for every table. In Day 4, "Exploring Database Fundamentals," you saw how to create primary keys (either natural or artificial—the latter by using identities or row GUIDs).

Domain Integrity

Domain integrity, sometimes also called *column integrity*, specifies the valid values for a specific column and whether NULL is allowed. Yesterday, you learned how to specify whether a column allows NULL in the table designer and how to specify a default value for a column. You can also specify CHECK() constraints where you implement validation rules. A CHECK() constraint allows you to define a validation rule for a column, enforcing domain integrity. CHECK() constraints allow you to perform data validation, such as ensuring that dates are logical (for example, birth date must be in the past). A CHECK() constraint can also be used to enforce business rules.

Just as in table creation, you can do this in the Visual Basic environment through the Data View window. Expand the SmallTownBank data link and expand the Tables folder. Right-click a table and select Design. This brings up the table design dialog you used in Day 4, shown in Figure 5.1.

FIGURE 5.1

The table Design dialog can be accessed from within the Visual Basic environment.

Column Name	Datatype	Length	Precision	Scale	Allow Nulls	Default Value	Identity	Identity Seed	Identity Increment	Is RowGuid
AccountKey	int	4	10	0			✓	1	1	
AccountNumber	char	20	0	0						
AccountTypeID	int	4	10	0						
CustomerID	int	4	10	0						
Balance	money	8	19	4						

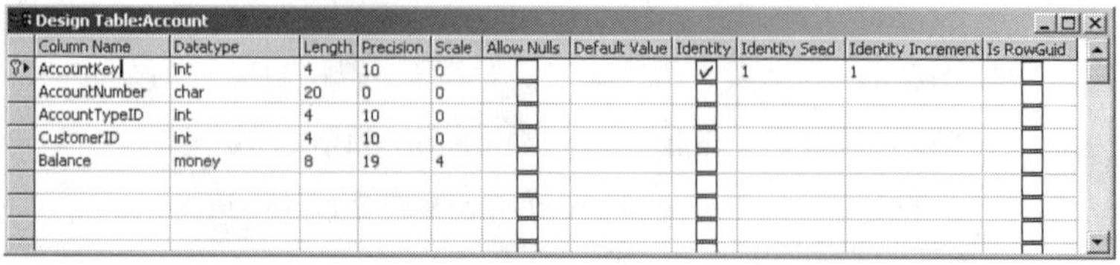

Right-click the empty area of the table design dialog and select Properties. This brings up the table Properties dialog, shown in Figure 5.2.

FIGURE 5.2

The table Properties dialog lets you define indices, set relation-ships, and create constraints.

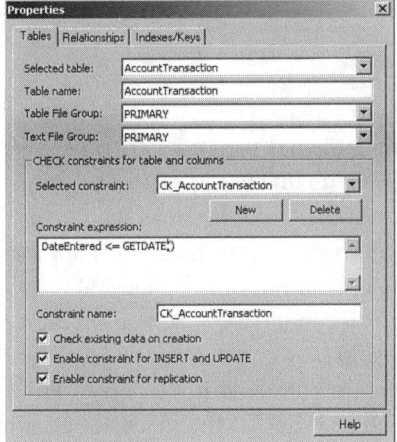

In Figure 5.2, you see an example of a CHECK() constraint using SQL Server GETDATE() function. As you can see, a CHECK() constraint can use other columns. Another popular form for CHECK() constraints, for example, might follow the format "State IN ('WA', 'OR', 'AK', 'AL')."

Referential Integrity

Referential integrity ensures that the relationship between two tables remains valid. This relationship is based on a master-detail relationship between the two tables, as you saw yesterday when we discussed primary and foreign keys. A master-detail relationship is a one-to-many relationship between two tables.

The often-cited example of a master-detail relationship is the order-master/order-detail relationship. A single order might comprise several items. (In the online bookseller scenario touched upon in Day 4, you can place an order for two or more books.) There is information specific to the order, such as shipping and billing information and information specific to each item being ordered, such as item code, quantity, and price. So two tables are needed to store the order information. Figure 5.3 shows an example of how two such tables might look. (You will notice that additional information is stored in more tables, but this is not relevant to our discussion of master-detail relationships.)

5

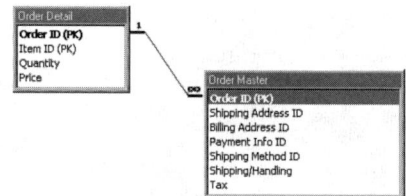

FIGURE 5.3

The Order Master and Order Detail tables share a typical master-detail relationship.

In Figure 5.3, the Order Master table has the Order ID (likely an identity column) as its primary key (PK). The Order Detail table has a composite primary key, comprised of the Order ID and Item ID. Of course, the Order ID links the Order Master and Order Detail tables. It is obvious that an Order Detail record that does not match any row in the Order Master table would be missing crucial information needed to fulfill the order. This is why you need referential integrity. You can tell SQL Server to enforce referential integrity by defining a foreign key relationship between the two tables, as shown in Day 4. SQL Server then helps enforce referential integrity in two ways. First, it will not allow you to enter an Item Detail record with an order ID that does not exist in the Item Master table. Secondly, it will not allow you to delete an Item Master record for which there are matching Order Details rows.

Stored Procedures

Stored procedures are precompiled SQL statements stored in the database. These statements can be used to insert, select, update, or delete data.

Stored procedures are the SQL equivalent of functions and subroutines in traditional programming languages. They can take and return user-supplied parameters. (Just like a function, a stored procedure is invoked by the application—not automatically by SQL Server.) Using stored procedures you can easily execute a batch of SQL statements in a single line, just as you can call a Visual Basic function or subroutine with a single line of code. This can reduce the amount of repeated code in your application and therefore make your application easier to maintain. This is a benefit subroutines and stored procedures share.

However, stored procedures have a unique benefit, because they are stored in compiled format in the database. When you create a stored procedure, SQL Server parses the statements and stores a compiled version of these statements in the database. Because of this, running a stored procedure is faster than running the statements contained in the stored procedure. Below you will find out how to create stored procedures.

Stored procedures can enforce business rules by ensuring that the rules are being followed prior to performing the action (inserting, updating or deleting). If the rules are not followed, the stored procedure can simply raise an error and refuse to do the action. Using a stored procedure to do this has the advantage that many client applications can call the stored procedures and that the business rule is implemented only once.

CREATE PROCEDURE Statement

Just as tables are created with the CREATE TABLE statement, so are stored procedures created with the CREATE PROCEDURE statement.

▼ SYNTAX

```
CREATE PROC[EDURE] procedure_name
[ ( parameter1 data_type_1 [OUT] [, parameter2 data_type_1 [OUT]] ... ) ]
AS
sql_statements
```

Here is an example of a CREATE PROCEDURE statement:

```
CREATE PROCEDURE sp_del_Customer
    (@CustomerKey INT)
AS
    DELETE FROM Customer
    WHERE CustomerKey = @CustomerKey
```

▲

Let us examine this example. The CREATE PROCEDURE is followed by the procedure name, sp_del_Customer. It is customary to use a prefix sp_ or pc_ for stored procedures. After the procedure name come the parameters enclosed in brackets and separated by commas. Parameter names start with the at sign (@). In our example there is just one parameter (@CustomerKey). Then, after the AS keyword, follow the SQL statements you want to execute as part of this stored procedure. Here there is only one statement, but stored procedures can contain many statements.

If you want to retrieve the value of a parameter after calling a stored procedure, simply put the keyword OUT after that parameter. You assign a value to this parameter by using SELECT @param = expression.

5

There are two types of stored procedures: row returning or non-row returning. The names give away the distinction. A non-row returning procedure only contains UPDATE, INSERT, or DELETE statements. The previous code snippet is an example of a non-row returning stored procedure. Listing 5.1 is an example of a row returning stored procedure. Row returning stored procedures contain a SELECT statement (causing the procedure returns statement).

LISTING 5.1   A Row-Returning Procedure Contains a SELECT Statement

```
 1: CREATE PROCEDURE sp_sel_Spouse
 2:     (@SpouseKey INT)
 3: AS
 4:     SELECT
 5:         SpouseKey,
 6:         FirstName,
 7:         MiddleName,
 8:         LastName,
 9:         SocialSecurityNumber
10:     FROM Spouse
11:     WHERE SpouseKey = @SpouseKey
```

The code for this stored procedure follows the same principles as the previous code.

Tip

Unlike triggers, discussed later in this chapter, you need to call stored procedures explicitly. However, it is possible to have SQL Server automatically execute a stored procedure at startup. Search the SQL Server documentation for sp_makestartup for more details on this handy feature.

Identity columns require special handling in stored procedures. Often when dealing with identity columns, you must know the value of the identity column for the newly inserted row. This is particularly true when dealing with master-detail relationships, as you need this value in order to insert the details. First you need to insert a row in the order master, then you need the value of the identity column to insert the foreign key in the order details table. SQL Server uses the @@IDENTITY keyword to give you this value. The @@IDENTITY keyword should be used immediately after the insert statement to ensure that the identity value is not lost. You can see in Listing 5.2 how you would use this keyword.

LISTING 5.2   You Can Retrieve the Value of the Identity Column Using @@IDENTITY

```
 1:
 2: CREATE PROCEDURE sp_ins_Account
 3:     @AccountNumber charCHAR(20),
 4:     @AccountTypeID INT,
 5:     @CustomerID INT,
 6:     @Balance MONEY = NULL
 7: AS
 8:     SET NOCOUNT ON
 9:
10:     INSERT Account
11:         (
12:         AccountNumber,
13:         AccountTypeID,
14:         CustomerID,
15:         Balance
16:         )
17:     VALUES
18:         (
19:         @AccountNumber,
20:         @AccountTypeID,
21:         @CustomerID,
22:         @Balance
23:         )
24:
25:     RETURN @@IDENTITY
26:
27:     SET NOCOUNT OFF
28: GO
```

In the stored procedure above, you find an insert statement. The Account table contains an identity column AccountKey. The INSERT statement implicitly adds a value for this column. You return this value by retrieving the @@IDENTITY value right after the insert statement.

Caution   Always retrieve the @@IDENTITY value as the first statement following the INSERT statement. If needed, declare a variable to store the identity value. For example,

```
DECLARE @AccountKey INT
INSERT Account
        (
        AccountNumber,
        AccountTypeID,
        CustomerID,
```

5

```
            Balance
            )
    VALUES
            (
            @AccountNumber,
            @AccountTypeID,
            @CustomerID,
            @Balance
            )

    SELECT @AccountKey = @@IDENTITY

    /* More statements … */

    RETURN @AccountKey
```

Tomorrow, you will see how to call stored procedures from VB using Active Data Objects. Listing 5.3 shows how you call a stored procedure from SQL.

LISTING 5.3 Calling a Stored Procedure from SQL Code

```
1:
2:      DECLARE @RetValue INT
3:
4:      EXEC @RetValue = sp_ins_Account '1000A1', 1, 102, 2000
5:
6:      PRINT @RetValue
```

You declare a variable of the proper type to receive the return value. You use the EXEC keyword to call the stored procedure and collect the return value. Finally, you print the returned value.

Triggers

A *trigger* is a special kind of stored procedure that is attached to a table and that is invoked (*triggered*) whenever an attempt is made to modify the data in the table. So triggers are invoked whenever an INSERT, DELETE, or UPDATE SQL statement is issued against the table. Constraints, such as foreign or primary key constraints, are checked prior to trigger execution. If you try to insert a row with a primary key that already exists, the primary key violation will stop the statement from executing, and the trigger will **not** be invoked. Unlike stored procedures, triggers are automatically invoked by SQL Server; they cannot be called directly and cannot take parameters. Each table can have up to three triggers—one associated with each action: INSERT, DELETE, and UPDATE. The syntax for creating a trigger is as follows:

▼ SYNTAX

```
CREATE TRIGGER trigger_name ON table_name
FOR { INSERT | UPDATE | DELETE }
AS
sql_statements
```

Here is an example of a CREATE TRIGGER statement:

```
CREATE TRIGGER CustomerKey_Update
        ON Customer
        FOR UPDATE
AS
    IF UPDATE(CustomerKey)
    BEGIN
        RAISERROR('Customer Key cannot be modified.',10, 1)
        ROLLBACK TRANSACTION
    END
```

▲

This trigger example shows a typical use of triggers: disallowing edit of a primary key. The IF UPDATE(*column_name*) is available within UPDATE and INSERT triggers to test whether a specific column was modified. RAISEERROR is a SQL Server function used to raise an error, the equivalent of Err.Raise in Visual Basic. ROLLBACK TRANSACTION is used to cancel the operation invoking the trigger.

Note

> A trigger is not the only way to disallow access to a column. The database administrator can also revoke privileges on the primary key column(s).

5

Triggers make the changes available to you through two special tables: "inserted" and "deleted". These tables are logical (conceptual) tables and have exactly the same structure as the table on which the trigger is defined. They hold a copy of the rows modified by the user.

When an INSERT statement is executed on a table protected with an INSERT trigger, new rows are added to both the trigger table and the "inserted" table. The "inserted" table contains a copy of the rows that have just been inserted. These rows are also present in the trigger table.

When a DELETE statement is executed on a table protected with a DELETE trigger, the rows are deleted from the trigger table and placed in the "deleted" table. The "deleted" table contains the rows that have just been deleted. These rows are no longer in the trigger table.

When an UPDATE statement is executed on a table protected with an UPDATE trigger, the original rows are deleted from the trigger table and placed in the "deleted" table. Then the modified rows are added to both the trigger table and the "inserted" table.

Listing 5.3 shows how you can use these logical tables. The Account_delete trigger prevents deletion of Account rows with a non-zero balance.

LISTING 5.3   A DELETE Trigger

```
1: CREATE TRIGGER Account_delete
2: ON Account
3: FOR DELETE
4: AS
5: IF (SELECT COUNT(*) AS Expr1
6: FROM Account
7: INNER JOIN deleted
8: ON Account.AccountKey = deleted.AccountKey
9: WHERE Account.Balance = 0) = 0
10: BEGIN
11:RAISEERROR('Account must have a zero balance to be deleted', 10, 1)
12: ROLLBACK TRANSACTION
13: END
```

ANALYSIS   The first four lines look familiar by now: the CREATE statement, followed by the name, followed by the AS keyword. Except for the use of TRIGGER instead of PROCEDURE, this is the same as with stored procedures. Then comes a fairly complex but typical query to determine whether the account balance is zero. The Account table is joined to the special "deleted" table to find which records are about to be deleted. (Almost every DELETE trigger will perform this join.) The WHERE clause restricts the rows being examined to those with zero balances. Finally, the COUNT(*) tells you whether or not the row being deleted has a zero balance. (As you can probably tell, this query does not work if multiple rows are being deleted simultaneously.) The ROLLBACK TRANSACTION statement is used to cancel the deletion.

Just as with stored procedures, triggers can be used for two purposes: keeping the data in the database consistent and enforcing business rules. Triggers are most often used for the former, while stored procedures are most often used for the latter. Later in this chapter, you will see an alternative to implementing the business rules in the data tier.

The Stored Procedure Wizard

SQL Server provides you with a great tool for creating the basic stored procedures needed for a DNA application. Since stored procedures execute faster than queries, you want to create up to four stored procedures for each table in the database—one for each of the DML statements: INSERT, UPDATE, DELETE, and SELECT. However, creating all these stored procedures is quite tedious. This is where the stored procedure wizard comes into play.

You access the stored procedure wizard from within the SQL Server Enterprise Manager. You can start it by selecting Tools, Wizards (there is also a wizard button on the toolbar). When the Select Wizards dialog pops up, expand Database, select the Create Stored Procedure Wizard, and then click OK. Click Next to go past the Welcome screen. In the Select Database screen, make sure the correct Database is selected, and then click Next. You now get a list of the tables in the database. You can check off for which DML statements (INSERT, UPDATE, or DELETE) you want to create a stored procedure, and then click Next. Figure 5.4 shows the final screen after the Customer table; all three types of DML statements have been selected.

FIGURE 5.4

The stored procedure wizard generated stored procedures to INSERT, UPDATE, *or* DELETE *rows in a table.*

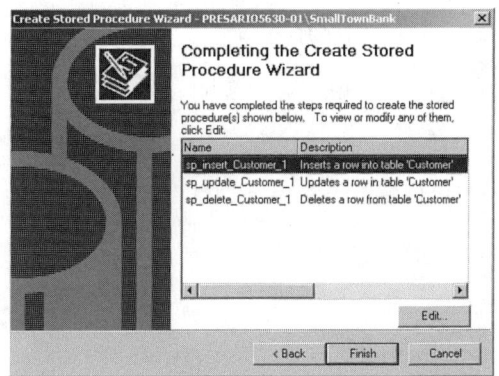

5

> **Tip**
>
> The SELECT statement is not an available choice. However, because you can edit the generated statements in the wizard, you can, for example, select INSERT, change the SQL statement to a SELECT statement, and rename the stored procedure accordingly.

In this final screen, you can—if you want—modify everything the wizard has done: the name of the stored procedure, the stored procedure parameters, and the SQL statements in the procedure. For the SmallTownBank application, you will remove the numbers after the names of the stored procedures and parameters. Highlight the sp_insert_Customers_1 procedure and click Edit. Change the name to sp_ins_Customer. Deselect the CustomerKey parameter (it is an identity column, so

SQL Server will automatically assign a value) and click edit SQL. Remove the numbers after the parameters and click OK. Check your edits against Listing 5.4.

LISTING 5.4   The Stored Procedure Wizard Can Reduce the Effort Required to Code a Stored Procedure

```
 1: USE [SmallTownBank]
 2: GO
 3: CREATE PROCEDURE [sp_ins_Customer]
 4:     (@FirstName      [char](50),
 5:      @MiddleName      [char](50),
 6:      @LastName      [char](50),
 7:      @SuffixName      [char](5),
 8:      @SocialSecurityNumber      [char](9),
 9:      @Address1      [char](50),
10:      @Address2      [char](50),
11:      @City      [char](50),
12:      @State      [char](2),
13:      @PostalCode      [char](10),
14:      @PhoneNumber      [char](20),
15:      @EMailAddress      [char](50),
16:      @UserID      [char](20),
17:      @SpouseID      [int])
18:
19: AS INSERT INTO [SmallTownBank].[dbo].[Customer]
20:     (
21:      [FirstName],
22:      [MiddleName],
23:      [LastName],
24:      [SuffixName],
25:      [SocialSecurityNumber],
26:      [Address1],
27:      [Address2],
28:      [City],
29:      [State],
30:      [PostalCode],
31:      [PhoneNumber],
32:      [EMailAddress],
33:      [UserID],
34:      [SpouseID])
35:
36: VALUES
37:     (@FirstName,
38:      @MiddleName,
39:      @LastName,
40:      @SuffixName,
41:      @SocialSecurityNumber,
42:      @Address1,
43:      @Address2,
```

```
44:        @City,
45:        @State,
46:        @PostalCode,
47:        @PhoneNumber,
48:        @EMailAddress,
49:        @UserID,
50:        @SpouseID)
```

ANALYSIS The stored procedure has the usual format, but this time uses more than 1 parameter.

You can check whether your code parses correctly by clicking the parse button. Change the name of the INSERT procedure to sp_ins_Customer. Deselect the CustomerKey column in the Include in the Set clause and click Edit SQL to remove the numbers after the parameters. Finally, change the name of the DELETE procedure to sp_del_Customer and remove the number after the parameter. Click Finish. SQL Server proudly announces it successfully created the three stored procedures.

Note

It is merely a matter of preference whether to leave the numbers after the parameters. We opted to delete the numbers as it makes the Visual Basic coding using ActiveX Data Objects (ADO) a bit less tedious (no need to look up the parameter numbers). You will learn about ADO objects tomorrow.

Where Do You Implement Business Rules?

5

If you write a distributed application, you must take care of minimizing network trips. Therefore, even if the database will reject invalid data, you should check as much as possible on the client side before going to the database. For example, you should ensure that all required data has been entered before even attempting to submit the data to the database. Similarly, if a column only accepts certain values (for example, a Gender column accepting only 'F', 'M', and '?'), you should check the validity of entered data at the client side. Of course, you cannot check everything without accessing the database—some checks require a database lookup, for example, to access the account balance.

As pointed out above, all the SQL statements discussed in this chapter serve two distinct purposes: keeping the data consistent and enforcing business policies. There are no good alternatives to the techniques presented in this chapter to keep the data consistent. Using SQL to enforce data integrity ensures that the data remains consistent no matter how the SQL statements are issued (for example, including statements issued by programmers).

However, you may opt to use Visual Basic components instead of SQL to enforce the business rules. When is Visual Basic better? Well, there are no hard and fast rules that dictate when VB is definitely better than SQL. However, since SQL has only limited control structures (IF THEN, loops, and so on), the more complex the logic is, the more suited Visual Basic is. The flip side of this is that simple rules (for example, those that can easily be expressed in a SQL statement) are best implemented in SQL.

Summary

In this chapter, you learned how to maintain data integrity by specifying the rules that SQL Server needs to enforce. You also learned how to create stored procedures (the equivalent of functions and subs) either manually or through the stored procedure wizard. Finally, you also learned how to use triggers to further control data integrity.

Tomorrow's lesson will look at ActiveX Data Objects (ADO). ADO is the cornerstone of Windows DNA's data access tier. It encapsulates the low-level details of database access and performs very well. Day 6 will guide you through the basics of ADO programming.

Q&A

Q Why are table names in stored procedures generated by the wizard preceded with `[SmallTownBank].[dbo]`?

A The first is the database; the second is the database owner. It is possible to access tables in different databases by using these prefixes. In most cases, however, these prefixes are redundant and not used when you write the statements with the help of a wizard.

Q What does `SET NOCOUNT ON/OFF` accomplish?

A When `SET NOCOUNT` is `ON`, the count indicating the number of rows affected by each SQL statement is not returned. When `SET NOCOUNT` is `OFF`, this count is returned. For stored procedures that contain several statements that do not return much actual data, this can provide a significant performance boost because network traffic is greatly reduced.

Q Data integrity seems to interfere with development. When do you add data integrity checks to the database?

A As soon as possible. If the developers try to insert invalid data, then they should be made aware of this as soon as possible. However, you need to create a set of consistent data to load into the database so the developers can use the database without getting errors due to missing data in lookup tables.

Workshop

The Workshop provides quiz questions to help you solidify your understanding of the material covered and exercises to provide you with experience in using what you've learned. Try to understand the quiz and exercise answers before continuing to the next lesson. Answers are provided in Appendix A.

Quiz

1. What are the three types of data integrity?
2. True/False. A CHECK() constraint is checked after the triggers.
3. Which DML statements can be turned into a stored procedure with the help of the stored procedure wizard?
4. How do you retrieve the value of the identity column after you insert a row in a table?
5. How do you pass a value by reference to a stored procedure?
6. True/False. In an UPDATE trigger, the modified values are stored in a logical table called "updated".
7. How do you access a trigger from within a stored procedure?
8. True/False. A stored procedure can contain more than one SQL statement.
9. How are stored procedures categorized?
10. How do you check if a column has been modified in a trigger?

Exercises

1. If you have Access, MSDE, or another database application, create a simple database and try to connect to it through ADO. Remember to create your DSN. Select some records out from it and display them on a form or debug window.
2. In Visual Basic or Visual Interdev, create a function that returns a recordset, which contains the results of a query.
3. Use the stored procedure wizard to create the following three stored procedures. You will need to modify the generated names and the parameters as explained previously.

5

Stored Procedure Listing 1

```
1: CREATE PROCEDURE sp_del_Account
2:     @AccountKey int
3: AS
4:     DELETE
5:     FROM
6:         Account
7:     WHERE
8:         AccountKey = @AccountKey
9: GO
```

Stored Procedure Listing 2

```
1: CREATE PROCEDURE sp_upd_Account
2:     @AccountKey int,
3:     @AccountNumber char(20),
4:     @AccountTypeID int,
5:     @CustomerID int,
6:     @Balance money
7: AS
8:     UPDATE
9:         Account
10:    SET
11:        AccountNumber = @AccountNumber,
12:        AccountTypeID = @AccountTypeID,
13:        CustomerID = @CustomerID,
14:        Balance = @Balance
15:    WHERE
16:        AccountKey = @AccountKey
17: GO
```

Stored Procedure Listing 3

```
1: CREATE PROCEDURE sp_ins_Account
2:     @AccountNumber char(20),
3:     @AccountTypeID int,
4:     @CustomerID int,
5:     @Balance money = NULL
6: AS
7:     SET NOCOUNT ON
8:
9:     INSERT Account
10:        (
11:        AccountNumber,
12:        AccountTypeID,
```

```
13:          CustomerID,
14:          Balance
15:          )
16:      VALUES
17:          (
18:          @AccountNumber,
19:          @AccountTypeID,
20:          @CustomerID,
21:          @Balance
22:          )
23:
24:      RETURN @@IDENTITY
25:
26:      SET NOCOUNT OFF
27: GO
```

4. Use the script found on the CD to generate the remaining stored procedures. You can use the SQL Query Analyzer (Programs, Microsoft SQL Server 7.0, Query Analyzer) to run the SQL statements. Make sure that the database selected in the DB combo box is the SmallTownBank database. Then select File, Open and locate the StoredProcedures.sql file on the CD. Run this script. Go to the stored procedures folder in Enterprise Manager and ensure that all procedures were created. (You might have to Refresh the list first.)

5

DAY 6

ActiveX Data Objects (ADO)

During the past few days, you have become familiar with SQL Enterprise Manager, creating tables and manipulating the database directly. You now want to learn how to interact with your database through your applications. How will you do this? The answer is using ActiveX Data Objects (ADO).

Expanding on what you learned of the DNA Architecture from the first two days, you are focusing on ADO in this chapter, which is the cornerstone of Windows DNA's data tier. Your business logic tier makes calls to your data tier where ADO is used. ADO enables access to your data stores in the data tier. To learn about ADO, this chapter will guide you through the basics of ADO programming and introduce you to the fundamental ADO objects: `Connection`, `Command`, and `Recordset`.

Using Visual Basic, you will learn to use these ADO objects to update and query a data store. You will notice that we use the term data store instead of database; the reason is that ADO can work with nearly any type of data.

Examples are flat files, mail repositories, directory services, and any other data provider you create. ADO is a universal data access technology. The best thing about this model is that from a programming perspective all data providers look the same. Today, you learn about

- The creation of a Data Source Name (DSN)
- DSN-less connections
- The difference between OLE DB and ODBC
- The Recordset, Connection, and Command objects
- Stored procedures and how to call them
- Other data stores

Creating a Data Source Name (DSN)

Before you can get into the actual programming of ADO, you first have to enter information about your data store by creating a DSN through the ODBC Data Sources applet in the Control Panel. This DSN, in combination with ADO, will allow you to easily connect to your data stores. When you create a DSN in this applet, you are not making a connection to the data, but entering information about the connection you will make. There are three different types of DSNs that you can make. Figure 6.1 shows the ODBC Data Source Administrator and the tabs of the three DSNs you can create. First, you will learn about each of the three DSN's. Next, you will create a System DSN. Fortunately, the steps you use to create a System DSN are the same steps you would use for creating the other types of DSNs.

FIGURE 6.1

The System DSN tab of the ODBC Data Source Administrator.

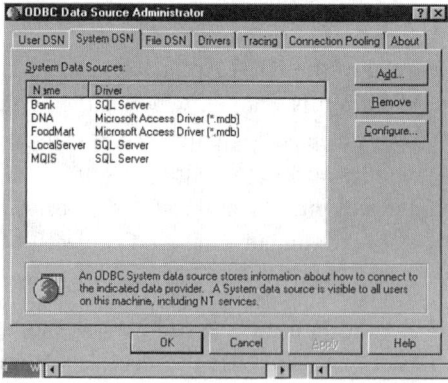

The first is a User DSN. A User DSN is available on a user-by-user basis. Therefore, in a case where client software is installed on a machine and you want only one specific person to access data, you could create a User DSN for that person. If another user logs in, that user would not have access to the DSN.

Next is a System DSN. A System DSN is available on a system whether or not someone is logged in. Often, for the scenario of a server where no one would be logged in, this still allows the DSN to be available. Typically, you might set up a System DSN on a Windows NT Server for a data-driven Web application. The Web application could then use the System DSN to learn where to access the data.

Finally there is the File DSN. A File DSN stores its information in a file. (It is nice to know that these names actually sometimes do make sense.) Typically, these files are stored somewhere under your Windows directory. You can find them by looking for files ending in .dsn. Unlike a System DSN, which is looked at every time your application makes a connection, the information from a File DSN might be read in once and then stored somewhere in the application. This occurs in Visual Interdev and IIS. If you set up a connection for a Web or subweb, the connection information is stored in the global.asa and the File DSN information is no longer referenced in the control panel. If you don't want to be referencing a System DSN from your application, but instead want to store all the connection information in your application, then choose a File DSN.

Tip

An advantage of a File DSN is that as you move the application from server to server, such as in a Web environment where you go from a development server to a production server, you will not have to recreate the DSN in the ODBC applet.

Follow these steps to make a DSN connection to the pubs database in MSDE. The pubs database is a sample database that comes with MSDE. The database is a publisher's database that includes information about fictitious publishers, authors, and books.

6

1. Open the ODBC Data Source Administrator in the Control Panel.
2. Select the System DSN Tab.
3. Click Add to add a new DSN.
4. Select SQL Server and click Finish.
5. For Name, enter **pubs_dsn**. Description is optional.
6. For Server, enter your machine name if you are running MSDE or type in the server you are connecting to. You can also select it from the drop-down.

7. Click Next.

8. The next choice involves SQL Server authentication. Authentication can be done through integrated security using NT authentication or SQL Server authentication. Choose SQL Server Authentication, which is more common. For the login, enter **sa** and for the password, leave it blank. sa is the default administrator account.

Note

You will still have to supply a valid login and password in your application. The login and password entered in for authentication is only for setting up the DSN.

9. Select Change the Default Database to and select the pubs database. Click Next.

10. Make no changes on this page. Click Next.

11. Click Finish. You can now click Test Data Source to make sure everything is fine and then click OK. Your newly created DSN should be present in the list of Data Sources.

After a DSN is entered, you can reference the DSN through a connection string in your code.

The following syntax is the format of a DSN connection string. This connection string will either be set to a ADO property or passed as a parameter with ADO methods. It will establish a connection between your application and the data store.

```
"[Provider=provider name;] { DSN=name | FileDSN=filename };
 ➥ [DATABASE=database;]UID=user; PWD=password"
```

Provider is the driver that provides you access to the underlying data. The default is MSDASQL, the ODBC OLE DB provider. The DSN (DSN=) or File DSN name (FileDSN=) corresponds to the name of the DSN in the ODBC administrator. The database name (DATABASE=) is the database you want to connect to. A valid user (UID=) and password (PWD=) is also required if security exists.

If you use a DSN or File DSN, it is created with the ODBC Administrator in the Windows Control Panel and referenced in applications. The following are examples of how you would reference the DSNs.

```
1: strConnectionString = "Provider=MSDASQL;FileDSN=pubs_filedsn;
   ➥Database=pubs;UID=sa;PWD="
2: strConnectionString = "Provider=MSDASQL;DSN=pubs_dsn;
   ➥Database=pubs;UID=sa;PWD="
```

▼ Line 1 is an example of a connection string with a file dsn. Line 2 is an example of a connection string with a system dsn. Both are connections to the pubs database with the
▲ same username, which in this case is sa.

Exploring DSN-Less Connections

DSN-less connections are similar to the File DSNs. After you create the File DSN, your application has the necessary connection string information to contact the Database. It no longer needs the settings in the ODBC Administrator. The application looks at the file where the DSN information is stored. Similarly, a DSN-less connection is a connection where all the necessary information is entered directly into the application, by-passing the ODBC Administrator altogether. In a Web environment, this can be very useful if you are working on Web server that is at a remote location. In this case you might not have physical access to the server to open the control panel and add a DSN. In this case you could still use a DSN-less connection in your application.

The following is the format of a DSN-less connection string:

```
"[Provider=provider name;] DRIVER=driver; SERVER=server; ➡

DATABASE=database;UID=user; PWD=password"
```

This is an alternative to setting a DSN. As with the DSN connection strings, you still specify a provider. You specify the ODBC driver (DRIVER=), such as "SQL Server," the server name (SERVER=), and the database name (DATABASE=). If necessary, you also supply a valid user (UID=) and password (PWD=) as seen in the lines below.

```
1: strConnectionString = "Provider=MSDASQL;DRIVER=SQL
   ➡Server;SERVER=(local);DATABASE=pubs;UID=sa;PWD=;"
2: strConnectionString = "DRIVER=SQL
   ➡Server;SERVER=(local);DATABASE=pubs;UID=sa;PWD=;"
```

Unlike the connection strings used with the DSNs, these strings reference no DSN. All the necessary information is in the string. Line 2 does not specify the provider, therefore
▲ it uses the default, which is MSDASQL, the ODBC OLE DB provider.

6

Comparing OLE DB and ODBC

ODBC (Open Database Connectivity) has been around now for many years and has allowed access to well-formed relational databases. It solves the developer's problem of how to access different databases easily from within an application. Now, from within an application you can access a delimited text file, a FoxPro database, and an Oracle database—as long as you have the proper drivers installed. Without ODBC, developers are required to know and understand the unique way data is stored in each of these systems.

NEW TERM   *ODBC* is an international standard whereby drivers can be created to access rela-
             tional data. This is why it is called open. As long as someone writes an ODBC
driver for the data, developers can access the data through standard objects such as ADO.
The qualification is that data has to be relational.

OLE DB is, in some ways, analogous to ODBC. OLE DB enables you access to data
stores by giving a standard interface into them, similar to ODBC. OLE DB comes in at a
lower level then ODBC, enabling developers to create providers to access all kinds of
data. Since it is at a lower level, it also enables faster access than ODBC. Also, Microsoft
has a OLE DB provider for ODBC, which you saw earlier called MSDASQL, enabling
you to access any ODBC data through it.

NEW TERM   *OLE DB* is a system-level programming interface to various types of data
             sources. This is how you can access directories, email folders, and any other type
of data that a provider is written for.

> **Note**
>
> You learned earlier that the ODBC OLE DB provider is the default provider in
> your connection strings. Why would you have an OLE DB Provider for ODBC?
> In doing so, ADO has to go through OLE DB, which goes through ODBC,
> which then accesses your data. This seems inefficient and slow. But by creat-
> ing this provider, it allowed the use of all the ODBC drivers that have
> already been created. Other OLE DB providers, such as SQLOLEDB, a
> provider for SQL Server, are also available. This type of provider will access
> SQL data directly through OLE DB.

Exploring the ADO Object Model

In ADO, the Connection, Command, and Recordset objects are the primary interfaces you
will use to access and manipulate the data. There are other objects you will be looking at
as well, but these are your primary objects to focus on. Figure 6.2 diagrams the Object
Model for ADO. This figure also shows the relationship that exists between the ADO
objects and collections.

Unlike its Microsoft predecessors, ADO objects are not dependent upon each other. You
can choose to use them together, but each may also be used independently as well, making them easier to use. This flexibility produces a number of different permutations to do
the same thing. You will look at some of these to give you a feel for the possibilities.
More important, your study will give you recommendations on how they can best be utilized.

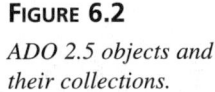

FIGURE 6.2

*ADO 2.5 objects and
their collections.*

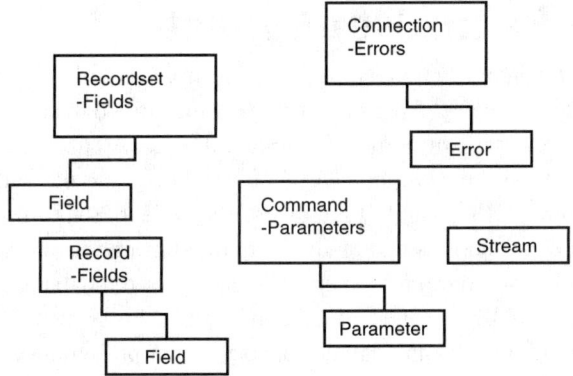

In a typical scenario for a Web-based application, you would use a Connection object to establish a connection to the database. A Command object would be used to call stored procedures to select, insert, update, and delete data. You would use a Recordset object to display them to the client. We will look at each of these three main objects and use each of them to get a Recordset back. After we have a basic understanding, we will look more into some of the other methods, properties, and parameters of these objects.

NEW TERM A *method* is an action that can be called on an object that the object will then execute. An object can have multiple methods.

NEW TERM A *property* is an attribute of an object.

NEW TERM A *parameter* is a value that is passed to an object while calling a method. A method can have 0 or more parameters.

There are some other objects as well. Table 6.1 gives a quick look at them. The new objects for ADO 2.5 are the Record and Stream objects, which we will touch on at the end of the chapter.

TABLE 6.1 More ADO Objects

Object	Function
Parameter Object	Sends the parameters for the store procedure efficiently.
Error Object	Contains information about an error, including number and description.
Field Object	Accesses or sets information about an individual field in a recordset.
Record Object	New for ADO 2.5. Accesses data in file or email systems or other non-relational data store.
Stream Object	New for ADO 2.5. Reads and manipulates stream data such as a file or email message.

6

Using the Recordset Object

The *Recordset object* is a collection of one or more records. A typical record would be the results of a SQL select from one or more tables in a database. But, it could also represent an email message or perhaps a file in a directory. The Recordset object is the primary object you will be using in ADO. You will become (and want to become) familiar with the different methods and properties of this object. You will pass these objects back and forth between functions and methods; iterate through it to display information to a user and add information to it to eventually save it to the database. And that's only the start! I might sound like a salesman here, but really this is the star in the ADO family. You will be using it to display data to the user in the presentation tier and also pass data between the different tiers. Tables 6.2 and 6.3 list useful methods and properties of the Recordset object.

TABLE 6.2   Recordset Methods

Method	Description
AddNew([*Fields*], [*Values*])	Adds a new record to the existing recordset.
CancelBatch([*AffectRecords*])	Cancels all pending records that had been added.
CancelUpdate	Cancels the prior record that had been added.
Close	Closes the Recordset object.
Delete([*AffectRecords*])	Deletes the current record in the recordset.
GetRows([*Rows*],[*Start*], [*Fields*])	Fills an array with multiple rows from a Recordset object.
Move(NumRecords, [*Start*])	Moves the position of the current recordset position.
MoveFirst, MoveLast	Moves to the first or last record of the recordset.
MoveNext, MovePrevious	Moves to the next or previous record of the recordset.
NextRecordset ([*RecordsAffected*])	If multiple recordsets were returned, it sets the next one to the current recordset.
Open([*Source*], [*ActiveConnection*], [*CursorType*], [*LockType*], [*Options*])	Opens the recordset.
Update([*Fields*], [*Values*])	Writes the record to the database that was added to the record with the AddNew method.
UpdateBatch(*AffectRecords*)	Writes all the records to the database that were added to the record with the AddNew method.

TABLE 6.3   Recordset Properties

Property	Values	Description
AbsolutePosition	Long	Ordinal position of the current record.
ActiveConnection	String	Connection object to which the Recordset object belongs.
BOF	Boolean	Beginning of file. Returns true if the current record position is before the first record.
CursorLocation	adUseClient| adUseNone| adUseServer	Client or server, location of data that is requested.
CursorType	adOpenDynamic| adOpenForwardOnly| adOpenKeyset| adOpenStatic| adOpenUnspecified	Type of cursor used for the Recordset object.
EOF	Boolean	End of file. Returns true if the current record position is after the last record.
Filter	Variant	Filter for the current data.
LockType	adLockBatch Optimistic| adLockOptimistic| adLock Pessimistic| adLockReadOnly| adLockUnspecified	Type of locking done while editing.
MaxRecords	Long	Limits the records returned from the open statement.
RecordCount	Long	Number of records in the recordset.
Source	String|Command object	Data source for a recordset.

6

In this chapter, you will be working with recordsets that get their information from data stores from, typically, SQL Select statements. The fields (columns) and the types of data in them are determined by the results received. This allows you the ability to receive information from a database and then display that data on a Web page.

The first method you will learn about is the Open method. Before that I want to define two important database concepts, locking and cursors.

New Term *Locking* in a database is the capability of a process to take control of a piece of data and restrict its access by any other objects. This is required in order to update records. Right before a record is inserted or updated, the table is locked by the object doing the action. When it is locked, no one else can insert a record in the same place or update the same record. When the action is complete, the lock is released.

This prevents the corruption of data. Otherwise you could have unpredictable results when you have two people try to update the same record at the same time. This locking is almost instantaneous; therefore, normal users will not notice the "lock" on the database.

The type of locking determines when and how the lock is done. Sometimes the lock might be applied as soon as the record has started to be edited or you might not do it until just before the update is written. It might lock just the field, or the record, or a block of records. Locking becomes important when considering scenarios of multiple users updating the same data. Your business rules will drive the type of locking that you require.

New Term A *cursor* is a copy of a set of records usually existing in a temporary format in memory. An ADO recordset is a type of cursor. It contains a set of records that came from a data source, which you can look at and change. Once you close it though, the cursor is gone.

The type of cursor then determines how you can manipulate and view the records in the cursor. It also determines how changes in the data store that are done by others are reflected in the cursor. You may be looking at a recordset that lists bank transactions. Depending on the type of cursor you have, if someone adds a transaction, you may or may not see the new transaction while you are working with the recordset.

With those new terms in mind, here is the format for the Open method.

```
recordset.Open Source, ActiveConnection, CursorType, LockType, Options
```

▼ **SYNTAX**

The open method allows you to open up a recordset. None of the parameters for this method are required. Source gives the source of the data for the recordset. Source is typically a SQL statement, such as "SELECT name FROM person", or a Command object. ActiveConnection defines the connection to the data. ActiveConnection is a Connection object or connection string. CursorType defines the type of cursor to be returned. CursorType is usually adOpenForwardOnly. LockTypes determine the type of locking. LockTypes are usually adReadOnly. CursorType and LockType are also Recordset properties and listed in Table 6.3. Options can tell the method what type of Source (for example, a SQL string rather then a call to a stored procedure.) If it is not a

▲ command object or that the Recordset should be restored from a previously saved file.

Take a look at what it takes to get some information back with the open method. The
Visual Basic code in Listing 6.1 will open a recordset for you.

LISTING 6.1   Opening a Recordset

```
1: Dim rst as ADODB.Recordset
2: Dim strConnectionString as String
3: Set rst = New ADODB.Recordset
4: strConnectionString = "DSN=pubs_dsn;Database=pubs;UID=sa;PWD="5: rst.Open
➥"SELECT au_lname FROM authors", strConnectionString
```

ANALYSIS   Lines 1 and 2 are the declarations. The first is an ADO Recordset object; the second is a string variable. Line 3 instantiates the recordset. At this point it has now
been created and is in memory. Line 4 defines our connection string. Here we do not
specify the provider. Therefore, we are using the default provider, MSDASQL, the
ODBC OLE DB Provider. It also specifies a System DSN called "pubs_dsn" and specifies a username and password. Line 5 takes all the parts and opens of a recordset. The
recordset is opened and filled with the data specified in the Source parameter,
"SELECT au_lname FROM authors".

This brings you to the point of having the data in an object. Next, you will need to get
the information out of the object and to its destination. Prior to that, you want to make
sure that data was actually returned. Otherwise, an error will occur if you try to access a
value in a record and there are no records in the recordset. To see if it is an empty
recordset, check to see if both EOF and BOF are true. Once that is done, loop through with
the MoveNext method, as seen in Listing 6.2

INPUT   LISTING 6.2   Looping Through with the MoveNext Method

```
1: If Not (rst.BOF And rst.EOF) Then
2:     Do While Not rst.EOF
3:         Debug.Print rst("au_lname")
4:         rst.MoveNext
5:     Loop
6: End If
7: Rst.Close
8: Set rst = Nothing
```

6

OUTPUT
```
Bennet
Blotchet-Halls
Carson
   . . .
Yokomoto
```

 Line 1 tests BOF and EOF. This is a little confusing because of the NOT operator. Table 6.3 lists the possibilities for the evaluation of this If statement.

TABLE 6.3 Possible Value for Not (rst.BOF And rst.EOF)

Condition	Expression Evaluates To
If rst.BOF is False, rst.EOF is False.	True
If rst.BOF is True, rst.EOF is False.	True
If rst.BOF is False, rst.EOF is True.	True
If rst.BOF is True, rst.EOF is True.	False

From the table, we can see, the only time the evaluation of the If will be false is when both BOF and EOF are true, which occurs when the recordset is empty. The recordset is empty when no records are returned from the data store. Line 2 begins a loop, which will continue until you reach the end of the recordset by testing the EOF property.

Line 3 prints a field to the debug window. You can reference each field in the recordset by name as shown in this line. You can also reference it by its ordinal value as shown in the following line:

```
Debug.Print rst(0)
```

Line 4 is critical, because if you forget it (as I have before) you will end up in an endless loop. The MoveNext method moves the current record pointer in the recordset to the next record. This allows us to iterate through all the values. Lines 5 and 6 close off the Do While and the If statements.

Finally, lines 7 and 8 are good programming practice which you should get in the habit of doing. Line 7 closes the recordset. If you have a connection open, this closes the connection. This is a good idea because each connection takes up resources.

Setting the recordset to Nothing tells Visual Basic to destroy the object and take it out of memory. This is supposed to be done implicitly by Visual Basic, but there are two advantages to doing it in code. One is that you are not keeping the memory used by the object any longer then you have to. If you wait for VB to do it, it could take longer. Secondly, Visual Basic (and this applies to ASP) might forget for some reason to release that object, which results in a memory leak since it will then never be released.

Commonly Used Properties

CursorType dictates what type of cursor is returned to the recordset and deals with how you can move through and modify the recordset. The CursorType property can be set as a property on a Recordset as shown in the following lines of code:

```
1: rst.CursorType = adForwardOnly
2: rst.Open "SELECT au_lname FROM authors", cnn
```

Line 1 sets the property; line 2 then opens up the recordset. You will notice that for the `ActiveConnection` parameter, there is no longer a connection string. Instead it is a `Connection` object, which you will be learning about in the next section.

Another way to set the `CursorType` is as part of the Open method as shown in this line:

```
3: rst.Open "SELECT au_lname FROM authors", cnn, adForwardOnly
```

In this line the `CursorType` is passed as the third parameter in the `Open` method.

In the two previous examples about the use of the `CursorType` property, the `CursorType` is `ForwardOnly`, which is the default value for it. This is one of four values. The following list explains each of the possible values for `CursorType`:

- `ForwardOnly` allows you to start at the beginning of the recordset and move forward. You can not move backwards or jump to another record. Also, `RecordCount`, which gives you a count of the records in the recordset, will return a value of `-1`, which means it is unknown. This is the fastest `CursorType`. Since it is forward only, internally the object does not have to remember anything about a record it has gone past. It also does not have to spend time counting the number of records.

- `OpenStatic` includes the same functionality as `ForwardOnly`, but you can also move back and forth through the records and get a record count.

- `OpenKeyset` adds the ability to see external changes that might occur to the data while you are viewing or manipulating it. For example, in a network environment another user could update one of the records in a recordset you are viewing. Also, deletes from other users will be inaccessible. This means that if a recordset is opened and a record from that recordset is deleted, when the record pointer moves to that record, the fields in that record will be inaccessible.

- `OpenDynamic` adds the ability to see additions. Others' deletes will be automatically removed from the recordset. This means that if a recordset is opened and a record from that recordset is deleted, the recordset will also have that record removed from it.

6

The decision on which to use is partly a tradeoff between functionality and speed. Going down through this list gives you more functionality, but less speed because of the overhead to support that functionality. Typically though, you will use `ForwardOnly` cursors for most of your recordsets since that provides all the functionality you need.

The LockType Property

▲ SYNTAX

The LockType property specifies the type of locking that is done on the records you retrieve in the recordset and what changes you can then make. The LockType property can also be set as a property on a Recordset just like the CursorType property, or you can also include it as part of the Open method as shown in the following line of code:

```
rst.Open "SELECT au_lname FROM authors", cnn, adForwardOnly, adReadOnly
```

In this line of code the LockType property is the fourth parameter of the Open method.

Like CursorType, there are also four possible values for LockType:

- adReadOnly doesn't allow updates or additions to the data. Also no locking is done. This is the default property.

- adLockOptimistic only locks the records at the time when the update occurs. It takes an optimistic view that it will not have any problem updating the record and will wait until the last moment to lock a record.

- adLockBatchOptimistic is the same as adLockOptimistic, but is selected when doing updates to multiple records at one.

- adLockPessimistic locks a record in order to ensure successful updates, typically as soon as the record is edited. This is the pessimistic view, assuming there might be trouble updating the records so the lock happens as soon as possible. Because of the length of the lock here, this method is not preferred.

▲

> **Tip** Be careful of the CursorType and LockType that you use. adForwardOnly and adReadOnly are the fastest and preferred methods. At times you may need to use other types, but you should be able to stick with these most of the time.

Using the Connection Object

The next object you will look at is the Connection object. This object allows us to communicate with the database. You can also specify where the information you get is retrieved to (client vs. server), timeouts for connections and response times, and also transactions that occur and where they begin and end. The ConnectionString property is the most important one, next to the actual open or execute method.

NEW TERM The *Connection object* creates an open connection to your data store. The Connection object allows you to create a connection to the database. It is opening a channel of communication.

Listing 6.3 is an example of how to make a connection to your database

LISTING 6.3   Connecting to Your Database

```
1: Dim cnn as ADODB.Connection
3: Set cnn = New ADODB.Connection
4: cnn.ConnectionString = "Provider=SQLOLEDB;DRIVER=SQL Server;
   ➥SERVER=(local);DATABASE=pubs;UID=sa;PWD=;"
5: cnn.Open
```

ANALYSIS   The first two lines declare and instantiate the object similar to what you saw in Listing 6.1. Line 3 sets the ConnectionString property of the connection to a valid Data Source. Notice this connection string is a DSN-less connection and uses the SQL OLE DB provider instead of the ODBC OLE DB provider as we did in earlier examples. The last line opens the connection to the database.

Tip

> The SQL OLE DB provider for Microsoft SQL Server will be faster than the ODBC OLE DB Provider. The reason is that it cuts out an entire layer of complexity by not having to go through ODBC.

Tables 6.4 and 6.5 list useful methods and properties of the Connection object.

TABLE 6.4   Connection Methods

Method	Description
Close	Closes the connection to the data store
Execute (*CommandText*, [*RecordsAffected*], [*Options*])	Executes a command on the connection
Open([*ConnectionString*], [*UserID*], [*Password*], [*Options*])	Opens a connection to a data store

TABLE 6.5   Connection Properties

Properties	Values	Description
CommandTimeout	*Long*	Time, in seconds, until a command times out
ConnectionString	*String*	Connection information about the data store
ConnectionTimeout	*Long*	Time, in seconds, until a connection times out

continues

6

TABLE 6.5   continued

Properties	Values	Description
CursorLocation	adUseClient| adUseNone| adUseServer	Client or server, location of data that is requested
DefaultDatabase	*String*	Database to connect to if one is not specified in the connection string
Provider	*String*	Provider name for a Connection object. Default is MSDASQL
Version	*String*	ADO version

Let's go ahead and make another connection in Listing 6.4. This time you will pass the connection string information in the Open method of the Connection object.

LISTING 6.4   Connecting to a Database via the Open Method

```
1: Dim cnn as ADODB.Connection
2: Dim rst as ADODB.Recordset
3: Set cnn = New ADODB.Connection
4: cnn.Open "Provider=SQLOLEDB;DRIVER=SQL Server;
   ➥SERVER=(local);DATABASE=pubs;UID=sa;PWD=;"
5: Set rst = cnn.Execute "SELECT au_lname FROM authors"
```

ANALYSIS   The first two lines declare the objects. Both a Connection and a Recordset object are being declared. Line 3 instantiates the Connection object. Line 4 opens this connection. Unlike in Listing 6.3 where the ConnectionString property of the connection was set, line 4 passes the connection string information as a parameter of the Open method; accomplishing the same task. This is a trade-off, where it is one less line of code, but probably more difficult to read. In line 5, the Execute method of the connection is called. This method returns a recordset, which we set to the recordset we declared earlier. The Execute method allows sending a command to the data store, a select statement in this example, which returns a set of records.

Exploring the Command Object

A *Command object* is used to execute commands against a data store. Ideally, we will use this object to do our calls to the database to call stored procedures. You can also use it to send *ad hoc* commands to the database, such as inserts or updates. For example, a SQL command like "UPDATE location SET city = 'Edmonds' WHERE county = 'King'" would be executed using a Command object.

Listing 6.5 gives an example of the Command object.

LISTING 6.5   The Command Object

```
1: Dim cmd as ADODB.Command
2: Dim rst as ADODB.Recordset
3: Set cmd = New ADODB.Command
4: cmd.ActiveConnection = "Provider=SQLOLEDB;DRIVER=SQL Server;
   ➥SERVER=(local);DATABASE=pubs;UID=sa;PWD=;"
5: cmd.CommandText = "SELECT au_lname FROM authors"
6: cmd.CommandType = adCmdText
7: Set rst = cmd.Execute
```

ANALYSIS   Lines 1 through 3 declare and instantiate objects. This time we are creating Command and Recordset objects. Line 4 sets the ActiveConnection property to a connection string. It can also be set to a Connection object that is open. Line 5 gives the text of the command to execute. In this case it is a Select statement. Line 6 sets the type of command that is set in CommandText. adCmdText is the value for an *ad hoc* text string that is to be executed. The type also can set to a stored procedure type, which tells ADO to treat the command text as a stored procedure name. Finally, line 7 executes the code. In this case the Execute method will return a result set and it will set it to rst, a Recordset object. Setting the command text to an update or insert command will cause the Execute method to not return a recordset. This makes sense since you are not requesting information, but telling the database to change information. Therefore, there is nothing to return.

This listing accomplishes the same action as the connection example in Listing 6.4. The idea here is to understand the flexibility you have with ADO. You were able to get a recordset back from the database by using the methods of different objects. There is not a set method to always use the objects.

In Day 5, "Putting Business Logic in the Data Tier," you learned about stored procedures and how those could be used in your database. Listing 6.6 demonstrates how you could call a stored procedure.

6

LISTING 6.6   Calling a Stored Procedure with the Command Object

```
1: Dim cmd as ADODB.Command
2: Dim rst as ADODB.Recordset
3: Set cmd = New ADODB.Command
4: cmd.ActiveConnection = "Provider=SQLOLEDB;DRIVER=SQL Server;
   ➥SERVER=(local);DATABASE=pubs;UID=sa;PWD=;"
5: cmd.CommandText = "reptq1"
6: cmd.CommandType = adCmdText
7: Set rst = cmd.Execute
```

continues

LISTING 6.6 continued

```
8: Debug.Print rst(2)
9: rst.Close
10: Set rst = Nothing
11: Set cmd = Nothing
```

OUTPUT 2.99

ANALYSIS The line to notice here is the `CommandText` property in line 5, which is set to a stored procedure name instead of a SELECT statement.

We will be looking more at calling stored procedures a little later today. After executing the command in line 7, line 8 prints the third column of the first record to the debug window. (Remember, the ordinal values are zero based: 0 is the first column, 1 is the second column, and so on.) The records are not looped through and, after printing this one value, the objects are closed and destroyed.

Tables 6.6 and 6.7 list useful methods and properties of the Command object.

TABLE 6.6 Command Methods

Method	Description
CreateParameter([Name], [Type], [Direction], [Size], [Value])	Use to add a parameter to the command object.
Execute([RecordsAffected], [Parameters], [Options])	Executes the command.

TABLE 6.7 Command Properties

Property	Values	Description
ActiveConnection	String	Connection object to which the Command object belongs.
CommandText	String	The command, which could be a table, stored procedure, or SQL command.
CommandTimeout	Long	Time, in seconds, before the command times out.
CommandType	adCmdUnknown| adCmdText| adCmdTable| adCmdStoredProc	Either a SQL statement, stored procedure, or table name.
Name	String	Name of a Command object.

Now that you are familiar with the most important objects in ADO, let's use them a little more so you can become more comfortable with them. You want to now look at how to do other things besides just selects. Finally, we'll look at the best practices method for calling stored procedures.

Tip

> When you declare a recordset object or any other object, it takes up memory on the system. Set your objects to Nothing after you have finished with them. An example of this is
>
> ```
> Set rst = Nothing
> ```
>
> If you don't, you could run into memory or other application errors. Also, it is good programming practice because you are getting rid of objects as soon as you are done using them. This releases the memory back to the computer to use for other tasks.

Performing Inserts, Updates, and Deletes

You have been retrieving data with our commands up to this point, but what if you want to affect data in some way. The methods are the same; the only difference is that you will typically not be returning a recordset.

All these commands encompass actions. None of them inherently return recordsets, therefore you can handle all of them identically. Listing 6.7 gives an example.

LISTING 6.7   SQL INSERT statement with the Command Object

```
1: Dim cmd as ADODB.Command
2: Set cmd = New ADODB.Command
3: cmd.ActiveConnection = "Provider=SQLOLEDB;DRIVER=SQL Server;
   ➥SERVER=(local);DATABASE=pubs;UID=sa;PWD=;"
4: cmd.CommandText = "INSERT INTO employee (emp_id, fname, lname)
   ➥Values('W-B33228M', 'Dennis', 'Richardson')" 5: cmd.CommandType = adCmdText
5: cmd.Execute
6: cmd.ActiveConnection = Nothing
7: Set cmd = Nothing
```

6

ANALYSIS   What changes here is in line 4. A SQL INSERT command is being set to the CommandText property. In line 5 it is executed. The INSERT command adds a new record to the employee table. To perform an insert on another table or change the values that are inserted, modify the command that is given here. Unlike Listing 6.6, which returned a recordset, this does not. Therefore, we do not even need a recordset object. After the command is completed, the object is cleaned up, meaning we close the connection in line 6, and then set the object to Nothing.

To execute a different command, simply change the `CommandText` to another valid SQL statement. Reviewing the `Connection` object, you could execute a similar command, without the `Command` object, as shown in Listing 6.8.

LISTING 6.8   SQL UPDATE Statement with the `Connection` Object

```
1: Dim cnn as ADODB.Connection
2: Set cnn = New ADODB.Connection
3: cnn.ConnectionString = "DSN=pubs_dsn;Database=pubs;UID=sa;PWD="
4:
5: cnn.Open
6: cnn.Execute "UPDATE employee SET fname = 'Brian' WHERE emp_id = 'W-B33228M'"
7: cnn.Close
8: Set cnn = Nothing
```

ANALYSIS   Line 3 is using our DSN instead of the DSN-less connection that have been used in the last few listings. Line 5 opens the connection. Line 6 uses the `Execute` method of the connection object and passes in a SQL UPDATE command for the `CommandText` parameter. This update command changes the name for the specified employee. This UPDATE command can be changed to modify another table or update other fields with different information. You could have also replace the INSERT statement in Listing 6.7 with the UPDATE statement in this listing. That would have worked also. Listings 6.7 and 6.8 show two different ways to send SQL commands to the database.

If there are two different ways to do the same command, the question then is, "Which should you use?". Listing 6.7, with the `Command` object, didn't require you to make a separate connection, although, it still made a connection implicitly when the command was executed. The second example, in comparison, has an explicit connection declared, which could be used for other database commands within the same code listing. Therefore, if you wanted to continue to work with the data store you could use a connection object and perform all the tasks that might have to be done. This might be an combination of SQL inserts, updates, and deletes. Otherwise, if just one command is being executed, the command object would work fine. At this point, don't get too hung up on where to use what object, focus more on understanding how the objects can be used.

For our last example, Listing 6.9 gives an example of a SQL DELETE command.

LISTING 6.9   SQL DELETE Statement with the `Command` Object

```
1: Dim cmd as ADODB.Command
2: Set cmd = New ADODB.Command
3: cmd.ActiveConnection = "DSN=pubs_dsn;Database=pubs;UID=sa;PWD="
```

```
4: cmd.CommandText = "DELETE employee WHERE emp_id = 'W-B33228M'
5: cmd.CommandType = adCmdText
6: cmd.Execute
7: cmd.ActiveConnection = Nothing
8: Set cmd = Nothing
```

ANALYSIS   Line 4 is where the SQL DELETE command is specified. It removes the record
we added in Listing 6.7 and modified in Listing 6.8 from the employee table.

This section gave examples on SQL inserts, updates, and deletes. By creating SQL commands in your code and executing them through ADO or through stored procedures, which you will learn about next, you can maintain the data in your database. Changing these commands allow you a great deal of flexibility. You can also construct these commands programmatically in your code. For example, if you had a label that was the value of an employee ID and a textbox which had the new value in it, you could execute the following line of code:

```
cnn.Execute "UPDATE employee SET fname = '" & txtFirstName & "' WHERE emp_id =
➡'" & lblEmpID  & "'"
```

This assumes a Visual Basic form that has a text box called txtFirstName and a label called lblEmpID. This constructs a SQL command on-the-fly by using information that has been entered by a user. The SQL command looks for an employee in the employee table who has an employee ID that matches the label. It would evaluate the text box and update fname field in the table for that record. Using ADO to maintain a data store gives us the power we need to create powerful applications. This knowledge will allow you to create the functionality you need in a data tier in the DNA architecture.

Calling Stored Procedures

In learning about the CommandText property of the Command object, you now know how to call stored procedures. You will now learn about some best practices for calling stored procedures.

6

Note

Remember, stored procedures will run faster than similar SQL commands that are executed with the Execute method of the Command or Connection objects. This is because they are already compiled. Stored procedures also allow you to separate your SQL into organized structures, making it easier to read and maintain.

Besides calling the store procedure as a text string where you set the `CommandType` property to `adCmdText`, you can also set it to `adCmdStoredProc`, which tells your data store that you are calling a stored procedure. This results in ADO not having to spend time figuring out what the string in `CommandText` is supposed to be: a table, a stored procedure, or a SQL command.

After telling ADO you will be calling a stored procedure, you have to tell it about the parameters for the stored procedure. Looking back on yesterday's material, you learned about how to create a stored procedure and how to pass parameters into the stored procedure when they are called. The parameters in the stored procedure declaration included the name of the parameter, the data type for it, and if it was an input or output parameter. It is this same information that you want to specify in ADO using the `CreateParameter` method of the command object. You will describe each parameter to ADO before you execute the stored procedure. The `CreateParameter` syntax for the command object can be seen below.

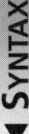

```
command.CreateParameter (Name, Type, Direction, Size, Value)
```

The first parameter, Name, can be anything. I used to always think this had to match the parameter name, but it can be anything you would like. It is used when you reference the parameter in the command object. `Type` is the data type such as `adVarChar` or `adInteger`.

Direction is either `adParamInput`, `adParamInputOutput`, `adParamOutput`, or `adParamReturnValue`. For example, you might have one parameter that is an input like an account number. Its direction would be `adParamInput`. Another parameter might be the account balance, that would be `adParamOutput`. Whether it is Input or Output or both depends on how it is defined in the beginning of the store procedure. A parameter that is set to `adParamReturnValue` would receive the return code that is specified inside the stored procedures.

Size is the maximum size in characters or bytes for the parameter. Finally, value is the value you are passing in for the parameter.

Here is an example of the `CreateParameter` method:

```
cmd.Parameters.Append cmd.CreateParameter("@person_id", adInteger, ➥

adParamInput, , intPerson_ID)
```

First, look at the parameters in the `CreateParameter` method. The name of the parameter is `"@person_id"`, which corresponds to its name in the stored procedure. It is an integer and an input parameter. The size does not need to be specified. This is required for character data, but not numeric data. Finally the value being passed in is a variable called `intPerson_ID`.

▼ Look at the rest of the line now. In this line of code, the Append method adds the parameter that is being created to the Parameters collection. You can add all your parameters with this same syntax. You only have to change the values passed in the CreateParameter method. You are required to append every parameter that is in the stored procedure.

Another way to write the line you just looked at would be

```
1: Set prm = cmd.CreateParameter("@person_id", adInteger, adParamInput, 4)
2: cmd.Parameters.Append prm
3: cmd.Parameters("@person_id").Value = intPersonID
```

Line 1 sets the parameter that is created with the CreateParameter method to a variable. Line 2 appends it to the Command object and line 3 sets the value for the parameter that
▲ was just appended.

Once you have appended every parameter to the command object, you can execute the stored procedure. The goal here is to explicitly tell ADO about the procedure that will be called and the parameters for the procedure. By giving ADO this information, it does not have to spend time figuring out the characteristics of the parameters.

Once you have added all the parameters to the command object, you are ready to call the stored procedure. Listing 6.10 shows how to call a stored procedures.

LISTING 6.10 Calling a Stored Procedure with Parameters

```
 1: Dim cmd as ADODB.Command
 2: Dim strName as String
 3: Set cmd = New ADODB.Command
 4: cmd.CommandText = "spSel_Person_Name"
 5: cmd.CommandType = adCmdStoredProc
 6: Set cmd.ActiveConnection = "DSN=pubs_dsn;Database=pubs;UID=sa;PWD="
 7: cmd.Parameters.Append cmd.CreateParameter("@person_id", adInteger,
     ➥adParamInput, , intPerson_ID)
 8: cmd.Parameters.Append cmd.CreateParameter("@name", adVarChar, adParamOutput,
     ➥50)
 9: cmd.Execute
10: strName = cmd("@name")
11: Set cmd.ActiveConnection = Nothing
12: Set cmd =Nothing
```

6

ANALYSIS Line 4 is the stored procedure to call and line 5 lets ADO know you are calling a stored procedure. Line 6 sets the ActiveConnection property. Lines 7 and 8 add parameters to the command object. The first parameter is an integer input parameter that is the person_id. A variable is also passed in, setting the value for this input parameter.

The second parameter is an output parameter. It is a character field with a size of 50. Line 8 executes it and line 10 sets the output parameter to a variable, strName. Lines 11 and 12 clean up the Command object.

This is one way you can use stored procedures, to return individual values. But, just like you used the Execute method to return recordsets with text strings, you can also do that with stored procedures. This is done by setting the recordset equal to the execute method of the command object. Listing 6.11 gives an example of this.

LISTING 6.11   Calling a Stored Procedure That Returns a Recordset

```
 1: Dim cmd as ADODB.Command
 2: Dim rst as ADODB.Recordset
 3: Dim strName as String
 4: Set cmd = New ADODB.Command
 5: Set rst = New ADODB.Recordset
 6: cmd.CommandText = "spSel_Person"
 7: cmd.CommandType = adCmdStoredProc
 8: Set cmd.ActiveConnection = "DSN=pubs_dsn;Database=pubs;UID=sa;PWD="
 9: cmd.Parameters.Append cmd.CreateParameter("@EmployeeID", adInteger,
    ↪adParamInput, 4, intPerson_ID)
10: Set rst = cmd.Execute
11: Set cmd.ActiveConnection = Nothing
12: Set cmd = Nothing
```

ANALYSIS   Lines 1 through 5 are declarations and instantiations of objects. The Recordset object is also declared since that will be holding our results. Lines 6 and 7 set the stored procedure name and the type of command. Line 8 makes a connection, and line 9 sets an input parameter. This is an employee ID. Line 10 differs from Listing 6.10 in that you are setting the return value to a recordset. Since the objects are independent of each other, lines 11 and 12 close the connection and destroy the object. The recordset is still around, and, at this point, its information could be displayed to the user.

Note   Whether or not a stored procedure returns a recordset is up to the stored procedure. You can design stored procedures to return one value or an entire set of records, depending upon your need. Refer to Day 5 and the SQL online documentation for more information on creating stored procedures.

Exploring Other Data Stores

At the beginning of the chapter, I discussed data stores and how ADO is part of Microsoft's Universal Data Access. You learned that with ADO, through the use of OLE DB, you can get at any type of data store out there. But, the examples, up to this point have been with SQL Server. Therefore, you will now learn about connecting to other data stores.

One specific example of an OLE DB provider that you can use with ADO is Index Server. Index Server is part of Internet Information Server and allows the user to set up indexes of Web pages that can then be searched on. This could include HTML pages as well as Word and Excel Documents among others. This is just one example that demonstrates that as long as you have a provider and correctly specify the provider in the connection string you can access the data. And you can access the data using all the ADO objects that you have been using in this chapter to access relational data.

The following listing gives an example of connecting to Index Server:

```
1: Dim cnn as ADODB.Connection
2: Set cnn = New ADODB.Connection
3: cnn.Open "provider=msidxs;"
```

Lines 1 and 2 are the same as we have seen. Line 3 makes a connection just like we have been doing with databases, but the difference being the provider name. It is not SQLOLEDB or MSDASQL, instead it is msidxs, which is the provider name for Index Server.

Another OLE DB provider that is available is one for ADS (Active Directory Service). Without getting into details, this can allow you access to physical directories on a hard drive, IIS Web sites, NT Domain and User accounts, and more. This is because ADS goes through another interface, ADSI (Active Directory Services Interfaces) to access this hierarchical data.

Here is an example of this connection:

```
1: Dim cnn as ADODB.Connection
2: Set cnn = New ADODB.Connection
3: cnn.Provider = "ADsDSOObject"
4: cnn.Open "Bank Ads Provider"
```

Line 3 sets the provider property on the Connection object instead of putting it in the parameter of the Open method.

6

Record and Stream Objects

New for ADO 2.5, the Record and Stream objects facilitate the use of data in data stores other then relational databases. More specifically, the Record object helps with data in file or email systems. You could use it to display an email message or update the contents of a document. The stream helps in working with a binary stream of bytes that make up a file or mail message.

A Record could be a row in a recordset, a file, or a directory. It can provide a way to navigate through hierarchical data. For this tree-structured data you could navigate through it, setting records to be subsets of the whole tree and then continue to move through them. With records you can perform a variety of functions including moving or copying files, set access permissions, or open up recordsets to view the subdirectories and files of the current record.

With the Record object you can then get at streams of data contained within the record. These streams may represent file contents or email messages. The Stream object allows you to manipulate the records or fields that contain these streams of information. Bytes can be read, written, iterated through, and further modified as needed. The Record and Stream object give you a way to get at non-relational data. Gives fields and streams a whole new meaning, doesn't it?

Summary

Today's lesson introduced you to the ActiveX Data Objects. After discussing and creating DSNs, you looked at the Recordset, Connection, and Command object. You saw how these can be used together or separately and when you might use each of these. You also looked at calling stored procedures. To do this you use the Command object, adding the necessary parameters and then calling the Execute method. Values may also be returned from here. Calling stored procedures like this will be integrated into our banking online application. For more information on ADO, see http://msdn.microsoft.com or http://www.microsoft.com/data.

Q&A

Q I have an application where I am constantly accessing the database. I think it would be easier just to make one connection; then I don't have to bother with making a new connection every time. Is this the best way?

A Actually, this would be a very costly process. You would be making a dedicated connection that no one else could use. You might think that it will cost more to make a connection every time, but, although your code may be calling a `Connection.Open`, connection pooling is going on in the background. This holds onto connections for a little time, even after the calling program may have closed them. If another user or application asks for that connection, it merely gives it the existing connection. This allows a much smaller number of connections to handle a much larger number of users.

Q Your examples had the connection string as part of the code. Wouldn't it be easier to put it into global variable and access that?

A Yes, definitely! In general, you don't want to be hard coding constants in your application. The examples in this chapter could have also been referencing a global constant, which also would have worked fine. This brings up an interesting point. Where do you store the connection string since it is not going to change and many times you will have only one string to access all your data? If you put your data access objects in a DLL, as you will in our banking application, a constant is one possibility. This gives increased speed, but that means you have to recompile the component if you change your connection string. It could also be stored in the registry. This gives you a lot more flexibility; if you move databases, just change the registry setting. Another option is to store it in a file. Site server does this with its configuration files. You just have to look at the various options and decide the best way for your application.

Workshop

The Workshop provides quiz questions to help you solidify your understanding of the material covered and exercises to provide you with experience in using what you've learned. Try to understand the quiz and exercise answers before continuing to the next lesson. Answers are provided in Appendix A.

Quiz

1. True/False. Connection strings always reference a DSN.
2. When would the `RecordCount` for a recordset always come back with -1?
3. What's the name of the default OLE DB Provider?
4. What object and corresponding method would you use to update a record?
5. What should you add to your command object when calling stored procedures and what methods do you use?
6. What are the two new objects with ADO 2.5?

6

Exercises

1. If you have Access, MSDE, or another database application, create a simple database and try to connect to it through ADO. Remember to create your DSN. Select some records from it and display them on a form or debug window.

2. In Visual Basic or Visual Interdev, create a function that returns a recordset, which contains the results of a query.

DAY 7

Database Transactions and the Distributed Transaction Coordinator

All relational databases use transaction rules to ensure data consistency. This chapter educates you on the transaction rules and components, and describes how you can participate in the transaction. You will cover distributed transactions and how you can increase the performance of your transactions. You will also learn about Microsoft's Distributed Transaction Coordinator (DTC), how DTC controls distributed transactions, and how you can use the DTC Admin Console to monitor and manage transactions. And finally, the chapter will touch on Microsoft Transaction Server (MTS) as it relates to database transactions. (Day 8, "Introduction to COM and MTS," will explore MTS in greater detail, and you'll add transaction support to your banking application in Day 10.)

In today's lesson, you will learn

- About transactions
- Rules for transactions

- About database and distributed transactions
- About Microsoft's Data Transaction Coordinator
- How to participate in the transaction
- How to increase the performance of your transactions
- About the role of Microsoft Transaction Server

Exploring Transactions

Transactions are the building blocks of processing in applications, and almost any operation an application performs can be considered a transaction. What makes transactions valuable is the capability to group a series of operations into a single unit of work. Loosely speaking, a transaction is a sequence of actions and operations that act as a single unit of work to transform the system from one consistent state to another consistent state.

Business rules within a system define which actions must be grouped together into a transaction. Can you think of some situations in the banking application in which you would want to perform a series of operations in a single unit of work? Table 7.1 lists some of these situations and explains why you might want to handle them with a transaction.

TABLE 7.1   A Listing of Some Good Transaction Candidates for the SmallTownBank Application

Situation	Transaction Description
New Customer	When a customer record is created, data may be inserted into many tables. If any of these inserts fails, the customer record should not be created in the database.
New Account	Account creation may insert data into many tables, so if any of these inserts fail, the whole account creation must fail.
New Customer and New Account	The application could create both a new customer record and a new account within the same transaction. If the new customer record fails, the account must not be added or there would be an account record without a customer (an orphaned record). In this case, if the customer insert worked, but the account insert failed, the customer insert would be rolled back, and must then be re-entered into the system.

Situation	Transaction Description
Transfer Funds Between Accounts	Transferring funds between accounts requires one account to be debited and another account to be credited. By combining these actions within one transaction, you are assured that both the credit and debit takes place or that neither takes place, and that the original account balances are preserved.
Remove a Customer	When removing a customer, all customer data, accounts, and history must be deleted from the database. If any of these deletions fail, the transaction must return the customer data to its initial state.

Now that you have a good idea of what transactions are, let's discuss the transaction rules used to characterize transactions.

Applying Transaction Rules

Transactions must follow four rules, called the ACID (Atomicity, Consistency, Isolation, Durability) properties. If any of these rules are violated, the sequence of operations does not qualify as a transaction.

 *ACID* is an acronym for properties that are used to characterize transactions (Atomicity, Consistency, Isolation, Durability).

Atomicity

Atomicity is the all or nothing rule for transactions. Transactions must be indivisible. What do I mean by indivisible? Remember that transactions are a sequence of actions—most often database actions such as inserts, updates, and deletes to the database tables. If one of these actions fails, none of them are applied to the database. The entire sequence of actions and operations performed within a transaction must finish before any changes are applied to the database. Once all actions complete, they are applied to the database.

 A transaction is *atomic* if it either completes the transaction, or returns the system to a state that is indistinguishable from the state it was in before the transaction began. Transactions that are atomic are designed to leave the database in a consistent state.

Consistency

Atomicity assumes the database is consistent before each transaction is executed (the data in each of the tables is *consistent* with the data in all the other tables). In Day 5,

7

"Putting Business Logic in the Data Tier," you learned about database rules, domain constraints, entity constraints, and referential integrity constraints. The SmallTown Bank data model states that the relationship between customer and accounts is one-to-many. A customer can have many accounts, but an account cannot belong to many customers. The database will maintain database consistency through a referential integrity constraint. The assumption that the database is consistent prior to execution of a transaction is realized through the use of these database integrity constraints.

NEW TERM A database is *consistent* if all associated semantic integrity constraints are satisfied. A transaction is consistent if it maintains this integrity throughout its successful completion (when it is *committed*) and in the case of failure (when it is *rolled back*).

During the execution of a transaction, the consistency constraint may be momentarily violated. In the earlier transaction example of transferring funds between accounts, the account containing the funds to be transferred may have its balance reduced before the account receiving the funds has its balance increased. That's fine as long as both steps of the transaction are completed. If the transfer failed before the second account receives the funds and the transaction was not rolled back, the account balance would change leaving the database in an inconsistent state. A transaction has consistency if, over the course of all actions, database integrity is maintained.

Isolation

Transactions have been discussed as if each was processed individually. If this were true, the cost per transaction of software and hardware would be extremely higher than it is today. Instead, many transactions are executed concurrently with other transactions.

That being said, even in a multiple user environment where many transactions can be executed concurrently, possibly affecting the same data, each transaction is executed as if it's the only transaction in the system. A system is *isolated* if each transaction is *serializable*. If each transaction is consistent, then any serial ordering of the transactions must be consistent. Even though transactions are executed concurrently, it appears to the transaction that the other transactions are executed either before or after it. The effects of one transaction are not visible to the other transactions until the transaction either successfully finishes (commits) or fails (rolls back).

NEW TERM *Isolation* is the capability to shield transactions from the effects of updates performed by other concurrent transactions.

NEW TERM *Serializable* transitions are a set of transactions that can be run in a series.

There are three ways concurrent transaction can violate the rule of isolation:

- Dirty Read   A database read operation that contains uncommitted data. For example, Transaction A changes a row. Transaction B reads the changed row before Transaction A commits the change. If Transaction A rolls back the change, Transaction B reads a row that is considered to have never existed.

- Lost Update   A lost update occurs when Transaction A reads a row, Transaction B updates the same row, and then Transaction A writes the row, overwriting the work Transaction B performed.

- Unrepeatable Read   An unrepeatable read happens when Transaction A reads a row, Transaction B overwrites the data with work it was performing, and then Transaction A rereads the row. The data Transaction A reads is not the same as the first read.

Transactions are guaranteed to be consistent if it can be shown that they avoid dirty reads, lost updates, and unrepeatable reads. You can show that your transaction avoids these pitfalls by adhering to these rules:

- Your transaction does not write data that is read by any other transaction before that transaction finishes.

- Other transactions do not read or write any data written by your transaction before your transaction finishes.

- Your transaction does not read dirty data from any other transaction, nor does it overwrite dirty data of any other transaction.

Enhancing Isolation with Database Locks

When two or more transactions access the same data concurrently, the database implements isolation by shared, update, and exclusive locks, as well as unlock operations.

TABLE 7.2   Different Database Locks and Situations to Use Them In

Lock	Situation
Shared	Used for operations that do not change or update data, for example, the SQL SELECT statement.
Update	Used when modifying a page; the update lock is later promoted to an exclusive lock before applying the changes.
Exclusive	Used for data-modifying statements, such as UPDATE, INSERT, or DELETE.

7

Locking prevents other transactions from accessing data. A transaction is said to be *well formed* if each read, write, and unlock action is controlled by a lock, and if every lock is released by the end of the transaction. Locking increases contention, and as such consumes resources. For this reason, isolation is sometimes compromised for performance reasons. For instance, queries of database tables sometimes run for long periods of time and touch many data rows. This, in turn, consumes many resources on a database by locking rows and deteriorating performance. You can increase performance in your application by applying varying levels of isolation within your transactions. In Table 7.3, each isolation level offers more isolation than the previous level, but does so by holding more restrictive locks for longer periods of time. Remember that when you set transaction isolation levels to be less restrictive, you trade data integrity for performance.

TABLE 7.3 Database Levels of Isolation

Isolation Level	Description
READ UNCOMMITTED	Directs the database to not issue shared locks and does not honor exclusive locks. At this level, you *can* experience dirty reads.
READ COMMITTED	Database uses shared locks while reading. At this level, you cannot experience dirty reads.
REPEATABLE READ, or SERIALIZABLE	Dirty reads, non-repeatable reads, and phantom values cannot occur.

To set the isolation level explicitly within your SQL statements use the following syntax:

```
SET TRANSACTION ISOLATION LEVEL [READ COMMITTED | READ UNCOMMITTED |
➡ REPEATABLE READ | SERIALIZABLE]
```

You can also improve performance in your applications and minimize locks by committing transactions as soon as they are finished. There are varying levels of locking you can specify, such as page level, row level, table level, and so on. To learn more about locking, refer to your Microsoft SQL Server documentation.

Durability

The database must preserve the effects of all committed transactions as well as database consistency in the case of system or media failures. The capability to do so is called *durability*. If a system fails while transactions are running, only the work done by the transactions in progress will be lost. The database will be able to reconstruct itself to its most consistent state prior to the failure.

To guarantee the durability of a transaction, the updates performed by a transaction must be recorded in some durable medium at the time of commit. Microsoft introduced row-level locking in SQL Server version 7.0. Every SQL Server database has a write-ahead transaction log that records changes made in the database. The log records the beginning and end of every transaction. When a request to modify the database is received, copies of both the old and new states of the database's affected portions are recorded in the transaction log. Microsoft SQL Server stores enough information in the log to either recreate (roll forward) or undo (roll back) the data modifications that make up a transaction when the system fails and a transaction is in progress. A transaction is a unit of work and a unit of recovery. By writing to the transaction log, SQL Server ensures database durability.

Working with Database Transactions

Any single SQL statement (a single unit of work), whether it affects one row or thousands of rows within a table, is considered to be a transaction. Therefore, in Microsoft SQL Server, transactions are implied in every SQL statement. However, as a SQL programmer, you may want to control your own transactions specifying that a series of SQL statements all be performed, or that the entire series be rolled back if any one of them fails. You can do this by specifying where a transaction starts and where it ends. You must also correctly handle errors that may occur and terminate transactions when necessary. Remember that transactions are started on a connection and managed at a connection level. What this means is that any statements executed on that connection are part of the transaction until the transaction ends.

Starting a Transaction

There are three ways to begin a transaction with Microsoft SQL Server: explicitly, with autocommit, or implicitly.

Starting Transactions Explicitly

Transact-SQL is the standard language for communicating between applications and SQL Server. Transact-SQL is made up of Structured Query Language (SQL), the ANSI-standard relational database language, as well as Microsoft's enhancements to the standard language. The Transact-SQL language can be used to create tables and indexes as you did in Day 4, "Exploring Database Fundamentals," as well as to define transactions. When you use the Transact-SQL statement BEGIN TRANSACTION in your SQL code, you are explicitly beginning a transaction. Every SQL statement that appears before a COMMIT TRANSACTION or ROLLBACK TRANSACTION statement is executed. Below is the syntax for the BEGIN TRANSACTION statement:

```
BEGIN TRAN[SACTION] [transaction_name | @tran_name_variable]
```

7

SYNTAX

Tip   In ADO, use the `BeginTrans` method on a Connection object to start an explicit transaction.

Notice that you can optionally name the transaction you are creating by placing a transaction name after the `BEGIN TRANSACTION` statement or by placing a variable, such as `@MyTran`, after the `BEGIN TRANSACTION` statement. Transaction names become important if you nest one or more transaction and want to specify which transaction you want to roll back to when errors occur. SQL Server permits nesting of transactions, but no actual nesting occurs. A nested transaction count is maintained for each open transaction. Each `BEGIN TRANSACTION` statement during an active transaction increments the nested transaction count by one, but has no other effect. Each `COMMIT` or `ROLLBACK TRANSACTION` statement during an active transaction decrements the nested transaction count by one. If and only if this decrement reduces the transaction count to zero, all updates are committed to the database. Therefore it is essential to issue `COMMIT` statements for every `BEGIN TRANSACTION` statement. You may ask why it's necessary to nest transactions at all, if all they do is to increment and decrement counts. First, you could roll back a nested transaction, and still complete the outer transaction and other nested transaction. Using explicit transactions in this manner gives you the most control over what set of statements makes up a transaction. Second, they also help clarify code for other programmers.

In the `SmallTownBank` application, account types are simply text descriptions that describe each type of account. Suppose you want to add new descriptions for the account types into the `AccountType` table, defining the types of accounts available for the SmallTown Bank. And you want to do so in one transaction. Listing 7.1 inserts three account type descriptions and performs a couple of select statements all in one transaction. You can execute this code using Query Analyzer.

LISTING 7.1   Explicit Transaction Example

```
 1: /* First explicit transaction started by BEGIN TRANSACTION statement */
 2: BEGIN TRANSACTION InsAccType
 3: GO
 4: INSERT INTO AccountType VALUES ('Joint Checking')
 5: GO
 6: INSERT INTO AccountType VALUES ('Joint Savings')
 7: GO
 8: SELECT COUNT(*) FROM AccountType
 9: GO
10: INSERT INTO AccountType VALUES ('Business Checking')
11: GO
```

```
12: SELECT * FROM AccountType
13: GO
14: COMMIT TRANSACTION InsAccType
15: /* Transaction is explicitly committed to the database*/
```

ANALYSIS   In Listing 7.1, line 2 creates the first transaction, which is named `InsAccType`. Then two `AccountType` descriptions are inserted in lines 4 and 6. Notice that I've included `SELECT` statements in lines 8 and 12 as part of the transaction, simply to illustrate that any SQL statements are part of your transaction until the transaction is committed or rolled back. When you execute this code, these `SELECT` statements also let you see the results of your inserts into the `AccountType` table. Normally, you would not include unnecessary statements in your transactions, such as these `SELECT`s because resources would be tied up until the transaction completes. Line 10 inserts the third description into the `AccountType` table. The transaction is then committed in line 14, which decrements the transaction count to zero and commits the changes to the database.

Beginning a Transaction via Autocommit

The default transaction mode for SQL Server is autocommit. Therefore you do not have to specify any SQL statements to control transactions. When autocommit is on, each individual SQL statement is committed when it completes. You may be wondering why you need to worry so much about transactions if autocommit is the default mode. Remember that this only applies to individual SQL statements, not a series of statements you define as in explicit transactions. If a statement fails, it is rolled back and all the statements up to that point are committed to the database. Listing 7.2 shows where autocommit transactions occur within the sample SQL code.

LISTING 7.2   Autocommit Transaction Example

```
 1: /* First autocommit transaction started by an INSERT statement */
 2: INSERT INTO AccountType VALUES ('Joint Checking')
 3: GO
 4: /* Transaction is automatically committed */
 5:
 6: /* Second autocommit transaction started by an INSERT statement */
 7: INSERT INTO AccountType VALUES ('Joint Savings')
 8: GO
 9: /* Transaction is automatically committed */
10:
11: /* Third autocommit transaction is started by a SELECT statement */
12: SELECT COUNT(*) FROM AccountType
13: GO
14: /* Transaction is automatically committed */
15:
```

7

continues

LISTING 7.2   Continued

```
16: /* Fourth autocommit transaction is started by a SELECT statement */
17: INSERT INTO AccountType VALUES ('Business Checking')
18: GO
19: /* Transaction is automatically committed */
20:
21: /* Fifth autocommit transaction is started by a SELECT statement */
22: SELECT * FROM AccountType
23: GO
24: /* Transaction is automatically committed */
```

ANALYSIS   Line 2 of Listing 7.2 shows the first transaction, which is implicitly started with the INSERT statement and completes when the INSERT of the description 'Joint Checking' occurs in the AccountType table. Additional INSERT statements in lines 7 and 17 also create implicit transactions, as do the SELECT statements in lines 12 and 22. It is important to notice that, with the autocommit option turned on in SQL Server, each statement—whether it modifies data or not—is an implicit transaction.

Tip

> In autocommit mode, it sometimes appears as if the entire batch of statements is rolled back, instead of just one SQL statement. This occurs when SQL Server encounters a compile error, not a runtime error. A compile error prevents the query parser from building a query execution plan, so nothing in the batch is executed. Although it appears as though all statements in the batch before the statement causing the error were rolled back, the error prevented anything in the batch from being executed. A quick way to determine which statement caused the error is to run each statement individually.

Listing 7.3 illustrates the difference between compile errors and SQL errors.

LISTING 7.3   Compile Errors Versus SQL Errors

```
1: /* Batch statements with a compile error.  None are executed /
2: INSERT INTO AccountType VALUES ('Joint Checking')
3: INSERT INTO AccountType VALUES ('Checking')
4: INSERT INTO AccountType VLAUES ('Joint Savings') /* Syntax Error */
5: INSERT INTO AccountType VALUES ('Savings')
6:  GO
7: SELECT * from AccountType /* Returns no rows */
8: Go
9:
10: /* Batch statements with a SQL error.  First Two are executed /
11: INSERT INTO AccountType VALUES ('Joint Checking')
```

```
12: INSERT INTO AccountType VALUES ('Checking')
13: INSERT INTO AcountType VALUES ('Joint Savings') /* Table Name Error */
14: INSERT INTO AccountType VALUES ('Savings')
15:  GO
16: SELECT * from AccountType /* Returns rows 1 and 2 */
17: Go
```

ANALYSIS   Listing 7.3 illustrates the difference between compile errors and SQL errors. Lines 2 through 5 insert rows into the AccountType table, however, the SQL key word VALUES is misspelled in line 4 as **VLAUES**. This causes the SQL Server compiler to generate an error, and, as the SELECT statement in line 7 shows by returning no rows, none of the statements in lines 2 through 5 will be executed. The INSERT statements in lines 11 through 14 attempt to insert four rows into the same AccountType table. This time, the AccountType table is misspelled in line 13 as **AcountType**. The misspelling of a table name generates a SQL error, not a compile error. Running lines 11 through 14 will insert both rows prior to the error, but not the row after or the row with the error. The SELECT statement in line 16 will display the first two rows only. What is important is that compile errors prevent an entire batch of statements from executing, but a SQL error will abort once the error is reached, and statements up to that point will be executed.

Starting Transactions Implicitly

Finally, you can start SQL transactions implicitly using the SQL SET statement. When the implicit mode is selected, SQL Server no longer automatically commits each statement. When implicit transaction mode is set, the next statement signifies the start of a new transaction. When it completes either through a COMMIT statement or a ROLLBACK statement, the next SQL statement starts a new transaction, and so on. To turn on implicit transaction mode, use the following syntax:

```
SET IMPLICIT_TRANSACTIONS ON
```

Listing 7.4 shows you how to use implicit transaction mode.

LISTING 7.4   Implicit Transaction Example

```
1: SET IMPLICIT_TRANSACTIONS ON
2: GO
3: /* First implicit transaction started by an INSERT statement */
4: INSERT INTO AccountType VALUES ('Joint Checking')
5: GO
6: INSERT INTO AccountType VALUES ('Joint Savings')
7: GO
8: /* Commit the first transaction */
```

7

continues

LISTING 7.4   continued

```
 9: COMMIT TRANSACTION
10: GO
11: /* Second implicit transaction is started by a SELECT statement */
12: SELECT COUNT(*) FROM AccountType
13: GO
14: INSERT INTO AccountType VALUES ('Business Checking')
15: GO
16: SELECT * FROM AccountType
17: GO
18: /* Commit second transaction */
19: COMMIT TRANSACTION
20: GO
21: SET IMPLICIT_TRANSACTIONS OFF
22: GO
```

ANALYSIS   The first line in Listing 7.4 turns implicit transaction mode on. The INSERT statement in line 4 actually begins the transaction implicitly. This same transaction is still open when line 6 inserts another row in the AccountType table. Line 9 then commits the first implicit transaction. Since there are no open transactions and implicit transaction mode is still turned on, line 12, which happens to be a SELECT statement, begins the second implicit transaction. Lines 14 and 16 are part of the second transaction as well, and line 19 commits the second transaction. Line 21 turns implicit transaction mode off. You can see that each form of transaction—explicit, autocommit, and implicit—handle the start and end of transactions differently. It's up to you to decide which is best for the transactions you create.

Ending a Transaction

There a two ways you can end a transaction, with either a COMMIT or a ROLLBACK statement. You commit a transaction when all statements finish successfully. A COMMIT statement guarantees all the transactions modifications are made a permanent part of the database, and frees resources your transaction consumed, such as locks. If an error occurs during your transaction, you can issue a ROLLBACK statement to cancel the effects of the transaction. The database is returned to the state of consistency that it was at prior to the start of the transaction, and resources are also released. Use the following syntax to designate the end of a transaction:

▼ SYNTAX

```
COMMIT [ TRAN[SACTION] [transaction_name | @tran_name_variable] ]
```

The COMMIT [WORK] parameter functions identically to the COMMIT TRANSACTION statement, except you cannot provide a transaction name, but can optionally supply the keyword WORK.

```
ROLLBACK [TRAN[SACTION] [transaction_name |
@tran_name_variable | savepoint_name | @savepoint_variable] ]
```

The ROLLBACK [WORK] parameter functions identically to the ROLLBACK TRANSACTION statement, except that you cannot provide a transaction name, but can optionally supply the keyword WORK.

▲

Tip In ADO, to end a transaction, call the Connection object's CommitTrans or RollbackTrans methods.

You have been introduced to transaction processing, now you will learn how to apply this knowledge to the SmallTownBank application.

Applying Transactions to the SmallTownBank Application

Let's think back to the sample transaction, transferring funds between accounts. Assume you have one customer who wants to transfer funds from her savings account to her checking account. To transfer funds between accounts, you must insert an AccountTransaction record, debit the balance of one account, and credit the balance of another. You want all of this to occur within a transaction you explicitly create. In order to focus on only the transfer funds transaction, let's assume you have a transaction type of 'Transfer Funds' in the TransactionType table, account types of 'Savings' and 'Checking' in the AccountType table, and a customer with each of these accounts in the Customer table. These are seen in Table 7.4.

7

TABLE 7.4   The `Customer`, `Account`, `TransactionType`, and `AccountType` Key Information

Table	Key Name	Value	Description
`Customer`	`CustomerKey`	100	Customer who requested a fund transfer between her savings and checking accounts
`Account`	`AccountKey`	10	Customer's savings account
`Account`	`AccountKey`	11	Customer's checking account
`AccountType` `'Savings'`	`AccountTypeKey`	1	Account type description for a savings account
`AccountType` `'Checking'`	`AccountTypeKey`	2	Account type description for a checking account
`Transaction Type` `'DEBIT'`	`Transaction TypeKey`	1	Transaction type description for debiting an account
`Transaction Type` `'CREDIT'`	`Transaction TypeKey`	2	Transaction type description for crediting an account

First, create a stored procedure called `PerformAccountAction` that can debit or credit an account when it is passed the `AccountID`, a dollar amount, and the action indicator of `'DEBIT'` or `'CREDIT'`. This can be seen in Listing 7.5.

LISTING 7.5   Stored Procedure Example to Debit or Credit an Account

```
 1: go
 2: CREATE PROCEDURE PerformAccountAction (
 3:    @AccountId As Integer,
 4:    @Amount As Money,
 5:    @Action As Char(10))
 6: AS
 7: BEGIN
 8:
 9:    If Rtrim(@Action) = 'DEBIT'
10:       Update Account
11:          Set Balance = Balance + @Amount
12:       Where AccountKey = @AccountID
13:    Else If Rtrim(@Action) = 'CREDIT'
14:       Update Account
15:          Set Balance = Balance - @Amount
16:       Where AccountKey = @AccountID
17:    Else
```

```
18:        RAISERROR ('PerformAccountAction expects an
           ➥@Action of DEBIT or CREDIT.', 16, 1)
19:
20: END /* Procedure PerformAccountAction */
```

ANALYSIS The PerformAccountAction procedure shown in Listing 7.5 accepts three parameters, an account ID (@AccountID) that is a unique key for a customer account, a dollar amount (@Amount), and text equal to either 'DEBIT' or 'CREDIT' as the action to perform (@Action). In line 9, the procedure checks to see if this is a debit to an account. If so, the account balance for the account passed to the procedure as @AccountID is decreased by the dollar amount passed to the procedure in the @Amount parameter. If the action to perform is not a debit, line 13 checks to see if the action is a credit. If so, the account balance is increased by the amount passed to the procedure. Line 17 is executed if the action text passed in is not equal to 'DEBIT' or 'CREDIT'. In this case, an error is returned using the Transact-SQL RAISERROR statement. This is a fairly simple procedure to increase or reduce the balance of an account.

Next, create a stored procedure called TransferFunds that will insert an AccountTransaction 'DEBIT' record for the checking account, and an AccountTransaction 'CREDIT' record for the savings account, debit the balance of the checking account (the source account), and credit the balance of the savings account (the destination account). To debit the checking and savings account records, this procedure will make use of the PerformAccountAction stored procedure you just created. This procedure must successfully perform all actions. If any one of these actions fail, the stored procedure must roll back the entire series of actions. This will ensure the funds get transferred (both the debit and credit occur) or, if errors occur, the database remains in the state it was in prior to executing the transaction. The following stored procedure, created in Listing 7.6, performs these tasks within an explicit transaction named FundTransfer.

LISTING 7.6   Stored Procedure to Transfer Funds Between Accounts

```
 1: CREATE PROCEDURE TransferFunds (
 2:     @CustomerID As Integer,
 3:     @SourceAccountId As Integer,
 4:     @DestAccountId As Integer,
 5:     @Amount As Money)
 6: AS
 7: BEGIN
 8:     DECLARE @TransferError integer
 9:     DECLARE @TransactionDescription VarChar(50)
10:     DECLARE @TransactionDate DateTime
```

7

continues

LISTING 7.6   continued

```
11:    DECLARE @DebitTransactionTypeId Integer
12:    DECLARE @CreditTransactionTypeId Integer
13:    DECLARE @ReturnValue Integer
14:
15:    Select @TransactionDescription = 'Transfer Funds'
16:    Select @TransactionDate = GetDate ()
17:    Select @DebitTransactionTypeId = (Select TransactionTypeKey
18:                                      from TransactionType
19:                                      where Rtrim(Description) = 'DEBIT')
20:    Select @CreditTransactionTypeId = (Select TransactionTypeKey
21:                                       from TransactionType
22:                                       where Rtrim(Description) = 'CREDIT')
23:
24:    BEGIN TRANSACTION FundTransfer
25:
26:    -- Debit receiving account
27:    EXECUTE @ReturnValue = PerformAccountAction @AccountId=@DestAccountId,
       ➥ @Amount=@Amount, @Action='DEBIT'
28:
29:    SELECT @TransferError = @@Error
30:
31:    IF @TransferError <> 0
32:       BEGIN
33:          ROLLBACK TRANSACTION FundTransfer
34:          Return
35:       END
36:
37:    -- Insert AccountTransaction record for Debit
38:    Insert Into AccountTransaction (AccountId, CustomerId,
       ➥ TransactionTypeID, Amount, Description, CheckNumber, Payee,
       ➥ DateEntered)
39:    Select @DestAccountId,
40:           @CustomerId,
41:           @DebitTransactionTypeId,
42:           @Amount,
43:           @TransactionDescription,
44:           Null,
45:           Null,
46:           @TransactionDate
47:
48:    SELECT @TransferError = @@Error
49:
50:    IF @TransferError <> 0
51:       BEGIN
52:          ROLLBACK TRANSACTION FundTransfer
53:          Return
54:       END
55:
```

```
56:    -- Credit source account
57:    EXECUTE @ReturnValue = PerformAccountAction
       ➥ @AccountId=@SourceAccountId, @Amount=@Amount, @Action='CREDIT'
58:    SELECT @TransferError = @@Error
59:
60:    IF @TransferError <> 0
61:      BEGIN
62:         ROLLBACK TRANSACTION FundTransfer
63:         Return
64:      END
65:
66:    -- Insert AccountTransaction record for Credit
67:    Insert AccountTransaction (AccountId, CustomerId,
       ➥ TransactionTypeID, Amount, Description, CheckNumber, Payee,
       ➥ DateEntered)
68:    Select @SourceAccountId,
69:           @CustomerId,
70:           @CreditTransactionTypeID,
71:           @Amount,
72:           @TransactionDescription,
73:           CheckNumber = Null,
74:           Payee = Null,
75:           DateEntered = @TransactionDate
76:
77:    SELECT @TransferError = @@Error
78:
79:    IF @TransferError <> 0
80:      BEGIN
81:         ROLLBACK TRANSACTION FundTransfer
82:         Return
83:      END
84:
85:    COMMIT TRANSACTION FundTransfer
86:
87: End /* Procedure TransferFunds */
```

ANALYSIS The TransferFunds procedure shown in Listing 7.6 is more complicated than the PerformAccountAction stored procedure shown earlier. In lines 2 through 5, the TransferFunds procedure accepts a customer key (@CustomerID) for the customer you are transferring funds for, a source account (@SourceAccountId) where the money being transferred currently exists, a destination account key (@DestAccountId) where the money is being transferred, and the amount to transfer (@Amount) as parameters. Lines 8 through 13 declare variables used in the stored procedure to store temporary values. Lines 15 through 20 set some of these temporary values. As their names indicate, they are used for errors, to store a description of the transaction, the date and time of the transaction, and so on. For instance, line 16 uses the Transact-SQL GetDate function to set the transfer date and time temporary variable, @TransactionDate.

7

Line 24 explicitly begins the FundTransfer transaction. Everything contained within the procedure, up to line 85 where the FundTransfer COMMIT is stated, must complete without error, or the entire transaction is rolled back and the database restored to the state it was in prior to calling the TransferFunds procedure. Line 27 calls the PerformAccountAction stored procedure to perform the account debit, and then line 29 checks to see if an error occurred during the debit. Remember that the PerformAccountAction stored procedure contains a RAISERROR statement if @Action is not equal to 'DEBIT' or 'CREDIT'. The RAISERROR statement will insert an error number into the system variable @@Error that you can inspect to see if an error has occurred. Also notice that system variables begin with @@. If an error occurs, line 33 rolls back the FundTransfer transaction. Lines 38 through 46 insert an AccountTransaction record to indicate that a transaction has occurred. You can use the AccountTransaction record to reconcile bank accounts or view the transaction history for an account. Lines 56 through 83 perform similar statements to credit the source account. The transaction is then committed, and the TransferFunds procedure is complete. This sample is fairly complex, but shows how you can use transactions to ensure database consistency.

Tip

> SQL Server tracks the number of transactions that are active for each connection in the database. The SQL variable @@TRANCOUNT returns the number of active transactions for the current connection.
>
> The BEGIN TRANSACTION statement increments @@TRANCOUNT by 1. ROLLBACK TRANSACTION decrements @@TRANCOUNT to 0, except for ROLLBACK TRANSACTION *savepoint_name*, which does not affect @@TRANCOUNT. COMMIT TRANSACTION or COMMIT WORK decrements @@TRANCOUNT by 1.
>
> SQL Server requires that a stored procedure or batch operation leave the transaction count the same as when the transaction started. If the transaction accounts are different, your code may have missed a commit transaction or rollback transaction.

You can also set a savepoint within your transaction. The savepoint defines a location to which a transaction can return if part of the transaction is conditionally canceled. Transaction savepoints and their usage are beyond the scope of this book. If you want to learn more about savepoints, refer to your Microsoft SQL Server Help files.

Now that you understand what transactions are and have successfully implemented database transactions, let's see how transactions can be applied across a distributed network such as the Windows DNA platform.

Distributed Transactions

Put on your thinking caps and remember back to Day 1, "Understanding Windows DNA." The Windows DNA architecture is defined as a framework introduced in 1997 as a means of integrating client/server and Web technologies in the creation of scalable, multitier applications delivered over an enterprise network. So far, you have limited your transaction discussion to actions and procedures occurring in one database. *Distributed transactions* are transactions that update data on two or more network-connected systems. Microsoft SQL Server supports distributed transactions, and allows you to create transactions that update multiple SQL Server databases, as well as other data sources. The Microsoft Distributed Transaction Coordinator manages distributed transactions and can be installed with SQL Server 7.0. You can access the MS DTC Administrative console in the Microsoft SQL Server 7.0 folder from the Start, Programs menus.

A distributed transaction involves

- *The application* The participant that requests the transaction. This could be your application or SQL Server itself.
- *The resource managers* The participants that contain the resources being operated on. A distributed transaction comprises local transactions in each individual resource manager. Each resource manager must be able to commit or roll back its local transaction in coordination with all the other resource managers in the distributed transaction.
- *The transaction manager* The participant in the transaction who controls the commit and rollback of a distributed transaction. The transaction manager coordinates with each resource manager to ensure that all the local transactions making up the distributed transaction are committed or rolled back together.

From an application perspective, a distributed transaction is managed in much the same way as a local transaction. When the transaction is complete, the transaction is either committed or rolled back. However the Transaction Manager must handle the commit of a distributed process differently to minimize the risk of failure. A commit of a large transaction across multiple, distributed resources can take a relatively long time as log buffers are flushed and freed. The commit process itself can also encounter errors initiating a rollback. If the transaction manager simply asked each resource manager to commit, it might get a success status back from some resource managers and then get an error from another resource manager. This creates a conflict because all the distributed

7

transactions should be rolled back, but parts are already committed. The transaction manager minimizes this risk by managing the commit process in two phases, the *prepare phase* and the *commit phase*. This so-called *two-phase commit* proceeds as follows:

1. The Prepare Phase

   The transaction manager sends a prepare-to-commit request to each resource manager. Each resource manager then performs all resource-intensive actions needed to complete the commit process, such as locking necessary records and flushing all log buffers. The resource manager only holds the minimum locks needed to maintain the integrity of the transaction, and then returns a success notice to the transaction manager.

2. The Commit Phase

   If all the resource managers return success notices to their prepare-to-commit requests, the transaction manager then sends COMMIT commands to each resource manager. Each resource manager then records the transaction as finished and frees their resources. If any resource manager returns an error to the prepare request, the transaction manager then sends ROLLBACK commands to each resource manager.

Starting a Distributed Transaction

Beginning and ending distributed transactions explicitly are much the same as beginning and ending local transactions. You can start a distributed transaction in one of three ways:

- When you start an explicit distributed transaction by issuing a BEGIN DISTRIBUTED TRANSACTION statement, you can also initiate a distributed query against a linked server. The SQL Server you are connected to calls Microsoft Distributed Transaction Coordinator (MS DTC) to manage the distributed transaction with the linked server. In addition, you can execute remote stored procedures as part of the explicit distributed transactions. For more information regarding linked servers, see "Configuring Linked Servers" in your Microsoft SQL Server Help files.

- While in a local transaction, you can execute a distributed query (a query containing data from multiple resources). When you execute a distributed query, your local transaction is escalated to a distributed transaction.

- If your application has a local transaction that calls a remote procedure on another SQL Server, and the option REMOTE_PROC_TRANSACTIONS is set ON, this escalates your local transaction to a distributed transaction.

Beginning a distributed transaction explicitly is much the same as beginning a local transaction. You issue the BEGIN DISTRIBUTED TRANSACTION statement and optionally provide a transaction name:

SYNTAX
```
BEGIN DISTRIBUTED TRAN[SACTION]
[transaction_name | @tran_name_variable]
```

Ending a Distributed Transaction

Once you have started a distributed transaction, you can perform distributed queries against linked servers or execute remote procedures against remote servers to perform the actions you desire. When the distributed transaction is complete, call the standard SQL statements—COMMIT TRANSACTION, COMMIT WORK, ROLLBACK TRANSACTION, or ROLLBACK WORK—to complete the transaction. For all distributed transactions, SQL Server automatically calls the MS DTC to manage the commitment and rollback of the transaction. In the next section, you will be introduced to the MS DTC. The sample code shown in Listing 7.7 inserts the 'Joint Checking' account type into tables residing in two different databases. You might want to perform distributed transactions to keep the two databases synchronized. If the INSERT completes successfully, both databases have the new record; otherwise, neither database does.

LISTING 7.7   Distributed Transaction Example

```
1: /* First explicit transaction started by BEGIN TRANSACTION statement */
2: BEGIN DISTRIBUTED TRANSACTION InsAccType
3: GO
4: INSERT INTO DNA..AccountType VALUES ('Joint Checking')
6: GO
7: INSERT INTO DNARemote..AccountType VALUES ('Joint Checking')
8: GO
9: COMMIT TRANSACTION InsAccType
10: /* Transaction is explicitly committed to both databases*/
```

ANALYSIS   The distributed transaction is started in line 2 explicitly by calling the BEGIN DISTRIBUTED TRANSACTION statement. Line 4 inserts the AccountType description into the DNA database, and line 7 inserts the same AccountType description into the DNARemote database. (The DNA database and the RemoteDNA database shown are arbitrary database names I made up on my SQL Server that you can modify to match your database names.) The transaction is committed just as local transactions are in line 9 with the COMMIT TRANSACTION statement.

Microsoft Distributed Transaction Coordinator

The Microsoft Distributed Transaction Coordinator (MS DTC) operates as a transaction manager that allows client applications to include several different sources of data in one

7

transaction. MS DTC coordinates committing the distributed transaction across all the servers engaged in the transaction.

SQL Server can participate in the transaction by calling stored procedures on remote servers running SQL Server, promoting the local transaction to a distributed transaction, and enlisting remote servers in the transaction, or by making distributed updates that update data on multiple OLE DB data sources. Figure 7.1 shows the promotion of a local transaction to a distributed transaction that enlists a remote server in the transaction. The MS DTC service on Server 1 coordinates this transaction with the MS DTC service on Server 2. The client in this situation is unaware the DTC service has escalated the transaction to a distributed transaction.

FIGURE 7.1

The MS DTC service promotes a local transaction to a distributed transaction.

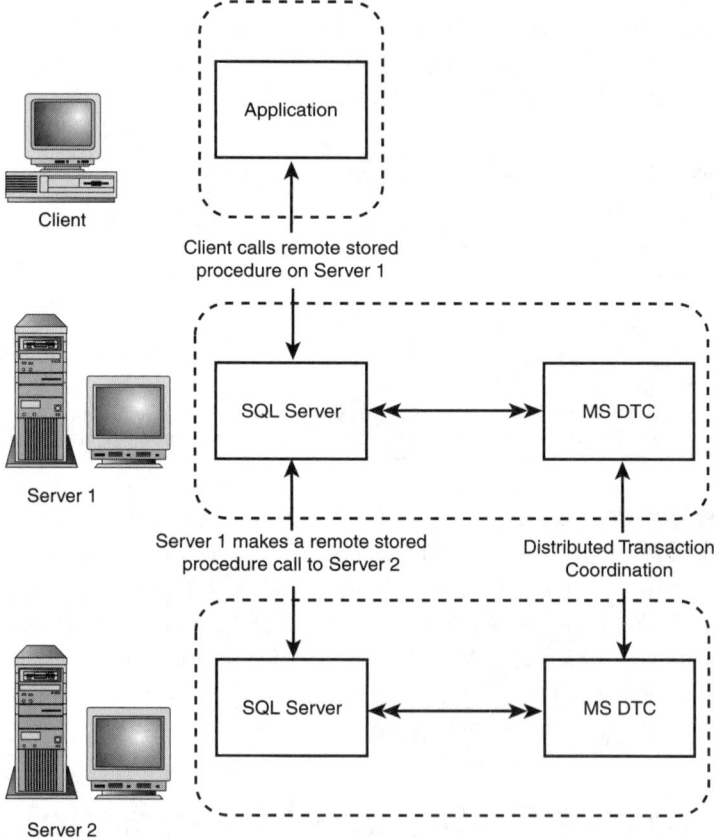

The client application can also explicitly start a distributed transaction. The MS DTC then manages the transaction and enlists other resource managers as needed to complete the updates performed by the client. Figure 7.2 shows the client application explicitly starting a distributed transaction.

FIGURE 7.2

Client application explicitly starts a distributed transaction.

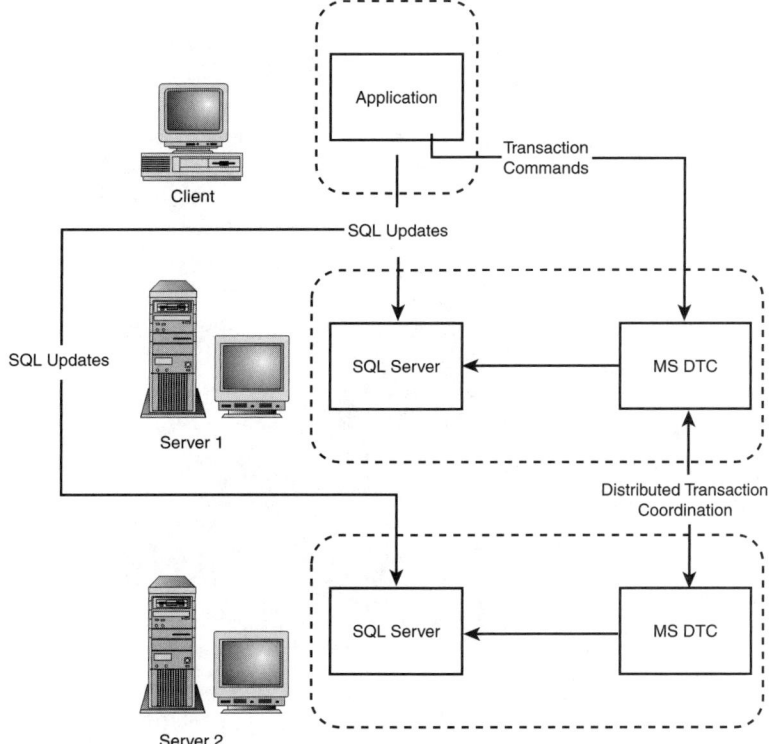

MS DTC allows SQL Server to act as an X/Open DTP resource manager and participate in distributed XA transactions. What this means to you is that SQL Server can be used by transaction processing (TP) monitors on Windows NT such as Tuxedo, TopEnd, and Encina. By using MS DTC and a TP monitor, customers can implement applications that span databases on other platforms such as Oracle, Sybase, or Informix on UNIX systems.

A key feature of MS DTC is an easy-to-use graphical administration interface called the DTC Admin Console (DAC). The DAC can be used to manage DTC systems and transactions and provides a simple interface for starting and stopping DTC, viewing MS DTC statistics, managing transactions coordinated by the MS DTC service, and managing the MS DTC log.

7

You can open the DAC by navigating to the Microsoft SQL Server 7.0 folder off your Start menu and selecting 'MSDTC Administration Console'. The DAC will appear with the General tab showing, as seen in Figure 7.3. From the General tab, you can stop and start the MS DTC service and view general information such as the version of the MS DTC.

 **Note**

> MS DTC is a snap-in to the Microsoft Management Console (MMC). The MMC is a universal container that Microsoft has established for all its system management components. You may notice that MS DTC looks very similar to the SQL Server 7 interface. This is no coincidence; they both use MMC. Into an MMC console you can add as many snap-ins as you want to provide your own custom central command center.

FIGURE 7.3

The MS DTC Admin Console General tab.

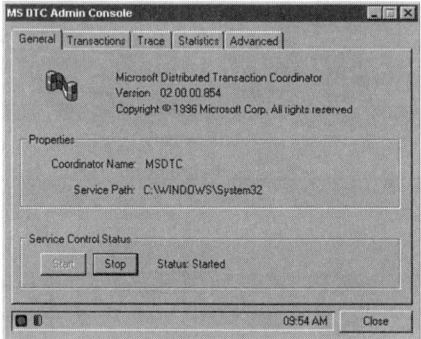

Managing Transactions with MS DTC

When you click the DAC Transactions tab, you can browse a list of the current MS DTC transactions. MS DTC will support thousands of concurrent transactions, so rather than displaying every transaction from MS DTC in the DAC, a set of rules is applied to which transactions show up in the transaction list.

To display in the list, either the transaction must be in doubt, or the transaction must have been in the active state for a period of time longer than that specified in the Advanced Property tab. You can view the transaction list as large or small icons, a simple list, or a detailed list. You can change the view by right-clicking a transaction and selecting the View Menu option. The Detailed List view is the only view that displays a transaction ID. Each view displays the transaction's status as an icon.

The transaction status can be Active, Preparing, Prepared, Committing, Committed, Indoubt, Aborting, Aborted, Heuristic Abort, Heuristic Commit, Heuristic Danger, or Heuristic Damage. I will discuss the Indoubt status and resolving those transactions in detail next. For explanations regarding other transaction status levels, consult your SQL Server documentation.

While a resource manager is prepared, it is "Indoubt" about whether the transaction is committed or rolled back. MS DTC keeps a sequential log so that its commit and roll-back decisions are durable. If a resource manager or transaction manager fails, they reconcile Indoubt transactions when they reconnect.

From the Transaction tab, you can also right-click any transaction and view its properties or resolve the transaction. The Properties dialog simply displays the transaction parent or subordinate ID for the transaction. You can then use the ID to trace through the open transactions and locate a transaction's parent or subordinate transactions (transactions controlled by the parent transaction). The Resolve menu allows you to force a transaction to commit or abort; you can also forget a transaction.

The Coordinator DTC

The Coordinator DTC is the MS DTC service on the system where the transaction was started. In the two-phase commit protocol, the Coordinator DTC makes the final commit or abort decision. It is never in doubt about the current status of a transaction, but it may be waiting to notify prepared resource managers of a commit decision and unable to deliver the commit request.

Subordinate DTCs

Subordinate DTCs are DTC services on systems, other than the coordinator, enlisted on a transaction owned by the coordinator DTC. When a subordinate receives a prepare request, it performs the prepare work, responds to the coordinator with a prepared status, and waits for the Coordinator DTC to notify it of a commit or abort decision. While the subordinate and coordinator perform prepare logic, all enlisted resources (SQL Servers) are asked to prepare. During this period, the data accessed by the transaction is still locked and cannot be accessed by other users. If the subordinate cannot communicate with the coordinator after a prepare request is received, the transaction is "in doubt."

Resolving Transactions

The following process is recommended for resolving an "Indoubt" distributed transaction on a subordinate DTC:

1. Go to the transaction list on the coordinator DTC and check the current status of the transaction.

7

2. If the transaction does not exist, then it must have aborted. Find all the subordinate DTCs and select the Abort option on the Resolve menu to mark the transaction as aborted.

3. If the transaction is shown as committed, go to all the subordinate DTCs and select the Commit option on the Resolve menu to mark the transaction as committed. Then go back to the coordinator and all the subordinates and select the Forget option on the Resolve menu to force the DTCs to forget about the transaction.

Figure 7.4 shows the Transaction tab, and the Resolve menu options.

FIGURE 7.4

The MS DTC Admin Console Trans-actions tab.

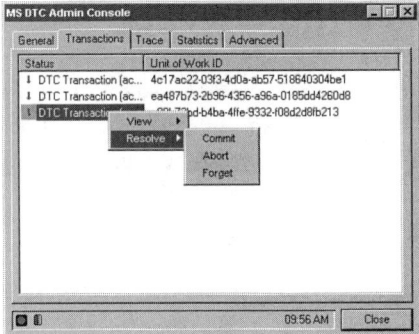

Viewing Transaction Statistics

The DAC Statistics tab provides current and aggregate statistical information for transactions controlled by the MS DTC service. It also displays the time the DTC service was started and the transaction response times. Figure 7.5 shows the DAC Statistical tab.

FIGURE 7.5

The MS DTC Admin Console Statistics tab.

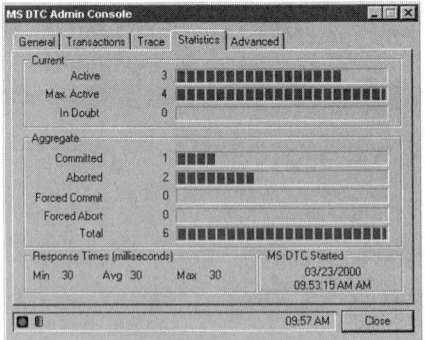

The DAC Advanced Options

The DAC Advanced tab allows you to control the transactions you are viewing. You can modify the refresh frequency, the age for transactions displayed, and the amount of transactions to trace. The Advanced tab also lets you change the location for the DAC log file, change the log file size, and erase the log contents by resetting the log. Figure 7.6 shows the DAC Advanced tab.

FIGURE 7.6

The MS DTC Admin Console Advanced tab.

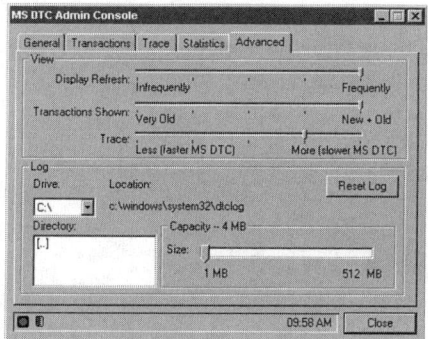

In summary, the graphical management of transactions the DAC provides eliminates many of the problems associated with database startup, recovery, and locking when the network connection is lost between servers or when a server is unavailable. In the next section, you will learn how to improve performance of your transactions and reduce contention between concurrent transactions.

Increasing Transaction Performance

Distributed transactions can become very complex, involving many data sources, and can consume valuable resources. You can create efficient transactions by keeping these guidelines in mind:

- Don't begin a transaction and then prompt for input from a user during the transaction. If you begin a transaction, then prompt for input, the transaction will block other transactions from finishing and will consume resources. Even if the user reacts immediately to the input request, his response time is significantly slower than an uninterrupted transaction. Prompt for all necessary input from users before beginning a transaction.

- Keep the transactions as short as possible. Do not open the transaction before it is required, and immediately commit or roll back changes after executing the transaction statements.

7

- Don't open a transaction while browsing data.

- Make use of lower transaction isolation levels. Many of your applications can be coded to use a read-committed isolation level. Not all transactions require the serializable transaction isolation level, but many developers use this default isolation level.

- Analyze your database structure and make sure it is normalized. If you have a few tables with many attributes, concurrency for the data in those tables will be high. However in a highly normalized database, the modifications will be spread over many, smaller tables, thus reducing concurrency. This helps you to access the least amount of data possible during a transaction.

In the next section you will be introduced to Microsoft Transaction Server (MTS). Keep in mind that most of these transaction performance concepts also apply to MTS.

Microsoft Transaction Server

Microsoft's definition of Microsoft Transaction Server (MTS) is *"a component-based transaction processing system for building, deploying, and administering robust Internet and intranet server applications."* You may be asking yourself, "What does that mean?"

It means that MTS provides many features to help you build distributed applications that can incorporate transactions and scale to meet usage demands. Included with MTS are the runtime environment, which manages the transactions; the MTS Explorer graphical user interface for deploying and managing application components; application programming interfaces (API); resource dispensers; and sample applications.

MTS applications are collections of components. With MTS you can encapsulate business logic into components. The components can reside on local or remote computers, and can be shared among different applications.

The MTS runtime environment is a middle-tier platform for running these components. The MTS runtime helps you develop, deploy, and administer applications by providing the following services:

- Distributed transactions

- Automatic management of processes and threads

- Object instance management

- A distributed security service to control object creation and use

- A graphical interface for system administration and component management

You can use the MTS Explorer to register and manage components executing in the MTS runtime environment. In Day 8, "Introduction to COM and MTS," you will be introduced to the component model used in MTS (COM), and how to begin using MTS.

Summary

Today's lesson teaches you about database transactions and the Microsoft Distributed Transaction Coordinator. Specifically, you were introduced to the ACID transaction rules. You also learned how to begin and end both local and distributed transactions. You had the opportunity to use the MS DTC and participate in distributed transactions. You learned how to increase the performance of your transactions. Finally, you were introduced to Microsoft's Transaction Server.

Tomorrow's lesson will take a closer look at Microsoft's Transaction Server. Specifically, you will learn about the component object model (COM), which is the foundation for all of Window's DNA-based development. You will also learn how to use the MTS runtime environment and MTS Explorer to put your components into MTS packages.

Q&A

Q How do I decide when to control transactions using ADO, as opposed to using Transact-SQL?

A Depending upon the situation, both are good choices. Much of your decision to use ADO or Transact-SQL depends upon the type of transaction being performed. If you are performing a distributed transaction over many data sources, such as a SQL Server and an Excel spreadsheet, or want to include Visual Basic code within a transaction, it is probably best to use ADO. Your SQL Server may not know the location and how to control the Excel spreadsheet, and definitely cannot produce Visual Basic code. On the other hand, if you are controlling only database transactions and would like the transaction code to be available to other applications (even those written in languages other than Visual Basic), SQL Server may be the correct choice, increasing performance and code reuse.

Q I only have one installation of SQL Server. How can I use distributed transactions?

A You can create two databases on SQL Server, each containing data you want to update in one transaction. Even without using a `BEGIN DISTRIBUTED TRANSACTION` statement and using the standard `BEGIN TRANSACTION` statement, SQL Server will escalate the transaction to a distributed transaction. The services of MS DTC will be invoked to perform the transaction that is distributed across databases.

7

Q Can I include Oracle and DB2 in a single transaction?

A Yes, any DBMS that supports the X/Open Architecture standard can participate in a distributed transaction.The examples in this chapter used Microsoft SQL Server exclusively. However, you can transact with any data store that supports the X/Open Architecture standard. The Distributed Transaction Coordinator works exclusive of SQL Server, so SQL Server does not need to be involved in order to use distributed transactions in your application.

Workshop

The Workshop provides quiz questions to help you solidify your understanding of the material covered and exercises to provide you with experience in using what you've learned. Try to understand the quiz and exercise answers before continuing to the next lesson. Answers are provided in Appendix A.

Quiz

1. What does the acronym ACID stand for and what is it used for?
2. How do you define an explicit, local transaction using Transact-SQL? How do you define an explicit, distributed transaction using Transact-SQL?
3. What does the durability property of a transaction mean?
4. What are some of the ways you can improve the performance of your transactions?
5. What role does the MS DTC assume in distributed transactions?

Exercises

1. Using Transact-SQL, create a stored procedure that performs a distributed transaction to transfer funds between two accounts for the same customer, where each account resides in a different database.
2. Create a batch of SQL Statements by altering your stored procedure created in exercise 1, so that the transaction is started, but does not end. Execute the batch of SQL statements using the Query Analyzer. Using MS DTC Admin Console, monitor your transaction. View the active transactions on the Transactions tab and statistics for all transactions on the Statistics tab. Try creating multiple transactions—some committed and some not—and view the output in the MS DTC Admin Console.

Week 1

In Review

You made it through this information-packed week. You should now have a good basic feel for what Windows DNA is all about and hopefully feel comfortable with the model (Days 1 and 2).

You learned where the Microsoft tools and technologies fit into Windows DNA. You learned how important Windows DNA is to Microsoft's development architecture and how it is the foundational model for all services, components, and development tools (Day 2).

You learned how to collect requirements, and how to use Visual Modeler to model a solution using Windows DNA (Day 3).

You learned about basic SQL and you developed the database that will be used by the banking project we are using to teach Windows DNA (Day 4).

You learned how to put business logic into the data tier and some guidelines regarding when you should do this, rather than put the logic into business components (Day 5).

You learned about Active Data Objects (ADO) and how it gives you a consistent interface across a broad range of data stores (Day 6).

You learned about transactions and the ACID test for all transactions. You also learned about Microsoft Transaction Server and the Distributed Transaction coordinator (Day 7).

1

2

3

4

5

6

7

WEEK 2

At a Glance

After the completion of Week 1, you now have a solid understanding of the data tier in Windows DNA. This includes creating the database and stored procedures to access data, receiving an introduction to ActiveX Data Objects, and gaining an understanding of transactions at the database level. You are now ready to build on this foundation and move into the business logic of creating an application.

This week you will work through the business logic tier, which is the middle tier between your data tier and the presentation tier. The business logic tier is the only way that the presentation tier and the data tier have access to each other. It communicates with both tiers, handling any business processes and rules involved. On one end, it communicates with the data store and knows how to initiate actions, which will update tables, insert records, and get information back. On the other end, it can take requests, process them according to the business requirements, and send back information that can be displayed to the user by the presentation tier.

The first three days of this week will be spent learning how to build objects into your application that can implement this business logic tier and how to deploy them on Windows NT. You will use Visual Basic to create these objects; Microsoft Transaction Server (MTS) will allow you to deploy them and allow the objects to be used efficiently by the system. MTS gives you great potential to handle transactions as well. You will also discover that MTS has far reaching capabilities when it comes to the scalability of your applications.

During the latter part of the week, you will have a chance to learn more about ActiveX Data Objects and some of the advanced features that are available in ADO. You will also learn how you can use ADO to send and receive data between the different tiers of Windows DNA. This will enable you to bring together the various application tiers.

In addition, you will have a look at COM+ in Windows 2000. You will learn about the additional benefits that COM+ gives you and why you will want to take advantage of this improved technology. Finally, your instruction on the business logic tier will be rounded out with an introduction to some of the other services that the Windows DNA platform provides. These include the ability to access legacy systems and Microsoft's queuing service, Microsoft Message Queue. After this week, you will have studied two of the three tiers and will be ready to move on to the presentation tier section, where you will learn to interact with the user.

DAY 8

Introduction to COM and MTS

On Day 7, "Database Transactions and Distributed Transaction Coordinator," you were introduced to Microsoft's Distributed Transaction Coordinator and Transaction Server (MTS). Today, you learn about MTS and the Component Object Model (COM). COM is the cornerstone of all Windows DNA development and thus important to understand. All of Microsoft's development tools are COM aware, which makes it extremely easy to develop COM components. We will explore COM to a depth of understanding that should enable you to work with the development tools. Later, on Day 13, "The Future: COM+," you will learn about COM+, the supercharged version that is packaged with Windows 2000. COM+ is a better, more integrated, version of COM that adds more capability without the need for you to do anything. Specifically, you will learn

- COM's history
- Threading models available to COM
- Whether COM is really object oriented

In addition to COM, you will learn more about MTS. In the MTS section of today's lesson, you will learn about

- Resource management
- Transaction support
- Security
- Hands on use of MTS and the MTS Explorer

Component Object Model (COM)

Microsoft's Component Object Model (COM) was covered briefly on Day 1, "Understanding Windows DNA." Today, we will examine COM in a little more detail to better understand its importance in Windows DNA. Let's begin by examining the history of COM.

A Brief History of COM

There are primarily two technologies that were the direct precursors to COM: Dynamic Data Exchange (DDE) and Object Linking and Embedding (OLE).

In November 1987, Microsoft introduced DDE in Windows 2.03. Although the ability to cut and paste was already incorporated into Windows, it was difficult to modify the pasted elements when the source data changed. DDE established a protocol for exchanging information between Windows-based applications and allowed elements pasted into an application to be updated using the interfaces of their native applications. Although helpful, DDE proved to be slow, difficult to use, and too resource intensive for the hardware of the day.

A little more than four years later, OLE was introduced in version 3.10 of Windows. In its first version, it facilitated the creation of compound documents. For example, this capability enabled an Excel spreadsheet to be inserted inside of a Word document (see Figure 8.1).

Changes could be made to the spreadsheet data while still inside of Word. In fact, it was not necessary to maintain two separate files for the spreadsheet and the word processing documents. The OLE specification allowed the data from the spreadsheet to be stored inside of the Word file itself. Although an improvement over DDE, the first version of OLE still suffered from performance problems related to its messaging-based architecture. Still, OLE 1.0 became a popular and well-used part of Microsoft Windows.

FIGURE 8.1

A compound document as it might have appeared using OLE.

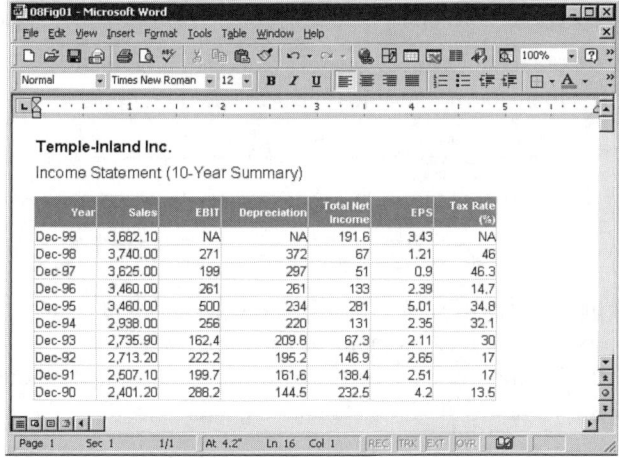

In 1993, Microsoft came to realize that the compound document problem addressed by OLE 1.0 was actually symptomatic of a larger problem. How should software components provide services to one another? To address this larger problem, Microsoft set out to provide this capability as part of the operating system, and COM was born. Microsoft initially believed that COM would primarily be used as the foundation for OLE 2.0 and other low-level system services. Software engineers inside the company however, were already beginning to understand that the technology that COM represented could result in an entirely new way to think about software development.

Although COM quickly became a technology that in many cases had nothing to do with compound documents, Microsoft continued to push the term OLE as the identity for technology that used COM. This continued until December 7, 1996.

It was Pearl Harbor Day when Microsoft officially announced that it "got" the Internet. It trimmed down the large OLE library to Internet size and re-christened the new technology ActiveX. As the term ActiveX began to be applied to capabilities previously described by OLE, it once again referred to the creation of compound. In late September 1997, Microsoft renamed ActiveX and the other elements of its Active Platform technology to Windows DNA. As you already know from Day 1, Windows DNA is not a product, but a collection of products and technologies that include COM. The latest enhancements to COM have resulted in yet another name for this technology, COM+. The capabilities added to this latest edition to the COM family are discussed in a later lesson (see Day 13).

Now that you have a general understanding of COM's origins, let's take a more detailed look at the technology itself.

COM Basics

Microsoft's Component Object Model is an open architecture that facilitates the cross-platform development of reusable object oriented components.

Note   If you need to review the concept of a component or an object see Day 1.

The most basic unit in COM is the component, which is represented in the operating system as a physical file (for example, .exe, .dll, .ocx, and so on) that contains one or more classes (see Figure 8.2). In Visual Basic a class can be thought of as the blueprint for an object including all the code and data elements that make up that object. Finally, an object is a specific instance of a class.

Tip   If you would like additional information on the concept of components and objects, they were first introduced on Day 1.

FIGURE 8.2

The relationship between a component and a class.

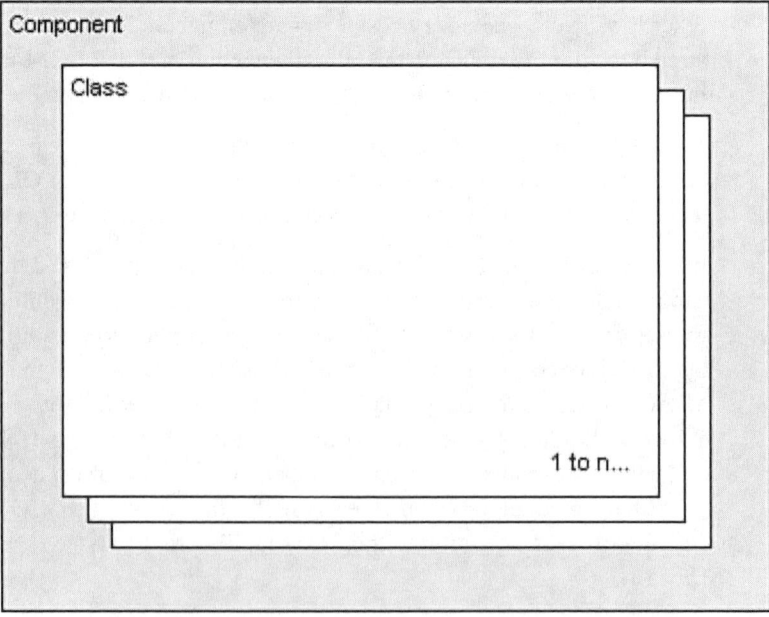

8

As mentioned earlier, Microsoft originally created COM to provide the capability for software components to provide services for each other. In order to do this, COM defines a set of interfaces that define how software components communicate.

A COM component can have one or more interfaces defined. Each interface represents an unchangeable contract between the component and its clients. For this to happen, the component and its clients must agree on a way to

- Determine the identity of an interface
- Describe how to construct an interface
- Discover which interfaces exist
- Expose the object's methods to the client.

It is important to be able to uniquely identify every component. COM provides this capability in two ways: first, by a name that meant for people to use (for example, IUnknown), and, second, by a Globally Unique Identifier (GUID, pronounced *goo-id*). A GUID is a 16-byte value that is guaranteed to be unique across the entire planet (although technically only until about 3400 A.D.). After an interface is defined, assigned a GUID, and published, it must not be changed. If your component changes in the future, you must create additional interfaces that contain any new capabilities. This is important so you don't cause compatibility problems with software that makes use of only the capabilities your original component contained.

In order for COM to work, a client needs to know exactly what is required to invoke a method. This means that the details behind constructing an interface need to be rigorously defined. COM defines a binary interface that every COM component must support for every interface. This binary standard means that a client can invoke a component's method regardless of the programming language that either is written in. This binary standard is implemented by a series of pointers to a memory structure called a VTable. A VTable contains the addresses of the functions that are implemented by the object. Luckily Visual Basic hides almost all this complexity behind a special VTable interface called IDispatch, which will be described later in this lesson.

But before we can call a method exposed in an interface, we need a way to determine which interfaces even exist. This is where IUnknown comes into play. The COM specification dictates that every COM object must support the IUnknown interface. This makes perfect sense, because there is no way for a client to know about the interfaces exposed by a component until it requests this information from IUnknown.

Finally, we need a way to both determine and then execute a component's methods. The IDispatch interface provides just this capability. IDispatch provides information about the methods that an object supports and can even execute them if required. These capabilities are used to provide Visual Basic and other scripting languages the capability to access COM components directly. Both the IUnknown and IDispatch interfaces are built for you behind the scenes in Visual Basic. In fact, there are many more interfaces built automatically by Visual Basic that are beyond the scope of this lesson. You will learn how to build your own COM components on Day 9, "Building COM Components in VB."

Threading Models

After a COM object is created, it executes in memory as part of a thread. A *thread* is a path of execution through a larger process or program. It is also the smallest unit of execution that Windows schedules. Because Windows is able to execute more than one thread in a single process it is called multithreaded.

COM supports multithreading by putting objects in the same process space into their own groups called *apartments*. COM supports two types of apartments:

- Single-Threaded Apartment (STA)
- Multi-Threaded Apartment (MTA)

The STA model enables a single thread to run within each apartment. A process can contain any number of STAs to provide multithreading for components that are not thread-aware. This is the only threading option that Visual Basic currently supports.

The MTA model enables multiple threads to execute within the same apartment, however, each process space can have just one MTA. This is not a limitation. Because an MTA can run any number of threads, there is really not a reason to have more than one MTA.

Is COM Object Oriented?

COM has much in common with other object-oriented technologies. As discussed on Day 1, it provides encapsulation, polymorphism, and inheritance. Although objects are at the core of COM, they aren't always exactly like other object-oriented systems.

So is COM really object oriented? Well, if you are asking if COM objects are exactly like C++ objects, the answer is no. But if the question is, does COM provide the principal features and benefits traditionally associated with objects, then the answer is a resounding yes.

At the end of the day, it is important to remember that the purpose of using COM is not to get caught up in endless debates that revolve around semantics, but to create better applications.

Microsoft Transaction Server (MTS)

Microsoft Transaction Server (MTS) is an extension of COM, which enables the development, deployment, and management of secure, high-performance, scalable, and robust applications. It is the easiest way to build and deploy industry-strength COM applications using development tools such as Visual Basic. MTS simplifies object use and reuse, and administrators can perform management tasks using the MTS Explorer. Three of the most important capabilities provided by MTS are

- Resource management
- Transaction support
- Security

Resource Management with MTS

MTS conserves server resources by keeping each instance of an object active only while it is in use by its client. This is known as *just-in-time activation* and enables the server where MTS is located to handle a greater number of clients than would otherwise be possible.

In addition, MTS can also enable the use of some resource dispensers (for example, ODBC) to pool resources to maximize the use of scarce resources. For example, when an ODBC connection to a database is released, the connection can be released to a pool instead of being closed. If another MTS object requests the same connection, it can be assigned from the pool rather than the much slower and resource-intensive action of creating the connection.

MTS Transaction Support

Applications today, especially in a distributed environment, can involve updating a data store. Often there is more than one object in the application that is also requesting changes to at least one data store and sometimes to multiple data stores simultaneously. MTS helps ensure that these update requests either completely succeed or completely fail. MTS helps ensure that transactions are not left in an inconsistent state.

Providing Security with MTS

Sophisticated applications typically involve more than a single user. Developers of distributed applications have traditionally had to spend a great deal of their time adding custom security routines to their applications.

MTS provides security by allowing you to define roles. A role contains a list of NT accounts that are allowed to use a component's interface. It is important to note that

MTS security is built on NT's native security, which makes it robust and easy to administer. As you will see later in today's lesson, it is not necessary to write any special code in your component to provide this level of security. It is provided automatically by MTS.

Putting COM Components into an MTS Package

The MTS Explorer is used to place COM components into MTS. The MTS Explorer is a Microsoft Management Console (MMC) snap-in. MTS Explorer enables the management of components and packages including

- Creating, deleting, or exporting a package
- Adding or deleting one or more components of an existing package
- Changing a package's properties, including its description, security settings, and identity and activation type
- Monitoring transaction statistics

In order to place a component into MTS, a package must first be created. A package is a group of DLLs (no .EXE or .OCX files) that are related to each other. The related DLLs might be part of the same application, or have similar security requirements (see Using Role-based Security).

To create an empty package, first load the MTS Explorer and double-click the computer where you want to create the new package. Next, right-click the Packages Installed folder and select New, Package from the pop-up menu, as seen in Figure 8.3.

FIGURE 8.3

Creating a new package using the MTS Explorer.

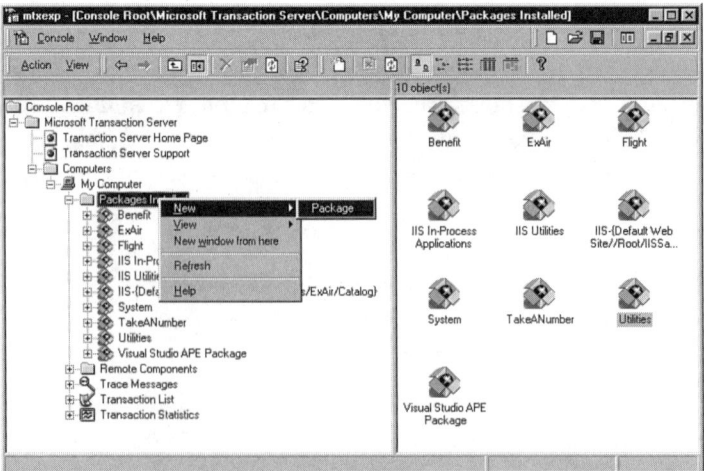

> **Tip**
>
> You can also click Action, New, Package from the toolbar.

The MTS Explorer invokes the Package Wizard, which will step you through the process of creating a new MTS package (see Figure 8.4). Click the Create an empty package button to continue.

FIGURE 8.4

Creating a new package with the Package Wizard.

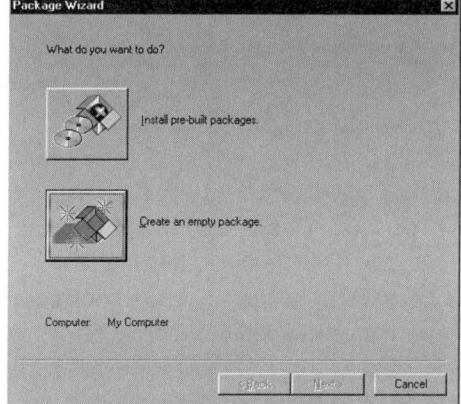

Now name your new package by typing a name (**SmallBank**) and clicking on the Next button. You must select which NT account will be used when components in the package are executed (see Figure 8.5). Select the This user radio-button and type the name of the NT Administrator account (Administrator) and its password.

> **Tip**
>
> If you choose not to use the administrator account, make sure that the account you select has appropriate rights to execute your component. For example, you should ensure that the account selected is able to log on as local and as a service.

> **Caution**
>
> It is usually better not to use the Interactive user radio-button because in many cases the execution of the component will fail unpredictably because of insufficient rights being granted to the currently logged on user. In fact, component access will also fail if no one is logged on to the server. This can be both frustrating and difficult to troubleshoot.

FIGURE 8.5

*Setting the package
identity.*

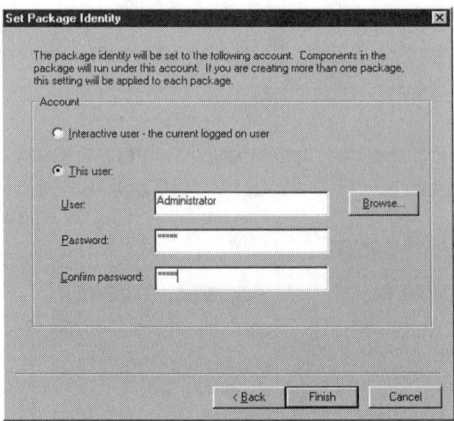

Next press the Finish button to add your new package to the MTS Explorer. Now that
you have created an empty package, you need to add an existing component to install a
new component into the package. Double-click the SmallBank package, and then click
the Components folder. Choose Action, New, Component from the toolbar. The
Component Wizard will appear, as depicted in Figure 8.6.

FIGURE 8.6

*Installing a new com-
ponent using the
Component Wizard.*

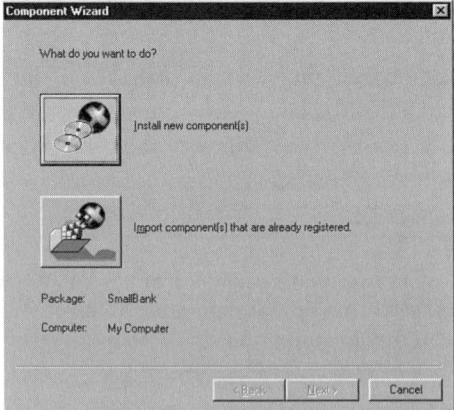

Click the Install new component(s) button to add a new COM DLL to the empty package. Click the Add files button, shown in Figure 8.7, to select an existing DLL on your
computer. Next, locate the BankBusiness.dll, which can be found in the Day 8 folder in
the Source directory of the CD that accompanies this book.

FIGURE 8.7

Selecting a file to install into MTS.

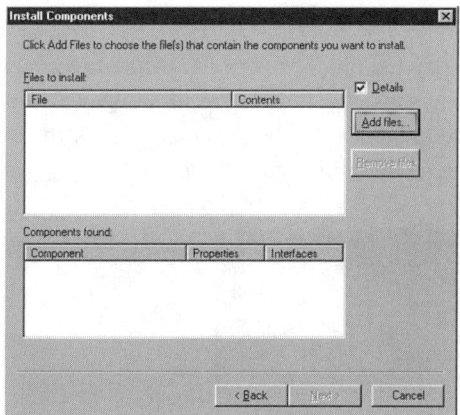

After you have located the DLL, click the open button and then the Finish button to add the component to the SmallBank package. Your screen will now look similar to Figure 8.8.

FIGURE 8.8

The MTS Explorer after successfully adding the COM component.

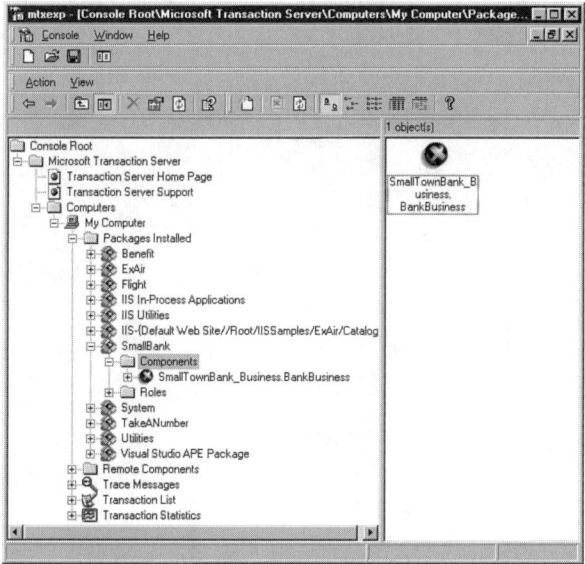

Finally, right-click the SmallTownBank_Business.BankBusiness component and select Properties from the pop-up menu. Click the Transaction tab and then the Requires a transaction radio-button. Click the OK button to save your changes.

Using the Transaction Monitor

You are now ready to verify the proper operation of the logon component. A sample application (logon.exe) has also been included in the Day 8 folder inside the Source folder on the CD that accompanies this book. Double-click the application in order to bring up the logon dialog, as seen in Figure 8.9.

FIGURE 8.9

Testing the proper function of the MTS component using logon.exe.

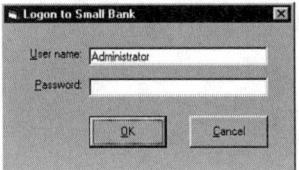

Leave the Password textbox blank and click the OK button. You will receive a message that the Logon to Small Bank failed. In this case, we want the logon process to fail so that we can track it in the Transaction Monitor. Press OK and then repeat this action again. At this point, your attempt to log on to Small Bank has failed twice. Switch to the MTS Explorer and click the Transaction Statistics node, located underneath the Computers folder (see Figure 8.10).

FIGURE 8.10

Viewing the Current and Aggregate statistics for MTS.

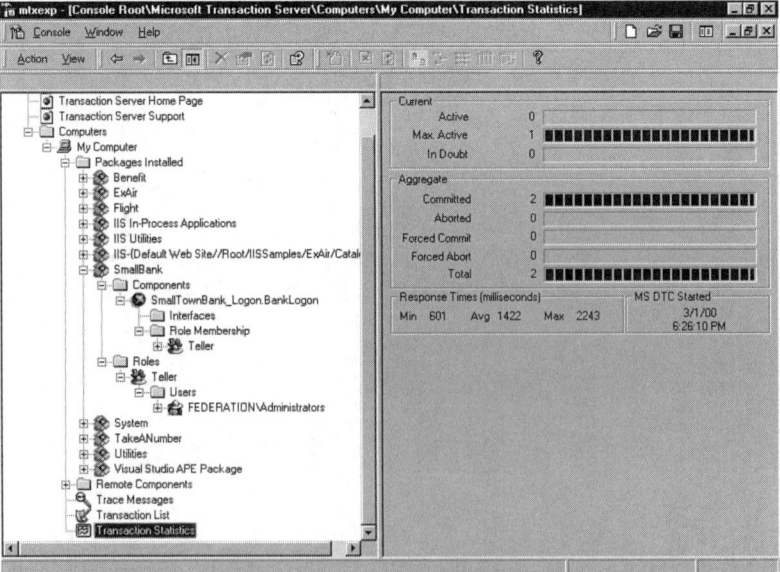

Assuming that this is the first time that you have executed a transaction since the Distributed Transaction Coordinator (DTC) was started, you will notice that the Aggregate statistics pane shows a total of two transactions committed and two transactions total.

Tip

> If the aggregate transaction numbers are all zero, look at the MS DTC Started date and time in the lower right-hand corner of the transaction pane. If it is blank, then that means that DTC has not been started. DTC must be started in order to record transaction statistics. Right-click the My Computer node and then select Start MS DTC from the pop-up menu. The logon.exe application will now generate information in the MTS Statistics pane.

To exit the logon.exe application, enter "password" in the Password textbox and press the OK button. You will be presented with a message that says the logon to Smalltown Bank succeeded. The Transaction Statistics pane will now show a total of four transactions completed.

The logon process provides a good deal of security for our Small Bank application, but how could we further restrict the capability of applications to even access our logon component? Luckily, we won't have to make a single change to our component. MTS provides built-in security for components using its role-based security.

Using Role-Based Security

As you develop sophisticated applications using MTS, you will likely need to secure your application against unauthorized access. Prior to MTS, it was not uncommon for applications to implement their own security mechanisms. Luckily, MTS has greatly simplified this process by including two types of security:

- Declarative security
- Programmatic security

Declarative Security

Declarative security is used to define user access based on roles defined at a package level. Declarative security does not require any changes to be made to the component itself. After you have implemented security for a package, you can specify access to individual interfaces or components within that package.

A *role* is a symbolic name that defines a group of related NT user and group accounts. For example, in the SmallTownBank application, the roles of teller and manager might be appropriate. After the manager and teller roles were defined, the MTS Explorer could be used to restrict the ability to use the Logon component to the manager or teller roles.

Tip

> Checking security takes time and consumes server resources. MTS attempts to minimize the use of these resources by only checking role security when a component is accessed from outside its package. When components inside a package invoke the methods of other components in the same package, they trust each other implicitly and do not check role security.

In order to implement declarative security for the logon component, you must first create a role. Locate the SmallBank package in the left pane of the MTS Explorer and double-click it. Next, click the Roles folder and then choose Action, New, Role from the toolbar. When the New Role dialog appears, enter "Teller" in the textbox and press the OK button (see Figure 8.1).

FIGURE 8.11

Adding a role to the SmallBank *package.*

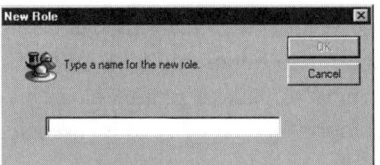

Now that you have defined a role for the SmallBank package, you next need to specify that the teller role be required to access the logon component. To do this, locate the logon component (SmallTownBank_Logon.BankLogon) in the left-hand pane and then double-click it. Now click the Role Membership folder and select Action, New, Role from the toolbar. When the Select Roles dialog appears (see Figure 8.12), click Teller and press the OK button.

If our SmallBank logon application were part of a commercial application, there would be no way to tell which NT accounts or groups were available when we were developing our application. This is precisely why we have only defined roles up until this point. When the SmallBank application was installed, the MTS Explorer would be used to associate NT accounts and groups with our predefined roles. This is exactly what we will do now.

FIGURE 8.12

Selecting a role.

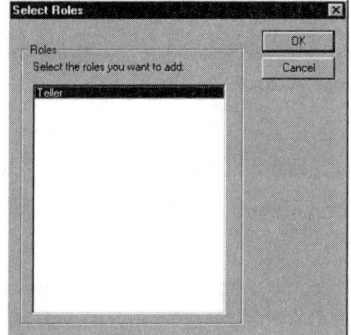

At this point, no one would be able to use the logon component because we have defined and assigned roles for the component, but have not yet assigned any NT accounts or groups to the roles.

Locate the logon component (SmallTownBank_Logon.BankLogon) and double-click it to reveal the Roles folder. Next double-click the Roles folder and also the Teller to reveal the Users folder. Click once the Users folder, and select Action, New, and then User from the toolbar. When the Add Users and Groups to Role dialog appears, select Administrators (or any other appropriate account or group) and click the Add button. To add the local group to the role, press the OK button, as seen in Figure 8.13.

FIGURE 8.13

Assigning the NT Administrators local account to the Teller role.

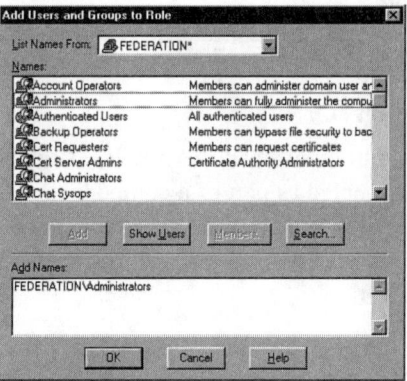

Now let's see if our declarative security works. First, locate and click the SmallBank package. Next, select Action and Shut down from the toolbar. This will make sure that all the changes we have made are reflected during our test.

Once again, run the sample application (logon.exe). Enter "password" in the appropriate textbox and click the OK button. You will see the Logon to Small Bank succeeded dialog. This means that security is in effect and the sample application was able to access the logon component.

Next, locate and click the Users folder (under the hierarchy SmallBank, Roles, Teller). Right-click the Administrators local group in the right-hand pane and select Delete from the pop-up menu. When the Confirm Item Delete dialog appears, click the Yes button.

In order to make sure that our security changes take effect, click the SmallBank package and choose Action and Shut down from the tool bar. Now load the sample application again and enter the appropriate password. This time, you will see a runtime error '70': Permission denied error dialog. Because you removed all the NT accounts and groups from the Teller role, the sample application did not have the required privileges to access the logon component. Finally, restore the appropriate NT accounts and groups back to the Teller role, as you did early in the lesson, to once again enable access to the logon component.

Tip

> If you can still access the logon component, you might not have security enabled on either the package or the component. Inspect the properties of the SmallBank package and the logon component by clicking the security tab of the property dialog. Enable authorization checking should be checked on both.

Programmatic Security

Programmatic security is used to indicate access privileges on a more granular level because this security is implemented as part of a components code. Using programmatic security, you can control access to any portion of the component. Programmatic security is often used to supplement declarative security, thereby providing an additional element of control in your MTS application.

Programmatic security is implemented in Visual Basic using the IsSecurityEnabled and IsCallerInRole methods. The IsCallerInRole method enables a component to check to see if the direct caller is a member of a role. The component is then able to function differently, based on this information. It accepts the role name as its only parameter and returns True if the caller is a member of the role. Otherwise, MTS raises the mtsErrCtxRoleNotFound error to indicate an error condition. This enables the Visual Basic program to use normal error processing logic to handle the error. Sample code that illustrates these points appears in Listing 8.1. It demonstrates logic that might have been used if our logon component had implemented programmatic security.

LISTING 8.1   Sample Code Implementing Programmatic Security for the Logon Component

```
 1: Public Function Logon(ByVal UserID As String, ByVal Password As String) As
Boolean
 2:
 3:     On Error Goto Logon_Error
 4:
 5:     Dim objContext As ObjectContext
 6:     Set objContext = GetObjectContext
 7:
 8:     If objContext.IsSecurityEnabled = False Then Goto Logon_Error:
 9:
10:     If objContext.IsCallerInRole("Teller") Then
11:         If UserID = "Administrator" Then
12:             If Password <> "password" Then
13:                 Goto Logon_Error
14:             End If
15:         End If
16:     End If
17:
18:     Logon = True
19:     Goto Logon_Exit
20:
21: Logon_Error:
22:
23:     Logon = False
24:
25: Logon_Exit:
26:
27:     Set objContext = Nothing
28:
29: End Function
```

You will notice in line 8 that if security is not enabled for this component, then the code branches to line 21, and the Logon function returns false for a failed logon attempt.

Next in lines 10 through 16, the code checks to see if the current role is Teller and if the UserID is equal to Administrator. If so, it expects the password to be password. If so, then the logon succeeds, otherwise it fails.

Summary

In today's lesson, you learned about MTS and how it implements resource management, transactions, and security. This included a hands-on look at the MTS Explorer and its capability to add components to MTS and configure their security. You also learned more about COM, its history, interfaces, and threading models. Although you didn't get a hands-on look by building a COM component in today's lesson, tomorrow you will do just that.

Q&A

Q Can some of my existing COM components make use of MTS without making any changes?

A Yes, but only if the COM components in question are implemented as DLLs. COM components implemented as .EXEs cannot be used inside of MTS. If your component maintains state (uses properties), it also might not gain the full benefit of MTS.

Q Can I use declarative security to control access between components in the same package?

A No. In order to conserve the resources of the server, MTS assumes that all components within a package trust each other. Security is only checked for requests that originate outside of a package.

Q Why can I not access my MTS component when I log off the NT server where MTS is running?

A It is likely that you have specified Interactive user as the account to be used when executing this component. This means that the account that is logged in to the NT server will be used when the component is accessed. When you log off the NT server, there is no valid account and component access failed.

It is usually better not to use the Interactive user setting. Access to the component might fail unpredictably because of insufficient rights being granted to the currently logged on user. In other cases, component access will fail if no one is currently logged on to the server.

Workshop

The Workshop provides quiz questions to help you solidify your understanding of the material covered and exercises to provide you with experience in using what you've learned. Try to understand the quiz and exercise answers before continuing to the next lesson. Answers are provided in Appendix A.

Quiz

1. What does COM stand for?

2. What two technologies were the immediate predecessors to COM?

3. True/False. COM objects are stored in special operating system files with a .com extension.

4. True/False. Microsoft application development tools such as Visual Basic, Visual C++, or Visual J++ are required to build a COM component.

5. What is the name of the only interface that is absolutely required for every COM component?

6. Name the threading model(s) supported by Visual Basic.

7. True/False. MTS security uses the concept of roles, which requires coding changes to be made to your component.

8. Name the two methods used to implement programmatic security in an MTS component.

Exercises

1. After adding a component to MTS, you decide to implement both package and component level declarative security. After carefully adding the new role underneath both the Roles and the Role Membership folders, you next add your NT account to the new role under the users folder.

   You verify that your component is operating correctly, and then delete your NT account from the users folder. Although you expect access to your component to be denied, it operates correctly as before.

   What two factors could be causing security to be bypassed?

2. You are creating a method inside a MTS COM component that should only be used by clients in the role of an administrator. How would you create this method in the form of a Visual Basic function called AdminsOnly?

DAY 9

Building COM Components in VB

Today you start writing code with the help of Microsoft Visual Modeler. You will see how Visual Modeler and Visual Basic work together to keep your design documents and application code coordinated. And finally, you will create a test harness so that you can test your component functionality. After today you will know how to

- Start and configure a Visual Basic project
- Import your Visual Modeler components
- Use SourceSafe
- Develop your project
- Utilize the Class Builder add-in
- Reverse-engineer your code back into Visual Modeler
- Create a test harness
- Test your components
- Store your finished code in Microsoft Repository

Getting Started with COM

Yesterday you were introduced to COM. Today, you want to learn how to implement COM using the developer tools Visual Modeler and Visual Basic. With them you will create your COM components. You can also implement COM technology with other tools such as Visual J++, Visual C++, or some other environment that can create a COM component.

One of the main advantages to using Visual Basic for development is its speed and ease of use. As you will see, all you need to do is tell Visual Basic that you want a COM component, add your methods and properties to it, and tell it to compile. That's it. It hides a lot of the complexity for you. This lets you concentrate on the current problem.

> **Note**
>
> In this chapter you will be using two Visual Basic add-ins that come with Visual Studio Enterprise Edition. This includes Visual Modeler, which you would have used on Day 3, "Architecting a DNA Solution," and also Visual Component Manager. If you discover these are not already installed while going through today's lessons, you may install them by running the Visual Studio setup and make sure they are selected under "Enterprise Tools."

In respect to Windows DNA, the COM components you are building today will fill in the business logic and data tiers of your application. The business components you are building implement the business logic of the SmallTownBank application. For instance, if a user asks for a withdrawal that is greater than the amount of money she has in her account, the business logic has to prevent this from occurring and send an error back. The data components are going to let you access your data store. Your business component would request an amount of money to be deducted from an account, and the data component would send the SQL commands to have that amount deducted in the database tables.

Starting a Visual Basic Project

Let's start Visual Basic. Go to Start, Programs, Microsoft Visual Studio 6.0, Microsoft Visual Basic 6.0. Upon startup, Visual Basic will pop up a New Project dialog.

From the New tab, select ActiveX DLL and select Open. Visual Basic will create a new project with an empty class module.

NEW TERM   A *class* module in an ActiveX DLL contains the methods and properties for that class. To access these methods and properties, the class can be instantiated within a program. For example, in ADO, a class would be Recordset and would be declared as

```
Dim rst as ADODB.Recordset
```

The Open method would correspond to a procedure in the class; the LockType property would correspond to a property in the class.

If necessary (and this will usually be the case), additional classes can be added to the project. Each represents a separate object that can be accessed in the code, which calls this COM component. In this case, Visual Modeler will be creating the classes for you. The only thing you need to make sure of is that Visual Basic is configured to enable Visual Modeler to create the project.

Configuring Your Project

Today you will be using Visual Modeler to generate a New Visual Basic project and place the project under source control. Before you can do this, you will need to configure Visual Basic to have the Visual Modeler add-ins and Source Safe add-in load on startup. This enables Visual Modeler to create the project automatically in Visual Basic and allows you to work with SourceSafe in Visual Basic.

NEW TERM   The *add-ins* for Visual Basic are available through the add-ins menu and provide additional design-time functionality to the Visual Basic development environment.

Working Around Add-In Bug

If you do not see the add-ins in the add-in dialog, it is probably due to a confirmed bug from Microsoft on this issue. For a work around, take a look at article Q190212 on the Microsoft Knowledge Base or go directly to the article at
`http://support.microsoft.com/support/kb/articles/Q190/2/12.ASP`.

In Visual Basic, you will make available three add-ins: Visual Modeler, Visual Modeler Menus, and Source Code Control. These enable integration between the Visual Modeler and Visual Basic and add the Visual Modeler menu items into Visual Basic. Visual Modeler comes as part of the installation of Visual Studio Enterprise Edition. The Source Code Control add-in is for Visual SourceSafe integration, which is described later. Follow these steps to load the add-ins:

1. From the add-ins menu, select Add-In Manager.
2. From the list of available add-ins, select Visual Modeler add-in.
3. In Load Behavior, make sure the Loaded/Unloaded check box and the Load on Startup check box are checked.
4. Repeat steps 2 and 3 for the Visual Modeler Menus add-in.

5. Repeat steps 2 and 3 for Source Code Control if it is not already done.

6. Click OK.

> **Note**   As long as you selected Load on Startup as the behavior for these add-ins, you will not have to go into the Add-In Manager again. The add-ins will be available to you from now on when you start up Visual Basic.

Click the add-ins menu. You will now see a Visual Modeler menu option with a sub-menu on it. The sub-menu has the following options on it:

- *Reverse-Engineering Wizard.*   Takes changes you have made in Visual Basic and incorporates them back into the model.
- *Browse Class Diagram.*   Allows you to select a diagram to view and then opens the model and displays the diagram in Visual Modeler.
- *About Visual Modeler Add-In.*   An about box giving a link to the Rational Software Corporation Web site.

In addition to the Visual Modeler menus, you will also see a SourceSafe menu under the Tools menu. At this point you are now ready to import your components into Visual Basic. Go ahead and quit Visual Basic and go back to the Model in Visual Modeler.

Importing Your Visual Modeler Components

You will be building on your earlier work in Visual Modeler from Day 3 in order to kick-start your Visual Basic project. Visual Modeler enables you to generate code to Visual Basic as well as to Visual C++. This lets you go straight from design to implementation. Diagrams in Visual Modeler can be easily cut and pasted into design documentation as well, giving a dual purpose for working with Visual Modeler.

After opening the SmallTownBank.mdl file (you created this on day 3, but also can get a copy of it from the CD), you will explicitly create a component in Visual Modeler. This mdl file should contain the Customer class from Day 3. Components you create in Visual Modeler correspond to components you will eventually generate in Visual Basic. Once created you will assign the Customer class to the component. The following steps will create the component and assign the Customer class to the component:

1. Start up Visual Modeler and open the SmallTownBank.mdl file that you have previously been working with on Day 3. If you would like to work with one that has all the changes up to today, you can get it from the CD in the \SmallTownBank\09\Start directory.

2. Open the view of the component diagram by selecting Component Diagram from the Browse menu. This will bring up the Select Component Diagram dialog.

3. Select the default, which should be Component Diagram: Component View/Main. Click OK. This brings up an empty diagram window.

4. You now want to add a component to this diagram. When you generate the code, this component will create an ActiveX DLL project in Visual Basic. The name of the component will correspond to the name of the Visual Basic project.

   From the Tools menu, select Create, and then Component. This is the same as selecting the Component toolbar button.

5. Move the mouse pointer over the Component Diagram window. Notice that the mouse pointer changes to crosshairs. Click in the window. A component name New Component appears.

6. Change the name of the component by clicking on the component name. Change the name to **SmallTownBank_Data**.

7. Right-click the component and select Open Specification.

8. For the Language, select Visual Basic and then click the Apply button. This will add an ActiveX DLL option to the stereotype drop-down. If ActiveX still doesn't show in the list, you can type in ActiveX DLL for the stereotype.

9. For the Stereotype, select ActiveX DLL. Figure 9.1 displays this dialog with these choices selected.

NEW TERM *Stereotype* represents a sub-classification of the class. With respect to Visual Basic, it allows you to specify whether your class represents a Visual Basic form, module, class, or some other type of file you might add to a Visual Basic project.

FIGURE 9.1

Component specifications for SmallTownBank_Data *component.*

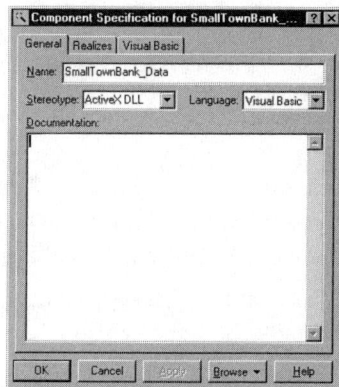

10. Click the Realizes tab. This lets you select the classes that will be part of this component.

11. Right-click the Customer class and select Assign. This places a red check box next to the class. Click OK to apply these specifications.

You have now laid out the name of the component within which your classes will be generated. The following steps will enable you to use Visual Modeler to generate Visual Basic code and create a new Visual Basic project based on this component.

1. Verify that your SmallTownBank_Data component is selected. If not, click the component.

2. From the Tools menu, select Generate Code. This will bring up the Code Generation Wizard Welcome window.

3. To skip this window in the future, select the Don't Show check box. Select NEXT.

4. The Select Classes window lets you pick which classes will be part of the component. You already assigned the Customer class to this component; therefore you don't have to do any more here. Select NEXT.

5. The Preview Classes window gives you an opportunity to further configure the class. Leave the default and click the NEXT button.

6. This window enables you to save the project before the code is generated and also to select some more generation options. Select the Include Comments and Generate New Collection Classes check boxes. Click NEXT.

7. The Finish window is your last opportunity to go back and make changes before the code is generated. Click FINISH. The wizard generates code for you and returns with a Delete Classes window.

Note

If it asks you to browse for a project file, select NO. This would occur if you use the .mdl file from the CD.

8. Form1 was added to the project when it was generated. This window tells you that the project will keep Form1 by default. Select Form1, which will move it to the Delete These Classes list and remove it from the Visual Basic project. Click OK.

9. The Summary window is the last window, letting you know what happened. The Log tab gives you additional details and indicates how long actions took. Click CLOSE.

Congratulations on successfully generating your Visual Basic project from Visual Modeler. By designing the components in Visual Modeler, you will now be able to go back and forth between applications. Visual Modeler enables you to view the design and architecture of your components and classes, whereas Visual Basic enables you to add the functionality to the classes. Later today, after making changes in Visual Basic, you will reverse engineer those changes back into your model.

Using SourceSafe

SourceSafe was introduced in Day 2, "Building a Windows DNA Application." This lets you work in a team environment by controlling who has access to important files, and also to track project files changes. Even in writing this book, I am using SourceSafe to track the changes to the chapters of the book as it is being written. No more need to have multiple directories for different copies of your projects. All this is kept in one place.

You might be wondering just how SourceSafe allows you to track your changes and work with files. In some respects you can think of SourceSafe as a public library. Just like you would check out a book from a library, you can check out a file from SourceSafe. Also like your library, SourceSafe tracks who has it checked out and while you have the file checked out, no one else can use it or modify it. When you are done with the file you check it back in so other people can use it. Only with SourceSafe there are no late fees.

This analogy breaks down as we talk about another feature of SourceSafe. That is the capability to track changes between check outs. Not only does SourceSafe track who has the file, but it also keeps of a copy of the file from each time it is checked in. If 10 people check out the file and make changes and check it back in, you can go into SourceSafe and look at the history and what the file looked like after each of those times it was checked back in. Of course when the next person checks it out, he or she gets the latest version. This actually brings in another feature. That is the ability to go back to any previous version of the check in file. This is known as rolling back the file. Again, if you have 10 versions of the file listed in the history and want to go back to the sixth time it was checked in, you can! Beware that if you do, you lose all the file versions that had been checked in after that.

Now that you have had a quick introduction to SourceSafe and before you go any further, you will add the `SmallTownBank_Data` project to SourceSafe to help you in your development efforts. In this situation, where you will probably be the only person using the components, the biggest advantage is being able to roll back to previous versions. Therefore, I encourage you to check in your items when you feel you have finished some area or task. As you move on to the next set of steps, you can feel confident knowing that, if your changes are too disruptive, you can check the file back in and roll back to your prior copy.

9

Now that you have a project, you will want to add it to SourceSafe, following these steps:

1. Under File, click Save Project. Save the files (SmallTownBank_Data.vbp and Customer.cls) to the same directory as the .mdl file. After saving the files, the Source Code Control dialog will appear.

> **Note** You are required to save the files before you can add them to SourceSafe. Once there is a physical file on the hard drive, it can be added to SourceSafe.

2. The dialog asks you whether or not to add it to source safe. Select the NO button.

3. From the File menu select Open Project. Select the project you just saved. You might be wondering where this is going. Good question! Because of the way the Visual Modeler removed Form1 from the project, you have to reload the project first before you can add it to SourceSafe. If you try to add it to SourceSafe before you reload the project you will receive an error.

4. From the Tools menu, select SourceSafe, Add Project to SourceSafe menu item.

5. The first thing SourceSafe asks you for is a login. This is the login to the SourceSafe database and is independent of Windows security. Type **Admin** for the username (default username) and leave the password empty (the default password for admin). The database is Common, which is the default database stored on your computer. In the future, in a team environment, this database might be on the network. In that case, you will click BROWSE and select the database from the network. Click OK.

6. It now asks you where in SourceSafe to add the project. The structure here mimics that of folders in Windows Explorer. You can put this project within another project folder similarly to nesting folders in Explorer. You will be putting this project at the top level. Type in **SmallTownBank_Data** for the Project name. Click OK.

7. SourceSafe will tell you the project doesn't exist and asks whether you would like to create it. Click YES.

8. The Add Files to SourceSafe dialog appears next which is shown in Figure 9.2. The File Type drop-down defaults to All. This will add all your files from the SmallTownBank_Data project to SourceSafe. Click OK. The files will be added and you will see a lock symbol appear next to each, which means they are now under SourceSafe control.

FIGURE 9.2

Add files to SourceSafe dialog.

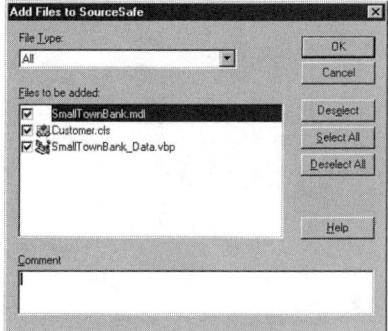

SourceSafe automatically adds the files to the SourceSafe Database. You can now check out (and check back in) the two files that are in this project, the Project file and the Customer class file. To check out the Customer class, right-click the class in the Project window and select Check Out. Notice the symbol changes from the lock symbol to a check symbol. Double-click the file to open it. You can now modify the file.

To check the file back in, use the following steps:

1. Right-click the file in the Project window and select Check In. This will bring up the Check In Files to SourceSafe dialog, as shown in Figure 9.3.

FIGURE 9.3

Check in files to SourceSafe dialog.

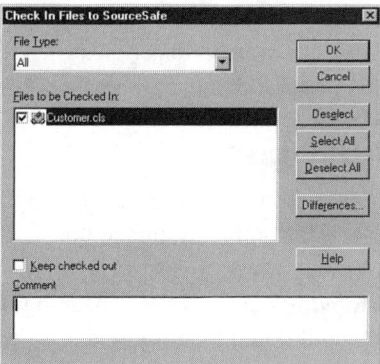

2. Because you are going to keep working with this file, select the check box Keep Checked Out. This enables you to save a version of the file to SourceSafe and to continue working on the file without having to check it out again.

3. Click OK to check in the file.

With SourceSafe enabled you are ready to continue working on your project.

9

> **SourceSafe Explorer**
>
> Although you have SourceSafe up and going for the project, you should also be aware that there is a standalone SourceSafe application called SourceSafe Explorer that you can also run. From it, you can check files out and in directly. To start it, select Microsoft Visual SourceSafe 6.0 from the Start, Programs, Microsoft Visual Studio, Microsoft Visual SourceSafe menu item.

Developing Your Project

Visual Modeler has given you the skeleton for the classes you are going to develop. Now you will learn how to configure your project properties and add both public and private functionality to the class. Properly configuring your project includes configuring how it will compile, setting the name of the component and other project level properties.

After configuring the project you will add public functionality to it, which involves creating the methods and properties of the class that are available to applications that use the component. An example of this would be a public GetAccountActivity function that a Visual Basic client application can call on to find the balance of an account.

Finally you will implement procedures that are available only to other procedures within the class. This private functionality includes internal functions, subs, and variables the component needs in order to get its work done. An example would be a function that a public method calls to retrieve the data store connection string. This function would not be available to other applications that use this component.

Configuring Project Properties

After a new project is created, you will want to configure it appropriately. This doesn't have to be done immediately, but it is good to do this at the start so you don't forget it later. Before doing this, check out the project file from SourceSafe because you will be modifying information that is stored in the .vbp file. Checking out the project allows you to update the file. Otherwise it would remain read-only and Visual Basic wouldn't let you make changes. Right-click the project file in the project window (SmallTownBank_Data.vbp) and select Check out. Go to the Project menu and select Properties at the bottom of the drop-down. The word "Properties" will be preceded by the name of the project. Upon selection you will see a display like Figure 9.4.

Let's take a look at a few of the important parts of this dialog. The first field you see is the Project Type. This was selected for you when you chose an ActiveX DLL project. You can look at the other types of projects available in the Project Type's drop-down box, but leave the choice as ActiveX DLL.

FIGURE 9.4

Project Properties dialog for ActiveX DLL.

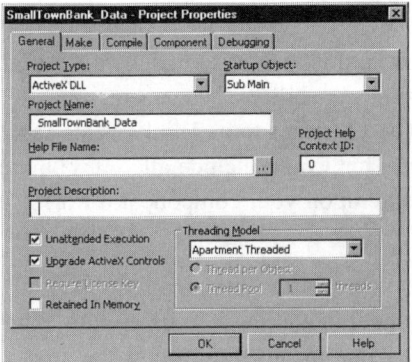

Project Name corresponds to the name of the project in the Properties window. You can change it in either place. Do not make the Project Name too generic, with names such as `Tools` or `DatabaseAccess`. Make your project names descriptive so that you, or another developer, will understand the purpose of the component during further development or at a later date. Examples of descriptive names are `SmallTownBank_Business` or `SmallTownBank_Data`, representing components on the business logic or data tier, respectively. The Project Description section describes the purpose of the component and allows you to give a better explanation than what the Project Name allows.

Should you want to reference a component in other projects (that is, select References from the Project menu and select a component), the References dialog will display the Project Description in the list of available references. If the Project Description section is left empty, the project name will be used as the reference name. You will have an opportunity to see this later when you test your component.

Another item to note is the Unattended Execution check box. This lets Visual Basic know that there will be no direct interaction with this project through items such as forms, dialogs, or other types of visual displays. Also, this component will be Apartment Threaded to enable better usage. Look at Day 8, "Introduction to COM and MTS," for more information on threading.

Some of the other properties on this page have no relevance since you are creating a DLL. Startup Object typically refers to the first form that is displayed. DLLs have no interface and there is not the same idea of a initial object that runs. Instead, another application can call any of a number of public methods and properties in any order they want. Therefore, this is not applicable. Also, the Help File Name and Project Help Context ID relate to having a user interface, which again is not applicable.

Version Compatibility

The last item you will look at in this dialog is version compatibility on the Component tab. Version compatibility is the capability of your component to maintain the same interfaces when you modify and add features to it. Think of interfaces as the way other applications call your component. This would include all your public methods and properties, because outside entities depend upon your component for these interfaces to remain the same.

This is important because as you create components and compile them into DLLs, it is the interfaces of your component that allow it to be used by other systems and applications. If the interface changes, that means the systems that used that interface must also change or else that application will no longer work. Imagine coming to your home and finding that the key to your home no longer works because all the locks have changed. The home is fine and the key is fine, but the way you access it has changed.

Look now at the compatibility options by clicking the Component tab. There are three version compatibility choices.

- *No Compatibility* assigns new identifiers to the project each time the project is compiled. Use this only if you will be changing the public methods, properties, and parameters of your component frequently.

- *Project Compatibility* keeps the same Type Library identifier, but Class identifiers will change. If you are the only person working on getting your component initially up and running, you can use this setting. You can recompile your component and also test it in your project without having to reset the reference to it. This is the default selection.

- *Binary Compatibility* keeps all identifiers the same, unless the interface is changed and then it will give a warning. Binary compatibility will enable you to update components without having to reregister them on the server or with other applications. For this reason, you will want to use Binary Compatibility in a multi-developer environment because other people will be dependent upon the component interfaces staying the same.

For this step, leave it set to Project Compatibility.

Whenever a component is created for the first time, it is registered automatically on the server on which it is compiled. Identifiers are given to the component to make it unique to the system. A Type Library ID is compiled into the component to identify it on the component level. Class identifiers are assigned to it to identify the various classes, and interface identifiers identify each of the public methods and properties. With this information you can be assured that when you call the component in code, you will be calling the correct DLL.

With compatibility set properly, you can make changes to your component and the identifiers for your component will not change. What breaks compatibility then? It is broken when you actually change the interface to a method or property. Let's say that you have an UpdatePerson method that you change from passing one parameter, Name, to two, FirstName and LastName. Because you are changing the interface to this method, you are forcing Visual Basic to give it a new interface identifier and thereby breaking compatibility with past versions of the DLL.

9

Note

How does keeping the same identifiers help you? By keeping the same identifiers, you can deploy the updated component, the physical DLL file, to the servers on which it resides without having to reregister it on the system or within MTS. This makes the component somewhat of a black box. The system is looking for a specific component; as long as the outside of the DLL looks the same, the system can still call it. Otherwise you will need to remove the old DLL from the system, remove any references to it, and then add the new component.

Do	Don't
DO plan ahead when you are first creating your component classes. Figure out all the methods, the method's parameters, and the method's return values. This will let you to keep binary compatibility.	**DON'T** start coding without knowing what the structure of your component will be like. With this structure, you will most likely run into time-consuming changes, having not only to change the interfaces to your classes, but also the code from other tiers of the Windows DNA platform that uses your classes.

Once you have set your project properties including the compatibility setting, you are ready to move on to writing the code in your class. In the next section you will add a function and two properties to your existing class that will be available to other components and applications that use your component.

Adding Public Methods and Properties of Your Class

Now that you have set up your project properties, you will now focus on adding functionality to your DLL. You will first add public functionality to your class, in other words, the functionality you will make available to other applications that use this component. For instance, if you added a public method to your class, another application could call it. Here is an example of calling a method in the ADODB component

```
Dim rst as ADODB.Recordset
Set rst = New ADODB.Recordset
rst.LockType = adReadOnly
rst.Open "Select Name From Person", strConnectionString
```

The class being used here, the `Recordset` class from the `ADODB` component, is referenced
in line 1. In line 3 a property, `LockType`, is set on the class. In line 4, the `Open` method is
called on the `Recordset` class. How you declare and call this ADO component is no different than how you will declare and call your own components. It is important to realize
how all components are structured in the same way. All components can have methods
and properties. `ADODB` just happens to be a component that Microsoft made.

Adding a Method

Here you will add a public method to your class in almost the same way that you would
add a procedure to a form or a module in Visual Basic. Simply create a procedure using
the `Function` or `Sub` keywords. The only extra step is adding the word `Public` to the
beginning of the procedure declaration. Add the output of Listing 9.1 to your Customer
class.

LISTING 9.1   Public Method in a Class Module

```
 1: Public Function GetAccountBalance(ByVal AccountID As Integer) As Currency
 2: Dim rst As ADODB.Recordset
 3: Dim strConnectionString As String
 4: Set rst = New ADODB.Recordset
 5: strConnectionString = "Provider=SQLOLEDB;DRIVER=SQL Server;
    ➥ "SERVER=(local);DATABASE=Bank_data;UID=sa;PWD=;"
 6: rst.Open "SELECT Balance FROM Account WHERE AccountKey = " & AccountID,
    ➥ strConnectionString
 7: If Not (rst.BOF And rst.EOF) Then
 8:     GetAccountBalance = rst(0)
 9: Else
10:     GetAccountBalance = 0
11: End If
12: rst.Close
13: Set rst = Nothing
14: End Function
```

ANALYSIS The declaration of the function is an important part, which is set to `Public` in line 1. Because it is a public function in a class module, it will be available from other applications when they instantiate this object (after it is compiled). Without the `Public` keyword, it would only have been available within the Customer class. `Public` tells the compiler that the component wants an interface (and an interface identifier) for this function to be created, enabling other applications to use it.

Lines 5 and 6 set a connection string and retrieve a recordset. After testing to make sure a record was returned, the function uses the ordinal value to reference the recordset in line 8 in the same way you might reference an array value. It sets the return value of the function to the balance.

> **Note**
>
> Because Listing 9.1 references the ADODB component, you will have to add a reference to it in the project. From the Project menu select References. Check the box next to Microsoft ActiveX Data Objects 2.1 Library and click OK. The DLL will not successfully compile without this reference.

A call to this method can display the value in a message box by executing the following line:

```
MsgBox objCustomer.GetAccountBalance(1234)
```

This would display the account balance for the account with an ID of `1234`.

Adding a Property by Making It Public

Properties can also be made publicly available in a similar way. By using the `Public` keyword instead of the `Dim` keyword in front of your variable declaration, you can make a property public, as in the following example:

```
Public SocialSecurityNumber as String
```

This property can be read or written to by users of your control. Unfortunately, by declaring a property this way, you have little control over what a user can set it to. Therefore, if you needed to have the value set within a particular range of values, you could not control this. An example would be a property named Gender, which could only be set to `M` or `F`. A public property doesn't allow you to control what values a user could set this to.

Suppose that you want to internally change the data type of the property to a `Single` data type instead of an `Integer` data type. For example, the user would always set it to an integer, but in the class, you perform calculations on the property value, which required decimal values to calculate correctly. You could not do this with a public property.

Finally, you also couldn't trigger other actions to take place when the property was changed or made to be read-only. Fortunately, to handle these shortcomings, there is an alternative and preferred method to implement properties and that is through property procedures.

Adding a Property with a Property Procedure

Property procedures are called when a property is read or written to. This lets the developer have full control over the property of the class.

NEW TERM   A *property procedure* is a procedure that uses special keywords—Let, Get or Set—and procedure declarations to implement properties in a class. Property procedures follow the same structure as a Sub or Function procedure, as seen in Listing 9.2.

LISTING 9.2 Declaring a Property Procedure

```
1: Property Get SocialSecurityNumber() as Integer
2:     SocialSecurityNumber = mstrSocialSecurityNumber
3: End Property
```

ANALYSIS   In line 1, you see the Get keyword being used. This keyword is the main difference between a Sub and a Function and can be Let, Get, or Set. It appears after the Property keyword and before the property name. The Get property procedure is called when a user of the class reads the value of the property. It would then set the value of the property to the value of another variable in line 2.

A Let property procedure is called when the user of the classes writes a value to the property. A Set property procedure is called when setting the value of a property to an object. This would be used instead of a Let property procedure.

You will use the Let property procedure most often, because you don't want to expose many properties as objects. Passing an object between your component and an application involves a lot of data relative to a number or text string and takes up system resources. This in turn impacts performance and therefore is undesirable.

Two properties are actually referenced. The user of the component references one property, which is publicly available, but the developer, through property procedures, can manipulate that property and store it to another private variable. Or if the user requests the value, the developer can again make changes to the private variable before sending the value back to the user.

To gain a better understanding of this, look at Listing 9.3. It declares a property with property procedures in a class. Go ahead and add this to the Customer class. This will enable you to set and retrieve the Social Security number for the class.

LISTING 9.3   Creating Property Procedures

```
1: Private mstrSocialSecurityNumber As String 'local copy
2: Public Property Let SocialSecurityNumber (strData As String)
3:      mstrSocialSecurityNumber = strData
4: End Property
5: Public Property Get SocialSecurityNumber () As String
6:      SocialSecurityNumber = mstrSocialSecurityNumber
7: End Property
```

9

ANALYSIS   Line 1 declares the private internal variable in our class. This variable is not available outside of this class. Line 2 is the declaration for the Let property procedure that is called when assigning a value to the property. As part of the Customer class, you can assign a value to it from another application in the following line of code:

```
Customer.SocialSecurityNumber = '111223333'
```

This would cause the Let SocialSecurityNumber procedure to be called, with a value of 111-22-3333 for the strData parameter. mstrSocialSecurityNumber is then set to the new value in line 3. The user might also want to assign the value to something else, like a text box as in the following line of code:

```
txtSocialSecurityNumber.Text = Customer.SocialSecurityNumber
```

This causes the Get property procedure in line 5 to be called. This sets the return value of SocialSecurityNumber equal to the private variable mstrSocialSecurityNumber, which in turn gets assigned to the text box in the prior line of code.

If you left the code like this, you would be implementing the same functionality that you would get with a public variable, but let's talk about some of the other tasks you might want to do. If you wanted to make this property read-only, you could just remove the Let property procedure. There would be no code then to assign the private variable a new value.

If you left the Let procedure in the class, you could also add more code to the procedure to update other properties, or perhaps to look up other information, such as name and address based on the Social Security number. Another possibility would be to validate the data that it is being sent to the Let procedure. Although you probably wouldn't do this for a Social Security number, you might do this for a credit card number and put it through a simple algorithm to make sure the number was valid.

Implementing properties through property procedures is good programming practice, and enables the greatest degree of freedom and protection for your class.

Private Functionality

You might already be familiar with this type of functionality. Procedures and properties that are not public will only be available within the class itself, that is, they will be *private*. A good example of a private procedure would be a function in a data tier class that returns the connection string to a database as shown in Listing 9.4. You certainly would need this information to reach the database, but would not want users of the component to know anything about the connection string. Also, you do not want to be hard-coding the connection string in every procedure that calls the database.

LISTING 9.4   Creating a Private Procedure

```
1: Function GetConnectionString() As String
2:     GetConnectionString = "Provider=SQLOLEDB;DRIVER=SQL Server;
➥ SERVER=(local);DATABASE=Bank_data;UID=sa;PWD=;"
3: End Function
```

ANALYSIS   Listing 9.4 returns a hard-coded string to the caller of the function. By calling this function from all your procedures, you have a single place to update if your connection string information changes. There is another advantage as well if later you want to store the connection string in the registry or some other, more dynamic location. You could change this function to get the string from another location without having to change any of the other procedures that call this function. This hides the complexity (or the lack of it in the prior listing) from other procedures that use it.

Utilizing the Class Builder Add-In

You have been looking at the various parts you can add to your COM component. Up to this point, you have done this by hand-coding or cutting and pasting the code in, but now you will learn about the Class Builder add-in. This add-in makes it easy to add methods and properties to your class by automatically generating code templates for your classes and also for the methods, properties, events, and enumerated values you add to your class. By having the class builder generate this code it saves you time in getting started with your class and also from making needless syntactical errors. The procedure we add in this section will continue to build on the Customer class that you have been working with. After you are finished with this section, you will get it synched up with the model in Visual Modeler.

First, follow these steps to make the Class Builder add-in available:

1. From the add-ins menu, select Add-In Manager.
2. From the list of available add-ins, select VB 6 Class Builder Utility.
3. In Load Behavior, make sure the Loaded/Unloaded check box and the Load on Startup check box are checked.
4. Click OK.
5. From the add-ins menu, select Class Builder Utility.

Because the Load on Startup check box was checked, the Class Builder menu item will be available to you from now on when you start up Visual Basic.

Figure 9.5 represents the Class Builder utility. For the current project, it lists all available classes on the left side. When you click a specific class, you can find out a class's methods, properties, and events in the right-hand side of the dialog.

FIGURE 9.5

The Class Builder utility enables you to add methods, properties, and events to your class.

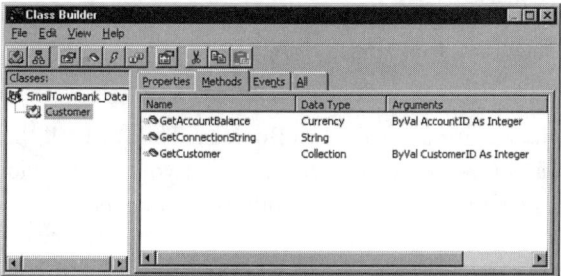

There are three different ways you can add methods, properties, and events to your class

• Select a class. Right-click that class to show a pop-up menu. From the New menu item, select the item to add.
• Select a class. From the File menu, select New and select the item to add.
• Select a class. Click the toolbar button corresponding to the new item you want to add.

You will add a new method to your Customer class called UpdateEMailAddress. This method enables someone to change his email address. The parameters for the method will be the customer ID and the new email address.

Use the following steps to create the new method:

1. Select the Customer class, right-click it, and from the new menu select Method. This brings up the Method Builder dialog. The Name field corresponds to the name of the method as it is declared in the Visual Basic code.

Arguments can be added, removed, or reordered by using the buttons on the right-hand side. Return Data Type determines whether the method will be declared as a function or a sub. Declaring as Friend makes the method available to other classes within the component. Finally, checking the Default Method check box sets the method to be implicitly used when the Class is used without specifying a method.

2. Enter UpdateEMailAddress for the name of the method.

3. Click the plus symbol. This will bring up the Add Argument dialog.

4. Enter **CustomerID** for the name.

5. Check the ByVal check box.

6. Set the Data Type to Integer.

7. Click OK.

8. Click the plus symbol. This will bring up the Add Argument dialog again.

9. Enter **EMailAddress** for the name.

10. Check the ByVal check box.

11. Set the Data Type to String.

12. Click OK.

13. Change the Return Data Type to Boolean. This will tell the caller whether the update was successful or not. At this point your dialog should look like Figure 9.6, which displays the new method with its arguments.

FIGURE 9.6

The Method Builder enables you to add methods to your class.

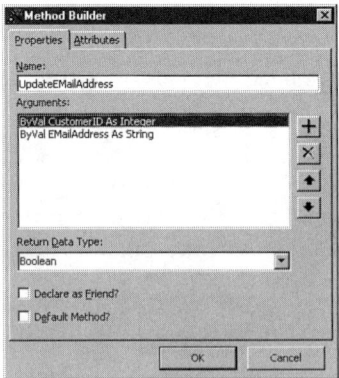

14. Click OK.

15. Close the Class Builder window.

16. You will be prompted to update the project. Click YES.

Looking at your class code, you now see the new method in your class called
`UpdateEMailAddress`. The Class Builder helps you create your class. This is especially
helpful when doing property procedures because it declares the `Let` and `Get` procedures
as well as the private property. This can save you from coding errors you might otherwise encounter if writing the procedures by hand.

> **Tip**
>
> If Visual Basic reports an error about no creatable component being detect-
> ed, make sure the class properties are set to Multiuse and not to Private.

9

Before finishing this section, compile your component into a DLL, using the following
steps:

1. From the File menu, select `Make SmallTownBank_Data.dll`.

2. In the Make Project dialog that appears, select where the DLL will be compiled.
   Leave it as the default directory and click OK.

The DLL is now compiled, unless there are compilation errors. If there are, you will have
to fix those before the DLL can be compiled. Make sure you have made a reference to
the `ADODB` component. For more information refer to the Note following Listing 9.1.

Reverse-Engineering Your Code Back into Visual Modeler

Now that you have made changes to your class, you need to synchronize it with your
model in Visual Modeler. You do this by reverse-engineering. This will take all the
changes you have made to the class in Visual Basic and incorporate them into the existing model in Visual Modeler. This actually enables you to go back from tool to tool and
make changes and keep files in both development environments up-to-date.

NEW TERM *Reverse-engineering* is the process of taking a developed entity and going back
and creating the plans for it. With regards to Visual Modeler, it is the ability to
take an existing Visual Basic project and import it into Visual Modeler creating a model
for the project.

Use the following steps to reverse-engineer the project back into Visual Modeler:

1. Save and check in all your files.

Note If you have closed both Visual Modeler and the model that you were working with earlier today, open the `SmallTownBank.mdl` file before proceeding. Reverse-engineering will not work unless the model is open.

2. From the Add-In menu, select Visual Modeler, Reverse Engineering Wizard. This will bring up the wizard.

3. If the wizard doesn't know which model to use, it will display the Selection of Model dialog. (If you do not see the model listed, you can click BROWSE and find it.) Select your model.

4. Click OK. This calls Visual Modeler and displays the Reverse Engineering wizard. This might seem a little convoluted, but remember that Visual Modeler is a program from Rational Software Corporation, while Visual Basic is obviously made by Microsoft. This results in two programs from two companies trying to communicate to each other, which probably makes complete integration difficult.

5. Click Next if necessary. You want to be on the Selection of Project Items window. This tells Visual Modeler which parts of the project to reverse-engineer. Make sure that the Customer class is selected and click NEXT.

6. This window enables you to tell Visual Modeler which tier your class should be in. Because your class is already in Visual Modeler, it will say it's assigned to Data Services. Click NEXT.

7. The finish window appears. Click FINISH. At this point Visual Modeler looks at the existing Visual Basic project and imports any changes that have been made to the model. When finished it will present a summary log of what it has done.

8. Click CLOSE.

You can now save your model file with the changes. At this point you could continue working in Visual Modeler or Visual Basic and then either generate more code or reverse-engineer back to the model again. By using both of these tools, you can quickly develop your application while still being able to keep track of the overall design of your components. I say component*s*, not component here, because although you have only been working with one component, you could easily add more classes and components in Visual Modeler to this same model to generate multiple projects with their own procedures and properties in Visual Basic.

Creating a Test Harness

Visual Basic groups allow you to easily run and debug components. You are able to do this without having to go to the trouble of actually deploying them to another machine, or put up a series of message boxes to check values.

NEW TERM A *Visual Basic group* is a container for one or more Visual Basic projects, which can include ActiveX DLLs. You will now add a new standard exe project to your existing Visual Basic group, which should at this time have only the Class module. You do not have to explicitly create a group or add the project to the group. Visual Basic will do this automatically when you choose to add a new project. Follow these steps to add a standard exe:

1. From the File menu, select Add Project.
2. From the Add Project dialog, select Standard EXE.
3. Click OPEN.

Note

> If Visual Basic asks you if you want to add this project to SourceSafe, say "No." Because this is just a test project that calls our component, there is no real need to have it in SourceSafe. This is not a hard and fast rule and open for the developer to decide.

Two obvious changes have occurred. The first is that the new project appears in the Project window with the previous ActiveX DLL project. The second change is that the Project window is now called the Project Group window. This is an indication that you are now working with a group of projects instead of a single Visual Basic project.

The first project in the window is the ActiveX DLL, which is the project you have been working on. The other is the new Standard EXE project, which you have just created. It has a name of Project1. Change the name to Harness. This new project will be the test harness from which you call the DLL project that is also part of this group. Next, change the name of the form to Test; it will be the form from which you will test the DLL. Do this by selecting Form1 from the Project Group window and changing the name in the Properties window.

Next, you want to reference your component in this new Standard EXE. You do this from the References dialog, following these steps:

1. In the Project Group window, select the Harness project.
2. From the Project menu, select References.

3. From the Available References lists, select the SmallTownBank_Data component that you have made.

4. Click OK.

The project, Harness, now has a reference to the SmallTownBank_Data DLL. This tells Visual Basic to make the methods and properties of the SmallTownBank_Data DLL available to you in the Harness project. At this point, you are now ready to add code to test your components.

Testing Your Components

You will now add some functionality to the form in the Harness project to have it call the DLL that you have previously compiled. This will let you to step through this exe and then call your component. As that component is called, it will automatically step into the exe as well. This enables you to easily debug your components.

You will be testing the method to get the account balance as well as the Social Security number property procedures. First you want to add controls to your form. In the Project Group window, under forms for the Harness project, double-click the Test form. This will bring up an empty form. Follow Table 9.1 and add the following controls to the form:

TABLE 9.1 Controls to Place on the Test Form

Control	Name	Caption/Label
Label	lblAccountID	Account ID:
Label	lblBalance	Balance:
Textbox	txtAccountID	
Textbox	txtBalance	
Button	cmdGetBalance	Get Account Balance
Label	lblSSN	SSN:
Textbox	txtSSN	
Button	cmdGet	Get SSN
Button	cmdLet	Let SSN

One you have finished adding the controls to the form, arrange them as shown in Figure 9.7.

FIGURE 9.7

Layout of the Test form for calling the SmallTownBank_Data *component.*

After the controls are added, the code behind the form can be developed. You will add code for each of the command buttons. Double-click the cmdGetBalance button to bring up the event procedure for the button's Click event. In the event procedure, add the code in Listing 9.5 to declare and instantiate your SmallTownBank_Data component and call methods and properties on it.

LISTING 9.5   Code for the cmdGetBalance Click Event

```
1: Dim objCustomer As SmallTownBank_Data.Customer
2: Set objCustomer = New SmallTownBank_Data.Customer
3: txtAccountBalance = objCustomer.GetAccountBalance(txtAccountID)
4: Set objCustomer = Nothing
```

ANALYSIS   Lines 1 and 2 create and instantiate the component. Line 3 calls the GetAccountBalance method of the component and sets it equal to the text box txtAccountBalance. The last line destroys the object.

Running the Test Form for the First Time

After you have added the code to the cmdGetBalance button, test the form. Before you run the form, there are a couple things you want to do:

- Set the Harness project as the startup project. Right-click the Harness project in the Project window and select Set as Start Up. If you don't do this, when you go to Start on the Run menu, it will run the first project that was in the project group, which is your component. This component has no interface and can only be activated from other applications. Nothing will happen and there will be very little excitement.

- Set the Test form as the Startup Object. Select the Harness project and from the Project menu, select Harness Properties. In this dialog, you can set the form as the Startup Object.

You are now ready to run the form. Hit the F5 key or under the Run menu, select Start. The form you have been working on will appear. Enter a valid AccountID integer into the first text box and then click the Get Account Balance button. This will fill in the Balance text box with the correct balance. If you don't put in an AccountID or the AccountID doesn't exist, you will get an error. At this point you might want to go to SQL Enterprise Manager and look up or enter some data to get a valid AccountID. You can stop the program by clicking End button on the toolbar.

That's it! You have successfully created and tested your first COM component. This also puts you well on your way to making DNA applications. With COM components you will continue to create and expand the business logic and data tiers in your application, adding more methods and properties.

Add the following line of code to the declarations section of the form code module. This code goes outside of procedures in the code window. To add the line, double-click the form to bring up the code window.

```
Dim mobjCustomer As SmallTownBank_Data.Customer
```

ANALYSIS This code declares a module level object, which will persist during the lifetime of the form, because it is in the declarations section of the module.

Next the object has to be instantiated. Add the following line to the Form_Load event:

```
Set mobjCustomer = New SmallTownBank_Data.Customer
```

ANALYSIS This creates the object when the form loads and will let the object be used while the form is running.

Next, add code to the cmdGet_Click and cmdLet_Click events procedures. Add the following line to the cmdGet Click event:

```
txtSSN = mobjCustomer.SocialSecurityNumber
```

ANALYSIS This assigns the value of the SocialSecurityNumber property to the text box.

Add the following line to the cmdLet Click event:

```
mobjCustomer.SocialSecurityNumber = txtSSN
```

ANALYSIS This sets the SocialSecurityNumber property to what is in the text box.

After you have added all this code to the various events, you will have a code module that looks like Listing 9.6.

LISTING 9.6   Code for the *cmdGetBalance* Click Event

```
 1: Dim mobjCustomer As SmallTownBank_Data.Customer
 2: Private Sub Form_Load()
 3:     Set mobjCustomer = New SmallTownBank_Data.Customer
 4: End Sub
 5: Private Sub cmdGet_Click()
 6:     txtSSN = mobjCustomer.SocialSecurityNumber
 7: End Sub
 8: Private Sub cmdLet_Click()
 9:     mobjCustomer.SocialSecurityNumber = txtSSN
10: End Sub
```

9

ANALYSIS   Listing 9.6 includes the declaration of the object `mobjCustomer` (in lines 1 and 3) and each of the event procedures. An additional line of code can be added in the form's unload event that destroys the object.

Run your form again. When you click the Get SSN button, nothing happens. You have to first type something in the SSN text box and click the Let SSN button to store a value to the object. Then clear the text box and click the Get SSN button. It will fill the text box with the value you just saved.

This property is not actually going to the database to get its information. Also, when the property is updated, it does not update the database. You will want to do both of these to make the database fully functional. By adding database functionality to the `Let` and `Get` property procedures, you will also get around having to keep the object in memory. Instead of having Social Security numbers stored in the objects memory, you would instead store them in the database. This will be talked about more in Day 10, "Adding Transactional Support."

Storing Your Finished Code in Microsoft Repository

Once you have completed development on your component, you will want to be able to store the project for future use and also allow others to be able to leverage work you have done. Furthermore, the project needs to be located in a central location so others will know where this component and other developed components can be found. Visual Component Manager and the Microsoft Repository allow you to do all of this and come as part of the installation of Visual Studio Enterprise Edition.

There are two ways to add your project to the repository. The first method is through the Visual Component Manager, which interfaces with the Microsoft Repository. The second method is to export directly to the repository. You would choose the latter if the other applications that want to use this component were not able to use the Visual Component Manager. In essence the two methods do the same thing, but the Visual Component Manager is a specialized interface into the repository specially designed for working with components.

In our case, we will be adding our project through Visual Component Manager, as follows:

1. From the Tools menu, select Publish, Source Files. This will bring up the Visual Component Manager Publish Wizard.

2. Click NEXT and then select the repository in which to store the component. Local Database is the default repository; select this. If you were working in a team environment, the repository could be out on a network where other developers could access it.

3. Create a new folder by clicking the New Folder button. The folder to store the project in can be one of the many default folders that are set up or, in this case, one of your own.

4. Call the folder SmallTownBank_Data and click NEXT.

5. The Title and Properties window contains information about the project, including name, file location, type, and author. Leave these as default selections and click NEXT.

6. The More Properties window lets you to put in additional information to help identify the project. Click NEXT.

7. The Select Additional Files window displays the files that will be added and lets you to select any others you might want to add. Click NEXT again.

8. This last window lets you to select the files that require COM registrations. If we had been publishing the DLL, you would need to make sure the DLL was checked here. Click NEXT.

9. The Finish page appears. Click NEXT.

You have successfully published your files to the repository. From the View menu, select Visual Component Manager or click the Visual Component Manager button on the toolbar. You will see your component under the SmallTownBank_Data directory on the Local Database repository.

This project is now available to anyone who wants to use it. The primary advantage in sharing it is reuse in your organization. Storing files in a central, organized place that is available to everyone encourages the type of reuse that can save you and others countless hours of reinventing the wheel.

Summary

Today's lesson taught you how to create a COM component in Visual Basic. You looked at some initial settings for a project and how to work with version compatibility. You added code, compiled the component, and successfully called it from a test application. Through this you also kept your model and your project synchronized between Visual Modeler and Visual Basic. SourceSafe was used to assist versioning, and finally the code was published to the Visual Component Manager. More information can be found on all these topics on Microsoft's MSDN Web site at http://msdn.microsoft.com.

Day 10 will look at the ability to add transactional support to your COM components. With business and data processes, this becomes vital. If two business processes are dependent upon one another, you can't have one business transaction occur and another not occur. This can ruin the integrity of your system. You have learned about how the DNA environment supports transactions in Days 7, "Database Transactions and Distributed Transaction Coordinator," and 8, "Introduction to COM and MTS"; tomorrow, you will learn how to use that environment in the Visual Basic environment.

Q&A

Q I have been creating Visual Basic applications for a while and do not see the reason to spend the extra time creating COM components. It seems much easier and quicker just to put the functionality right there in the code. Am I missing something here?

A I would agree that at first creating COM components does seems to add unnecessary complexity and time. In reality, after you get used to creating COM components, it really becomes quite easy. Additionally, as you will see in the coming days, it enables you to change out one of your DNA application's tiers, without having to rewrite the whole application. With MTS, your COM components also become more scalable. Reuse is, of course, another advantage. Even for small projects, COM components just make things easier in the long run.

Workshop

The Workshop provides quiz questions to help you solidify your understanding of the material covered and exercises to provide you with experience in using what you've learned. Try to understand the quiz and exercise answers before continuing to the next lesson. Answers are provided in Appendix A.

Quiz

1. When opening a new project, what kind of project do you want to select to create a COM component?

2. What property procedure would you have if you wanted to make a property read-only?

3. What are two advantages to using SourceSafe with project development?

4. What keyword in the procedure declaration is required to make your component's procedures accessible by other applications?

Exercises

1. Create a simple component that has a method that takes a number and returns its square. Call this component from a Standard EXE application.

2. At this point, you need to update your existing project to include more of the functionality that you will have in the finished application. The accompanying CD-ROM contains the SmallTownBank files for tomorrow's lesson. Copy the files to your local hard drive and take a look at the additional projects, classes, and methods that have been added. There is also an updated SmallTownBank.mdl file to look at. The files are located at \SmallTownBank\10\Start.

DAY **10**

Adding Transactional Support

Today we revisit transactions and add the code that enables you to participate in a transaction. Are you starting to get the impression that transactions are important to a Windows DNA enterprise solution? They are, and today, you will learn why and how to enable your components to be transactional. We will discuss the design rules and code that enable your components to work well under a transaction server. We will return to the transaction console, install components, and see how to monitor component transactions. After today, you will know how to

- Add transactional support to your components
- Configure objects for transactions
- Complete and abort transactions
- Create and install a package of components into Transaction Server
- Monitor your components as they transact
- Raise errors
- Handle updates to your components
- Design considerations

Adding Transactional Support to Your Components

On Day 7, "Database Transactions and Distributed Transaction Coordinator," you learned about database transactions and the part the Distributed Transaction Coordinator (DTC) plays in transactions. You had an opportunity to work with the Microsoft Transaction Server (MTS) on Day 8, "Introduction to COM and MTS." Now you will leverage that knowledge by adding transactional support to your components and enabling your components to take advantage of everything that MTS offers.

When I talk about transactional support, remember that being able to put your database updates within one transaction is only one benefit of MTS. Before you move on, here is a quick recap of Day 8 and the benefits that MTS brings to your application:

- *Scalability*   Components and the resources they use are managed well, making it very easy to create a new instance when another client calls a component. Also resources are managed such as memory and database connections to enable a greater number of concurrent users.

- *Isolation*   Components can run in their own processes so as not to be harmful to other parts of the system.

- *Security*   Roles can be defined as to who can call a component. Users can be defined for the identity that a component runs under.

- *Concurrency*   Multiple users can use a component without having to worry about handling simultaneous calls.

- *Flexibility in location*   Components can physically be placed on different servers in different areas without the user of the application needing to be aware of the locations.

As you can see, there are many more advantages to using MTS besides transactional support. By keeping these additional benefits in mind, you can see that MTS makes sense even if you don't plan to run your components inside transactions. Therefore, as you learn about placing components in MTS today, don't think about how you can just place components there that require transactions. Instead, be considering it for all your components.

Now let's focus on the task at hand. Adding transactional support involves two parts: component configuration and code modifications. For component configuration you have four options when selecting the type of transactional support. These can be set in your component in Visual Basic or within MTS Explorer. These options are listed in Table 10.1.

TABLE 10.1 Transaction Support Types

Support Type	Description
Requires a transaction	Component must run in a transaction. If a transaction is already running, it will run in that transaction; otherwise, it will begin its own.
Request a new transaction	Component must run in a transaction that it starts itself. It will start a new transaction that it will run in whether a transaction is running or not. After it has started a new transaction, other components can join that transaction.
Supports transaction	If a transaction is already running, it will run in that transaction; otherwise, it will not be in a transaction.
Does not support	Component will not run in a transaction, whether or not one transaction is running already.

Here are some examples that further explain these different support types. In the examples, consider two actions that have to be accomplished. Each will be carried out by separate methods in two different components. The first action, adding a new customer for the bank, will be implemented by a method called NewCustomer. It will always be called first. The second action, adding a new account for the new customer, will be performed by a method called NewAccount, (sorry to be so predictable). It will be called second.

Each of these methods, NewCustomer and NewAccount, can involve multiple inserts and updates to multiple tables and databases. Also, each circle in the Figures 10.1 through 10.5 represent another transaction.

Figure 10.1 represents the context of the transaction if both components are set to "Requires a transaction." NewCustomer, because it requires its own transaction, will start up a transaction. NewAccount also requires a transaction, but because NewCustomer already created one, NewAccount will run within that transaction. If NewAccount failed, then neither a new customer nor a new account would be created.

FIGURE 10.1

Both objects "Require a transaction."

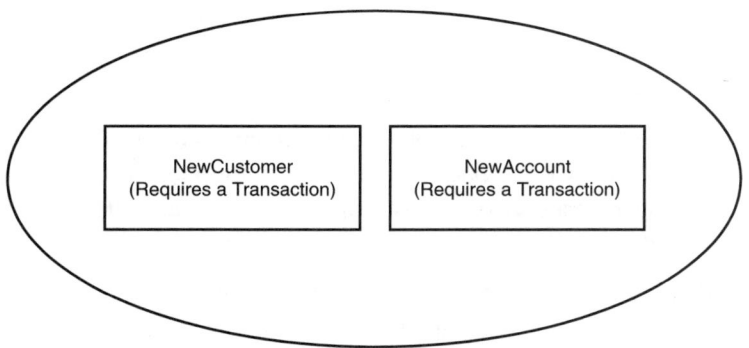

Figure 10.2 displays what happens when NewCustomer requires a transaction and
NewAccount requests a new transaction. In this scenario, if either action failed, the other
action may still succeed. Therefore, an account could be created, but the customer might
not be. This, of course, could be a very bad situation, which is why planning how your
components interact is so important.

FIGURE 10.2

NewCustomer *and*
NewAccount *run in sep-*
arate transactions.

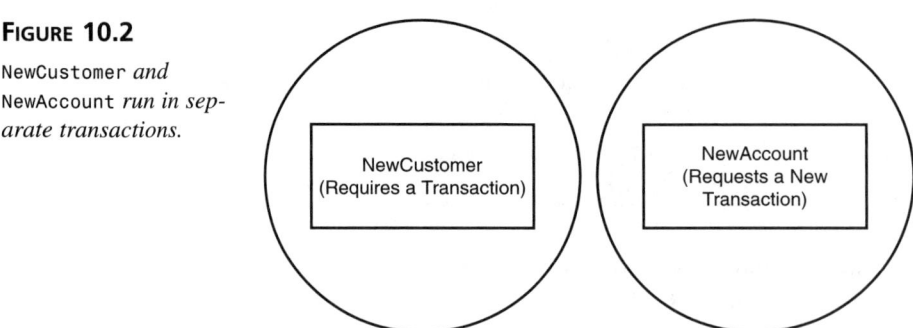

Next, we see Figure 10.3 has NewCustomer set to "Supports Transactions," whereas
NewAccount is set to "Requests a new Transaction." In this case, only NewAccount runs in
a transaction. Although NewCustomer supports transactions, it will not create one if one is
not started.

FIGURE 10.3

Only NewAccount *runs*
in a transaction.

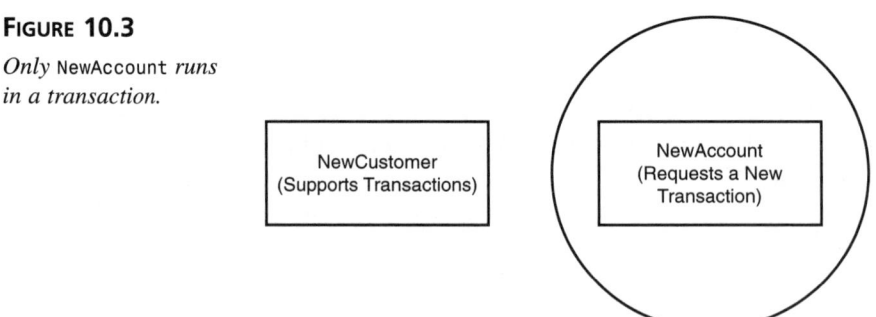

In Figure 10.4, NewCustomer is set to "Requests a new Transaction." Therefore it makes a
transaction, whether one is running or not. NewAccount, on the other hand, is marked to
not support transactions. This results in it not taking part in the transaction NewCustomer
started.

Realistically, how you set up transactions will be driven by your business requirements.
If you were actually adding a customer and setting up a bank account for them, there

are probably a couple different possibilities that you might actually implement. One possibility is to have NewCustomer either require a transaction or request a new transaction and NewAccount to require a transaction. This assures that they will be in the same transaction and, if one fails, they both fail.

Figure 10.4

Only NewCustomer runs in a transaction.

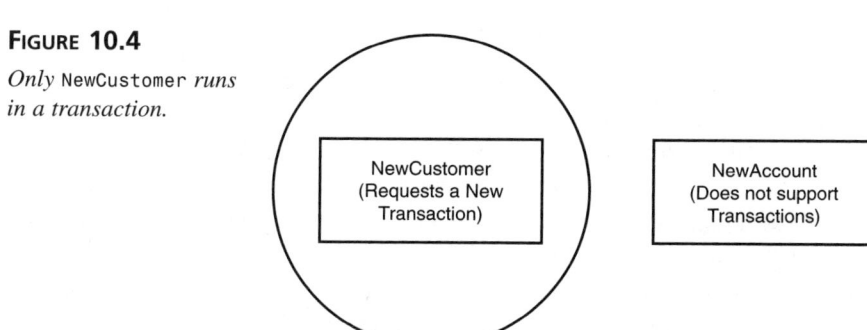

Another possibility is to have them both set to request a new transaction. If NewAccount fails, you do not have to enter in the Customer information again. But you would have to make sure that you do not call NewAccount if NewCustomer fails, otherwise you would have this Account with no Customer associated with it. You could accomplish this through error handling.

Now that you have a good idea of the types of transactional options available, you can configure your component.

Configuring Objects for Transactions

The first thing you will need to do is set a reference to the Transaction Server Library. This library enables you to reference the various methods, properties, and events from Transaction Server in your application.

Follow these steps:

1. Open the SmallTownBank_Data project. This can be the project that you have been creating or you can copy the Visual Basic project from the \SmallTownBank\10\ Start directory off the CD-ROM and onto your local hard drive.

2. From the Project menu, select References.

3. From the Available References lists, select the Microsoft Transaction Server Type Library.

4. Click OK.

5. Open the `SmallTownBank_Business` project, adding it to the same project group as the data component. You can also copy this from the CD-ROM in the same location referenced in step 1.

6. Repeat steps 2 through 4.

You can now reference the MTS objects in your components.

The next step is to set the `MTSTransactionMode` property for each class in the components. Click the class in the Project window. The `MTSTransactionMode` will display as one of the properties in the Properties window. The possible values for it are `NotAnMTSObject`, `NoTransactions`, `RequiresTransaction`, `UsesTransaction`, and `RequiresNewTransaction`. Except for the first value, these correspond to the transaction support types that you can set in MTS Explorer, listed earlier in Table 10.1. In fact, when the components are installed in MTS Explorer, it will look at the `MTSTransactionMode` property to determine how to set the transaction support in MTS.

In the Small Town Bank application, each project has only one class. This makes it easier to determine the transaction support, but, regardless of the size of the application, it requires planning to determine how you want the components to behave and how they will interact with each other. Do components belong to the same transaction? Is the completion of one action dependent on the other? In what order will the components be called? These are all good questions to ask as you work on adding transaction capabilities to your component.

Specifically, in dealing with the banking application, transactions are very important when dealing with money amounts. You certainly can't have one part of a transaction occur (for example, debiting an account) while another part fails (for example, crediting an account). Therefore, you will modify your component to enable the transferring of funds in the same transaction.

For your two components, `BankData` and `BankBusiness`, mark both of them as requiring a transaction. Do this by clicking on the drop-down for `MTSTransactionMode` and selecting 2 - Requires transactions. You are now ready to modify the code in the components.

In general, you will select "Requires a transaction" or "Supports a transaction" to give you the most flexibility with components. There could be cases where you want a component to start a new transaction, such as the `TransferFunds` method. Other times it might join an existing transaction, such as with the `DebitAccount` method. In that case, you would not want to mark the component as "Requests a new transaction." If `TransferFunds` first called `CreditAccount`, you would not want `DebitAccount` to start up and create its own transaction when one was already running. At this point you now have projects and classes that are configured to allow for transactions. To actually have your components run in transactions you will also have to add some Visual Basic code, which you will do next.

Getting the Object Context

Object context—the idea of having an object and keeping track of its context—is very important with MTS. Trying to understand everything a component may be doing without knowing its object context is akin to walking in on two people who are in the middle of deep conversation or going into a movie 15 minutes late. Without the context of the people's conversation or the setting for the movie, you are lost. In the same way, MTS keeps track of how a component is being used.

By being able to keep track of the context within which a component is running, MTS can quickly enable components to be discarded and created. MTS keeps the context of the component, yet releases the actual component. The component is then free to be used by whomever needs it, without having to go through the expensive process of being destroyed and created again.

NEW TERM *Object context* is the information regarding how a component is created and used. This is a wrapper around which a component can be placed in and taken out of.

Figure 10.5 demonstrates how multiple users can reuse components. Three customers want to transfer money at their local bank, by using their Web browser from home to access the bank's Web site. Customer A enters the appropriate information and the computer starts the transfer. This first transfer takes a little longer, because the object has never been created. Once it has spun-up (you'll see what I mean by this when we look at Transaction Monitor later today), the object can quickly be called again. Now, when Customer B does the same action for her account, she can quickly use the cached object. If Customer C does a transfer, while B's transfer is still running, another object will have to be created. You will now have two objects instantiated. These will persist in memory until a timeout has been reached and the object and its resources are released.

FIGURE 10.5

Component reuse with MTS.

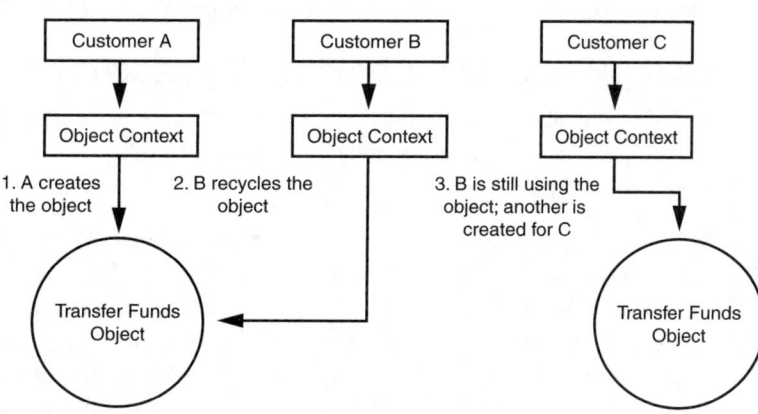

MTS saves the context within which the component is created and called. By keeping track of the context, it can swap new instances in and out of the component as needed.

In the previous example, two components were created instead of three. Not a big savings. But when using Windows DNA to scale from a hundred to thousands of users, the savings can be much more. Before MTS, a component had to be made for every user on a 1:1 ratio. Now, they can be reused over and over again in a 1:2 ratio, a 1:10 ratio, or an even higher ratio.

Note

> Realistically, users are not constantly using up processor time; they might be reading a Web page or deciding how much money to transfer. The actual processor time can probably be calculated down into seconds or maybe even milliseconds. With this in mind, it is easier to see how components can be passed from one user to the next.

Now that you have learned how an object has a context under MTS, let's look at how you can actually release those components. Releasing components enables the component instance to be freed and then MTS can give that instance to the next client that calls that component. To release a component, you first get a context reference to your component. To do so, you would add the following lines of code to your components' public methods:

```
1: Dim objContext as ObjectContext
2: Set objContext = GetObjectContext
```

Line 1 declares a variable of type `ObjectContext`. This is an object type defined by MTS. Line 2 gets the current context of the object. Once you have this object context, you continue on with the procedure. The next step in releasing the components will be covered in the next section, which takes you through completing and aborting the transaction.

Completing and Aborting Transactions

In order to complete or abort a transaction, which in turn enables MTS to recycle the component, there are two methods that you call from the `ObjectContext` object: `Set Complete` and `Set Abort`.

▼ SYNTAX

`SetComplete` tells MTS that the component has completed its action successfully and is ready to release the object and have it recycled by MTS. The component that created the object has not destroyed it and still holds a reference to the object. Also, MTS has the context of the object. Therefore, the component could reference another method on the object and the component would enlist MTS to give it another instance of the object. But for now the component is done. You will want to do `SetComplete` as often as possible in order for MTS to be able to recycle the instantiated object.

▼ The following line demonstrates the use of `SetComplete`:

```
objContext.SetComplete
```

▲ By calling the `SetComplete` method on `objContext object`, it indicates to MTS that the transaction was successful.

SYNTAX

`SetAbort` also releases the component to be recycled, but it tells MTS that the transaction was not completed successfully and that it should roll the entire transaction back. You will only do one `SetAbort`; after performing a `SetAbort`, you will want to exit the function and send back an appropriate error.

▼ The following line demonstrates the use of `SetAbort`:

```
objContext.SetAbort
```

▲ By calling the `SetAbort` method on `objContext object`, it indicates to MTS that the transaction failed. Typically you would use these in conjunction with error handling. If an error is returned from a stored procedure, you call a `SetAbort` to abort the transaction.

10

With the ability to use the ObjectContext object and the SetAbort and SetComplete methods, you can now add the code to the `BankData` classes and allow the BankData component to use transactions. Follow these steps to enable the component to take part in transactions:

1. Double-click the BankData class in the project window to view the code.

2. Go to the top of the `CreditAccount` function.

3. After the `Dim` statements, add the following lines:
   ```
   Dim objContext As ObjectContext
   Set objContext = GetObjectContext
   On Error GoTo CreditAccount_Err
   ```

   This declares the `ObjectContext` object, which can then be used later.

4. Just before the `End Function` line, add the following code:
   ```
   objContext.SetComplete
   Set objContext = Nothing
   Exit Function
   CreditAccount_Err:
       objContext.SetAbort
       Set objContext = Nothing
   ```

   If everything was successful, the `SetComplete` will complete the transaction. The reference to the object context is destroyed, and the function is exited. Otherwise, if an error was encountered, it will go to the error handler label, `CreditAccount_Err`, and abort the transaction. After that it will destroy the object reference and then the function will end.

5. Go to the top of the `DebitAccount` function.

6. After the `Dim` statements, add the following lines:

```
Dim objContext As ObjectContext
Set objContext = GetObjectContext
On Error GoTo DebitAccount_Err
```

7. Just before the `End Function` line, add the following code:

```
objContext.SetComplete
Set objContext = Nothing
Exit Function
DebitAccount_Err:
    objContext.SetAbort
Set objContext = Nothing
```

8. Recompile the component.

At this point you have made all the necessary programmatic changes to enlist the `CreditAccount` and `DebitAccount` methods in a transaction, but you still have to modify the `TransferFunds` method (part of the `BankBusiness` class) to enable it to participate in a transaction.

Unlike the `CreditAccount` and `DebitAccount` methods, which call the database, the `TransferFunds` method calls other components you are creating. These components also need to be included in the same transaction. To do that you use the `CreateInstance` method of the `ObjectContext` object.

▼ SYNTAX

`CreateInstance` returns a new object of the type specified in the `CreateInstance` parameter. The new object will participate in a transaction if it is able to participate in a transaction and does require a new transaction.

The following line demonstrates the use of `CreateInstance`:

```
Set objData = objContext.CreateInstance("SmallTownBank_Data.BankData")
```

▲ This creates an object that runs within the current transaction.

What you will need to do then is to call the BankData component with the CreateInstance method. This will allow the DebitAccount and CreditAccount methods to both be in the same transaction. Open up the `BankBusiness` project and go into the `TransferFunds` function. Replace the existing code for the function with the updated code segment in Listing 10.1

LISTING 10.1 Updated Code for the `TransferFunds` Function to Work with
INPUT MTS

```
1: Dim objData As SmallTownBank_Data.BankData
2: Dim objContext As ObjectContext
3: Set objContext = GetObjectContext()
```

```
4:  On Error GoTo TransferFunds_Err
5:  Set objData = objContext.CreateInstance("SmallTownBank_Data.BankData")
6:  TransferFunds = False
7:  If Not objData.DebitAccount(CustomerID, FromAccount, Amount) Then
8:      objContext.SetAbort
9:      Set objData = Nothing
10:     Set objContext = Nothing
11:     Exit Function
12: End If
13: objContext.SetComplete
14: If Not objData.CreditAccount(CustomerID, ToAccount, Amount) Then
15:     objContext.SetAbort
16:     Set objData = Nothing
17:     Set objContext = Nothing
18:     Exit Function
19: End If
20: TransferFunds = True
21: objContext.SetComplete
22: Set objData = Nothing
23: Set objContext = Nothing
24: Exit Function
25: TransferFunds_Err:
26: If Err <> 0 Then
27:     objContext.SetAbort
28:     Set objData = Nothing
29:     Set objContext = Nothing
30: End If
```

10

ANALYSIS Lines 1 though 3 declare variables and get the object context. Line 4 sets the error handler. Line 5 calls the CreateInstance method and returns a BankData object. Lines 7 through 12 and 14 through 18 call the DebitAccount and CreditAccount methods. If they return false, it is assumed that the call failed and a SetAbort is called and the function is exited. Line 13 and line 21 call SetComplete to let MTS know it can recycle the component. If anything goes wrong, the function jumps to the error handler in line 25 and the transaction is aborted.

By configuring components to run in a transaction and by using the CreateInstance method to instantiate objects within components, both the components and the objects they instantiate will be part of the same activity.

NEW TERM *Activity* involves one or more MTS objects that are involved in the same transaction. Therefore, even in the BankData component, when it runs by itself, it is still part of an activity.

After you have finished adding this code, recompile the BankBusiness component.

Working with State and Components

Although the context of the object is kept, it does not keep track of the internal settings of the component. This is known as the state of the component. Therefore, if you have public properties set on the component and then tell MTS that you are finished with the component (by a `SetComplete` or `SetAbort`), it will not know about those properties the next time you use the component. The alternative is to not tell MTS that you are finished until the very end of your procedures. The disadvantage is that MTS cannot reuse this resource until you are finished, which in turn can affect your scalability.

NEW TERM   *State* involves the internal data of a component. This typically involves information that is stored in a component between calls to the component. An example would be a public property. Components can then be referred to as being *stateful* (that is, they contain state) or *stateless* (that is, they do not contain state).

In the following, state would be lost:

```
MyObj.MyProperty = propvalue
ObjectContext.SetComplete
MsgBox MyObj.MyProperty
```

The message box for this property would be empty because the `SetComplete` method has released the object instance. If you look back to Figure 10.5, the context of the object still exists, but the SetComplete allows the object to be used by another customer.

One of the items you really want to consider in your components is state. An object that maintains state is an object that depends on information being in the object from call to call. If you had one method that initialized a number of public properties on the object, and then called other methods that used those properties to complete actions, that object would be stateful. This comes at a cost; the component cannot be reused as needed by MTS. You would have to hold on to that instance of the component, because if you lost it, you would also lose the data in the object. If you call a `SetComplete` or a `SetAbort`, then you are telling MTS that you don't need this information any longer.

Therefore, to be able to scale better and have MTS work better for you, you do not want to make your components stateful. Here are two rules you can follow to do this:

- **Do not have public properties.** This will require the object to persist the information between calls to it.
- **Pass all the information that your object needs in through parameters.** Two ways to do this are through recordsets and XML.

Your underlying goal is to isolate your component methods from one another. In other words, one method doesn't need to know anything that would have been gathered in another method.

Creating a Package and Installing Components into Transaction Server

Before adding in components to MTS, you will create a package for the components to reside in. You looked at packages, earlier on Day 8. They enable you to logically organize your COM components and assign security. Use the following steps to make a package for the banking components:

1. Create a directory on the hard drive called COM. This gives you a central place to put all your installed COM components. You can place them anywhere, but I like to keep things organized.

2. Create a subdirectory underneath it called SmallTownBank. If you have different applications on the same computer, you can make a different subdirectory for each application. This directory is where you will put all the SmallTownBank components you might create.

3. Copy the SmallTownBank component to the SmallTownBank directory. You can use a component that you created yesterday or from the CD-ROM that is located in \SmallTownBank\10\Start.

4. Open up MTS Explorer and drill down to the Packages Installed on your local computer by clicking on the plus signs to the left of Microsoft Transaction Server, then Computers, then My Computer and finally Packages Installed.

5. Right-click Packages Installed and select New Package. Figure 10.6 displays the first Package Wizard window.

FIGURE 10.6

Adding a new package to MTS.

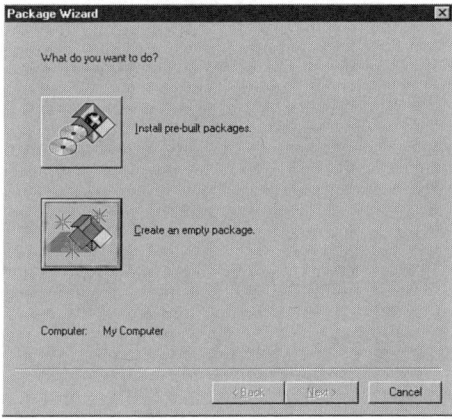

10

6. Select Create an Empty Package. If you had exported the package from another computer, you could select Install Pre-built Packages.

7. Enter **SmallTownBank** for the name of the package.

8. Select Interactive User. Later, if you would like, you can apply the knowledge you learned on Day 8 about roles and role-based security, but for now we will stay with the interactive user.

9. Click Finish. This will install your empty package in MTS.

Adding the Components

You will now have a chance to install your component into MTS. There are two ways to do this. One is through the machine on which you create the component; this would be your developer machine that is running Visual Basic. You can also install components into MTS via the machine on which you will run the component (a staging or production server).

Whenever you compile your component in Visual Basic, it automatically registers itself on the machine on which it is compiled. It becomes available for immediate use by applications, but you will still need to add it to MTS. When installing the component into MTS on your own machine, it will reregister the component.

After testing the components on your own machine, you will most likely copy the components to your development server. Tying this into Windows DNA, this development server will host your middle-tier components. After copying the physical files to the server, you will add the components to MTS, which will register them.

There are a few different ways to add your components to MTS (as with everything in Windows), but I will show you how I typically do it. This first method is for installing a COM component into Transaction Server where it is already registered. This is what you would do to load your component into MTS on your development machine:

1. Click the SmallTownBank package to display the Component folder.

2. Click on Components.

3. Right-click Component and select New.

4. Select Import Components That Are Already Registered. This will display all the registered components on the local machine. An example of this is in Figure 10.7.

5. Select the SmallTownBank classes from the list.

6. Click Finish. The component(s) will display in the right-hand pane, as seen in Figure 10.8.

FIGURE 10.7

Adding components to MTS that are already registered.

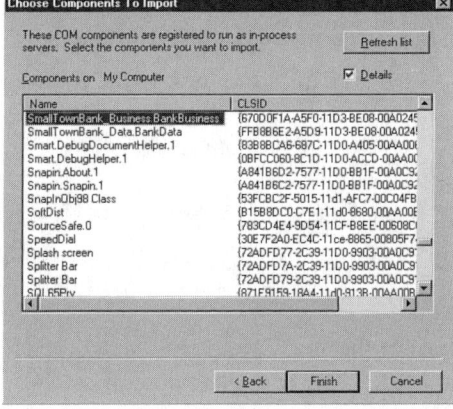

FIGURE 10.8

SmallTownBank *package with* SmallTownBank *components in MTS.*

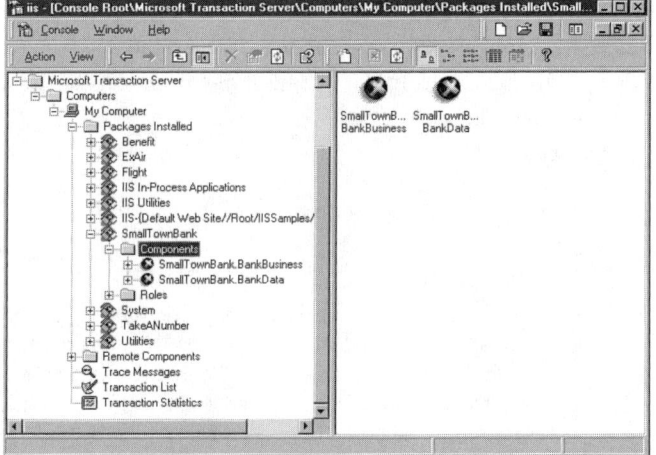

The second method installs a COM component on a machine where it has not been compiled and on which the component is not registered. This would be the case if you wanted to install the component on your staging or production servers. Follow these steps:

1. Copy the component to the machine where it will be installed into MTS. You might want to create a folder called COM. Create another folder underneath that called SmallTownBank. You would make another subfolder under the COM folder for each of your future projects.

2. Click the SmallTownBank package to display the Component folder.

3. Click on Components. This brings up an empty pane on the right representing the installed components for the SmallTownBank package. At this point you could right-click Component and select New. Instead you will drag the component into MTS.

4. From Windows Explorer, drill down the directory to which the component was copied. If you used the suggestion in step 1, it would be in \COM\SmallTownBank.

5. Click and drag BankData.dll from Explorer to the right-hand pane of the MTS Explorer window. This will automatically register the component with MTS. The component will now show up in the right-hand pane.

Adding Transaction Support to the Components

Now that the component is installed in MTS, you will need to specify how it will work in transactions:

1. In the right-hand pane of the SmallTownBank_Data project, right-click the SmallTownBank.BankData class and select properties.

2. Click the Transaction tab. This will display the different transaction support that you can select for your component.

3. Select Requires a Transaction If It Is Not Already Selected. The initial setting for this option is taken from the setting it has in the Visual Basic developer environment for the class properties.

4. Click OK.

The components are now ready to be part of a transaction.

Note

These steps could be unnecessary if you already specified the information in the MTSTransactionMode property in Visual Basic, which you looked at in the section Configuring Objects for Transactions. MTS will look at this property when the component is installed and set the transaction support to the corresponding property. There is an exception to this. If you install components into MTS by selecting Import Component(s) That Are Already Registered, it will not pick up this setting.

Monitoring Your Components as They Transact

Along with all the other features that MTS gives you, you can also observe what the installed components are doing in MTS. There are two different views that will tell you whether they are running in MTS and what transactions are going on.

> **Tip**
>
> If you have your components in a Visual Basic group along with your testing harness, you might have trouble testing the components with MTS when you start up your test harness. The problem is that when debugging components in Visual Basic, MTS is not aware of the components and therefore GetObjectContext doesn't return a reference. Then when you go to call a method on the Context object, an error occurs. If you receive the error, "Object variable or with block variable not set," here are a couple suggestions:
>
> - If you want to be able to view your components in the transaction monitor in MTS, close the project group and open only the test harness project. You will now be able to call your components and view them in MTS.
> - If you want to be able to step through your components, then you can add a registry key, which enables you to debug your components. The key is
>
> HKEY_LOCAL_MACHINE\SOFTWARE\Microsoft\Transaction Server
> ➥\Debug\RunWithoutContext
>
> To add this automatically, double-click the file RunWithoutContext.reg found on the Windows DNA CD-ROM in the \SmallTownBank\10 directory. Be careful when editing the registry. This will enable you to step through the code of the components, but then none of the MTS commands such as SetComplete or SetAbort have any transaction support. You also can remove the key by using RegEdit.

10

The first view to look at is the components themselves. If you click the Components folder of the SmallTownBank package, you will see the installed components. By running the components from a test harness, you will see they become activate. You can click various views on the toolbar and know the component is active by seeing the globe spin in the right-hand pane. Clicking the Status View toolbar button gives you additional information.

To give you a better overall picture, check out the Transaction Statistics window for Transaction Server. This is located under My Computer in MTS Explorer. Click Transaction Statistics, and the right-hand pane will display aggregated numbers of what is going on in MTS for the computer. This includes committed and aborted transactions as well as the number of active components. There are other statistics listed, as shown in Figure 10.9.

FIGURE 10.9

Viewing transaction statistics in MTS.

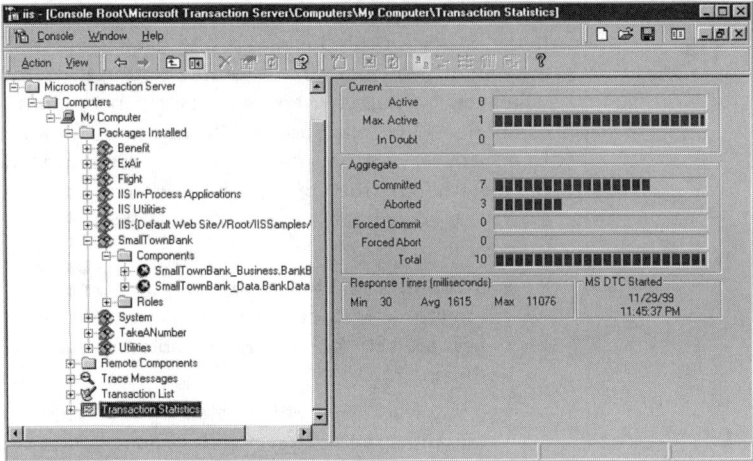

Raising Errors

In the code that you have incorporated into your components today, you have had an error handler for each of the functions. The error handler is called if an error occurs and then proceeds to exit out of the function. The function traps the error and then returns a value of false indicating the action failed. This is one way to handle errors, but, instead of suppressing the error, you might want to pass the error back to the caller of the function. You can do this through the `Err.Raise` method in Visual Basic.

▼ SYNTAX

The `Raise` method on the `Err` object generates an error, which is passed back to the calling application. It has the following syntax:

```
Err.Raise number, [ source], [ description], [ helpfile], [ helpcontext]
```

number is required and must be a long integer. It is your error number added to the vbObjectError, which is the Visual Basic error constant. Your error number can be any number from 513 to 65535. Numbers lower than this can conflict with system error numbers.

source is optional and is a string indicating the object that is generating the error. *description* is another optional string and tells what the error is. *helpfile* is an optional string that contains the path of the help file and *helpcontext* is an optional string specifying the corresponding topic in the help file. An example of the `Raise` method is

```
Err.Raise vbObjectError + ERR_INV_DATA, "CreditAccount", "Invalid data has
➥been entered."
```

▼ ERR_INV_DATA is a constant that has already been defined. "CreditAccount" describes
the source that is generating the error and the last parameter is the description, which
▲ tells what the error is.

Errors that you raise in one component will bubble up to the next component. It is then
either handled there or bubbles up once again. It continues to do this until it displays to
the user or is handled.

Handling Updates

During the course of your development, you will need to perform many updates to your
component. In Day 9, "Building COM Components in VB," you looked at how project
and binary compatibility helps you when you recompile your DLL. Now after it is
recompiled, you will need to replace the old DLL with the new one.

There are actually some tricks to this. It is not as easy as just copying over a file. You
often times must shut down a service or process so that the file is no longer in use before
you can delete or copy over it. This occurs with MTS—which might have the object in an
activity—or with Internet Information Server, if you are working with a Web application.

Removing and Updating

You can use a couple different methods to remove a package. One is to shut down the
processes in MTS; the other is to shut down and restart IIS if you are using this in a Web
application. By doing this you are forcing MTS or IIS to release its use of the object.

Use the following steps when you want to remove and update the component:

1. From the MTS Explorer, right-click the computer where the component will be
   updated and select Shut Down Server Processes. This will stop all the instances of
   the components that are running.
2. Right-click the computer again and select Stop MS DTC.
3. Go to the directory in Windows Explorer where DLL is located and delete or
   update the file.

If this is an Internet application and it still can't be deleted, use the following steps:

1. Go to Control Panel Services.
2. Stop the IIS Admin Service by clicking the service and then clicking the Stop button. It will warn you that one or more other services are also stopping. Remember
   these other services.
3. Start the IIS Admin Service by clicking the Start button.

4. Start the World Wide Web Publishing Service by clicking the service and clicking the Start button.

5. Repeat step 4 for any other services that were stopped when you stopped the IIS Admin Service.

6. Try to delete the file again.

Tip

Often when working with COM and IIS, you might have a need to stop and start the Web service or some other services. Instead of constantly having to go to Control Panel, make a text file and give it a `.cmd` extension. Put the following code in the file:

```
REM Services to stop
NET STOP "IIS Admin Service" /y
REM Services to start
NET START "World Wide Web Publishing Service"
```

NET STOP stops the service, whereas NET START starts the service back up again. If you need to stop or start more services, just add them using the same syntax. The "/y" suppresses the screen confirmation. You can list all the services that are running by typing **NET START** from a command line. If they are dependent upon one another, make sure that you put them in the correct order (for example, FTP service will start after the IIS service).

Save this file and then, whenever you want to restart the service, simply double-click the file from Explorer or make a shortcut to it on your desktop and in your Start menus. An example of this file is on your Windows DNA CD-ROM. The file is called `RestartIIS.cmd` and is located in the `\Day\10` directory.

There might still be times when you have to actually restart the computer when you want to update the component, but that should be rare.

Considering Design

Here are a few tips to consider when designing your components. This will help your components scale better in the Window DNA architecture:

- Call SetComplete as often as you can. This tells MTS that it is free to recycle the component. The sooner MTS can recycle a component, the sooner it can give the component to another user.

- Create database connections as late as possible and release them as soon as possible. Connection pooling is still going on, but you want to help that out even more by limiting your connect time.

- Create references to objects as soon as possible. This has little impact on performance. For example,

```
Dim rst AS ADODB.Recordset
```

creates a reference, but doesn't allocate any resources to the actual object. This enables you to instantiate as soon as you need to do so. When you do instantiate the object, do so as late as possible. For example,

```
Set rst = New ADODB.Recordset
```

This creates the object.

Summary

Today's lesson taught you how to add transactional support to your COM components. This included placing the components in a transaction and then enabling them to complete or abort. You gained an understanding of the importance of this in business and data processes. If two business processes are dependent upon one another, you certainly can't have one business transaction occur and another not occur. You also looked at how to update and monitor your components in Microsoft Transaction Server. Finally, you saw how to raise errors and saw some guidelines for using your components.

Tomorrow's lesson will look at ADO. You were introduced to ADO on Day 6, "ActiveX Data Objects (ADO)," but in Day 11, "Interacting with the Database—ADO Revisited," you will dig deeper into its capabilities. One important area is the passing around of disconnected recordsets in components. Datashaping is also another technique you will learn, which enables you to work with hierarchical recordsets. Another part is to look at the XML capabilities that the current version of ADO has as well as the XML capabilities of ADO 2.5. All this will be in the context of sending information back and forth through your DNA layers, going from the presentation layer, to the business logic layer, and finally to the data layer and then sending the information back through to the user again.

Q&A

Q How many different classes and components should I have? Do I put everything into one component? Should I have one class?

A In organizing your components, you certainly will want to separate out your business components from your data components. This keeps the logic physically separate and also enables you to easily move the physical location of the component to another machine.

Regarding how many components and how to organize classes within components, there isn't one correct answer, but there are a few different approaches. One approach is to organize components and classes by process. You can have a separate class for all your transaction methods, another one for your accounts, and another for the customer. Later, you can put these in separate components if they grow too big. If it is a large application, you can have some standard components that you use in different parts of your application, perhaps to send email messages or get registry settings. Place these in separate components that can be reused over and over again.

Another approach is to organize classes by usage. If you have certain methods that are being called constantly, put those in their own component. Don't unnecessarily add to the component size by putting in methods that are called infrequently; instead put those in their own component as well. This makes method handling more efficient because only methods that are going to be used right away are loaded into memory.

Whichever approach you choose, make sure you plan ahead. This will be your greatest help to make components that are logical to use and scalable.

Q Do I really need to put everything into Microsoft Transaction Server? What if I don't even use transactions?

A A resounding yes comes to mind. Even if you don't use transactions you will still want to use Transaction Server for the other benefits it brings, which has been outlined at the beginning of today's material. Furthermore, Transaction Server offers you an easier way to handle your components, both in terms of updating them and moving them to different servers. As you have seen today, dragging and dropping DLLs into MTS Explorer certainly provides an easy way to install components. Finally, COM and Transaction Server are being combined in Windows 2000 into COM+ and Microsoft Component Services. In order to leverage yourself for these latest technologies, MTS will prepare you today for what you will most certainly be using in the future.

Workshop

The Workshop provides quiz questions to help you solidify your understanding of the material covered and exercises to provide you with experience in using what you've learned. Try to understand the quiz and exercise answers before continuing to the next lesson. Answers are provided in Appendix A.

Quiz

1. How many times will you call SetComplete and SetAbort while working with a transaction?

2. Where can you look to see what your components are doing?

3. How can you create an object within a component to place in the same transaction as that component? For instance, Component A is running in a transaction. It calls Component B, which needs to run in the same transaction.

4. Where do you set the transaction support for a component?

5. What are the different types of transaction support?

Exercise

1. Using the SmallTownBank components, change the types of transactions that the components support, specifically the BankData class. Look at the AccountTransaction table to see what effect that has.

10

DAY **11**

Interacting with the Database—ADO Revisited

Today you will build out the classes that interact with the database using ADO. You will cover best practices for interacting with the database by managing database connections, using commands and stored procedures, and using disconnected recordsets and batch updates. Following today's lesson, you will know about

- Using best practices for working with data
- Bringing data into your component
- Sending data to requesting components
- Receiving data back from another component
- Transactional properties
- Handling errors

Best Practices for Working with Data

Our banking application is continuing to evolve. Today you want to mature the data tier almost to the point where it should be in the final product. The data tier will be responsible for managing all the connections to the database and making all the calls to the database. Likewise, you will continue to work with the business logic tier in being able to interact properly with the data tier.

The business logic tier will send requests for data and send data to be updated, going through the data tier. Keep in mind that you want to be sure to keep the data tier and the business logic tier separate. Why do we want to do this? If we ever decide to move the data to a different type of data store, we can do this easily. All we have to do is switch the data tier out to use another type of data store. The business logic tier should ideally not have to be touched at all. The business logic tier just knows that, if it has to update a record in a table, it just has to call a particular procedure and pass the appropriate parameters to the data tier.

Today, four decisions will be made for the `SmallTownBank` application:

- How will you access the data store to get the data into your data tier?
- How will you send the data back to the calling components (in this case, the business logic tier)?
- How will your business logic tier receive the data?
- How will you send data back to the data store?

Each of these questions will help you get an idea of how your data and business logic tier components will be implemented. Also, each plays a part in the Windows DNA architecture. Some of the questions will be easier to answer than others. You will get a fair exposure to each situation and the possibilities that are available to you.

Before you get into these questions in more depth, some primer information has to be covered to give you a better idea of what the possibilities are. This information applies to all the questions and, therefore, is valuable to know before you go farther.

Choosing the Correct Object: Commands Versus Recordsets

The Command object and Recordset object will be your best friends as you implement the Windows DNA architecture. Recordsets will enable you to pass information back and forth between different parts of your application.

Learning about the Command and Recordset objects on Day 6, "ActiveX Data Objects (ADO)," you saw that Command objects were used for calling stored procedures, whereas recordsets were used to receive information back from the data store. If you were not using stored procedures, you would more likely use a Recordset object, but you still could get away with not using it. Simply set the CommandText property of the command object to the SQL query string. Listing 11.1 gives an example of this.

LISTING 11.1   Using the Command Object

```
1: Dim cmd as ADODB.Command
2: Set cmd = New ADODB.Command
3: cmd.ActiveConnection = "Provider=SQLOLEDB;DRIVER=SQL Server;
      ➥SERVER=(local);DATABASE=Bank_Data;UID=sa;PWD=;"
4: cmd.CommandText = "UPDATE Customer SET FirstName = ""Jonathan""
      ➥WHERE (FirstName = ""Jon"") AND (LastName = ""Moons"")"
5: cmd.CommandType = adCmdText
6: cmd.Execute
```

ANALYSIS Line 3 sets the connection and line 4 is the actual command. After specifying adCmdText for the CommandType, all that is left to do is call the Execute method (line 6). This will update any records that meet the WHERE criteria—all without using the Recordset object.

In reality, which objects you use is up to you. Whichever way you choose, be consistent in how you access the data store.

11

Referencing ADOR

When working with components, you will be adding references to ActiveX Data Objects in Visual Basic. In the references dialog it is helpful to know the difference between Microsoft ActiveX Data Objects 2.x Library and Microsoft ActiveX Data Objects Recordset 2.0 Library. The later is a subset of the ADO library, which contains a streamlined version of the ADO objects without the Connection and Command objects. This is a lightweight version to help with size and speed for clients that are only going to be manipulating recordsets. Also, it is referenced as ADOR, instead of ADODB.

Disconnected Recordsets

Up to this point you have been looking at recordsets that have a live connection with the data store. Now you will learn about being able to take a chunk of data in a recordset and have it disconnected from the source of its data. This enables you to manipulate the data as you would like, which includes reading and updating records.

Disconnected recordsets also enable you to define the types of fields in the recordset and then proceed to populate the recordset with information. A connected recordset gets its structure and data from a query to a data store to which it is connected. A disconnected recordset can be defined programmatically or get its information from the data store.

NEW TERM A *disconnected recordset* contains a snapshot of the data and does not have a connection to a data store. Its schema and data can be defined from a SQL command or be defined programmatically by the developer.

Let's first look at a case where you actually define the schema for a disconnected recordset. For example, you can set the first column to an integer value. The next column can be a character value, and so on. After the disconnected recordset is defined, you can set the values for the columns. Finally, you can pass the recordset between the different tiers of your application, enabling you to update or insert records in the data store.

To create a disconnected recordset, you use the Fields collection. Within the Fields collection is the Apppend method, which enables you to specify the schema for a recordset. This includes the field name, the data type, and the length.

The Append method enables you to add fields to the disconnected recordset. The syntax for it is

```
Fields.Append Name, DataType, [FieldSize], [Attribute]
```

Name is the name of the field and corresponds to the name, which will reference it using the Recordset object. *DataType* designates the type of field that it is (for example, Char, Integer, or DateTime). *FieldSize* is an optional field specifying the size in characters or bytes. *Attribute* enables you to specify attributes for the field for characteristics such as whether it enables Null values or whether it is a primary key.

Examples of this method would be

```
rst.Fields.Append "Password", adChar, 6, adFldIsNullable
```

By instantiating a recordset you can append all the necessary fields to the recordset. The only other stipulation is that you must set the CursorLocation of the recordset to adUseClient, forcing the recordset to be created on the machine from which the code is being run. The other option for this is adUseServer. For a connected recordset, this would indicate the cursor is on the SQL Server machine. For a disconnected recordset, it does not apply. Listing 11.2 gives an example of creating a disconnected recordset based on the Spouse table in our SmallTownBank application.

LISTING 11.2   Creating a Disconnected Recordset

```
1: Dim rs As ADODB.Recordset
2: Set rs = New ADODB.Recordset
3: rs.CursorLocation = adUseClient
4: rs.Fields.Append "SpouseKey", adInteger, 16, adFldRowID
5: rs.Fields.Append "FirstName", adChar, 50
6: rs.Fields.Append "MiddleName", adChar, 50
7: rs.Fields.Append "LastName", adChar, 50
8: rs.Fields.Append "SocialSecurityNumber", adChar, 9
```

ANALYSIS   Lines 1 and 2 declare and instantiate the ADO recordset object. The CursorLocation property is set next in line 3. After that all the fields are added to the recordset. You will notice on line 4 that the adFldRowID attribute is set for the field. This indicates the field is an identity column and cannot be written to.

After you have created the recordset, you can add data to the record in the same way that you would to a connected recordset. This is with the AddNew method, which was mentioned in Day 6. Listing 11.3 is an example of adding data to a disconnected recordset.

LISTING 11.3   Adding Data to a Disconnected Recordset

```
1: rs.AddNew
2: rs("FirstName") = "Carolyn"
3: rs("MiddleName") = "M"
4: rs("LastName") = "Foster"
5: rs("SocialSecurityNumber") = "111223333"
6: rs.Update
```

ANALYSIS   Line 1 uses the AddNew method to add a record to the end of the recordset. Lines 2 through 5 add in the information to the new record. Typically you have been reading information from recordset fields. The difference here is that, instead of reading from them, you are writing to the fields. Line 6 calls the Update method, which then actually does the write to the recordset.

Next, instead of having to do the work of defining the schema of the recordset, you can also issue a SQL command against the data store and get a disconnected recordset back. To make the recordset disconnected, you have to use the CursorLocation, LockType, and CursorType properties of the Recordset object. CursorLocation is used for specifying the cursor will reside on the client computer that is creating the recordset, instead of on the computer with the data store on it. LockType is set for batches to enable multiple records to be updated, and CusorType is set to be static to be able to have a snapshot of the data Recordset. Listing 11.4 is an example of a disconnected recordset that is created from a data store.

LISTING 11.4 Creating a Disconnected Recordset from a Data Store

```
1: Dim rs As ADODB.Recordset
2: Set rs = New ADODB.Recordset
3: rs.CursorType = adOpenStatic
4: rs.LockType = adLockBatchOptimistic
5: rs.CursorLocation = adUseClient
6: rs.Open "SELECT * FROM Account WHERE CustomerID = 1", cnn
7: rs.ActiveConnection = Nothing
```

ANALYSIS   Line 3 through line 5 set the previously mentioned recordset properties. Line 6 opens up the recordset and assumes there is already a Connection object created called cnn. Line 7 closes the connection, but because of the properties that were set before opening the recordset, all the information is still there.

By using disconnected recordsets, you have another medium available to you for manipulating data besides individual variables, arrays, and collections. Not only can you manipulate the data in the recordset, but you can also pass information to another tier. The recordset also affords you a lot of meta information about the data that it stores, such as the data type, the size, and other attributes. This helps the developer, but it also makes this medium for temporarily containing data somewhat large. This is a trade-off to keep in mind. If you are concerned about keeping the data you pass between tiers light-weight, then you might not want to use recordsets.

Batch Updates

Although you have already learned how to update individual records, you will now learn how to update multiples or "batches" of records. This uses the disconnected recordset information that you just learned about and takes you past just creating the recordset to manipulating and writing the information back to the data store.

In looking at the Windows DNA architecture, this enables you to bring down a set of records to the presentation tier. When changes are made to the data in this tier, the information is sent back through the business logic tier to the data tier.

You start with the same steps that created a disconnected recordset in the previous listings. When you have the data in the recordset, you can manipulate the records. This would typically be done through a client interface involving textboxes or a grid, if multiple records are involved. Listing 11.5 gives an example of updating a disconnected recordset created from the Account table and writing the information back to the data store.

LISTING **11.5**　Using UpdateBatch with a Recordset

```
1: rs("Balance") = intNewBalance1
2: rs.MoveNext
3: rs("Balance") = intNewBalance2
4: rs.ActiveConnection = cnn
5: rs.UpdateBatch
6: rs.Close
7: Set rs = Nothing
```

ANALYSIS　Line 1 sets a new value to the Balance field of the first record. Line 2 moves to the next record, and line 3 sets a value to the Balance field of the second row. After all the updates are done, the connection is reestablished in line 4. The UpdateBatch method is called in line 5 and writes the changes back to the data store. Finally the connection is closed and the object is destroyed.

Although only a couple changes were made in the Listing 11.5, in reality, you could have been dealing with a complex grid that involved account transfers, bills to be paid, and other financial transactions. Then, all at once, all these changes would be written back to the data store.

A presentation like this significantly cuts down on the round trips to the server and, therefore, cuts down on network traffic. For someone with a slow connection or a server with limited bandwidth, this can be very advantageous.

11

Bringing Data into Your Data Tier Component

Now that we have covered some important primer information, you can now address the first question in today's lesson. It asked what methods you specifically want to employ in getting data into your data tier in the SmallTownBank application. Figure 11.1 shows what part of the DNA architecture is being focused on.

FIGURE 11.1

Retrieving data from the data store into your data tier.

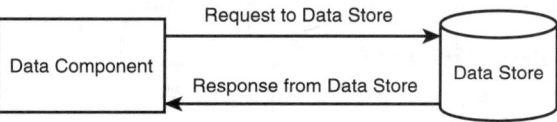

You've got ADO at your disposal with a complement of methods that can be used with it to access data. You already know many of these methods; you now have a chance to learn a few more and to put them together in your data tier.

Data Interaction Methods

When retrieving information from the data store, you will most often want to use stored procedures, which you learned about on Day 6. The alternative to using stored procedures is to send a SQL string directly when the recordset is opened. This is slower, but it does give you more flexibility to build ad hoc queries and also enables you to take advantage of some additional features of ADO, which you will look at later.

Whichever method you choose, there are different options available to you with recordsets. A couple properties that you have looked at already on Day 6 are the `CursorType` and `LockType` properties. Setting the `CursorType` to `adOpenForwardOnly` and the `LockType` to `adLockReadOnly` will be the fastest method of retrieving data. These are the default settings; use these unless you need to have them set to something else. One example would be, if you were doing the batch updates that were outlined earlier today, then you would need to use `adOpenStatic` and `adLockBatchOptimistic`, respectively. `CursorLocation` defaults to `adUserServer`. Use this unless you need a disconnected recordset. Again, this was described earlier.

There are a couple more properties to be aware of. When doing batch updates, the `MarshalOptions` property can specify whether to return all rows or only rows that have been modified back to the server. When working with client-side cursors, a property called `Update Criteria` (with a space) enables you to specify how ADO determines whether a record has been updated since the recordset was created. This gives you control over how to handle issues of simultaneous updates to the data. Although beyond the scope of this book, you can find more information on these two properties at Microsoft's MSDN site, `http://msdn.microsoft.com`.

Stored Procedures Revisited

On Day 6, you learned how to call stored procedures. You can now see how that will look inside your components that you have created. In addition to the code that you have already used to call the stored procedures, you will add in the procedure declaration, connection string information, some variables, and return some type of result. When you have that, you can easily call store procedures from your components.

When creating procedures to call stored procedures, the primary decision is whether or not a recordset will be returned. Performing inserts, updates, and deletes, your business logic tier will just want to know whether or not it was successful. As long as a Boolean value is returned that will hopefully be satisfactory. With an insert you might have to actually return the new identity of the record that was inserted. If you do need to return the identity you can have your function return it as an integer. Listing 11.6 gives an example of calling one of these types of stored procedures.

LISTING 11.6   A Method That Inserts a Record

```
 1: Public Function Ins_AccountType(ByVal rs As ADODB.Recordset,
    ➥Optional ByVal strConnection As String) As Boolean
 2:     Dim cmd As ADODB.Command
 3:     Set cmd = CreateObject("ADODB.Command")
 4:     If strConnection = "" Then
 5:         strConnection = GetConnectionString
 6:     End If
 7: With cmd
 8:     .ActiveConnection = strConnection
 9:     .CommandText = "sp_ins_AccountType"
10:     .CommandType = adCmdStoredProc
11:     .Parameters.Append .CreateParameter("@AccountTypeKey",
    ➥adInteger, adParamReturnValue)
12:     .Parameters.Append .CreateParameter("@Description",
    ➥adChar, adParamInput, 50)
13:     cmd("@Description") = rs("Description")
14: End With
15:     cmd.Execute
16:     rs("AccountTypeKey") = cmd("@AccountTypeKey")
17:     Set cmd.ActiveConnection = Nothing
18:     Set cmd = Nothing
19:     Set Ins_AccountType = True
20: End Function
```

11

ANALYSIS   Line 1 declares Ins_AccountType as a public function, which makes it available to other applications. Therefore, by adding this function to your Data class, it will actually become a method that is available to the business logic tier components. Notice the return item is a Boolean value. After the Command object is created, it checks to see whether the connection string was passed in strConnection in line 4. If it was, the Command object will use that value; otherwise, it will call GetConnectionString to obtain the connection string to the database.

The With command in line 7 enables you to bypass having to specify the Command object. Lines 8 through 13 set various properties, which include the stored procedure name and the parameters to pass to the stored procedure. Line 15 executes the stored procedure. After the execution the new identity value is stored back in the recordset that was originally passed in. Notice that this was passed by reference, so the value written to it will exist in the procedure that called this function.

Lines 17 and 18 clean up and then a True value is set for the function to return in line 19. This indicates the insert was successful. Additional code in this function can include error handling to be able to trap the error and have the function return a value of False.

Listing 11.6 can be slightly modified to also handle updates and deletes. Next, look at Listing 11.7, which will give an example of a method that returns a recordset. Data is not being modified, but, instead, it is being fetched from the data store. This will typically be implemented in the database with a Select statement. One thing you will need to be sure of is that you are not closing the connection to the recordset. You still want to clean up and not leave objects instantiated that don't need to be.

LISTING 11.7   A Method That Returns a Recordset

```
 1: Public Function Sel_AccountType(ByVal AccountTypeKey As Integer,
    ➥Optional ByVal strConnection As String) As ADODB.Recordset
 2:     Dim cmd As ADODB.Command
 3:     Set cmd = CreateObject("ADODB.Command")
 4:     If strConnection = "" Then
 5:         strConnection = GetConnectionString
 6:     End If
 7: With cmd
 8:     .ActiveConnection = strConnection
 9:     .CommandText = "sp_sel_AccountType"
10:     .CommandType = adCmdStoredProc
11:     .Parameters.Append .CreateParameter("@AccountTypeKey",
    ➥adInteger, adParamInput, 16)
12:     cmd("@AccountTypeKey") = AccountTypeKey
13: End With
14:     Set Sel_AccountType = cmd.Execute
15:     Set cmd.ActiveConnection = Nothing
16:     Set cmd = Nothing
17: End Function
```

ANALYSIS The declaration differs slightly from the Listing 11.6. This function has a return value of an ADO recordset instead of a Boolean. Lines 2 through 5 declare a Command object and get the connection string. Lines 8 through 12 set the necessary properties.

Up to now, the functions in Listings 11.6 and 11.7 have been very similar. The big difference is in line 14 of Listing 11.7 where the Set statement is used. When the command executes, it will call the stored procedure and return a result set, which is in the form of a recordset. In line 14, the return value of the function is set to this recordset. Lines 16 and 17 destroy the Command object, but that will not affect the recordset that was just returned. You would not want to close the recordset, because that would cause you to lose your results.

Encapsulating database actions such as inserts, updates, and deletes within functions allows you to reuse the functions over and over again. Other functions that you create on the business logic tier might need to perform a similar database action, but employ different business logic. For example, one function might insert a record of a table because of a transfer of funds, while another function might make an insert into the table to add in monthly interest. Write the insert function once and then call it from each of these business logic functions.

Data Shaping—Hierarchical Recordsets

Relational databases offer us *n*-dimensional views of our data. You could have a store with many clients. Each client could have many orders; each order, many items. The items, in turn, could be stored in many warehouses. Data such as this can be very easily represented in a relational database.

Difficulties come in though when there is a need to represent data in a hierarchal manner. For example, the directory structure in your computer would be very difficult to place into a relational structure. And if you did put it into a relational database, it would be very difficult to understand the structure by simply looking at the physical entities database. Something like this is much better suited to a hierarchal view. This gives you another option for bringing your data into the data tier.

With ADO 2.x, you have the ability to actually obtain hierarchal recordsets from a SQL data store using Data Shaping. This is accomplished by using the ADO SHAPE command when making SQL calls. The SHAPE command enables you to specify a recordset with additional recordsets appended on as fields in rows.

NEW TERM *Data shaping* is one or more data updates, inserts, or deletes grouped as a single entity. By grouping the actions together, the actions can either all occur or else no actions occur.

▼ SYNTAX

The SHAPE command has the following syntax:

```
SHAPE {parent entity } [´ parent-alias]
APPEND ({child entity} [´ child-alias]
RELATE parent field TO child field)
```

What is being created here is a recordset with fields that contain more recordsets. This is similar to a folder, which would contain another folder inside of it. Here is an example of the syntax that would be used with the SHAPE command:

```
SHAPE {SELECT * from Customer}
APPEND ({SELECT * from Account} AS Accounts
RELATE CustomerKey to CustomerID)
```

Customer is the parent entity in this case. This simple SQL command can be replaced with a much more complex command, which includes joins, WHERE clauses, and other

▼ valid SQL syntax. In this case, it simply returns every field from the Customer table.

11

▼   In addition to the regular Customer fields, it will also have another appended field called
     Accounts, as specified in the second line. This is the purpose of the APPEND keyword.
     This field will contain a recordset corresponding to the second Select statement; the
     recordset contains all the fields in the Account table. The condition, specified by the
     RELATE keyword, is that the child recordset for each row will only contain the records
     that match the CustomerKey for that record. The recordset will essentially give you all
▲   the bank accounts for each customer.

The preceding syntax is the simplest form of the SHAPE command. It can also be used to
create multiple nesting of recordsets inside each other. In other words, one recordset can
contain a field that contains a recordset; that recordset can contain another field that
holds a recordset, and so on. Also, aggregate functions can be returned with a field that
contains a recordset that makes up the aggregate.

If you look at the tables for the SmallTownBank application, the SHAPE command can be
used for creating a recordset with a list of customers and their accounts. Figure 11.2 is an
example of what a result set would look like that uses the SHAPE command with the
Customer and Account tables.

FIGURE 11.2

Result set of using the
SHAPE *command with*
the Customer and
Account tables.

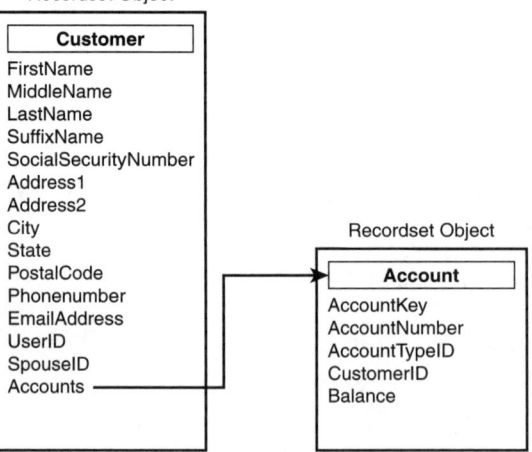

The SHAPE command enables you to return recordsets in a hierarchal method. Visual
Studio has graphical tools that can help you generate your SHAPE commands. Visual
Basic has controls that can display hierarchal recordsets. Instead of using the SHAPE command, the results can be returned in a single recordset, but lots of redundancy would
exist. For every child row, the data in the parent row would be repeated.

The one disadvantage to using the SHAPE command is that, if you are working with a SQL database, you cannot put it into a stored procedure. The SHAPE command is part of ADO, not part of the SQL syntax. It is ADO that manipulates records as they come back from the data store and puts them into an hierarchal form. As a result, you are relegated to passing the code in a SQL string. This decentralizes your data commands because now, instead of having all your SQL commands in your stored procedures, they are now also in your middle tier components. Finally, command execution can be slower then stored procedures because the commands are not compiled.

Sending Data to Requesting Components

After your data component has obtained the requested information, it will need to send the information back to the business logic tier. If you need to send back an individual value, such as an identity value from a newly inserted record, you can pass that as the return value for the function. If you are dealing with a result set consisting of many rows or even a single row of data with multiple columns, you will handle this differently—either with a different return type or parameters that are passed by reference. The two recommended possibilities for this are a disconnected recordset or an XML string. Figure 11.3 displays what you are attempting to do in this section. The data has to go from the data component to the business component.

11

FIGURE 11.3

Sending data back to the business component in Windows DNA.

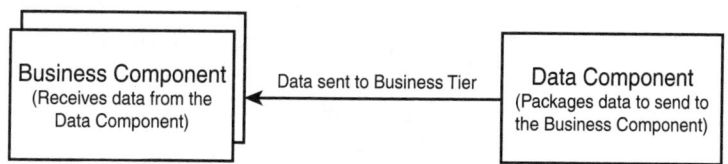

With either a disconnected recordset or an XML string, you will need to pass the object back appropriately so that object is valid. Take a look first at returning a recordset, and then look at what must be done for an XML string.

Returning a Disconnected Recordset

In Listing 11.7, the return value for the function was set directly by executing the Command object:

```
Set Sel_AccountType = cmd.Execute
```

Instead of doing this directly, you can make sure that records were returned from the execution of the store procedure. Listing 11.8 is an example of making this operation a little more robust.

LISTING 11.8 Returning a Recordset

```
1: Set rst = cmd.Execute
2: If not (rst.BOF And rst.EOF) Then
3:     Set Sel_AccountType = rst
4: Else
5:     Err.Raise vbObjectError + 1, "No records", "No records were returned."
6: End If
7: Set rst = Nothing
```

ANALYSIS Line 2 checks the recordset that is returned to see whether there are records in it. If there are records, then the function will set the return value to rst. Otherwise it will raise an error. This will bubble up to the calling component, in which case, the calling component can handle and possibly raise another error. Regardless, this allows you to make sure that a recordset with records is being returned. Of course, there might be a case, where returning no records is perfectly fine. For instance, a customer might not be married and therefore not return a record from the Spouse table. But if you are looking up a customer and her ID doesn't return a record, then that is a problem.

Returning an XML String

With XML you will still want to make sure the object is a recordset and that it has records. But, you will additionally have to go through the process of converting the recordset to a string. ADO 2.1 provides the capability to save an ADO recordset to a file as XML. You can then read the file to get the XML string. In ADO 2.5, the file is bypassed and now you can use a stream object to place it into a string as XML. The function in Listing 11.9 is an example of how to do this.

LISTING 11.9 Obtain an XML String from a Recordset

```
1: Public Function ADOToXML(rst As ADODB.Recordset) As String
2:     Dim str As ADODB.Stream
3:     Set str = New ADODB.Stream
4:     rst.Save str, adPersistXML
5:     ADOToXML = str.ReadText(adReadAll)
6:     Set str = Nothing
7: End Function
```

ANALYSIS The function passes in a recordset and immediately declares a Stream object. As mentioned on Day 6, the stream object is new in ADO 2.5. By using the recordset Save method in line 4, you can store the recordset in the Stream object and then use the stream's ReadText method to return a string. In this case, it is set to the return value of the function.

If you wanted to incorporate this call into your Select statement, you would first need to change the data type of the function's return value to a string. You can then return a string by adding the following line at the end of the function:

```
Sel_AccountType = ADOToXML(rst)
```

With that line of code, you would call the function, which would return the recordset as string. This is relatively easy, but you would want to make sure that this extra function call in each Select does not affect scalability.

Receiving Data Back from Another Component

When data is sent to another component, the next tier has to be able to receive it. This takes you to the third part of moving data through the tiers and represents the business logic tier being able to handle the data it receives. You can look again at Figure 11.3, in which you will be focusing on the business logic tier.

Data can be received back from the user in a variety of ways. If it is an individual value, it can be the return value of a function. Fine for one value, this kind of data transfer is used for many built-in functions such as Date(), IsNumber(), IIF(), and others. But if more then one value is returned, you have to think of other options.

When it comes to data, you can easily pass the information back as a recordset. This allows you the flexibility to return one record with one column or a thousand records with 10 columns. The only disadvantage to this is that an ADO recordset will not be recognized on systems that do not support Microsoft's Data Access technologies.

For a more generic solution, you might want to use XML. A string in XML can be understood by any system. You can use a parser if there is one for that operating system, which should not be a problem given XML's popularity. Otherwise, using string manipulation, you can read the XML yourself. The following two sections take a brief look at handling each of these.

Getting Information Back as a Disconnected Recordset

In receiving the data back from the data component, you will want to make sure that you can handle cases, in which the recordset is empty. For instance, if you are retrieving data from a lookup table to determine whether an account is a checking or a savings account and it doesn't return any records, you will want to raise an error. This error would signal that the account type is not valid. Other times, if no records are returned, it might be acceptable. A customer may have just opened an account and might not have any account transactions yet. In this case, no records being returned is acceptable. Listing 11.10 shows how to work with a recordset returned from a data component.

LISTING **11.10**   Working with a Recordset Returned from a Data Component

```
1: Dim rst as ADODB.Recordset
2: Set rst = objSTB.Sel_AccountType(intAccountTypeKey)
3: If Not (rst.BOF and rst.EOF) Then
4:     txtDescription.Text = rst("Description")
5: End If
6: rst.Close
7: Set rst = Nothing
```

ANALYSIS   Prior to calling the method in the data component, a recordset is declared, but not instantiated. The method will then return a recordset and set it to the declared recordset object, rst. Line 3 checks to see whether records are in the recordset. If there are records, the description in the text box is set to a field in the recordset. After the records have been retrieved, the recordset can now be closed in line 6 and destroyed in line 7.

Tip   If you want to be able to handle the case of the method not returning a recordset, you will want to trap for error 91, "Object variable or With block variable not set." You can modify Listing 11.10 to look like the following:

```
 1: Sub GetAccountType(intAccountTypeKey)
 2: Dim rst as ADODB.Recordset
 3: Dim objSTB As SmallTownBank_Data.BankData
 4: On Error GoTo GetAccountType_Err
 5: Set objSTB = CreateObject("SmallTownBank_Data.BankData")
 6: rst = objSTB.Sel_AccountType(intAccountTypeKey)
 7: If Not (rst.BOF and rst.EOF) Then
 8:     txtDescription.Text = rst("Description")
 9: End If
10: rst.Close
11: Set rst = Nothing
12: Exit Sub
13: GetAccountType_Err:
14:     If Err.Number = 91 Then
15:         Err.Raise 91, "No recordset", "A valid recordset was
 ➥not returned. Please enter a valid AccountTypeKey."
16:     Else
17:         Resume Next
18:     End If
19: End Sub
```

ANALYSIS The On Error statement in line 4 directs the function to the
GetAccountType_Err label when an error occurs. In the Error
handler in line 14, the function checks for the error number. If the error is
91, then you know a valid recordset was not returned, in which case you can
raise an error back to the presentation layer. Error handling such as this
enables you to better inform your users of what is occurring and also
enables you to take an appropriate action when an error does occur.

Getting Information Back as XML

If you are receiving the data back as an XML string, you will either manipulate the XML
string directly or transform it back into an ADO recordset. By working with the string
directly, you will most likely want to use Microsoft's XML Parser, a new feature with
Internet Explorer 5.0. You will be learning more about this parser in Day 12, "The Power
of XML." One thing to keep in mind with the XML Parser though is that it has not
scaled well in the past. Fortunately, Microsoft realized this and fixed or improved many
of the scalability shortcomings. An improved version of XML Parser has been made
available with the release of Windows 2000.

In order to access the XML, you would use the parser to load the XML string into an
XML Document Object Model (DOM). Listing 11.11 gives an example of how you
would do this.

LISTING 11.11   Loading an XML String with the XML Parser

```
1: strXML = objSTB.Sel_AccountType(intAccountTypeKey)
2: Set XMLDoc = Server.CreateObject("Microsoft.XMLDOM")
3: XMLDoc.async = False
4: XMLDoc.loadXML strXML
```

ANALYSIS Here you are assuming the Sel_Account method returns an XML string.
Eventually you will have the ability to tell the methods to return either an XML
string or an ADO recordset, based on the parameter information that you pass. When you
have the string, you create the XMLDOM object in line 2. Setting the async property to
False in line 3 stops processing until the XML string is loaded. Line 4 loads the XML
string. At this point you can access the data in a variety of ways, which you will learn
about tomorrow.

Sending Data Back to the Data Store

When updates, inserts, or deletes have to be made, the information to perform those changes must go across the various DNA tiers. Figure 11.4 displays what is accomplished in this step and completes the round trip for the data coming from and going back to the data store. You can see that the presentation layer initiates an action to send data back to the business component. The business component sends that to the data component and that is finally sent to the data store.

FIGURE 11.4

Sending data back to the data store in Windows DNA.

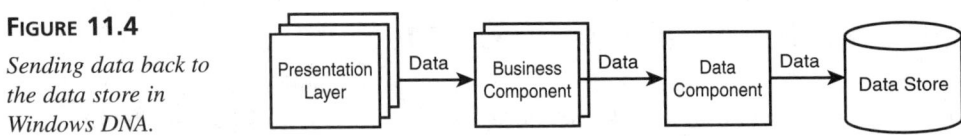

In getting the data to the data store, there are two different scenarios that you have to handle:

- Updates, inserts, and deletes to single records
- Update, inserts, and deletes to multiple records

To handle single records, one of the easiest ways to do this is by passing the information to the data store as parameters to a procedure. This enables you to easily call the procedure without having to do a lot of intermediary steps. Here is an example of a function header that contains the information to be inserted in a record as individual parameters:

```
Public Function DebitAccount(ByVal CustomerID As Integer,
➡ByVal AccountID As Integer, ByVal Amount As Currency) As Boolean
```

This function passes in `CustomerID`, `AccountID`, and the amount to debit the account. This makes this function easy to call and also makes it easy to read the information. The three values passed in can be easily inserted into the stored procedures' parameter values.

Using Recordsets to Pass Information

Instead of sending single records to the data store as individual parameters and multiple records as recordsets, you can do it all with recordsets. By placing new record's information into a recordset and passing that as a parameter, you already have data typing enforced. An example of this would be

```
Public Function DebitAccount(ByVal rstDebitAccount As ADODB.Recordset)
➡As Boolean
```

Also, if your schema changes later on, you will not need to change the interface of your components. The parameter list is still a recordset.

There is some additional work in that you have to create a disconnected recordset, define the fields, and set the values every time you want to perform some type of action on your data store. This can add extra overhead that can be undesirable. Also the data that is marshaled between your components increases because of the extra information that the recordset contains.

In order to handle multiple record updates, you will need to employ a recordset. Most likely you will be using a recordset that was created from the data store. Changes would have been made to more then one record and now you need to write the updates to the data store. At this point you would perform a batch update as was described earlier in today's lesson under "Best Practices for Working with Data."

Exploring Transactional Properties

You have used the Connection object to create a connection with the data store and also to execute SQL statements. Another key feature of the Connection object is the transactional properties that it provides. Through the BeginTrans, CommitTrans, and RollbackTrans methods, you can manage transactions. This is very similar to what you have already done with MTS, but this is specific to a single connection, where MTS can span multiple connections and components.

New Term In the context of a database, a *transaction* is one or more data updates, inserts, or deletes grouped as a single entity. By grouping the actions together, the actions can either all occur or else no actions occur.

Here are explanations of the different transactional methods in the Connection object:

- BeginTrans starts the transaction. After you call this method, all modifications to the database become part of the transaction.

- If at some point you run into a problem, calling the RollbackTrans method will undo all the database changes, back to the point where the BeginTrans was called. This will also end the transaction.

- If all database changes are successfully accomplished, then call CommitTrans. This method commits the changes and also ends the transaction.

In order for transactions to work, they do have to be supported by the provider. The provider would be the source of your data. Two common providers that support transactions are Microsoft SQL Server and Oracle. Listing 11.12 is an example of using the transaction properties of the Connection object.

11

LISTING **11.12**   Creating a Transacted Connection Object

```
 1: Dim cnn as ADODB.Connection
 2: On Error GoTo GetAccountType_Err
 3: Set cnn = New ADODB.Connection
 4: cnn.ConnectionString = "DSN=pubs_dsn;Database=pubs;UID=sa;PWD="
 5: cnn.Open
 6: cnn.BeginTrans
 7: cnn.Execute "UPDATE employee SET fname = 'Brian' WHERE emp_id = 'W-B33228M'"
 8: cnn.Execute "INSERT INTO employee (emp_id, fname, lname) ➥
Values('W-B32218N', 'Charles', 'Smith')"
 9: cnn.CommitTrans
10: cnn.Close
11: Set cnn = Nothing
12: Exit Sub
13: GetAccountType_Err:
14:        cnn.RollbackTrans
15:        cnn.Close
16:        Set cnn = Nothing
17: End Sub
```

ANALYSIS   Line 6 turns on transaction processing with the BeginTrans method. Lines 7 and
8 execute two SQL statements. If these are successful they will continue to line 9
and execute the CommitTrans method. If an error occurs it will go the error handler and
issue a RollbackTrans in line 14.

Handling Errors

ActiveX Data Objects gives us the ability to store a collection of the errors that occur for
a connection and to cycle through them at any given point. This information is stored in
the Errors collection, which is part of the Connection object. Using a For Each command you can loop through the errors.

This is different from looking at the Err object in Visual Basic, which contains only one
error. If a database command that is executed generates multiple database errors, the
Errors collection can be looped through.

It is possible that an error might not get added to the Errors collection, but the application does raise an error in Visual Basic. In this case you might just want to stick with the
Err object. The errors might not be as clear, but it will make error handling easier; you
will not have to check both the ADO Errors collection and the Visual Basic Err object.

Listing 11.13 is an example of looking at the errors collection after the Execute method
is called.

LISTING 11.13   Checking the Errors Collection

```
1: On Error Resume Next
2: Set rst = cmd.Execute
3: If cnn.Errors.Count > 0 Then
4:    For Each objErr in cnn.Errors
5:        strMsg = strMsg & "; " & objErr.Number & ": " & objError.Description
6:    Next
7: End If
```

ANALYSIS   Listing 11.13 assumes that there is a Connection object, cnn, which exists. It checks the count property of the Errors collection in line 3 and, if it is 1 or more, it loops through all the errors and appends them to a string called strMsg in line 5. This string can be taken, and an error can be raised.

Error handling is a requirement for any robust application. The benefits of giving customers appropriate errors and enabling the system to gracefully recover easily justifies the extra work error handling takes. Besides deciding on how to handle errors, there are other items to consider as well. You may also want to develop a coding standard for your team, a method of documenting your code, and a schedule for doing code reviews of other developer's code. Like any part of Windows DNA, these items will take planning before you begin your development, but increases the chances of your project being a success.

Summary

Today's lesson expanded your knowledge on ActiveX Data Objects. It gave you the knowledge you needed to be able to construct your data and business components. Specifically, you learned how you should retrieve data from the data store and how to send data back to requesting components. You also learned how the requesting components can receive the data and finally how to send data back to the data store. In this process you learned about disconnected and hierarchal recordsets in ADO 2.x and also how to do batch updates.

Day 12 will look at the capabilities of XML. You will learn about XML syntax and also about how XML can have schemas defining how a XML document is constructed. Accessing data in an XML document will be covered and also how ADO 2.x works with XML data.

11

Q&A

Q I am trying to use the `RecordCount` property with a recordset, but it just returns a –1. Why?

A If you open a recordset with the default `CursorType` and `LockType`, it will return –1, indicating the record count is unknown. This is because with a forward-only, read-only cursor, ADO cannot cycle through the recordset to get the record count. Change the `CursorType` and `LockType` to get a record count. For instance, set them to be static and use optimistic locking. The penalty you pay for this is speed, so you might want to be careful and only do this when necessary.

Q When my component receives the recordset from the data component, it is empty or Null. What's wrong?

A Make sure you are not using the `Close` method on the recordset in the calling component. Most likely the component is being closed and therefore the calling component gets no data back. The following code will close the recordset that gets returned:

```
Set rst = cmd.Execute
Set Sel_AccountType = rst
rst.Close
```

Remove the `rst.Close` to successfully return the recordset.

Q What happens if I retrieve some records and while I am modifying them someone else updates the record(s)? Then when I go to update them, the previous updates are lost.

A This is known as a *collision*. People have often managed this by having a "Date When Last Modified" column in each table, and checking to see whether this date changes between retrieving the record and doing an update. Fortunately, ADO can handle this for you with the `Update Criteria` property. Combined with the `Resync` method and the `Filter` property, this enables you to successfully navigate an environment in which multiple users might be updating the same record.

Workshop

The Workshop provides quiz questions to help you solidify your understanding of the material covered and exercises to provide you with experience in using what you've learned. Try to understand the quiz and exercise answers before continuing to the next lesson. Answers are provided in Appendix A.

Quiz

1. What's the difference between ADODB and ADOR?
2. What collection and method do you use to add additional columns to a recordset you are creating from scratch?
3. What does the CursorLocation property need to be set to for a disconnected recordset?
4. What is the new object in ADO 2.5 that enables you to easily convert a recordset to an XML string?
5. What is the command that enables you to return a hierarchal recordset?

Exercises

1. Create a Visual Basic group that has an ActiveX DLL project and a Standard EXE. In the DLL, add a method that calls the pubs database and retrieves a record. Have the form display the results in a text box.

2. Modify the SmallTownBank components. If you look at the SmallTownBank\11\ Start, some changes have been made to the project. Many of the functions that contained only a function declaration in both the SmallTownBank_Data and the SmallTownBank_Business components have been filled in with code. A comment has been added to the procedures designating the code has been added for Day 11. Also, there has been an error handler that has been added to the SmallTownBank_Business component that can be called to easily raise errors.

   Your first task is to add in functions to handle all the standard stored procedures calls that will insert, update, delete, and select all the records from the tables. The code for these will be added to the BankData class of the SmallTownBank_Data component and can be cut and pasted from Standard procedures for BankData class.txt. This will also add in a function to use as a standard error handler and also a function to replace GetConnectionString. Modify CreditAccount and DebitAccount to use the error handler. The new GetConnectionString function will get information from the registry.

   Next, in the DownloadAccountActivity and DownloadAccountBalance procedures in the BankBusiness class add in an If...Else statement that checks the Integer parameter, FileFormat, on whether to return a recordset or an XML string. For now, you will just be returning a recordset. Therefore, you don't have to add any code for the XML case right now.

   Finally, modify the procedures Sel_AccountsByCustomerID and GetCustomer in the BankData class to check whether records are returned. If there are no records returned, raise an error.

11

DAY **12**

The Power of XML

Today we cover how to work with XML in the business components using the XMLDOM object and the ADO 2.x XML capabilities. We will build business objects that work with XML. XML is a very powerful way to move data across the Internet because it is self-defining and technology independent. XML is quickly becoming the standard for moving data between systems, and thus it is important that you understand how to work with it. XML is purely a way to describe and structure data. It needs a supporting language, definitions, and technology to be usable. We will cover all these topics in this chapter.

NEW TERM   *eXtensible Markup Language (XML)* is a way to represent data using tags. The XML tags define the element name and attributes, thus XML is self-defining. XML elements can be nested within each other allowing hierarchical structures to be represented. The specific details and examples of XML are the basis of this chapter.

You will learn how to load XML-encoded data into a document tree and then work with the elements of that tree. You will also learn how to use ADO 2.x to create, load, work with, and save XML data.

This chapter is not intended to teach you everything you need to know about XML—the subject is a book unto itself. We want to give you insights and lessons learned to make working with XML easier. We are covering the Microsoft XML engine: Other XML engines work similarly but might have slight differences in their object models. Everything you need to know about XML can be found at `http://www.w3.org` or `http://msdn.microsoft.com/xml`.

In fact, because of the constantly changing standards on the Internet, it is better to have a Web site than a bound book for specific details. After today, you will have learned

- What XML is and its related technologies
- Why you should use XML
- When to use XML
- How to use XML

Microsoft's Push to Be a Leader in XML

Microsoft has built XML capabilities into every 2000 product. At the base of all of the 2000 product releases is Windows 2000 which has native XML support. The XML subsystem is constantly being updated to support the emerging standards and to improve performance. Within Microsoft's line of servers, all of them are being updated to work with XML as a native data transport and storage format. Internally within a Microsoft system you can expect that XML is to be the preferred data format for interoperability between the server products. In fact, Microsoft is adding a new BizTalk server which is responsible for transforming data between disparate formats and XML. XML will then be the native format that it and other server products work.

Microsoft Office 2000 can use XML as a native format. When you select to save a document as HTML, a combination of HTML and XML is written to the file system. The reason that XML is used is because HTML does not have the capability to store all the information needed to preserve the document's fidelity. When you view an HTML document created with Office 2000 in Internet Explorer 5.0, it looks as if you are viewing the document in the native application. And, in fact, the native application (Word, Excel, PowerPoint) can read and write the document without any loss in quality or functionality. This is a good example of how XML is being used to solve real-world problems. In the case of Office 2000, now documents can be created and posted on the Internet, and anyone with Internet Explorer can view the document with all the formatting intact without having to own the application that created the document.

Introducing Hierarchical Data Structures

Hierarchical data structures are everywhere in computing yet, until recently, you have not had an easy way to work with them. What are hierarchical data structures? They look like trees (see Figure 12.1). You use them every day when you use the Windows operating system. Mapped into the namespace of Windows are directory trees. The Windows Explorer represents all the objects in your system as a tree view. Expand and contract the tree (click the [+] and [-] symbols, respectively), and you can view the various nodes of that tree. This sort of hierarchical view has become very commonplace yet the traditional forms of storing and representing data have not improved to work with this data—that is, not until recently with the addition of XML engines to relational databases.

As you recall from Day 4, "Exploring Database Fundamentals," data is represented in tables in the form of rows and columns. In order to have hierarchical representation, you need to create other tables for the associated data using keys to link them. So far, so good. Now when you want to retrieve a resultset that uses joins between multiple tables, what happens? A single row column table is returned with all the results. In the join process, the relational database management system (RDBMS) denormalizes the data and repeats data values to fill empty cells. This is not the best way to return data if you want it represented as a tree. In this chapter, you will see how XML can preserve the normalization of the data by being able to represent data hierarchically. Often times XML is panned because it is verbose because everything is represented as text, however, the fact that it can represent data hierarchically allows it to reduce data duplication and thus with complex dataset it can produce a smaller resultset.

Tip

> Get comfortable working with hierarchical data. It is a fantastic way to create order in a complex environment. All Microsoft products will eventually represent their data structures hierarchically, if they do not already. All these products will either use or have the capability to use XML as a native format.

The XML Data Tree

The best way to understand how data is represented within XML is to see it as a tree (see Figure 12.1). It is very intuitive to see that everything starts from a root element and then branches out with the end nodes typically representing the data. The reason I say typically is because the root and branch nodes can contain data in the form of attributes.

12

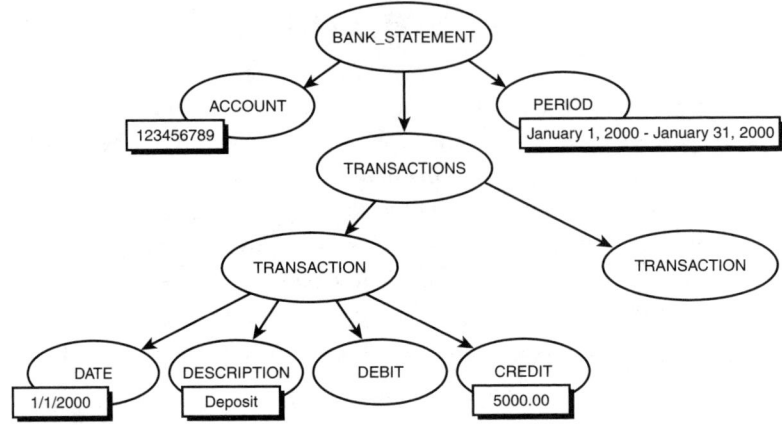

Exploring XML Syntax

The XML syntax is the same as HTML, but stricter. This strictness is a good thing because it has caused the HTML standard to be updated to XHTML, which is no surprise. By having HTML that complies with XML standards, you no longer are tied to the browser for rendering HTML. The problem has been that the loose standards around HTML required all sorts of exceptions in the code to try to render the pages. XHTML actually makes the pages more universal, which is what HTML was supposed to be in the first place.

The XML syntax has the following rules:

- The first standard for XML is that all tags must have a closing tag. No exceptions. HTML was known for having unary tags such as <p>, <br>, and <hr>. To be compliant with the XML standard, they must be well formatted and now must have a closing tag such as <p></p> and
</br> or use the short hand <p /> and <br />.

- The next area in which XML tightens the HTML standard is that all attribute values must be contained in quotes, for example, <TAG MYATTRIB="RED" />. The attribute MYATTRIB has a value of RED.

- XML requires that all tags be contained within a single root node so that it can know when the XML data should end. For example, we see in Listing 12.1:

LISTING 12.1   XML Data Tree

```
 1: <BANK_STATEMENT>
 2:      <ACCOUNT>123456789</ACCOUNT>
 3: <PERIOD>January 1, 2000 to January 31, 2000</PERIOD>
 4: <TRANSACTIONS>
 5:           <TRANSACTION>
 6:                <DATE>1/1/2000</DATE>
 7:              <DESCRIPTION>Deposit</DESCRIPTION>
 8:               <DEBIT />
 9:               <CREDIT>5000</CREDIT>
10:         </TRANSACTION>
11:        <TRANSACTION>
12:                <DATE>1/3/2000</DATE>
13:              <DESCRIPTION>Check 101</DESCRIPTION>
14:              <DEBIT>123.45</DEBIT>
15:              <CREDIT />
16:         </TRANSACTION>
17:... (continue repeating for all transactions)
18:      </TRANSACTIONS>
19: </BANK_STATEMENT>
```

- All tags must nest completely. If the tags are not properly nested, the parser will fail to understand the data and will generate an error.

  For example, the following code will not work:

  ```
  <BANK_STATEMENT><ACCOUNT>123456789<PERIOD>January 1,2000 - January 31,2000
      ➥</ACCOUNT></PERIOD></BANK_STATEMENT>
  ```

  You can see that the <ACCOUNT> and <PERIOD> tags overlap. This is not allowed.

  The nesting needs to look like this:

  ```
  <BANK_STATEMENT>
  <ACCOUNT>123456789</ACCOUNT>
  <PERIOD>January 1,2000 - January 31,2000</PERIOD>
  </BANK_STATEMENT>
  ```

  The use of line breaks and indentation can help keep the tags from overlapping.

- The XML document must start with a special line called an XML declaration. The XML declaration tells the receiver of the document that what follows is XML rather than HTML or some other markup text. Because XML is an open standard, it is possible that an HTML keyword could be used as a markup tag. Without the XML declaration, the browser would see and render the tags it knew as HTML and discard the rest. The XML declaration is

  ```
  <?xml version="1.0"?>
  ```

12

The XML declaration might optionally include the character encoding being used. To specify UTF-8 (an 8-bit encoding of 16-bit Unicode), for example, you do this:

```
<?xml version="1.0" encoding="UTF-8"?>
```

Notice that the single XML declaration is identified by being enclosed in the `<?xml` and `?>` delimiter pair, and by having a version attribute. In addition, the word `xml` must be in lowercase.

- XML is case sensitive. This is an area that can cause a great deal of trouble because not only are the tags case sensitive, but the parameters to the methods you use to work with XML data are as well. For example, I spent hours one day getting the case correct in a directory path. As you know, you can have mixed case in an NT file path, and it can take some time to get the exact path case correct. I mention this because the errors you get don't point to the fact that the case does not match. This could cause you much aggravation when trying to resolve the problem. In our case, the problem showed up when the application was moved from stage to production. This is frustrating because you are "live" with a "dead" application, and you don't know why. Fortunately, Microsoft has fixed this problem with Windows 2000; however, you should still be aware of it because you might run into an old MSXML.DLL that exhibits this behavior.

You can check out the official W3C specification for XML at `http://www.w3.org/TR`. Microsoft has also developed an XML specification site at `http://www.microsoft.com/xml`.

Exploring XML Elements

Like HTML elements, XML elements are the items that make up the structure of the file. An element consists of the opening tag, the attributes (if any), the data, and the closing tag. If the element contains nested sub elements, they are considered to be part of the element in a parent/child relationship.

 Note

> Valid element names must start with an alphabetic character (A to Z or a to z) or an underscore (_). The remainder of the name can consist of letters, digits, hyphens, underscores, or periods. Strings that begin with xml or XML (or any combination of upper- or lowercase) are reserved and should not be used. Case is significant, so make sure that you are consistent.

Element Attributes

As in HTML, you can use attributes within the opening tag to attach specific values to an element. Unlike HTML, XML attributes are case sensitive and must be enclosed in quotes. Data can be represented in the element as an attribute or as the text between the tags. When we look at the Document Object Model (DOM), you will see that these two types of data are represented differently within the document tree and are thus accessed differently. There are no rules for where to place data. However, you will find that it is easier to retrieve values from the element attributes. An example of an XML statement with its attributes defined follows:

```
<TAG ATTRIB1="ATDATA">Data</TAG>
```

XML Schemas and Namespaces

An XML schema defines the tag hierarchy for a specific XML file. XML allows for great flexibility in the definition of the tags and how they are nested. This open structure is a double-edged sword because the disadvantage of such flexibility is that it is difficult for the receiving program to add any context to the data. The receiving program has to add a great deal of logic to understand the relationships and structure of the data. We will see how schemas solve this problem.

Namespaces allow multiple schemas to be used at the same time within a document. It is not hard to see that as you do more with XML, you will eventually be working with multiple XML documents. Namespaces are a way to keep these documents logically separated. We will look at how namespaces are implemented.

12

Data Type Declaration (DTD)

The traditional way to define a schema is to develop a Data Type Declaration (DTD). The DTD defines the valid tags that are contained within an XML document, the location of those tags within the documents XML tree, and the data type of the values contained within the tags. XML data is represented as text so that it can easily transmit across the Internet; however, not all data is text. DTD allows you to specify the data type and acceptable values. In this way, the application receiving the XML data can retrieve the DTD and know how to apply it so that data validation rules to the XML data.

A DTD specification might look like

```
<!DOCTYPE BANK_STATEMENT [
<!ELEMENT ACCOUNT(#PCDATA)>
<!ELEMENT PERIOD(#PCDATA)>
```

```
<!ELEMENT TRANSACTIONS (TRANSCATION)>
<!ELEMENT TRANSACTION (DATE DESCRIPTION,
         ➥DEBIT, CREDIT)>
<!ELEMENT DATE (#PCDATA)>
<!ELEMENT DESCRIPTION(#PCDATA)>
<!ELEMENT DEBIT(#PCDATA)>
<!ELEMENT CREDIT(#PCDATA)>
]>
```

What you see is that an XML data set of type BANK_STATEMENT looks like Listing 12.2.

LISTING 12.2 XML Data Set

```
 1: <BANK_STATEMENT>
 2:   <ACCOUNT>123456789</ACCOUNT>
 3: <PERIOD>January 1, 2000 to January 31, 2000</PERIOD>
 4:      <TRANSACTIONS>
 5:         <TRANSACTION>
 6:             <DATE>1/1/2000</DATE>
 7:             <DESCRIPTION>Deposit</DESCRIPTION>
 8:             <DEBIT />
 9:             <CREDIT>5000</CREDIT>
10:         </TRANSACTION>
11:         <TRANSACTION>
12:             <DATE>1/3/2000</DATE>
13:             <DESCRIPTION>Check 101</DESCRIPTION>
14:             <DEBIT>123.45</DEBIT>
15:             <CREDIT />
16:         </TRANSACTION>
17:      </TRANSACTIONS>
18: </BANK_STATEMENT>
```

The data type is very loosely defined as any character data. This book is not going to get into the specifications for the DTD language. The purpose is to illustrate that the DTD syntax is very different from XML syntax.

If you want to learn more about DTD, visit http://www.w3.org/ or http://msdn.microsoft.com/xml/. You will need to drill around to find information specific to DTD as other specifications are starting to win approval.

XML Schema

The problem with using DTDs is that they defeat the goal of XML being self-contained. To use a DTD, the application must know how to read and enforce the DTD. As you can see, the DTD syntax is not at all like XML and thus requires different rules to interpret the code. DTD syntax is very complex because it needs to be to define complex document structure in SGML. Standard Generalized Markup Language (SGML) is the parent of HTML and XML. XML and HTML are subsets of SGML. HTML is an application of SGML and thus has a very complex DTD that defines its syntax. You can find the DTD for HTML at http://www.w3c.org. The best analogy I could come up with to describe the relationship of DTD to XML is a situation in which each person would receive a French-German translation dictionary with every French document, but everyone speaks English. This would require everyone to know three languages in order to understand the letter. With XML schemas, the dictionary is French-English, which requires only two languages to understand the document.

To resolve this situation, Microsoft has proposed and submitted a specification for XML-based schemas. The XML schema is as complex as any DTD schema; however, it is written in XML so that it is easier to understand because it follows the same syntactical rules. The XML schema for the previous DTD example looks like Listing 12.3.

LISTING 12.3 XML Schema

```
 1: <?xml version="1.0"?>
 2: <Schema name="bankStatementSchema"
 3:     xmlns="urn:schemas-microsoft-com:xml-data"
 4:     xmlns:dt="urn:schemas-microsoft-com:datatypes">
 5: <ElementType name="ACCOUNT" content="number" model="closed">
 6:     <description>The account number</description>
 7: </ElementType>
 8: <ElementType name="PERIOD" content="textOnly" model="closed">
 9:     <description>The dates the statement covers</description>
10: </ElementType>
11: <ElementType name="DATE" content="date" model="closed">
12:     <description>The transaction date</description>
13: </ElementType>
14: <ElementType name="DESCRIPTION" content="textOnly" model="closed">
15:     <description>The transaction description</description>
16: </ElementType>
17: <ElementType name="DEBIT" content="number" model="closed">
18:     <description>Filled if the transaction is a debit</description>
19: </ElementType>
20: <ElementType name="CREDIT" content="number" model="closed">
21:     <description>Filled if the transaction is a credit</description>
22: </ElementType>
23: <ElementType name="TRANSACTION" content="eltOnly" model="closed">
24:     <description>The details of a transaction</description>
25:     <element type="DATE" />
26:     <element type="DESCRIPTION" />
27:     <element type="DEBIT" />
28:     <element type="CREDIT" />
29: </ElementType>
30: <ElementType name="TRANSACTIONS" content="eltOnly" model="closed">
```

12

continues

LISTING 12.3   continued

```
31:     <description>The list of transaction</description>
32:     <element type="TRANSACTION" />
33: </ElementType>
34: <ElementType name="BANK_STATEMENT" content="eltOnly" model="closed">
35:     <description>The bank statement data</description>
36:     <element type="ACCOUNT" />
37:     <element type="PERIOD" />
38:     <element type="TRANSACTIONS" />
39: </ElementType>
40: </Schema>
```

ANALYSIS This schema is more verbose than the DTD schema, but it is more understandable. The first couple of lines in the schema are required in order to locate the schema specifications. After that everything is described in element type blocks. This is a very simple example of a schema. There are many more attributes that can be used to describe the elements. Take a look at the `bankstatement.xml` for Day 20, "Office 2000 and Web Components," and you will see many more attributes being used.

One topic that is not going to be covered in depth here, however, you should be aware of is the XML Data Reducer (XDR) specification. XDR is a short-hand specification for communicating data-types and other attributes within an XMLSchema. By employing XDR the size of the schema can be reduced and thus make the stream smaller which improves transportation and processing efficiency. For more information on XMLScema and XDR, see `http://msdn.microsoft.com/xml/reference/schema/start.asp`.

To tell the XML parser to use the schema, modify the opening tag for the block as follows:

```
<BANK_STATEMENT xmlns="x-schema:bankStatementSchema.xml">
```

The `xmlns="x-schema:bankStatementSchema.xml"` designates to the parser to use the defined schema when evaluating the XML document's validity beyond being well formatted.

Namespaces

Because XML allows users to define their own tag names, it is possible that two XML schemas will have tags with the same name. To resolve this, you can assign each schema to its own name space.

Suppose that you want to use both of the following XML files in an application, as seen in Listing 12.4.

LISTING 12.4   XML Document Without Namespaces Added

```
 1: <JOB>
 2: <TITLE>Consultant</TITLE>
 3: <EMPLOYEE>
 4:         <FIRST_NAME>John</FIRST_NAME>
 5:         <LAST_NAME>Doe</LAST_NAME>
 6: </EMPLOYEE>
 7: </JOB>

 8: <BOOKS>
 9:    <BOOK>
10:        <TITLE>Sams Teach Yourself Windows DNA in 21 Days</TITLE>
11:        <AUTHOR>
12:            <FIRST_NAME>Michael</FIRST_NAME>
13:            <LAST_NAME>Rockwell</LAST_NAME>
14:        </AUTHOR>
15:    </BOOK>
16: </BOOKS>
```

You will notice that TITLE, FIRST_NAME, and LAST_NAME have name conflicts. The program might be confused as to which element in which schema you are referring. The way to resolve this problem is to add a namespace to the XML document. The new XML documents would look like Listing 12.5.

LISTING 12.5   XML Document with Namespaces Added

```
 1: <JOB xmlns:job="http://www.somecompany.com/ns/job/">
 2: <job:TITLE>Consultant</job:TITLE>
 3: <job:EMPLOYEE>
 4:         <job:FIRST_NAME>John</job:FIRST_NAME>
 5:         <job:LAST_NAME>Doe</job:LAST_NAME>
 6: </job:EMPLOYEE>
 7: </JOB>
 8:
 9: <BOOK xmlns:book="http://www.somecompany.com/ns/book/">
10:    <book:TITLE>Sams Teach Yourself Windows DNA in 21 Days</book:TITLE>
11:    <book:AUTHOR>
12:        <book:FIRST_NAME>Michael</book:FIRST_NAME>
13:        <book:LAST_NAME>Rockwell</book:LAST_NAME>
14:    </book:AUTHOR>
15:</BOOK>
```

12

ANALYSIS   You can see that all the elements have a prefix that designates the namespace to which it belongs. Now when you access an ambiguous element programmatically, you can be specific by using the namespace prefix.

Using the XML Document Object Model

When you load an XML document, it is mapped into a document tree. This document tree has an associated object model that allows you to navigate and access elements programmatically. The majority of your programming time will be working within this document object model, so we will cover it in some detail. The concept of an XML Document Object Model (XMLDOM) is relatively new. The XMLDOM is similar to the DHTML DOM found in Microsoft Internet Explorer. We will be using the XML2 Document Object Model found in Internet Explorer 5.0. Actually, XML2 can be installed separately from IE5 because it is not exclusive to the Web browser. The XMLDOM can be used in any program. See the following Note on installing XML2.

> **Note**
>
> XML2 is officially named Microsoft XML Parser. The parser can be found at http://msdn.microsoft.com/downloads. Select Tools and then select Microsoft Downloads, MS XML Parser. A newer more efficient version is also in the works so don't be surprised to find XML3 or later available. The standards around XML are evolving very quickly and Microsoft is updating its parsers to keep current with these evolving standards.

We first need to make some distinctions between client-side and server-side processing of XML.

Client-Side XML

Currently Internet Explorer 5.0 is the only browser that can work with client-side XML. This is because the XML2 parser is integrated with IE5. The types of things that you do on the client side are generally related to the display of data from an XML document or Data Island. A data island is XML that has been embedded within the HTML/DHTML document.

If you send just the XML to the IE5 browser, it will be displayed in a List view like the one seen in Figure 12.2.

XML can be formatted for display in a number of different ways. The typical way is to use Cascading Style Sheets (CSS), tabular data binding, and eXtensible Style Language (XSL).

Cascading Style Sheet Formatting

The easiest way to format XML data is to use Cascading Style Sheets. A style sheet allows you to define a set of style properties for named element name. A style sheet allows you to separate the presentation attributes from the formatting and the data.

Presentation characteristics can be based upon an element's name or attributes. The three elements that come together are XML for the data, HTML for the formatting, and CSS for the presentation attributes. In the following example, we are going to leave out the HTML component because you have not covered it. HTML will be covered on Day 17, "Using DHTML for the Presentation Tier," and Day 19, "Thin HTML—Reach Clients." In Figure 12.3, you can see how the CSS has styled the XML.

Figure 12.2

IE5 XML List view.

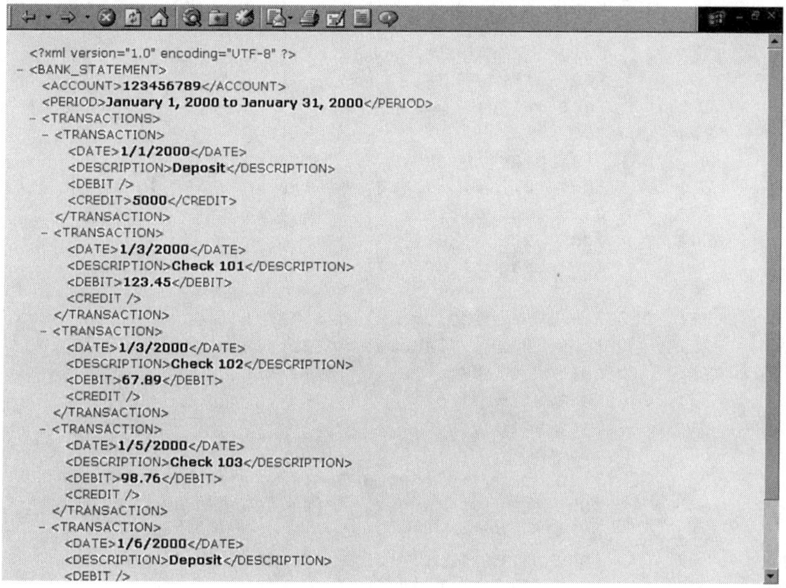

A style sheet for the bank statement's XML document would look something like Listing 12.6.

Listing 12.6 Bank Style Sheet

```
1:   BANK_STATEMENT          { display:block; margin:10px }
2:
3:   ACCOUNT        {display:inline;
4:       font-family: Tahoma, Arial, sans-serif;
5:       color: black;
6:       font-size: 14pt;
7:       font-weight: bold }
8:
```

continues

LISTING **12.6**   continued

```
 9:   PERIOD  {display:block; margin:10px;
10:       font-family: Tahoma, Arial, sans-serif;
11:       color: darkgray;
12:       font-size: 14pt;
13:       font-weight: bold }
14:
15:   TRANSACTION  {display:block; margin:10px;
16:       font-family: Tahoma, Arial, sans-serif;
17:       color: darkgray;
18:       font-size: 12pt;
19:       font-weight: bold }
20:
21:   DATE {display:inline;
22:       font-family: Tahoma, Arial, sans-serif;
23:       color: purple;
24:       font-size: 12pt;
25:       font-weight: bold }
26:
27:   DESCRIPTION {display:inline; margin:10px;
28:       font-family: Tahoma, Arial, sans-serif;
29:       color: black;
30:       font-size: 12pt;
31:       font-weight: bold }
32:
33:   DEBIT {display:inline;margin:10px;
34:       font-family: Tahoma, Arial, sans-serif;
35:       color: red;
36:       font-size: 12pt;
37:       font-weight: bold }
38:
39:   CREDIT {display:inline;margin:10px;
40:       font-family: Tahoma, Arial, sans-serif;
41:       color: green;
42:       font-size: 12pt;
43:       font-weight: bold }
```

You need to tell the XML parser to use the CSS to format the data as specified by the CSS. You do this by including the following instruction at the top of your XML file after the `<?xml version="1.0"?>` declaration:

```
<?xml-stylesheet type="text/css" href="bankstatement.css"?>
```

This tells the parser to load the CSS. The resulting document looks like Figure 12.3.

FIGURE 12.3

CSS-formatted XML.

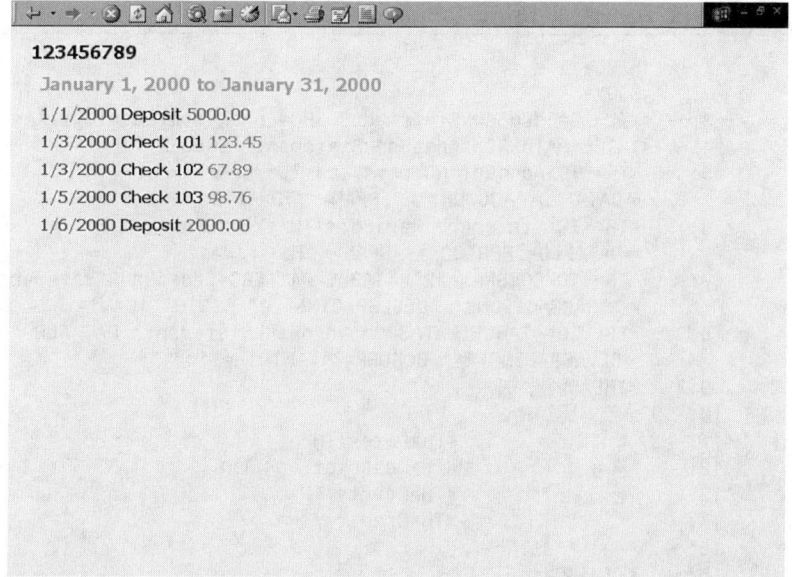

123456789

January 1, 2000 to January 31, 2000

1/1/2000 **Deposit** 5000.00

1/3/2000 **Check 101** 123.45

1/3/2000 **Check 102** 67.89

1/5/2000 **Check 103** 98.76

1/6/2000 **Deposit** 2000.00

Tabular Data Binding

Note

> The material in this section is an enhancement to HTML, which you will not learn until Day 17. You may want to come back to this section after Day 17. Or you can read through it to get a sense of how tabular data binding works.

12

Tabular data binding extends the capabilities of the table HTML tags to display XML data. Tabular Data Binding is a capability only found in IE 4 and IE 5. New attributes have been added to the table markup syntax to allow XML to be automatically displayed in HTML tables. Within the TABLE tag, the DATASRC (data source) attribute designates which XML data source to use for the entire table. This sets up the binding between the table and the data source. It is possible to use multiple DATASRCs, in which case, you would specify the DATASRC within the SPAN. (A span is a way to section off parts of a HTML page.) Within the TBODY (table body) section, the data rows are repeated for each instance of the data within the XML data source. Within the TD (table data) tag, you specify the element within a SPAN or DIV (another way to section off parts of a HTML page) using the DATAFLD (data field) attribute (see Listing 12.7).

LISTING 12.7   HTML Using Tabular Data Binding

```
 1:   <HTML>
 2:   <BODY>
 3:   <XML ID="dsoBankStatement" SRC="bank_statement.xml"></XML>
 4:   <TABLE DATASRC="#dsoBankStatement" BORDER="1">
 5:    <TR><TD>Account Number</TD><TD><SPAN
      ➥DATAFLD="ACCOUNT"></SPAN></TD></TR>
 6:    <TR><TD>Statement Period:</TD><TD><SPAN
      ➥DATAFLD="PERIOD"></SPAN></TD></TR>
 7:    <TR><TD COLSPAN="2"><TABLE DATASRC="#dsoBankStatement" DATAFLD=
      ➥"TRANSACTIONS"  CELLSPACING="0" WIDTH="100%">
 8:    <TR><TD><TABLE DATASRC="#dsoBankStatement" DATAFLD="TRANSACTION"
      ➥CELLSPACING="1" BORDER="1" WIDTH="100%">
 9:    <THEAD>
10:         <TR>
11:                 <TH>Date</TH>
12:                 <TH>Description</TH>
13:                 <TH>Debit</TH>
14:                 <TH>Credit</TH>
15:         </TR>
16:    </THEAD>
17:    <TBODY>
18:         <TR>
19:             <TD><SPAN DATAFLD="DATE"></SPAN> </TD>
20:             <TD><SPAN DATAFLD="DESCRIPTION"></SPAN> </TD>
21:             <TD><SPAN DATAFLD="DEBIT"></SPAN> </TD>
22:             <TD><SPAN DATAFLD="CREDIT"></SPAN> </TD>
23:         </TR>
24:    </TBODY>
25:    </TABLE>
26:    </TD></TR>
27:   </TABLE></TD></TR>
28:   </TABLE>
29:   </BODY>
30:   </HTML>
```

The use of the TBODY (table body) or THEAD (table heading) tags is not mandatory. IE will be able to repeat the bound elements automatically. However, in terms of style, it helps to set apart the repeating elements from the static elements.

Another attribute that is not used in the example is DATAFORMATAS. This attribute allows you to specify either TEXT, which is the default or HTML, which specifies that the browser should display any HTML content within the value. Note that HTML cannot be included in an XML document unless it is marked up in a special way. For example, to represent <B>Hello</B>, you would need to write it to read <B>Hello</B>. Special characters in HTML have an alternate representation; in this example, < has < as its alternate representation. If the less than or greater than symbol had been included in the XML element data, the parser would have difficulty determining if the symbol was part of the element data or the tag.

Another issue with binding to XML is that it can be hierarchical. To accommodate this you would include another table within a TD element to represent the child elements. The child elements will then repeat for each child within that table. You can see in our example that we have done this twice—first with the TRANSACTIONS tag, and then again with the TRANSACTION tag because it contains the DATE, DESCRIPTION, DEBIT, and CREDIT tags.

You tell the browser how to load and display the XML document by specifying the ID and source of the XML document within the new XML HTML tag as we have done in this example. The XML tag is a new HTML tag that was introduced with IE 5.0. It is an HTML tag, not an XML tag, so it requires that you use HTML syntax. Within this tag, you could include a data island or a reference to an external XML file as we have done by using the SRC attribute. Figure 12.4 shows you the final result. The source code is available on the CD-ROM accompanying this book.

FIGURE 12.4

Data bound output.

Account Number	123456789
Statement Period:	January 1, 2000 to January 31, 2000

Date	Description	Debit	Credit
1/1/2000	Deposit		5000
1/3/2000	Check 101	123.45	
1/3/2000	Check 102	67.89	
1/5/2000	Check 103	98.76	
1/6/2000	Deposit		2000

12

NEW TERM   A *data island* refers to the embedding of the XML document within the HTML document. This is done by placing the XML code within the XML tags.

Data binding is also supported within IE 4.0 through the use of a Java class. You can invoke this Java class with the following code:

```
<APPLET CODE="com.ms.xml.dso.XMLDSO.class"
    ID="dsoBankStatement" WIDTH=0 HEIGHT=0 MAYSCRIPT=true>
    <PARAM NAME="URL" VALUE="bankstatement.xml">
 </APPLET>
```

This is an introduction to XML data binding. You can find more information at `http://msdn.microsoft.com/xml/c-frame.htm?946332275020#/xml/xmlguide/default.asp`.

eXtensible Style Language (XSL)

XSL is a very large topic and at the time of the writing of this book was still being formalized by the W3C. XSL and the associated XML Query Language (XQL) allow you to control how XML data is displayed. The final standard is expected to include techniques for styling output to a number of different devices such as printers and various page readers. XSL is more than just a styling language; it is a transformation language. Typically you will be transforming XML into HTML; however, XSL can transform the XML data into any format you would like. XSL can create new elements or remove existing ones, so you are not tied into the current Cascading Style Sheet model of applying style to existing elements. XSL has condition and iteration logic that enables it to do very sophisticated things with the XML data.

To tell the browser to process the XML data using the XSL template, add the following directive:

```
<?xml-stylesheet type="text/xsl" href="bankstatement.xsl" ?>
```

This should look very similar to the directive used for the CSS. We are not going to be able to cover this exciting topic; to do so to any real depth could easily take another book. For the specifics on this new styling language, check http://www.3w.org or http://msdn.microsoft.com/xml/.

eXtensible Style Language Transformation (XSLT)

eXtensible Style Language Transformation (XSLT) is a subset of XSL. The way that XSLT came about was that the specification for XSL is very extensive and thus the module for processing XSL is very complex. Microsoft needed a very efficient transformation engine, primarily for BizTalk Server, and thus developed and proposed that the transformation specification should be broken out of the XSL specification. The W3C agreed and thus the creation of XSLT.

XML transformations are very important for the ability for heterogeneous systems to manipulate the XML data into a format that is understandable by different systems. XSLT thus needs to be very efficient in the processing of the data because a modern business system may be dealing with hundreds of transformations per second.

Server-Side XML

The XMLDOM can also be used on the server side to allow your program to be able to work with XML data easily. Naturally you could do your own parsing or use another parser; however, the Microsoft parser is fully COM compliant and loaded with useful methods. The real challenge when getting started is learning the XMLDOM structure and the object hierarchy.

The highest level object is the document. Within the document, you have nodes. The nodes can nest many levels deep. All nodes have a parent-child relationship. Another object that exists is the NodeList, a collection object that allows you to enumerate and iterate through the nodes. A variation on the NodeList is the NamedNodeMap, which allows you to locate and reference nodes by name rather than by index. The NamedNodeMap allows you to iterate through child nodes that are not from the same parent. Without this capability, you would need to traverse all the branches looking for all the nodes you were interested in working with. I find that the NamedNodeMap capability makes easy work of working with XML data.

Note

There are two versions of the Microsoft.XMLDOM: a rental (apartment-threaded) version and a free-threaded one. The rental version is designed for single-threaded programming and the free-threaded version is designed for multiple-threaded access. When using the XMLDOM on the server side, you will want to use the free-threaded version. It is instantiated by calling `CreateObject("Microsoft.FreeThreadedXMLDOM")`. The performance is not as good as the single-threaded version, but you will avoid bottlenecks because of resource contention. Your overall throughput will be better.

Server-Side XSL Usage

As you recall, XSL is made up of templates that apply patterns and filters against the XML data. The XML data that matches the pattern is then transformed as specified to a new output format. Instead of transforming the XML to HTML, you could use XSL to transform the XML to another XML document with a different schema or any other format you need. This makes XSL useful at any tier in the Windows DNA model.

XSL is instantiated in the same way you instantiate the Microsoft XMLDOM. The Microsoft XMLDOM fully understands the XSL syntax, and it is simple to transform data. The following code snippet is all that is required to read and transform XML based on an XSL style sheet:

```
1: set objxml = createobject("Microsoft.XMLDOM")
2: set objxsl = createobject("Microsoft.XMLDOM")
3: objxml.async = false
4: objxsl.async = false
5: objxml.load("bankstatement.xml")
6: objxsl.load("bankstatement.xsl")
7: strResult = objxml.transformNode(objxsl)
```

12

You create an object instance of the XMLDOM for both the XML (line 1) and XSL (line 2) documents, you then load them (lines 5 and 6), and finally you transform the XML document based on the XSL template (line 7). The strResult variable contains the transformed data. Typically, strResult is an HTML stream that can be sent to any browser.

You could also, for example, check the browser type and version. If the browser is Internet Explorer 5.0, you would not need the listed server-side code. You could simply return the XML and XSL files and let the browser process the files on the client side. If the browser is not IE 5, you would run this code, process the files on the server side and then return the resulting HTML.

You are not limited to just using XSL to format XML into HTML: You can also use XSL to do XML conversion to any thing you want. This capability gives you tremendous flexibility in programming and processing because the data transformations are contained in the XSL rather than the program logic. For example, you can allow your creative people to work with just the XML and XSL, and they will not need to touch the mainline processing code.

Working with XML

The way you work with XML is through the XML Document Object Model or the capabilities of the other services that offer XML support that can be found in ADO 2.1 and later. XML support is provided by the MSXML.DLL. To create an instance of the root class, you will instantiate Microsoft.XMLDOM or Microsoft.FreeThreadedXMLDOM, depending on the location and type of application being developed.

There are many different ways in which you can get XML data on the server, including the following:

- Using ADO 2.1 or later to get XML information directly from any database that supports ADO
- Reading data from a database or other source and constructing an XML tree using the DOM
- Loading an XML file using the XML control's load method
- Constructing a string and loading it into the XML control using the loadXML method
- Constructing an XML text string directly, without building an XML document object on the server

Constructing an XML Tree Using the DOM

You can create or alter XML trees programmatically using the API's of the DOM. The following code builds an XML tree:

```
set xmldoc = createobject("Microsoft.XMLDOM")
set newnode = createobject("Microsoft.XMLDOM")

set newnode = xmldoc.createNode("element","MyData","")
xmldoc.appendChild(newnode)
set newnode = xmldoc.createNode("element","Item","")
newnode.text = "This is the data"
xmldoc.appendChild(newnode)
... continue to add nodes until your XML document is built
```

You can see that two things are happening: You create an instance of the XMLDOM for the XML document, and an instance which you use to construct the node. After the node is constructed, you append it to the XML document. You do not need to worry about closing XML tags because the APIs handle that automatically for you. After you have constructed your XML document, you can persist it by calling the save method:

```
xmldoc.save("MyFile.xml")
```

Alternatively, you could stream the file to its destination using Response.Write (covered on Day 18, "Active Server Pages").

Loading the XML from a File

The easiest way to populate your XMLDOM is to load it from a file. The following two lines are all that are required to load an XML file into the DOM.

```
set xmldoc = createobject("Microsoft.XMLDOM")
xmldoc.load("MyFile.xml")
```

When loading an XML document, it is always good practice to check for parsing errors, as outlined in Table 12.1. You can do this by adding code similar to following:

```
Set myErr =  xmldoc.parseError
 If (myErr.errorCode <>  0) Then
      Print "An error occurred in the XML document"
    Print "Error code: " & myErr.errorcode
    Print "Error reason: " & myErr.reason
    Print .. Other error values listed in the table below.
 End If
```

12

TABLE 12.1   A Complete List of Parser Error Information

Available Error Information	Description
errorcode	Returns the error code number in decimal
filepos	Returns the absolute file position where the error occurred
line	Returns the number of the line where the error occurred
linepos	Returns the character position where the error occurred
reason	Returns the reason for the error
srcText	Returns the full text of the line containing the error
url	Returns the URL of the XML file containing the error

Manually Constructing the XML Document

If you want to construct the XML stream without using the Microsoft.XMLDOM object, you can construct the XML document manually. For example:

```
dim xmlstr as string

xmlstr = xmlstr & "<?xml version=""1.0""?>"
xmlstr = xmlstr & "<MyData>"
xmlstr = xmlstr & "<Item>Data Goes Here</Item>"
xmlstr = xmlstr & "</MyData>"
```

Here you are simply building a text stream that contains the XML instructions. Often times this is the only way to get what you want; however, be aware of all your options before using this blunt approach. The following section, "Using ADO to Create an XML File or Stream," should be used if you are rendering an ADO recordset because it is easy and very complete. See the bankstatement.xml file on the CD-ROM for an example of the output.

Using ADO to Create an XML File or Stream

With ADO 2.1 and later, functionality has been added to persist a recordset as an XML string. This can be seen in Listing 12.8.

LISTING 12.8   Code to Convert an ADO Recordset to XML

```
1: Dim rs1 As ADODB.Recordset
2: Dim stm As New ADODB.Stream
3: Dim xmldoc as New Microsoft.XMLDOM
4:
5: rs1.Open   "SELECT * FROM authors", "DSN=pubs;uid=sa;pwd=;", _
6:            adopenStatic, adLockReadOnly, adCmdText
```

```
 7: rs1.Save "c:\myfolder\mysubfolder\myrs.xml", adPersistXML
 8: rs1.Save stm, adPersistXML
 9:
10: xmldoc.load(stm)
```

You simply need to tell the recordset to save itself (line 7), specify a location, and tell it you want it to be saved as XML by specifying `adPersistXML`. In the first example, we specify the location as a file (line 7), and in the second example, we specify a stream (line 8). Streams are new with ADO 2.5: They represent a stream of binary or text data. The important thing to note is that the recordset must be saved somewhere before you can work with it. In our example, we saved it to a stream before loading it into the XML-DOM.

Using an Active Server Page to Create XML

Another way to output XML is by using an Active Server Page to send the XML to the response object, as seen in Listing 12.9. Active Server Pages will not be covered until Day 18 so you might want to come back to this section after you read Day 18.

LISTING 12.9   Using an Active Server Page to Return XML

```
 1:   <%
 2:   response.ContentType = "text/xml"
 3:
 4:   ' Create and open a recordset.
 5:   Set rs = Server.CreateObject("ADODB.Recordset")
 6:   rs.Open "select * from authors", "dsn=pubs;uid=sa;pwd=;"
 7:
 8:   ' Save recordset directly into output stream.
 9:   rs.Save Response, adPersistXML
10:
11:   ' Close recordset
12:   rs.Close
13:   Set rs = nothing
14:   %>
```

In Listing 12.9, we set the HTML header's ContentType to be `text/xml`. This will ensure the browser knows that it is receiving XML data. The code then retrieves a recordset , and finally it is saved to the `Response` object .The `Response` object is an intrinsic ASP object that returns information to the client.

Note

> It should be noted that for all of the benefits of XML it has some usage limitations. For example it is not good for representing large datasets. In the previous code you just loaded the entire XML dataset into memory and you will be working with it in memory. This has a profound impact upon system resources and can severely limit scalability. If you do find that your XML data streams are large then you may want to find a way to break them into smaller data sets or you may want to move the data into a relational database and then use the capabilities of the RDBMS to work with the data.

Working with the XMLDOM

Now that you have the XML document loaded, you need to work with the XML tree. You have a couple of ways to proceed: You could traverse the XML tree by processing each branch recursively, or you could use the getElementByTagName or NamedNodeMap methods to have the XMLDOM locate the elements you are interested in working with and give you a collection with those nodes and their children. Both methods are covered in this section.

The first way is to walk through the entire XML tree looking for the information of interest to you. This kind of approach is good if you are collecting metadata about the XML tree or perhaps producing a report on the tree or executing a loosely defined search. The code to traverse an XML tree would look like Listing 12.10.

LISTING 12.10 Code to Traverse and Report on an XML Tree

```
 1: Dim xmldoc as New Microsoft.XMLDOM
 2: Dim objNode as New Microsoft.XMLDOM
 3:
 4: xmldoc.load("mydoc.xml")
 5: showChildNodes(xmldoc)
 6:
 7: sub showChildNodes(ByVal xmlNode as string)
 8:     Dim intCount as integer
 9:     Dim intNode as integer
10:     Dim intAttr as integer
11:
12:     Print "Node name = " & xmlNode.nodeName
13:     Print "Node type = " & getNodeType(xmlNode.nodeType)
14:     Print "Node value = " & xmlNode.nodeValue
15:     'Show Attributes
16:     objAttrList = xmlNode.attributes
17:     if objAttrList != Null then
18:         intCount = objAttrList.length
19:         if intCount > 0 then
```

```
20:                  for intAttr = 0 to intCount - 1
21:                      Print "Node name = " & objAttrList(intAttr).nodeName
22:                      Print "Node type = " & objAttrList(intAttr).nodeType
23:                      Print "Node value = " & objAttrList(intAttr).nodeValue
24:                  next
25:             end if
26:         end if
27:         'Check for child nodes
28:         intCount = xmlNode.childNodes.length
29:         if intCount > 0 then
30:         for intNode=0 to intCount - 1
31:             showChildNodes(xmlNode.childNodes(intNode))
32:          next
33:
34: end sub
35:
36: sub getNodeType(byVal intType as integer)
37:     Dim strType as string
38:
39:     switch(intType)
40:         case 1:    strType = "ELEMENT (1)"
41:         case 2:    strType = "ATTRIBUTE (2)"
42:         case 3:    strType = "TEXT (3)"
43:         case 4:    strType = "CDATA SECTION (4)"
44:         case 5:    strType = "ENTITY REFERENCE (5)"
45:         case 6:    strType = "ENTITY (6)"
46:         case 7:    strType = "PROCESSING INSTRUCTION (7)"
47:         case 8:    strType = "COMMENT (8)"
48:         case 9:    strType = "DOCUMENT (9)"
49:         case 10:   strType = "DOCUMENT TYPE (10)"
50:         case 11:   strType = "DOCUMENT FRAGMENT (11)"
51:         case 12:   strType = "NOTATION (12)"
52:     end switch
53:     getNodeType = strType
54: end sub
```

12

We see a number of things happening in this code. First of all, we are processing the tree from top to bottom, left to right, by walking down each of the branches until we hit a terminating leaf. Every time the showChildNodes function sees that it is not a leaf node, it calls itself with a pointer to the next child node (line 31). This is called *recursive processing* because the sub-routine is calling itself each time it is not a leaf node. Calls to the showChildNodes routine are stacked up until it reaches a leaf, then it completes the current instance of showChildNodes and unstacks itself one level. Every time it hits the end of a collection it completes the current instance of showChildNodes and unstacks one level. Recursion is a very efficient way to handle processing hierarchical structures like an XML tree. As we visit each node, we output the node name (line 12), type (line 13), value (line 14), and attributes (lines 16 through 26). You will notice that the node type is simply an integer that we convert to a string (line 13 and lines 36 through 54). You will also notice that we have to loop through the list of attributes to display their values (lines 20 through 24). Other things to notice are that everything in XML is represented in the tree as evidenced by the 12 node types (lines 40 through 51). You should also notice that the XMLDOM has all the enumerators you would expect from any COM collection. The standard enumerators of any collection are length, item(index), nextNode, and _newEnum() which supports the for each node in Visual Basic Scripting syntax. The enumerations are provided through the NodeList Interface. We obtain a node list by making a call to childNodes (line 31). You now have two methods (item(index) (line 31) and nextNode, which is not used in this example) and one property (length) (line 28) enable you to navigate the nodes in the list.

Note

> In this example we are using recursion to walk through the XML tree. Recursion is where you call yourself in order to process data, in this example line 31 calls showChildNodes from within itself. The effect is that the state of the current call is pushed upon the stack to make room for the new call. When the routine finally hits a leaf node it will return and the state of the previous call will be pulled off of the stack. This approach is very compact and elegant at the expense of system resources, primarily the stack. For processing large complex XML datasets recursion is not the best solution. In this case you may want to consider SAX, which will be cover a bit later in this chapter.

Navigating the XML Document Tree

In the previous example, we navigated the document tree in one direction. In reality, you have methods to allow you full navigational control. The node list has properties that allow you to get pointers to the parent, siblings, and children of the current node. Table 12.2 lists the attributes and the values they provide.

TABLE 12.2 Node Methods and Properties for Navigating the Node Tree

Method/Property	Description
firstChild	A read-only property that returns the first child node. If the node has no children, firstChild returns Null.
lastChild	A read-only property that returns the last child node. If the node has no children, lastChild returns Null.
previousSibling	A read-only property that returns the node immediately preceding this node in the children of this node's parent. Null is returned if no such node exists.

Method/Property	Description
nextSibling	A read-only property that returns the node immediately following this node in the children of this node's parent. Null is returned if no such node exists.
parentNode	A read-only property that returns a pointer to the parent node.

After you have the pointer to the desired node, you can, as we did in the example, return its name, type, value, and attributes by accessing the properties seen in Table 12.3.

TABLE 12.3 Information Available on Each Node

Property	Description
attributes	A read-only property that returns a NamedNodeMap containing attributes for this node.
dataType	A read-only property that indicates the node type.
nodeName	A read-only property that indicates the name of the node.
nodeType	A read-only property that indicates the type of node.
nodeTypeString	Returns the node type in string form.
nodeTypedValue	A read/write property for the typed value of the node.
nodeValue	A read/write property for the typed value of the node.

A few of these properties return the same value; for example, nodeTypedValue and nodeValue generally return the same value. As you recall, XML is represented as text; however, it is possible to specify a data type. For example, if we had the following node:

```
<AGE dt:integer>28</AGE>
```

nodeTypedValue would return the number 1, whereas nodeValue would return the character one.

The dataType property would return integer for our example.

The nodeType is represented by a numeric value. The nodeTypeString property returns a string with the node type. The mapping is as seen in Table 12.4.

TABLE 12.4 Node Type Values

Node Type	Name	Numeric Value
NODE_ELEMENT	element	1
NODE_ATTRIBUTE	attribute	2

continues

12

TABLE 12.4 continued

Node Type	Name	Numeric Value
NODE_TEXT	text	3
NODE_CDATA_SECTION	cdatasection	4
NODE_ENTITY_REFERENCE	entityreference	5
NODE_ENTITY	entity	6
NODE_PROCESSING_INSTRUCTION	processinginstruction	7
NODE_COMMENT	comment	8
NODE_DOCUMENT	document	9
NODE_DOCUMENT_TYPE	documenttype	10
NODE_DOCUMENT_FRAGMENT	documentfragment	11
NODE_NOTATION	notation	12

We need to tell you about one more method of the document interface, getElementByTagName(tagName). This method will return a collection of all the elements with the specified tagName with all their child elements. You can then iterate through the collection as we have done in our example. Here is a quick code snippet to demonstrate:

```
nodeList = xmldoc.getElementsByName("TRANSACTION")
 for i=0 to nodelist.length - 1
Print "Date = " & nodeList(i).getNamedItem("DATE")
    Print "Description = " & nodeList(i).getNamedItem("DESCRIPTION")
    Print "Debit = " & nodeList(i).getNamedItem("DEBIT")
    Print "Credit = " & nodeList(i).getNamedItem("CREDIT")
 loop
```

In this example, we get a collection of all the TRANSACTIONs in the XML document, and then we proceed to print the first and last names. A new method is also used in this example, getNamedItem. The getNamedItem method is much better to use than item(index) because it ensures that you are accessing the correct node.

Modifying the XML Document Tree

Now that we have covered navigation and retrieving information from the XML document tree, we will cover modification of the XML document tree by creating, updating, and deleting nodes.

The creation of nodes actually requires two XMLDOM objects, one for the XML document to be modified and one for the new node(s) to be added. The process is simple. First, navigate to the location in the XML document tree where you want to insert the new node. Next, create the new node using the methods available in the document interface. Finally, insert the node. Here is an example:

```
set xmldoc = createobject("Microsoft.XMLDOM")
set newnode = createobject("Microsoft.XMLDOM")

set newnode = xmldoc.createNode("element","MyData","")
xmldoc.appendChild(newnode)
set newnode = xmldoc.createNode("element","Item","")
newnode.text = "This is the data"
xmldoc.appendChild(newnode)
.. Continue to create and append nodes to the XML document
```

The methods for creating nodes are seen in Table 12.5.

TABLE 12.5 Methods to Create a Node

Method	Description
createAttribute(name)	Creates a node of type ATTRIBUTE with the name supplied.
createCDATASection(data)	Creates a node of type CDATA_SECTION with the node value set to data.
createComment(data)	Creates a node of type COMMENT with the node value set to data.
createDocumentFragment	Creates a node of type DOCUMENT_FRAGMENT with the context of the current document.
createElement(tagName)	Creates a node of type ELEMENT with the nodeName of tagName.
createEntityReference(name)	Creates a node of type ENTITY_REFERENCE where name is the name of the entity referenced.
createNode(type, name, namespaceURI)	Creates a node of the type specified in the context of the current document. Allows nodes to be created as a specified namespace.
createProcessingInstruction (target, data)	Creates a node of type PROCESSING_INSTRUCTION with the target specified and the nodeValue set to data.
createTextNode(data)	Creates a node of type TEXT with the node value set to data.

12

You will quickly notice that these methods relate directly to the 12 node types specified in Table 12.4.

After you have created the node to be added, you need to add it to the XML document tree. You have the methods shown in Table 12.7 available to you.

TABLE 12.7   Adding/Updating Nodes

Method	Description
appendChild(newChild)	A method to append newChild as the last child in the node.
insertBefore(newChild, oldChild)	A method to insert newChild as a child of this node. oldChild is returned. oldChild must be a child node of the element, otherwise an error is returned. If newChild is Null, then oldChild is removed.
replaceChild(newChild, oldChild)	A method to replace oldChild with newChild as a child of this node.

To update a node, you can either use the replace method if you have built a new node, or you can simply change the properties in Table 12.8 for the current node.

TABLE 12.8   Node Properties

Property	Description
dataType	A read/write property that indicates the node type.
nodeTypedValue	A read/write property for the typed value of the node.
nodeValue	A read/write property for the node value.
text	A string representing the content of the element and all descendants.

If you want to remove a node, you can use the insertBefore method with a Null value for the newChild and specify the node to be removed in the oldChild value. Also, there is a removeChild method, which is described in the following sidebar.

 A *removeChild(child) method* removes a childNode from a node. If childNode is not a child of the node, an error is returned.

The XMLDOM has a great number of other attributes and methods that you can use to work with the XML data. In this chapter, we have touched on about 20% of them, covering the most useful attributes and methods. The purpose of this chapter is to familiarize you with the XMLDOM so that you can start working with it, as well as for you to understand the terminology and concepts enough so that you can understand the complete documentation. You can access the complete documentation at http://msdn.microsoft.com/xml. The May/June 1999 issue of MSDN News has a poster outlining the top-level Internet Explorer 5.0 XML Object Model. It is available at http://msdn.microsoft.com/msdn-online/voices/news/xml_objm.asp.

Simple API for XML (SAX)

Simple API for XML (SAX) is a standard interface for event-based XML parsing. SAX offers a fast, low-memory alternative to processing XML documents using the Document Object Model (DOM). When the DOM is used to parse an XML file, it builds a complete tree of a document in memory. SAX, in contrast, traverses the document and informs the calling application of parsing events, such as the start or end of a new element. One of the best reasons for using SAX is for parsing long documents. With a SAX parser, for example, an application can monitor events as they occur and read into memory only the necessary parts of the document. SAX implements an event driven processing model which is familiar to programmers because Windows programming is essentially event driven. Using SAX is an advanced topic beyond the scope of this book. I wanted you to be aware of it so that if you feel that it can help you in solution development you can pursue more information on the subject. A recent article on the subject can be found at `http://msdn.microsoft.com/workshop/xml/articles/joyofsax.asp`.

Summary

XML is a powerful and friendly way to represent data in a very transportable format. XML is simple, yet powerful; any type of data can be represented with XML. Hierarchical data structures are required to represent the complex data structures that are everywhere in modern computing environments. XML is very adept at representing and working with hierarchical data structures.

XML is a very important technology to Microsoft and is a core capability of all of their 2000 products. .NET Platform utilizes XML extensively in its platform and thus you should get very familiar with XML and comfortable working with it. XML is a rapidly evolving standard and thus you should expect that new features and standards will be emerging in the future.

12

You learned about providing schemas for XML document using DTD and XML schemas. You saw where both of these schema definition languages fit and why XML schemas are best for day-to-day schema definition because such definition uses the same syntax as XML.

You learned about namespaces and how they are used to insulate XML documents from each other and to provide a way to eliminate ambiguity in the parser.

Finally, you learned how to create, load, save, and work with XML documents using the Microsoft XML Document Object Model. We covered the basics of the XML DOM. You will want to get a good reference book or bookmark the Microsoft XML Web site for more in-depth details.

The use of XML is rapidly finding its way into Microsoft products, so check the online resources frequently for the latest information at `http://msdn.microsoft.com/xml`.

Q&A

Q If I work with XML, will I be limiting the browsers I can reach?

A No, IE5 is the only browser at this time that supports native XML; however, you have the option of either using a Java class to render the XML on the client side or render the XML into HTML on the server before sending it to the client.

Q Where can I use the Microsoft XMLDOM?

A The Microsoft XMLDOM is a COM component, so it can be used anywhere that a COM component can be instantiated. This includes any Windows programming language (Visual Basic, Visual C++, Visual Java, and so on), Windows Scripting Host, and anywhere that VBScript is supported (Microsoft Office 2000, Active Server Pages, and so on).

Q XML looks verbose. Won't that affect performance?

A Not really. XML is in an Internet transferable format; it can be sent without any intermediate conversion. This is not the case with binary data that needs to be UU or MIME encoded before it can be sent across the Internet. Another factor is hardware compression that occurs between modems. XML can achieve a high level of compression because of its schema.

Q Are there standard XML templates I should be using?

A Yes. Work is underway to define standard industry schemas that allow for easy interchange between systems. Before defining your own schema, you should check to see if a schema already exists. If you are working with a specific application or software suite, check with the vendor. Also, two Web sites are acting as clearinghouses for this information: `http://www.xml.org` and `http://www.biztalk.org`. Check out these sites for schemas and other related information.

Q Can everything be represented in XML?

A In theory, yes, but in reality, no. Text, numbers, dates, and currency are well represented by XML. Images, audio files, and other binary data do not translate well. However, it is possible to include pointers and links within XML files that would allow this type of information to be accessed via XML.

Workshop

The Workshop provides quiz questions to help you solidify your understanding of the material covered and exercises to provide you with experience in using what you've learned. Try to understand the quiz and exercise answers before continuing to the next lesson. Answers are provided in Appendix A.

Quiz

1. What are the key areas in which XML syntax is stricter than HTML?
2. What is the purpose of eXtensible Styling Language (XSL)?
3. What are the ways you can present XML data?
4. What are the differences between DTD and XML schemas?
5. What are the two versions of the Microsoft XMLDOM, and when would you use each?

Exercises

1. Create an XML document using Notepad and then open it with Internet Explorer 5.0. Did it parse correctly? Now mangle the XML document and then open it again with IE 5.0. Notice the parser errors. Fix the document for the next exercise.
2. In this exercise create a Cascading Style Sheet to display your XML data. Add a reference to the style sheet in your XML document file. Now open the XML document in IE 5.0. Did it display the way you wanted?

12

DAY 13

The Future: COM+

COM+ is correctly named since it is largely COM, which you learned about on Day 8. If you have not read this lesson, you should do so before you continue. While COM+ is an extension of COM, two huge improvements have been added. The first is an updated version (3.0) of Microsoft Transaction Server (MTS). MTS is no longer separate from COM. The combined COM and MTS team has updated and integrated MTS into COM so they now function as one. Along with the MTS/COM merger, this lesson will cover quite a few features now available in COM+ including:

- Just-in-Time activation
- Resource pooling
- Queued components
- Events
- Automatic transactions
- Threading
- Constructor strings

These features continue the maturation process of Windows DNA by providing additional infrastructure elements in the operating system itself. This allows the programmer to focus on building sophisticated solutions. In fact, most of the new capabilities discussed in this lesson focus on the business logic and data tiers of the Windows DNA architecture. These enhancements make it much easier to develop advanced n-tier applications in a fraction of the time previously possible. Let's begin by looking at Just-in-Time activation.

Activating Objects with Just-in-Time Activation

Just-in-Time (JIT) activation describes the capability of COM+ to activate an object just prior to its use. This allows server resources to be used much more efficiently. This is particularly true when you are attempting to scale your applications to a high number of transactions per minute.

As would be expected, COM+ also attempts to deactivate the object as quickly as possible for the same reason. *Activation* in this case means that the object is being either instantiated for the first time, or merely obtained from a pool of objects (see "Reusing Objects via Resource Pooling," later in this lesson). Conversely, *deactivated* means either destroyed or returned to the pool.

It is important to note that when COM+ deactivates an object it only does so on the server side. As far as the client is concerned, it still has a valid reference to the object. The next time that the client invokes a method on the object, which it still believes is active, COM+ silently activates the object, just in time.

Activating Client-Side Objects Through JIT

Not only does JIT benefit the server, it helps the client as well. In the past, it was held that client applications should create objects as late as possible and then destroy them quickly. This practice caused a great deal of thrashing on the client side, as objects were constantly created, and then destroyed.

JIT allows the clients to hold a reference to an object as long as necessary without having to worry about consuming resources on the server. This in turn reduces thrashing because objects, once created, can remain active for as long as they are needed.

Note

The use of JIT is optional for components that do not require a transaction, but mandatory for components that do require a transaction.

Of course, JIT only makes sense if your components do not hold state. This is because an object's state is lost each time it is deactivated. In addition, if your component requires a transaction, it cannot maintain state across a transaction boundary. This would be violating the isolation of the transaction.

Enabling JIT on Your Components

To enable JIT on an existing component, you must first load the Component Services administration by clicking on the Start button, Programs, Administrative Tools and finally Component Services. Next, locate the SmallTownBank application, and then the SmallTownBank_Business.BankBusiness component. Right-click this component and then select Properties from the pop-up menu. When the Properties dialog appears, click the Activation tab and then select the Enable Just In Time Activation check box. Finally, click the OK button to save your changes.

 **Caution** You should only configure a component for JIT activation when the component is correctly written to support JIT. In fact, if a component maintains state, you should probably disable JIT activation to ensure that the component continues to function properly.

The bottom line is that JIT activation improves performance on the client by allowing object references to remain active, helping to reduce the trashing associated with rapid activation and deactivation. Minimizing memory usage and encouraging the reuse of objects also improve server performance. This, of course, brings us to resource pooling.

Reusing Objects via Resource Pooling

JIT activation on the server means that objects are created and destroyed with great frequency. There is a great deal of time and CPU cycles expended each time a COM+ object is created. This is the reason that COM+ has introduced the concept of a resource pool. Instead of destroying an object, COM+ simply returns it to its original state and places it in a pool. The next time a client request an object, COM+ simply retrieves it from the resource pool and does not have to re-create it.

13

Monitoring Pool Usage with Component Services

You can configure and monitor the usage of the pool at a component level. Using the Component Services administrative tools, you're able to define the minimum and maximum size of the pool as well as timeout values. When the application is running, COM+

handles all the details of object activation and reuse according to the criteria you have specified for the pool (see Figure 13.1).

FIGURE 13.1

Monitoring the usage of the pool.

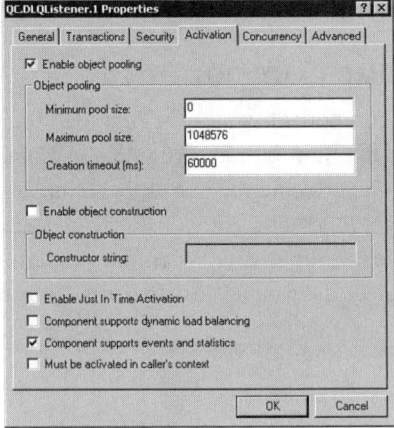

It is important to note that objects that are pooled cannot be bound to a particular thread, as is the case with objects that make use of the Apartment threading model. Unfortunately, the Microsoft Visual Basic development environment can currently create only Apartment model components. This means that Visual Basic components cannot be pooled.

This limitation might be removed in a future version of Visual Basic, so it can support the creation of objects that make use of a Neutral Apartment threading model.

Queued Components

COM requires an in-depth knowledge of marshaling in order to queue, send, receive, and process asynchronous messages. COM+ introduces Queued Components, which automatically marshal data in the form of a Microsoft Message Queue (MSMQ) message. Because Queued Components support is built-in support for transactions, a server failure will not result in inconsistent data. Overall, Queued Components allow objects to be invoked either synchronously or asynchronously without any special programming.

As seen in Figure 13.2, Queued Components consist of

- Recorder
- Queue
- Listener
- Player

FIGURE 13.2

*Message flow for a
Queued Component.*

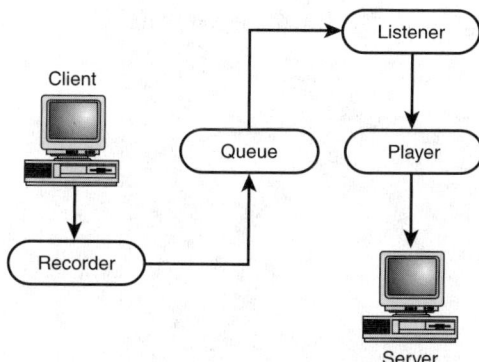

When a client creates a queued component, the client is connected to a special object called the *recorder*, rather than the actual object. The client application makes calls as usual, but they are recorded on the client rather than immediately being sent via RPC (Remote Procedure Call) to the server. After the object is deactivated, a series of messages is sent asynchronously to the server where the object resides using a MSMQ queue.

The listener on the server takes note of the incoming messages in the queue and then invokes the player, which actually creates the target object, and plays the recorded messages to it.

What is important to note is that, as the programmer, you don't have to worry about MSMQ at all; COM+ takes care of all the details. You simply make use of the component as you normally would and COM+ makes sure everything works correctly, even though the client and server objects are not even running at the same time.

Just as important is the fact that writing these components in Visual Basic is just as easy. You create your components as you always have, with just a few restrictions. For example, as you might expect, it is not possible to use output parameters in your method calls. Instead, you simply install the component into COM+ and mark its interfaces as queued. COM+ then takes care of listening for incoming MSMQ messages from remote clients and calling the component in turn using the player.

Enabling Queuing

To enable Queuing, load the Component Services administration and right-click on the application folder, then select Properties from the pop-up menu. When the Properties dialog appears, click the Queuing tab. Finally, select the Queued check box to allow the application to be reached by an MSMQ queue, as seen in Figure 13.3.

13

FIGURE 13.3

Enabling queuing for a COM+ application.

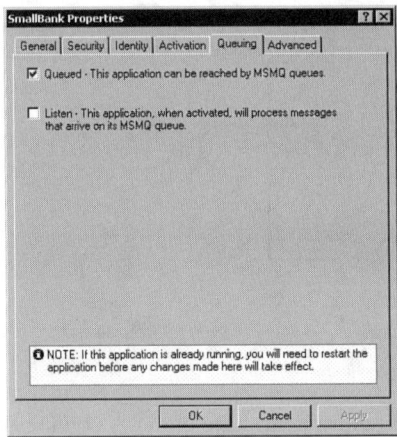

If the Listen box is checked, it tells COM+ that when the application is launched, COM+ should also activate the listener service to receive calls through MSMQ.

Once you have configured a queued component, it simple to use it in a Visual Basic application. For example, let's assume that the component is called SmallBank.Account and has a method called Credit. In this example, the Credit method requires an account number and a dollar amount in order to perform its task. The Visual Basic code for such a component would be very straightforward, as seen in Listing 13.1.

LISTING 13.1 Using a Local Queued Component

```
1: Set qAccount = GetObject("queue:/new:SmallBank.Account")
2: qAccount.Credit ("123-45-6789", 1000)
3: Set qAccount = Nothing
```

In this example, the queue is located on the same computer as the component. If you require queuing, the target component will likely reside on another computer in the network. Luckily, it is surprisingly simple to add this logic to your Visual Basic program as seen in Listing 13.2.

LISTING 13.2 Using a Queued Component on Another Computer

```
1: Set qAccount = GetObject("queue:computername=SBAccounts/new:
   ➥SmallBank.Account")
2: qAccount.Credit ("123-45-6789", 1000)
3: Set qAccount = Nothing
```

The only change was the addition of the computer name to the GetObject function. Only a few years ago, it would have seemed fanciful to even suggest that queuing could be implemented so easily in an application.

Events

Another new feature of COM+ is events. An *event* is a single call to a method on a COM interface, originated by the publisher and delivered by the COM+ Event service to the correct subscriber(s). A *publisher* is any program that makes the COM calls that initiate events. A *subscriber* is a COM+ component that receives calls (representing events) from a publisher. The subscriber implements an interface as a COM server; the publisher makes calls on that interface as a COM client (see Figure 13.4).

Events represent a programming model that is able to support the concept of late-bound method calls between a publisher and a subscriber, using the COM+ event subsystem. Prior to COM+, a component might repeatedly poll the server to see if an event had taken place. But now, using COM+ Events, the event system is able to notify interested subscribers proactively.

FIGURE 13.4

Publisher communicating to a subscriber using the COM+ Event subsystem.

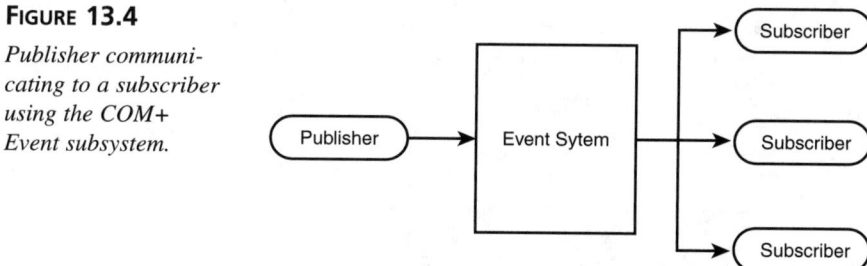

Registering a New Event Class

In order to register a new event class, you must first load the COM+ Component Services application. Locate the Components folder inside the application where you want the new event class to reside. Select Action, New, and then Component from the toolbar to invoke the COM Component Install Wizard. Your screen will look similar to Figure 13.5.

Press the Install New Event Class(es) button to create a new class. Click on the Add button to locate the DLL file of the component you wish to install as seen in Figure 13.6.

Click the Next button and then the Finish button to create the new event class. You will not notice much difference between a regular component and an event class, except on the Advanced tab of its Properties dialog (see Figure 13.7).

13

FIGURE 13.5

Creating a new event class.

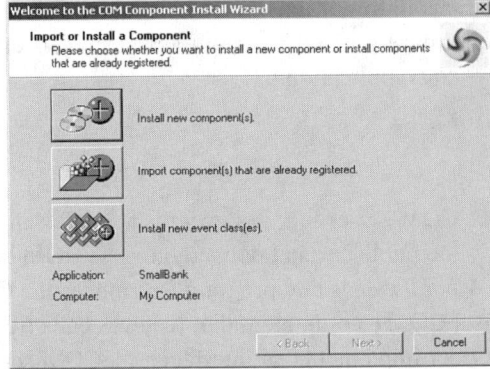

FIGURE 13.6

Installing a DLL as an event class.

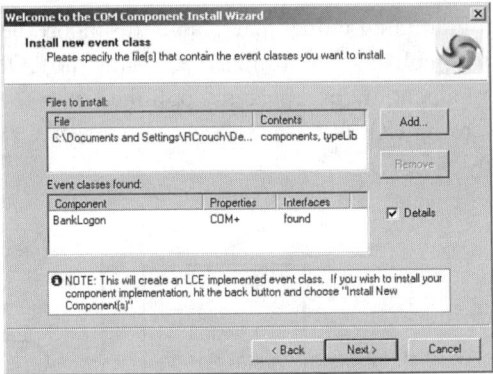

FIGURE 13.7

Configuring Publisher ID for an Event Class.

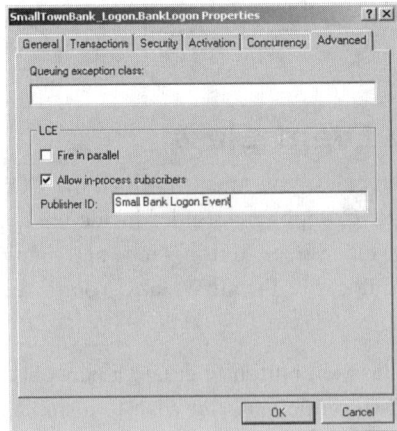

In this case, I entered Small Bank Logon Event as the Publisher ID. This is all that needs to be done to allow a subscriber to locate the event class and subscribe to it. It is also all that is necessary for a publisher to create an object of the event class and fire it. Next, you only need to add one or more subscriptions using the Subscriptions folder located under the event class.

Using Automatic Transactions

In prior versions of MTS, it was the responsibility of the programmer to obtain a context for an object and then invoke either the SetComplete or SetSetAbort methods. COM+ introduces the capability to automatically start and end a transaction under specific conditions. A transaction is started when

- A non-transactional client calls a component that requires a transaction or a new transaction.
- A transactional client calls a component that requires a new transaction.

Conversely, COM+ ends a transaction by either committing or aborting it when any one of the following conditions occurs:

- The root object of the transaction finishes its work and is released by COM+.
- The transaction exceeds the timeout value specified for the component.
- The client releases the root object.

Keep in mind that any client can call a component that isn't transactional, but because COM+ activates the object instance outside a transaction, none of the resources touched by the object will benefit from transaction protection. A component that is not transactional can never participate in a transaction, and yet it still incurs the entire overhead of context creation. On the other hand, a programmer can disable a component's transaction requirement and eliminate the overhead of context creation. Disabling a component's transaction requirement is useful to programmers who prefer to use the COM+ framework without making their application transactional.

Of course, you will still need to communicate the success or failure of some transactions programmatically. This is especially true when business logic is involved, and you need to complete or abort a transaction based on these business rules. Listing 13.3 contains a very basic example of controlling a transaction programmatically.

13

LISTING 13.3 Indicating Success or Failure of a Transaction in a Component

```
 1: Option Explicit
 2:
 3: Public Sub Credit(ByVal strAccount As String, _
 4:                    ByVal curAmount As Currency)
 5:
 6:    Dim objcontext As ObjectContext
 7:    Dim contextstate As IContextState
 8:
 9:    If Not GetObjectContext.IsInTransaction Then
10:      ' Throw an error since we want to make sure that this component
11:      ' is in a transaction.
12:      Err.Raise 99999, "SmallBank.Account:Credit", "I need a transaction!"
13:    End If
14:
15:    ' Handle any errors
16:    On Error GoTo UnexpectedError
17:
18:    ' Get our object context
19:    Set objcontext = GetObjectContext
20:
21:    ' Get the IContextState object
22:    Set contextstate = objcontext
23:
24:    ' VERY Simple Account Validation
25:
26:    If Len(strAccount) <> 11 Then 'xxx-xx-xxxx
27:      Err.Raise 99999, " SmallBank.Account:Credit",
28:        "Account Number: Incorrect Length"
29:    End If
30:
31:    If curAmount < 1 Then 'Must be positive
32:      Err.Raise 99999, " SmallBank.Account:Credit",
33:        "Amount: Must be positive"
34:    End If
35:
36:    '
37:    ' Add logic here to update account information.
38:    '
39:
40:    ' Everything works!
41:
42:    contextstate.SetMyTransactionVote TxCommit
43:    contextstate.SetDeactivateOnReturn True
44:    Exit Sub
45:
46: UnexpectedError:
47:    ' There's an error
```

```
48:    contextstate.SetMyTransactionVote TxAbort
49:    contextstate.SetDeactivateOnReturn True
50:
51: End Sub
```

Lines 9 through 13 demonstrate the capability of a component to verify that it is part of a transaction and to raise an error if it is not. Next, line 16 turns on error handling to make sure all errors are processed by the error handler. Lines 26 through 36 perform some very basic validation to make sure that the account number and credit are okay.

Assuming everything went well to this point, line 37 would normally contain the logic necessary to credit the account. In this case, the code only contains a placeholder for brevity's sake.

Lines 42 and 43 tells COM+ that everything went alright by voting for the transaction to succeed. As expected, the error handling routine located in lines 46 through 49 asks COM+ about the transaction since an error of some kind occurred.

The code in lines 43 and 49 simply tell COM+ that the object can be deactivated, which allows it to be used by other callers, ensuring optimal performance.

Threading: Neutral Apartments

COM+ introduces a new threading model called *neutral apartments* to simplify programming in multithreaded environments. Neutral apartments are the preferred model for components with no user interface. In the past, to prevent bottlenecks and to maintain server scalability, COM developers were forced to implement free-threaded components. However, free-threading models were complicated to implement because they must deal with synchronized access. In neutral apartments, objects follow the guidelines for multithreaded apartments but can execute on any kind of thread. Future versions of Visual Basic will allow the use of neutral apartments, which, for the first time, will allow components built with it to be pooled.

13

Constructor Strings

Many COM components are able to make use of configuration information that has traditionally meant the use of the registry entries or INI files. This configuration information typically included things like the ODBC DSN name. COM+ allows this type of information to be specified right in the Component Services snap-in, using something called an *object constructor*.

To use a constructor string in your Visual Basic program, your object must be configured within COM+ Use Component Services to navigate to your component. Right-click the component and select Properties.

In the Activation tab, select Enable Object Construction and type the string in the Constructor String text box. This can be a DSN, the name of some computer or queue, or some other information that your application needs to function that is administration-related.

Retrieving the String with Visual Basic

Now that the administrative stuff is out of the way, you still need to retrieve this string using Visual Basic. First, make sure your project has a reference to "COM+ 1.0 Services Type Library".

In your class module, beneath any Option statements, add the following line of code:

```
Implements IObjectConstruct
```

You can also add a private class-level variable to hold the string:

```
Private mstrObjectConstructor As String
```

In the scope list box in your code editor, where it reads (General), you should have a new item called IObjectConstruct. When you select it, the IObjectConstruct_Construct function will be added to your class.

Add the following code to it so the function looks as follows:

LISTING 13.4   Retrieving a Constructor String

```
Private Sub IObjectConstruct_Construct(ByVal pCtorObj As Object)
    msConstructorString = pCtorObj.ConstructString
End Sub
```

This retrieves the ConstructString and stores it in your private variable.

Configuring COM+ Application

The MTS Explorer used to place COM components into MTS has been replaced by the COM+ Component Services snap-in, used to configure all COM+ components.

The COM+ Component Services snap-in allows the management of components and component applications including

- Creating, deleting, or exporting an application
- Adding or deleting one or more components in an existing application
- Changing an application's properties, including its description, security settings, and identity and activation type
- Monitoring transaction statistics

Note

The MTS term *package* has been replaced in COM+ by the term *application*.

In order to configure a component in COM+, an application must first be created. An application is a group of DLLs that are related to each other. The DLLs might be part of the same application, or they might have similar security requirements.

To create an application, first load the Component Services snap-in and double-click the computer where you want to create the new application. Next, right-click the COM+ Applications folder and select New, Application from the pop-up menu, as seen in Figure 13.8.

FIGURE 13.8

Creating a new application using the Component Services snap-in.

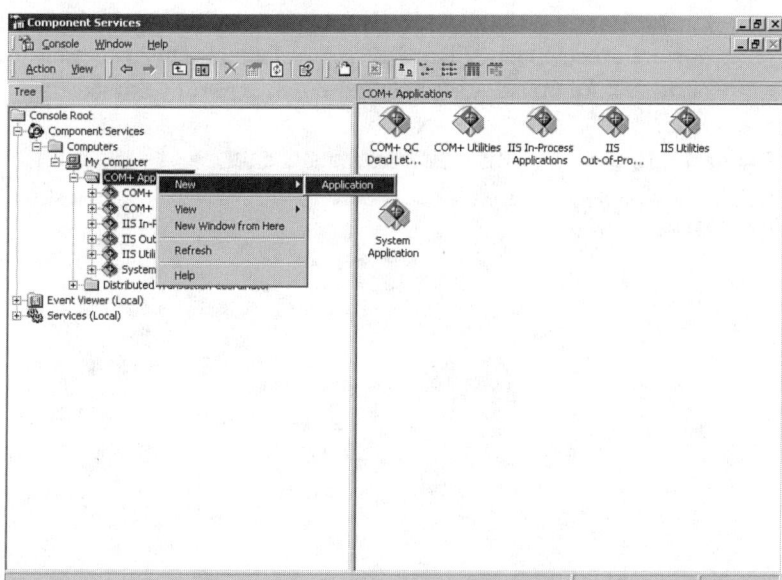

13

> **Tip**   You can also click Action, New, Application from the toolbar.

The Component Services snap-in invokes the COM Application Install Wizard, which will step you through the process of creating a new COM+ application (see Figure 13.9). Click the Create an empty application button to continue.

FIGURE 13.9

Creating a new application with the COM Application Install Wizard.

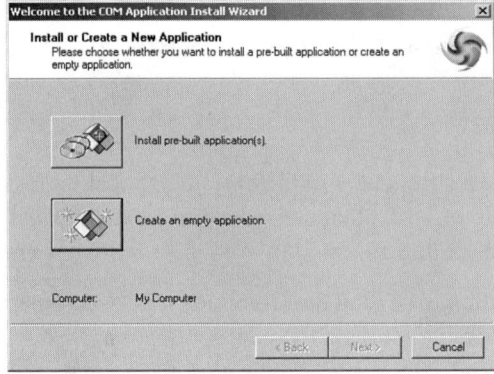

Now name your new application by typing a name (SmallBank) and clicking the Next button. You must select which NT account will be used when components in the application are executed (see Figure 13.10). Select the This user radio-button and type the name of the NT Administrator account (Administrator) and its password.

FIGURE 13.10

Setting the login for the COM+ application.

It is usually better not to use the Interactive user radio-button because in many cases the execution of the component will fail unpredictably because insufficient rights have been granted to the currently logged-on user. In fact, component access will also fail if no one is logged on to the server. This can be both frustrating and difficult to troubleshoot.

Press the Finish button to add your new application to the Component Services snap-in. Now that you have created an empty application, you next need to add an existing component to configure a new component into the application. Double-click the SmallBank application, and then click the Components folder. Choose Action, New, Component from the toolbar. The COM Component Install Wizard will appear, which is depicted in Figure 13.11.

FIGURE 13.11

Installing a new component using the COM Component Install Wizard.

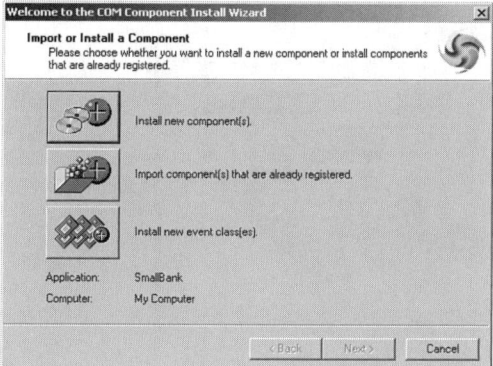

Adding Components to Your Applications

Click the Install new component(s) button to add a new COM DLL to the empty application. Click the Open button shown in Figure 13.12 to select an existing DLL on your computer. Next, locate the BankBusines.dll, which can be found in the Day 13 folder in the Source directory of the CD that accompanied this book.

After you have located the DLL, click the Open button and then the Finish button to add the component to the SmallBank application. Your screen will now look similar to Figure 13.13.

Finally, right-click the SmallTownBank_Logon.BankLogon component and select Properties from the pop-up menu. Click the Transaction tab and then the Requires a transaction radio-button. Click the OK button to save your changes.

13

FIGURE 13.12

Selecting a file to install into the COM+ application.

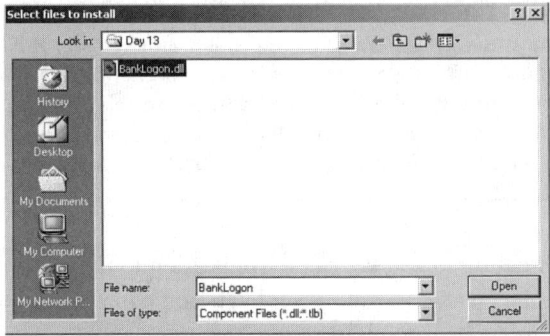

FIGURE 13.13

The Component Services snap-in after successfully adding the COM component.

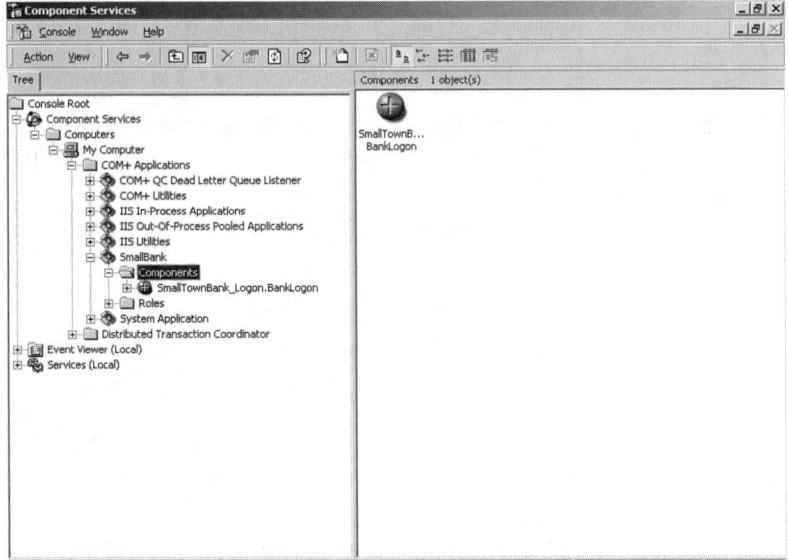

Summary

COM+ is clearly the next stage in the evolution of Microsoft's component-based middle-ware. It integrates and extends the features of COM and MTS, making it easier to design, develop, implement, and administer component-based solutions. In short, under COM+ the distinction between COM and MTS disappears.

Q&A

Q **It seems like Just-in-Time (JIT) activation helps the server primarily. Is this correct?**

A No, JIT helps both the server and the client. JIT allows the clients to hold a reference to an object as long as necessary without having to worry about consuming resources on the server. This, in turn, reduces thrashing because objects, once created, can remain active for as long as they are needed.

Q **Can I still use COM components developed for MTS?**

A Yes, COM+ completely supports components developed for COM and MTS. You might have to make changes to your component if you want to take advantage of some of the advanced features of COM+.

Q **My components do not make use of transactions. Is there any reason to install them into the COM+ subsystem?**

A Yes, even if your components do not use transactions, they can take advantage of Just-in-Time activations to improve performance and scalability.

Q **I have heard that a COM+ component should not maintain state. Is this correct?**

A Yes, in many cases a component that maintains state cannot take full advantage of COM+ capabilities such as Just-in-Time activation.

Workshop

The Workshop provides quiz questions to help you solidify your understanding of the material covered and exercises to provide you with experience in using what you've learned. Try to understand the quiz and exercise answers before continuing to the next lesson. Answers are provided in Appendix A.

Quiz

1. True/False. When COM+ deactivates an object, it does so on both the client and the server.
2. True/False. The use of JIT is optional for components that do not require a transaction.
3. What is the best way to create a pooled object using Visual Basic 6.0?
4. Name the four services that allow queued components to operate under COM+.

13

5. Events represent a programming model that is able to support the concept of late-bound events or method calls between a _____ and a _____, using the COM+ event subsystem. Fill in the blanks.

6. Using automatic transactions in COM+, when is a transaction considered to be started?

7. What is the name of the new COM+ threading model?

8. True/False. Constructor strings can be used to administratively define generic information (such as an ODBC DSN) that can be passed to an object at the time it is created.

Exercise

1. Create a role called Teller and assign that role to the Logon component that was configured for COM+ in today's lesson.

DAY 14

Best Practices and Other Services

Today we cover a number of miscellaneous topics that either do not fit into the other days or are designed to meet specific system requirements not used in our sample application.

We will discuss interacting with other systems. Using COM TI to interact with mainframe systems, such as CICS and IMS. Using Microsoft Message Queue to provide asynchronous communication between processes. Using BizTalk to send XML based messages between systems across the Internet. Using Simple Object Access Protocol (SOAP) for distributed object communication via the Internet. And finally, we will conclude with a discussion of Visual Studio.NET.

We will discuss

- Interacting with other systems
- Using COM TI to interact with older mainframe systems, such as CICS and IMS
- Using Microsoft Message Queue to provide asynchronous communication between processes

- Using BizTalk to send XML-based messages between systems across the Internet
- Using Simple Object Access Protocol (SOAP) for distributed object communication via the Internet
- Using Visual Studio.NET

Asynchronous Communications—Working with Message Queues

Most programmers are not used to working with queues because, in the past, one either had to develop the capabilities themselves or purchase and learn an expensive and complex package. Microsoft has changed this by delivering a free queue capability with Windows NT Option Pack 4. In this section, we are going to look at what queues are and why would you want to use them.

Why Use Queues?

A *queue* enables you to asynchronously send information between processes. The queues act as in and out message boxes for the various processes servicing the queues.

There are several situations in which it makes sense to use queues. The first is when you have process intensive tasks that need to be performed on some types of data. In the past these tasks would be stored away and then run in batch mode during an off time, such as in the middle of the night. In today's 24/7 processing environment, this sort of work usually does not make sense. Rather, it is better to put work into prioritized work queues. Other processes then monitor these queues and service the messages as they come into the queue. The benefit of using queues are

- Messages in a queue can be prioritized as high-priority, they are serviced before low-priority messages.
- The queuing process does not need to wait for the work to be completed, it can return control to the user more quickly.
- A number of work tasks are being queued, processors and resources can be better used.
- Queues can be made available network wide, it is much easier to enlist multiple computers—each running an instance of the service routine to handle peak demands. This ability to have multiple instances of processing routines servicing a queue makes scalability very easy.

The queue management systems do a great deal of work to ensure that queued messages are delivered only once, that they are robust enough to survive system failure, and that they are secure. Other features provided by queue management systems include logging, encryption, and namespace integration.

Microsoft Message Queue (MSMQ)

Microsoft Message Queue is an incredibly rich service made available to developers. Microsoft has added many features one would want in a queuing product, while keeping it simple to use. MSMQ basically consists of five methods: Open, Close, Read, Write, and Listen. MSMQ is dual interfaced so that it can be used by Visual Basic, Visual C++, Visual J++, Microfocus COBOL, and scripting environments such as ASP. MSMQ provides a comprehensive set of functionalities, consisting of

- **Reliable, resilient message delivery.** MSMQ uses sophisticated techniques to ensure that messages are recoverable and are dynamically routed at least cost to their intended destinations. This enables developers to focus on the business logic, rather than communication, issues. The Message Queue Information Store (MQIS) allows messages to be stored physically within a database so that the messages are resilient between system outages.

- **One-time, in-order message delivery.** System reliability requires that messages be delivered only once and in the intended order. Imagine what would happen to our banking application if this did not happen.

- **Transaction support.** MSMQ can participate in transactions, ensuring that messages are part of a transaction and thus that the effects of these messages follow the ACID rules.

- **Automatic message journaling.** MSMQ can make journal entries of all messages sent or received by an application. Journals provide audit trails and simplify recovery from many types of failure.

- **Notification service.** MSMQ can notify the sending program of a message's successful or failed delivery so that the program can take appropriate action.

- **Message priority support.** MSMQ enables an application to assign priorities to messages and queues. MSMQ delivers messages in priority order. Priorities allow applications to process important messages first when there is a backlog.

MSMQ has the following scalability, interoperability, availability, and manageability capabilities:

- **Hierarchical, directory service–based architecture.** Having a centralized directory of all queues and machines allows for better scalability because queue and machines can be added from a central location. Processes can send messages across process and machine boundaries without preconfigured routes.

14

- **Connectors to other queuing systems.** The MSMQ Connector enables MSMQ to interoperate with other queuing systems. This enables MSMQ to participate in heterogeneous environments where messages need to be sent to processes running under non-NT services.

- **Message routing services.** MSMQ uses the lowest cost routing available. When a route is broken, MSMQ will reroute messages in an attempt to deliver them.

- **Management console.** The MSMQ console is integrated into the Microsoft Management Console so that it can be part of a unified management interface.

MSMQ is integrated with Windows NT and other Microsoft products, enabling it to provide a higher level of functionality. Some of this functionality is described in the following list:

- **MTS integration.** MSMQ offers seamless integration with MTS, enabling transactions to include MSMQ operations.

- **Clustering support.** MSMQ supports operation on clustered Windows NT servers that enables MSMQ to automatically fail-over, making it fault tolerant.

- **IIS Active Server Page (ASP) support.** MSMQ is dual interfaced so that active server pages can send and receive messages with MSMQ.

- **MAPI and Microsoft Exchange integration.** Integrating MSMQ and Exchange makes it easier for developers to send messages and forms via MSMQ.

With MSMQ's integrated security, developers can ensure that only users with the appropriate permission can send and receive messages. Messages can also be digitally encrypted and signed, providing a secure way to move messages confidentially between systems. The following list describes these features in more detail:

- **Windows NT Access Control List (ACL) integration.** By being integrated with Windows NT, ACL access to all queue functions can be precisely controlled.

- **Built-in message encryption and signature support.** MSMQ can use the Microsoft Crypto API to automatically encrypt, protect, and sign messages. This protection prevents messages from being viewed or changed during transmission.

- **Windows NT security log integration.** Administrators can specify which MSMQ events get tracked in the Windows NT Security Log. Logging events enables the organization to track the changes and events that affect their mission-critical applications.

MSMQ Programming Model

When two applications want to communicate with each other using MSMQ, one must act as a sender and the other as a receiver. After the requesting application has sent a message, and the target application has received and processed the message, the two applications can reverse their roles. For example, Application A can send a request message to Application B. Application B receives the request, performs some processing, and then sends a response message back to Application A. Application A then becomes a receiver to retrieve the response message. In fact, most operations require programmers to use just five simple API calls: Locate, Open, Send, Receive, and Close. See Figure 14.1 for an illustration of how messages flow through MSMQ.

FIGURE 14.1

Message flow through MSMQ.

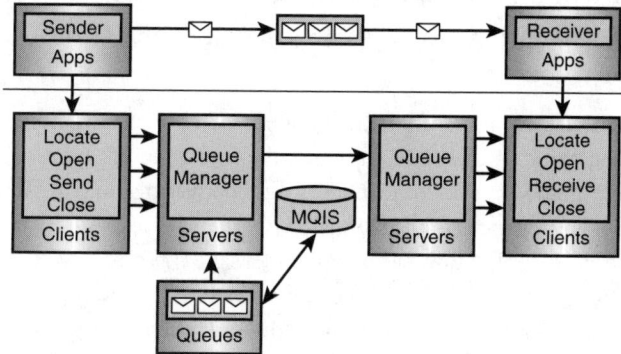

Applications Acting as a Sender Through MSMQ

When an application wants to send a message using MSMQ, the normal procedure using the MSMQ COM implementations is to

1. Create an instance of a MSMQQueueInfo object, set the PathName property equal to the name of destination queue, and invoke the Open method on the object. This method returns an MSMQQueue object that represents an instance of an open MSMQ queue (or, a queue to which the sending application can send messages). The MSMQQueue object is used only by Microsoft Message Queue Server to identify the destination queue locally to the sending MSMQ Server. The Open operation does not establish an actual connection to the destination queue, and the destination queue does not have to be reachable over the network to be opened by the sender.

2. Create an instance of a MSMQMessage object and provide values for properties such as Body (which normally holds the application-specific content of the message) and Label (which describes the message and can be viewed by administrators through the MSMQ Explorer). If desired, the sender can set additional message properties, such as message timeout values, delivery modes, and the name of a response queue (if required).

14

3. Send the message by invoking the Send method on the message along with the MSMQQueue object representing the appropriate destination queue as a parameter.

4. Close the instance of the MSMQQueue object by invoking its Close method.

If the application anticipates sending additional messages to the same queue, it can leave the queue open and close it later. Avoiding frequent Open Close calls to the same target queue will improve performance greatly.

Applications Acting as a Receiver Through MSMQ

When an application wants to receive a message using Microsoft Message Queue Server, the normal procedure is to

1. Create an instance of a MSMQQueueInfo object, set the PathName property equal to the name of queue from which the message will be received, and invoke the Open method on the object. This method returns an MSMQQueue object that represents an instance of an open MSMQ queue (for example, a queue from which the receiving application can receive messages). To receive a message, the destination queue must be located on the same machine as the receiving application or be reachable over the network through an available network connection.

2. Invoke the Receive method on the MSMQQueue object. Microsoft Message Queue Server will pass back an instance of an MSMQMessage object containing the message at the head of the queue (or at the *cursor* position, if cursors are being used). The object will include the body of the message (in the Body property) along with other information such as the name of any response queue. It is the responsibility of the receiving application to decide what to do with all messages that it receives (including sending any required response messages).

3. Close the instance of the MSMQQueue object by invoking its Close method.

As before, if the application anticipates receiving additional messages from the same queue, it can leave the queue handle open and close it later.

Tip

> If you package messages together into a single MSMQ message you will get better performance than using several individual messages. This is some thing to consider when architecting scalability into your application.

Advanced Receive Options

Microsoft Message Queue Server supports a number of advanced receive options. For example, developers can request *nondestructive* receives, and MSMQ will return an

MSMQMessage object containing a copy of the message at the head of the queue (or at the cursor position) but will not remove the message from the queue. This enables receivers to decide whether they want to process a given message or leave it for another application. Microsoft Message Queue Server also supports *blocking* and *nonblocking* receives. With blocking receives, control is not returned back to the requestor until a message is available in the queue. Nonblocking receives enable applications to check for messages but continue processing if none are available.

You have only touched upon the basic capabilities of MSMQ in this chapter. MSMQ is a product full of features, and you are encouraged to investigate further the other capabilities available if it looks like queues will help you. Many of the capabilities address specialized needs of certain system types. Entire books are written on the subject. The intent of this section was to get you familiar with the basic queuing process.

Interacting with Legacy Systems—COM TI

If you are familiar with mainframe environments, you will know that the mainframe has been message based and transactional for a long time. Also, a great deal of business logic is built in to these systems. Often times it does not make sense to rewrite this business logic because it is extremely complex, the source code is out of date, or for a host of many other reasons. Fortunately, Microsoft SNA Server has a component called COM TI (Transaction Integrator) that enables Windows NT systems to participate in a CICS or IMS transaction. If you have the need to work with processes on legacy systems, then you will want to check out the capabilities of SNA Server and COM TI.

Integrating Legacy Systems with Host Integration Server

Microsoft has come to realize that it cannot be everywhere, at least not all at once. There are too many systems currently in place that would take too much time, effort, and money to just switch over. Although some of these systems are years old, corporations rely on these for their daily operations. To help its customers keep these older legacy systems around and still use the latest features of Microsoft technology, Microsoft is coming out with Host Integration Server 2000. This will enable enterprise organizations to not lose their huge investments in existing infrastructure, but to still create new, mission-critical applications on the .NET Platform platform that can pull data from these legacy systems.

14

Host Integration Server provides a multitude of services for the enterprise organization. Network and Security Integration will enable one password to be used for multiple systems. Data Integration will enable database information to be read from various systems, regardless of the platform on which the data resides. Applications will also be able to interact by using both Microsoft's messaging technology and COMTI. Host Integration Server can use MSMQ and COMTI to create new systems that encapsulate existing business logic and applications. By enabling Microsoft technologies to interact and work with IBM mainframe, AS400, and UNIX platforms, Host Integration Server opens up many new possibilities and potential customers for the Windows DNA platform. The beta for Host Integration Server is scheduled to be available mid-year 2000.

Getting to Know BizTalk Server 2000

Now that you understand XML (refer to Day 12, "The Power of XML") and asynchronous message-based development models, we are ready to discuss BizTalk. BizTalk provides a framework that uses XML, XML schemas, and MIME to enable systems to communicate between applications and organizations in an open, independent format.

NEW TERM *Multipurpose Internet Mail Extensions* (MIME) is a standard way to encode binary data for transport across the Internet. MIME is used extensively by e-mail packages to encode attachments.

BizTalk is a message format that uses XML to represent the message content. BizTalk specifies a message container format, much like an envelope contains a letter.

The BizTalk framework relies upon information to be represented in XML. The information must have an accessible XML schema that can be used to provide context to the data.

BizTalk is capable of translating many different types of data into and out of and XML schema. For example BizTalk can read X.12 EDI formatter data, delimited flat files, MSMQ, COM, and any other formats that you can define. BizTalk comes with a tool to help you define the translators for various message formats. This capability gives you the ability to work with other systems very easily. BizTalk works at the business layer of the Windows DNA platform. Often times you will need to interoperate with packages or other systems. In the past you had to do extensive development to accommodate the required interfaces. BizTalk gives you a tool that allows you to build these interfaces, called adapters, very quickly and easily.

Introducing BizTalk Server 2000 Terminology

BizTalk introduces a new set of terminology. The following sections briefly define these new terms.

Business Document

The *business document* is an XML stream containing the business transaction data. This transaction data can represent a purchase order, invoice, sales forecast, or any other business information. A business document forms the payload of a message. The business document is also referred to as the *body* of the BizTalk message.

The BizTalk framework does not prescribe the content or structure (schema) of individual business documents. The details of the business document content and structure, or schema, are defined and agreed upon by the solution implementers.

Schema

A *schema* is the metadata used to describe the content and structure of a business document. This formal description is used by application developers to create systems to process corresponding business documents, or by parsers that validate a business document's conformance to the schema at runtime.

Organizations can publish their schemas in the library on http://www.biztalk.org, or through other means.

Note

> Schemas for business documents do not contain any BizTags (see the next section), as described in the specification. A schema contains only those tags required to support the business transaction, as designed by the publishing/ implementing organization. General requirements and guidelines for schema implementations are defined in the BizTalk Schema Guidelines document available on http://www.biztalk.org/Resources/schemasguide.asp.

BizTags

BizTags are the set of XML tags (both mandatory and optional) used to specify business document handling. The BizTags are added as an XML envelope or wrapper for a business document by an application or application adapter. They are processed by the BizTalk server, or by other applications facilitating the document interchange. The XML envelope format is discussed in detail a bit later in this chapter.

BizTalk Document

A *BizTalk document* is a business document with the handling BizTags. It is a single, well-formed XML stream.

14

BizTalk Message

A *BizTalk message* is the unit of interchange between BizTalk servers. BizTalk messages are used to send BizTalk documents, and any related files, between BizTalk servers.

The details of the BizTalk message's wire encoding are transport specific. For example, an FTP transport can implement the message as a single BizTalk document in XML. Alternatively, an HTTP implementation can encode the BizTalk document within a MIME message.

BizTalk Server

A *BizTalk server* is represented by the set of services providing the processing functionality defined in the BizTalk framework specifications.

BizTalk Adapter

A *BizTalk adapter* is the component that provides the translation between messaging formats. Standard adapters are provided in the BizTalk server implementation. Specialized adapters can be custom developed to support specific formatting requirements. Microsoft provides a BizTalk JumpStart kit which is basically a set of wizards to generate adapters based upon mapping BizTalk messages to database schemas. The JumpStart kit is discussed later in this chapter.

Application

An *application* is the line of business system(s) where the business data or logic are stored and executed. An application also includes any additional adapters that might be required to emit or consume XML and communicate with the BizTalk infrastructure.

Sending a BizTalk Server 2000 Message

BizTalk is about sending messages between systems. BizTalk servers act as the translators for the various systems to allow BizTalk messages to be transformed to a format required by the respective systems. BizTalk servers communicate using the BizTalk XML-formatted messages between each other. When communicating with other systems, BizTalk servers translate the messages to the format required by the partner system.

Figure 14.2 shows the series of processing steps triggered by an event within a business application:

1. An event occurs within a business application.
2. The application, or the application adapter, creates a BizTalk document. This document is structured according to the schemas published for both BizTalk messages and implementation-defined business documents.
3. The application transmits the BizTalk document to the BizTalk server.

4. The sending BizTalk server adds any required transport-specific envelope information, and transmits the BizTalk message to the destination server.

5. When the message is received by the destination BizTalk server, it can be validated and staged for processing by the destination applications.

FIGURE **14.2**

Sending a BizTalk message.

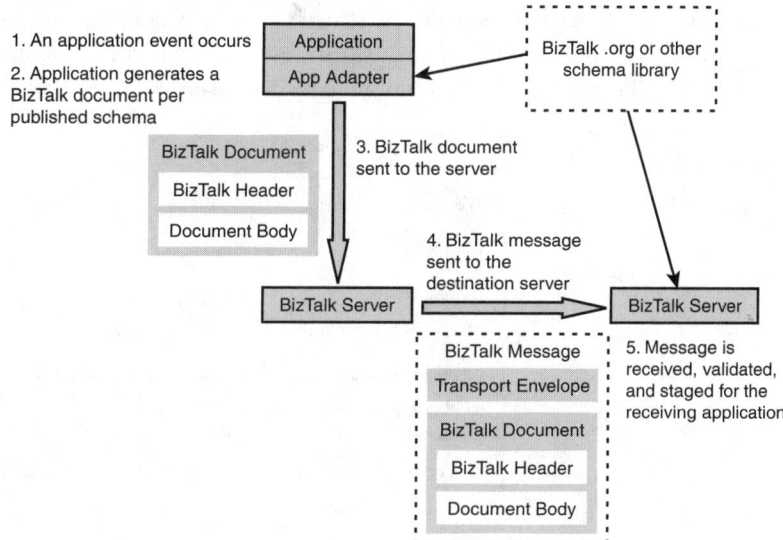

BizTalk Server 2000 Architecture and Message Format

The BizTalk architecture and associated message format is relatively simple. It consists of three layers: the application, the BizTalk server, and data communications. At each layer, the message is wrapped in a container that is appropriate for that layer, as shown in Figure 14.3.

FIGURE **14.3**

BizTalk message flow.

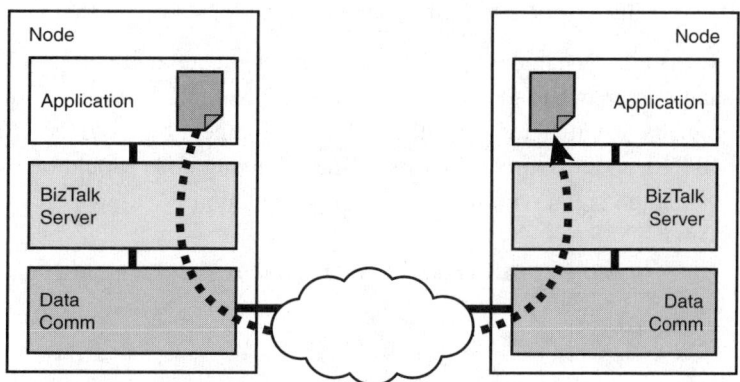

14

The application format is specific to the particular application. It is formatted in XML, and the schema is published to a commonly accessible location, such as `http://www.biztalk.org`.

At the BizTalk layer, the business data is encapsulated in an XML structure that adds information, known as BizTags. These BizTags will be used by BizTalk servers to deliver the business data. This envelope structure contains document-routing and handling information. Figure 14.4 illustrates the various sections of a BizTalk message. The specifics of each layer in this format will now be discussed.

FIGURE 14.4

BizTalk message layers.

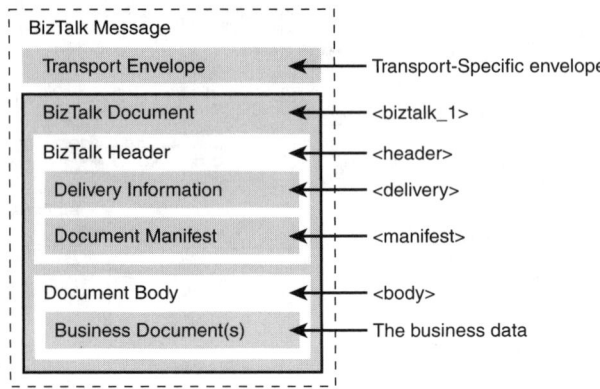

BizTalk XML Formatting Rules

BizTalk follows the strict formatting rules of XML. Recall from Day 12 that XML

- Is case sensitive
- Must include fully nested pairs of element tags
- Requires that attributes be contained in quotes
- Must have an XML header, for example, `<?xml version="1.0" ?>`

A BizTalk Document (version 1.0) must begin and end with the XML tags `<biztalk_1>` and a reference to the BizTalk namespace. Note that Universal Resource Names (URN) registry specifications are still under development by the Internet Engineering Task Force (IETF), so the approach shown in the following code should be used when direct schema validation is not required for the implementation:

```
<biztalk_1
        xmlns="urn:biztalk-org:biztalk:biztalk_1">
    …
</biztalk_1>
```

The `<biztalk_1>` tag is also known as the *root tag* for the XML document. These outer tags define a document as being a BizTalk version 1.0 document, using element declarations from the BizTalk framework namespace. This namespace reference makes it clear that the message envelope is defined by the BizTalk Framework Independent Document Specification and permits a BizTalk server or receiving system to validate the structure and content of the message as it is processed.

For a document to be labeled a BizTalk Framework-Compliant Document, the outer tags must begin and end as shown in the previous code snippet. Without these tags, the server that is processing a document to extract its data will be unable to locate further information specified within the BizTalk Framework.

Within the outer envelope are two major sections—the `<header>` and `<body>`—which are similar to those found in HTML documents. However, when these elements are contained within a BizTalk document, they have completely different meanings.

We do not have enough pages to cover the full tag specification in each of these sections, so we will just cover the highlights. For the full specification, tools, and so on, visit `http://www.microsoft.com/biztalk`. Listing 14.1 shows an example BizTalk message. The implementation detains for each section will be covered at a high level following the listing.

LISTING 14.1   Sample BizTalk Message

```
 1:    <?xml version="1.0" ?>
 2:  <biztalk_1 xmlns="urn:biztalk-org:biztalk:biztalk_1">
 3:  <header>
 4:  <delivery>
 5:  <message>
 6:     <messageID>8230948204820</messageID>
 7:     <sent>1999-01-02T19:00:01+02:00</sent>
 8:     <subject>Bank Statement</subject>
 9:     </message>
10:  <to>
11:     <address>http://www.smalltown.com/statement.asp</address>
12:  <state>
13:     <referenceID>123</referenceID>
14:     <handle>7</handle>
15:     <process>bankStatement</process>
16:     </state>
17:     </to>
18:  <from>
19:     <address>...</address>
20:     <state>...</state>
21:     </from>
```

14

continues

LISTING 14.1 continued

```
22:    </delivery>
23: <manifest>
24: <document>
25:    <name>smalltown_Statement_1</name>
26:    <description>Bank Statement</description>
27:    </document>
28:    </manifest>
29:    </header>
30: <body>
31:    <docType xmlns="urn:..." />
32:    </body>
33:    </biztalk_1>
```

ANALYSIS The header element (lines 3 through 29) has a number of child elements; among these are <delivery> (lines 4 through 22) and <manifest> (lines 23 through 28). The delivery element has child elements such as <message> (lines 5 through 9), <to> (lines 10 through 17), <from> (lines 18 through 21), which provide information about the source and destination systems, as well as meta information about the business data message. The message element is required as well as its children <messageID> (line 6) and <sent> (line 7). The message ID is a unique sequential number or GUID. The sent element contains a time stamp.

The <to> (lines 10 through 17) and <from> (lines 18 through 21) elements are also required. They both contain required child elements, <address> (line 11) and <referenceID> (line 13). The address is the URI of the source and the destination for the message; the referenceID is again a unique number that references the interchange the message is associated with.

The <manifest> (lines 23 through 28) element contains information about the document. It is intended as a place to communicate information about the content of the message. <manifest> is not a required element, however, if you do use it you will need certain required elements.

The <document> (lines 24 through 27) element is a required child element of the manifest. Within the document element is a required *<name>* (line 25) element, the name or type of the root element of the XML business document, for example, "SmallTown_Statement_1". This value corresponds with the root tag or schema name of the business document schema passed.

The <body> (lines 30 through 32) element contains the actual business data. The contents of the body will be dictated by the BizTalk schema for the respective application.

BizTalk Messages with Base-64 or MIME

A BizTalk message can contain non-XML data if it is encrypted as base-64 or multi-part MIME. The provision of the capability to transmit binary data is included for completeness. Binary data *can* substantially increase the size of the BizTalk message. For example if you wanted to send pictures in a BizTalk message you would MIME encode them. On the other hand you would not send a recordset MIME encoded because the recordset would be smaller and more accessible if it were converted to XML before transmission.

The transport layer is typically HTTP or MSMQ, however, any network format can be used. The transportation envelope is outside of the BizTalk specification.

Introducing the BizTalk Server 2000 JumpStart Kit

To help you get up-to-speed on BizTalk, Microsoft has developed the BizTalk JumpStart Kit. The kit includes documentation, a sample application, and Visual Basic plug-ins to make the creation of BizTalk documents easy through the creation of BizTalk adapters. The adapters created map an XML document to a Visual Basic class. By doing this, the Visual Basic application can interact with any other system that can receive BizTalk documents. Ideally these documents will be communicating through BizTalk servers as opposed to directly between applications. Another plug-in provided is used to map a BizTalk document to a database schema. This BizTalk-to-database mapping allows for a complete end-to-end, system-to-system interaction because both the packaging and translation of the data being exchanged between applications is handled by these tools. If you have ever had to do this type of plumbing work in the past you will appreciate the amount of work that these tools save you.

The JumpStart Kit Architecture

The BizTalk JumpStart Kit is a sample application programming tool set designed to show technicians, administrators, and software designers a simple way to create an XML layer that links different applications. As such, it is distributed as source code, white papers, PowerPoint slide shows, and tools. After it's compiled, the software itself consists of four different parts. The first part is known as the core services. The second part is a set of utilities. The third part consists of programming tools used by software developers to create the software components that manage the XML and applications being integrated. Finally, the JumpStart Kit ships with a sample application that demonstrates the concepts required for using the JumpStart Kit.

14

Architecture Pieces

In this architecture, a programmer is provided with a complete environment for creating, deploying, and managing software components that manage XML, database access, and business logic. The BizTalk JumpStart Kit makes it possible for programmers who know the XML format they need to manage to easily create components that fit into this architecture. The programmer who starts with a BizTalk XML schema that describes the XML, uses the tools provided to create an application adapter, a message management "plug-in," and, if required, data access components that reach into any relevant relational databases. If you are dealing with application-specific data, you may very likely not have a BizTalk XML schema defined for your application. In this case you will need to define a schema first. Once you have your schema then the tools will automate the creation of the COM and database interfaces for your schema.

Programmer Responsibilities

To extend the JumpStart Kit, the programmer will need to create two—and possibly three—kinds of components. In Figure 14.5, these components are shown on the right. Each of the component types are explained in the following sections.

FIGURE 14.5

BizTalk JumpStart Kit architecture.

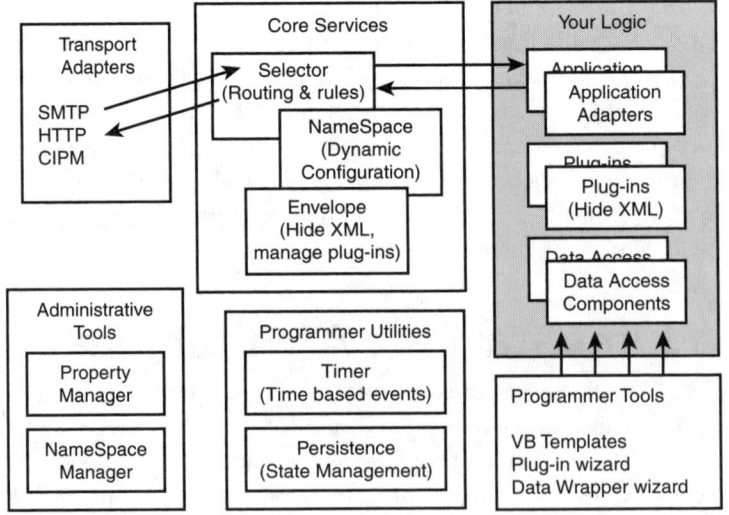

Application Adapters

An application adapter consumes an incoming message. When a message arrives via a transport adapter (refer to left side of Figure 14.5), it is passed to the selector. The selector decides if the message has arrived at the right place and, if so, hands the message to the appropriate application adapter. When planning to accept and process a particular message type, the programmer using the JumpStart Kit needs to plan on creating an application adapter for each message type that can come in.

The adapters are used to reach into applications or databases, or to perform specific business logic. The exact nature of the application adapter is dependent on the tasks that must be accomplished to properly process a given message. After they are created, adapters are installed in your production or prototype environment in a two-step process.

The first step is to copy the component into the desired Microsoft Transaction Server instance on whatever computer is appropriate. The second step is to use the administrative tool to configure the Namespace. The Namespace is a core service used by the selector to dynamically invoke the correct application adapter whenever a particular type of XML message is received.

Plug-Ins

The purpose of a plug-in is twofold and depends on whether the application needs to create or consume a specific XML structure. Plug-ins work with the core envelope object design to completely hide the underlying XML from the programmer. These two object types ease the burden of having to learn about XML—a learning step that you might not want to invest in too broadly before you get started. Together, the envelope and plug-in architecture enable a programmer to choose whether to create or consume XML messages.

Because most integration or commerce scenarios involve a simple pattern of sending a request and getting back a response (or the converse of getting a request and sending a response), the JumpStart Kit is optimized to let you use XML in these situations.

Microsoft provides a code generator, the toolkit provides source code and compile scripts for a Visual Basic source code generator that can read an XML schema. It can generate all the source code required to make a plug-in without manual coding.

Plug-ins can also be created manually as code by following the directions in the white paper called "Envelopes and Plug-ins Explained." This white paper is provided with the JumpStart toolkit so that architects, designers, and programmers can better understand what is happening inside of the envelope and plug-in code.

The premise that lets the code generator—and most message interchanges in general—work is that the design of the messages is well known. The BizTalk Framework defines a mechanism for describing messages, called an XML schema. XML schema describe XML data structures in a highly technical but accurate manner. The BizTalk.org XML schema library is an excellent source for obtaining schemas that describe the many different software applications which use XML. The Plug-In Wizard—a code generator that

14

works with Visual Basic—reads schemas and creates plug-ins that are compatible with both the schema and the envelope object that the selector uses to encapsulate the XML information received.

Plug-ins take the pain out of processing messages by hiding the details of the underlying XML, as well as the XML parser object interface, from the business programmer. The result of using envelopes and plug-ins in your application adapter is that the programmer gets to use a normal object interface—with properties, classes, and collections. Used with Visual Basic or Visual InterDev, the envelope and plug-in objects enable the programmer to take advantage of programmer productivity features such as IntelliSense, data tips, and type-ahead.

Data Access Components

In many instances, to complete the activities required in an application adapter component, the programmer will need access to tables in relational databases. In Windows DNA, the data tier is separate from the business logic tier. Because the application adapters represent the business logic layer of the message interface between your partner applications, the usual approach would be to make another component layer that manages the actual database connections, SQL query logic, and database management tasks.

The JumpStart Kit comes with source code for a tool that automates the creation of simple data access components. The source is provided so that your programmers can extend the concept of code generation for handling repetitive tasks (such as creating data access components) to suit the needs of your own business. This code generator (or *wizard,* as they're commonly known) can be compiled and used as is to create data access components as well. The sample application data access components were created in this way.

The result of using this wizard is a component that is fully transactional and compatible with the Microsoft Transaction Server. The code generated by the wizard itself is also a great source of best coding practice for using technologies like ActiveX Data Objects (ADO), Microsoft Transaction Server, and Visual Basic.

The BizTalk JumpStart Kit has a number of additional tools, samples, and utilities that can be used to configure your environment. If you are interested in using BizTalk, you will want to download the BizTalk JumpStart Kit.

Exploring the Simple Object Application Protocol (SOAP)

Simple Object Application Protocol (SOAP) is a specification for conducting inter-process communication using XML over HTTP. SOAP is a protocol, not an API, so it can be implemented on any platform. Why is SOAP cool? To understand it, we need to discuss the two alternative IPC formats, CORBA and DCOM. Both of these formats are intended to enable objects on any system to work with objects on any other system. The problem with using the formats lies in the complexities of the standards and their implementation. Both formats are relatively closed within their own respective constituencies. SOAP breaks these limitations by bringing communication down to two universally accepted formats: HTTP and XML. In fact, you will notice that HTTP and XML are fundamental to many of Microsoft product updates. More about this when we discuss Visual Studio.NET.

SOAP facilitates interoperability among different programs and platforms. This open interoperability makes existing applications accessible to a wider range of users. SOAP is basically a network protocol that has no specific programming model. Rather, it relies upon the HTTP and XML specifications.

SOAP uses XML as an encoding scheme for requests and response parameters, using HTTP as a transport. SOAP deals with a small number of abstractions. A SOAP end point is simply a HTTP-based URL that identifies a target for method invocation. SOAP, like BizTalk, uses an <envelope> XML element that contains a <body> element to contain call elements. Listing 14.2 is an example request message formatted using the SOAP protocol.

LISTING 14.2   SOAP Request Message

```
 1: POST /my_server/my_object  HTTP/1.1
 2: Host: 123.123.12.1
 3: Content-Type: txt/xml
 4: Content-Length: 175
 5: SOAPMethodName: urn:bank-com:IAccount#balance
 6:
 7: <Envelope>
 8:   <Body>
 9:       <m:balance xmlns:m='urn:bank-com:IAccount'>
10:           <theAccountNumber>56789</theAccountNumber>
11:       </m:balance>
12:   </Body>
13: </Envelope>
```

ANALYSIS   The SOAPMethodName (line 5) header must match the first child element (line 9) under the <Body> element; otherwise, the call will be rejected. Notice the syntax between lines 5 and 9 differs in that the method comprises of XML block (lines 9 through 11). Contained within that block are the [in]put parameters required for the method. The rest of the lines in this code sample are standard HTTP protocol lines.

14

The SOAP response format, Listing 14.3, is similar to the request format. The response payload will contain the [out]put or the [in]put/[out]put parameters as child elements of a distinguished response element. The parameter values are not marked specifically as input or output but rather are determined by their position in the XML hierarchy. This element name is the same as the request call element concatenated with the `Response` suffix (lines 7 and 9). Listing 14.3 is the minimum SOAP response to the previous call.

LISTING 14.3   SOAP Response Message

```
 1: 200 OK
 2: Content-Type: text/xml
 3: Content-Length: 123
 4:
 5: <Envelope>
 6:    <Body>
 7:       <m:balanceResponse> xmlns:m='urn:Bank-com:IAccount'>
 8:          <result>$234.76</result>
 9:       </m:balanceResponse>
10:    </Body>
11: </Envelope>
```

ANALYSIS   Notice that the response element is named `balanceResponse` (lines 7 and 9), which is simply the method name followed by `Response`.

Anything can be serialized into an XML payload, which is then exchanged using HTTP protocol. There is a bit more that can be said about data typing, various parameter-passing scenarios, and fault codes. You can learn about these areas at `http://msdn.microsoft.com/soap`.

Exploring Application Center 2000 Server

As the size of Web sites increase, systems engineers find their paradigm changing. They are moving from administering a couple computers that host Internet Information Server and SQL Server to having an entire Web farm of computers that are able to handle an enormous user base. Network Load Balancing, which was an add-on to NT 4.0 and is now part of Windows 2000 Advanced Server, enables you to create these Web farms by having multiple computers all support the same Web site. This fits in with Windows DNA by taking you to the next level of spreading your presentation, business logic, and data tiers horizontally in your Web site.

With all these computers making up a Web site, there is a tremendous burden to balance all this hardware and keep it running and in sync with everything else. This is where

Application Center 2000 Server will come in. It will enable you to manage the computers and monitor what is currently going on. You can easily replicate content and data to other machines to get them quickly online to participate in the Web farm. Also, diagnostics will help you isolate problems more quickly. App Center Server will help streamline the process of working with load-balanced machines.

Application Center 2000 adds back a feature that was in the beta versions of Windows 2000 but was pulled before it was released. The feature is component load balancing. Component load balancing gives operations the ability to specify that certain components can be balanced across multiple computers. With the previous mentioned Web Load Balancing the network traffic is distributed across up to 32 computers. What the Component Load Balancing (CLB) services do is allow the components in a system to be run on a number of computers. In the current architecture a COM component can be run locally or remotely using DCOM but not both. CLB resolves this limitation by adding the capability to do both.

The way that CLB works is that one computer acts as the CLB service. Its job is to know about what components it can balance and onto what computer the components can be invoked. When the CLB dispatches a component to be invoked in a remote system, the remote system adds some additional monitoring of the component so that it can report its status and resource usage to the CLB Server. The CLB Service uses this information to determine on which computer to run components.

The other capability that Application Center 2000 works with is the Clustering Service. Computers that are configured in a cluster are identical in terms of configuration and look to the system as a single system. Work is balanced across the clustered system. The clustered systems communicate amongst themselves keeping each other informed of the work they are performing. By doing this, if a machine in the cluster fails the other machine can assume the processing.

These capabilities help with scalability and reliability of the system. The cost associated with planning, deploying and managing will go down as systems are made to work together better AppCenter Server represents another accomplishment for Microsoft, reaffirming its capability to create Web sites on the Windows DNA platform that have high performance and are highly scalable.

Visual Studio.NET

14

Visual Studio.NET has been updated to support the new services exposed by Windows 2000 and add development capabilities to create XML, BizTalk, and SOAP-enabled applications. Visual Basic, one of the tools in Visual Studio, has been substantially updated with many new object-oriented features, better error handling, and free threading capabilities.

Visual Studio.NET is specifically designed to support Windows DNA programming on the .NET platform. Scalability, durability, and ease of maintenance are major focuses of this release of the development suite.

The hot new capabilities of Visual Studio.NET are Web Applications and a better Visual Basic. Some of the capabilities are new, others build upon existing capabilities of Visual Studio 6. You will learn where you can prepare today for these new capabilities.

Web Applications

Web Forms and Web services are a new way to develop Web-enabled applications.

ASP+ Web forms are a language-independent way to construct user interfaces. Web forms execute on the server, enabling them to adapt to different user browser capabilities. Web forms are built with the exact same technology that you have used previously to develop user interfaces. For performance reasons, Web forms are made up of two parts, HTML pages and compiles executable code, both run on the Web server. The creation of Web Forms is identical to the way that forms are created in Visual Basic. The developer creates a form and then drags controls off of a palette onto the form and sets the controls' properties. The code behind the form controls is compiled into a separate, executable module to maximize performance.

Web Forms, WebClasses, and ASPs

Previous versions of Visual Studio tools have attempted to simplify Web development for desktop developers. For example, Visual Basic provided support for DHTML clients and WebClasses whereas Visual InterDev eased development of Active Server Pages (ASPs). Although these are all powerful tools for Web development, the overlap in their functionality is confusing. Developers have asked for more direction in choosing a particular Web technology.

Web Forms are the fundamental way to build Web applications with the next generation Visual Studio tools. Web Forms represent an evolution of ASP and WebClasses providing the best of both models. Regardless of what language you choose, Web Forms will be central to your Web architecture.

Microsoft is committed to continuing support for both Web Classes and ASPs. The applications you build today will continue to work in the future.

Preparing for Web Forms

To prepare for using Web Forms, Microsoft recommends that you build your applications on a multitier architecture. The core business functionality should be placed in middle-tier components authored with any Visual Studio development language. These components should be connected to an ASP page using Visual InterDev with minimal script.

The majority of the logic should *not* be in the script, but rather in the business object. If you follow this design pattern, you'll be well-positioned for the future. We will cover the presentation layer in Week 3, so you might want to refer back to this section after you finish the book.

Middle-tier business functionality exposed via standard Web protocols is known as *Web services*. Web services are a combination of XML and binary applications on the Web server that use XML and HTTP to exchange information between themselves and the client application. Because they use these standard protocols, they can easily pass information through corporate firewalls and interoperate with XML-enabled client applications. Because Web services use standard protocols, they can be developed on any platform—for example, Apache running on top of UNIX. However, if you develop on top of NT, you will find that Visual Studio has a number of features that will make the job easier by automatically creating and assembling these services.

After a Web service has been built, both the compiled code and an XML file describing the public methods of the service are published to the Web server. The Web service can now be invoked via HTTP, and XML can be used to pass data to and from the service, as we saw in the SOAP example.

More information about these types of applications will appear in Week 3, especially in Day 20, "Office 2000 and Web Components," and Day 21, "Implementing Digital Dashboards in Windows DNA Applications."

If you develop your Web applications using the Windows DNA model discussed in this book, you will be in a good position to easily convert your components to use these new features.

A Better Visual Basic

Visual Basic is a widely used language for rapidly developing applications. Its history dates back to the beginning of Microsoft. Yet, you could not do everything with Visual Basic that is possible with C++, and thus developers had to know both languages. Many of these limitations have been resolved in Visual Basic.NET. Visual Basic.NET now has more object-oriented features, free threading, type safety, and structured exception handling.

Object-Oriented at Last

The object-oriented capabilities of Visual Basic, up until now, have been limited to encapsulation and interface inheritance. Now inheritance, encapsulation, overloading, polymorphism, and parameterized constructors have been added to the language.

14

Inheritance

The number one, most-requested feature for Visual Basic is support for implementation inheritance. Developing in Internet time requires rapid assembly and massive reuse. To facilitate implementation inheritance, the Inherits keyword has been added to the language.

Developers can use the new keyword Inherits or the class property sheet's Inherits property to derive from an existing class.

The INHERITS statement supports all the usual properties associated with inheritance:

- Instances of the derived class support all methods and interfaces supported by the base class.
- The derived class can override methods defined in the base class using the *Overrides* keyword.
- The derived class can extend the set of methods and interfaces supported by the base class.

Encapsulation

Encapsulation means that developers can contain and hide information about an object, such as internal data structures and code. It isolates the internal complexity of an object's operation from the rest of the application.

Overloading

Overloading is a feature that will enable an object's methods and operators to have different meanings depending on their context. Operators can behave differently depending on the data type, or class, of the operands. For example, x+y can mean different things depending on whether x and y are integers or structures. Overloading is especially useful when your object model dictates that you employ similar names for procedures that operate on different data types.

Polymorphism

Polymorphism refers to the capability to process objects differently, depending on their data type or class. Additionally, it provides the capability to redefine methods for derived classes.

Parameterized Constructors

Parameterized constructors (or more simply, *constructors*) enable you to create a new instance of a class while simultaneously passing arguments to the new instance.

Constructors are essential for object-oriented programming because they enable user-defined construction code to be passed parameters by the creator of the instance. They simplify client code by enabling a new object instance to be created and initialized in a single expression.

Free Threading

Today when developers create applications in Visual Basic, the code that they write is *synchronous*, that is, each line of code must be executed before the next one. When developing Web applications, scalability is key. Developers need tools that enable concurrent processing.

With the inclusion of free threading in Visual Basic.NET, developers can spawn a thread, which can perform some long-running task, execute a complex query, or run a complex calculation while the rest of the application continues, providing asynchronous processing.

Structured Exception Handling

Developing enterprise applications requires the construction of reusable, maintainable components. One challenging aspect in past versions of Visual Basic was its support for error handling. In the past, developers had to provide error-handling code in every function and subroutine. Developers have found that a consistent error-handling scheme means a great deal of duplicated code. Error handling using the existing On Error GoTo statement sometimes slows the development and maintenance of large applications. Its very name reflects some of these problems: As the GoTo implies, when an error occurs, control is transferred to a labeled location inside the subroutine. After the error code runs, it must often be diverted to another cleanup location via a standard GoTo, which uses yet another GoTo or an EXIT out of the procedure. Handling several different errors with various combinations of RESUME and NEXT quickly produces illegible code. It also leads to frequent bugs when execution paths aren't completely thought out.

With Try…Catch…, finally you can execute a code block as seen here:

```
Try
    Any block of code


Catch
    if something goes wrong this code is run
```

14

Finally, these problems go away. Developers can nest their exception handling, and there is a control structure for writing cleanup code that executes in both normal and exception conditions.

Type Safety

Today the Visual Basic language is very liberal in the implicit type coercions it will generate. For assignment and for parameter passing other than by reference, the Visual Basic compiler will enable nearly any data type to be converted to any other type by generating runtime coercion. The runtime coercion operation will fail if the value that is to be converted cannot be converted without data loss. Through the addition of a new compilation option, Visual Basic.NET can generate compile-time errors for any conversions that might cause an error at runtime. Option Strict improves type safety by generating errors when a conversion is required that could fail at runtime or when an unexpected type conversion—like the automatic conversion between numeric types and strings—occurs.

Summary

Microsoft has a number of services that, in Windows NT 4, were separate components like MSMQ. With Windows 2000 and COM+, message queuing is built in to the operating system.

As the size and complexity of systems increase along with the need for around-the-clock service, the need to asynchronously process data increases. With a queuing process, services can be brought online and taken offline without affecting the rest of the system.

New protocols such as BizTalk and SOAP enable heterogeneous systems to interoperate using standard industry protocols like HTTP and XML. As Microsoft evolves the Windows DNA model and tool set, it is clear that Internet standards and protocols are the new foundation for work. All Microsoft products, services, and platforms are being Internet-enhanced to the point that XHTML is a native format for all services and applications. This is not to say that XML and HTTP will replace all other protocols. Rather, these protocols are at the touch points with other systems. Internally, highly typed, binary coupling will still exist between components and services.

Visual Basic continues to emerge as a major language in the Microsoft tool set. With the addition of more C++–like capabilities, more powerful applications will be developed more rapidly using Visual Basic as the primary language.

Q&A

Q **Why are some of the protocols used by Microsoft, such as XML schema, not industry standards? And should we wait until a standard is set?**

A The need for capabilities is far outpacing the W3C's ability to research, get consensus, and establish a standard. To address this, Microsoft has developed de facto standards in conjunction with others in the industry that it then implements in new products. These standards are then submitted to the W3C for adoption. For the most part, Microsoft's standards have been adopted, sometimes with minor changes. When such standards are adopted, Microsoft usually provides tools to convert code to the standard. If you need the capabilities a de facto standard provides, it is best to start using the standard now. You might have to make adjustments later, but they will be minor in comparison to the effort following the standard will save you.

Q **Where can I get programming help?**

A Microsoft makes specifications, JumpStart Kits, examples, and documentation available through its Microsoft Developers Network (http://msdn.microsoft.com).

Q **Are there any additional capabilities we should know about?**

A All the protocols discussed today have extensive documentation, examples, and white papers to help you get up to speed on them and to start using them. Today was an introduction to the technologies so that you will be aware of the capabilities. You will want to review the complete documentation before diving in.

Q **Will I have to go back and change all my interfaces to use these new capabilities?**

A No, Microsoft still supports all the old interfaces and has made an effort to enable the older interfaces with the new capabilities. Microsoft realizes that it takes time to learn the new ways. Besides, a great deal of intellectual capital exist in components developed in previous architectures.

Moving forward, you will want to use the new interfaces where they make sense.

Workshop

The workshop provides quiz questions to help solidify your understanding of the material covered, as well as exercises to provide you with experience in using what you have learned. Try to answer the quiz and exercise questions before checking the answers in Appendix A.

14

Quiz

1. What capabilities does MSMQ give the developer?

2. What are the five basic methods in MSMQ?

3. What are the three layers in BizTalk?

4. What are the protocols used by SOAP?

5. What is the new way that Visual Studio 7 will handle presentation tier elements?

Exercises

1. This is all new technology that is changing and being enhanced as this book is being written. Go to the Microsoft Web site and search on these technologies to see the latest information on these capabilities.

   Tip: Microsoft keeps its developer-related information at http://msdn.microsoft.com. And more technical information can be found at http://www.microsoft.com/technet.

WEEK 2

In Review

You have just completed the second week of learning about Windows DNA. Congratulations on making it through two of the three weeks. By completing this week, you have moved from application design and the database implementation to creating the business logic tier of an application. This tier contains all the business's information that is vital to the application working successfully.

Looking back at this week, you have achieved a number of accomplishments. After gaining an understanding of COM and MTS, you had an opportunity to open up new ActiveX DLL projects in Visual Basic and create COM components. The properties of an ActiveX DLL project were covered, including important aspects such as the threading model and binary compatibility. You also had a chance to incorporate transactions into the component.

This was all done in the SmallTownBank application that you have been working on throughout this book. You began by creating two components, SmallTownBank_Data and SmallTownBank_Business. The first component contains the data access methods that you use to contact the data store. It contains very little business logic, but it does contain information on the stored procedures to interact with SQL Server. By creating this component, you can change the data store without having to re-create the entire middle tier. You only have to rework this data component. Two of the methods in SmallTownBank_Data, CreditAccount, and DebitAccount allow you to modify account balances by crediting and debiting an account. Both methods insert and update records.

The second component, SmallTownBank_Business, contains business logic. A method you added in this component, TransferFunds, coordinates the two methods in the data component, DebitAccount and CreditAccount. TransferFunds transfers amounts from one account to another. This method starts up a transaction which DebitAccount and CreditAccount become part of. This allows you to have both the credit and debit occur or to have neither occur. Within these components you implemented a series of methods. In order to make this run in a transaction, you placed the components in Microsoft Transaction Server and set the components to run in the same transaction. By incorporating the transactional capabilities of MTS, you ran these all in a transaction, thereby assuring that the account balances will remain correct.

After working with MTS, you had a chance to look again at ActiveX Data Objects and dig more into the capabilities of it. You learned about how to implement ADO in your components and move data in between the DNA tiers. You had a chance to work with stored procedures some more and also learned about how you can have ADO return hierarchal recordsets with the SHAPE command. You looked at disconnected recordsets and how to handle errors in ADO using the Errors collection.

Another great part of this week was the introduction to XML. You learned about the syntax of XML and how to make an XML document. You had a chance to learn about schemas and DTDs and how those can define what is in an XML document. Additionally you used the XMLDOM object to load an XML document and format the data with an XSL file as well as to look at the data programmatically. Finally you had a chance to see how ADO is integrated with XML.

To round off the week, you looked at the COM+, which offers the latest in COM technology. You learned about various improvements that COM+ has brought with it to Windows 2000, including queued components, component load balancing, component server, and object pooling, to name a few. By looking at MSMQ, you saw how you could communicate with disparate systems that normally couldn't work together. You also saw how MSMQ could be used for asynchronous communications. Finally, you got a sense of some of the new capabilities that will be delivered in development tools that will support the .NET platform (the platform that will replace the Windows DNA platform by 2002).

With this knowledge you are now ready to work with the presentation tier. In this tier, you design an interface to work with a user; it will complete your introduction to Windows DNA.

WEEK 3

At a Glance

You have now reached a point in your learning about Windows DNA where you are ready to put a face on your product. Up to this point, there hasn't been any work on what the users of the system will actually use. Week 3 brings you to the presentation tier of the Windows DNA platform.

With the Internet, the presentation to users has changed drastically over the past few years. Instead of working with an application that the user or an administrator installs on his machine, the user now finds himself navigating through a Web site application. The Internet has also created a number of different ways to deliver the presentation tier. A Web application is one possibility, but you can also create a rich client in Visual Basic and use various technologies to communicate over HTTP to a server that can be physically located anywhere as long as it is hooked to the Internet. This gives a lot of possibilities to look at this week. You will begin with looking at richer clients, such as a Visual Basic client application, and end the week by looking at thinner clients, such as a Web page with only HTML in it.

Visual Basic client applications offer lots of rich functionality. This includes custom windows, specialized controls, and an extensive programming language, which allows a client application to be created that works well for the client. You will learn about the pros and cons of using Visual Basic as a client. More importantly you will learn how to connect your Visual Basic application in with the business logic tier of your application. Next you will have a chance to work with ActiveX controls. These are custom controls that you can imbed in a Visual Basic form and that allow you to move the application to the Web easily because the controls can also be imbedded on a Web page.

15

16

17

18

19

20

21

The next part of the week will look specifically at what you can do in a browser such as Internet Explorer. You will start with how you can add in capabilities to the page on the client by using DHTML. This allows you a lot of functionality without having to return to the server for more information. This will also give you an introduction to JavaScript. You will then learn how to do processing on the server with Active Server Pages. With this information, combined with information you will learn about HTML, you will be able to make Web pages that, by themselves, contain very little functionality and instead shift most of the processing and functionality to the Web server. Active Server Pages will do this processing for you, allowing your Web pages to change accordingly to a user's actions.

You will finish off the week by looking at exciting new technologies that are beginning to gain more momentum. One of those technologies is the Web components that come with Windows 2000. These components can help you with analyzing data and working with spreadsheet information. Anyone with Office 2000 can bring these components up in a Web browser. Finally the Digital Dashboard, which is contained within Outlook 2000, will also be introduced. This allows you to create a customized interface that can manage your information and allow you to easily access it.

This week covers the final and third tier of the Windows DNA platform. By rounding off your knowledge with information on the presentation tier, you will be able to start working on your own applications and envisioning how they can work within Windows DNA. Continue your education as you go through this week and gain momentum as you move from learning about Windows DNA to implementing Windows DNA. Enjoy this next week!

DAY 15

A Rich Native Windows Client

Today, you will build a rich Visual Basic presentation layer. When most people think of developing an Internet application, they assume that the Web browser is the only user interface available. This is not the case, and, in fact, the Windows DNA platform works very well with the standard Windows executable applications that you are used to developing. The important thing to remember is that the client in this model is for presentation and emissary processing only. All business and data processing should occur at the other two tiers. The issue then becomes, how do you connect to these services? Microsoft has provided four technologies for doing this:

- Windows Sockets (WinSock)
- Distributed COM (DCOM)
- Remote Data Services (RDS)
- Microsoft Internet Transfer Control (WinInet)

In this chapter, the user will use WinSock, DCOM, RDS, and the WinInet component to communicate with server-side business components. The advantages and disadvantages of each technology will be discussed.

Building a Rich Client

You build a rich Windows client in the same way that you have been developing personal productivity desktop applications and client/server applications. The difference is that you use business objects that exist on another computer, rather than on the local system. Microsoft has released several technologies over the past few years to address this capability. Each have their own advantages and disadvantages, which we will discuss in this chapter.

Building the Client

You build your client with the same development tools that you have used to develop other applications, including other Windows DNA components. In our case, you will be using Microsoft Visual Basic to develop this sample application. The first thing you need to do is develop the forms that you will be using to build out these examples.

Begin by opening Visual Basic and creating a new project called `SmallTownBank`. Now create two forms with the listed fields seen in Tables 15.1 and 15.2.

TABLE 15.1   Form `frmAccountBalance`

Control Type	Control Name
WinSock	tcpClient
MSHFlexGrid	mshfgAccountBalance
TextBox	txtOutput
CommandButton	cmdDownloadAccountActivity

TABLE 15.2   Form `frmServer`

Control Type	Control Name
WinSock	tcpServer
TextBox	txtOutput

The forms should look something like Figures 15.1 and 15.2. You will use these forms throughout this chapter to show you how to use the various connection methods.

FIGURE 15.1

Account Balance form.

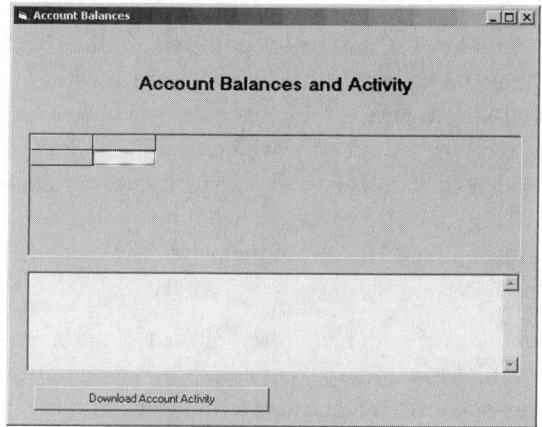

FIGURE 15.2

WinSock Server form.

Using WinSock to Connect to Business Objects

Windows Socket programming is a relatively mature way to communicate using TCP/IP. Socket-based programming is very old in terms of how you develop programs that work across the network. The first question is, what is a socket? It is a TCP/IP port. What is a TCP/IP port? In addition to the IP address, the port designates the service that one wants to run. Typically when using a browser to access Internet services, a prefix designates the well-known port to use. For example, http://1.2.3.4 is really calling port 80 at IP address 1.2.3.4. In the example, port 80 is the well-known port for the http www service. Many of the Internet services operate on their own well-known ports. For example FTP runs on port 21, Telnet runs on port 23, Kerberos on port 88, Network Printing on port 92. For a complete list of well known ports visit http://www.isi.edu/in-notes/iana/assignments/port-numbers. The first 1024 ports are reserved for these well-known services. The port numbers above 1024 are not reserved and therefore can be used by applications you develop. Another way to fully specify the sample address is `http://1.2.3.4:80`. The port designation at the end of the IP address is optional. You would use this optional parameter if the Internet service was running on a different port than its typical well-known port. So, for example, you have a secret Web server running on port 8080. The only way to access it would be to designate `http://1.2.3.4:8080`. So an Internet address has thousands of port on which services can be run. Some of these ports, 1 through 1024, are well known and should only be used for the well-known services assigned to those ports. The rest of the ports are available to you for your particular applications use.

WinSock can communicate with either the well-known ports or the ports specific to your application. The architecture of a socket-based program requires a server that listens on a specific port and an application that can communicate with that port. If you are communicating via a well-known port, then you most likely have a server service running that is listening on that port. You could also develop your own server service, in which case you might want to use a port number that is greater than 1024. Your application would listen on the specified port. Clients that wish to communicate with your applications would then need to communicate using that application specific port.

When you communicate with WinSock, you need to follow the handshaking rules and protocols established between the server and client. With the well-known ports, these protocols are standardized by the Internet Engineering Task Force (IETF). You will recall that in Day 14, "Best Practices and Other Services," you saw some of the HTTP protocol information being used. For your own applications you can use an established protocol or define your own protocol. A protocol is simply an agreed upon set of messages and responses to those messages that are established between two systems. A typical transaction is very similar to the one you laid out for message queuing. The server opens a port and listens. When a client sends a message on the given port, the server reads the message, does some processing based upon the messages instructions, and then writes back the results to the client. The server then returns to a listening state, and the process repeats itself.

Advantages and Disadvantages of WinSock

The advantages of using WinSock are

- Freedom to communicate on any TCP/IP port. You have total freedom to communicate with any service that uses TCP/IP ports.

- You have a greater degree of control over the details of the transactions. This low-level control gives you the ability to work closer with the protocol implementation details.

The disadvantages of using WinSock are

- You must know the specific protocols for a given port. Winsock only gives you very basic, low level capabilities to open, listen, read, write, and close a port. You must implement and comply by the protocol established for the systems to transact. Later in this chapter you will learn about the Inet control which is designed to handle the HTTP, FTP, and GOPHER protocol details for you.

- The client and server must be kept in sync for the processing to work. Because the conversation between the client and the server process are controlled by each party taking turns in the conversation to send and receive messages, it is possible that one of the parties abnormally ends a conversation possibly leaving the other party in an unresolved state. The system that is waiting for a specific message might be blocked from working with other clients until it completes its conversation. This statefulness of a conversation can make a system unstable if the state is not maintained correctly by ensuring that the conversation completes. As you recall this was one of the benefits of using MSMQ in that it ensured that messages would be delivered in the proper sequence.

LAB: Connecting via WinSock

Creating a connection via WinSock is fairly straightforward. You first need to open your test VB client application. You are now going to create a function to open a WinSock connection with the Web server and request results from a server component. In this lab you will retrieve the information from both a well-known port as well as an application defined port. The application that uses the well-known port will open a port on the Web server, and the application that uses an application-defined port will use a server application you build to service the request.

Client Request to a Well-Known Port

You are first going to connect to the Web server and retrieve data using the results from an Active Server Page. To do this, add the code in Listing 15.1 to the frmAccountBalance you created earlier.

LISTING 15.1   WinSock to Web Server

```
1: Private Sub Form_Load()
2:     tcpClient.RemoteHost = "localhost"
3:     tcpClient.RemotePort = 80 'using the web server
4: End Sub
5:  Private Sub cmdDownloadAccountActivity_Click()
6:     Dim txtSendHTTPData As String
```

continues

LISTING 15.1   continued

```
 7:      If tcpClient.State <> sckConnected Then _
 8:          tcpClient.Connect
 9:      Do While tcpClient.State <> sckConnected
10:          DoEvents
11:      Loop
12:      txtSendHTTPData = "GET /smalltown/accountactivity.asp  HTTP/1.1" &
        ↪vbCrLf & _
13:                      "Host: localhost" & vbCrLf & _
14:                      "Content-Type: txt/html" & vbCrLf & vbCrLf
15:      tcpClient.SendData txtSendHTTPData
16: End Sub
17:  Private Sub tcpClient_DataArrival _
18: (ByVal bytesTotal As Long)
19:     Dim strData As String
20:     Dim XMLData As String
21:     Dim rsOutput As New ADODB.Recordset
22:     Dim pos As Integer
23:     Dim pos2 As Integer
24:     Dim length As Integer
25:     Dim myStream As New ADODB.Stream
26:      tcpClient.GetData strData
27:     txtOutput.Text = strData
28:     pos = InStr(strData, "Content-Length:")
29:     If pos > 0 Then
30:         pos = pos + Len("Content-Length:")
31:         pos2 = InStr(pos, strData, vbCrLf)
32:         length = Val(Mid(strData, pos, pos2 - pos))
33:         XMLData = Right(strData, length)
34:     Else
35:         XMLData = strData
36:     End If
37:     myStream.Open
38:     myStream.WriteText XMLData
39:     myStream.Position = 0
40:     rsOutput.Open myStream
41:     Set mshfgAccountBalances.Recordset = rsOutput
42: End Sub
```

ANALYSIS Listing 15.1 adds three pieces of functionality to the page. The first is the Form_Load event for the form. When the form loads, it specifies to the WinSock control the RemoteHost and RemotePort that will be used by the application. In this example, it is using the local computer, localhost (line 2). The Web service is running on the local computer. The RemotePort is set to 80 (line 3), which is the well-known TCP/IP port for WWW service.

The next routine `cmdDownloadAccountActivity_Click` (line 5) is what starts the interaction with the Web server. The first thing you do after dimensioning our string to hold the command (line 6) is check to see if a connection is open (line 7). If the connection is not open, it requests a connection (line 8). You then need to wait until you are connected (lines 9 through 11) before you can transact on the connection. Please note the DoEvents within the loop—this enables the system to process other messages in the queue. The effect is that the display will be updated, and events such as closing the program will be processed. The next three lines (lines 12 through 15) construct the HTTP message you are going to send to get the results from the backend Active Server Page. In this message you are requesting that the `accountactivity.asp` page within the `smalltown` virtual root be run. You use the `GET` command and are using the HTTP/1.1 protocol (line 12). Line 13 indicates the hostname, and line 14 indicates the Content-Type, which in this case is txt/html. The extra carriage return, a line feed at the end, is very important because it tells the Web server that you are done with the command. The last thing that this routine does is send the data to the server (line 15).

The final routine in this listing handles the data arrival event for the WinSock control (line 17). You first dimension the variables that are going to be used in this routine (lines 19 through 25). The data type that might be new to you is the stream object (line 25). A stream acts much like a file handle when dealing with other controls. It will be discussed in detail later in this analysis. The first thing you do is `Get` the data and put it into a temporary variable (line 26). The program then outputs the data to the `txtOutput` control so that you can see what has come back (line 27). The data will be much easier to decipher if you set the properties of the TextBox control to multiline and have a vertical scrollbar. Because the data is coming back from a Web server, it will have header information in the data stream. When you run this program, you will see this header information. You need to strip off the body text if it is coming from a Web server. To do this you search for the `Content-Length`, that is what line 28 is doing. If it finds the `Content-Length` string, the position will be greater than zero (line 29) in which case the length value needs to extracted (lines 30 through 32). You then know how many characters of the return value represent the body data (line 32). You now take that many character from the right side of the return string to get the body data (line 33). Lines 34 through 36 assume that you just got data back, which will be the case with the server application you will develop later.

Now we get into working with the stream. A *stream* is an object that acts like an in-memory file system. The reason you are using a stream is so that you can load the data into a recordset so that the FlexGrid control can render the data. This is admittedly a convoluted process because you are loading the data into a stream object so that it can then be loaded into a recordset object that is then represented in a MSFlexGrid control. This exercise is good in that it shows how to coerce data into various formats so that it can be used in different ways. In Day 20, "Office 2000 and Web Components," you will learn about some controls that can accept the XML data directly. The first thing you do is open your stream (line 27). You then write the data you received into the stream (line 38). Next you reposition the stream position to the beginning (line 39). Now you can load the stream into the recordset (line 40) by using the Open method against the stream. When you see the ASP code in Listing 15.2, it will be clearer how this is working. Finally, you load the FlexGrid using the recordset (line 41).

Web Server Code

In order to run this example, you need to have a page on the Web server that will return data to you. Listing 15.2 is the Active Server Page that is being called by Listing 15.1.

LISTING 15.2   Active Server Page to Provide Data to the WinSock Client (accountactivity.asp)

```
 1: <%@ Language=VBScript %>
 2: <%
 3: set cn = server.CreateObject("ADODB.Connection")
 4: set rs = server.CreateObject("adodb.recordset")
 5: adOpenStatic = 3
 6: adLockReadOnly = 1
 7: adUseClient = 3
 8: adPersistXML = 1
 9: sql = "select * from AccountTransation where AccountID='1'"
10: rs.CursorLocation = adUseClient
11: cn.Open "DSN=SmallTownDSN"
12: rs.Open sql,cn,adOpenStatic,adLockReadOnly
13: rs.Save Response, adPersistXML
14: %>
```

ANALYSIS   Listing 15.2 is a quick page that returns an ADO Recordset in XML format. The first thing that you do is create your connection and recordset objects (lines 3 and 4). Next are definitions for ADO constants (lines 5 through 8). Unlike VB, ASP pages do not know how to access COM object constants. Because the number of constants being used in this example is small, they are defined inline. If you were to use many constants, then you might want to include the adovbs.inc at the top of your page. The adovbs.inc file includes all the constants used by ADO. To use this file you need to copy it to the same directory as your ASP page. To locate the file, run Start—Find and search your system for the adovbs.inc file. When you find it, copy it to the directory where your server page is located. The constants are being used instead of their numeric representations to make the code more readable. Next, the SQL query statement is constructed (line 9).

15

The recordset cursor location (line 10) is being set to the client so that you can be assured that all the data comes to us open. This will speed performance for what you will be doing. Now the connection to the database is opened (line 11). A system Data Source Name has been created to point at the SmallTown Bank data. Next the recordset is opened (line 12) thus retrieving the data. Finally the recordset is sent back to the client in XML format by calling the Save method of the recordset object and specifying the Save format as adPersistXML (line 13). The second parameter is interesting in that you are using the intrinsic Response object as the save destination. This has the effect of streaming the XML data directly to the client. As was mentioned in the Listing 15.1 analysis, the Open of the data stream into the recordset is the counterpart to this Save operation.

You now have all the pieces to run this application. Make sure that in VB the startup form is set to frmAccountBalance and that you are pointing to the accountactivity.asp page. You can test the ASP page by calling it with your browser. If it works, you will get a white page, to see the XML. Right-click and select to View Source. If an error occurs, then an error message will tell you where to correct the error.

If all goes well you should see a screen similar to Figure 15.3.

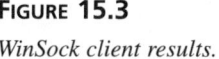
FIGURE 15.3

WinSock client results.

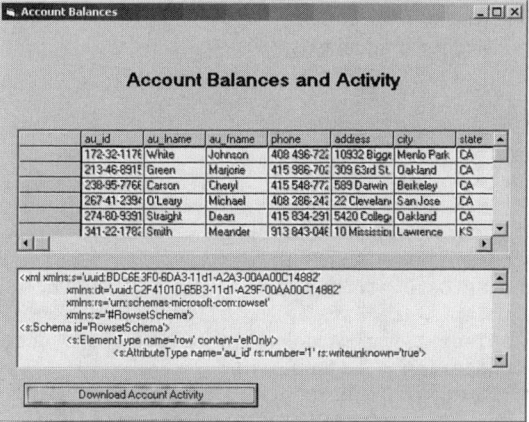

Client Request to a User-Defined Port

This client is very similar to the well-known port request with two variations. First the port number is different; you will use port 1001. The other difference is that you do not need the HTTP protocol header information. You can simply send a request for the information. To prepare the client for this example, change line 3 in Listing 15.1 to have a port number of 1001. You will not change lines 13 through 15, though in reality, you would set up your own protocol with the server. The server you build will respond to anything being sent. If you want you can change lines 13 through 15 to send a different message to see that no protocol is being used.

Server Application

In order to test our new client, you need to have an application on the server which is listening on the given port and which can service the request. You have already created the frmServer at the beginning of this section. You are now going to add the code in Listing 15.3 to the form.

LISTING 15.3   WinSock Server Code

```
 1: Private Sub Form_Load()
 2:     tcpServer.LocalPort = 1001
 3:     tcpServer.Listen
 4:     frmAccountBalance.Show
 5: End Sub

 6: Private Sub tcpServer_ConnectionRequest _
 7: (ByVal requestID As Long)
 8:     If tcpServer.State <> sckClosed Then _
 9:     tcpServer.Close
10:     tcpServer.Accept requestID
11: End Sub

12: Private Sub tcpServer_DataArrival _
13: (ByVal bytesTotal As Long)
14:     Dim strData As String
15:     Dim rs As New ADODB.Recordset
16:     Dim cn As New ADODB.Connection
17:     Dim myStream As New ADODB.Stream
18:     tcpServer.GetData strData
19:     txtOutput.Text = strData
20:     sql = " select * from AccountTransation where AccountID='1'"
21:     rs.CursorLocation = adUseClient
22:     cn.Open "DSN=SmallTownDSN"
23:     rs.Open sql, cn, adOpenStatic, adLockReadOnly
24:     myStream.Open
25:     rs.Save myStream, adPersistXML
26:     tcpServer.SendData myStream.ReadText
27: End Sub
```

ANALYSIS   Listing 15.3 is all that is needed to return the same results as the accountactivity.asp page without involving a Web server. The first routine (line 1) is run when the form is loaded. In this case, it sets the LocalPort property of the WinSock control to 1001 to match the port that will be used by the client (line 2). The

WinSock control is then placed in Listen mode (line 3). Finally, the client form is loaded (line 4). This is just for our demonstration purposes; in reality, the server would run on a server system and the client, on its own system. Because you can have only one startup form, you will change the startup form to be frmServer. It will load and then load the frmAccountBalance.

The next routine (lines 6 through 11) handles ConnectionRequests to the WinSock control. It first checks to see if the socket is open, not closed (line 7). If it is open, then it closes it (line 9). The port is closed because if it is open it indicates that it is in conversation mode with another client. By closing the port and then accepting a request the communication will be setup properly between the client and the server. Finally, it accepts the new request (line 10).

The final routine handles the DataArrival event for the WinSock control (lines 12 through 27). This routine is very similar to the accountactivity.asp. The major difference is that you need to use a stream object to persist and return the XML data because a Response object does not exist in this context. Line 24 opens the stream object. Line 25 saves the recordset object in XML format to the stream. Finally, line 26 sends the stream data as text to the client. At first the method ReadText might not make sense because you are writing it to the client. However, the notion is that you are reading the XML as text from the stream object and sending it to the client.

The client will then receive the XML data and process and display it in the same way that the data from the ASP page was handled. As you recall from Listing 15.1, lines 30 through 37, if no HTTP header information is found, you assume that the entire response is XML data.

You are now ready to run the example against your new server. Make sure that you set the startup form to be frmServer. You will see a couple different things when you run this example. First, there will be a server form in addition to the client form. When you press the account activity form, you should see the request show up in the text box on the server form, in this case, the HTTP request. In the client form you will see that no HTTP header information is in the response data.

You now have two ways to interact with the server using the WinSock control.

Using DCOM to Connect to Business Objects

Distributed COM is a way to invoke objects remotely using the COM specifications. The DCOM works by registering the remote object in your system registry with a pointer to the remote system where the object actually exists. When the object is called from the client, the system creates what is known as *proxy*, which handles all the communication between the local system and the remote system. In this architecture you develop your application as if the COM component is on the local system. All the work to move the request to the remote system and return the response to the client is handled by Windows.

DCOM enables component applications to operate across the Internet. DCOM provides the following attributes and capabilities:

- Transport neutrality—DCOM enables components to communicate with each other over any network transport, both connection-oriented and connectionless, including TCP/IP, UDP/IP, IPX/SPX, AppleTalk, and HTTP.
- Provision of Distributed Java—Because DCOM is language neutral, Java applets can communicate directly with each other over the Internet (and with any ActiveX component, regardless of authoring language).
- Evolutionary technology—In addition to Java support, DCOM enables components written in other languages, including C, COBOL, Basic, and Pascal, to communicate over the Internet, providing a growth path for existing applications to support Web technology.
- Common components for the browser and Web server—Because ActiveX components can be embedded into browser-based applications, DCOM enables a rich application infrastructure for distributed Internet applications using the latest browser technology.
- Security—DCOM integrates Internet certificate-based security with rich Windows NT-based security, combining the best of both worlds.

If you are strictly working in a Microsoft environment, then DCOM has a number of benefits that you can leverage out of the box. As was mentioned in Day 14, SOAP is the up and coming standard for heterogeneous interoperability. Until Microsoft enables all their products to use SOAP, DCOM is your next-best solution for distributed computing.

Advantages and Disadvantages of DCOM

The advantages of using DCOM are

- All the communication between the systems is handled by the operating system. By having all the underlying plumbing handled by the system you can focus on developing your solution.
- A very granular security schema exists to enable you to tightly control who and how your components are accessed. A tight control over security is always a good thing when working across the Internet.

- The components can operate in multiple modes so that, if the component actually resides on the local system, the local object will be used, as opposed to the remote object. This is the best of both worlds in that the system will use the component that will provide the best performance.

- Client distributed components can communicate over any network protocol, not just TCP/IP. The ability to work across many different network protocols allows the client to work in many environments.

The disadvantages of using DCOM are

- The COM component must be registered in the clients' registry so that it is capable of being invoked remotely before it can be used. This is an added complexity to the configuration.

- The technology is limited to Windows systems. Although, some companies have developed implementations of COM and DCOM that can run on UNIX systems, this capability is not widely implemented. For all practical purposes you are restricted to using DCOM between Windows based systems.

LAB: Connecting via DCOM

In order to invoke a COM component via DCOM, you need two computers. You are not going to remote a component in this lab, rather we are going to tell you how you can make any COM object remotable using Visual Basic. First, you need the Enterprise edition of VB. Open your project, which contains the COM components you want to invoke remotely. Now select Project-Properties and select the Component tab. In the middle of the tab you will see a check box that says Remote Server Files. If this check box is selected, the files will be created to enable you to register the component so that it can run on a remote server. DCOM is that simple; it is simply a registry setting that points to the component on a remote server.

When DCOM is installed on your computer, a utility is also installed to enable you to easily configure your DCOM connections. That utility is called DCOMCNFG.EXE. Go to Start—Run; enter DCOMCNFG and press Enter. The utility should run. What you will see listed are all the DCOM applications your system knows about. On the Applications tab select an entry and press the Properties button. You will be given a set of tabs that contain information about that object. Select the location tab and notice the three options you have for remoting a component. They are Run application on the computer where the data is located, Run application on this computer, and Run application on the following computer. You can see that you have a number of options for invoking components remotely. You can now look around at the other tabs to see the degree of control you have over the DCOM-enabled components.

Using Remote Data Services (RDS) to Connect to Business Objects

Remote Data Service (RDS) predates XML and is a technology to remote a recordset onto a client's IE browser. The problem with sending an ADO recordset across the Internet is that it is binary data that does not easily move across the Internet without using special encoding. In our WinSock example, you converted the ADO recordset into XML before you sent it across the Internet. Besides the technical problem, the idea of passing the recordset to the client violates the Windows DNA rule that a tier is to only communicate with the tier next to it. The goal of RDS is to gain access to and update data sources through an intermediary such as IIS. In a RDS solution the business tier, which is running in conjunction with IIS, owns the recordset. The data is then optionally processed on the server side before being sent to the presentation tier. The data needed by the presentation tier is packaged in an Internet-friendly way and sent to the client. The data is proxied at the client so that the client can interact with the local data representation as it were on the local system and have those interactions communicated to the server process transparently. The server process actually uses ADO to perform commands on the client's behalf, optionally do additional processing, and return the data to the presentation tier. On the client, the data is put into a form that can easily be understood by visual controls.

This programming model contains certain convenience features. If you don't need a complex server program to access the data source, and if you provide the required connection and command parameters, RDS will automatically retrieve the specified data with a simple, default server program.

However, if you need more complex processing, you can specify your own custom server program. For example, because a custom server program has the full power of ADO at its disposal, it could connect to several different data sources, combine their data in some complex way, and then return a simple, processed result to the client application.

Finally, if your needs are somewhere in between, ADO now supports customizing the behavior of the default server program.

The programming model specifies the sequence of activities necessary to accomplish this goal. The object model specifies the objects whose methods and properties affect the programming model.

15

RDS provides the means to perform the following sequence of actions:

1. Specify the program to be invoked on the server, and obtain a way (a proxy) to refer to it from the client (RDS.DataSpace).

2. Invoke the server program. Pass parameters to the server program that identifies the data source and the command to issue (proxy or RDS.DataControl).

3. The server program obtains a Recordset object from the data source, typically by using ADO. Optionally, the Recordset object is processed on the server (RDSServer.DataFactory).

4. The server program returns the final Recordset object to the client application (proxy).

5. On the client, the Recordset object is put into a form that can be easily used by visual controls (visual control and RDS.DataControl).

6. Changes to the Recordset object are sent back to the server and used to update the data source (RDS.DataControl or RDSServer.DataFactory).

The following are key elements of the RDS programming model:

- RDS.DataSpace
- RDSServer.DataFactory
- RDS.DataControl
- Event

RDS.DataSpace

Your client application must specify the server and the server program to invoke. In return, your application receives a reference to the server program and can treat the reference as if it were the server program itself.

The RDS object model embodies this functionality with the RDS.DataSpace object. The RDS object does some optimization depending upon whether the client-to-server connection is via the Internet or an intranet. For our purposes you will just cover the Internet scenario.

RDSServer.DataFactory

RDS provides a default server program that can either perform an SQL query against the data source and return a Recordset object, or take a Recordset object and update the data source.

The RDS object model embodies this functionality with the RDSServer.DataFactory object.

In addition, this object has a method for creating an empty Recordset object that you can fill programmatically (CreateRecordset) and another method for converting a Recordset object into a text string to build a Web page (ConvertToString).

With ADO, you can override some of the standard connection and command behavior of the RDSServer.DataFactory with a DataFactory handler and a customization file that contains connection, command, and security parameters.

In addition to the direct data connection capability, you can write your own custom business object that can perform complicated data access, validity checks, and so on. This is the preferred method in the Windows DNA model.

RDS.DataControl

RDS provides a means to combine the functionality of the RDS.DataSpace and RDSServer.DataFactory, and also enable visual controls to easily use the Recordset object returned by a query from a data source. RDS attempts, for the most common case, to do as much as possible to automatically gain access to information on a server and display it in a visual control.

The RDS object model embodies this functionality with the RDS.DataControl object.

The RDS.DataControl has two aspects. One aspect pertains to the data source. If you set the command and connection properties of the RDS.DataControl, it will automatically use the RDS.DataSpace to create a reference to the default RDSServer.DataFactory object. Then the RDSServer.DataFactory will use the connection property value to connect to the data source, use the command property value to obtain a Recordset from the data source, and then return the Recordset object to the RDS.DataControl.

The second aspect pertains to the display of returned recordset information in a visual control. You can associate a visual control with the RDS.DataControl (in a process called *binding*) and gain access to the information in the associated Recordset object, displaying query results on a Web page in Internet Explorer. Each RDS.DataControl object binds one Recordset object, representing the results of a single query, to one or more visual controls (for example, a text box, combo box, grid control, and so forth). There can be more than one RDS.DataControl object on each page. Each RDS.DataControl object can be connected to a different data source and contain the results of a separate query.

The RDS.DataControl object also has its own methods for navigating, sorting, and filtering the rows of the associated Recordset object. These methods are similar, but not the same as the methods on the ADO Recordset object.

15

RDS Events

RDS supports two of its own events, which are independent of the ADO event model. The onReadyStateChange event is called whenever the RDS.DataControl ReadyState property changes, thus notifying you when an asynchronous operation has successfully completed, terminated, or experienced an error. The onError event is called whenever an error occurs, even if the error occurs during an asynchronous operation.

Note

Microsoft Internet Explorer provides two additional events to RDS— onDataSetChanged (the recordset is functional but still retrieving rows) and onDataSetComplete (the recordset has finished retrieving rows).

Advantages and Disadvantages of RDS

The advantages of using RDS are

- Provides functional compatibility with ADO Recordsets. By being functionally compatible with ADO, the learning curve is substantially reduced and the effort to switch between the two protocols is trivial.

- Achieved efficiencies by having the recordset manipulation occur jointly between the client and server. Only changes are exchanged. This reduces the network traffic and thus improves the efficiency of the system. Since processing is shared between both systems, each system can handle the processing needs of the respective systems.

- The transport is negotiated by the RDS based upon the type of network connection being used. This means that the components are network aware and are capable of utilizing specific features intrinsic to the particular network protocol to improve efficiency. All these efficiencies are handled automatically by RDS.

The disadvantages of using RDS are

- Added complexity by having to go through a proxy. The more participants you have in any system, the more you increase complexity. Certainly a direct connection from the presentation tier to the database would be more efficient, however, this would violate the Windows DNA architecture.

- Multiple objects need to be invoked to retrieve, transfer, and display the data. An increased number of objects that need to be involved also increases complexity and resource usage.

LAB: Connecting via RDS

Connecting to RDS can be simple or complex. In this lab you will make a simple connection to a Web server and execute the default RDSServer.DataFactory. Listing 15.4 is all the code you will need.

LISTING 15.4   RDS Code

```
 1: Private Sub cmdDownloadAccountActivity_Click()
 2:     Dim DS As New RDS.DataSpace
 3:     Dim RS As ADODB.Recordset
 4:     Dim DC As New RDS.DataControl
 5:     Dim DF As Object
 6:     Set DF = DS.CreateObject("RDSServer.DataFactory", "http://localhost")
 7:     Set RS = DF.Query("DSN=SmallTownDSN", "Select * from AccountTransation
        ➥where AccountID='1'")
 8:     DC.SourceRecordset = RS
 9:     mshfgAccountBalances.Recordset = DC
10: End Sub
```

ANALYSIS   Listing 15.4 will replace the code under the Download Account Activity button. The first thing that happens is that you dimension your variables (lines 2 through 5). You will notice that the DataSpace is created as it is dimensioned (line 2). The next thing that occurs is that a connection is set up between the client and the data factory on the server (line 6). The two parameters are the program id of the object to invoke on the server that will be providing the data. In this example, you are using the default RDSServer.DataFactory. The next parameter is the server on which to invoke the object. In this example, it is being invoked via HTTP. The data space and the data factory determine how to send the data depending upon the protocol being used. Next the actual query is being sent to the remote data factory (line 7). Then the program sets the RDS.DataControl object SourceRecordset to be the recordset returned by the data factory (line 8). Finally the FlexGrid object's recordset property is set to the data control causing the data to be displayed in the control.

If you wanted to have a user-defined server object act as a data factory, then you would create and register it on the server. You then replace RDSServer.DataFactory on line 6 with the program id of your object.

Using the Windows Internet Components to Connect to Business Objects

15

The WinInet component encapsulates the complexities of interacting with a Web, FTP, or Gopher server. WinInet enables you to operate at a higher level than does WinSock, in which you have to handle TCP/IP and the HTTP protocol. With the WinInet control you can actually create your own simple browser. The control handles the HTTP header creation for you and takes off the header after the data is returned. An added, nice feature is the capability to communicate via HTTPS, which is a secure Internet session. The complexities of secure Internet communications are handled within the control.

Advantages and Disadvantages of WinInet

The advantages of using the WinInet control are

- It provides high-level access to HTTP and TCP/IP so you don't need to format your own HTTP headers and then strip them off the returned data. By eliminating the need for the developer to implement the communication protocol details you allow the developer to work on the business solution. Also the implementation details of the HTTP protocol are rather specific and complex which translates into extra development and debugging work for the developer.

- The control can process secure (HTTPS) Internet transactions. HTTPS uses Secure Socket Layer (SSL) protocol which has a fairly complex series of messages that need to be exchanged between the client and server to establish a secure communication channel. By encapsulating these implementation details within the control you again free the programmer to work on the specific business solutions. Having the ability to handle secure Internet communications allows you to engage in conducting sensitive transactions over the Internet.

The disadvantages of using the WinInet control are

- You are restricted to interactions with a Web, FTP, or Gopher server. You cannot develop your own server unless, of course, it is one of the three that are supported servers. The Inet control is designed to work with the most common Internet protocols and servers. If you need to interact with other types of servers or use other types of protocols you will need to use the Winsock control or another third-party control to implement it.

- You are limited to using the defined protocols. As stated in the previous disadvantage, if you want to use a protocol other than the three supported ones you will need to use the Winsock control or another third-party control to implement it.

LAB: Connecting via the WinInet Component

In this lab you are going to now modify your sample application to use the Microsoft Internet Transfer control. First, add the WinInet Control to your tools pallet by right-clicking the pallet and selecting Components. Now scroll down and check the Microsoft Internet Transfer Control 6.0. The control should now be on your pallet. Now open the frmAccountBalance and add the Inet control onto the form. Don't worry about the placement; it will be invisible at runtime. Change the name of the control to MyInet. You are now ready to add the code in Listing 15.5.

LISTING **15.5**   WinInet Code

```
 1: Private Sub cmdDownloadAccountActivity_Click()
 2:    MyInet.Protocol = icHTTP
 3:    MyInet.RemoteHost = "localhost"
 4:    MyInet.URL = "http://localhost/smalltown/accountactivity.asp"
 5:    MyInet.Execute , "GET"
 6: End Sub

 7: Private Sub MyInet_StateChanged(ByVal state As Integer)
 8:    Dim strHTML As String
 9:    Dim vtData As String
10:    Dim rsOutput As New ADODB.Recordset
11:   Dim myStream As New ADODB.Stream
12:    Select Case state
13:    Case icResponseCompleted
14:       vtData = MyInet.GetChunk(1024, icString)
15:       Do While LenB(vtData) > 0
16:          strHTML = strHTML & vtData
17:          vtData = MyInet.GetChunk(1024, icString)
18:       Loop
19:       txtOutput.Text = strHTML
20:       myStream.Open
21:       myStream.WriteText strHTML
22:       myStream.Position = 0
23:       rsOutput.Open myStream
24:       Set mshfgAccountBalances.Recordset = rsOutput
25:    End Select
26: End Sub
```

ANALYSIS   Listing 15.5 is all the code you will need to achieve the same results as you did with the WinSock examples. The code has been broken out into two functions. The first function is the one that you have been modifying throughout this day, cmdDownloadAccountActivity (lines 1 through 6). In this function you set the properties of the MyInet control (lines 2 through 4) and then you execute using the GET command

15

(line 5). You could have also chosen to set the control properties (lines 2 through 4) in the form load event, as you did in other examples.

The next routine handles the StateChanged event for the MyInet control (lines 7 through 26). This routine will get the data that is returned to the MyInet control. The first thing the routine does is dimension the variables it needs (lines 7 through 11)—nothing special here. The next thing it does is ensure that the response is completed by using a single-case select statement (lines 11 through 25). By doing this it ensures that the program waits until all the data is available before processing it. When all the data is available, it loops through the data 1024 bytes at a time building a local string (lines 14 through 18). Finally, it displays the data in the txtOutput field on your form (line 19). Lines 20 through 24 are the exact same lines used in the WinSock examples to load the data into a stream, which is then loaded into a recordset used to populate the FlexGrid.

This again is a fairly simple example to get you familiar with this control. You will notice that the control knows how to remove all the HTTP header information and also knows how to format an HTTP packet. If you are using the HTTP protocol instead of TCP/IP, this is the best control for this type of interaction.

Advantages and Disadvantages of a Native Windows Client

A native Windows application offers a number of benefits to the developer. The developer has ultimate control over how information is presented, manipulated, and communicated. You have a large number of ActiveX controls at your disposal, as well as other code libraries, which have been developed over the years. Native Windows applications tend to have better performance because they can take advantage of local system resources. Native Windows applications tend to be the least expensive to develop because the applications have the capabilities to do their own emissary processing and thus do not need to integrate complex workflows between Web pages. The ability to include input validation at the field or form level substantially improves the user experience because they are immediately alerted to a problem. Because all the processing is self-contained within the Windows application, complex work flows are not required as is the case with HTML-based solutions.

Despite all these advantages there are a few disadvantages. The first is size, Native applications tend to be larger than a page that can be displayed in a browser. Actually, pages in browsers take up no more additional room than the browser, unless ActiveX controls are being downloaded. The next disadvantage is portability. Native Windows applications can only run on Windows systems, whereas HTML pages can run on any system with a browser that supports the page features.

Determining if you should use a native Windows-based presentation or a browser-based presentation will depend upon the required reach and richness. These requirements will come out during your analysis and design phase. It does not need to be an exclusive solution either. For example, you could provide the bank employees with a native Windows application while supplying the customers with a browser-based solution. Because of the way that Windows DNA separates the presentation tier from the business logic and data tiers, it is not uncommon to offer several interfaces based upon user needs.

Summary

With all the talk of the Internet you might think that native Windows applications are dead. Not the case—they still provide the richest, most powerful solutions available at a reasonable cost. In this chapter you learned about four ways that you can connect to the business logic and data tiers from your native Windows applications. You learned about WinSock, Distributed COM (DCOM), Remote Data Services (RDS), and the Microsoft Internet Transfer Control (WinInet). You developed a sample application using these capabilities and explored the advantages and disadvantages of using these communications methods.

WinSock gives you great flexibility to communicate with anything via TCP/IP. You learned how to communicate with well-known services like a Web server as well as to communicate with servers you build.

DCOM gives you a way to extend the COM architecture across many systems. You learned that this architecture is basically limited to Microsoft platforms. DCOM gives you a great deal of granularity and security and is easy to implement.

Remote Data Services is an older technology that enables a recordset to be extended across a network. The client establishes a proxy to a recordset or a data factory on a server. The transportation of that data across the network is automatically managed by the RDS components.

Finally you looked at the Microsoft Internet Transfer Control. The WinInet control handles the specifics of the protocols for HTTP, HTTPS, FTP, and Gopher. This enables you to focus on the things that you need to do without having to handle the protocols.

Q&A

Q Are there other way to get this information?

A Yes, a new protocol called SOAP is currently emerging that will enable objects to be run on other servers, and all the communications will be in XML via HTTP. Day 14 covers this protocol.

Q I noticed that the WinSock and Inet components are implemented as controls. Is there any way to implement them as components?

A No, not these particular controls. However, you can find third-party components that will provide similar functionality. For today's discussion, we talked about implementing the presentation tier so it is okay that these capabilities are implemented as controls.

Q How is security handled with these components?

A The security is the same as you would have with any server-based component. Each control implements security differently based upon its particular architecture. WinSock is the loosest, in that you need to pass the user id and password within the format prescribed by the particular protocol you are using. DCOM has a very granular security model implemented at the system level. RDS uses the security of the data factory for authentication. And the WinInet control has property fields that enable you to provide the security information.

Workshop

The Workshop provides quiz questions to help you solidify your understanding of the material covered and exercises to provide you with experience in using what you've learned. Try to understand the quiz and exercise answers before continuing to the next lesson. Answers are provided in Appendix A.

Quiz

1. What is the key benefit of using the WinSock control?
2. What is the key disadvantage of using the WinSock control?
3. How do the WinSock and WinInet controls compare?
4. What is the role of RDS in the Microsoft data architecture?
5. In what situation would you most benefit from using DCOM?

Exercises

1. Create a secure connection to a Web server using the WinInet control.

2. Extend the WinSock with a custom server sample program to service a number of commands.

DAY **16**

Using ActiveX Controls to Move Business Logic from the Server to the Client

Today, you will learn how to build ActiveX controls and deploy them to a client. This process enables you to encapsulate the functionality of a Visual Basic form and reuse it in any container that can handle ActiveX controls. A *container* is an application that can act as a host to the ActiveX control and enable it to run. The two containers you will be using with your ActiveX controls today will be a Visual Basic Standard EXE and an HTML page in Internet Explorer. Today, you will learn about

- ActiveX controls
- Deciding when to use ActiveX controls
- Using Visual Basic to build ActiveX controls
- Signing and marking your controls safe to run
- Deploying your controls

What Are ActiveX Controls?

ActiveX controls are a few years old already and are the third version of OLE Controls, from which the .OCX extension comes. When ActiveX controls are compiled, they still receive an .OCX extension.

ActiveX controls, you will notice, are very similar to the ActiveX DLLs that you learned about earlier in this book. But there are a couple of primary differences between the two when it comes to the Windows DNA platform:

- ActiveX controls typically contain a visual interface with which the user interacts.
- ActiveX controls run on the client, whereas you typically would use ActiveX DLLs on a Web server. You could have DLLs installed and run on the client as well, but that is not typically how they are implemented in a Web environment.

Because ActiveX controls can run on a client browser, they are a great option when creating a rich presentation tier using Windows DNA. Many of the limitations of HTML and even Dynamic HTML (which you will learn about in Day 17, "Using DTHML for the Presentation Tier") can be overcome with the richness of ActiveX controls. Most of the functionality that you can get in a Visual Basic form can be mimicked in an ActiveX control. This enables you to use controls like the Tree control or a grid control, which aren't easily duplicated using HTML and DHTML. One popular example of this is the Portfolio control in MSN's MoneyCentral Investor (http://moneycentral.msn.com/investor/home.asp). This enables you to track your stock portfolio all on one page. It includes functionality such as resizable columns, the capability to add stock symbols, automatic updates, and saving of data files. It would not be possible to get the same amount of functionality that you get in this control through HTML or Dynamical HTML.

If you have been using Visual Basic, controls are not a new concept to you. You have been using controls whenever you create a form in Visual Basic. You add on a text box control, then maybe a label control, after that possibly a command control. All these are controls. They are, by default, a part of the toolbox in Visual Basic. By creating ActiveX controls in Visual Basic, you can actually add your controls to the toolbox and use them just as you would a standard control.

One of the best parts of an ActiveX control is that it is reusable. This again corresponds to how ActiveX DLLs work. If a control contains common functionality, it can be reused over and over again. Also, although ActiveX controls reside on the client, they can be automatically updated when new versions become available on the server from which they originated.

As with your standard controls, there are two modes within which ActiveX controls operate. These are Design mode and Run mode. Both of these modes have to be considered as you create your control. You will take a closer look at these next.

Design Mode

Typically, when you hear the word *design*, you are probably thinking of creating the control. In this context, Design mode occurs after you have created your control and are now implementing it in another environment, whether that is a Visual Basic form or an HTML page.

Therefore, in Visual Basic, *Design mode* is when you are using the Visual Basic development environment to size a control, change its properties in the properties window, and perform other actions that determine how you want a control to look and behave, by default, when the application is run. This is just how you would configure standard Visual Basic controls. For a combo box, you would set a property for how many items display in the list when the drop-down arrow is selected. For a text box, you would set what the font of the contents will be.

The Design mode would be focused on public properties or initial data in the control. As part of creating a control, you can spend a lot of time just designing the interface that users will use to set up the control. If you add a standard Visual Basic tab control to a form and right-click it to bring up its properties, it has its own set of property pages. You can add property pages to your ActiveX control as well. As you can see with the tab control, this type of configuration is pretty involved and would take a considerable amount of time just to create the property pages. Both property pages or other external properties could be set in your control while it is in Design mode.

Run Mode

Run mode is how the control actually operates when the application is running. For instance, a combo box displays items in its list when it is clicked or a button triggers an event when you click it. If you created a mortgage interest calculator, the control would fill information in a results area after the specified information is entered. These actions would be more focused on setting the methods in the control.

In all, there are three steps in the life of an ActiveX control that you create:

1. Design and create the ActiveX control.

2. Design and create a Visual Basic form or HTML page and add the ActiveX control to it. Add the code necessary to have the container and control interact.

3. Run the Visual Basic form or HTML page, and see them run.

16

With this knowledge about ActiveX controls, you will now learn about when it is appropriate to use ActiveX controls on a page. This will enable you to better architect your application.

Deciding When to Use ActiveX Controls

In figuring out when to use ActiveX controls, you need to consider a number of things. One of them is who your audience is. This is important because the user must have an application that can run the ActiveX control. As mentioned earlier, a Visual Basic Standard EXE and Internet Explorer both natively support ActiveX controls. Therefore, for a Web-based application in which you can specify the client browser, ActiveX controls make a lot of sense. This would apply to an intranet or extranet that you can be assured will be able to run the ActiveX control. If you want to deploy an application on the Internet to a wide audience using a variety of browsers, then ActiveX controls might not be as practical.

Note

Netscape has a number of different vendors that make a plug-in which enables ActiveX controls to run in Netscape Navigator. For more information, go to http://www.netscape.com and search for ActiveX Plug-In on the home page. Netscape users wanting to run an ActiveX control need to do an additional download and install before their ActiveX controls will work.

Another item to consider is bandwidth. This is primarily a concern only when a user first comes to the site and needs to download your control. If the control has a lot of functionality in it and is relatively large in file size, users could have to wait five minutes for it to download. On the other hand, this only happens the first time they download the control and after that, only when you update the control on the Web site. Again, you have to figure out if the slow bandwidth would dissuade users from using the control. Another option, especially when you are distributing a Windows native client, is to include your ActiveX control(s) in the distribution package. This way, the controls will be installed on the client, and the client will have a faster startup time. You will still be able to have new versions automatically download in the future.

Finally, you have to consider what you have to get done. Does it make more sense to use an ActiveX control instead of doing it with HTML? With an ActiveX control, you get can get a lot more functionality, but it can also take more development time. The control I mentioned earlier on MoneyCentral Investor enables you to track investments and provides a rich client interface that couldn't easily be done any other way.

This is the end of the discussion on the *What* and *Why* of ActiveX controls. Next we will tackle the *How*. This will take you through creating an ActiveX control for the `SmallTownBank` application that you have been working on. You will have a chance to implement it on a Visual Basic form and then at the end of tomorrow's lesson, you will place it on a Web page.

Using Visual Basic to Build ActiveX Controls

16

As you go through this next section, you should notice the similarities with ActiveX controls and ActiveX DLLs. In fact, all your knowledge about public and private properties and methods comes into play here. The `Public` keyword enables functions and methods to be called from outside of your control just as they can be with a DLL.

The ActiveX control that you will make will let you view the account transaction history that has gone on for any customer. You will tell the control what customer you want, and the control will then load the accounts into a drop-down list box and retrieve the account details.

First, you will create an ActiveX control project and add on a couple of standard Visual Basic controls. This will give you a framework from which to build. From there you will add on properties and events to give more functionality. When that is finished, you can create a test harness that lets you try out your control and see how it works. The test harness will serve the same purpose as the test harness that was created on Day 9, "Building COM Components in VB," in the section, "Creating a Test Harness." Follow these steps to create your ActiveX control project:

1. Start Microsoft Visual Basic and, from the New tab, select ActiveX control.
2. Click Open. This will give you a new project with one control called `UserControl1`.
3. Select the project you just created.
4. In the Properties window, change the project name to **Account**.
5. Select the user control you just created.
6. In the Properties window, change the control name to **Transactions**.
7. From the Project menu, select Components. This will cause the Components dialog to appear.
8. In this dialog, check the Microsoft DataGrid Control 6.0 and click OK. This will add the DataGrid control to the Visual Basic toolbox.
9. From the Project menu, select References. This will cause the References dialog to appear.

10. Select Microsoft Remote Data Services Server 2.1 Library and click OK. This will enable you to connect to the data store on the server from your client application and retrieve data.

11. Double-click the Transactions ActiveX control to view the control. This will look very similar to an empty form, but without a border. In fact, adding other controls to the ActiveX control works in the same way as adding them to a form.

   You are now going to add three controls from the toolbox to your new ActiveX control.

12. Add a label to the control and call it **lblAccount**. Change the label to say **Select an account:**.

13. Add a combo box and call it **cboAccount**.

14. Add a data grid control and call it **grdTransactions**.

Congratulations! At this point you have created the framework for the control that you will build. After you have added this last control, your Transactions ActiveX control should look something like Figure 16.1.

FIGURE 16.1

The Transactions ActiveX control.

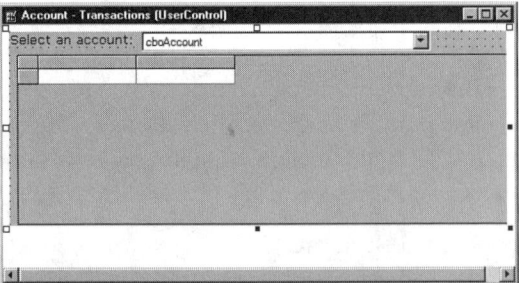

Next, you will add public properties to your control. These public properties will enable other applications, such as an HTML page, to set these properties.

Adding Public Properties to Your Control

You will quickly notice that creating public properties for ActiveX controls is the same as creating them for ActiveX DLLs. By using the Public keyword to declare a variable, it makes it available to programs outside of the ActiveX control. You will be creating three different public properties. Two of them are for RDS to be able to know the server to contact and how the server connects to the data store. The third property will let you specify the CustomerKey. For each of these properties, you will be specifying a Let and a Get. If you would like to review how a Let and a Get work, refer to the section "Adding a Property with a Property Procedure" in Day 9.

The first two properties you will be implementing are the ServerName and ConnectionString for the ActiveX control. ServerName will enable RDS to specify the server with which it has to connect. ConnectionString is the command for that server to connect to the data store. By specifying both a Let and a Get procedure for both of these, you will enable other applications to both read and write to these properties, which, in this case, makes sense. Both of these obviously need to be written to so you don't have to re-create the component every time you change servers or data stores. By being able to read these properties, you can check to see what the current values are and if they have been set.

The other property is CustomerKey, which is the current Customer identity value displayed in the control. This value is used to load the control with the correct customer information. It will be used by the LoadCustomer method that will be added later. Follow these steps to add these three properties:

1. From the Project window, right-click the Transactions control and select View Code. This will give you an empty code window.

2. At the top of this window, add the following code:

```
Dim m_ServerName As String
Dim m_ConnectionString As String
Dim m_CustomerKey As Long
```

These are all module level variables. They will maintain the value of the ServerName, ConnectionString, and CustomerKey variables while the control exists. The duration of the existence of a control depends on the container for it. In a Visual Basic form a control exists while the form is open. In a Web page, a control exists while the user has that page displayed in a browser window.

3. Add in the property procedures, as shown in the following code snippet. These procedures will enable ServerName, ConnectionString, and CustomerKey to be read and set by the Visual Basic form or Web page that hosts the control.

```
' Server Name
Public Property Get ServerName() As String
    ServerName = m_ServerName
End Property
Public Property Let ServerName(ByVal New_ServerName As String)
    m_ServerName = New_ServerName
End Property
' Connection String
Public Property Get ConnectionString() As String
    ConnectionString = m_ConnectionString
End Property
```

16

```
Public Property Let ConnectionString(ByVal New_ConnectionString As String)
    m_ConnectionString = New_ConnectionString
End Property
' Customer Key
Public Property Get CustomerKey() As Long
    CustomerKey = m_CustomerKey
End Property
Public Property Let CustomerKey(ByVal New_CustomerKey As Long)
    m_CustomerKey = New_CustomerKey
End Property
```

These are the same types of procedures that you saw on Day 9, "Building COM Components in VB." The Get procedures retrieve the value of the variables, m_ServerName, m_ConnectionString, and m_CustomerKey. The Let procedures set the values of m_ServerName, m_ConnectionString, and m_CustomerKey.

You have now added three public properties to your ActiveX control. These will be all the public properties for the control, but you will still add another public method as well as an event routine. Specifically, the next section demonstrates how to add code to your control that will use RDS and enable you to contact the server and get results from the database.

Adding Public and Private Methods to Your Control

In this section, a couple methods will be added to the code window of your Transactions ActiveX control. The public method will be used to load the customer accounts into the combo box on the control. The other method that will be added will be a click-event that is triggered when a user selects an account from the combo box. This click-event will load the transaction history into the grid.

This is also where you will be using RDS to contact the SmallTownBank database on the server. RDS, or Remote Data Service, was introduced in Day 15, "A Rich Native Windows Client." You will be using the DataSpace and Datafactory objects to connect to the data store.

Add Listing 16.1 to the code window of the Transactions control. This listing is the public method, which will load the combo box that you added earlier. This code can also be found by opening the Account.vbp file in today's material on the CD-ROM accompanying this book.

LISTING 16.1   Runs a Query and Loads a Combo Box with a List of Accounts

```
 1: Public Function LoadCustomer() As Boolean
 2: Dim rs As Object    'Resultset
 3: Dim ds As Object    'RDS.DataSpace
 4: Dim df As Object    'RDSServer.DataFactory
 5: Dim strSQL As String
 6: Set ds = CreateObject("RDS.DataSpace")
 7: Set df = ds.CreateObject("RDSServer.DataFactory", m_ServerName)
 8: strSQL = "SELECT A.AccountKey, AT.Description, A.AccountNumber " & _
 9:     "FROM Account A INNER JOIN AccountType AT ON " & _
10:     "A.AccountTypeID = AT.AccountTypeKey " & _
11:     "Where A.CustomerID = " & m_CustomerKey
12: Set rs = df.Query(m_ConnectionString, strSQL)
13: cboAccount.Clear
14: cboAccount.AddItem ""
15: cboAccount.ItemData(cboAccount.NewIndex) = 0
16: If Not (rs.BOF And rs.EOF) Then
17:     Do While Not rs.EOF
18:         cboAccount.AddItem Trim(rs("Description")) & " #" &
            ➥Trim(rs("AccountNumber"))
19:         cboAccount.ItemData(cboAccount.NewIndex) = rs("AccountKey")
20:         rs.MoveNext
21:     Loop
22: End If
23: rs.Close
24: Set rs = Nothing
25: Set ds = Nothing
26: Set df = Nothing
27: End Function
```

16

ANALYSIS   Line 1 declares the function with the Public keyword, which makes it accessible to outside applications. Line 6 creates a DataSpace object, and this is used in line 7 to create a DataFactory object. Notice the module level variable, m_ServerName is passed along in the CreateObject call. After the SQL SELECT statement is put together, the recordset is retrieved with the RDS Query method in line 12. The SELECT statement doesn't retrieve all the accounts, only the accounts for a particular customer. Also, the connection string is passed in through the module level variable, m_ConnectionString. This gives information about the data store and is the same information you would supply for an ADO connection string.

After the recordset is retrieved, the data needs to be placed into the combo box. Line 13 clears any information that might already be in the combo box. Line 14 adds a blank entry to it. The ItemData property, which you see in lines 15 and 19, is used to associate integer values with the items in the combo box. In this case, you can use the ItemData property to assign each of the AccountKey values to entries in the combo box. Lines 16 through 22 go through the recordset and add an entry into the combo box for every account a customer has. Cleanup work is done after the function is finished.

The LoadCustomer method is not called just once. You can call it anytime you want to use the control to access the account information of another customer. This is what you will eventually do in both the test harness program and the Web page that uses this control.

Now it is time to add the other procedure. This will be an event procedure, which will get called every time the user selects an account from the combo box. Listing 16.2 contains the code for this event.

LISTING 16.2   Event Procedure for Loading the Data Grid Control with Account History

```
 1: Sub cboAccount_Click()
 2: Dim rs As Object      'Resultset
 3: Dim ds As Object      'RDS.DataSpace
 4: Dim df As Object      'RDSServer.DataFactory
 5: Dim strSQL As String
 6: Set ds = CreateObject("RDS.DataSpace")
 7: Set df = ds.CreateObject("RDSServer.DataFactory", m_ServerName)
 8: strSQL = "SELECT TT.Description, " & _
 9:     "AT.Amount, AT.Description AS [Transaction Description], " & _
10:     "AT.CheckNumber, AT.Payee, AT.DateEntered " & _
11:     "FROM TransactionType TT INNER JOIN AccountTransaction AT " & _
12:     "ON TT.TransactionTypeKey = AT.TransactionTypeID " & _
13:     "WHERE AT.CustomerID = " & m_CustomerKey & _
14:     "AND AT.AccountID = " & cboAccount.ItemData(cboAccount.ListIndex)
15: Set rs = df.Query(m_ConnectionString, strSQL)
16: Set grdTransaction.DataSource = rs
17: Set ds = Nothing
18: Set df = Nothing
19: End Sub
```

ANALYSIS   After declaring the procedure and the variables, Listing 16.2 executes the same code as Listing 16.1 in creating the DataSpace and DataFactory objects. The SELECT statement in lines 8 through 14 is different in this procedure though. It uses two criteria. The first is the CustomerKey, and the second is the account that is currently selected in the combo box on the control. This enables you to drill down to a specific account. After the recordset is retrieved, all that is left is to set the grids DataSource property to the recordset that was returned in line 16. One difference from the previous listing is that the recordset is left open because that is the source of data for the grid.

16

ActiveX Control Interface Wizard Add-In

Another add-in available to you in Visual Basic is the ActiveX control Interface Wizard Add-In. This wizard guides you through creating the properties, methods, and events for your ActiveX control. This is similar to the Class Builder Add-In that you looked at when you were creating COM components in Day 9. To load the ActiveX control Interface Wizard Add-In, select Add-In Manager from the Add-Ins menu, select the ActiveX Control Add-In, and then select Loaded from the Load Behavior radio buttons.

This ActiveX control is almost complete. There are only a couple housekeeping procedures left to make your control work a little better for the user. One of them is to add scrollbars to the grid control. This property can only be set at runtime. Therefore this will be added to the Initialize routine of the control. Add Listing 16.3 to the code window.

LISTING 16.3   Setting the `ScrollBars` Property

```
1: Private Sub UserControl_Initialize()
2:    grdTransaction.ScrollBars = dbgBoth
3: End Sub
```

ANALYSIS By setting `ScrollBars` to `dbgBoth` (line 2), there will be both horizontal and vertical scrollbars on the grid. You can also choose to have one scrollbar or the other, or have them done automatically.

The second housekeeping procedure, shown in Listing 16.4, will resize the grid when the control is resized. This will enable the grid to fill in any unused space that would otherwise occur when its controls are resized.

LISTING 16.4   Resizing the Grid Control

```
1: Private Sub UserControl_Resize()
2:    grdTransaction.Move 0, grdTransaction.Top, ScaleWidth, ScaleHeight -
      ➥grdTransaction.Top
3: End Sub
```

ANALYSIS The `Move` method (line 2) actually is more like a new size method. It enables you to set the size of the grid control in the following order: left, top, width, and height. The left and right borders will correspond to the left and right sides of the control. The top of the grid will remain constant and will be wherever you place it on the `Transactions` control. To see the grid control's current setting, click it and then look for the `Top` property in the properties window.

The bottom boundary is a simple calculation. Because the grid is starting a certain distance from the top of the control, that amount (grdTransaction.Top) must be subtracted from the total height of the control. That gives you the new bottom boundary for the grid control. To really understand this, it might help to draw the control and grid out on a piece of paper and give it values. (Reminds me of a story problem....)

> **Note**
>
> The UserControl object is a self-reference that enables your ActiveX control to respond to events from the container object. Recall that an ActiveX control must run within a container object. In order for an ActiveX control to be a good citizen, it must have some way that it can respond to events which are sent to the container object or to events raised by the container object. The UserControl object is the interface that allows this notification to occur ActiveX controls can also send events to the container object, which the container can choose to handle as well. You will see some of this interaction in Day 20, "Office 2000 and Web Components."
>
> The UserControl event-handling capability is one of the two capabilities that differentiates ActiveX controls from ActiveX components. The other capability is the ability to have a presentation layer. When you think about it, it makes sense. The presentation items need some way to tell the rest of the components of changes to the items.

You have now completed your first ActiveX control. But, does it actually work? To test your ActiveX controls, you will use the same method that you used for testing your DLLs on Day 9. You will create a test harness program and call the ActiveX control from there. Instead of instantiating it, as you did with DLLs, you will add it to a form from the toolbox.

Creating a Test Harness

A *test harness* enables you to easily test whether your control is working and doing what it should. It also enables you to step through the code of the control and easily find problems that might exist. Again, these are the same reasons you want to do this with your COM components that you create on Days 9 and 10. You can follow these steps to get the test harness started, and then you can switch to the code window and add in the code listings that follow:

1. With the ActiveX control still open, select Add Project from the File menu.
2. Select Standard EXE and click Open. An empty form will appear.
3. Select the project you just created. It should be called Project1.

4. In the Properties window, change the project name to **Harness**.

5. Select the form from the project window.

6. In the Properties window, change the form name to **frmMain**.

7. From the Project menu, select Components. This will cause the Components dialog to appear.

8. In this dialog, check the Transactions control that you just finished creating. You will find it under the project name **Account**. This will add the Transactions control to the Visual Basic toolbox.

9. From the Project menu, select References. This will bring up the References dialog.

10. In this dialog, check the **SmallTownBank_Data** component and the Microsoft ActiveX Data Objects Recordset 2.1 Library. This will enable you to use these components in the Harness project.

11. Double-click **frmMain** in the project window to display the form.

   You are now going to add three controls from the toolbox to your new ActiveX control.

12. Add a label to the control and call it **lblCustomer**. Change the label to say **Select a customer:**.

13. Add a combo box and call it **cboCustomer**.

14. Add the Transactions control and call it **ctlTransactions**.

Note

> Now that you have added the Transactions control to frmMain, you are working with the Transactions control in Design mode, which you learned about earlier today. The control is now one object; it is no longer a separate label, combo box, and grid control. If you want to change how the control looks, you will need to modify the Transactions ActiveX control project.

This takes you trough creating the graphical part of the Harness project. It should look something like Figure 16.2. Next, you will add the necessary code to make the test harness interact with your ActiveX control.

This test harness will load all the customers into the combo box when the form loads. A user will be able to select a customer from the combo box. This will cause the CustomerKey property on the control to be set, and the LoadCustomer method will be called. Listing 16.5 contains the code for the Form_Load event, which will populate the combo box. This code can be found by opening the Harness.vbp file in today's material on the CD-ROM accompanying this book. Add this listing into the code window of the form.

FIGURE 16.2

The test harness to test the ActiveX control.

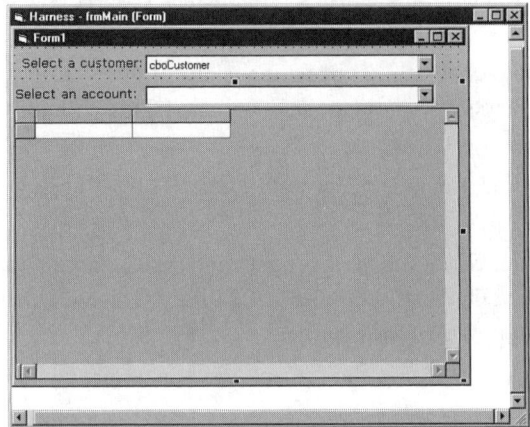

LISTING 16.5   Loading the Combo Box

```
 1: Private Sub Form_Load()
 2: Dim objSMTData As SmallTownBank_Data.BankData
 3: Dim rs As ADOR.Recordset
 4: ctlTransactions.ServerName = "http://mycomputer"
 5: ctlTransactions.ConnectionString = "Provider=SQLOLEDB;DRIVER=SQL Server;
    ➥SERVER=(local);DATABASE=Bank_data;UID=sa;PWD=;"
 6: Set objSMTData = New SmallTownBank_Data.BankData
 7: Set rs = objSMTData.Sel_All_Customer
 8: cboCustomer.Clear
 9: cboCustomer.AddItem ""
10: cboCustomer.ItemData(cboCustomer.NewIndex) = 0
11: If Not (rs.BOF And rs.EOF) Then
12:         Do While Not rs.EOF
13:         cboCustomer.AddItem Trim(rs("LastName")) & ", " &
            ➥Trim(rs("FirstName")) & " #" & Trim(rs("SocialSecurityNumber"))
14:         cboCustomer.ItemData(cboCustomer.NewIndex) = rs("CustomerKey")
15:         rs.MoveNext
16:     Loop
17: Else
18:     MsgBox "Listing customers failed."
19: End If
20: rs.Close
21: Set rs = Nothing
22: Set objSMTData = Nothing
23: End Sub
```

ANALYSIS In lines 2 and 3, the `BankData` object and a `Recordset` object are declared, respectively. Lines 4 and 5 set public properties of your Transactions ActiveX control. The control will use these settings when it uses RDS to connect to the server. In line 7, all the customers are retrieved.

Lines 8 through 19 fill the combo box with the appropriate customer information. The combo box is cleared in line 8, and the recordset is looped through in lines 12 through 16. The combo box will display last name, first name, and a customer's social security number. Objects are then cleaned up in lines 20 through 22.

Next, you just have to add a piece of code to call the `LoadCustomer` method on the ActiveX control when a customer is selected from the combo box. Listing 16.6 contains the click-event code to add to the `frmMain` code window.

LISTING 16.6   Event to Load New Customer Information

```
1: Private Sub cboCustomer_Click()
2:     ctlTransactions.CustomerKey = cboCustomer.ItemData(cboCustomer.ListIndex)
3:     ctlTransactions.LoadCustomer
4: End Sub
```

ANALYSIS This piece of code sets the `CustomerKey` in line 2 and then calls the `LoadCustomer` method in line 3. The `CustomerKey` is taken from the `ItemData` property of the combo box that is set when the combo box is loaded.

In the final step, Listing 16.7 will make the control work smoother. It will resize the control as the form is resized. This works in conjunction with the resize code you added to the control to resize the grid in the ActiveX control.

LISTING 16.7   Resizing the Control

```
1: Private Sub Form_Resize()
2:     ctlTransactions.Move ctlTransactions.Left, ctlTransactions.Top,
   ➥frmMain.ScaleWidth, frmMain.ScaleHeight - ctlTransactions.Top
3: End Sub
```

ANALYSIS This event has one piece of code in it, the `Move` method. Again, this is the same method that was used when resizing the grid in Listing 16.4. It sets the left and top borders and then specifies the width and height of the `ctlTransactions` control.

You have now completed both the ActiveX control and the harness test application and are ready to test the control. Before you do, set the Harness project as the startup project

16

by right-clicking the Harness project in the Project window and selecting Set as Start Up. To test the control in Run mode, select Start from the Run menu. When it starts up, you should see something like Figure 16.3.

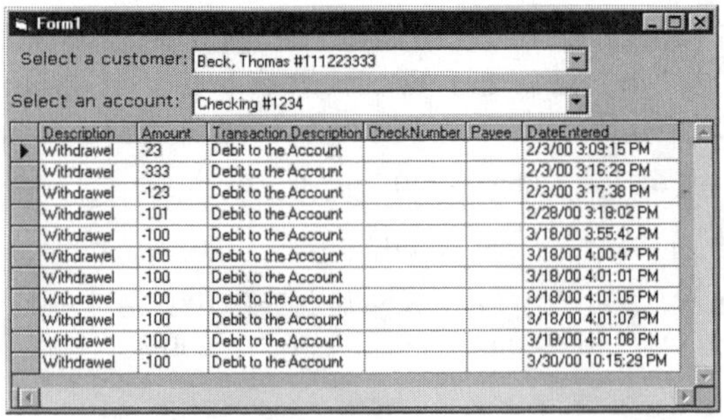

FIGURE 16.3

Running the Transactions ActiveX control.

At this point, you'll want to deploy your control. Because the Transactions control will eventually be deployed on the Internet, there are a few extra steps to take to ensure that users can trust that the control will not harm their systems. This includes marking your control as safe and signing your control so that users will have trust in whoever is making this control available to download. You will look at these issues next, as well as how to use the Package and Deployment Wizard.

Deploying Your Controls to the Internet

You have created an ActiveX control, and now the challenge is to send it out to the people who will be using it. Although the ActiveX control is a program, it is not something that you have to install on clients before they use it. With the Internet, you can place a tag on a Web page, which will cause a browser that supports ActiveX controls to check to see if the control is already on the client's system. If it is not, the tag will automatically download the new control.

These next sections will walk you through what you have to consider before you deploy your control and how to package your control for deployment.

Marking Your Controls Safe to Run

You surf to a page on the Internet that you heard about somewhere, and suddenly a window pops up, asking you if you want to download and install a control. If I can't be sure who created the control, then my first instinct would be to say "No." On this basis, you can make the greatest control in the world, but if no one thinks it is safe to use, then you are lost. There will be two things you can do to make users feel good about installing your control. The first one is to make sure the control is both Safe for Initialization and Safe for Scripting.

Controls Marked Safe for Initialization

An ActiveX control can be marked as *Safe for Initialization* when its vendor can guarantee that it will not perform any harmful actions to the user's computer when it initializes. This includes no writing to .INI files, registry settings, or other files that are specified in initialization parameters. Internet Explorer will not download files that have not been marked as Safe for Initialization.

Controls Marked Safe for Scripting

An ActiveX control can be marked as *Safe for Scripting* when its vendor can guarantee that it cannot perform any harmful actions to the user's computer by any scripting actions that are possible with it. This means none of the public methods and properties can be set that would enable writing to any script-defined .INI file settings, registry settings, or access to script-specified files on the user's computer. For example, as a vendor, you could have a specific data file used to persist information in your ActiveX control. That would be safe. On the other hand, it would be unsafe if the name of the data file could be specified through a setting or parameter on the ActiveX control.

 **Caution**   The surprising note about marking your controls as "safe" is that there is no automatic software test of your component to make sure it really is safe. Someone could create a control that is completely harmful, but still mark it as "safe." It is just a matter of a check box getting checked. Therefore, before you download a "safe" component from an unknown or questionable source, you might want to think twice.

To actually mark the controls as "safe," you will use the Package and Deployment Wizard. But, before we discuss the wizard, let's take a look at signing your control.

Signing Your Controls

Signing your control enables a user to verify who makes the control or who is packaging the control to be downloaded. This gives the user an avenue for recourse should something bad happen to his system as a result of installing the control.

The other advantage to signing your control is that, if your control has been signed and then is tampered with by anyone else before the user gets it, the browser will detect the tampering. This stops people from turning an ActiveX control into a Trojan horse of sorts.

You'll use a technology called Authenticode to sign your control. Authenticode enables the user of the control to verify who the distributor or author of the control is and also that he is who he says he is. It also prevents others from tampering with the code or impersonating someone else. To use Authenticode with your control, you need a certificate from a Certificate Authority.

NEW TERM A *Certificate Authority* is a reliable third party that can distribute certificates to individuals and groups and also vouch for the authenticity of those individuals or groups. Its role is similar to that of a mortgage broker in the sale of a house. The broker acts as a middle agent between the buyer and the seller to ensure that both parties' interests are protected. To make sure the deal goes through, both parties rely on the broker.

In the case of a certificate, the browser will automatically contact the Certificate Authority to make sure that the control is from whom it says it is from. If everything is okay, then the Certificate Authority will display this additional information to the user. This will assure the user of who is responsible for the control and give the user a source of recourse should anything bad happen.

To sign your control, you will need the Platform SDK (Software Developer Kit). This is a relatively new SDK and is a combination of various other SDKs from the past. This contains a utility called SignCode, which will enable you to run a wizard to sign your control. If you have Internet Explorer 5.0 and Windows NT SP4 or later, there is a wizard that you can run instead of the command line tool.

You can download the Platform SDK from the Internet at `http://msdn.microsoft.com/downloads/sdks/` or receive it with a MSDN Universal subscription. When you install the Platform SDK, choose custom setup to install the security tools.

Using the Package and Deployment Wizard

Now that you have looked at some issues concerning the safety of the component, you can go through the Package and Deployment Wizard and create a `.CAB` file. A `.CAB` file is a *cabinet* file, which packs in all the information necessary to install the ActiveX control over the Internet. The following steps show how to package the control into a cabinet. The cabinet file can then be placed on a Web server to be made available to users.

1. Close up your existing ActiveX control project.
2. From the Start menu, go to Programs, Microsoft Visual Studio 6.0, Microsoft Visual Studio 6.0 Tools, and select Package & Deployment Wizard. This will bring up the wizard dialog, as shown in the Figure 16.4.

FIGURE 16.4

Visual Studio 6.0 Package and Deployment Wizard.

3. Click Package to create the .CAB that can be deployed over the Internet.

4. The wizard might ask you to compile the .OCX file again. Say OK to this. This will ensure that the control includes your latest changes.

5. On the Package Type dialog, select Internet Package and click Next.

6. On the Package Folder dialog, leave the default, which is the same location as where the ActiveX control project is located. Click Next.

7. If the wizard asks you to create a folder called Package, click OK to create it. This is where it will place the .CAB and .HTM files.

8. If the wizard asks if you want to include the Property Page DLL, say No. This DLL should be selected only if you will use it in other design environments.

9. In the Included Files dialog, leave the default selections and click Next.

10. In the File Source dialog, leave the defaults. This tells the package where the source of the files is located. Notice that all the files—except for Account.ocx, which is your ActiveX control—are available for download from Microsoft. This enables the package to be very small. Click Next.

11. The Safety Settings dialog, which you can see in Figure 16.5, appears. Select Yes for both of the drop-downs and click Next.

12. The final dialog lets you specify the name of the script. Enter **Transactions** for the script name and click Finish. This script name is used internally by the wizard and will not affect the output that it creates in the .HTM file.

13. When it is finished creating the package, it will display a report summary. Click Close.

14. Click Close again to exit the Package and Deployment Wizard.

16

FIGURE 16.5

Safety Settings dialog.

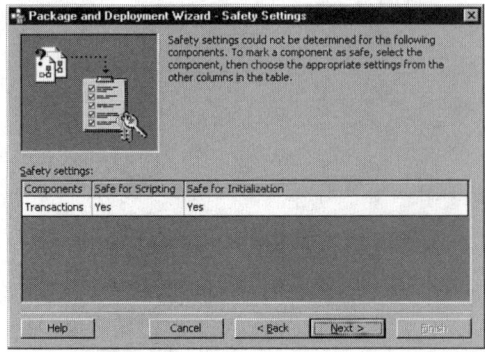

Good job on completing the wizard and creating a package! If you open up the .HTM file that the wizard created for you in the Package folder, you will see the HTML tag in Listing 16.8.

LISTING 16.8   Wizard-Generated OBJECT Tag

```
1: <OBJECT ID="Transactions"
2: CLASSID="CLSID:21218C60-073E-11D4-BE55-00A02458DD9C"
3: CODEBASE="Account.CAB#version=1,0,0,0">
4: </OBJECT>
```

ANALYSIS   Line 1 is the beginning of the tag and identifies the name that you gave the control in Visual Basic. Use this name to refer to the control in the HTML page where it's located. The name corresponds to a control name in Visual Basic. The CLASSID attribute is a unique identifier for the ActiveX control. If you build your own control, your CLASSID will be different because each one is uniquely generated. For more information, look at the "Version Compatibility" section in Day 9.

The CODEBASE attribute is the associated .CAB file to download that contains the control to be installed. If the version changes in the control, it can also be changed here in the <OBJECT> tag. This will signal the browser to download an updated version of the control.

You can now copy the .CAB and .HTM files that the wizard created and copy them to a Web site. From there you can call up the .HTM file, and you should be able to successfully bring up the control. To actually make the control function, you will need some additional code. You will have an opportunity to do this in tomorrow's exercises as you learn about client scripting and JavaScript.

The Package and Deployment Wizard is a great help in deploying your components. If you would like some more information on using this, you can check out "Downloading ActiveX Components" at the following link:

```
http://msdn.microsoft.com/library/devprods/vs6/vbasic/vbcon98/
➥vbconDownloadingActiveXComponents.htm
```

This takes you to the end of deploying your control. You looked at packaging the control, as well as issues surrounding the safety and authenticity of your control.

16

Summary

Today's lesson taught you how to create your own ActiveX control. Around this topic you learned what ActiveX controls are and when to use them. You also learned how to add public properties and methods to an ActiveX control. After your control was created, you had a chance to learn about signing your control and making it safe for users to download. Finally, you looked at deploying your control across the Internet.

Tomorrow's lesson will look at DHTML. Specifically, JavaScript will be introduced because that is the primary scripting language for DHTML. You will learn about the Document Object Model and how to access elements on a page with it. You will also learn how to add events to a page so it will call JavaScript functions. At the end of tomorrow, you will also have a chance to take the ActiveX control that you created today and work with it in an HTML page.

Q&A

Q My control has diagonal lines across it in the form I placed it on and looks disabled. Why is that?

A You currently have the ActiveX control project open and the User Control displayed. Because changes to your control will affect how it looks on a form, Visual Basic automatically places the lines through it, signifying it might not be displayed correctly. When you are done with your control and close the control, Visual Basic will update the control on your form and remove the lines.

Q I have updated my control and placed it on the Internet, but users are not getting the updated control. What is wrong?

A You will need to update the control's version on the Properties dialog, which is found under the Project menu. On the Properties dialog, click the Make tab and increment the version number. The next time you build the .OCX and run the Package and Deployment Wizard, the wizard will generate a new .HTM file and update the CODEBASE attributes in the OBJECT tag with the new version.

Workshop

The Workshop provides quiz questions to help you solidify your understanding of the material covered and exercises to provide you with experience in using what you've learned. Try to understand the quiz and exercise answers before continuing to the next lesson. Answers are provided in Appendix A.

Quiz

1. What is the new type of Visual Basic project that you learned to create today?

2. What is the extension of the file that your control is packaged in for distribution over the Internet?

3. What does Safe for Initialization mean?

4. What does Safe for Scripting mean?

5. What tag does the Package and Deployment Wizard create on an HTML page to display a control?

6. How would you make a public ActiveX control property be read-only?

Exercises

1. Modify the `LoadCustomer` Transactions control to take in an optional long parameter. This will contain the `CustomerKey` and enable users to call the `LoadCustomer` method without first having to set the `CustomerKey` property. Test the control with the Harness project to make sure it works.

2. Create an ActiveX control that uses the Tree control, which is part of Microsoft Windows Common Controls 6.0 component. Add a public method called `AddNode` that enables you to add items to the tree. Add another public property called `LabelEdit`, which enables you to toggle the `LabelEdit` property of the Tree control back and forth. The `LabelEdit` property allows or disallows a user to manually edit the items in a tree. Create a harness program that calls this public method and property.

Day 17

Using DHTML for the Presentation Tier

Today you will take the logic and presentation layers from the Native Windows client and implement them in DHTML. You will learn about the Document Object Model (DOM) and how to use JavaScript to implement client-side logic. You will also learn how to interact with the ActiveX controls discussed in Day 16, "Using ActiveX Controls to Move Business Logic from the Server to the Client."

Dynamic Hypertext Markup Language (DHTML) is a client-side scripting technology that enables the objects in the presentation space to interact. DHTML creates a richer, more exciting experience for the user. With DHTML, it's as if the user was using a native application. One of the main advantages of DHTML is that it works entirely on the client side, so there are no communication links left open to the server. This is very valuable to users because they no longer have to wait for a delayed response anytime they interact with the user interface. When you finish today's lesson, you will know about

- Writing JavaScript
- Scripting compatibility issues between Netscape and Internet Explorer

- Client-side versus server-side scripting
- The differences between JavaScript, JScript, and ECMA Script
- Interacting with the Document Object Model
- Working with ActiveX controls on a Web page

Distributing the Presentation Layer

For the past couple days, you have been learning about how to implement a rich presentation layer on the Windows DNA platform. The client has been a Visual Basic application, though. What happens if you want to put this on the Web? Will you have to give up all the richer features? Fortunately, because of the capabilities of today's browsers like Netscape Navigator and Internet Explorer, moving to a Web-based presentation layer doesn't necessarily mean that you have to give up all the functionality that you are used to. Specifically, Dynamic HTML (DHTML) gives the developer the ability to enhance a Web site's functionality and generate a better experience for the user.

NEW TERM *Dynamic Hypertext Markup Language* (DHTML) combines regular HTML with events and objects. This enables the developer to create an HTML page that can interact with the user and change a page's content or layout based on a user's choices.

DHTML is not a language; instead client-side scripting languages like JavaScript or VBScript implement DHTML. It is DHTML that sets the framework for the scripting languages. The results are dynamic Web pages.

If you have already been creating forms in Visual Basic, you will be familiar with the concepts of what DHTML can do. Let's say you create a form with a text box and a button. The user fills in a username and clicks the button to log in to an application. In a Visual Basic form you can program the click event of the button to read the username from the text box control and then verify that the username is valid. DHTML enables you to perform the same type of activities. You can have events that are triggered by users as well as access all elements that are on the Web page. With a regular HTML page, this would not be possible on the client.

Note

For creating the DHTML pages, I will assume that you are using Visual Interdev. There are numerous other editors out on the market, which are also very popular, that you can also use to edit HTML and DHTML pages. These include HomeSite, UltraEdit, and Notepad to name a few. Therefore, please feel free to use what is easiest and most productive for you.

Implementing DHTML on a page does take more work than creating a client in Visual Basic. One of the reasons for this is that the development environment in Visual Interdev is not as mature as that of Visual Basic. Therefore, it takes more time to develop in Visual Interdev than in Visual Basic. This makes sense, considering that Visual Basic has been around for many more years than Visual Interdev. I remember making a Visual Basic application back in 1992; in comparison, my first Visual Interdev application was in 1997. Five years is a lot of time. In the future I believe you will see Interdev become more sophisticated and seamless for developing Web-based applications.

Another reason for the extra work is the scripting language. VBScript is a subset of Visual Basic and does not have all the capabilities of Visual Basic. Error handling is just one example that makes Visual Basic applications preferred over DHTML pages. Fortunately, because of the extensibility of COM/COM+, much of the functionality that is lacking in VBScript or JavaScript can be made up for in external components. This is seen in everything from third-party components to components that come with Site Server 3.0, Commerce Edition.

In this day, you will learn about how you can leverage the various parts of the browser environment on the client to create robust applications. Specifically, you will look at how to implement DHTML with JavaScript (you will learn about VBScript tomorrow) and the Document Object Model (DOM). This knowledge will enable you to enhance the user experience in a Web browser. I won't be covering all the features of DHTML, but instead the ones that will probably give you the greatest benefit. If you do want more information, I will direct you to some additional resources both during, and at the end of, the day.

The bottom line is that implementing DHTML allows you to create a great presentation layer on the Windows DNA platform and still have the application accessible through the Web. The next section will introduce you to JavaScript, the scripting language you will use to be able to leverage DHTML.

Up and Running with JavaScript

Before you look more at DHTML, you will learn the basics of JavaScript, which is a scripting language you can use to implement DHTML. In this section, you will learn JavaScript fundamentals, which will enable you to move on to more complicated examples. If you are already familiar with Visual Basic, you will be able to quickly pick up on how JavaScript works. Comparisons will be made as often as possible to help you get a feeling for the similarities and dissimilarities.

First, look at how to write a statement that will declare a variable. You use the `var` keyword instead of the `Dim` keyword that you would use in Visual Basic. Also, statements in JavaScript end in a semicolon. Look at the following line:

```
var strWarning;
```

This declares a variable `strWarning`. One big difference from Visual Basic is that JavaScript is case sensitive. Therefore, if you had typed **VAR** or **Var**, you would receive an error.

If you wanted to assign a value to a variable, you would use the equal sign:

```
strWarning = 'You must enter your first name.';
```

This assigns the text string to the variable `strWarning`. Notice that you can use single quotes. If you did this in VBScript, the VBScript engine would think part of the line was a comment. To add a comment in JavaScript, use two forward slashes:

```
//This is a warning message.
```

Unlike Visual Basic, which has two types of procedures, JavaScript has only functions. Another difference is that you set the return value for the JavaScript function with the `return` keyword, instead of setting the return value to the name of the function, as in Visual Basic. Listing 17.1 is an example of a JavaScript function.

LISTING 17.1   A JavaScript Function That Returns a String

```
1: function GetWarning() {
2:         //This is a warning message.
3:         var strWarning;
4:         strWarning = 'You must enter your first name.';
5:         return strWarning;
6: }
```

ANALYSIS   After declaring and assigning a value to the variable, `strWarning`, this function returns the string back to the calling function. This is done with the `return` keyword. Braces designate the beginning and ending of the function. Braces are used to encapsulate not only functions but various other blocks of code in JavaScript as well.

One common example of using braces is in an `if…else` statement. There is no `Then` keyword or `End If`, as in Visual Basic. Only the words `if` and `else` are used, with their statements enclosed in braces. This is demonstrated in Listing 17.2.

LISTING 17.2   An if…else Statement in JavaScript

```
1: if (blnReceiveMailer == true) {
2:     //True
3:     alert('Value is true.');
4:     }
5: else {
6:     //False
7:     alert('Value is false.');
8:     }
```

ANALYSIS   The if statement in line 1 tests whether the value of the variable, blnReceiveMailer, is true or not. If it is, it calls the alert box— which is similar to the Visual Basic MsgBox function—and displays a message. If it is false, it displays another message. Both the if statements (lines 2 and 3) and else statements (lines 6 and 7) are enclosed by braces.

Besides the if…else, there are other ways to control the flow of your JavaScript. These include the do…while statement, which executes a loop until a condition is met, and the for statement, which iterates a set number of times through a loop.

Another important aspect of any language is calling built-in functions. With Visual Basic, you might call the IsNumeric function to see if a value can be evaluated to a number or Date function to get the system date. In this respect, JavaScript is very similar to Visual Basic, with its own set of functions. For example, Javascript also has a function called Date.

One big difference between the languages is that JavaScript treats certain items as objects, whereas Visual Basic treats them as variables. This applies to both strings and dates. Whenever you create a string in JavaScript, you are actually creating an object. This String object has methods that you can then call. This results in fewer built-in functions because they now become methods for these special JavaScript objects. For example, to get the length of a string in Visual Basic, you would use the following line of code:

```
strFirstName = "Jeff"
intLength = Len(strFirstName)
```

The Len function returns the length of the variable strFirstName and assigns the length to intLength. In JavaScript, you would perform this same function by

```
strFirstName = "Jeff";
intLength = strFirstName.length;
```

17

Instead of calling the Len function, you call the length method. Dates in JavaScript work similarly. Instead of a Month function, you call the method getMonth, which is shown in Listing 17.3.

LISTING 17.3   Using the getMonth Method

```
1: var dtmToday;
2: dtmToday = new Date();
3: intMonth = dtmToday.getMonth() + 1;
4: alert('Month: ' + intMonth);
```

ANALYSIS   After declaring a variable, it retrieves the system date in line 2. Notice that it uses the new operator. This is not necessary for the String objects, but is for Date objects. In line 3, the getMonth method is called, which returns the month number. 1 is added to the result because the month numbers returned are zero-based, ranging from 0–11. An alert box is then displayed with the correct month.

You have now been introduced to some of the main concepts of the JavaScript scripting language. To remember some of the subtleties of JavaScript, Table 17.1 lists some differences between JavaScript and Visual Basic that have been covered.

TABLE 17.1   Differences Between JavaScript and Visual Basic

Difference	JavaScript	Visual Basic
Case sensitive	Yes	No
Comments	//	'
Equality operator	==	=
Character at end of statement	;	None
Declaring Variables	var	Dim

This is a quick overview of JavaScript. For more information, there are many Web sites that give information about JavaScript. One of those is at Microsoft at http://msdn.microsoft.com/scripting/. Next you can take a look at a couple key benefits of DHTML. You will also see examples demonstrating how you can take advantage of those benefits.

Benefiting from DHTML

The following two sections will cover two key features of DHTML. The first is the reduction of round-trips to the server. This enables you to shift the load from the server to the browser to enable better scalability. The section after that, "Selectively Augmenting the User Interface (UI)," will cover enhancements that you can make to the user interface, resulting in a richer experience for the user.

Reducing Round-Trips to the Server

When the World Wide Web was first taking off in 1995, browsers were very limited in what they could do. They were, in fact, pretty close to being almost "dumb terminals." Besides understanding the limited set of HTML commands, they didn't do much more. Therefore any validation or database updates had to be done on the server that was hosting the Web site. This made for a lot of submissions to the server and additional pages sent back to the user in order to perform relatively straightforward tasks such as filling out a payment form. These round-trips to the server caused the user to have to wait each time.

With DHTML, developers gained the ability to create smart Web clients. This enabled them to place more of the burden on the client's browsers, which could easily handle the additional processing.

With DHTML, larger sets of data could be downloaded to the client and manipulated by them. This is made easier with XML and XSL style sheets, which you learned about on Day 12, "The Power of XML." With XML you can download a chunk of data and then manipulate it in the client's browser using the XML parser.

By using DHTML you greatly enhance the capabilities of the client. The ability to run client-side scripts enables anything, from simple validation of a zip code to some complex programs, to be implemented. (Believe it or not, there is a DHTML version of Asteroids that you can find on the Microsoft site.) This allows the user to do much more between trips to the user, which results in a better user experience.

One simple example is checking to see if a user has filled in a field or not. This can be checked on the client with JavaScript or on the server with some ASP. Two of the files in the Day 17 folder are called `validate_client.asp` and `validate_server.asp`; they demonstrate these two approaches. `validate_client.asp` checks to see if the user has filled in the text box before it submits the form to the server. The `validate_server.asp` file sends the information to the server, and then the server checks to see if the user entered information in the text box. Add these functions to a Web page and try them out. Look at the source code and try to see what is going on. If you are not familiar with all the tags, the ASP will be covered in Day 18, "Active Server Pages," and HTML will be covered in Day 19 "Thin Client—Reach Clients."

> **Tip**
>
> If you look at `validate_client.asp`, you will see the line
>
> `if (frmMain.FirstName.value == '') {`
>
> Unlike with Visual Basic, you must surround the conditional statement in the `if` statement with parentheses or else you will receive an error.

Selectively Augmenting the User Interface (UI)

Besides reducing round-trips, DHTML also allows you to add extra functionality on-the-fly to the User Interface. This can include all kinds of cool effects, from drop-down boxes that show menus to explanatory text that appears on the page when a user clicks on a term. You can control this according to the user or the browsers.

Listing 17.4 causes Internet Explorer browsers to change the color of text as the mouse pointer moves over the text. The code uses events to trigger the color change, which you will be learning about later today. This is the `mouse_over.htm` file on the CD-ROM accompanying this book; it uses functionality specific to Internet Explorer.

LISTING 17.4   Change the Color of Text with a `mouseover` Event

```
 1: <HTML>
 2: <SCRIPT LANGUAGE="JavaScript">
 3: <!--
 4: function ChangeColor() {
 5:      window.event.srcElement.style.color = "red";
 6:      }
 7: function ChangeBack() {
 8:      window.event.srcElement.style.color = "black";
 9:      }
10: -->
11: </SCRIPT>
12: <BODY onmouseover="ChangeColor()" onmouseout="ChangeBack()">
13: <H1>This H1 text will become RED.</H1>
14: <H2>This H2 text will become RED.</H2>
15: <H3>This H3 text will become RED.</H3>
16: <H4>This H4 text will become RED.</H4>
17: </BODY></HTML>
```

ANALYSIS   Line 1 indicates that this is an HTML page. Skip over to the `<BODY>` tag in line 12. This sets the events. Because the events are declared in the `<BODY>` tag, they will apply to every element in the page. This is known as a top-down event and will be covered later today. The onmouseover and onmouseout events are set in the `<BODY>` tag to call two JavaScript functions. Two functions are ChangeColor and ChangeBack. One sets an element to red; the other, to black. This is similar to Visual Basic, where you would write an event procedure, which would react to some user-initiated event such as clicking a button. The `<SCRIPT>` tags enclose the JavaScript functions in lines 2 through 11. The key here is the `srcElement` property, which is the element that originally triggered the event and corresponds to the H1, H2, H3, or H4 element for this page. The rest of the page is regular HTML.

By incorporating the five lines of JavaScript code in Listing 17.4, that page was able to change its look on-the-fly with DHTML. The JavaScript on the page can make simple changes—as you just saw—or very complicated ones. This gives you, the developer, many options when creating a Web site.

One of the next issues to look at is the compatibility of the two major browsers in the market today, Netscape and Internet Explorer. You will learn about some of the differences and hopefully be able to figure out solutions when you find that a page works in one browser, but not the other.

Scripting Compatibility Issues—Netscape Versus Internet Explorer

The three recommendations I can make to you if you are going to be implementing client-side scripting and want it to work for both Netscape and Internet Explorer is to test, test, and test. You will need to test not only the oldest version of the browser you are supporting, but each version after that as well, if you want to cover all the angles.

This is even more important if you are working with the 3.0 versions of the browsers. Netscape and Microsoft's 3.0 browsers contained their first implementation of some client-side scripting functionality. Although both companies tried to follow a standard, each used its own implementations. By the 4.0 versions, the browsers were much closer to each other in functionality. What I found with these past versions is that, what worked on Netscape 3.0 and 4.0 and IE 4.0 might not work on IE 3.01. What worked on IE 3.01 and 4.0 and Netscape 4.0 might not work on Netscape 3.0. If it sounds confusing, it's because it is.

Specifically, the problems lie in the fact that the different browsers implement different versions of JavaScript as well as different functionalities specific to their browsers. Table 17.2 displays the browsers and their JavaScript versions.

17

TABLE 17.2 A Listing of the Different JavaScript Versions That the Browsers Support

JavaScript Version	Implemented in Netscape	Implemented in Internet Explorer
1.0	2.0	3.0
1.1	3.0	NA
1.2	4.0	4.0
1.3	4.06	5.0

As you can see, both were up to JavaScript 1.2 in version 4.0 of their browsers. Also, JavaScript version 1.2 included a lot of functionality that has become pretty common. As a result, it is easier to make the 4.0 versions of the browsers compatible, compared to early versions. Nevertheless, the subtle differences in how Netscape and Microsoft implement their scripting can add significantly to development time.

If you are going to create an Internet application, you will need to account for both Microsoft and Netscape browsers. This needs to be considered during the design, analysis, development, and testing phases. Now that the two major browsers have been discussed, you will take a look at scripting on the client versus scripting on the server.

Note

In the section, "Interacting with the Browser," there are a couple links provided to both Microsoft and Netscape on the objects and properties each supports. Also, the rest of today will provide examples, in which some work on both browsers and some only work with Internet Explorer. Both of these will give you a chance to see what works and what doesn't. For an additional resource, check out Danny Goodman's JavaScript Pages at http://www.dannyg.com/javascript/index.html.

Client-Side Versus Server-Side Scripting

With the additional capabilities of DHTML available to you, you need to make a choice of where you will do your processing. You can choose the client or the server. Using the client enables you to handle the requests of a user more efficiently and in less time. At the same time, client-side processing requires the browser to have a certain amount of intelligence.

If you decide to use the client, it doesn't mean that everything has to be done there. You will most likely balance out processing activity, choosing the location that makes the most sense. If someone wants a mortgage calculator, you could probably put all that in a client script. When the person applies for a loan though, that information will need to be processed on the server.

For today, you will take the approach that the browser can handle the scripting and controls that you send to it. In Day 19 though, you will have the opportunity to have only HTML on the client and move all the processing to the server. In the next couple days, you will be reading about this topic again as you learn more about the server-side possibilities. For now, look at the next section where you will have a chance to see some specifics about JavaScript and the differences between similar scripting languages.

JavaScript, JScript, and ECMAScript

All three of these languages, JavaScript, JScript, and ECMAScript, are part of the same family. They are all part of a scripting language that enables you to write a script once and have it work across different browsers and different platforms, as long as all the browsers conform to the standard. You could also easily write a piece of code, which would conform to all three scripting languages.

Out of the three, JavaScript was the first iteration of a scripting language standard and was put out by Netscape. JScript followed and is Microsoft's enhanced version of JavaScript. As a result JScript has functionality that will not be available in non-Microsoft browsers. One example of that functionality is the all collection, which gives you information about every element on a page. This would enable you to loop through it and find all the TD tags on a page.

In addition to Microsoft and Netscape being involved, ECMA has also entered the language competition. ECMA is a group dedicated to standardizing information and communication systems. As a result, ECMA published a standard for scripting called the ECMAScript Language Specification, which drew from both JavaScript and JScript. Microsoft and Netscape have since added additional functionality that goes beyond the ECMA standard. In addition, they have recommended that ECMA adopt some of these additions. The ECMAScript standard can be found at http://www.ecma.ch/stand/ecma-262.htm.

17

JavaScript and JScript

I will point out that, when I mention *JavaScript*, I might actually be referring to JScript or to both JavaScript and JScript. I use *JavaScript* because it is the commonly accepted term to refer to the ECMAScript standard in client-side scripting.

As you might imagine, scripting development is an ongoing process in which standards are updated continually. As soon as one recommendation is incorporated, additional recommendations are made. It is up to ECMA to decide which additions are helpful to the global community. As a result of this process, there is currently quite a bit of overlap between the three different standards for scripting.

In addition, JScript and JavaScript have their own additional features, which they hope will become standard as well. If you are developing for a specific browser and version (which might be the case for an intranet site, for example, a Web site for employees in your company), this gives you some extra functionality to experiment with. But, if you are developing for an Internet site where you don't have control over the client browser, extra testing must occur to make sure the client-side script works across various browsers.

Note   Through the rest of today, I will try to reference functionality that is common to a recent version of both Internet Explorer and Navigator. Where that is not that case, I will try pointing it out.

In general, when developing client-side scripts, determine what browsers the Web application must support during the design and analysis phase. In development, be aware of the limitations and differences between the different browsers and their versions. In testing, try all the different browsers that are supported in the specification. Without determining these requirements beforehand, you could spend countless hours rearchitecting your presentation layer. This covers the various areas of JavaScript. You will now move onto the Documents Object Model (DOM) and learn how you can reference the elements in a page and associate events with them. In this next section, you will also have a chance to learn about specific differences between the browsers.

Interacting with DOM

Up to this point, you have been focusing mainly on JavaScript, the language you will use to implement DHTML. Now, you will learn about two more concepts that you have to understand to be able to take advantage of DHTML. One is the object model that is available to you. The other is an understanding of how events work with DHTML. When you combine knowledge about the object model and events with JavaScript, you will be on your way to using DHTML with your client-side scripts.

If you have used VBA with any of the Office 2000 components, you have worked with an object model. For instance, if you used Visual Basic for Applications to access a schedule in someone's Outlook folder, you would have referred to Outlook as an object. In the work you have done in this book with ActiveX Data objects, you have also worked with another object model. If you have programmed with Excel, you might have used Excel's object model to manipulate worksheets. As with all these applications and COM Components, your browser has its own object models. As soon as you learn them, you will have the ability to access anything that is currently on a Web page.

Learning About the Document Object Model

DHTML exposes you to the Document Object Model. The root of the DOM is the *document* object. From this object you can access everything that is on a document, by following the object model hierarchy. You can use the various collections that are available to you through the document object. One of the collections you will probably be using the most is the forms collection. The forms collection gives you access to your form and all the input tags within the form. By using this reference you can validate data before it is submitted.

NEW TERM The *Document Object Model* (DOM) is the object model for the current document. With an HTML page, the DOM gives you access to all the elements that make up the Web page. These include text boxes, drop-downs, and various other controls on a form as well as the regular text on the page.

SYNTAX

To reference the forms collection or any other collection from the document object, use the following syntax:

```
document.collectionname("formname").fieldname
```

Notice the document object and the collection separated by a period. The specific item in the collection can then be referenced by parentheses and quotes after the collection name. For a form called frmRegistration with a text box called FirstName, you could reference it with the following line:

```
document.forms("frmRegistration").FirstName
```

This would give a reference to FirstName, which you could then read in the value, validate, display in a alert box, or do whatever else you needed to do with it.

The syntax section showed you how to drill down to a specific text box on a Web page. Another way to think about this is like a tree. Starting at the top of the tree, you can branch down to its various parts until you reach the point you are looking for. Figure 17.1 gives an example of the path that was taken to reach the FirstName text box.

17

FIGURE 17.1

Branching to the
FirstName *text box.*

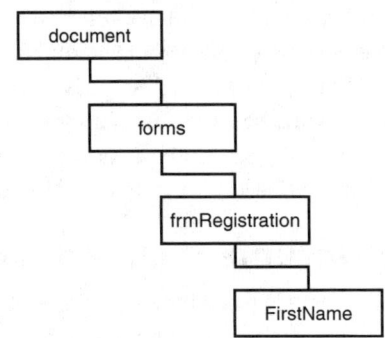

When you have the input object, FirstName, you will probably want to the look at what
was entered. You can do this by looking at the value property:

```
strFirstName = document.forms("frmRegistration").FirstName.value;
```

This assigns the value that is currently in the FirstName text box to the variable
strFirstName. At this point you would write some more JavaScript to validate the entry.
Validation could include any number of things, testing for minimum length, maximum
length, making sure that only alphabetic characters are entered, or whatever else your
business requirements might necessitate.

By starting off with the document object, you have access to the elements in the Web
page. Besides the forms collection, there are other collections (including the anchors,
links, and images collections), which allow you access to other elements as well.

In addition to being able to access elements of the page through the collections, you can
access elements directly if they are not part of a collection and they have an ID attribute
as part of their tag. For instance, to use DHTML to access a paragraph tag, you would
declare it as

```
<P ID="Description"> Product Description </P>
```

This would allow you to access this element in your client-side JavaScript. With the ability to access the element as an object, you can now change the properties of that object.
Two useful actions you can do now are to dynamically change the content of the object
and to dynamically change its style.

You can use four different properties to change the content of the object. Unfortunately,
these properties are specific to Internet Explorer version 4.0 and higher. I will show how
to mimic one of the properties in Navigator. The first one of these is the innerHTML property. This property enables you to set or retrieve the text between the elements tags. Any
HTML tags you replace the text with will be interpreted as HTML. innerText also

replaces the text between the element tags, but it does not interpret any of the text as HTML. To change the text in the paragraph element with an ID of `Description`, you could use the following command:

```
Description.innerHTML = "Washer and Dryer";
```

This would replace `Product Description` with `Washer and Dryer`. Using the `innerText` property would produce the same results in this case because there is no HTML in the text that is being replaced. If you used the following line of code and replaced the text with HTML tags, it would appear differently to the user:

```
Description.innerHTML = "<B>Washer and Dryer</B>";
```

The `<B>` tags would make `"Washer and Dryer"` appear in bold with the `innerHTML` property, but `"<B>Washer and Dryer</B>"` would appear with the `innerText` property. Take a look at the `dynamic_content.htm` file in today's material on the CD-ROM accompanying this book. It has an example with these properties.

As I said earlier, this only works in Internet Explorer. You can mimic this in Navigator by using the `document.write` method, which writes to the specified area. You would also need the `document.close` method, which forces this information to display:

```
document.Description.document.write = "<B>Washer and Dryer</B>";
document.Description.document.close();
```

The `write` method sends the information to the area called `Description`. The `close` method tells Navigator that there is no more information coming and that the information should be displayed.

Changing the content of the page might not be the only thing you want to do. You might also want to change the style of the page. This is another feature of the DOM and is implemented using style sheet syntax. Style sheets will be covered in Day 19, "Thin HTML—Reach Clients," but you will get a quick look at them here. You'll learn how to set a couple style sheet properties dynamically, enabling you to set other style sheet properties later on as you learn more about them.

You will first look at how to change the font dynamically and then how to show and hide text.

To change any style in Internet Explorer, you will want to use the style object. If you want to change the font, you would set the font property of the style object:

```
Description.style.font = "bold 16pt Verdana";
```

This would set the text inside of the `Description` element to be Verdana font, 16 pt. in size, and bolded. To do the same thing in Navigator, you would use

```
Description.font = "bold 16pt Verdana";
```

17

One difference is that the `style` object doesn't exist in Navigator, and is not needed with it. Another is that the command for Navigator belongs inside of `<STYLE>` tags and occurs when the page is loaded. Internet Explorer enables the font and other style properties to be changed at any time. The code that shows this is on the CD-ROM in `dynamic_styles.htm`.

One other useful style sheet property to look at is the `display` property. This property determines whether the text inside the element will display or not. When the text is displayed, no space is reserved in the page for the text. The three display property values are

- `none`   Text is not displayed; no space is reserved for it.
- `inline`   Text is displayed in the same line as whatever might precede or go after it.
- `block`   Text is displayed as a separate block. Other text will be displayed on separate lines.

To show the contents of a tag that had an ID of `Description`, use the following command:

```
Description.style.display = 'block';
```

When the `display` style is set to `block`, the text will display to the user. This property enables you to have more information show up when a user performs some action. For instance, a user could click a product to get a full description of the product. display.htm, which works in Internet Explorer only and is in today's material on the CD-ROM accompanying this book, gives an example of the `display` property.

As you have seen, the DOM allows you to find the values of various objects and elements in your page. Furthermore, not only can you read the values of elements, but you can also change the content and style of the elements. Next, you will have a chance to gain knowledge of the browser through the DOM.

Interacting with the Browser

Besides being able to look at a document, you can also look at the browser that is hosting the document. This has already been talked about earlier today, but now you will have a chance to use some of the methods and properties that it exposes to you. In general, the browser object enables you to programmatically do most things you typically do by clicking around in your browser. This includes moving back and forth between pages, jumping to other pages, and seeing what type of browser is running.

Just as the `document` object allows you a starting point to access the rest of the document, to access the browser information you use the `window` object as the root. From this, you can access all the parts of the browser. Figure 17.2 shows the various objects that are available to you from the `window` object. These objects are common to both Internet Explorer and Navigator.

FIGURE 17.2

Objects to access the browser and its contents.

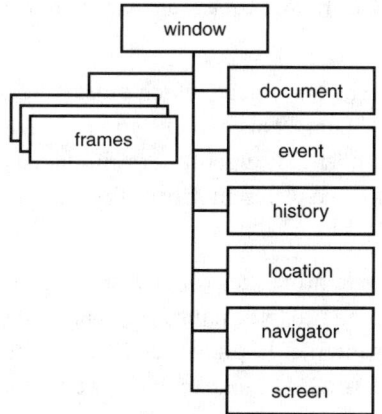

17

The following list is an explanation of the objects and collections that are accessible from the `window` object:

- `location`   Sets or retrieves information about the current URL.
- `document`   Provides access to the current page.
- `history`   Retrieves information about the URLs the client has visited.
- `screen`   Retrieves information about the client's screen.
- `event`   Retrieves information about the current event.
- `navigator`   Retrieves information about the client's browser.
- `frames`   Contains a collection of HTML frames, if any, in the browser window.

We'll look more closely at two of these objects: the `location` object and the `navigator` object. These are both useful to know about, in order to perform common client-side scripting techniques.

The `location` object allows you to look at or change the current URL. This enables you to programmatically have the user jump to another page. A common scenario for this is to have the client-side script validate the data, and, based on what the user has entered, the user is taken to one page or another. Another possibility is to have a user pick from a drop-down list. Based on what he picks, he is sent to a particular page.

There are various properties of the location object that tell you about the current URL, but it is the href property that gives you the entire URL. By setting this property to another URL, you can cause the browser to jump to another page:

```
location.href = 'http://www.microsoft.com/dna'
```

Setting the href property to the new string causes the browser to jump to the Windows DNA site at Microsoft. On the CD-ROM, location.htm demonstrates setting the location.href property.

Another useful object is the navigator object, which gives you information about the current browser that the client is using. This enables you to build sophisticated scripts that only execute code if the browser can support it, or, in the case of Navigator and Internet Explorer, if the code has two different scripts that can run, depending on the browser.

The navigator object has a couple properties for determining this: the appName and the appVersion property. The appName property returns the name of the browser. Internet Explorer will return "Microsoft Internet Explorer" and Navigator will return "Netscape." If you look at the files on the CD-ROM, dynamic_content.asp uses the appName property.

appVersion gives you the version number and platform of the browser. If you are implementing technology that occurs in the latest browser version and not in earlier browser versions, then appVersion will enable you to differentiate between them. You can access appVersion with the following line:

```
alert(navigator.appVersion)
```

This will cause the appVersion property to display in the browser. The file location.htm demonstrates this.

There are many more objects and properties available to you in the browser and the document. If you want more information on them, go to Microsoft's Web Workshop at http://msdn.microsoft.com/workshop/ and look at DHTML. Also, you can open the Netscape site at http://developer.netscape.com/docs/manuals/js/client/jsref/index.htm and look at the Object Reference section.

You now want to move onto events. Although you have already seen some pages that implement client-side events in them, you will be able to learn how to use them yourself in the next section.

Allowing Events to Work for You

Now that you know how to reference any object on a page, you can now learn how to use events to run your scripts. This is crucial, because it is the events that will trigger the scripts to make your dynamic page changes for you. In order to add an event to an element on your page, you will need to set the event handler for that element.

▼ SYNTAX

In order to attach an event to an element, add the event as an attribute of the element:

```
<ElementName LANGUAGE=javascript EventName=EventHandler>
```

`ElementName` refers to any valid HTML element, such as a button (`<INPUT>` tag) or a paragraph (`<P>` tag). The script language is set to JavaScript with the `LANGUAGE` attribute. Event names correspond to any valid event that that element supports. `onclick` is a very common event that most elements support. Others include `onchange`, `onload`, and `onmouseover`. The event handler is a valid JavaScript command or JavaScript function.

An example of attaching an event to an element is

```
<INPUT type="button" value="appVersion" id=cmdVersion name=cmdVersion
➥LANGUAGE=javascript onclick="return cmdVersion_onclick()">
```

▲ This is an HTML `<INPUT>` tag that displays a button. The `onclick` attribute has the button call the function `cmdVersion_onclick` when it is clicked.

Take a closer look at `location.htm` if you have not already done so. The `onchange` event has been set for it. Listing 17.5 displays the HTML for the drop-down box.

LISTING 17.5   HTML Drop-Down Box with an `onchange` Event

```
1: <SELECT id=cboWebSite name=cboWebSite LANGUAGE=javascript
   ➥ onchange="return cboWebSite_onchange()">
2: <OPTION></OPTION>
3: <OPTION value=http://www.microsoft.com>Microsoft</OPTION>
4: <OPTION value=http://www.netscape.com>Netscape</OPTION>
5: </SELECT>
```

ANALYSIS   Line 1 is the critical line. The `LANGUAGE` attribute is set to JavaScript, and the `onchange` event is set to call the function `cboWebSite_onchange`. There are three options listed for this drop-down. The first is empty and is declared in line 2. The second and third are `Microsoft` and `Netscape`, respectively. The value of the drop-down box becomes either Microsoft's or Netscape's URL if either of the two are selected. After the event has been set, the corresponding function must be included or an error will result. Listing 17.6 shows the `onchange` event.

17

LISTING 17.6   The onchange Event for the Drop-Down Box

```
 1: function cboWebSite_onchange() {
 2:     if (document.frmMain.cboWebSite.value == '') {
 3:         alert('No value selected.');
 4:         }
 5:     else {
 6:         objCurrent = document.frmMain.cboWebSite;
 7:         alert(objCurrent.options[objCurrent.selectedIndex].value);
 8:         location.href = objCurrent.options[objCurrent.selectedIndex].value;
 9:     }
10: }
```

ANALYSIS   The function is declared in line 1. Line 2 is an if statement. If the first value—the empty string—was selected in the drop-down box, then the alert in line 3 will open telling the user that a value was not selected. Otherwise, if the value of the drop-down is not an empty string, the script will display an alert displaying the selection chosen in line 7. In line 8, the script will cause the browser to jump to the new URL that was selected in the drop-down box.

You might be wondering about line 6. objCurrent is a temporary variable that the drop-down box is being assigned to. This allows you to reference the drop-down box in lines 7 and 8 without having to write out document.frmMain.cboWebSite. It also makes your code a little more succinct.

Tip

Remember that JavaScript, when testing for equality, uses the two equal signs. This is equivalent to the phrase, "is equal to." The following line

```
a.value == true;
```

would test to see if the value of variable a is equal to true. When assigning values, use one equal sign. This is equivalent to the word *becomes*. In the line

```
a.value = true;
```

the value of a *becomes* true. This is different from VBScript and Visual Basic and has caused me frustration many times when I forgot this difference.

By following the same approach that was used for the drop-down box, you can add a valid event to any element on a Web page. Find the element to which you want to add an event. Add a LANGUAGE attribute. Set the event name to a function and write the function. Now that you know how to add events to an individual element, you will get a chance to take a look at a couple subtleties in how Navigator and Internet Explorer handle events.

Top-Down or Bubble-Up?

Not only do elements have events that occur when an action is taken upon them individually, an action can originate from other elements as well. In this area, Navigator and Internet Explorer take two different approaches to event handling. In Navigator, when you perform an action, it starts at the topmost hierarchy, such as the body tag, and works its way down until it hits the individual element that triggered the event. For instance, if someone clicked a button on a form, Navigator would first look for an event handler set on the body, then it would look for one on the form, and then for one on the button. This would be a top-down approach, which starts at the top and works its way down.

An alternative to this is to allow events to bubble up and let event handlers along the way handle them. For instance, you could attach a mouse-over event to your body tag. When a user moved the mouse pointer over anything within that body, a mouse-over event would bubble up to the body tag, where the event would then be called. Likewise, you can also issue a command to stop the bubbling-up process at any point as it moves up through the hierarchy.

A good way to see the differences in how these event-handling approaches work is to attach two different events to two different elements on a page and see in what order they get called when you trigger an event. Listing 17.7 gives an example of how you can do this.

LISTING 17.7 Handling Events in a Web Page

```
 1: <HTML><HEAD>
 2: <SCRIPT LANGUAGE=jscript>
 3: <!--
 4: function TestArea_onclick() {
 5:     alert('onclick_TestArea event');
 6: }
 7: function BodyArea_onclick() {
 8:     alert('onclick_BodyArea event');
 9: }
10: //-->
11: </SCRIPT>
12: </HEAD>
13: <BODY ID="BodyArea" LANGUAGE=javascript onclick="return BodyArea_onclick()">
14: <P>This is before.</P>
15: <P ID="TestArea" LANGUAGE=javascript onclick="return TestArea_onclick()">
16: Click Me!</P>
17: <P>This is after.</P>
18: </BODY></HTML>
```

17

ANALYSIS Line 2 starts the <SCRIPT> block. There are two onclick() functions, one in lines 4 through 6 and one in lines 7 through 9. They both throw up alert boxes. Each of these are attached to separate events. In line 13, the <BODY> tag has an onclick event attached to it. In line 15, a <p> tag has the other onclick event attached to it.

When this file is displayed, if you click the "Click Me!" in Internet Explorer, because it bubbles up, it will execute TestArea_onclick first. If this file is opened in Navigator, it will execute BodyArea_onclick first. This file is called event_flow.htm on the CD-ROM.

Internet Explorer offers an additional feature to actually stop the bubbling up. If at any point you don't want the event to bubble up anymore, you set the cancelBubble property to false and it will stop. Add the following line to the function TestArea_onclick() function:

```
window.event.cancelBubble = true;
```

If the <P> tag that has an event attached to is clicked, the body event will not be executed. The event has not bubbled up any further after setting the cancelBubble property to true.

The differences between the two browsers aren't as great as they first might seem. If you have multiple events going on for a single action—for instance, one at the body level and one at the paragraph level—you might run into problems. However, if you have just one event, it will get triggered when appropriate, whether it is from the top down or bottom up.

Next you take a look at ActiveX controls. DHTML offers some great features, but you can enhance DHTML even more with ActiveX controls, which you learned about on Day 16. You will now learn how to place these controls in your own Web page.

Interacting with ActiveX Controls

ActiveX controls enable you to place a lot of functionality in an interface that can be reused over and over again. One good example of an ActiveX control that could be used on the Web is a tree view control. This would enable you to display hierarchical data on a Web page without having to create the control from scratch with DHTML.

As you learned in Day 16, you can create an Internet package and deploy your controls to the Internet using the Package and Deployment Wizard. When you create a package, the wizard produces a .CAB file and an .HTM file. Looking inside the HTML file, you will see the code that creates the ActiveX control on the screen. Listing 17.8 is an example of an ActiveX control on a page.

LISTING 17.8	The <OBJECT> Tag Adding the `tvCatalog` Control to a Web Page

```
1: <OBJECT ID="tvCatalog"
2: CLASSID="CLSID:9E16FC50-DF6C-11D3-BE4D-00A02458DD9C"
3: CODEBASE="Menu.CAB#version=1,0,0,0">
4: </OBJECT>
```

ANALYSIS	The begin <OBJECT> tag includes attributes which specify the control to use. An ID is given to the control. This is how the control will be referenced in the page with DHTML. The CLASSID is the unique identifier for the control. The CODEBASE attribute identifies the .CAB file to download if the client does not already have the control installed on her machine. The version corresponds to the version you can set for the properties in Visual Basic under project properties. That way, if the user has an earlier version that is installed, the browser will go ahead and install the new version.

With this tag on the page, you can now use a client-side script to reference the control. With the control in Listing 17.8, there is one method and one property of the control that you will interact with. There is an AddNode method that enables nodes to be added to the Tree View control that is part of the ActiveX control. There is also a LabelEdit property, which can be set to 0 or 1. This toggles the capability on and off to be able to edit the contents of the tree in the control. To interact with the method and property, you would treat them just as you would a COM component you instantiated with the Server.CreateObject method. Simply use the object name followed by the method or property. Listing 17.9 gives an example of JavaScript that interacts with the tvCatalog control.

LISTING 17.9	A Client-Side Script to Access the ActiveX Control

```
 1: function cmdLoad_onclick() {
 2: tvCatalog.AddNode("", 4, "ID1", "Stereos");
 3: tvCatalog.AddNode("ID1", 4, "ID2", "Sony KJ11");
 4: tvCatalog.AddNode("ID1", 4, "ID3", "Panasonic ERP");
 5: }
 6: function cmdToggleEdit_onclick() {
 7: if (tvCatalog.LabelEdit == 1)
 8:     tvCatalog.LabelEdit = 0;
 9: else
10:     tvCatalog.LabelEdit = 1;}
```

ANALYSIS	The first function is an onclick event that adds three nodes to the ActiveX control. Lines 2 through 4 add the three nodes using the public method AddNode. This will build the contents of the hierarchical tree view control. The second function is also an onclick event. It reads the public property LabelEdit from the ActiveX control.

17

Line 7 tests whether or not LabelEdit is equal to 1. If it is, the script sets LabelEdit to 0, if it isn't, the script sets LabelEdit to 1. The control and the Web page that loads the control and has the events in Listing 17.9 can be found at the folder for Day 17. The file is called activex_control.htm. You will also need the .CAB file called Menu.CAB.

Using this same approach, you can access any public methods or properties on your ActiveX control or other ActiveX controls as well. You now have the basic knowledge to work with ActiveX controls in your Web pages. Utilizing DHTML, you can treat the ActiveX control as another object. This takes you through the last of DHTML today. This is just a start, and I encourage you to continue to investigate the possibilities for using DHTML on your Web sites.

Summary

Today's lesson taught you DHTML. Specifically, some of the main concepts of JavaScript were introduced. You also looked at the Document Object Model and how you could access elements on a page with it. You had the opportunity to add events to elements on a page and saw how to tie this to JavaScript functions. Finally, you learned how to add ActiveX controls to a page and have your page interact with them. For more information on DHTML, take a look at Microsoft's Web Workshop on DHTML at http://msdn.microsoft.com/workshop/author/default.asp.

Tomorrow's lesson will look at HTML and how you can make the client very thin. You'll first take a closer look at some of the common tags in HTML and how to use them and then learn how to work with just HTML in a page without DHTML. This results in moving the logic from the client to the server. You'll find out what this means to you, the developer, and how to work around the limitations of an HTML-only client.

Q&A

Q How do I decide when to use JavaScript on a page when not all browsers support it?

A There are a couple different approaches you can use. One approach is to determine the minimum browser requirements. You could say this is Internet Explorer 4.0 and Navigator 4.0, or you could set the version lower or higher. Create the site to that standard and make sure it works.

The other approach is to create sites for multiple browser types and detect the browser and then execute the appropriate code. You can detect the browser at the client, as you learned about in this chapter, or you can detect the browser on the server, as you will learn about tomorrow. This way you could support two or more versions of the application. With each additional presentation layer, there comes a price in terms of longer development time and longer testing time.

Q I already know VBScript. Why can't I use that on the client?

A Keep in mind, VBScript only works natively in Internet Explorer. Navigator doesn't support it. Nevertheless, there might be times when you can choose to use VBScript on the client. One case is on an intranet, when you can dictate the browser that will be used. Another is if you are creating administration pages and you can require that the administrator use Internet Explorer. Although there is a plug-in for Netscape Navigator to support VBScript, it is not built in. Therefore, use JavaScript in order to make your script compatible with the most clients.

Workshop

The Workshop provides quiz questions to help you solidify your understanding of the material covered and exercises to provide you with experience in using what you've learned. Try to understand the quiz and exercise answers before continuing to the next lesson. Answers are provided in Appendix A.

Quiz

1. If you had a text box named `txtStartDate` on a form that was named `frmMain`, how could you read the value in JavaScript in order to validate the entry?

2. What property could you set to cause the client browser to jump to another page?

3. Given the button

   ```
   <INPUT TYPE=BUTTON NAME=cmdTotal VALUE="Total Your Order">
   ```

   add an `onclick` event to it to call the function `GetTotal`.

4. In Internet Explorer, how do you cause an event to stop bubbling up?

Exercises

1. Using client-side JavaScript, create a page that checks to make sure a number is between two values, 5 and 11. Display an alert box indicating whether the value is valid or not.

2. In Day 16, you created an ActiveX control for your Visual Basic presentation layer. As you learned today, these controls can also be used in browsers. Add a page with the appropriate scripting that will load and use the ActiveX Control from Day 16. To get started, you can use the code from the test harness application and convert that over to an HTML file.

DAY **18**

Active Server Pages

Today you will be introduced to using Active Server Pages to manage the presentation layer and to interact with the business logic components. Active Server Pages enable you to create dynamic content for Web sites and communicate with business logic tier components. With the help of ASPs, you can create HTML that is custom-tailored to each user.

Keep in mind, the topic of ASPs is enormous. There are entire books as well as whole Web sites dedicated to the topic of ASP programming. Therefore, the goal of today is not to teach you all there is to know about ASP, but to introduce you to ASP and enable you to get started with some initial pages. There are many intrinsic objects and functionalities available to the Active Server Pages programmers that allow you to rapidly create dynamic Web pages. You will look at some of these objects and point out their strengths and weaknesses. After today, you will have learned

- Introducing server-side scripting
- Creating Active Server Pages (ASPs)
- Adding script tags to ASPs

- Using built-in objects
- Gluing together components
- Scripting objects and server components

Introducing Server-Side Scripting

Active Server Pages (ASPs) has been a tremendous help in building dynamic Web sites. The ease of use that it brings enables rapid development and quick updates of pages. With a small snippet of code, you can call a component and display information to a user. Nothing has to be compiled and the pages build on languages most people know already. It is an ideal solution.

 *Active Server Pages* are files that are parsed by Microsoft Internet Information Server and then sent out to the user. An ASP contains script blocks, which begin and end with the <% and %>. IIS looks for and processes the code in these blocks of code. Script blocks can contain any supported language. By default, they support VBScript and JavaScript. There are add-ins that also enable support for Perl and other languages. ASPs are only limited by the language that they are written in, that is, the developer of the scripting engine can build whatever functions he wants into it. This is similar to the idea that, if your scripting engine (like VBScript) doesn't support some functionality, you can build components to do that work.

The other advantage to using ASPs has to do with the fact that they are "server" pages. The scripts are run on the server enabling them to be browser independent. Whether the browser is Internet Explorer, Netscape Navigator, or Browser X, as long as it can display an HTML page, the ASP will work. This is in contrast to what you learned yesterday about DHTML. For DHTML to function, the browser must support it.

> **Caution**
>
> Because of the ease of creating ASPs, developers might be tempted to put the majority of their business and data logic in Active Server Pages, instead of placing it into components. Although ASPs are easy to put together, they are really meant to be only the glue between applications. An ASP is made of non-compiled code, which is parsed and executed on-the-fly on the server. This is certainly slower then using pre-compiled components under MTS.

Therefore, as you go through today's lesson, remember that ASPs are not an end unto themselves, but merely a structure to organize your application. In other words, if you find yourself writing pages with a 1,000 lines of ASP code (and, yes, I have done this myself), you might want to rethink what you are doing. Perhaps it would be better to place the code in one or more components.

Where Did ASPs Come From?

When I first started creating content for the Internet in the beginning of 1995, there were not many options for publishing to the Internet. Static HTML files were the primary medium for displaying content. Even then the number of HTML files were amazing, but information quickly went out of date. Files on the Internet had to be continually updated manually.

The process involved using your favorite HTML editor, which at that time might have been Notepad. A file would be edited, and then an FTP program would transfer the file up to a Web server. The content would be updated, and you would be done.

This didn't last long though. As soon as more people started using the Internet, they wanted more from their browsing experience. Also data stores needed to be accessible and able to be displayed to the user. One way to achieve this (which many Web sites did) was to create a static Web page for each item in a data stores. If you had 2,000 items, you would have 2,000 pages. Imagine if you wanted to change the standard header on the pages. It was very cumbersome.

In order to have more interaction with the user, Common Gateway Interface (CGI) evolved, enabling more robust programs to be called that could deliver dynamic content and relieve some of the tedious tasks.

Common Gateway Interface (CGI) is a standard that enables a user, when they request a Web page, to activate a program. This program is a separate executable or uncompiled script. Most often GGI is written in PERL, which is a scripting language. This enables Web sites to have interactive pages, that is, pages display information based on user input. One of my first experiences with CGI was a searchable listing for businesses in my area. People could select a category, and the page would process the selection and display all the matching businesses. Not a big deal, but back in 1995, there wasn't much else like it.

The problem with CGI programs is they run as a separate process. Every time a person requests a page, another application will start, process the request, and quickly shut down. Imagine starting another instance of your word processor every time someone accessed your Web server. This gets pretty intense for the machine.

18

Instead of using a separate program, developers seeking alternatives to CGI started to evolve a parsed file that combined HTML and program commands. Although Microsoft wasn't the first to think of this idea, it was first to incorporate the concept into its IIS 2.0, using .IDC and .HTX files. The .IDC files contained SQL database commands, which retrieved a set of records. The records were displayed using the .HTX files. The .HTX files were template files, which had HTML tags and scripting tags designating where the fields in the records should go. Unfortunately, this was very structured and there weren't a lot of options if you wanted to do more then display records.

In IIS 3.0, Microsoft introduced Active Server Pages (ASPs). Again, ASP-type technology had already been around in other flavors, but Microsoft brought dynamic Web page development to the mainstream by doing two things. First, Microsoft incorporated ASPs into its Web server, which was gaining popularity. This immediately gave ASPs a large base of users. Second, Microsoft leveraged its existing VB developer base by using a subset of the VB language called VBScript as the primary language in ASPs. This greatly reduced the learning curve for those users.

With VBScript, ASPs enabled use of a robust language. This included the capability to draw information from any data store out there by using ADO—the exact same ADO that we have been using since Day 6 in this book.

Of course, VBScript doesn't do everything. One thing added into VBScript was a Replace command, which Visual Basic lacks. This command enables you to search for a piece of text in a string and replace it with another piece of text. This was a common command in PERL that Visual Basic lacked. There is also a Split command in VBScript. This command allows you to take a delimited string and assign the substrings of the string to an array. Both the Replace and the Split function might have been brought about by the strong need for string manipulation. Perl was great at this and could handle regular expressions. VBScript now does this, too, with the help of a component.

How Do ASPs Work with IIS?

ASPs work with IIS through ISAPI (Information Server Application Programming Interface) filters. As page information is sent in and out of IIS, it goes through the ASP ISAPI filter, as seen in Figure 18.1. The ASP filter looks for script blocks in between the <% and %>. It processes the information as appropriate. When sending a page back to the user, the page includes both a header and body. The header information lets the client's browser know what type of information is being sent. It describes the format for the body of the page.

FIGURE 18.1

How ISAPI filters work in NT Server.

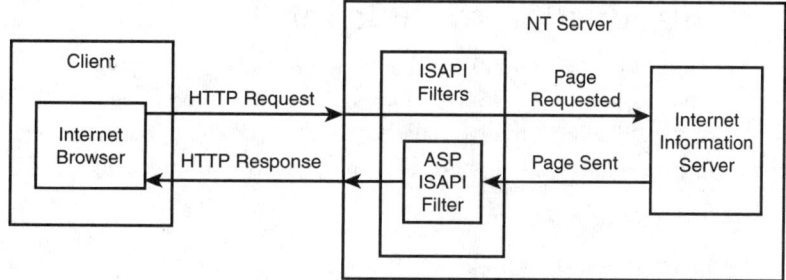

An *Information Server Application Programming Interface* (ISAPI) filter is a compiled file that reads through pages sent from and to IIS. By default, the ASP filter checks any pages with an .ASP extension. This can be configured in IIS. Before the ASP ISAPI filter reads through the file, a line would look like

```
<% = "<H1>Hello World!</H1>" %>
```

After going through the filter, the client would receive it as

```
<H1>Hello World!</H1>
```

ISAPI filters are very powerful. If you wanted to build your own, you could have a filter do whatever you wanted to information coming to or from your server. One example would be to look at any URLs being sent to users and replace them with another if you wanted the location to change. For instance, you could change a URL from microsoft.com to yourcompany.com. The ASP ISAPI filter processes the ASPs, but you will now take a look at what actually goes into an Active Server Page.

Creating Active Server Pages (ASPs)

Creating ASP files is relatively easy. They are text files and you can use notepad to create or modify them, which is what a lot of people used to do when ASP first came out. Today you have a lot of choices with one example being the editor the comes with Visual Interdev 6.0. It includes color-coding for your files while you edit them, auto-complete features for commands or components it recognizes, and a toolbox to easily add tags to your pages. These are just a few of its features and is a good tool to use when developing ASPs.

With the editor to get you started, you will now look at VBScript, which is the scripting language that you use in Active Server Pages. By placing VBScript in your pages, you can then produce the dynamic pages that you are working towards.

18

Introduction to VBScript

Assuming that you already know Visual Basic, you'll find very few differences between Visual Basic and VBScript. One important difference is that all variables in VBScript are of the type `Variant`. No data typing is used when you `Dim` variables or declare variables in procedure headings. For example, in VB you might declare a variable as

```
Dim strState As String
```

In VBScript, this would be

```
Dim strState
```

In Visual Basic, there is no `As` keyword.

Another difference is in how you instantiate objects. To do this in VBScript, you would use the built-in Server object, which you will learn about later today.

Script Tags

Script tags tell IIS when it has to process script commands, which occurs before it sends back HTML to the client. Whenever the ASP filter hits these tags, it activates the appropriate scripting engine and runs the script. When it hits the end tag, it turns off the scripting engine.

There are three ways to add scripts to your ASP.

The first method is to use the `<SCRIPT>` tag and place your code between the begin and end tag as shown in the following example:

```
<SCRIPT LANGUAGE=VBSCRIPT>
' Insert VBScript commands here
</SCRIPT>
```

The first line is the begin tag; it tells the ASP filter that scripting is starting. The `LANGUAGE` attribute tells it which script engine to run. After that you will put in your script commands. After you have finished, you end the block of code with the end script tag.

You have already seen the next method, which uses the percentage (%) sign, as shown here:

```
<%
' Insert Script commands here
%>
```

The opening tag tells the ASP filter to begin processing script commands. Notice that with this tag there is no option to specify the type of language to use. Therefore it will use the default language, which can be specified at the top of the page with the following line:

```
<%@ Language=VBScript %>
```

The @ sign specifies that this is a processing directive. A processing directive gives instructions to the ISAPI filter on how to read through the page. The LANGUAGE directive tells what scripting language is being used. The language can also be specified in IIS itself.

The other difference, which is not readily apparent, is that the <SCRIPT> tag is not necessarily processed in the order that it appears on the page. Therefore, if you have a script block that does some processing and displays a value, it might not appear where you place it in the ASP. If you do use the <SCRIPT> tag, only place functions in the script block. Then you can call the functions from where you use the <% and %> tags.

The last way to place <SCRIPT> tags in an ASP is with the inline tag, which is similar to the <% and %> tags. The only difference is that it has an equals sign and that it merely writes whatever the script in the tag evaluates to. Listing 18.1 is an example of using this tag.

LISTING 18.1   Use HTML and ASPs to Display a Line with Today's Date

```
Today's Date is <% = Date() %>.
```

OUTPUT   Today's Date is 6/17/00.

ANALYSIS   The equal sign tells the ASP filter to evaluate what comes after it and display it to the user. This can be a concatenated string; it can call a procedure, like the preceding example, or even call a custom procedure.

Tip

Try to keep the number of <SCRIPT> tags to a minimum in your ASP. Each time IIS hits a script block, it must switch from HTML to whatever script engine is being specified. This switch back and forth takes time. Therefore, try to keep your scripts in blocks as opposed to using an inline method.

Up to this point, you have been looking at small snippets of code. Listing 18.2 will let you see how these snippets can come together in an entire page. It contains a simple ASP with just a few lines of ASP in it. You can find this page on the CD-ROM as `hello_world.asp` under today's directory.

LISTING 18.2   A Basic Active Server Page

```
1: <%@ Language=VBScript %>
2: <HTML><HEAD></HEAD>
3: <BODY>
4: <P><% = "<H1>Hello World!</H1>" %></P>
5: <P>Today's Date is <% = Date() %>.</P>
6: </BODY></HTML>
```

ANALYSIS   If you have looked at an HTML page before, you will notice that it looks very similar. The first difference is in line one with the Language processing directive. Next is the script block in line 4, which prints out 'Hello World!' The script block in line 5 prints out the current date. Although this page contains only two script blocks, many more could be included in it as well.

As you begin to look at the built-in objects that are available in ASP, you can plug code snippets into this page if you want. Also, you will have a chance to look at other ASPs on the CD-ROM.

Exploring Built-In Objects

Now that you have seen how Active Server Page script blocks can be added to a Web page, you will learn how to use the objects that are automatically available to you in an ASP. *Built-in objects* are objects that are automatically available to you in your ASP. You use these just as you would any other COM component, but you don't have to declare or instantiate them. There are five built-in objects available to you in ASP scripts, which are described in Table 18.1.

TABLE 18.1   Active Server Pages Built-In Objects

Object	Description
Response	Used to send various types of information back to the user. This can be in the form of HTML, setting a cookie, or even changing the header. You can also affect the way data is sent back by sending data a little at a time or all at once.
Request	Used to read information that is coming from a user. This is most often used to get information a user inputs on a form or information from a link they click. It can also be used to read information about the user's browser type or information about the server itself.
Server	Used primarily to instantiate COM components.

Object	Description
Session	Used to store session level information. A session is an individual user's visit to a Web site. This is similar to going to the local grocery store. If you went there three times in one day, that would be three sessions. After a specified time period of inactivity on the user's part, the session will end and session information will be lost.
Application	Similar to a session except on the application level. An application lasts while a Web site is running and does not end until the application is stopped in IIS. Application information is available to everyone who is using the Web site.
ObjectContext	Used for page level transactions. The options for this correspond to the different types of transaction support that can be set in Microsoft Transaction Server.

With these objects available to you, you have the ability to create Web sites with a multitude of functionality. You can access in other objects whatever you don't have available. All the objects you have been creating in the past week are readily available. As long as the objects are properly registered, your ASPs will be able to use them.

Now that you have an overview of the objects, you can dig into specifics on how to actually use them. You will look at code examples and then use the information to create your own ASPs.

The Response Object—Sending Information to the Client

The Response Object will be used to send information back to the user. The most often used method of the Response object is the `Write` method. This would be equivalent to a print statement that would send text back to the user.

SYNTAX

The `Write` method sends the information back to the user to display in her browser. The syntax for the Write method is

```
Response.Write < String Expression >
```

▲ It will send the *String Expression* to the user. The expression can be any valid string including function calls, literal strings, and string concatenations.

For example, the following line shows an actual write statement:

```
Response.Write "<H1> Windows DNA 2000 </H1>"
```

This would display the following in the browser:

```
Windows DNA 2000
```

This would display in the appropriate font format for the H1 tag. If you were to view the source code of the page, you would see

```
<H1> Windows DNA 2000 </H1>
```

With the `Write` method, you are creating a Web page on-the-fly for the user. This dynamic enables you to customize information to the user to give them a unique experience at your site. The information you send back doesn't have to be HTML only. It can also include JavaScript, which you learned about yesterday on Day 17, "Using DHTML for the Presentation Tier." For example, Listing 18.3 will send a client-side JavaScript function to the client's browser, which can then be called by a page event. On the CD-ROM, `java2.asp` implements this code.

INPUT   **LISTING 18.3**   Server-Side ASP Script Generates Client-Side JavaScript

```
1: Dim vbCrLf
2: vbCrLf = chr(13) + chr(10)
3: Response.Write "function FormatDate(d) {" & vbCrLf
4: Response.Write "var sDate" & vbCrLf
5: Response.Write "sDate = (d.getMonth() + 1) +""/"" +
   ➥d.getDate() + ""/"" + d.getFullYear();"& vbCrLf
6: Response.Write "return sDate;" & vbCrLf
7: Response.Write "}" & vbCrLf
```

OUTPUT

```
function FormatDate(d) {
var sDate
sDate = (d.getMonth() + 1) +"/" + d.getDate() + "/" + d.getFullYear();
return sDate;
}
```

ANALYSIS   Lines 1 and 2 declare a line feed for the code that is written out, making it easier to see in the client browser. Line 3 is the function declaration. Line 5 contains double quotes in it. This enables you to put quotes inside of a string without Visual Basic thinking it is the end of the programmatic string. It continues until the function is closed off in line 7 with the ellipses. The output of the code snippet is what you would see in the source of the client's browser.

In Windows DNA applications, the `Write` method will be used to send information back from the data store. In the banking application that you are working on, the user will request information about a particular bank account and the script in the Web page will display that information to the user. The Web page will be dynamic based on what the user enters. Listing 18.4 assumes a recordset has been retrieved that contains a customer's information.

INPUT **LISTING 18.4**   Displaying Information from a Recordset

```
1: Response.Write "Name: " & rs("FirstName") & " " & "LastName")
2: Response.Write "<BR>"
3: Response.Write "Phone: " & rs("Phone") & "<BR>"
```

OUTPUT
```
Name: Jonathan Moons
Phone: 5035551212
```

ANALYSIS Line 1 uses the Write method to display a concatenated string, using string literals to display a label and also put a space in between the first and last name. It then uses the recordset to display the name. Line 2 sends back the
 HTML tag to display the next information on the next line. Line 3 displays the phone number and sends another <BR> tag.

The great thing about this code is that it is very similar to what you used in your Visual Basic presentation layer. Your business logic and data layers do not have to change when you use the Windows DNA architecture. Because you don't have to rebuild the entire back-end infrastructure, this enables you to rapidly develop multiple presentation layers. Next you will take a look at some various properties and methods that are available to you as part of the Response object.

Redirecting a Client

Besides the Write method, another method on the Response object that is available to you is the Redirect method. There might be times when you want to jump to another page. Based on a user's input, you might send him to another page, or maybe because a user hasn't logged in yet, you need to force her to log in or register. In any case there is a method called Redirect that enables you to do this. The following is an example of it:

```
Reponse.Redirect "login.asp"
```

The method takes only one parameter, the page you want to redirect the user to.

Buffering and Sending Information

Typically, page content is sent to the user as soon as you issue your Response.Write commands. This is as if you are on the phone. As soon as you speak, the person on the other end of the line hears your voice. There is no delay involved. The person on the other end doesn't have to wait until you have finished a sentence before they hear what you have said.

18

If you wanted to delay the page content going back to the user, you could use the Buffer property on the Response object. If this property is set to True, none of the content is sent over HTTP to the user until the entire page has been processed. Instead, the data is stored in a temporary buffer.

Why would you want to use the Buffer property? When a Web server sends a page to a browser, there are two parts to it. Before the browser can display a page, it must have the header information. This includes what type of content is in the body, if there any cookies that need to get set, and if a secure connection has to be made among other things. Therefore, as soon as the first Response.Write or HTML is sent to the user, the header is sent right before it. The second part is the body of the page, which is the HTML that the user sees in a browser window. Usually it is not a problem to keep buffering set to False. But, suppose you want to do something that affects the header (like set another cookie or redirect a user to another page) and you have already used the Response.Write method. You will not be allowed to do this because the header has already been sent. In fact, if you try to do this, you will receive the following error message:

```
The HTTP headers are already written to the client browser. Any
HTTP header modifications must be made before writing page content.
```

By setting the Buffer property to True, you can still make changes to header information without receiving this error. This may not be needed very often, but you may have a situation where you do need to do it. One possibility is if you hit an error and want to redirect someone to an error page. Another is if you need to set a cookie.

Besides the Buffer property, there are other Response properties and methods, which control the flow of the page. These as well as the Buffer property, are listed in Table 18.2.

TABLE 18.2   Response Properties and Methods That Control the Output of Data to a Client

Name	Description
Buffer	True or False. Buffers content until the ASP is finished.
Flush	Sends everything in the page buffer.
Clear	Empties out the contents of the page buffer.
End	Ends processing of the page.

Take a look at how this will actually work in a page. Listing 18.5 gives an example of using the Buffer command. If you removed line 1 in the following listing, you would receive an error.

LISTING 18.5   Using the Buffer Command

```
1: Response.Buffer = True
2: Response.Write "Hello"
3: Response.Redirect "default.asp"
```

ANALYSIS   Line 1 turns on buffering. The Write in line 2 is not sent to the browser, but is held in memory. By setting Buffer property to True you will be able to write text to the body and still issue other commands like the redirect in line 3, which affect the header.

Writing Cookies to the User

Cookies are a great way to keep track of users as they visit your site—not only during a current visit to your site that day, but also during different visits that might span weeks or months. One of the first times I used cookies was with a site that tracked when a user last visited the site and how many times they had visited the site. The site would post news bites of the most recent information that had been added to the site since a user's last visit. If the user visited twice in one day, he might not see anything new; if it had been a week since the last visit, then he probably would.

In order for you to send cookies to the client, you would use the Response object. Of all the methods on the Response object, I would say that this is one that could cause you some grief if you are not careful. Either they don't get written when you think they will or they expire too soon are a couple problems that might occur.

The actually Cookie is stored on the user's hard drive as a small text file. The maximum information that a cookie can hold is 4 KB. Browsers such as Internet Explorer or Navigator give you the option to receive cookies, prompt you to receive cookies or not accept cookies at all. Most sites, especially commerce sites, expect you to have cookies, therefore turning them off is not really an option. For example, I have to have cookies turned on to access my financial accounts. Also, since it is just a file, you can go into Windows Explorer and physically delete the file. Search for a folder called Cookies in your Windows directory and you will find the cookie text files. If you delete these, your cookies are gone.

18

Note

> Cookies are a useful way for Web sites to keep track of visitors. Cookies can track how often you visit, what pages you look at, and even how long you stay on a page. This is very useful information for the Web site operators, but some people do not want to give up this information. As a result, the user cannot access the site or finds his experience is not as personalized. There is definitely some give-and-take here. You have to be willing to give information to get a benefit.
>
> This is very similar to the many grocery stores in the city where I live (Portland, OR) that have been issuing cards. With these cards you no longer have to clip coupons to save on your purchases; you just have the stores swipe the card. Very convenient and it saves money, but you are enabling the store to track your buying habits and those of your family. From this they can extract a huge amount of information.
>
> My only point here is that tracking systems like cookies are not isolated to the Internet, but have been around for a long time. Just think of all those warranty cards you filled out, which ask you about your three favorite hobbies. As time goes by and people get used to using the Web, people wanting to reject cookies will be less of an issue.

SYNTAX

To write out a cookie for a user, use the following syntax:

```
Response.Cookies("FirstName") = "Terese"
```

The name of the cookie is "FirstName" and the value for it is "Terese".

By setting the cookie value and doing nothing else, the cookie will only persist until the user closes her browser. In order to have the cookie for a longer period of time, use the `Expires` property:

```
Response.Cookies("FirstName").Expires = Date + 365
```

This will persist the cookie for 365 days. At the end of that time, the cookie will expire and will no longer be available. To expire the cookie immediately, simply set the `Expires` property to today's date. To see an ASP that works with cookies, take a look at `cookie.asp` on the CD-ROM for today's material.

Now you that have looked at a variety of ways to send information to the user, you will next take a look at how to get information from the user with the `Request` object.

The Request Object—Getting Information from the Client

Just as the `Response` object sends information to the user, the `Request` object reads information from the user. Whenever a user submits a form, clicks on a link on a page, or enters a Web site, the Request object can be used to gather that information and process it in a Web page. To gather this information, the Request object has a series of *collections*, as shown in Table 18.3.

TABLE 18.3   Collection in the Request Object

Name	Description
Form	The form variables submitted by a form.
QueryString	The querystring variables submitted by a link or a form. The querystring cannot be longer than about a 1,000 characters.
ServerVariables	The variables which contain server and user information.
Cookie	Cookie information on the user's computer.

If you want to access a value that is returned from a user, you will use the following syntax:

```
strFirstName = Request.Form("FirstName")
```

This will store the FirstName form variable in the string, strFirstName. You can also use an ordinal value to read a value:

```
strFormValue = Request.Form(0)
```

This will read the first value into the variable strFormValue. This is generally not used though, because you cannot depend on the order of the variables. But you could loop through all the variables using a For loop, as shown in Listing 18.6.

LISTING 18.6   Looping Through the Forms Collection

```
1: For Each Item in Request.Form
2:     Response.Write Item & ": "
3:     Response.Write Request.Form(Item) & "<BR>"
4: Next
```

ANALYSIS   Line 1 starts the loop by going through each of the items in the Forms collection. Line 2 displays the name of the variables, and line 3 displays the value of the variable. Line 4 closes off the For-Next loop.

In the previous examples, you have been accessing the Forms collection specifically. There might be times though when you don't know which collection the variable will be in. If you do not know, or want the Request object to look at all of the collection, do not include the collection name when you specify the variable:

```
Request("FirstName")
```

18

This line will cycle through the collections in the following order: QueryString, Form, Cookies, ServerVariables. As soon as it finds the variable, it will stop.

Tip

> Do not get in the habit of excluding the collection name. Although it is easier, it takes the Request object time and effort to look through all the collections. Also your code is not as easy to read because another developer will not readily know where the variable is coming from.

Retrieving Information with the Forms Collection

The Forms collection lets you process forms that a user submits. Forms are created using the HTML <FORM> tag along with various <INPUT> tags. Every form must also have a way to submit the form so the information will get sent back to the server. Listing 18.7 displays a simple HTML form. This page can be found on the CD-ROM and is called form.asp.

LISTING 18.7   Displaying a Form

```
1: <FORM ACTION="form.asp" METHOD="POST">
2: <INPUT TYPE=TEXTBOX NAME=FirstName>
3: <INPUT TYPE=SUBMIT NAME=cmdSubmit VALUE="Submit">
4: </FORM>
```

ANALYSIS   Line 1 declares the beginning of the form. All the input tags (for example, text boxes, drop-downs, radio buttons, submit button, and so on) must be located between this <FORM> tag and the end </FORM> tag in line 4. The ACTION property specifies the page to which the form will be posted, which can be the same or a different page. METHOD is how the information is sent. Forms, for the most part, use POST for the type of METHOD, but you can also set this to GET. (GET would be sent as a querystring.) Line 2 declares an input box with the name FirstName and line 3 displays a submit button.

To retrieve the information from this form you will use the Forms collection to retrieve an individual field. Listing 18.8 is how you would get the first name.

LISTING 18.8   Retrieving a Field

```
1: <%
2: Dim strFirstName
3: strFirstName = Request.Form("FirstName")
4: Response.Write "Your name is : " & strFirstName
5: %>
```

OUTPUT `Your name is : Jonathan`

Line 3 set the variable to the value that the user entered in the form. Line 4 echoes the information back to the user with the `Response` object. The Forms collection is one way to get information back from the user.

Retrieving Information with the `QueryString` Collection

The `QueryString` collection contains the variables that are passed along with the URL. Here is some clarification: When a user sends a request to the server, he sends more then just a command saying, "Give me this page that I want." He also sends information about his cookies associated with the site, and about his browser. If applicable, the user might send information in an input form, as well as other information. Included in this "other information" is something called the `querystring`. If you are at a site and you look at the URL you just clicked, it might look something like the following:

`http://mdsn.microsoft.com/default.asp?vara=1&varb=2&varc=3`

The `querystring` is all the information after the question mark. The ampersands separate out name value pairs. This `querystring` is sent along as a separate part of the HTTP header as is the "Form" information. Both are in the form of name value pairs.

NEW TERM A *name value pair* is an entity (consisting of two values, which make up a pair), a variable name, and the value of the variable. A series of pairs can be passed along in a form:

```
Cow    Holstein
Dog    Greyhound
Cat    Siamese
```

Each of these pairs has a name (for example, Cow, Dog, Cat) and a value associated with it (for example, Holstein, Greyhound, Siamese).

If this were passed along in a `querystring`, it could look something like

```
http://www.windowsdnaworld.com/samples/
➥animals.asp?Cow=Holstein&Dog=Greyhound&Cat=Siamese
```

where the question mark starts the `querystring` and the ampersands separate the pairs.

18

> **Caution**
>
> Querystrings are limited to 1,024K in length (around 1,000 characters). Therefore, do not get too carried away as you create your `querystrings`. Keep their length limited.

Listing 18.9 is an example of how to use the Request object to retrieve the querystring information. This listing can be found on the CD-ROM in querystring.asp.

LISTING **18.9**   Requesting Information from a querystring

```
1: Dim A,B,C
2: A = Request.QueryString("VarA")
3: B = Request.QueryString("VarB")
4: C = Request.QueryString("VarC")
5: Response.Write "Using the Request object is as easy as "
6: Response.Write A & ", " & B & ", " & C & ".<BR>"
```

 **OUTPUT**   If you called the page with the URL

```
http://mdsn.microsoft.com/default.asp?VarA=1&VarB=2&VarC=3
```

it will display

```
Using the Request object is as easy as 1, 2, 3.
```

 ANALYSIS   After declaring the variables, lines 2 through 4 retrieve the querystring information and place the values into the variables. Lines 5 and 6 print out the variables.

> **Tip**
>
> If you will be using links on a page using the <A> tag, you will be using the QueryString collection to process the pages when a user clicks them. If you will be using forms with submit buttons, you will be using the Forms collection to process the pages.

Accessing Information with ServerVariables

Another part of the Request object are ServerVariables, which give you access to whatever other information might be passed on with the user request as well as specific server information. This might include items like UserName if you are on an intranet, or possibly the physical path to a file.

The syntax for the ServerVariables collection is the same as the Form and QueryString collections:

```
strPath = Request.ServerVariables("<Server Variable Name>")
```

strPath will contain the value for *ServerVariable*.

If you want to see all of them, the For-Each loop will enable you to do so. Listing 18.10 will allow you to access all the ServerVariables available. This listing can be found on the CD-ROM in server_variables.asp.

LISTING 18.10   Displaying All the ServerVariables

```
1: Response.Write "<table border=""1"">"
2: For Each SrvrVar in Request.ServerVariables
3:     Response.Write "<tr><td>" & SrvrVar & ":</td><td> "
4:     Response.Write Request.ServerVariables(SrvrVar) & "</td></tr>"
5: Next
6: Response.Write "</table>"
```

ANALYSIS   These variables are placed in a table and the name and value is listed in each row. Line 1 starts the table, lines 2 through 5 loop through the ServerVariables collection, and line 6 closes the table.

If you ran the previous example, you can see that ServerVariables give you a lot of information. Some of it is useful; some of it isn't. You do want to keep this information in mind though, because there might be a time when you do need it, such as if you want to display the values for any collection.

One of the more useful variables is USERNAME, which I have used on intranets before. When IIS is properly configured for NT authentication, USERNAME will return who is currently logged in, allowing you to customize the browser experience. For instance, if you display a list of employees, you can link the current user's name to a page where he can update his employee information.

Another useful variable is the path variable. If you will be writing files with the FileSystem object, which is discussed later today, you can use the path variable to get back a valid path.

Getting Cookies from a User

Using the Request object to get cookies from a user is a little more straightforward then writing them out with the Response object. You don't have to worry about the expiration date or other information; either the cookie is there or not.

Here is an example of reading back the cookies that you set earlier:

```
intCustomerID = Request.Cookies("CustomerID")
```

You can check whether the variable intCustomerID has a value that is greater then 0. If it does, then the user has been at a site before and their name can be looked up. If it doesn't, then this is a new user, whom you can prompt to register or log in.

18

The Server Object—Working with the Server

Now that you have seen the Request and Response objects, you will look at the Server object, which enables you to call other COM components. You can call any of your custom COM components, as well as any others that are loaded on the system. This includes ADO components, Site Server components, SMTP components, or anything else. The possibilities are almost limitless. Need extra functionality that VBScript can't provide? Use another language to create a COM component and call that from your ASP.

To call your components with the Server object, use the CreateObject method. By passing in the string that corresponds to the object name and the class, you can instantiate the object.

The CreateObject method enables you to instantiate COM components. It has the following syntax:

```
Server.CreateObject(<ObjectName.ClassName >)
```

ObjectName will correspond to the name of the DLL project in VB, either SmallTownBank_Business or SmallTownBank_Data. *ClassName* corresponds to one of the classes in the DLL project—either BankBusiness or BankData in the components you have been building. The method will return an object if it is successful.

Using the Server object, you can instantiate an object with the following lines of code:

```
Dim objCustomer
Set objCustomer = Server.CreateObject("SmallTownBank_Business.BankBusiness")
```

▲ After declaring the object, you can set it to the Banking Data component.

Gluing Together Components

By utilizing the Response, Request, and Server objects, you have the ability to use any of your components. This also enables you to tie into the Windows DNA architecture. The Response and Request objects let you interact with the presentation layer, whereas the Server objects enable you to tie into the business logic layer, which in turn accesses the data layer.

Listing 18.11 demonstrates how you can use ASPs as glue between your components. VBScript will instantiate a component, pass information to a method, and return a true or false.

LISTING 18.11 Using ASPs to Glue Together Components

```
 1: Dim objSTB
 2: Dim blnSuccess
 3: Set objSTB = Server.CreateObject("SmallTownBank_Business.BankBusiness")
 4: blnSuccess = objSTB.TransferFunds(Request.Form("txtCustomerID"),
    ➠Request.Form("txtAccountFrom"), Request.Form("txtAccountTo"), Request.Form
    ➠ ("txtAmount"))
 5: If blnSuccess Then
 6:   Response.Write "Transfer Succeeded"
 7: Else
 8:   Response.Write "Transfer Failed"
 9: End If
10: Set objSTB = Nothing
```

ANALYSIS This might remind you of the SmallTownBank Visual Basic application that you have been working on. In fact, all I did was cut the code and paste it into the ASP and then clean it up so it will be VBScript instead of Visual Basic code.

Application, Session, and Page Objects—Scoping Variables

18

When someone uses a browser to connect to a Web server and access a Web page, he does not retain the connection to the server. This is different from traditional client/server applications in which a user might be running a Visual Basic EXE on her computer, which will then access a SQL server database. While in the application, the person will have a particular logon and every access to the SQL server could be traced to the user. The application will know what the person just did and what they could do next. This is vastly different from the Internet.

With a page request from a Web server, a page is sent back to the user. When the page request is finished, the server is done. When another page request comes in from the same user (or a different user), the server sends back the page and once again it is done. It doesn't know whether the page request was from the same or a different person. It does what was asked for, but there is no constant connection. Therefore, if a user put in a name and phone number two pages ago, there is no way to have that information available on the current page. In Visual Basic you would just set this to a persistent object or a global variable, but on the Web this isn't possible.

Because of these shortcomings and the desire to be able to give a richer Internet experience and to prevent forcing someone to put in the same information on every page, various methods have evolved. One possibility is to set cookies manually on your Web site. You can set a customer ID cookie and then read that when they access a page. With that ID, their information can be looked up in the data store.

An alternative to this is to use the scoping methods that are available to you within IIS. Scoping methods give you the ability to set variable scope at the application, session, or page level.

You have already looked at page level variables. These are variables declared on an ASP using the VBScript convention of

```
Dim <VariableName>
```

Remember there is no data typing of variables in VBScript because all variables are variants.

Session variables are particular to one user's visit to a site. When a user has not accessed anything on the site for a set amount time (the default is 20 minutes), the variables will be released. This is tracked by storing a temporary cookie on the client. Application variables are available to anyone accessing the site. Therefore, one variable will be accessible by everyone.

To declare session and application level variables, you use the `Session` and `Application` objects. These object do not have methods associated with them such as the `Response`, `Request`, and `Server` objects. Instead they are more like the collections in the `Request` object, like the `Form` and `QueryString` collections. The following line is an example of how to set a value to a session level variable:

```
Session("FirstName") = "Mary"
```

The session variable, `FirstName`, is set. This variable will be available from this page or any other consecutive page within the site. Therefore, if a user named Mary clicks another page and the following line existed in the ASP:

```
Response.Write "Your name is " & Session("FirstName") & ".<BR>"
```

it will display as

```
Your name is Mary.
```

To assign objects to session level variables—which is not recommended (see Do/Don't in the following section)—you will use the `Set` command:

```
Set Session("rs") = rstCustomer
```

`rstCustomer` will be a recordset that contains customer information. This recordset could be accessed from now on; you won't have to make the database call each time for this. But this advantage is more than outweighed by the extra resources that the recordset takes up.

The `Application` object works in the same way. The difference is that, instead of the variable being accessible only within the session for that one user, the variable is now available to anyone within the application. Here is an example:

```
Application("CompanyName") = "Macmillan"
```

After that is set, any other user who requests a page from the same site will have access to that variable. The line

```
Response.Write "Your company is " & Application("CompanyName") & ".<BR>"
```

will display as

```
Your company is Macmillan.
```

Do	Don't
DO instantiate objects at the page level. MTS is designed to give out these instances efficiently. As soon as you are done with them, set them to Nothing.	DON'T instantiate objects at the Session or Application level. This wastes resources on the server, which could be better used elsewhere. For instance if you declare a Session level ADO object, it will not go away until the session times out, which is 20 minutes by default. If you declare the object at the Application level, users will have to wait and use that one Application object, one user at a time. User A would use it. When she is done, User B could use it, and so on. It creates a huge bottleneck.

The ObjectContext Object—Creating More Transactions

Hopefully, by this time you are comfortable with the idea of transactions and how components and database calls can run in the same transaction. This enables changes to data stores to either all occur or not occur. Another feature of IIS enables you to place an Active Server Page within a transaction. All objects in that page can then become part of the same transaction. If you would like to review transactions briefly, take a look at Day 7, "Database Transactions and Distributed Transaction Coordinator," to read about database transactions or Day 10, "Adding Transactional Support," to look at how you added transactional support to your COM components.

18

This is done through a directive located at the top of the page. You can add this through Visual by following these steps:

1. Open or create the ASP that you want to make into a transacted ASP.

2. Right-click the page and select properties. The Properties page as shown in Figure 18.2 will be displayed.

FIGURE 18.2

Creating page transactions.

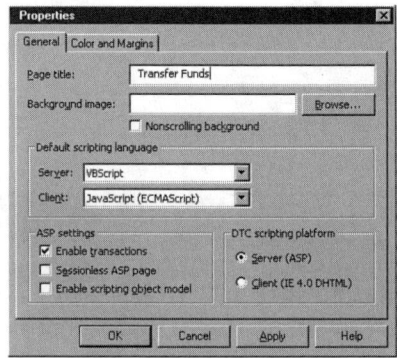

3. Select Enable Transactions.

4. Click OK.

If you look at the top of the page, you will see the following line:

```
<%@ Transaction=required Language=VBScript %>
```

Instead of following the preceding steps, you can also type directly on the page. The Properties window is convenient to use if you forget the syntax.

After transactions are set for the page, you can now call components in that page and they will be enlisted in the transaction.

This is also where the ObjectContext object comes into play. It has two methods: SetComplete and SetAbort. These correspond to the same methods in Visual Basic. SetComplete can be called multiple times, but, the first time SetAbort is called, the entire transaction is called back.

Unlike in Visual Basic, there is not an alternative way to instantiate an object such as the CreateInstance method. You will still use the CreateObject method from the Server object. Take a look at Listing 18.12 to see how a transactional page might be put together. This code was taken from the business component that you created on Day 9, "Building COM Components in VB," and Day 10. This function can be found in business.asp on the CD-ROM.

LISTING 18.12   Transacted ASP That Calls Components

```
 1: Function TransferFunds(CustomerID, FromAccount, ToAccount, Amount)
 2: Dim objData
 3: Set objData = Server.CreateObject("SmallTownBank_Data.BankData")
 4: TransferFunds = False
 5: If Not objData.DebitAccount(CustomerID, FromAccount, Amount) Then
 6:    ObjectContext.SetAbort
 7:    Set objData = Nothing
 8:    Exit Function
 9: End If
10: ObjectContext.SetComplete
11: If Not objData.CreditAccount(CustomerID, ToAccount, Amount) Then
12:    ObjectContext.SetAbort
13:    Set objData = Nothing
14:    Exit Function
15: End If
16: TransferFunds = True
17: ObjectContext.SetComplete
18: Set objData = Nothing
19: End Function
```

ANALYSIS   Line 1 gives the function declaration, which is the same as the Business component you created. After the `Dim` statement in line 2, line 3 creates the object. Lines 5 through 9 debit the account and lines 11 through 15 credit the account. To test the transaction capability of the page, pass in an incorrect account ID to transfer to. It will return a false in line 11 and call the `SetAbort`, which will roll back the previous insert in line 5. If everything is fine, line 17 calls the `SetComplete` and line 18 cleans up.

Creating HTML On-the-Fly

Now that you have been introduced to all the built-in objects, it is time to see how they all work together.

Listing 18.13 does two things. First, it displays a page enabling the user to indicate what to transfer. Again this is very similar to the harness application you created on Day 10. After the user submits the page, the second action the page takes is to update the account. It does this by reading in the entered values with the `Request` object and passing them to the `BankBusiness` component.

18

LISTING 18.13   A Complete Active Server Page

```
 1: <%@ Language=VBScript %>
 2: <% If Request.Form("intAction") <> "" Then
 3:     intAction = CInt(Request.Form("intAction"))
 4: Else
 5:     intAction = 0
 6: End If %>
 7: <HTML><HEAD>
 8: <TITLE>Transfer Funds</TITLE>
 9: </HEAD>
10: <BODY>
11: <% If intAction = 0 Then %>
12: <P><form method="POST" action="transfer.asp">
13: <input type="hidden" name=intAction value="1">
14: <table border="1" width="400">
15:  <tr><td>Customer ID:</td>
16:   <td><input type="text" name=txtCustomerID size="20"></td></tr>
17:  <tr><td>Transfer from Account ID:</td>
18:   <td><input type="text" name="txtAccountFrom" size="20"></td></tr>
19:  <tr><td>Transfer to Account ID:</td>
20:   <td><input type="text" name="txtAccountTo" size="20"></td></tr>
21:  <tr><td>Amount to Transfer:</td>
22:   <td><input type="text" name="txtAmount" size="20"></td></tr>
23: </table></P>
24: <P><input type="submit" value="Transfer Funds" name="B1">
    ➥<input type="reset" value="Reset" name="B2"></P>
25: </form>
26: <% Else
27: Dim objSTB
28: Dim blnSuccess
29: Set objSTB = Server.CreateObject("SmallTownBank_Business.BankBusiness")
30: blnSuccess = objSTB.TransferFunds(Request.Form("txtCustomerID"),
    ➥Request.Form("txtAccountFrom"), Request.Form("txtAccountTo"),
    ➥Request.Form("txtAmount"))
31: If blnSuccess Then
32:   Response.Write "Transfer Succeeded"
33: Else
34:   Response.Write "Transfer Failed"
35: End If
36: Set objSTB = Nothing
37: End If %>
38: </BODY></HTML>
```

ANALYSIS   The first thing to notice is that the transaction is not set in line 1. All the data modifications occur within the business component, SmallTownBank_Business. This component is under MTS already and therefore will run in a transaction. Line 2 requests a form variable. This value will only be set if the user is submitting the page. If it is empty, the page is being called for the first time. Based on the value, or lack thereof, it sets intAction appropriately. By setting the variable once, you will not need to call the Request object each time.

The rest of the page is split into two parts by the If/Then statement in line 11. If intAction is 0 (indicating that the user hasn't been to this page yet), it will display an HTML form in lines 12 through 14. You will take a closer look at HTML in Day 19, "Thin HTML—Reach Clients." After the user fills out the information and submits the form, intAction is set to 1. That will cause the Else part to be executed.

In the second part, the business component is instantiated in line 29 and the TransferFunds method is called in line 30. After that, the success or failure of the transfer is reported back and the page finishes on line 38. MTS components along with the Response, Request, and Server objects in ASPs allow you to transfer funds between accounts.

Using Includes Files

Up to this point we have been looking at code that is located either in your COM components or right in the ASP page. COM components are, of course, easy to reuse over and over again and ASPs can tie them together, but what if you want to be able to access an ASP function or constants from every page? For instance, if you want to have a constant for a carriage return vbCR, but didn't want to put that declaration at the top of every page, how would you handle it? This is particular to ASP, therefore, it wouldn't apply for a component.

The solution is to use an Include file. An *Include file* gets inserted into the ASP, before the ASP filter processes it. This makes the Include file an ideal location for code that needs to be reused.

SYNTAX

The syntax for the include is

```
<!--#INCLUDE FILE ="include/i_adovbs.asp"-->
```

The # sign represents a pre-processor directive, something that occurs before the ASP filter executes the script in the page. *FILE* is a parameter, which gives the location of the file. This will typically use a relative path.

▲

Here are a couple examples of using the Include directive:

```
<!--#INCLUDE FILE="i_adovbs.asp"-->
<!--#INCLUDE FILE="../include/i_adovbs.asp"-->
```

The first example includes a file that is in the same directory as the page that has the Include directive. The second example specifies a file that is in another directory (include). The "../" indicates that IIS first moves up one directory and then looks into the `include` directory, which is at that level. In other words the file with this reference would be `\websites\Macmillan\bank\transfer.asp` and the `include` file would be `\websites\Macmillan\include\i_adovbs.asp`. The advantage to using these relative paths versus hardcoded paths like `C:\InetPub\`... is that the page will still work if you move it to another location or another server.

Note

> `i_adovbs.asp` is the `adovbs.inc` renamed. It is from Microsoft and contains all the data constants that you need to work with ADO and SQL Server.

Tip

> I used to follow the Interdev 1.0 way and give my include files an extension of `.inc`. The problem with that is that the Editor doesn't recognize it and doesn't color code the file. There used to be a workaround to this in 1.0, but in Interdev 6.0 it is no longer possible. Therefore, I now use a naming scheme I picked up in Site Server, which is to have an `.asp` extension on the include files, but prefix the files with an `i_`. An example would be `i_global.asp`.

Include files are very useful because they enable you to reuse code that you already have. It also gives you a place to put items that do not belong in components. When you `include` a file, remember to place your script tags in the appropriate place. It is just like cutting and pasting the code into the file. Therefore, be sure not to leave out or double up on your script tags.

Do	Don't
DO be purposeful in what you put in `include` files. Ask yourself whether that is the appropriate place to put it.	DON'T place items, especially functions, in `include` files if it would be better to have them in components.

Using Scripting Objects and Server Components

Besides the core parts of ASPs that you have already learned, there are a number of other capabilities available in both scripting objects and server components. Scripting objects are part of the VBScript language, whereas server components are additional components that have been included with IIS. Unlike with built-in objects, you do have to declare and instantiate these server components.

Some of these make up for the lack of functions in VBScript—functions that are normally available in Visual Basic. An example of this is the `FileSystemObject` object, which gives you access to your files, folders, and drives. Others give you functionality that is specific to the Web. An example of this is the Browser Capabilities component. This can tell you what a browser supports, such as cookies or JavaScript.

In this section you will be learning about two different scripting objects, the `FileSystemObject` object and the `RegExp` object (for regular expressions). For the other scripting object and server components, such as the Ad Rotator, Tools, and Counter components, a brief summary will be presented and additional resources mentioned.

By learning about the various standard components, you will have more resources available to you to make dynamic and powerful Web sites. Also, after you have used a few components such as the ADO components, using others just becomes a matter of knowing the syntax. Therefore, we will stick with descriptions and then you can decide which ones you want to investigate further.

The FileSystemObject

The `FileSystemObject` object enables access to the file system. Whether you want to read files, get file dates, or create a list of files in a directory, this object will enable you to do this and more.

The `FileSystemObject` is part of the scripting component and is instantiated in ASPs using the following syntax:

```
Set objFile = Server.CreateObject("Scripting.FileSystemObject")
```

This line instantiates a `FileSystemObject` object. There are numerous other methods and properties available with this object. One that will enable you to write to a file is the `CreateTextFile` method. It has the following syntax:

```
objFileSystemObject.CreateTextFile(FileName, [Overwrite[, Unicode]])
```

`FileName` is the full path and file that you want to create. `Overwrite` is a Boolean value specifying whether to overwrite an existing file if it is present. The default is False. `Unicode` is a Boolean value indicating whether the file is created as a Unicode or ASCII file. The default is ASCII.

In this section, you will learn how to create and write information out to a file. To do this, use the `TextStream` object. This object is used to enable access to a file. Listing 18.14 demonstrates a use of the `FileSystemObject` object. You can also find this code in file_system.asp on the CD-ROM.

◀ SYNTAX

18

LISTING 18.14   Using the FileSystemObject to Create and Write Data Out to a File

```
1: Sub WriteFileShort(strFileName, strData)
2: Dim objFSO, objTS
3: Set objFSO = CreateObject("Scripting.FileSystemObject")
4: Set objTS = objFSO.CreateTextFile(strFileName)
5: objTS.Write strData
6: objTS.Close
7: Set objFSO = Nothing
8: End Sub
```

ANALYSIS In lines 1 and 2, two parameters are passed in: the name of the file which includes the physical path and the data to write to the file. Line 3 instantiates the FileSystemObject object and line 4 uses the CreateTextFile method. This method creates the file and also returns back a TextStream object. Line 5 uses the Write method of the TextStream object to write the data. The file is closed in line 6 and, after cleaning up, the function ends.

As stated previously, the FileSystemObject object handles all your file needs. There is enough functionality with it to deserve a chapter all by itself. Take a look at the other resources mentioned later in this chapter to find out more about the FileSystemObject object.

Regular Expressions, the RegExp Object

Along with Internet Explorer 5.0 came the release of VBScript version 5.0. This included support for regular expressions with the RegExp object. Using regular expressions gives the developer some powerful functionality for string searching and manipulation that has long been around in other languages such as Perl.

NEW TERM A *regular expression* is a method for string searching and manipulation through pattern matching. The patterns themselves take a while to understand if you have not used them before.

SYNTAX

The syntax for RegExp is as follows:

```
Set < object name> = New RegExp
```

RegExp is the name of the regular expression class. After the object is instantiated, you can use the Replace or Execute methods. The Replace method replaces text and the Execute method finds all the matches for a pattern. The pattern can be anything from a ZIP code (for example, 12345-6789) to looking for the word *DNA*, to looking for all the spaces in a string.

▼ Prior to calling these methods the `Pattern` property must be set to a regular expression. Once it is set you can call either method. The Replace is called by

```
strNew = objRegExp.Replace(strStart, strReplace)
```

`strStart` is the string to be searched using the regular expression in the `Pattern` property. `strReplace` replaces the strings that are found. The new string is returned from the method. To call the `Execute` method, use the following syntax:

```
Set objMatches = objRegExp.Execute(strSearch)
```

▲ `strSearch` is the string being searched by the pattern. `objMatches` is a collection of the matches found as a result of the search.

Here are some examples to look at. Listing 18.15 is an example of using the `Replace` method. Both Listing 18.15 and Listing 18.16 can be found in `regexp.asp` on the CD-ROM.

LISTING 18.15   Replacing Text Using a Regular Expression

```
1: Function RegExpReplace(strSearch, strPattern, strReplace)
2: Dim objRegExp
3: Set objRegExp = New RegExp
4: objRegExp.Pattern = strPattern
5: objRegExp.Global = True
6: RegExpReplace = objRegExp.Replace(strSearch, strReplace)
7: End Function
```

ANALYSIS   In line 1 the function is declared to take three parameters. The first is the string being searched. The second is the pattern that is used to search the string, and the third is the string to replace the matches. After creating the regular expression, the function calls the `Replace` method in line 6. This will search the string and replace the matches. The return value is the results of the `Replace`.

Another example uses the `Execute` method, demonstrated in Listing 18.16.

LISTING 18.16   Function to Find a Pattern Match

```
1: Function RegExpExecute(strPattern, strSearch)
2: Dim objRegExp, objMatches
3: Set objRegExp = New RegExp
4: objRegExp.Pattern = strPattern
5: objRegExp.Global = True
6: Set objMatches = objRegExp.Execute(strSearch)
```

continues

18

LISTING 18.16 continued

```
 7: If objMatches.Count > 0 Then
 8:   RegExpExecute = True
 9: Else
10:   RegExpExecute = False
11: End If
12: End Function
```

ANALYSIS Line 1 declares the function to take two parameters. The first is the pattern; the second is the string being searched. The function sets the pattern and calls the `Execute` method in line 6. This method returns a collection of the matches. Line 7 checks to see of any matches were found. If there were, it returns a true in line 8. Otherwise it will return a false in line 10.

A function like this can be useful for all types of validation. You can check to see whether a credit card number has the right number of digits, whether a phone number is entered correctly, or that an email has the right format. There are many possibilities that save you from having to parse through a string by hand.

Other Components

Besides the two you have just covered, a variety of other components exist. A good resource for finding more information on these is your local help on your IIS Web server. Typically you can reach it by going to `http://localhost/IISHelp`. Another good resource is the Microsoft Script Technologies site at `http://msdn.microsoft.com/scripting/`. Table 18.4 is a list of server components available in IIS.

TABLE 18.4 Additional Server Components Available in IIS

Component	Description
Ad Rotator	Cycles through advertisements. Enables you to specify the schedule.
Browser Capabilities	Enables determination of what a browser can and can not do.
Content Linking	Creates an object enabling you to link together pages of a Web site much like pages in a book.
Collaboration Data Objects for NTS	Enables you to send email from a page.
Tools	Miscellaneous utilities too small to separate into their own component.
MyInfo	Contains personal information about the site administrator.
Counters	General purpose counters; you increment them manually.

Component	Description
Content Rotator	Rotates through content in a designated text file. Enables you to rotate through links and images.
Page Counter	Page counter, which keeps track of the number of visits to a page.
Permission Checker	Enables you to test whether a user has permission to access a page before he selects the links.

These additional components give great additional functionality to tasks you might commonly have to do. Keep these in mind as you are creating more robust Web sites in order to save yourself hours of development time.

Summary

Today's lesson taught you about Active Server Pages. You learned about how IIS processes ASP pages and the script tags that the ISAPI filter looks for in a page. You also read about the built-in objects that are available on a page such as the `Request` and `Response` objects. State was also addressed by talking about `Session` and `Application` objects as well as cookies. Finally page transactions were discussed along with how to add transactional capabilities to your Web page.

Day 19's lesson will look at HTML. The basics of HTML will be discussed, along with what is available to you for creating a slimmed down presentation layer. You used HTML today to display information; tomorrow you will see some more of the options. You will then move to a thin client, where the work is done on the Server in ASPs and the HTML results sent to the client.

Q&A

Q I have been creating ASPs, and it seems best to put everything into the page itself. Why do I want to get involved with components and `include` files?

A When you are used to the Windows DNA paradigm, creating applications that use components and segment out functionality becomes second nature. Window DNA is built upon the idea of separating out functionality for the purposes of reuse and scalability. As a DNA application, the same principles apply here. Even `include` files with functions offer a great stepping-stone if you want to move those to components later.

18

Q **Yesterday we learned about JavaScript; today we covered VBScript. Do I need to use both? Which is better?**

A There is no real reason to use both or one instead of the other, except if you favor specific features. VBScript offers a couple of useful functions such as `Replace` and `Split` that aren't available in VB. There is also an add-in for regular expressions. JavaScript has similar features though. Also, JavaScript's language is more structured (I often find myself making syntax errors, but that is probably because of my VB background. If you are starting from scratch and want to use one language for client and server script, JavaScript would be the choice, because only IE clients natively support VBScript.

Workshop

The Workshop provides quiz questions to help you solidify your understanding of the material covered and exercises to provide you with experience in using what you've learned. Try to understand the quiz and exercise answers before continuing to the next lesson. Answers are provided in Appendix A.

Quiz

1. What would be the syntax to read a variable named `txtCity` from a page that could be either from a form or a `querystring`?

2. What command would you use to cause IIS not to send content until the entire ASP was finished?

3. How do you instantiate an object in ASPs?

4. How do you require page transactions?

5. What server variables contain the filename of the current ASP?

6. Using the `FileSystemObject` object, what command could you use to open a new file?

Exercises

1. Up to this point, you have been placing logic on the client. You now can move that logic to run on the server and have it process the information.

   Using the `SmallTownBank` application, take the code from Listing 18.12 and create a Web page that mimics the account transfer form that was made on Day 9. Experiment with the form that will take in account numbers and an amount to transfer; execute the server-side code, which moves the money around.

On the CD, you can find the file on Day 18. It is called `transfer.asp`. You will have an opportunity tomorrow to learn more about the HTML tags involved. Try experimenting with the transactional settings, removing the component from MTS and trying it. Use invalid data for the form and see what happens then as well.

18

DAY **19**

Thin HTML—Reach Clients

Today, you will degrade the DHTML presentation layer to use only HTML on the client for the presentation tier and ASP on the server for implementing the business logic tier. I do want to mention that this chapter is certainly not an exhaustive look at HTML. Highlights will be mentioned today, as well as tips that can be useful in your pages. To further your HTML knowledge, you can find additional information on HTML on the Web, including on Microsoft's MSDN site. I encourage you to look at it at `http://msdn.microsoft.com` or `http://www.usheen.com/html/home.html` for further information on HTML.

After today's lesson, you will have learned about

- HTML fundamentals
- Using ASP to check browser compatibility
- Creating a static presentation layer with HTML

HTML–The Basics

A friend of mine introduced me to the World Wide Web in the fall of 1994. In January of 1995, I opened my first Internet account, and I have been surfing the

Web and posting content ever since. The one thing I remember about going on the Web is that so many of the Web pages were "gray." That used to be the default background color for the browsers. This can be very plain and very boring. In the same way, the content was plain as well. It was static, text-based content that changed when Webmasters found time to do it. Over time, this has all changed, allowing dynamic Web sites to take their place. This was accomplished in part by implementing technologies like those in Windows DNA.

The amazing thing is that, although the back-end processes have grown tremendously with data stores, COM, and XML, the same language is still being used to display the content: Hypertext Markup Language (HTML). Although XML, as you have learned on Day 12, "The Power of XML," can replace writing HTML, the XML is still using HTML to display content to the user. Nevertheless HTML will still be around just because of its sheer volume, if nothing else, for years to come. Today, you will learn about HTML and the basics of an HTML page. HTML is a great layer for your Windows DNA presentation tier and, at the end of today, you will have an opportunity to create a thin client to support the `SmallTownBank` application.

Using HTML Tags

How do you use HTML? Here is a quick overview. HTML tags are used to mark items in your Web document that will indicate the items' style, format, or both. For example, if you wanted to emphasize some text, you would use the `<EM>` tag as follows:

```
<EM> Emphasized Text </EM>.
```

This has marked up the text `Emphasized Text`. When I say that text is *marked up*, I mean it has a begin tag (`<EM>` in this example) and an end tag (`</EM>` in this example), around the text. Any word processor performs a similar action when you modify the look of the text by changing the font or font size. The difference is that you cannot see the tags in the word processor. Here are couple rules about using HTML in your Web pages:

- Every begin tag should have a corresponding end tag.

- All tags must be properly nested.

Closing HTML Statements with End Tags

It is always good practice to close your tags. This is especially important with items such as tables, but also something I would recommend for paragraph and line breaks. For example, the `<BR>` tag is used for a line break. One way I often do this is to just use the `<BR>` tag at the end of the line:

```
Here is a line break.<BR>
```

This works fine, but another way to do it is

```
<BR>Here is a line break.</BR>
```

By using this second method, it makes your code easier to read. It also allows you to identify that portion of text more easily when reviewing your source code. This will help you with both DTHML and Cascading Style Sheets (as seen later in this chapter).

Properly Nesting HTML Tags

The second rule of using tags is that all tags must be properly nested. Tags cannot overlap each other. Once you place a begin tag, both the begin and end tags for any other tags that you include must come before the initial end tag that you used. To make this clearer, here is an example of what will not work:

```
<BLOCKQUOTE><B>Here is an indented text.</BLOCKQUOTE></B>
```

The bold end tag (`</B>`) must come before the `</BLOCKQUOTE>` end tag. The problem is that the browser will not know exactly what to do with this line of HTML and it is much harder to code as well as read and understand. This is especially true as you start doing pages with more complicated layouts. Depending on which browser you are using, the overlapping of tags may still work, but you could run into problems later on and spend a lot of time tracking down the incorrect placement. Here is the example written correctly and formatted so it is easy to read:

```
<BLOCKQUOTE>
        <B>Here is an indented text.</B>
</BLOCKQUOTE>
```

In this case the bold tag, B, has both its beginning and ending tag within the BLOCKQUOTE tag.

Besides the tag name, you may also need to include further information for a tag by specifying attributes for a tag. This attribute information goes within the < and > symbols. For example, to use the link tag, <A>, you must specify where the link jumps to with the HREF attribute. Here is an example:

```
<A HREF="tables.htm">Go to tables page.</A>
```

The HREF attribute is set to `"tables.htm"`, which tells the browser to jump to that page if the link is clicked. Attributes are also very important when creating tables, as you will see later today, and also for many other tags like the image tag, <IMG>.

Now that you have a good idea of how tags and attributes work, let's take a look at how these would fit in a page. Listing 19.1 shows the basic structure of a page.

19

LISTING **19.1** Structure of a Web Page

```
1: <html>
2: <head>
3: <title></title>
4: </head>
5: <body>
6: </body>
7: </html>
```

ANALYSIS The HTML tag in line 1 indicates that the page contains HTML. This is a standard tag. Within that you can see two distinct parts. The <HEAD> tag and the <BODY> tag. The information in the <HEAD> tag doesn't display on the page. This is information about the page and what it contains. For instance, the <TITLE> tag goes in the title bar of the browser. This is also a place where your ASP code could go. The <BODY> tag in line 4 indicates the start of the actual content of the document, which will be displayed to the user. This continues until the BODY end tag, which is seen as </BODY> in line 6.

The Presentation Tier: HTML's Domain

In a large portion of this book, you have been focused on content. This has involved data access components that receive and send data back from the data store, as well as business components that also send and receive data, performing the appropriate tasks while following the specific rules for the business. HTML, though, is not concerned with content, but with how to present the content or information to the user. HTML controls how the data fields look on the page.

In these next sections, you will have a chance to focus on various parts of HTML and how each part is used to present information to the user. Specifically, you will look at style sheets, tables, forms, and frames. At the end of these sections you will be able to implement each of these on your own pages.

Style with Cascading Style Sheets

With recent releases of Internet Explorer and Netscape Navigator, the use of Cascading Style Sheets has allowed content developers the ability to easily change the look of their site without having to change every individual field.

Cascading Style Sheets (CSS) are templates that allow you to specify the look and feel for a page or pages. They also allow you to separate the look and feel from the content of the page. By defining the look and feel in one place, you can allow that to cascade to many other pages.

For instance, if you have a <BOLD> tag, this would typically cause the text to be bolded. By defining the bold tag in a style sheet, this allows you to cause the text that is within the `<BOLD>` and `</BOLD>` tags to look however you want. You could decide to make the text 14 pt. Arial Italic. By defining this in one place (the style sheet), every place that references the style sheet will format this text the same way.

Cascading Style Sheets

Cascading Style Sheets came from a limitation of browsers to describe how content should look. When people first started using the Web, they had only the limited set of HTML tags available to them. There was no way to choose a font and if you didn't like the point size that the H1 through H6 tags produced, you were out of luck. In response to this situation, Microsoft added the `<FONT>` tag to its browser. Internet Explorer could then read this tag and, depending on the setting, make the font larger or smaller. It could also make other format changes such as the typeface or font color.

The problem with this is that the `<FONT>` tag had to be entered into each piece of text, and it cluttered up the page you were working with. If you generated the pages on-the-fly with ASP, there were lots of extra tags to keep track of, and again these forced the ASP to generate both content and style. It is out of this that Cascading Style Sheets eventually evolved, allowing developers to once more only worry about content. Although I will not be going deep into detail on Cascading Style Sheets, you can find more information online at the Microsoft site at `http://msdn.microsoft.com/workshop/author`.

There are a few different ways to implement style with Cascading Style Sheets. There are linked style sheets and embedded style sheets where you have specific sections that define all the styles for a page and also inline styles, which define the style for individual tags. You will look at each of these next.

Linked Style Sheets

One way to add styles to a page is to have a *linked* style sheet in which the style sheet is its own physical page and is referenced from an HTML page. The HTML page would reference the sheet, as demonstrated in the following line:

```
<link REL="stylesheet" HREF="main.css" TYPE="text/css">
```

The `<link>` tag allows you to reference a linked style sheet. This allows you to easily keep style settings separate from your HTML tags. You could use this same line in as many HTML pages as you wanted and all of them would then point to the same style sheet. This tag uses the `HREF` attribute to specify the file `main.css`, which would contain the style sheet rules. An example of this file could look like the following:

```
<STYLE>
H1{font: 18pt Comic Sans MS}
H2{font: bold 16pt Verdana }
</STYLE>
```

19

ANALYSIS The style tags delimit the beginning and ending of the style information. The style rule applies to the H1 and the H2 tags and indicate the font properties for the tags. main.css can be found on the CD-ROM accompanying this book.

With the linked style sheets, the following syntax is used to declare a style rule:

```
tag {property1:value; property2:value; ...propertyn: value}
```

The tag corresponds to any valid HTML tag. The property is the style sheet property and the value is an acceptable property value. For example

```
TD{font: bold 10pt Verdana;text-align:left;vertical-align: top}
```

This would cause table elements to have a bolded 10pt Verdana font, to be horizontally aligned left, and vertically aligned to the top.

▲

Embedded Style Sheets

Another way to implement styles in a page is through an embedded style sheet in which you have both the style sheet information and the HTML tags within the same physical page. With an embedded style sheet, you take an HTML page and add the style sheet information to the <HEAD> section of the page. You use the same syntax as linked style sheets to declare the style rules. Listing 19.2 is an example of an embedded style sheet in an HTML page.

LISTING **19.2**   Using an Embedded Style Sheet

```
 1: <html>
 2: <style type="text/css">
 3: <!--
 4: H5 {font:  bold 12pt Verdana; text-align="left";}
 5: H6 {font: 10pt Verdana; text-align="left";}
 6: -->
 7: </style>
 8: <head>
 9: <title>Embedded Style Sheet</title>
10: </head>
11: <body>
12: <h5>This is the H5 tag.</h5>
13: <h6>This is the H6 tag.</h6>
14: </body>
15: </html>
```

ANALYSIS Line 2 uses the <style> tag to designate the start of the style sheet. The </style> end tag in line 7 designates the end of it. HTML comment tags are included in lines 3 and 6. By tagging the style rules as comments, you will not inadvertently display the information contained between the <style> tag if the browser doesn't support the style sheet syntax. Lines 4 and 5 declare the style rules to be used on this page. These rules set the default font for the H5 and H6 tags, which are standard HTML header tags. Lines 12 and 13 display two lines using the heading tag. Figure 19.1 displays how this page looks when viewed in a browser.

FIGURE 19.1

Using an embedded style sheet.

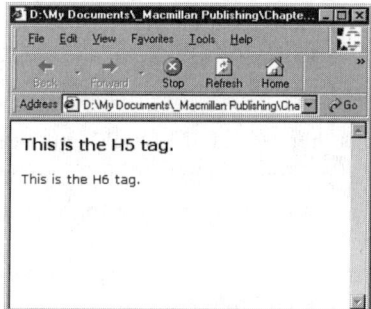

Editing Style Sheets

To edit a style sheet file, you have a couple options. You can do it through a text editor like Notepad, which is often my preference for style sheets. Another option is to use the CSS editor built in to Visual Interdev. This assists you in building style sheets when you are starting from scratch and gives you the correct syntax for the styles. In order for Visual Interdev to use the editor when you double-click the file, give it a .css extension when you add the file to the Web site in Visual Interdev. The CSS editor is shown in Figure 19.2.

19

FIGURE 19.2

The CSS editor in Visual Interdev.

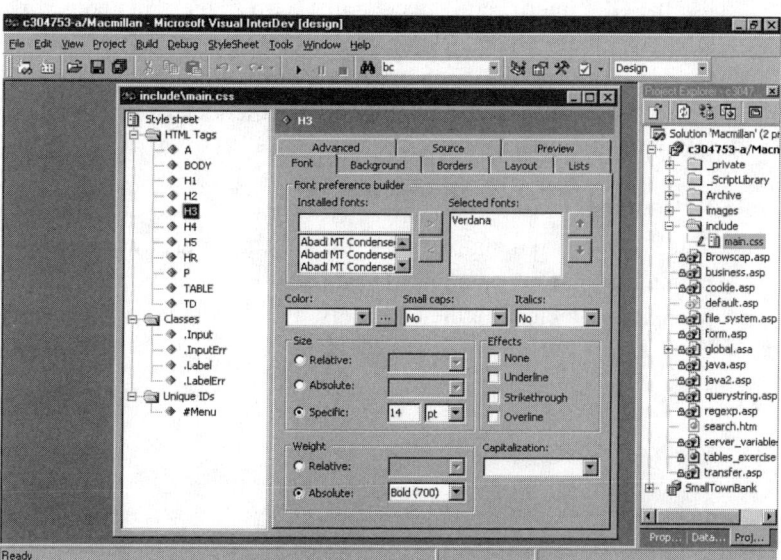

Inline Styles

The third way to define style rules in a HTML page is to use inline styles. These allow you to apply a style on a tag-by-tag basis. An example of this is

```
<I STYLE="font: italic Arial; color: blue;">Italic Text</I>
```

The resulting text would not only be italicized, but also it would be blue in the Arial font. Inline styles are useful at times, but don't overuse them since, again, they make your HTML cluttered and harder to change in the future.

There is much more to style sheets then this, and I would encourage you to look at the many online resources available to get more information. As mentioned earlier, the MSDN (`http://msdn.microsoft.com`) is a great place for additional information.

Page Layout

Now, style sheets alone will not allow you to be successful in having great-looking pages. You will need to combine style sheets with the proper page layout. When using HTML tags, be selective in which ones you use and be consistent from page to page. If you use the H2 tag at the top of a page to designate a primary heading, make sure you use that same tag on all the related pages. This enables you to change the linked style sheet and have the change take effect on all your pages. You might want to take a look at some Web sites that you like and view the HTML source, which is typically a menu selection from your browser. See what they use to implement style.

When working with an HTML editor such as FrontPage, make sure you are not inadvertently putting in many <FONT> tags by mistake. FrontPage will add the <FONT> tag if you use the GUI interface to create your HTML page. This will work against you later on when you make changes in the style sheet. The <FONT> tag will override the changes forcing you to go into each page and remove or modify the <FONT> tag. By laying out your pages well, you can quickly update the look of the site, but, as with anything, it takes planning ahead.

Creating Tables

Tables serve two main purposes. Initially, table tags were created for the purpose of displaying tabular information. If you had a list of names and addresses, you could easily place it in a table with the table tags, and it would neatly display on your screen.

Subsequently, users discovered that you could treat your whole page as a table, and thereby be able to place pieces of data in different places on your screen. This gives more of a newspaper-type look to your HTML page. Creators of Web content continued to use tables by nesting them inside one another. This gave further control over the layout of the page.

Tables are a great way to lay out your page. Yet, there have been a number of occasions when I had to spend a good deal of time tracking down a stray table tag because it would not display in Netscape Navigator. Although there are tools out today that can help you check this, you still want to be careful that you don't carelessly miss a required tag.

> **Tip**
>
> Internet Explorer and Netscape Navigator take two very different approaches to displaying content. Internet Explorer is very forgiving when it comes to tags. It doesn't complain if you miss a tag or put information in the wrong place and will still display the page content. This is NOT the case with Netscape Navigator. Netscape's browser will simply not display anything at all. Instead you will be left with a blank screen (unless you view the source) and no idea why it happened.
>
> I think there are valid reasons for both of these approaches. Your responsibility as you develop HTML pages lies in knowing that they both exist.

The basic structure of a table involves the table declaration and table rows. Within each row are one or more cells. Tables 19.1 and 19.2 give a list of table tags and some of the more popular attributes used with them.

19

TABLE 19.1   HTML Table Tags

Tag	Name	Description	Attributes
TABLE	Table definition	Specifies a table	BORDER, WIDTH
TR	Table Row	Specifies a table row	ALIGN, VALIGN, WIDTH
TH	Table Header	Table header cell (centered and bold)	ALIGN, VALIGN, WIDTH
TD	Table Data	Table cell	ALIGN, VALIGN, WIDTH, COLSPAN, ROWSPAN

TABLE 19.2   Attributes Referenced in Table 19.1

Attribute	Values	Description
BORDER	Integer	Width in pixels of the border
WIDTH	Integer [%]	Width in pixels of the object or, if followed by a percent, the width as a percentage of the parent object
ALIGN	Left, center, right	Alignment of the text within the object
VALIGN	Middle, bottom, top	Vertical alignment of the text with the object
COLSPAN	Integer	Number of columns for the row to span
ROWSPAN	Integer	Number of rows for the cell to span

Now that you have seen the tags that make up a table, you are ready to create one for yourself. Listing 19.3 gives a table declaration.

LISTING 19.3   Page with a Two-Column, Three-Row Table

```
1: <HTML>
2: <HEAD><TITLE>Tables</TITLE></HEAD>
3: <BODY>
4: <TABLE BORDER="1">
5:    <TR><TH>Header A</TH><TH>Header B</TH></TR>
6:    <TR><TD>Data A1</TD><TD>Data B1</TD></TR>
7:    <TR><TD>Data A2</TD><TD>Data B2</TD></TR>
8: </TABLE>
9: </BODY></HTML>
```

ANALYSIS   Line 3 declares the table with a border of 1. The default is 0. Line 4 designates the first row. This row contains two header cells, Header A and Header B. The next two rows are normal data rows, each with two <TD> tags in them. After the last row is closed at the end of line 7, the <TABLE> end tag is inserted, and the page is finished.

Listing 19.4 is a more complicated example. This one involves nesting a table within another table and using some of the ROWSPAN and COLSPAN attributes.

LISTING 19.4   Nested Tables

```
1: <HTML>
2: <HEAD>
3: <TITLE>Nested Tables</TITLE>
4: </HEAD>
5: <BODY>
6: <TABLE BORDER="1" WIDTH="500">
7:    <TR>
```

```
 8:        <TD COLSPAN="2">Page Header</TD>
 9:      </TR>
10:      <TR>
11:        <TD WIDTH="150">Menu Area</TD>
12:        <TD>
13:        <TABLE BORDER="1" WIDTH="400" HEIGHT="300">
14:          <TR>
15:            <TD ROWSPAN="2">Two Rows</TD>
16:            <TD>Data A</TD>
17:          </TR>
18:          <TR>
19:            <TD>Data B</TD>
20:          </TR>
21:        </TABLE>
22:        </TD>
23:      </TR>
24:      <TR>
25:        <TD COLSPAN="2">Page Footer</TD>
26:      </TR>
27: </TABLE>
28: </BODY>
29: </HTML>
```

ANALYSIS   This example starts off with the first table declaration. The first row is displayed in lines 7 through 9. This uses the COLSPAN attribute, causing the cell to span two columns. In the next row (defined in lines 10 through 14), there are really only two <TD> tags. This makes sense, since the <TD> tag in the first row spanned two columns. This first row could be the menu area for a page.

The next <TD> tag makes things a little complicated. Instead of there being text inside this <TD> tag, there is actually another table declaration. This next table contains a couple rows. The first element in line 15 has its ROWSPAN property set to 2. The next element in line 16 looks normal. The row in lines 18 through 20 only has one <TD> tag in it because the first cell is being taken up by the element in line 15, which spans two rows. After the TABLE end tag is hit in line 27, the <TD> end tag for the row in the first table may be included. We then finish the page with a footer (line 25), which like the header, spans two columns.

This example is easier to understand if you take a look at its output in Figure 19.3.

Tables give you a lot of flexibility when laying out your page. Too many nested tables can also slow your page down, so don't get too carried away with it. Also, don't use nested tables if you don't have to.

19

FIGURE 19.3

Displaying nested tables.

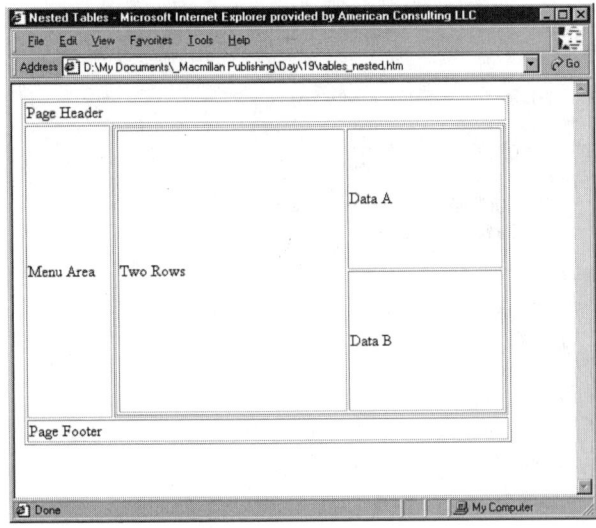

Tip

When specifying the width of a table, you want to be careful in whether you use pixels or a percentage. Realize that, if you specify width as a percentage, the table can grow automatically as the user resizes the window. This can often create disarray on the page if the window happens to be sized too small or too large. By specifying a pixel width, you will know how the table will be sized and can place the items to look best in that size of a table.

Forms

If it weren't for forms, your HTML experience would primarily be unidirectional. You would request to look at a page, and the server containing that page would send it back to you. You would request another page, and that page would be sent to you as well. This method generates many requests for information on your part, but you are not sending any data back to the server. Realistically, this is the majority of your browsing experience, perhaps 90% or more for a lot of people. But if you want to send information back—such as to sign up for an email list, to register for a membership, to send feedback to someone, to submit your VISA information to purchase items, or to complete any of a number of business-to-business activities—you need to have some mechanism for doing that. That's what forms are all about, generating a two-way exchange of data between a client and a server.

 A *form* utilizes the `<FORM>` tag along with one or more `<INPUT>` tags allowing users to send useful information back to a Web server.

Forms were briefly discussed on Day 18, "Active Server Pages," with the `Forms` collection in ASP. You will now learn about some of the various types of input on a form and how to use them. The contents of the form are encapsulated inside of the `<FORM>` tags. Take a look at Table 19.3, which lists the various attributes of the `<FORM>` tag.

TABLE 19.3   `<FORM>` Attributes

Attribute	Description
ACTION	This specifies the page to submit the form to.
METHOD	Either GET or POST.
NAME	The name of the form. This is useful when using DHTML and would be used as the object name.

`ACTION` and `METHOD` should always be set. The `ACTION` can be the full or relative path to the page that will process the form. The `METHOD` for the form should always be `POST`. A form that uses the `GET` method will be sent along the querystring, which was discussed on Day 18. This is not recommended primarily because the querystring has a limited length and therefore imposes a limit to the information that can be sent on a form.

 Note

> One thing to remember is that you can have multiple forms on a page, but you cannot nest them.

19

Within the `<FORM>` tags will be all the `<INPUT>` tags. `<INPUT>`tags allow you to display various controls on your form including text boxes, radio buttons, and check boxes. You can have any of the other HTML tags inside the form as well, but only the `<INPUT>` tags, which are in between the begin and end `<FORM>` tag will be submitted with the form. Which `INPUT` control is displayed is determined by what you set the `TYPE` attribute equal to on the `<INPUT>` tag. Table 19.4 is a list of the possible values for the `TYPE` attribute.

TABLE 19.4 Values for the TYPE Attribute

Value	Description
Button	Displays a button. Typically used for client-side scripting to activate a script.
Checkbox	Used to select Boolean options, which will either be Yes or No.
Hidden	Used to set information that you do not want to have displayed on the form, such as ID values.
Password	Used for password fields. The characters in the field will be masked with asterisks.
Radio	Used when a user can pick only one of two or more options, such as a shipping method.
Reset	Button that causes the input controls on the form to be set back to their original values, which may or may not be blank.
Submit	Button to submit the form to the page specified in the ACTION attribute.
Text	Typical input box to enter any type of text data.

Each of the INPUT TYPES in Table 19.4 has attributes associated with it. The two primary ones are NAME and VALUE. These correspond to the name value pairs, which were discussed on Day 18. When referring to the INPUT TYPES, you use the NAME attribute. You most often do this with the REQUEST object in an ASP.

The VALUE attribute may or may not have to be set to a value. It functions a little differently for each of the controls. For buttons, like the Button, Submit, or Reset INPUT TYPES, it is the text that displays on the button. For Checkbox and Radio INPUT TYPES, it is the value that the control gets set to if the box is checked or a radio button is selected on a page. For Hidden INPUT TYPE, it is the value that gets passed when the form is submitted. For Password and Text INPUT TYPES, it is the default value in the text control.

Here is an example of a TEXT INPUT TYPE:

```
<INPUT TYPE="TEXT" NAME"txtFirstName" VALUE="Phil">
```

This will cause a text box control to display on the Web page with "Phil" displaying in the control. Here is an example of a radio button:

```
<INPUT TYPE="RADIO" NAME="Account" VALUE="Checking">
<INPUT TYPE="RADIO" NAME="Account" VALUE="Savings">
```

Notice that for the user to be able to pick only one of the items, the radio input controls must have the same name. The user can select either one. If the user selects the second one, "Savings" would be the value of "Account".

A couple other popular controls that you typically see on Web pages that have not yet been mentioned are drop-down lists and list boxes. To create drop-down lists and list boxes, you will use the <SELECT> and <OPTION> tags. The <SELECT> tag has a NAME attribute, but unlike the <INPUT> tag, not a VALUE attribute. The <SELECT> tag has the following syntax:

```
<SELECT NAME="name of control" [SIZE="rows to display"] [MULTIPLE]>
```

The SIZE and MULTIPLE attributes apply to list boxes only. The value of SIZE is the row size of the list box. MULTIPLE is not assigned a value. If it appears in the <SELECT> tag, it allows users to shift-click to select multiple items in the list box.

The items that appear in a list are included between the begin and end <SELECT> tags using the <OPTION> tag. The <OPTION> tag has the following syntax:

```
<OPTION VALUE="option value" [SELECTED]> value to display in list
```

SELECTED would apply to only one item in the list and designates the default or "selected" item in the list when the form is originally displayed.

Here is an example of a simple drop-down list box:

```
<SELECT NAME="AccountType">
<OPTION VALUE="1">Savings</OPTION>
<OPTION VALUE="2">Checking</OPTION>
</SELECT>
```

"AccountType" would have a value of 1 or 2, depending on whether the user selects Savings or Checking in the drop-down list.

Now that you have read about the various types of controls in a form, let's take a look at a sample form and see how it works. Listing 19.5 displays an example of a simple response page.

19

LISTING 19.5   Form with Various INPUT TYPES

```
 1: <HTML><HEAD><TITLE>Sample Form</TITLE></HEAD>
 2: <BODY>
 3: <FORM METHOD="POST" NAME="frmMain" ACTION="form.htm">
 4: <INPUT TYPE="HIDDEN" NAME="txtSource" VALUE="ResponsePage">
 5: <BR>Name: <INPUT TYPE="TEXT" NAME="txtName">
 6: <BR>Age: <INPUT TYPE="TEXT" NAME="intAge" SIZE="5">
 7: <BR>State: <SELECT NAME="cboState">
 8:    <OPTION VALUE="OR">Oregon</OPTION>
 9:    <OPTION VALUE="CA">California</OPTION>
10:    <OPTION VALUE="MO">Missouri</OPTION>
11: </SELECT>
```

continues

LISTING 19.5   continued

```
12: <BR>Heard about us from:
13: <INPUT TYPE="RADIO" NAME="cboHeardFrom" VALUE="Radio">Radio
14: <INPUT TYPE="RADIO" NAME="cboHeardFrom" VALUE="Email">Email
15: <BR><INPUT TYPE="CHECKBOX" NAME="chkMailingList" VALUE="True" CHECKED>
16: Check here to receive email updates.
17: <BR><INPUT TYPE="SUBMIT" NAME="cmdSubmit" VALUE="Submit Response">
18: <INPUT TYPE="RESET" NAME="cmdReset" VALUE="Reset Values">
19: </FORM>
20: </BODY></HTML>
```

ANALYSIS   The <FORM> tag in line 3 declares the start of the form. There is a "HIDDEN" variable in line 4, which would tell a page processing this form that txtSource is equal to "ResponsePage". Lines 5 and 6 display simple text boxes. Lines 7 through 11 display a drop-down list box for state selection. Notice the display is the full state name, but the value that is set is the state abbreviation. Next, radio buttons allow a user to choose one of two choices (lines 13 and 14). The check box in line 15 is simply a yes or no question. Lines 18 and 19 display the buttons to submit the form or reset the form back to its original state. Finally the form is closed with the end <FORM> tag. Figure 19.4 displays the output of the HTML.

FIGURE 19.4

An HTML form.

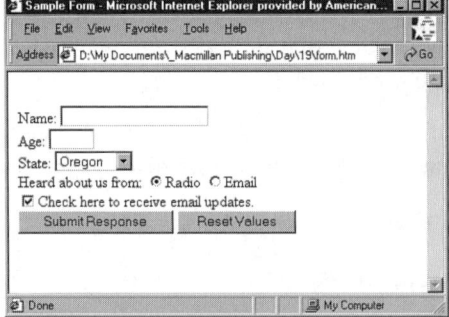

Copy the file form.htm from the CD-ROM accompanying this book; make changes to it and see what happens. You can use the ASP skills you learned in Day 18 to process the form and display the submitted values. Once you understand how to create forms, this will help you in both being able to make effective and useful forms on a page as well as making it easier to write ASPs that process the forms.

Frames

Frames have never been a favorite with me, but, if you have an existing set of HTML files, it is an easy way to give a common look and feel to your entire Web site without having to modify each and every page. Frames allow you to display one or more Web pages inside a single browser window. This would allow you to have a menu page on the left, while the user navigates through the site and displays the content pages on the right.

Frames work by having a default document that contains references to the documents you want to display in the frames and what dimensions the frames are. For example, a file called default.htm could set up a frame and declare one HTML page to span the top quarter of the browser window and have an ASP fill in the lower three-quarters of the window. Neither the HTML page in the top window nor the ASP page in the bottom would know anything about each other or have to have any special coding. That is all done using a <FRAMESET> tag in default.htm.

The <FRAMESET> tag with the COLS and ROWS attributes uses the following syntax:

▼ SYNTAX

```
<FRAMESET COLS="ColumnWidth1, ColumndWidth2, ColumnWidthN"
➥ROWS="RowHeight1, RowHeight2, RowHeightN">
        <FRAME SRC="SourcePage1" NAME="FrameName1">
        <FRAME SRC="SourcePage2" NAME="FrameName2">
        <FRAME SRC="SourcePageN" NAME="FrameNameN">
</FRAMESET>
```

The COLS and ROWS attributes specify the width and height, respectively, of each of the frames in the page. Height and width can be expressed in pixels (for example, 10, 400), as a percentage (for example, 10%, 50%), or as ratios to the other columns or rows (for example, *, 3*). You can mix and match these as well, sometimes with unpredictable results. When using the relative size, it calculates the amount used for pixels or percentages and then allocates the rest for the relative sizing. If you had a setting of

```
COLS="30, *, 2*"
```

the first column would be 30 pixels, and the second would be one-third of the remaining space. The third column would take up the other two-thirds, or the remaining space.

The <FRAME> tag requires you to specify the initial file for the frame in the SRC attribute. The NAME attribute is used to differentiate the page from other FRAMEs when you want frames to work in conjunction with each other. This is explained a little later in this section.

▲

A typical example of using a <FRAMESET> tag would be to have a menu on the left-hand side of the window and the sites pages display on the right-hand side. Take a look at Listing 19.6 for an example of a page with a <FRAMESET> tag. This is on the CD-ROM accompanying this book and is called frameset.htm.

19

LISTING 19.6 Using the <FRAMESET> Tag

```
 1: <HTML>
 2: <HEAD>
 3: <TITLE>Sample FRAMESET</TITLE>
 4: </HEAD>
 5: <FRAMESET COLS="160,*">
 6:   <FRAME SRC="css_embedded.htm" NAME="menu">
 7:   <FRAME SRC="tables_nested.htm" NAME="main">
 8:   <NOFRAMES>
 9:   <BODY BGCOLOR="WHITE">
10:   <H1>Your browser must support frames.</H1>
11:   </BODY>
12:   </NOFRAMES>
13: </FRAMESET>
14: </HTML>
```

ANALYSIS This page has two frames. The first has a width of 160 pixels; the second uses the balance of the width available in the browser. The two pages are named in lines 6 and 7. Lines 8 through 12 use the <NOFRAMES> tag to display text if the browser doesn't support frames. The <FRAMESET> is ended in line 13.

What's with <NOFRAMES>?

The idea here is that any page that understands frames knows to ignore anything in between the <NOFRAMES> tag. Therefore, if a browser didn't know about frames, it also wouldn't know about the <NOFRAMES>tags and would display the HTML between the <NOFRAMES>tags.

One more detail to look at is how to update the contents in the right-hand side of the frame by clicking on links in the left-hand side. This is done with the TARGET attribute in the <A> tag. Here is an example:

```
<A TARGET="main" HREF="tables.htm">
```

By placing this link in menu.htm, it will cause the target of the link to be in "main", which is the name of the right-hand window in the frames.

Frames are easy to implement and offer a quick way to get some standard look to a sight. The downside is that a user can also get lost if he happens to have a link to one of the pages that is normally in a frame. He may get a standalone page with no reference to the rest of the site. Also the look and feel of a site with frames is not nearly as smooth as one without them. The user experience seems to suffer. This is exemplified by the fact that most large-scale Web sites do not employ frames. Therefore, I am not saying, "Rule them out," but I am saying, "Make sure they serve the right purpose for you."

Checking Browser Compatibility in ASP

With an HTML-only presentation layer, you can offer users two choices. One is an HTML thin client. The second is a rich client that provides functionality right on the client browser. In an ideal world, you really want to give each user the best possible Web page experience. You don't want to necessarily program to the lowest common denominator. Therefore, if a browser can support the requirements for a richer client, such as JavaScript and ActiveX controls, then you should probably use these rich client features in your development to take full advantage of the browser's capabilities. Otherwise, if the browser in question can't support rich client capabilities, your best option is to give users a thin HTML client. In order to figure this out programmatically, you can use the Browser Capability component, `BrowserType`. This component resides on the IIS Server and is another Server Component in addition to the `FileSystemObject` and `RegExp` components that you learned about on Day 18. The Browser Capability component will tell you what type of browser the user has and what their browser supports.

The Browser Capability component reads in the browser name (also known as the user agent) and then performs a lookup in a text file called `Browsecap.ini`, which is located on the Windows NT IIS Server in the \WINNT\system32\inetsrv folder. This is a lookup file that contains information on what specific browsers do and do not support. Listing 19.7 is a sample listing from that file.

LISTING 19.7   Sample from the `Browsecap.ini` File

```
 1: [IE 5.0]
 2: browser=IE
 3: Version=5.0
 4: majorver=5
 5: minorver=0
 6: frames=True
 7: tables=True
 8: cookies=True
 9: backgroundsounds=True
10: vbscript=True
11: javaapplets=True
12: javascript=True
13: ActiveXControls=True
```

19

Among other things, the `Browsecap.ini` has information on whether the browser can support JavaScript, cookies, tables, frames, and ActiveX controls. In order to use the Browser Capability component, you need to instantiate an instance of the component and then merely reference the items from Listing 19.7 as attributes of the object. Listing 19.8 is an example of ASP code that uses the Browser Capability component.

LISTING 19.8   Finding Browser Properties

```
1: Set objBrowser = Server.CreateObject("MSWC.BrowserType")
2: If objBrowser.javascript = True Then
3:    Response.Write "This browser supports client-side validation."
4: Else
5:    Response.Write "Cannot use client-side validation with this browser."
6: End If
7: Set objBrowser = Nothing
```

ANALYSIS After the object is instantiated, it tests to see if the browser supports JavaScript or not. Based on this condition, it displays a message. Instead of displaying a message, you would probably include JavaScript code. Another possibility is to just jump to an entirely different page. You also could execute the code in Listing 19.8 when they first come to the site and then have an HTML site and a HTML/Scripting site.

This component is able to determine what the client browser is by looking at the `HTTP_USER_AGENT` from the `ServerVariables` collection. For additional information on `ServerVariables`, you can look at Day 18. The Browser Capability component compares this value to the headings on the `Browsecap.ini` file. Therefore, if your clients' requirements for browser capabilities are straightforward, you may want to simply retrieve the server variable and add your own logic to see if the browser supports the required functionality. Listing 19.9 gives an example of using this value.

LISTING 19.9   Determining the Browser with HTTP_USER_AGENT

```
1: <% Dim strBrowser
2: strBrowser = Request.ServerVariables("HTTP_USER_AGENT")
3: If Instr(strBrowser, "MSIE") Then %>
4: <link REL="stylesheet" HREF="include/menu.css" TYPE="text/css">
5: <% End If %>
```

The `Instr` function determines whether the browser is Internet Explorer or not. If it is, then a linked style sheet is added to the page. If it is not, then nothing is done. An additional change to this might be to try to determine the version of the browser. If the version of Internet Explorer were too old, then the code would also do nothing.

Whether you use the Browser Capability component or look at the value of HTTP_USER_AGENT, you have the ability to control what content is sent to the client. This allows you to better customize the experience for the client. The downside of this is that it requires extra work to meet the requirements of different browsers. Whether you create a rich interface or just use HTML is a design decision that has to be weighed along with time, cost, and complexity.

HTML—A Static Presentation Layer

The implications of using HTML are both detrimental and beneficial to our Windows DNA architecture. You have to see if you can meet the requirements of the application, given what the client browser is capable of doing. This is especially important as Web applications are getting more and more advanced in the services they offer customers. With some commerce sites, you are able to make a purchase in a few clicks if you are already registered. In stock transactions, you can be automatically notified of stock price fluctuations. With subscription services, you can select which content you want and how you want it delivered to you. All these raise the expectations of users as they go to other sites. You have to make sure you are meeting these expectations as well, or your site will be passed over in lieu of other Web applications.

In order to address this issue, take a look at what HTML does and doesn't do for you. On one hand, you can allow other types of client browsers to access your application that would otherwise not be able to use it. On the other hand, you have to figure out how to handle clients that do not have JavaScript support or the ability to use ActiveX controls. This presents two challenges: added workflow complexity and maintaining client state.

19

Handling Added Workflow Complexity

One of the great things about client-side scripting is that you are able to validate user input before making a return trip to a remote server. This enables you to get all the required information from a user, and get it in the correct format, before submitting a form back to a server. Validation could include a date having the correct format, having 16 digits for a credit card number, enter only alpha characters for a name, or entering a valid state to name a few.

If the browser doesn't support JavaScript and therefore client-side scripting is not available, this does not mean that you can not validate a user's input. This simply means that the validation will now occur on the server, as opposed to on the client. The result of this server-side validation is that more round-trips must be made between the server and the client. If the input in one or more fields is entered incorrectly on a form, the server must read in the input from the user, figure out which input is incorrect, and then send the form and the partially correct information back to the user. The user then makes changes and submits the form again. If there is still a problem, the form is returned again. This continues until the form is correctly filled out.

During these round-trips, two things are occurring. First, greater demand is being placed upon server resources because the server is now providing validation to user input, whereas the client used to do this. This increased load can have an effect on large sites that have many concurrent users. Also, the time required to fill out the form is lengthened for the user because she must wait for a response each time the server validates the response.

Maintaining Client State

Another issue with using an HTML client is the difficulty to track client state, which revolves around who the user is and what they are doing. Through an ActiveX control, more work can be done on the client on a single page. Multiple records can be reviewed and updated and it is easy to know who the user is and what they are doing. Without ActiveX controls, a new query must be called each time to get the additional record or records. Each update might only handle one record at a time. This requires extra ASP code to handle these additional situations. The page is not sending out a control and recordset and processing updates. Instead, multiple pages are used to display multiple records as well as individual records. Update pages are required as well as pages for each step of the process. This adds process complexity to a site. With Active X controls, everything was captured on one page, whereas, with an HTML client, records could now be on multiple pages.

User-Friendly Validation

I would encourage you, if you take this approach, to send back any information that the user has already filled in. This will allow her to pick up where the problem has occurred, instead of having to fill out the entire form again. It certainly irritates me when I must start an entire form over again if I forgot one field or left out a number on my phone number by mistake.

If information is very complicated, you could have a form span multiple pages. In this case, you will want to maintain the client's state, tracking what information they have entered and what they still need. One way to do this is to insert the record into a database table. This would represent a partial record. As more information is filled in, you can update the database. In order to track the client between calls, you can save the identity of the new record as a cookie on the client and look for this next time.

If you are not using cookies, you can still pass the identity as a hidden field on the form or as a name value pair on a querystring. A hidden field might look like the following line of code:

```
<INPUT TYPE="HIDDEN" NAME="CustomerID" VALUE="1234">
```

If this was part of a querystring, it might look like this:

```
<A HREF="NextPage.asp?CustomerID=1234>Next Page</A>
```

You would generate this HTML on-the-fly by ASPs. For example, after doing an insert into the customer table, the ID that is returned would be added to the HTML. If this were on a form and the new ID were assigned to a variable called intCustomerID, you could generate the HTML with this line:

```
Response.Write "<INPUT TYPE=""HIDDEN"" NAME=""CustomerID""
➥VALUE=""" & intCustomerID & """>"
```

In making the client thinner, you have, in essence, made the server fatter. The processing has been shifted from client to server. As with every part of an application, this to has to be planned out. As long as good design and analysis are followed, and you realize the limitations of the client browser, you can successfully deliver an application even to the most limited browser.

Summary

Today's lesson teaches you how to use HTML in the DNA presentation layer. This includes use of style sheets, frames, forms, and tables. You created a thin client that is compatible across a variety of browsers. The trade-off, as you learned, is a sacrifice of the client-side functionality and an increased workload on the server.

Tomorrow's lesson will give you a look at Office 2000 and the Web components that you can utilize on your Web site. These components are available on any machine that has an Office 2000 license, which makes Office 2000 Web components great for intranets and extranets. The components include a spreadsheet, a chart, and a PivotTable. You will also look at using a data control for quickly creating data-aware pages.

19

Q&A

Q **I want every browser to be able to view my pages and have my Web site look good. Why is that so difficult?**

A There are many browsers out there. Every time you create a new Web site or do some major work on an existing one, you have to ask yourself, "Who will be viewing the site?" Do you make the site a richer experience for the 80% of people who will come, making it not nearly as good for that other 20% whose browsers don't support richer client capabilities? The other option—do you degrade the site so it works for everyone, but so that 80% group doesn't have nearly as good of an experience? If the larger group isn't coming back again, then that is a problem. The bottom line is, don't try to please everyone. Do some research and make a good business decision on what to do.

Q **I want to be able to have a drop-down box from which users select options, resulting in another drop-down whose contents are based upon the first selection. Can I do that?**

A The quick answer is no, not in HTML. What you are requiring is for some event handling to occur and for dynamic data to fill up the drop-down box. To do this in HTML, you would have to have one drop-down per page. The alternative is to use DHTML to trigger an event, which would fill the other drop-down.

Q **I created a set of radio buttons, but the users can select more then one at time. Why isn't it working correctly?**

A The NAME attribute in the radio buttons is apparently set to different names. Make sure each radio button has the same name.

Workshop

The workshop provides quiz questions to help solidify your understanding of the material covered, as well as exercises to provide you with experience in using what you have learned. Try to answer the quiz and exercise questions before checking the answers in Appendix A.

Quiz

1. What cell attribute do you use to make a cell's contents display at the top of a cell?
2. How do you instantiate the Browser Capabilities component?
3. How do you set the default item in a drop-down list?
4. What server variable can you use instead of using the Browser Capabilities component?

5. What type of style sheet would you use to have the same style for every page in a Web site?

6. How would you make all the links in one frame show up in another frame?

Exercises

1. Create a page with tables that looks like Figure 19.5. Once you have done that, create it with both frames and tables.

FIGURE 19.5

Nested tables, or a frame and table.

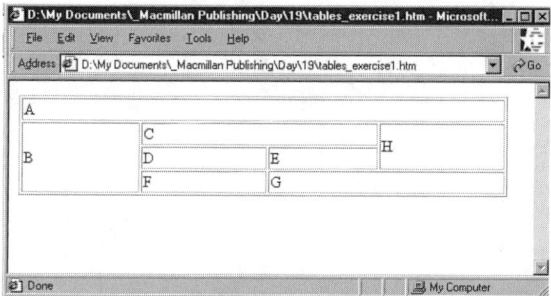

2. Utilizing the SmallTownBank components, create two ASP's to view and modify customer information. Give them the ability to add and update records in the Customer table. Use server-side scripting to do all of the processing and validation of the data. For the validation check to make sure that certain fields are filled in. Have the first file, customers.asp display a list of all the customers that the bank has. This file will allow you to drill down to the second file, customer.asp, which will give a detailed look at one customer.

19

DAY 20

Office 2000 and Web Components

Today you will learn about using Microsoft Office 2000 to create Web content. We will explore the Office Web Components (OWC) and how they can be used to enhance a solution. You will use DHTML to do some quick OWC work. This chapter prepares some components that will be used in our Digital Dashboard in Day 21, "Implementing Digital Dashboards in Windows DNA Applications."

The Microsoft Office Web components fit nicely into the presentation tier of the Windows DNA platform. They are ActiveX components and therefore are on the rich side of the capability spectrum. However, they make easy work of spreadsheet-based presentations, graphs and charts, or PivotTable information. Today you will see how these components can be used in your solution. If you don't understand some of these terms, not to worry—you will understand them by the time you finish today's chapter.

I would like to point out that these components are a very good indication of what is to come from Microsoft in the way that their products will be integrated into the Web. As you learned on Day 14, "Best Practices and Other Services,"

XML plays a big part in the future of Microsoft products. These components make good use of XML today.

After today, you will have learned

- The four Microsoft Office Web Components
- Incorporating OWCs into your solutions
- Interacting with the Office Web Components

Office Web Components

There are four components collectively known as the Microsoft Office Web Components; they are the Spreadsheet, Chart, PivotTable, and Data Source Component. They are designed to bring interactive spreadsheet modeling, database reporting, and data visualization to control containers that support ActiveX. Remember that COM and ActiveX are one and the same, so these terms are interchangeable. The best containers are Internet Explorer 5.0 and 4.01, Office 2000, Visual Basic 6.0, and FrontPage 99. Other containers can be used; they just have not been tested thoroughly.

The Office Web Components are delivered as part of Microsoft Office 2000, because some of the same developers who developed Office also developed the Web components to act as mini-versions of Excel and Access. The programming model for OWC is the same as for Excel and Access with some exceptions. In fact, when you ask Excel or Access to save content as HTML, they use these controls.

An important factor in the use of Office Web Components is licensing. In order for a client to legally be able to use the Office Web Components, he must have a license for Office 2000. This restriction keeps the applications that can be deployed to the confines of an intranet or perhaps an extranet. With these restrictions, why bother to use these components? The answer is speed—these components are fast and powerful. I have tried to get the same functionality with Java components and find them extremely slow in comparison. These components make easy work of delivering powerful applications. If you had to try to develop the same functionality with DHTML, it would take years. With OWC, you can have solutions done in days instead of months.

The "Web" in the OWC name is misleading because Office Web Components are certainly useful in other applications. A restriction is that they can currently only be hosted in Internet Explorer 5.0. You might be familiar with products that enable you to host ActiveX components in Netscape. However, they do not give you access to the DHTML programming model that enables you to programmatically interact with the controls.

The "Components" part of the OWC name does not give the whole story either, because often times the components will be acting as controls. The individual OWC are identified as both "components" and "controls" in this chapter, depending on usage. The official names define them as components, however, they are implemented as ActiveX controls. (You learned about this on Day 16, "Using ActiveX Controls to Move Business Logic from the Server to the Client.") The Spreadsheet, Chart, and PivotTable controls are built to be used as controls as well as in-memory server objects. This allows you to use these components at either the client side or the server side.

Let's take a closer look at each of these components.

Spreadsheet Component

The Spreadsheet component (see Figure 20.1) is truly impressive. Imagine having the full power of Excel embedded in your Web page—that is what you get with the Spreadsheet control. It is like a small version of an Excel spreadsheet that can be embedded in your Windows DNA application. It contains a recalculation engine that supports nearly all the calculation functions available in Excel 2000. The Spreadsheet control can write its data into an XHTML file format that can be read and written by Excel 2000. Because the format is HTML, it can be streamed across the Internet, allowing the data to either be embedded or be loaded from a URL.

NEW TERM *XHTML* is a refined version of HTML that complies with the strict formatting rules of XML. Microsoft uses a combination of HTML and XML in order to provide the metadata needed to better work with the information. It should be noted that the format, although open in terms of syntax, is somewhat proprietary to Microsoft in terms of the meaning of the data.

Using the Spreadsheet control is a very easy way to provide input forms that have automatic recalculation capabilities. A sample application that would use this control would be a mortgage calculator. Figure 20.1 shows you the Spreadsheet control.

We will be using this control to provide an online bank statement. The cells of the Spreadsheet control can be bound to other objects on a DHTML Web page so that, when one is updated, the other will be as well. This makes it possible to feed real-time data to the control and have the numbers automatically update.

20

Chart Component

The Chart component (see Figure 20.2) makes easy work of delivering your data in a graphical format. The Chart control supports nearly all the two-dimensional and Polar chart types of the chart control in Excel 2000. The OWC Chart control can be data-bound to the Spreadsheet control, the PivotTable control, XML, or an ADO Recordset object. It also can be filled with literal data values. When the Chart control is bound to a data source, the Chart control will update whenever the source data changes.

FIGURE 20.1

The Spreadsheet control.

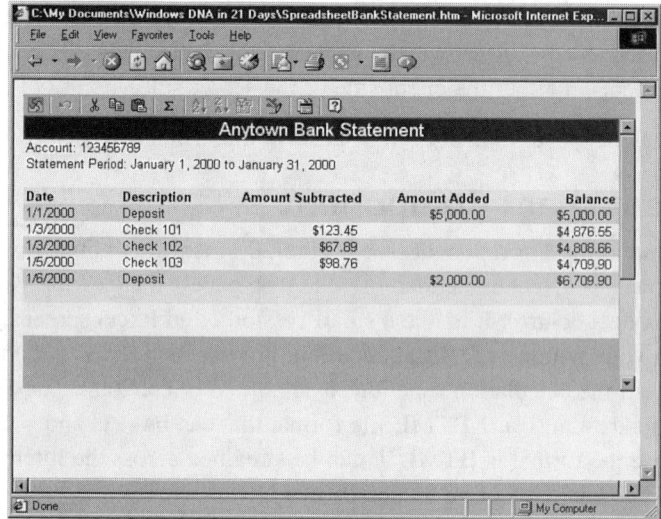

FIGURE 20.2

The Chart control.

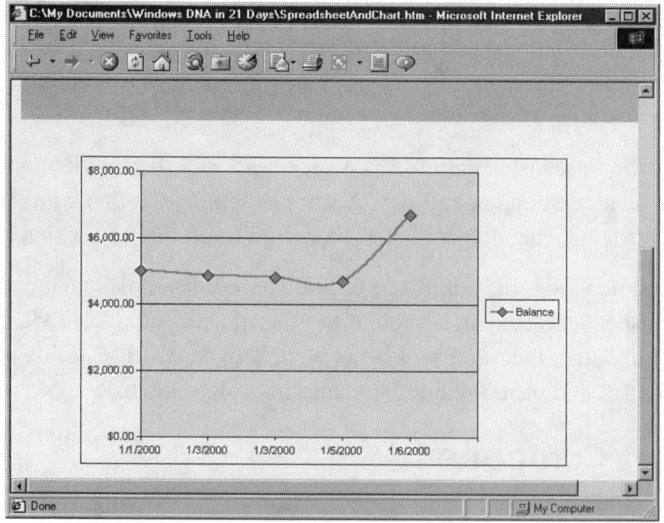

The Chart control is useful anytime you need to display data graphically. Because it has a programming model, you can have the Chart control respond to events, enabling you to do some cool things. We will use the Chart control to show account balances over time.

PivotTable Component

Online Analytical Application Processing (OLAP) servers are becoming commonplace in the business environment. These OLAP services deliver data in a multidimensional format known as a *cube*. The PivotTable component (see Figure 20.3) lets you rotate, slice, and roll up detail, or expand detail in the cube by simple dragging elements around in the control. The PivotTable control is truly impressive in its capability to let the user manage the display of data.

FIGURE 20.3

The PivotTable component.

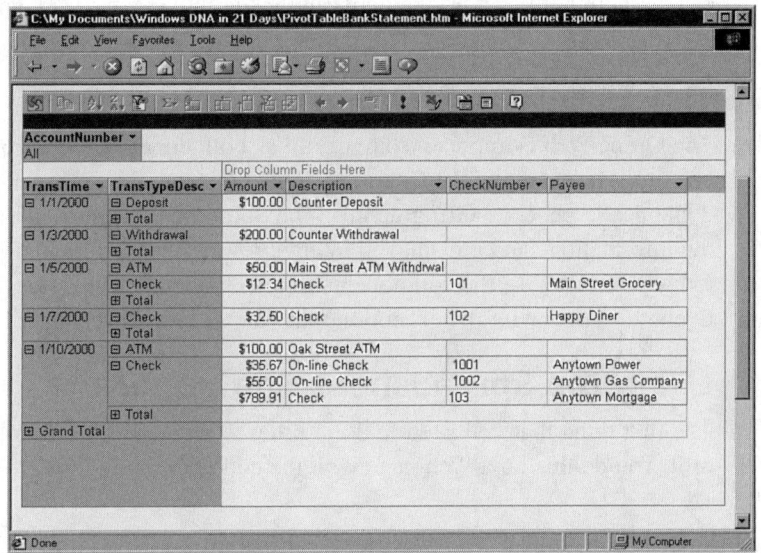

Another impressive capability of this control is that it can take tabular data and process it into a cube on-the-fly. Normally cubes are pre-built by an OLAP server before they get to the control. The capability to build cubes on-the-fly from tabular data means that you do not need an OLAP server to get this sort of data view capability. Naturally, you would not use this on-the-fly capability for complex multidimensional cubes consisting of millions of rows of data, because of the excessive latency that would be involved while the cube is built at the client computer. This capability does enable you to prototype solutions without the need to invest in an OLAP server up-front.

20

Data Source Component

The Data Source component does not have a user interface. Its purpose is to work behind the scenes managing data. The Data Source component is the backbone for controls that require data from external sources. It is used to retrieve, manipulate, and bind data to controls. If you have used Access 2000 you might have noticed that it has the capability to make data available on the Web in several ways. This is accomplished through the Data Source component. Almost every time other Access components retrieve data from an external source, the Data Source component is involved.

However, the Data Source component also has its own programming model that you can use to build and manipulate hierarchical recordset objects. You might have noticed that hierarchical data is a major enabler to powerful Windows DNA applications. This control can be thought of as a bridge between tabular and hierarchical data representation.

Using the Controls in a Solution

The Office Web Components are useful as both client-side controls and server-side components. For example, the Chart and PivotTable components can be used on the server to dynamically generate GIF graphics. The Spreadsheet control can return HTML, so that the information can be displayed in any browser that supports HTML 3.2. Our focus today will be to use the components as client-side controls. The server-side usage is relatively the same, with the exception that you will not have a user interface.

Using the Spreadsheet Component

The first thing that you need to do in order to work with a control is to create an instance of it. You do this on a Web page with the code in Listing 20.1.

LISTING 20.1   Inserting a Spreadsheet Control into a Web Page

```
 1: <div id="divSpreadsheet" align="center" LANGUAGE="javascript">
 2: <object
 3: align="top"
 4: classid="CLSID:0002E510-0000-0000-C000-000000000046" height="333"
 5: id="objSpreadsheet"
 6: name="Account"
 7: style="HEIGHT: 333px; LEFT: 97px; TOP: 19px; WIDTH: 461px" width="461">
 8: <param NAME="HTMLURL" VALUE>
 9: <param NAME="HTMLData" VALUE>
10: <param NAME="DataType" VALUE="HTMLDATA">
11: <param NAME="AutoFit" VALUE="-1">
12: <param NAME="DisplayColHeaders" VALUE="-1">
13: <param NAME="DisplayGridlines" VALUE="-1">
```

```
14: <param NAME="DisplayHorizontalScrollBar" VALUE="0">
15: <param NAME="DisplayRowHeaders" VALUE="-1">
16: <param NAME="DisplayTitleBar" VALUE="0">
17: <param NAME="DisplayToolbar" VALUE="0">
18: <param NAME="DisplayVerticalScrollBar" VALUE="0">
19: <param NAME="EnableAutoCalculate" VALUE="-1">
20: <param NAME="EnableEvents" VALUE="-1">
21: <param NAME="MoveAfterReturn" VALUE="-1">
22: <param NAME="MoveAfterReturnDirection" VALUE="0">
23: <param NAME="RightToLeft" VALUE="0">
24: </object>
25: </div>
```

ANALYSIS You see several things in this example. The first is that the entire Spreadsheet object is contained within a division <div> (lines 1 through 25). This provides a way to refer to the space occupied by the entire spreadsheet within the DHTML object model. The <div> has an id of divSpreadsheet. Next is the declaration of the actual spreadsheet object. The classid (line 4) and id (line 5) are the important values in this declaration. The classid refers to the Global Unique ID (GUID) for the spreadsheet control. The id is the name you are going to use in your scripts to refer to the spreadsheet. We are calling our spreadsheet objSpreadsheet. All the other parameters simply specify the initial property values the Spreadsheet component will have when it initially loads. These values can then be changed programmatically from within the page or interactively by the user.

The DataType (line 10) parameter tells the Spreadsheet component which of the properties to use for loading data. You can choose from HTML data, comma-separated values, or text. We specified that we will be working with HTML data. When working with HTML data, you can specify the URL where to get the data in the HTMLURL (line 8) property. You can also supply the data yourself with the HTMLData (line 9) property. In fact, if you create an HTML page with Excel 2000, the majority of the page will be data in this property.

After you have your control loaded you can now start interacting with it programmatically. Two events that you will most likely be using are the OnLoad and OnExit events. The OnLoad event fires after the page is loaded; this is a good time to programmatically load your spreadsheet with data and to apply programmatic formatting. The OnExit event provides a good opportunity to persist the data before the page is unloaded. See Listing 20.2, line 79, for an example of how the onLoad event is used.

20

The easiest way to develop an interactive Spreadsheet control is to use Microsoft Excel 2000 to do the modeling and to set up your layout and HTML file. See the `BankStatement.xls` on the CD-ROM accompanying this book for the prototype. After you have the page prototyped, you will want to save it as HTML. Select File, Save As, and then select Save as type of Web page (*.htm,*.html). You will see the dialog box in Figure 20.4. Select the Publish button.

FIGURE 20.4

The Excel Save As dialog box.

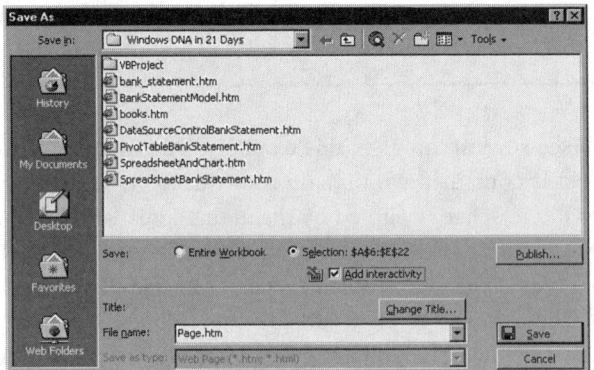

You will now be presented with a Publish as Web Page dialog box (see Figure 20.5). In the items to publish, choose a range of cells and then select the part of the spreadsheet you want included. Don't worry if you are not sure about how many rows you will need because we will cover dynamically adding rows later. In the Viewing Options section, select Add Interactivity with Spreadsheet Functionality. Select the Open Published Web Page in Browser button. Give your page a name and select Publish. The page will be saved and then opened in your Web browser. You will see your spreadsheet published using the OWC Spreadsheet control.

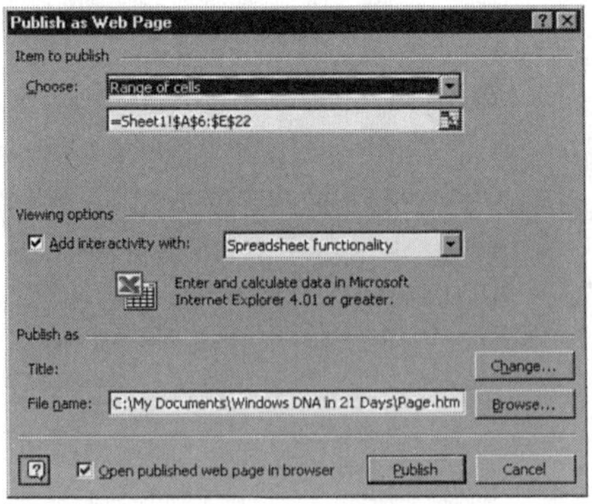

FIGURE 20.5

The Publish dialog box.

The next step is to set the basic properties. Right-click the OWC Spreadsheet control and select Property Toolbox. This toolbox gives you the ability to manage how cells are formatted, as well as limited control over the display. Select Show/Hide and then click Row Headers and Column Headers. The row and column headers should be toggled off. Please explore some of the other options available to you. You will notice as you select other cells in the spreadsheet that the properties change in the toolbox, indicating that they are referring to that cell. This is all that we want to do in Excel and the browser.

Using Visual InterDev 6.0 to Enhance Your Spreadsheet Components

We now move to Visual InterDev 6.0, where we will do more work on the formatting and add DHTML interactivity. Open the htm file you created and select the spreadsheet in the Design view. Notice all the properties that are available in the properties box. You will want to change the following:

- **id** should be **objSpreadsheet**. Excel automatically generates long control names. You want to keep them simple yet clear.

- **AutoFit** should be **False**. This will ensure that the user will be able to see the full spreadsheet in the browser without needing to use the Spreadsheet scrollbars.

- **AllowPropertyToolbox** should be **False**. This will keep the user from bringing up the property toolbox and changing the spreadsheet formatting.

- **DisplayColHeaders** should be **False**. You might want to keep column headers on during development but make sure you turn them off before moving the page out of development.

- **DisplayHorizontalScrollbar** should be **False**. We want to only use the browser scrollbars.

- **DisplayPropertyToolbox** should be **False**.

- **DisplayRowHeaders** should be **False**. You might want to keep row headers on during development but make sure you turn them off before moving the page out of development.

- **DisplayTitlebar** should be **False**. This will keep the spreadsheet small.

- **DisplayVerticalScrollbar** should be **True**.

- **DisplayToolbar** should be **True**. This will enable the user to open the spreadsheet in Excel as well as cut and paste portions to another application.

- **EnableAutoCalculate** should be **True**. This will ensure that calculations will be correct whenever values change.

- **EnableEvents** should be **True**. This will ensure that your application knows when the spreadsheet changes.

20

We now want to set the viewable size properties. This is most easily done by selecting the control and dragging the sizing handles. One tip is to drag the handles approximately to the width of any scrollbars you might be using. Save and open your page in IE5 to see how it will display. Make any adjustment to the size until it looks correct.

These are the major properties that need to be set. Now switch to the Source view so that you can see what the code looks like and so we can start adding our VBScript. You will notice that Excel has actually created a nice shell with all the necessary HTML and even exception code, in case the user does not have the component or a browser capable of hosting the OWC control. At this point, I like to add carriage returns between elements to make them more readable. You will notice that the entire control is hosted in a `<div>`. Change the id of the `<div>` to divSpreadsheet. Now break up the parameters for the Spreadsheet control so that each parameter is on a new line. You will notice that many of the values we set in the Design view are represented here. You will also notice a very long line for HTMLData. This HTMLData parameter is actually the XML that describes the spreadsheet. We are going to replace this parameter with code which will be smaller and more efficient.

Initializing and Formatting Your Spreadsheet

Add the code in Listing 20.2 to the head section of the HTML page and point the body onLoad event to this code. What we are doing in this script is formatting and loading the spreadsheet data.

LISTING 20.2 Programmatically Setting the Spreadsheet Control's Parameters

```
 1: <script ID="clientEventHandlersVBS" LANGUAGE="vbscript">
 2: <!--
 3: sub DefaultData()
 4: set XMLData = dsoBankStatement.recordset
 5: AccountNumber = XMLData("ACCOUNT")
 6: Period = XMLData("PERIOD")
 7: with objSpreadsheet.ActiveSheet
 8:     .Protection.Enabled = false
 9:     .UsedRange.Clear
10:     .ViewableRange="A1:E8"
11:     set myRange = .Range("A" & .Range(.ViewableRange).Rows.Count -1)
12:     .Range("A1:E1").Merge
13:     .Cells(1,1).halignment = objSpreadsheet.constants.ssHAlignCenter
14:     .Cells(1,1) = "Anytown Bank Statement"
15:     .Cells(1,1).Font.Size="14"
16:     .Cells(1,1).Font.color="white"
17:     .Cells(1,1).Interior.Color="Navy"
18:     .Range("A5:B5").halignment = objSpreadsheet.constants.ssHAlignLeft
19:     .Range("C5:E5").halignment = objSpreadsheet.constants.ssHAlignRight
```

```
20:     .Range("A5:E5").Interior.Color="yellow"
21:     .Range("A5:E5").Font.Bold =true
22:     .range("A1").ColumnWidth=100
23:     .range("B1").ColumnWidth=120
24:     .range("C1").ColumnWidth=130
25:     .range("D1").ColumnWidth=130
26:     .range("E1").ColumnWidth=130
27:     .Cells(2,1) = "Account: " + AccountNumber
28:     .Cells(3,1) = "Statement Period: " + Period
29:     .Cells(5,1) = "Date"
30:     .Cells(5,2) = "Description"
31:     .Cells(5,3) = "Amount Subtracted"
32:     .Cells(5,4) = "Amount Added"
33:     .Cells(5,5) = "Balance"
34:     'Load data from XML data island
35:     I = 6
36:     set theXMLDoc = document.all("dsoBankStatement").XMLDocument
37:     set objNodeList = theXMLDoc.getElementsByTagName("TRANSACTION")
38:     for k =0 to objNodeList.length - 1
39:         for j=0 to objNodeList(k).childNodes.length - 1
40:             select case objNodeList(k).childNodes.item(j).nodeName
41:                 case "DATE"
42:                     .Cells(I,1) = objNodeList(k).childNodes.item(j).text
43:                     .Cells(I,1).halignment = objSpreadsheet.constants.
                        ➥ssHAlignLeft
44:                 case "DESCRIPTION"
45:                     .Cells(I,2) = objNodeList(k).childNodes.item(j).text
46:                 case "DEBIT"
47:                     .Cells(I,3) = objNodeList(k).childNodes.item(j).text
48:                     .Cells(I,3).NumberFormat="Currency"
49:                 case "CREDIT"
50:                     .Cells(I,4) = objNodeList(k).childNodes.item(j).text
51:                     .Cells(I,4).NumberFormat="Currency"
52:                 end select
53:         next
54:     .Cells(I,5).NumberFormat="Currency"
55:     if I = 6 then
56:         .Cells(I,5).Formula ="=D" & cstr(I) & "-C" & cstr(I)
57:     else
58:         .Cells(I,5).Formula ="=E" & cstr(I-1) & "-C" & cstr(I) & "+D"
            ➥& cstr(I)
59:     end if
60:     myRange.InsertRows(1)
61:     I = I + 1
62:     next
63:     'shade alternate lines
64:     for L = 6 to I step 2
65:         .Range("A" + cstr(L) + ":E" + cstr(L)).Interior.Color="0xe0e0e0"
66:     next
67:     'example of using Range as a collection
```

20

continues

LISTING 20.2   continued

```
68:     Set myrng = .Range("A" & cstr(I) & ":E" & cstr(I)).Cells
69:     For Each mycell In myrng.Cells
70:         mycell.Interior.Color = "yellow"
71:     Next
72:     .Protection.Enabled = True
73: end with
74: end sub
75: //-->
76: </script>
77: </head>
78:
79: <body onload="DefaultData()">
```

ANALYSIS   In this sample code we see a number of things happening when the HTML page is loading. The `onLoad` event (line 79) fires the `DefaultData` function (line 3), which takes the following actions. An XML recordset is set up (line 4) and then two variables (`ACCOUNT` (line 5) and `PERIOD` (line 6)) are populated from an XML data island, which has been instantiated as an ADO recordset (line 4). Not shown in the example is the XML data island that was sent with the page. (It is included, however, with the example on the CD-ROM accompanying this book.) It is nice and easy to work with XML as if it were a recordset because it enables you to use well-known methods and properties.

The next block of code (lines 7 through 33) sets up spreadsheet formatting. In this code example you will notice that a number of different techniques are used to format the spreadsheet. This is so you can have examples of the various techniques and methods available. If you are like me, you like to have working code examples that you can dissect and reuse for your projects. For example, you will notice that `Range` (lines 12 and 18 through 26) and `Cells` (lines 13 through 17 and 27 through 33) methods are used interchangeably. The difference that you will notice is that `Range` takes a traditional `Alphabetic` column identifier and a numeric row. Ranges can specify a single cell or a block of cells within your spreadsheet. `Range` is also passed as a string value. `Cells`, on the other hand, takes a numeric column and row as its parameters. One thing that you will notice about the `Range` method is that it has a `Cells` property. In this instance `Cells` is an enumerator for the cells within the range so that you can use the selected `Range` as a collection. I have included an example of this at the end of the code block.

Finally, data is loaded into the spreadsheet from the XML data island (lines 36 through 53), this time by working with the XMLDOM. You may notice that the XMLDOM is not explicitly loaded in the client code. This is because the DOM is the native client environment. On the server we had to create a virtual DOM so that we could manipulate the code programmatically. What you might find interesting is that you have to do very little to make the XML data accessible.

Another thing you will notice in the code is how we have access to enumerated constants through the `constants` property (lines 13, 18, 19, and 43). This is a really cool capability that I hope shows up in other Microsoft APIs. Typically VBScript does not have access to enumerated constants because of the way that controls are bound. This capability fixes this problem.

Saving Data

The next topic is how one would save data collected using a spreadsheet. We are not collecting data to save in the sample code, however, here are sample code listings (in Listing 20.3) for your information. The best way to save the data is to move an entire spreadsheet to the server as HTML. Fortunately, the Spreadsheet control has a single property that renders an entire spreadsheet as HTML. That property is called `HTMLData` (line 4). Listing 20.3 shows how to save data.

LISTING 20.3   Saving Component Data

```
1: sub changepage(URL)
2:     dim frm
3:     set frm=frmSaveData
4:     frm.MyData.value = objSpreadsheet.HTMLData
5:     frm.NextPage.value = URL
6:     frm.submit
7: end sub
8: <form name="frmSaveData" action="SaveData.asp" method="POST">
9:     <input type="hidden" name="MyData">
10:     <input type="hidden" name="NextPage">
11: </form>
```

ANALYSIS   The technique involves having a hidden form on the page (lines 7 through 10) that I can use to push the data to the server using the POST method. The reason we want to pass the data to the server in a form, instead of as command line arguments, is because the data can be quite large and the length of a query string is limited in some browsers. Anyway, you have this hidden form with two hidden fields MyData, (line 8) and NextPage (line 9). The MyData field will contain the actual `HTMLData` (line 4). The NextPage (line 5) field is the page that you want the Save routine to redirect you to after the data is saved. The SaveData ASP page (line 8) is simply a page that persists the data on the server; it has no presentation elements. This technique is good when you have multiple pages of data you are collecting and you don't want to be moving all the data between each page.

20

The data is actually saved from the page when the changepage sub-routine is called. All the links on the page set their onclick event to call this changepage routine (lines 1 through 7). Here is an example:

```
<input type="button" value="Go On" onclick="changepage('NextPage.asp')">
```

You can call the changepage routine from any element in which you can have an event fire the changepage routine. The changepage routine takes in the next page parameter, populates the hidden form fields, and then fires the form's submit event.

You will need to write your own SaveData routine. You need to make a few choices. Where do you want the data persisted (saved)? Keeping in mind the Windows DNA scalability issues, it is best that you NOT persist the data in memory. You might also find that you do not have enough memory to save the HTMLData there. My suggestion is to send it off to the database. How many forms will the user be filling out? Where and how you save the data depends upon how much data is being collected. If, for example, the user is filling out several worksheets that will then be submitted in a final process, then you might want to simply persist the HTMLData for each form and then process all the worksheets in a final submission routine. The other option is to pull out the data you need from the spreadsheet on each page change with the SaveData routine. I prefer to use a generic SaveData routine, which saves the HTMLData. A final submission routine does the final parsing and processing of all the orders spreadsheets. This works well because, if the user wants to return to a page, you simply need to send the HTMLData for the page back as a parameter to the spreadsheet control. It is automatically redisplayed.

LISTING 20.4   Saving Component Data Server-Side

```
1: <%
2: 'Code to save the data to a database
3: set objHTMLDataHandler=server.CreateObject("BusinessTier.PersistHTMLData")
4: Success = objHTMLDataHandler.SaveHTMLData(Request.Form("MyData"),
session.SessionID)
5: 'Go to the next page
6: Response.Redirect(Request.Form("NextPage")
7:  %>
```

ANALYSIS   Listing 20.4 gives you a quick snippet of code to show how you might save data. First, you create an instance of your business tier component, which will do the actual data save (line 3). Remember IIS is at the presentation tier and that you should never make a direct call to the data tier nor should you manipulate the database directly. The business object has a method called SaveHTMLData (line 4), which takes two parameters—the data and the current session ID—so that the data can be matched to the proper user. The scenario is that the data is temporarily stored in the database until it is committed by some final routine. In the `Session_OnExit` routine, a method is called in this object to clear out that user's temporary data. This way the application is relatively stateless and self-managing in terms of its data. This is just one possible scenario; you use what works for you. Finally the page redirects to the NextPage (line 6).

It's easy to extract data from the `HTMLData` at the server. You simply create an instance of the spreadsheet component in the server memory and then load the `HTMLData` into it. You can then access the data in the cells of the spreadsheet using the `Cells` and `Range` methods as we did earlier. Listing 20.5 gives you an example of how this is done.

LISTING 20.5   Server-Side Object Instantiation

```
1: <%
2: 'Code to load data into a server-side instance of a spreadsheet
3: set objSpreadsheet = server.CreateObject("OWC.Spreadsheet")
4: objSpreadsheet.HTMLData = Request.Form("MyData")
5: 'now work with the data
6: .. do something here
7: %>
```

ANALYSIS   In Listing 20.5, you are creating an instance of the Spreadsheet component (line 3). You then load that control with the data that you received from the changepage routine (line 4). After this you work with the data in the same way that you did for the client side.

Reacting to Events

You might want to react to user interaction with the spreadsheet. This is possible by reacting to events that the spreadsheet raises. You must have set the property `EventsEnabled` to `true` for the spreadsheet control and then you must write a handler for the event. Previous examples did not contain handlers, so Listing 20.6 is a snippet from another project provided as an example.

20

LISTING 20.6   Client-Side Event Handling

```
1: sub objSpreadsheet_EndEdit(spinfo)
2:     if (spinfo.range.row = 14) and (spinfo.range.column = 2)
   ➡ then
3:         FileNumber.innerHTML = spinfo.EditData
```

continues

LISTING 20.6 continued

```
4:      end if
5:      if (spinfo.range.row = 15) and (spinfo.range.column = 2) then
6:          CustomerPONumber.innerHTML = spinfo.EditData
7:      end if
8: end sub
```

ANALYSIS Every time the user moves to a new cell, the EndEdit event is fired. The event passes a SpreadsheetEventInfo object (spinfo) (line 1), which contains data about the changes in the cell the user just left. You can then look at the information in the spinfo collection and make a determination whether you need to act upon the user's action. In this example, row 14, column 2 (line 2) is a field that contains the user's File Number and row 15 (line 5) is the user's Purchase Order Number. The event handler checks the spinfo collection to see what row and column have been changed and whether they match the criteria. A DHTML element is set with the new value (lines 3 and 6). This is a fairly trivial example, however, it gets you going with event processing. The SpreadsheetEventInfo object is used for many different events, and it contains much more information than was used in this example. IntelliSense and the online developer documentation will help you understand the other events you can handle.

Using the Chart Component

The Chart component can be used alone or in conjunction with the other components. At first, the Chart component might seem like a fairly simple component. In fact, you will find that charting is a very granular process that requires several parameters to be set in order to produce a graph. Charting also has a language of its own, which, if you are not familiar with it, can be very confusing. This subject can clearly take an entire book to teach. For this reason I will not be able to cover all the details of charting in this section. Rather, I will show you how to bind the OWC Spreadsheet component from our previous section's example to the Chart control. At the end of this chapter I will give you a reference to an excellent book on programming with the Office Web Components.

Working with any of the OWC Web Components is very similar from component to component. So I will not be going over things that have already been covered. Once you work through a few of these examples, you should have enough knowledge to learn other capabilities on your own.

Instantiating the Chart Component

Before we can use the Chart component, we need to create an instance of it. Just as with the Spreadsheet control, the Chart can be instantiated as a control with a visual display or as a component with only service functions. As a server service, the Chart control can dynamically create a chart that is then returned in GIF format to a client whose browser is incapable of hosting the Chart control. Of course, you will need to check the user's browser capability to determine if you should use the server-side control or the client-side control.

NEW TERM *ChartSpace* is the term used to describe where the Chart control will render its chart. The ChartSpace is capable of rendering multiple graphics, all within a single chartspace. Most of the methods provided in the Chart control deal with manipulating the ChartSpace.

The easiest way to start a ChartSpace is to prototype it in Excel and then save it as an HTML page as we did with the spreadsheet. When you look at the page created, you will see, at minimum, the following object declaration:

```
<object
 id="objWebChart"
 classid="CLSID:0002E500-0000-0000-C000-000000000046" width="100%" height="350">
</object>
```

As with the Spreadsheet control, you will programmatically set the parameter values.

You can see that a Data Source Control is also created. Because you can use a Spreadsheet component as a data source, we will not be using the DSC in this example.

Binding a Spreadsheet to the Chart Control

Often you will use the Chart control in conjunction with the Spreadsheet and PivotTable controls to give data a graphical look. The secret to doing this is to put in place event handlers that update the Chart when a spreadsheet changes. Listing 20.7 binds the sample bank statement information to a chart.

LISTING 20.7   Binding a Spreadsheet Control to a Chart Control

```
 1: Sub BindChartToSpreadsheet(chartspace, spreadsheet, srngSeries,
    ➥ srngCategories, srngValues, fSeriesInCols)
 2:     ' Local variables
 3:     Dim myChart
 4:     Dim mySeries
 5:     Dim rngValues
 6:
 7:     set c = chartspace.Constants
 8:     chartspace.Clear
 9:     set chartspace.DataSource = spreadsheet
10:     set myChart = chartspace.Charts.Add()
11:     myChart.HasLegend = True
```

20

continues

LISTING 20.7   continued

```
12:     myChart.type= c.chChartTypeSmoothLineMarkers
13:     myChart.SetData c.chDimSeriesNames, 0, srngSeries
14:     myChart.SetData c.chDimCategories, 0, srngCategories
15:     'loop through the different series in the range
16:     set rngValues = spreadsheet.Range(srngValues)
17:
18:     for each mySeries in myChart.SeriesCollection
19:         if fSeriesInCols then
20:             mySeries.SetData c.chDimValues, 0, _
21:                 rngValues.Columns(mySeries.Index + 1).Address
22:         else
23:             mySeries.SetData c.chDimValues, 0, _
24:                 rngValues.Rows(mySeries.Index + 1).Address
25:         end if
26:     next 'mySeries
27:
28: End Sub
```

ANALYSIS   You call the BindChartToSpreadsheet function at the end of the DefaultData routine to cause the chart to be loaded with the bank account balance information.

```
BindChartToSpreadsheet objWebChart, objSpreadsheet, "e5", "a6:a" & cstr(I),
➥"e6:e" & cstr(I), True
```

The BindChartToSpreadsheet routine takes six parameters. The first parameter (chartspace = objWebChart) is a reference to the chart space. The chartspace is where the chart(s) will be created. The chartspace is the chart object you declared in your page. The second parameter (spreadsheet = objSpreadsheet) is the spreadsheet that will provide the data. The third parameter (srngSeries = "e5") is a string-based reference to the range of cells that will provide the series information. The example has just one, the account balance. The fourth parameter (srngCategories = "a6:a" & cstr(I)) is a reference to a string-based range that provides the categories—in our example, the transaction dates displayed on the X axis. You will notice that we are dynamically adding the final row number. The fifth parameter (srngValues = "e6:e" & cstr(I)) is the string-based range of the values for the chart—the range of account balances displayed on the Y axis. Again we are setting the bottom row dynamically. The sixth parameter (fSeriesInCols = True) tells the routine whether the series values are in a column or row.

The code in Listing 20.5 takes the values passed to it and sets the parameters in the associated ChartSpace. You should note that the code sets a reference to the controls' Constants (line 7) so that it can use the enumerated constants for various settings. This reference is only needed in VBScript routines; VBA routines know how to access the enumerated constants.

This routine is simply setting the chartspace parameters so that it can display the spreadsheet data. First, it makes sure that the chartspace is clear (line 8). It then associates the spreadsheet as the ChartSpace's DataSource (line 9). It proceeds to add a chart to the ChartSpace (line 10). Remember that you can have multiple charts within a ChartSpace. The rest of the code is simply setting the chart's parameters. The only complex part of the code is where the range data is being plotted (lines 18 through 26). A local variable (rngValues) is associated with a spreadsheet's range (line 16). Next the code loops through the chart's mySeries collection, setting the values (lines 20 and 23).

This has been a brief introduction and example of how to use the Chart control. The code is included on the CD-ROM accompanying this book. I encourage you to start playing around with the attributes and methods to familiarize yourself with the control's capabilities. If you are new to Visual Basic, I want to point out a few features that make this exploration easier. First, the entire object model is included in the MSDN documentation that comes with Visual Studio and is available from the Web site. Once you have set a reference to an object, the Intellisense capabilities of VB will do statement completion by giving you pick lists of the methods and properties available. If you want to know more about a property or method, press F1, and the online help should come up for that item.

Using the PivotTable Component

The PivotTable component enables us to easily work with hierarchical data. In today's example, we will replace the Spreadsheet control with a PivotTable control. We will also change the XML so that it is a persistent version of an ADO recordset. Back in Day 12, "The Power of XML," we covered how to persist an ADO recordset in an XML format. In those examples, we persisted the data to a file, a stream, and a response object. I have persisted an ADO recordset from the database we created in this book. Doing so places the metadata required by the PivotTable control into the XML structure. You can look at the BankStatement.xml file on the CD-ROM to see all the metadata provided by the persistence method of the recordset object. The PivotTable control needs this information to know how to work with the data.

20

> **Tip**
>
> You should be using the ADO, SQL Server 2000, BizTalk, and other system capabilities to return XML, rather than creating your own when you are working with bound controls. The bound controls use the schema information that is sent with the XML to know how to work with the XML data. When OWC controls are bound to each other, they exchange the necessary schema data in their HTMLData streams.

Instantiating the PivotTable Component

As with the other Office Web Components, the PivotTable control is created by declaring the object:

```
<OBJECT classid="clsid:0002E520-0000-0000-C000-000000000046" height=384
➥id=objPivotTable
    style="LEFT: 0px; TOP: 0px" width=518 VIEWASTEXT>
    </OBJECT>
```

You will notice that the declaration is relatively simple. Much of the control's format will be set automatically by the incoming data based upon the Schema information sent. The initial style property is used for the initial rendering of the control. This is optional; it can be changed by you programmatically and by the associated schema from the XML.

Binding to the PivotTable Component

The process of setting up the control and binding data to the PivotTable is very straight-forward. You can see from Listing 20.8 that not much work is needed to use this control.

LISTING 20.8   Loading a PivotTable with Data

```
 1: Sub Window_onLoad()
 2:     objPivotTable.AutoFit = False
 3:     objPivotTable.height = "70%"
 4:     objPivotTable.width = "100%"
 5:
 6:     ConnectToXML objPivotTable, "BankStatement.xml"
 7:
 8:     ' Show all result columns in the report
 9:     objPivotTable.ActiveView.AutoLayout
10:
11:     ' Format the numbers
12:     set pview = objPivotTable.ActiveView
13:     pview.FieldSets("Amount").Fields(0).NumberFormat = "$#,##0.00"
14:     pview.FieldSets("CheckNumber").Fields(0).NumberFormat = "#,##0"
15:
16: End Sub
17:
```

```
18: Sub ConnectToXML(ptable, sURL)
19:     ptable.ConnectionString = "provider=mspersist"
20:     ptable.CommandText = sURL
21: End Sub
```

ANALYSIS When the page loads we set some of the attributes of the PivotTable (lines 2 through 4). We then call the ConnectToXML (line 6) function to load the XML data. We pass the function two arguments: The first is a pointer to the current instance of the PivotTable (objPivotTable), and the second is the path to the XML data ("BankStatement.xml"). In this example the data is coming from a static .xml file in the current directory. In a real application the data would be coming from a data island, stream, or response object. The ConnectToXML routine (lines 18 through 21) does two things; it sets the data provider type (line 19), and it associates the data with the control (line 20). This syntax should look very familiar; it is the same as with how you set ADO data sources. In our example we are using the Microsoft XML persistence format (mspersist). The connection string can be set to any valid ADO connection string. After the data is loaded, we can then refer to the columns by name and set formatting (lines 9 through 14).

More examples of how you would change aspects of the PivotTable programmatically are provided on the CD-ROM. Again, this is a very powerful control. Take some time to work with the examples and see what effects your changes have on the control's behavior.

This is a brief introduction to this control. You will want to dig more into the MSDN documentation or get a book that covers this subject more extensively to learn about more of the capabilities of this control. Behind the control is the whole world of data warehousing and Online Analytical Processing (OLAP). If you are into the data tier, then you probably know something about OLAP. If you are not into manipulating and warehousing data, no problem; you can consume the data provided by the data tier using the PivotTable control very easily (lines 19 and 20).

Using the Data Source Control Component

The Data Source Control component does not have a user interface. Rather, it is a helper control that makes it easy to connect to data sources, bind to controls, execute commands, and retrieve results. The Data Source Control is the workhorse behind Access 2000. When you use the Data Source Control with the other Office Web Components, you actually use very little of its functionality. Most of the functionality exists to support Access 2000.

20

In this section we will use the Data Source Component with our PivotTable example. In actuality we were using the Data Source Component in our previous example; we just did not see it. The PivotTable Control creates a hidden Data Source Component in memory when it needs to render data. In this example, by explicitly creating the component we gain access to the other functionality of the component.

Instantiating the Data Source Component

The declaration for the Data Source Component is

```
<object id="objDataSourceControl"
 classid="CLSID:0002E530-0000-0000-C000-000000000046" VIEWASTEXT>
</object>
```

You should always place this declaration in the HEAD section of your HTML file. You can see that this is a straightforward object declaration, nothing special here.

How to Use Data Source Components in Your Solution

We actually need to make very few modifications to our PivotTable sample code to make it work with a Data Source Component. The only real changes are in the ConnectToXML routine:

```
ConnectToXML objPivotTable, objDataSourceControl, sURL
```

The first change is to add a parameter to the function that points to the Data Source Control. The second parameter is new, as seen in Listing 20.9.

LISTING 20.9   Loading a PivotTable with Data Using the Data Source Control

```
1: Sub ConnectToXML(ptable, dsc, sURL)
2:     dsc.RecordsetDefs.AddNew sURL, dsc.Constants.dscCommandFile, "PivotData"
3: set ptable.DataSource = dsc
4:     ptable.DataMember = "PivotData"
5: End Sub
```

In the ConnectToXML routine, we define a new recordset using the XML data that has been passed to the routine (line 2). We then associate the Data Source Control with the PivotTable (line 3). And we tell the PivotTable to use the "PivotData" member of the Data Source Control (line 4).

You now have updated the PivotTable example to explicitly use the Data Source Component. By using the Data Source Control explicitly, you are now able to add calculated fields and server filters, and use parameters against the control. Many relation database systems allow you to include calculated fields as part of your SQL statement.

However, these statements are quite complex. Other data stores do not have this feature. The DSC gives you an easy way to get this functionality by allowing you to add calculated fields to a RecordsetDef object. Here is an example that will add an account balance field to each row:

```
sub AddEndingBalance(dsc)
   dsc.RecordsetDefs.PageFields.Add "[BEGININGBALANCE]-
   [DEBIT]+[CREDIT]",dsc.Constants.dscCalculated, "EndingBalance"
end sub
```

This routine takes a pointer to a data source control and then adds a new calculated field called EndingBalance to each field in the recordset. This is a pretty simple example, and it does not really work with our XML data because we don't have the fields referenced. However, it does illustrate what a calculated field is.

The DSC exposes the Data Shape Provider's capability to create calculated fields in your recordset object. It does this by evaluating the calculated expression at the client using the Jet expression service. The Jet expression service exposes all the "safe" VBA runtime functions, allowing you to build some complex expressions.

Server filters are another feature of the DSC. When you add a RecordsetDef object, you can simply use the name of a table or view, instead of a full SQL statement. The server filter acts like a WHERE clause in that it will limit the number of records returned from the server.

Adding the following command to our DSC definition would restrict the range of checks returned to between 1000 and 2000.

```
Dsc.RecordsetDefs.ServerFilter = "CheckNumber Between 1000 and 2000"
```

The DSC is allows you to easily manipulate the data set you are using. I have only touched upon the capabilities of this control. I felt that you needed to have some exposure so that if you needed the capabilities mentioned you would know where to find them.

20

Summary

The Office Web Components that come with Microsoft Office 2000 are an easy and powerful way to add spreadsheet, chart, and PivotTable functionality to your application. To use this functionality the client needs two things: an Office 2000 license and a host capable of containing ActiveX/COM components. Spreadsheets can be fully interactive at the client, or they can be created at the server and sent to the client as HTML.

The Spreadsheet control gives you an embeddable version of Microsoft Excel. The functionality of this control is nearly identical to the full-blown application. It comes complete with a recalculation engine.

The Chart control is another powerful control that provides you with charting capabilities. You have a wide range of charts that you can create, with complete control over how the charts are rendered. Charts can be rendered at the client or on the server, and then sent to the client as a GIF image.

The PivotTable control is a very powerful way to display hierarchical data to the user. With its capability to work with XML, OLAP cubes, or flat relational data, this control gives you great flexibility in presenting data. Not only do you have programmatic flexibility, but the end user has the ability to reshape the data by dragging and dropping columns on the various drop zones.

Another component included with the Office Web Components is the Data Source Control. This control works behind the scene managing data on behalf of the other Web components. This component is primarily used by Access 2000 to publish forms on the Web. It does give you full access to the "safe" functionality of the Jet expression service, allowing you to add calculated fields to your DSC.

We have just touched the regarding what these components are capable of doing. If you want complete coverage of the subject, Microsoft has provided a great deal of information in the MSDN documentation and a number of examples on its Web site. I know of at least one good book on the subject. I am sure if you searched on "Programming Microsoft Office 2000 Web Components," you would get a good hit.

Q&A

Q What happens if you do not have the Office Web Components on your computer, but want to use them?

A You need to add a codebase directive to the object declaration similar to the following:

```
codeBase=file:\\appserver\office2000\
msowc.cab#version=9,0,0,2710
```

Notice the file path to an application server. The component is not intended for Internet download because of the licensing issues. You will need to install an entire Office 2000 image on the application server. There is no provision to add just the Office Web Components. To create your installation image, run `setup.exe /a` from the Office 2000 CD. It will consume about 554MB of disk space.

Q Where can I get programming help?

A The Office Web Components development help is included with Microsoft Office 2000. You can also find help at `http://msdn.microsoft.com`. If the components are installed on your computer, you should get IntelliSense statement completion support in your Microsoft development environment.

Q When I create an interactive spreadsheet from Excel, it creates a very large file that takes a long time to load across the Internet. Why is this, and what can I do to reduce download time?

A Excel saves the format of each and every cell as `HTMLData`. If you have done much formatting, this `HTMLData` string can be quite large. You will want to replace the `HTMLData` with your own onload-programmed formatting logic. In most cases you will be able to shrink the size of your page substantially. We, in fact, did this with the examples in this book.

Q The COM syntax looks complex. How will I ever be able to understand it?

A Yes, at first glance, the COM syntax looks complex. However, you will find that after you work with it for a while, it starts to make sense. Microsoft is fairly consistent with its naming conventions. Use the Object Browser to view the methods, attributes, enumerators, and relationships of each of the components. Having a copy of the object model also helps. You can find the object model in the Office 2000 online programming documentation (`MSOWCVBA.CHM`). IntelliSense will also help you to ensure that your syntax is correct.

Workshop

The Workshop provides quiz questions to help you solidify your understanding of the material covered and exercises to provide you with experience in using what you've learned. Try to understand the quiz and exercise answers before continuing to the next lesson. Answers are provided in Appendix A.

Quiz

1. Where do you install the Web components from?
2. What types of data sources can the PivotTable control use?
3. Where can Office Web Components be hosted?
4. What is the native format for Office Web Component data?
5. How do you interact with the components?

20

Exercises

1. Open the `SpreadsheetAndChart` HTML page and change the chart type to be `chChartTypeColumnStacked`. How did the graph change? Now try `chChartTypeArea`.

2. Open the `PivotTableBankStatement` HTML page and experiment with moving various columns onto the drop zones. How did the PivotTable change? Did you get any different insights into the data?

DAY 21

Implementing Digital Dashboards in Windows DNA Applications

Today we will pull together a digital dashboard contained within Microsoft Outlook 2000. You will be exposed to information and content management solutions. A complete banking shell is provided but only the bank statement link will be built using the bank statement from Day 20, "Office 2000 and Web Components." You can use the information presented to add the rest of the functionality from other presentation examples to the dashboard.

This chapter shows you how you can use other product capabilities to enhance your Windows DNA solutions. Today you will be learning how to blend Outlook and the Web by exposing Outlook capabilities via DHTML Web pages and how to host Web pages within Outlook. In Day 16, "Using ActiveX Controls to Move Business Logic from the Server to the Client," you learned about how to develop ActiveX controls to add functionality. Outlook provides four ActiveX control through which you can expose its content. You will learn to use these controls today. Clearly your common operating environment needs to be using Outlook 2000 in order to take advantage of this capability fully. If you are using only DHTML then you may want to take advantage of the information nugget code you will be learning about in this chapter.

Today you will learn

- What a digital dashboard is
- How to create a digital dashboard
- How to include intrinsic Outlook 2000 information in your digital dashboard

Digital dashboards are solutions designed to help knowledge workers access the information and experience they need to work smarter. By delivering information from a broad variety of sources into the tools that people are familiar with, a digital dashboard enables knowledge workers to make faster, better business decisions.

A *digital dashboard* is a consolidated view of information for knowledge workers—it consolidates personal, team, corporate, and external information with single-click access to analytical and collaborative tools. Microsoft delivers this capability in the container of Outlook 2000. Why Outlook 2000? Because Outlook 2000 is familiar to many users, and it is easy to use. Outlook 2000 has the capability to present its content (email, calendar, tasks, contacts, personal files, and so on) in a Web format. In addition to these personal task and scheduling information features, you can also incorporate any other Internet-accessible information.

A digital dashboard makes it easy to access the information important to you in a single view. Whether this is business metrics, email, team tasks, industry news, or weather, your valuable data can all be focused and presented in a personalized digital dashboard. You can use the Office Web Components in a digital dashboard solution to provide various ways to view the data. For example, you can use the PivotTable and Chart controls to give you unique views into your data.

By seamlessly integrating with accounting and other line-of-business systems, digital dashboards enable you to dynamically interact with critical business information. This gives you the power to transform information to help spot trends that can unearth opportunities, and avoid pitfalls.

Digital dashboards are based on the powerful, familiar tool that most knowledge workers use today: Microsoft Office. Built-in collaboration tools enable teams to easily manage projects in a central location.

Digital dashboards take advantage of the capabilities of Microsoft Outlook 2000 and Microsoft Exchange Server to take mail, documents, discussions, and Web pages offline. This enables you to get the right information exactly when you need it, whether on an airplane, at the office, or with a customer.

Let's face it—we live in an age when we are being bombarded with information. Digital dashboards enable us to categorize and manage this information so that we can be more organized and productive with our time.

Digital Dashboards and Outlook 2000—An Information Management Container

Outlook 2000 has been updated to work with Web-formatted data. We are rapidly becoming a world where the Internet is the dominant data exchange medium and the formats used on the Web are becoming the standards by which we work with and communicate information. Outlook can work with Internet-based information from several sources, as well as call upon its own data sources (email, calendar, tasks, contacts, personal files, and so on) to provide a consolidated information view. This consolidated view is known as a digital dashboard.

Outlook works with its own data stores, with group and corporate data stores (via Exchange), and with Internet-based information. All of these information spaces are brought together using Outlook 2000 as a personal portal to this information.

Digital dashboards also promote collaboration and an easier flow of knowledge. Utilizing the team-oriented capabilities of Outlook 2000 and Exchange 5.5, knowledge workers can easily create shared documents, discussions, project tasks, and other collaborative solutions. Vital corporate information such as sales and customer data can be intelligently filtered into a digital dashboard to alert knowledge workers of potential problems or opportunities. Knowledge workers can also get a wide range of work-related information found outside their companies on the Web, such as research material, news and stock tickers, and targeted news feeds covering specific industries.

Microsoft Outlook is the application that ushered in the common hierarchal folder list view that is very common in applications today. Many applications use the folder list view down the left side of the screen, with multi-pane folder content and a detail view on the right side (see Figure 21.1).

21

FIGURE 21.1

The Outlook 2000 user interface.

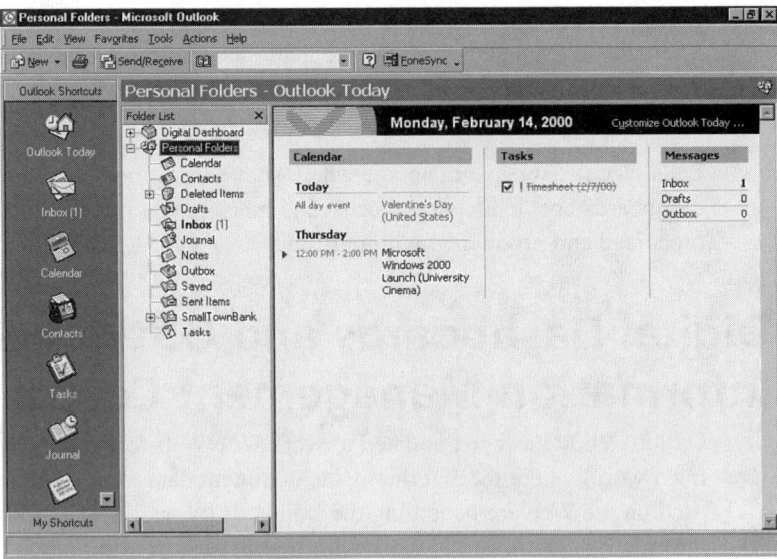

Outlook 2000 Personal Productivity Applications

Outlook provides several personal productivity applications. The first is a robust email client that can work with a wide range of servers. This is the application that most people instantly associate with Outlook. It should be noted that two versions of Outlook exist: the full version and Outlook Express. Outlook Express is essentially a Mail and NNTP Newsgroup reader that is installed with Internet Explorer. The mail capabilities in the full version of Outlook support all the latest Internet mail protocols as well as the enhanced capabilities of Microsoft Exchange. The full version of Outlook comes with Office 2000 or can be purchased as a standalone product.

Outlook 2000 Calendar

Another productivity tool in Outlook is the calendar where a user can keep her schedule. The calendar provides several different views, alerts, and integration with other Microsoft technologies such as NetMeeting.

Outlook 2000 Contacts List

The contacts list is where you store all the information about the people you communicate with. The type and amount of information you can store about a contact is vast. Because of the variable way that Outlook stores data, not only do you have many predefined pieces of information that you can store but you are also able to define your own data fields.

Outlook 2000 Tasks List and Journal

The tasks list is your to-do list. Again all the bells and whistles are included so that you can track a great deal of information about tasks. The journal capabilities in Outlook are similar to the task list, in that its role is to automatically track the timeline of tasks performed by the user. For example, you might know that you were working on a document last week but you don't remember the name and how long you spent working on it. If the journal has been configured to track documents, you could simply go to the journal and that information will be there.

Outlook 2000 Notes Feature and Outlook Today

The two final features are the notes folder, which is equivalent to electronic post-it notes, and Outlook Today, which is a consolidated view of your messages, calendar, and tasks. We will see how to build upon the Outlook Today folder to extend this capability.

Building a Digital Dashboard

A digital dashboard is nothing more than a DHTML Web page that contains personalized content. One can have a number of these personalized pages organized within Outlook's folder structure to make up a very powerful personal information portal. Adding to the power of these pages is the power to access Outlook's intrinsic functionality such as email, contacts, calendar, tasks, and folders. We will see later how we access this content from a DHTML page.

Information Nuggets

Microsoft uses the term *information nugget,* or *nugget,* to provide a way of thinking about the discrete types of content found in a digital dashboard. A *nugget* is a unit that is used within a digital dashboard to contain a certain type of content, for example, email, contacts, or tasks. Nuggets can contain an ActiveX control, an Active Server Page (ASP), or an XML data stream. Nuggets can come from various Microsoft data sources, such as Outlook 2000, SQL Server 7.0 data warehouse, or a Web server. Figure 21.2 shows you three information nuggets. Both the To Do and Messages nuggets are expanded, and the Calendar nugget is rolled up. You will learn how to create these nuggets later.

The nugget window is a container that enables the nugget to be expanded and rolled up on the digital dashboard. The nugget window gives the user the control and ability to display many nuggets on a single dashboard.

You will come across these terms in Microsoft's documentation about digital dashboards.

21

FIGURE **21.2**

Information nuggets.

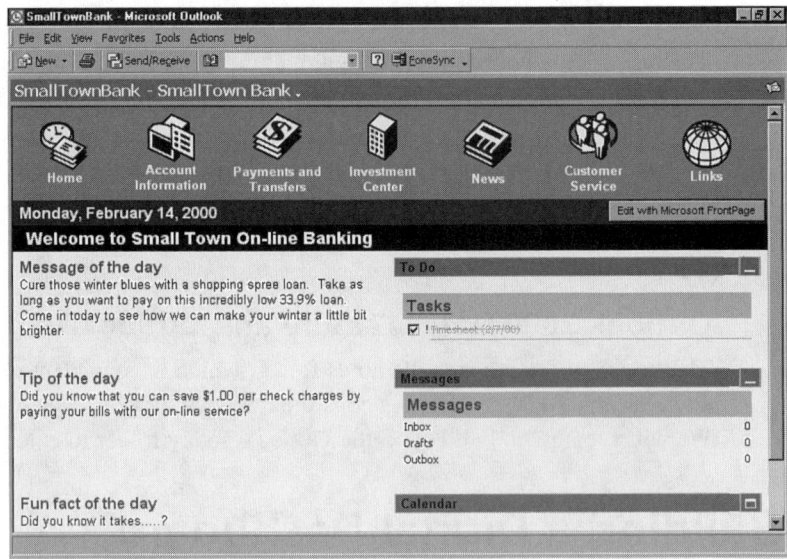

Working with Outlook Today

Outlook Today is a digital dashboard that contains a consolidated view of the calendar, tasks, and messages folders. If you go to your Outlook Today folder, you will see that you have the ability to customize the content and display in a limited fashion (see Figure 21.3).

FIGURE **21.3**

Outlook Today.

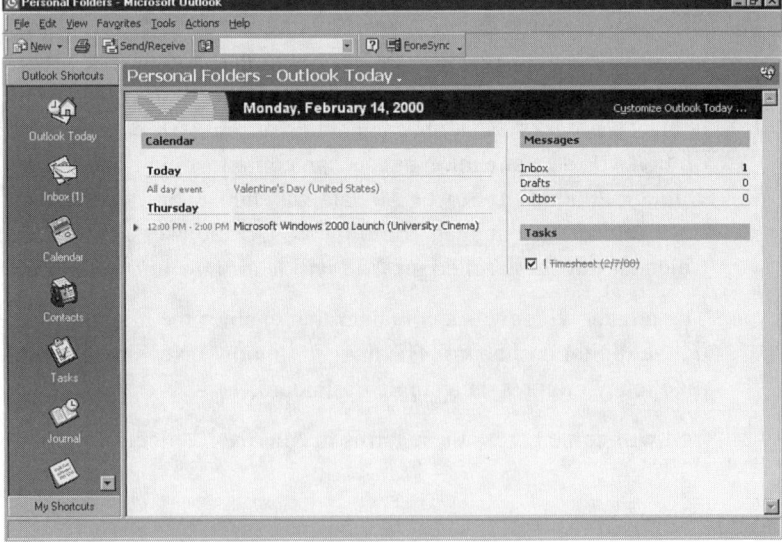

The Outlook Today page is actually a DHTML page contained in a DLL. Our first task will be to pull this page out of the DLL and to create a modified version.

To locate the original Outlook.htm file, enter the following URL in the Address box in Internet Explorer:

```
res://C:\Program Files\Microsoft Office\Office\1033\Outlwvw.dll/Outlook.htm
```

You might get a scripting error message; just answer no to debugging it.

To save a copy of Outlook.htm, follow these steps:

1. On the View menu, click Source to open a copy of the `Outlook.htm` source file in Notepad.
2. On the Notepad File menu, click Save As.
3. In the Filename box, type **Outlook.htm**.
4. Be sure to save the file as an HTM file, and not as a TXT file.
5. Search for the text `display:none` and replace all three instances with the text **display:**.

The source file was designed to take advantage of performance enhancements that are only available when the file is saved as a DLL. Because you are saving the file as an HTM or ASP file instead, you must change this property.

Outlook Today uses the `Url` string value entry in the Windows registry to determine which page to display. This setting is located in the `HKEY_CURRENT_USER\Software\Microsoft\Office\9.0\Outlook\Today` subkey. By modifying this setting, you can point users' computers to your customized version of Outlook Today.

To modify your registry to show your `Outlook.htm`, follow these steps:.

1. Start the registry editor by selecting Start, Run, and then enter **Regedit.exe**.
2. Navigate to `HKEY_CURRENT_USER\Software\Microsoft\Office\9.0\Outlook\Today`.
3. Select Edit, New, String Value, and type **url**.
4. The new key will show up. Select the url key and right-click and then select Modify.
5. Enter the path to your html page, for example, **C:\Outlook.htm** in the value data field.
6. Exit out of the registry editor.
7. Open Outlook and see if your page loads.

21

The display might not show some of the icons that are embedded within the DLL. Not to worry—they are available in the Microsoft Office Resource Kit Toolbox. The ORK can be downloaded from Microsoft at `http://www.microsoft.com/office/ork/2000/appndx/toolbox.htm`.

The toolkit contains a file called OutExmple.exe, which is an archive that contains all the pages and graphics for the Outlook Today page. You can also download just the OutExmple.exe file from the Microsoft Office download site at `http://officeupdate.microsoft.com/downloadCatalog/dldoutlook.asp`. The `OutExmple.exe` download extracts the files seen in Table 21.1 to your computer.

TABLE 21.1   Components of the Web Page Version of Outlook Today

Filename	Description
Outlook.htm	Source of Outlook Today page
Custom.htm	Source of Customize Outlook Today page
OutExmpl.htm	Sample of a customized Outlook Today page
Clock.gif	Source of the clock image file used in Outlook.htm and Custom.htm
Gap.gif	Source of gap image file used in Outlook.htm and Custom.htm
Thumb0.gif	Thumbnail image used in Custom.htm
Thumb1.gif	Thumbnail image used in Custom.htm
Thumb2.gif	Thumbnail image used in Custom.htm
Thumb3.gif	Thumbnail image used in Custom.htm
Thumb4.gif	Thumbnail image used in Custom.htm

Accessing Content

You now have a working HTML page that is working with Outlook to display content. We are now going to delve into the code that allows us to access the Outlook data.

If you open up the Outlook.htm page we just created, you will notice several object references which relate to the messages, calendar, and task list in the page. These are ActiveX controls that give you access to the various information in Outlook. You can use these objects or you can use an even more powerful ActiveX control that was released after Outlook 2000 shipped, called the Outlook View Control. The control does everything that the other separate ActiveX controls do and more, all in a single control. The View Control allows you to show any folder in any defined view contained within

Outlook. You will learn how to use this control later in the chapter. The control is installed with the Digital Dashboard Starters Kit or the Team Productivity Update. Both of these updates are available from `http://officeupdate.microsoft.com/outlook`.

The Dashboard Startup Kit will install the Outlook View Control as well as several sample dashboards. We are going to borrow code and graphics from these samples, along with the code from the Office Web Components stuff we developed, for a sample banking dashboard for SmallTown Bank. The sample dashboard is included on the CD-ROM accompanying this book. You might want to install the Team Productivity Update because it contains the documentation for the View Control.

Integrating Your Content with Outlook 2000

The first obvious question is, how do we get the dashboard into Outlook? A dashboard is nothing more than an Outlook 2000 folder with a default associated Web page. This type of folder is called a Folder Home Page. To illustrate this, let's add a folder home page for Microsoft Developers Network, following these steps:

1. Start Outlook 2000.
2. Select Outlook Today.
3. Select File, Folder, New Folder.
4. Give the folder a name of **MSDN**.
5. When your new folder shows up on your folder view, right-click the MSDN folder and select Properties.
6. Select the Home Page tab and enter **http://msdn.microsoft.com** for the address.
7. Choose to show the home page by default for this folder.

If you are connected to the Internet, you will see the MSDN Web site when you select this folder.

Folder home pages are similar to the Outlook Today folder, with the added capability to associate the home page with any public or private folder. Each page in your dashboard is an Outlook folder. Folders can be nested within folders, so you can create a hierarchy for your dashboards. With this in mind, let's get down to building your SmallTown Bank dashboard. Create a folder tree in Outlook under your Personal Folders tree. To do this, right-click the SmallTownBank folder and select New Folder. You will be asked for the Name of the folder. Use the following list to name the new folders. You should have created the following six folders under the `SmallTownBank` folder:

21

SmallTownBank Folders

Account Information

Payments and Transfers

Customer Service

Investment Center

Links

News

 **Caution** | Spelling counts! The menu in the sample dashboard included on the book's CD is based upon the folder names.

Now copy the sample application from the Day 21 Start folder on the CD-ROM to your system so that you can modify the samples as you go through the rest of this chapter. Copy the entire Dashboard folder and all subdirectories. You should see a start and Finish subdirectory. Each of these subdirectories has files and the following subdirectories: borders, common, and images. It does not matter where you copy the files because you will be creating the address links for the folders next.

Create the following folder links to the Dashboard folder with these steps:

1. Right-click each of these folders in turn:
    - SmallTownBank—Default.htm
    - Account Information—AccountInfo.htm
    - Payments and Transfers—PandT.htm
    - Customer Service—CustomerService.htm
    - Investment Center—InvestmentCenter.htm
    - Links—Links.htm
    - News—News.htm

    For each, select Properties.

2. Select the Home Page tab and enter the associated Web page as detailed in the list for the address.

3. Choose to show the home page by default for this folder.

Be sure to check the box to show the home page by default. The SmallTownBank folder structure can be seen in Figure 21.4.

Note

You will see some files with a 2 appended to the filename, for example, bankstatement2.htm and News2.htm. These are enhanced versions of the files, for which you might want to change the folder home page links later in the chapter. For now, link to the base versions.

FIGURE 21.4

The SmallTownBank *folder structure.*

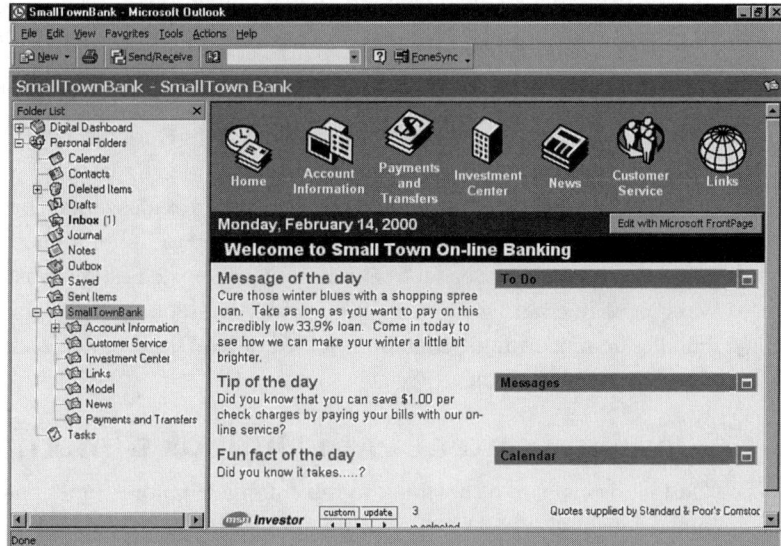

You should now see the dashboards for SmallTownBank. A button has been added to each page, enabling FrontPage 2000 to be loaded and to edit the page. You can actually use Visual InterDev to work with the pages as well, however, the examples were created with FrontPage 2000 using some of the features such as shared borders. We will be working with the ActiveX controls, so it is recommended that you stick with one of these editors, preferably FrontPage 2000.

Editing Your Content

You will notice a navigation bar at the top of each page. This navigation bar is contained in a FrontPage shared border. We want to open this page and take a look at the URLs. Open FrontPage and load the SmallTownBank project you copied over from the CD. Expand the _borders directory; you should see top.htm. If you do not see top.htm,

21

don't panic. FrontPage hides some files. You can unhide the files by following these steps:

1. Select the Tools menu.
2. Choose Web Settings.
3. Select the Advanced tab.
4. Check Show Documents in Hidden Directories.

The page should show up. Open `top.htm` and switch to the HTML tab. Notice the HREF tags; the URL is `outlook://Personal%20Folder/SmallTownBank/<sub-folder>`.

This is how you navigate between folders within Outlook. If you were to change the URL to point to the actual Web page, you would get a runtime error because we are getting the date and time from Outlook. Outlook provides some special features to Web pages that are associated with folders. It is okay to link to outside pages; however, pages with `<iframe>` and `<frameset>` will not work hosted in Outlook because of the special version of Internet Explorer that is used by Outlook. In order for Outlook to efficiently handle the rendering of content, a scaled down DLL version of Internet Explorer was developed for Outlook.

Viewing Content with Outlook's Internet Capabilities

Outlook is capable of hosting the full Internet Explorer functionality at a small performance penalty. When Outlook displays a Web page or folder home page, it uses the complete version of Internet Explorer. The complete version enables back and forward buttons, full Iframe support, and, most important, support for the Internet Explorer offline cache.

Viewing Your Content with the Full Version of Internet Explorer

More sophisticated digital dashboard solutions will require the full version of Internet Explorer. The full version enables a much greater degree of development flexibility and the ability to take the page offline, even if hosted on a Web server. You can use the full version of Internet Explorer to display Outlook Today by adding two settings to the Microsoft Windows registry. Open your registry using Regedit.exe and find the current user key. You'll then want to change the URL property to point to your digital dashboard Web page, and you want to change the navigate value to "yes". Steps 1 through 3 that follow show the proper registry key you should open and demonstrate the URL property value changes and the navigation value changes described previously.

1. `HKEY_CURRENT_USER\Software\Policies\Microsoft\Office` `\9.0\Outlook\Webview\mailbox`

2. "url"= `http://digidash/home.htm` (Enter the location of your digital dashboard here.)

3. "navigation"="yes"

Note

> If you switch to the full version of Internet Explorer, you lose all the performance enhancements associated with using a DLL. For example, the RENSTA-TICTABLE tables are no longer displayed when the page first loads, and your data is displayed more slowly.

Adding Functionality to Your Dashboard

It is now time to add functionality to our digital dashboards. The pages contain placeholders for what you will be adding to the dashboards. Please follow the directions carefully; we will be adding similar functionality in different ways on different pages.

Our first exercise will be to add a calendar, task, and message control to the default page for `SmallTownBank`. If you open up the `default.htm` page, you will see that three nuggets are defined on the page for you. Each has a placeholder string of text that tells you the type of control that needs to be inserted in its place. Select the Insert Tasks Here string. From the FrontPage menu, select Insert, Outlook Controls, My Tasks. Your task list should show up. If it does not, make sure you have tasks in your Personal Folders, Tasks folder. Repeat this process for the messages and calendar controls. Now save your page and switch to Outlook to test your work.

If the page is open, press the Refresh button, or right-click and select Refresh. Expand and collapse the nuggets. Cool stuff. This covers these three controls, which are quite simple. Refer to Figure 21.4 for a picture of what this dashboard looks like.

Let's take a look at the nugget code. Switch back to FrontPage and switch to HTML view. You will notice that the nugget code is bracketed by comments. Get a nugget in view on the screen and let's talk about the code. You will notice two divisions; the outer division contains the nugget container, which looks like Listing 21.1.

21

LISTING 21.1   Information Nugget Code

```
 1: <div class="wholeNugget" ID="nug_messages_1">
 2: <table CELLPADDING="1" CELLSPACING="0" BORDER="0" WIDTH="100%">
 3: <tbody>
 4: <tr TITLE="Messages" STYLE="height:17px; font:bold 10pt arial">
 5: <td NOWRAP ID="title" CLASS="NuggetBar" STYLE="padding-left:5px;
    ➥border-left-style:solid; border-left-width:1px; border-top-style:solid;
    ➥border-top-width:1px; border-bottom-style:solid;
 6: border-bottom-width:1px;">
<span style="overflow: hidden" ID="text">Messages</span></td>
 7:
 8: <td NOWRAP ID="drag" CLASS="NuggetBar" STYLE="border-top-style:solid;
    ➥border-top-width:1px; border-bottom-style:solid;
    ➥border-bottom-width:1px"></td>
 9: <td NOWRAP ID="disp" TITLE="Hide" CLASS="NuggetBar"
    ➥onclick="displayNugget(nug_messages_1)" STYLE="border-top-style:solid;
    ➥border-top-width:1px; border-bottom-style:solid; border-bottom-width:
    ➥1px; border-right-style:solid; border-right-width:2px;border-
    ➥left-style:solid; border-left-width:2px;width:16px">
    ➥<img SRC="images/open.gif" width="17" height="13"></td>
10: </tr>
11: </tbody>
12: </table>
```

ANALYSIS   This code looks a bit complex. In actuality, it is very straightforward. The entire table consists of the actual nugget title and the expand and collapse button. The expand and collapse button calls a script function called `displayNugget`, which handles the expansion and collapse of the nugget. The displayNugget is JavaScript code, which is contained in the common directory.

Following the nugget title bar code is another division, which contains the actual content; it looks like Listing 21.2.

LISTING 21.2   Information Nugget Content Division

```
 1: <div ID="content" CLASS="Nugget" STYLE="display:none; padding:2px;
    ➥ position:relative; top:-2; width: 100%; overflow-x:auto;
    ➥margin:1px; border-top-width:0px">
 2: <table border="0" width="100%">
 3: <tr>
 4: <td id="msgs1" width="80%">ActiveX Control is in here </td>
 5: </tr>
 6: </table>
 7: </div>
```

ANALYSIS   This code is again fairly straightforward. Generally you should be able to cut and paste nugget code where you want to use it. Put your content where it says `ActiveX Control is in here`. You can play around with the style attributes later if you are so inclined.

Using the Microsoft Outlook View Control

Now we examine the fourth ActiveX control on the Insert, Outlook Controls menu, Outlook View Control.... When you see ellipses after a control name, you know you are in for a complex control. The View Control contains all the functionality of the previous three controls and a great deal more. The View Control can be thought of as an ActiveX version of Outlook 2000, much like the Spreadsheet Control is an ActiveX version of Excel.

The Outlook View Control gives an Outlook folder home page the capability to display the contents of an Outlook folder; to control folder views; and to create, open, print, and delete folder contents. With the control, the folder home page also can open the Outlook Address Book. Because of security restrictions, the Outlook View Control is recommended for use only on Web pages displayed by Outlook as folder home pages.

You are now going to use the View Control to add the same functionality as we did with the three separate controls to the News page. You will then explore the enhancement that this control brings.

Switch to the News page and select Edit with Microsoft FrontPage. This will bring up the `News.htm` file. You will see placeholders for the various View Controls to add. Select the Add Tasks Here text and then select Insert, Outlook Controls, Outlook View Control.

You will be presented with a directory tree from Outlook. Select the Tasks folder under your Personal Folders. The Task View will show up in the place of the selected text. Right-click the new view control and select ActiveX Control Properties. Select the Parameters tab and notice that the View is Active Tasks. This is the default view for this folder.

Note   Later in this chapter, we will explore how to change views within a folder using the Outlook View Control properties. For now, let's finish adding the other View Controls to the page.

21

To finish adding View Controls to the page, select the text Add Messages Here and again insert the Outlook View Control, this time selecting the Inbox folder as the content. If you check the properties of the control, the view should be set to Messages. Finally,

replace the Add Calendar Here text with an Outlook View Control pointing to the
Calendar folder. See Figure 21.5 for what the finished control will display. If you inspect
the ActiveX Control Properties, the View should be set to Day/Week/Month. You will
notice that this control has been set to span the entire width of the browser so that the
calendar can be shown.

FIGURE 21.5

*An example of the
View Control.*

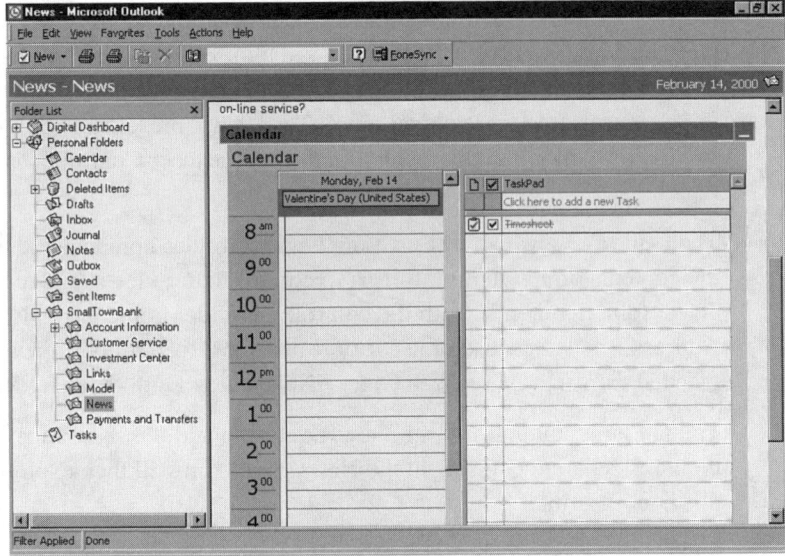

It should be clear to see that the View Control can display any folder within Outlook.
This is a really terrific functionality because it allows you to develop your own folders
and views within Outlook and then be able to display them in a Web page via the View
Control. The next thing that we want to do is add the capability to switch Views from
our digital dashboard.

Switching the View Out of Digital Dashboard

Because the View Control is a standard ActiveX control, you can change the view by
simply changing the View Property. You might have noticed when you inspected the
ActiveX Control Properties that all the properties are free form text. This is because the
control can support any folder or view that the user can create in Outlook. This is a very
powerful capability; however, if you misspell a view or folder name, the control will
revert back to the default view, which is the message folder. If you see that your folder
changed to a message folder, this is a good indication that you got a parameter incorrect.
The best way to determine folder names and views is to bring them up in Outlook.

In this next set of exercises, you will modify the News.htm file to switch views on your messages. Figure 21.6 shows what you can expect to see when you complete this exercise.

FIGURE 21.6

Message View bar.

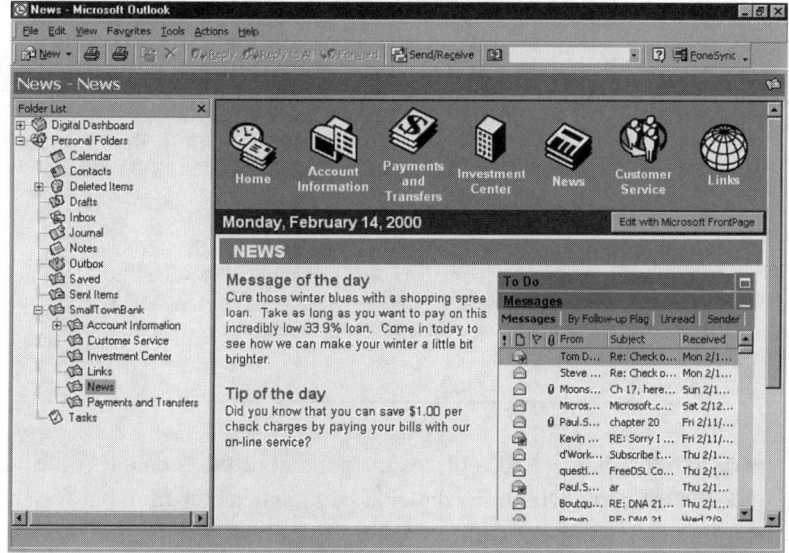

The process of switching views is quite simply a process of changing the view property of the Outlook View Control, as seen in Listing 21.3.

LISTING 21.3   Adding a View Bar

```
 1: <table id="tblTopNavBar" border="0" cellpadding="0" cellspacing="0"
 2: ➥style="width:100%;">
 3: <tr>
 4: <td valign="top" nowrap id="tdNavBar"><span class="topBarSpan"><span
 5: ➥<id="spanMessages4"
 6: onclick="HighPriorityMessages.view=L_MESSAGES_TEXT;
 7: ➥changeMessagesTab(this);" xonblur="LoseFocus" xonFocus="changeFocus"
 8: ➥id="FolderBtn2" class="btnFolder" style="font-weight:bold">
 9: ➥ Messages</span><span id="spanMessages3" onclick="HighPriorityMessages.
10: ➥BYFOLLOWUPFLAG_TEXT; changeMessagesTab(this);" xonblur="LoseFocus"
11: ➥view=L_]xonFocus="changeFocus" id="FolderBtnHome" class="btnFolder"
12: ➥style="width:0px; ">By Follow-up Flag</span> <span id="spanMessages5"
13: ➥onclick="HighPriorityMessages.view=L_UNREADMESSAGES_TEXT;
14: ➥changeMessagesTab(this);" xonblur="LoseFocus" xonFocus="changeFocus"
15: ➥id="FolderBtn5" class="btnFolder">Unread</span>
```

continues

21

LISTING 21.3   continued

```
16: <span id="spanMessages2" onclick="HighPriorityMessages.view=L_BYSENDER_TEXT;
17: ➥changeMessagesTab(this);" xonblur="LoseFocus" xonFocus="changeFocus"
18: ➥id="FolderBtn3" class="btnFolder">Sender</span>
19: </span><!--End Folder Button Bar-->
20: </td>
21: </tr>
22: </table>
23: <div style="HEIGHT:200px;MARGIN-BOTTOM:0px;MARGIN-LEFT:0px">
24: <object ID="HighPriorityMessages" CLASSID="CLSID:0006F063-0000-0000-C000-
25: ➥000000000046"style="width:100%;height:100%" codebase="../outlctlx.CAB#
26: ➥ver=9,0,3024" width="192" height="192">
27:                 <param NAME="View" VALUE>
28:                 <param NAME="Folder" VALUE="Inbox">
29:                 <param NAME="Namespace" VALUE="MAPI">
30:                 <param NAME="Restriction" VALUE>
31:                 <param NAME="DeferUpdate" VALUE="0">
32: </object>
33: </div>
```

ANALYSIS   Listing 21.3 replaces the content of the "content" division. This code creates a table within the division that contains a button bar for changing the view. Following it is the Outlook View Control. Notice that the ID of the View Control is "HighPriorityMessages" and that the action for each of the buttons is to change the view property of this object. The views referenced are local constants contained in a script block in the header of the page. This is seen in Listing 21.4.

LISTING 21.4   An Example of Using Local Constants

```
 1: <script>
 2:
 3: //Localization Variables - Replace with Outlook View Names from Local
 4: ➥Version of Office
 5:
 6: L_MESSAGES_TEXT='Messages'
 7: L_BYFOLLOWUPFLAG_TEXT='By Follow-up Flag'
 8: L_BYSENDER_TEXT='By Sender'
 9: L_UNREADMESSAGES_TEXT='Unread Messages'
10:
11: </script>
```

ANALYSIS   You will notice that the values of the localized values are the same as the view names within Outlook. No magic here. You will also notice that a JavaScript function called `changeMessageTab` is called after the view property is set (refer to Listing 21.3). This function simply switches the font to bold for the selected view, as seen in Listing 21.5.

LISTING 21.5   The `changeMessageTab` Function

```
 1: <script language="javascript">
 2:
 3: function changeMessagesTab(currentdiv)
 4: {
 5:      spanMessages2.style.fontWeight="normal"
 6:      spanMessages3.style.fontWeight="normal"
 7:      spanMessages4.style.fontWeight="normal"
 8:      spanMessages5.style.fontWeight="normal"
 9:      currentdiv.style.fontWeight="bold"
10: }
11:
12: </script>
```

Note

> If you look at this code in FrontPage Normal view, you will see that it breaks up the view change buttons. This is a problem with FrontPages' capability to accurately represent the HTML in this view. If you select the Preview tab, it will show the buttons correctly.

Using XML in Your Digital Dashboard

The next enhancement to this page is to not use an Outlook view at all for the Calendar nugget. Instead we will access the data using the data binding capabilities of the table HTML tags, similar to what you learned in the XML chapter. Figure 21.7 shows how this calendar will look in your digital dashboard. Listing 21.6 is the HTML code used to display the calendar.

LISTING 21.6   Code to Use XML to Display the Calendar Information

```
 1: <table border="0" cellspacing="1" cellpadding="1" valign="top"
    ➥name="ItemCol" datasrc="#CalList">
 2: <tr>
 3: <td nowrap valign="top" width="10" align="left"></td>
 4: </tr>
 5: <tr>
 6: <td>
 7: <div datafld="Next" DATAFORMATAS="html">
 8: </div></td>
```

continues

21

LISTING 21.6   continued

```
 9:  <td valign="top" nowrap width="120">
10:  <div DATAFLD="StartEnd" DATAFORMATAS="html" class="CalendarStartEnd">
11:   
12:  </div>
13:  </td>
14:  <td valign="top" width="100%">
15:  <div datafld="SubjectLocation" DATAFORMATAS="html" class=
     ➥"CalendarSubjectLocation">
16:   
17:  </div>
18:  </td>
19:  </tr>
20:  </table>
```

ANALYSIS   The code in Listing 21.6 again replaces the content of the content division for the calendar nugget. This code uses the databound fields from the Outlook calendar to create a three-column HTML table. The first column (lines 6 through 8) is an arrowhead that points to the next appointment in the calendar. It will appear as a red triangle and has the name "Next". The second column (lines 9 through 13) shows the start-to-end date, and it has the name "StartEnd". And the third column (lines 14 through 18) is the subject and location. The data field is called SubjectLocation. All of these data fields are returned as Outlook Web Access (OWA) HTML.

FIGURE 21.7

The XML display of the calendar.

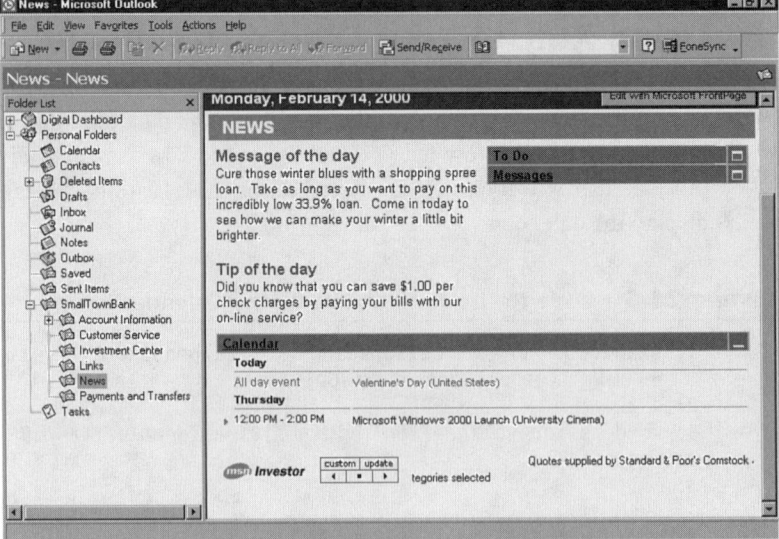

NEW TERM *Outlook Web Access* (OWA) is a capability that has been part of Outlook since Outlook 95. OWA enables Outlook content to be rendered by a Web browser. It is actually very complex; fortunately the details are hidden by the rendering engine. The URL is a long, unique, alphanumeric value that points to a specific record in the Outlook data store. When the URL is accessed, Outlook is instructed to take you to that specific record.

Make the code change yourself or load News2.htm to see the two changes at work. You can start to get a feel for the control that you have using the Outlook View Control within your dashboard.

Adding Office Web Components into Your Digital Dashboard

Our next exercise will be to take the bank statement that we created in Day 20 with the Office Web Components and to build it into a dashboard. The first step, as you learned earlier in this chapter, is to create a folder under Account Information called Bank Statement. Next, set the folder's properties to point at the bankstatement.htm file in the sample files for Day 20. Figure 21.8 shows you what this page should look like.

FIGURE 21.8

Bank Statement Version 1.

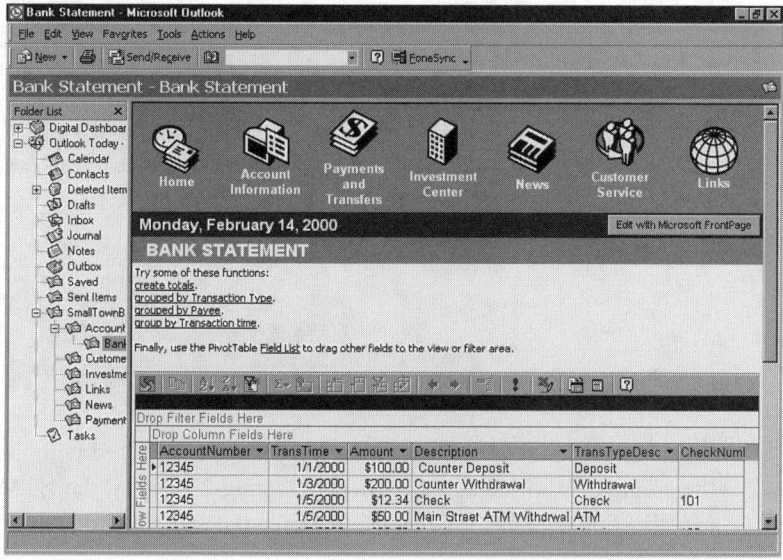

You will see the file is essentially the same as PivotTableBankStatement.htm from Day 20. Two changes had to be made to the file to make it work as expected. First, the size of

21

the PivotTable Control had to be changed to an absolute height, rather than a percentage. The following line is changed in the Window_onLoad event handler subroutine:

```
objPivotTable.height = "384"
```

The next change was to get the Window_onLoad subroutine to fire when the page is loaded. Outlook does not fire this event when the page is loaded. The resolution in this case was to fire the subroutine with an inline script. By adding a call to Window_onLoad within a script block in the body of the HTML, the script will be run as soon as that line is loaded. Please note that, because the script is running inline, you must not call the script until all the dependent controls are loaded. For this reason most of the inline script comes at the bottom of the HTML.

Next you can dress up the page with the various nugget and control button techniques you learned with the previous examples. Figure 21.9 is the dressed up version of the file.

FIGURE 21.9

Bank Statement Version 2.

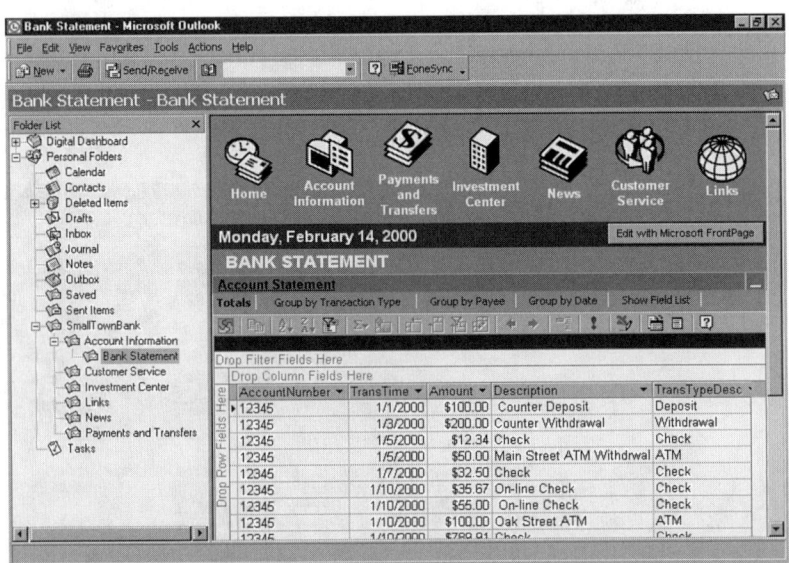

Wrap the Account Statement in the nugget code. I started with the messages code from the previous example and modified it. Listing 21.7 is all the HTML for the example. You can also find it in `bankstatement2.htm` in the sample code on the CD-ROM.

LISTING 21.7   Nugget Code to Wrap the Bank Statement

```
 1:<!------ Begin Bank Statement Nugget---->
 2:
 3:<div class="wholeNugget" ID="nug_statement_1"
   ➥href="http://www.microsoft.com">
 4:
 5:<table CELLPADDING="1" CELLSPACING="0" BORDER="0" WIDTH="100%">
 6:<tbody>
 7:<tr TITLE="BankStatement" STYLE="height:17px; font:bold 10pt
 8:➥arial" WIDTH="100%">
 9:<td NOWRAP ID="title" CLASS="NuggetBar" STYLE="padding-left:5px;
   ➥border-left-style:solid; border-left-width:1px; border-top-style:solid;
   ➥border-top-width:1px; border-bottom-style:solid; border-bottom-width:
   ➥1px; text-decoration:underline"><span ID="text">Checking Account -
   ➥12345</span></td><td NOWRAP ID="drag" CLASS="NuggetBar" STYLE=
   ➥"border-top-style:solid;border-top-width:1px; border-bottom-style:
   ➥solid; border-bottom-width:1px"> </td>
10:<td NOWRAP ID="disp" TITLE="Hide" CLASS="NuggetBar"
   ➥onclick="displayNugget(nug_statement_1)" STYLE="border-top-style:solid;
   ➥border-top-width:1px; border-bottom-style:solid; border-bottom-width:
   ➥1px;border-right-style:solid; border-right-width:2px;border-left-
   ➥style:solid; border-left-width:2px;width:16px"><img SRC="close.gif"
   ➥width="17" height="13"></td>
11:</tr>
12:</tbody>
13:</table>
14:<div ID="content" CLASS="Nugget" STYLE="display:block; padding:0px;
   ➥position:relative; top:-2; width: 100%; overflow-x:auto; margin:1px;
   ➥border-top-width:0px">
15:<table id="tblTopNavBar" border="0" cellpadding="0" cellspacing="0"
   ➥style="width:100%;">
16:<tr>
17:<td valign="top" nowrap id="tdNavBar">
18:<span class="topBarSpan"><span id="spanStatement5"
   ➥onclick="vbscript:CreateTotals()" xonblur="LoseFocus"
   ➥xonFocus="changeFocus" id="FolderBtn1" class="btnFolder"
   ➥style="font-weight:bold">Totals</span>
19:<span id="spanStatement4" onclick="vbscript:GroupByTransactionType()"
   ➥xonblur="LoseFocus" xonFocus="changeFocus" id="FolderBtn2"
   ➥class="btnFolder" style="font-weight:bold">Group by Transaction Type
   ➥</span>20:
21:<span id="spanStatement3" onclick="vbscript:GroupByPayee()"
   ➥xonblur="LoseFocus" xonFocus="changeFocus" id="FolderBtn3"
   ➥class="btnFolder" style="font-weight:bold">Group by Payee</span>
22:<span id="spanStatement2" onclick="vbscript:GroupByDate()"
   ➥xonblur="LoseFocus" xonFocus="changeFocus" id="FolderBtn4"
   ➥class="btnFolder" style="font-weight:bold">Group by Date</span>
```

continues

21

LISTING 21.7   continued

```
23:<span id="spanStatement1" onclick="vbscript:ShowFieldList()"
    ➥xonblur="LoseFocus" xonFocus="changeFocus" id="FolderBtn5"
    ➥class="btnFolder" style="font-weight:bold">Show Field List</span>
24:<!--End Folder Button Bar-->
25:</span>
26:</td>
27:</tr>
28:</table>
29:<div style="HEIGHT:200px;MARGIN-BOTTOM:0px;MARGIN-LEFT:0px">
30:<!-- PivotTable Control -->
31:<OBJECT classid="clsid:0002E520-0000-0000-C000-000000000046"
    ➥height=384 id=objPivotTable
32:style="LEFT: 0px; TOP: 0px" width=518 VIEWASTEXT>
33:<param name="XMLData" value="&lt;xml
    ➥xmlns:x=&quot;urn:schemas-microsoft-com:office:excel&quot;&gt;
34: &lt;x:PivotTable&gt;
35:  &lt;x:OWCVersion&gt;9.0.0.2710&lt;/x:OWCVersion&gt;
36:  &lt;x:CacheDetails/&gt;
37: &lt;/x:PivotTable&gt;
38:&lt;/xml&gt;"></OBJECT>
39:</div>
40:</div>
41:</div>
42:<!--End Nugget-->
```

ANALYSIS   You can see several things in this code. First, the nugget division is wrapped around the PivotTable control. Next you see that a navigation bar replaces the html links from Listing 21.6. All the code from Listing 21.6 has been reused. Because the code from Day 20 is VBScript and the `changeMessagesTab` code was in JavaScript, I changed the onClick action to simply call the VBScript code, which in turn managed the button state. The following code shows the changed `changeMessagesTab` function which is now called `clearStatementTab`. Two lines were then added to all the functions that are called by the `onClick` event. The first line calls the `clearStatementTab` function and the second sets the tab that was clicked to bold. Another slight addition was to call `clearStatementTab` at the end of the `Window_onLoad` routine, so that the tab would be in a cleared state:

```
sub clearStatementTab()
    spanStatement1.style.fontWeight="normal"
    spanStatement2.style.fontWeight="normal"
    spanStatement3.style.fontWeight="normal"
```

```
    spanStatement4.style.fontWeight="normal"
    spanStatement5.style.fontWeight="normal"
end sub

Function CreateTotals()
    clearStatementTab
    spanStatement5.style.fontWeight="bold"
    ...
End Function
```

This should give you a good starting point for developing your own digital dashboards. Refer to the sample code that was provided by this book, as well as the sample code that comes with the Digital Dashboard Starters Kit, for examples and starting points for building your own digital dashboards.

Summary

Microsoft Outlook 2000 provides a great deal of functionality that you can use to build custom views into the data which it manages, as well as data from other data sources through the use of Office Web Components and Web technology.

Digital dashboard pages are hosted within Microsoft Outlook 2000. They are enhanced through the integration with Outlook's capabilities to manage messages, tasks, and calendars. Three ActiveX controls give you quick and easy access to these areas. A fourth ActiveX control, the Outlook View Control, gives you access to any folder and view within Outlook.

Digital dashboards can link into Outlook in two ways. The first way is to augment or replace the Outlook Today page, which is at the root of every Outlook user's tree of folders. Using the Outlook Today folder is an easy, simple way to ensure consistency within an organization. The second way is to create Outlook folder home pages with digital dashboards as their default content. In this way you can create groups of folders that are used for specific purposes.

Digital dashboards introduce the concept of information nuggets, or nuggets. These nuggets are DHTML containers that enable more control and management of the dashboards' presentation space. By enabling content to be collapsed and expanded, nuggets allow more information to be made available in a specific dashboard. Multiple dashboards can be grouped together to form a suite of dashboards, which work together. In such a grouping you link between Outlook folders rather than to the specific URLs for the pages.

21

Q&A

Q **Why use Outlook as a container for digital dashboards? Couldn't this be done with plain DHTML pages?**

A Digital dashboards are DHTML pages and, for the most part, can be viewed using Internet Explorer. The benefit of hosting them in Outlook is that you get an optimized version of Internet Explorer, a hierarchal structure in which to place your pages, and access to intrinsic Outlook content such as calendar, messages, and tasks.

Q **Where can I get programming help?**

A The documentation for the View Control is included with the Team Folder Enhancement, which can be downloaded from Microsoft's Outlook home page.

Q **Are there any additional capabilities I should know about?**

A Yes, the Outlook 98 Deployment Kit will enable you to compile your pages into a DLL. Compiled pages are faster and more secure than the text-based versions we created today. You might need to make modifications to your files in order for them to work properly within the DLL. For more information, download the Outlook Deployment kit from Microsoft.

Q **Will these capabilities work with previous versions of Outlook?**

A No not really. Many of these capabilities are new to Outlook 2000. The release of Office 2000, which includes Outlook 2000, ushered in a tremendous array of Web components and support for Web technologies. Digital dashboards use much of this new Web technology.

Workshop

The Workshop provides quiz questions to help you solidify your understanding of the material covered and exercises to provide you with experience in using what you've learned. Try to understand the quiz and exercise answers before continuing to the next lesson. Answers are provided in Appendix A.

Quiz

1. What package installs the Outlook View Control?
2. What is an information nugget?
3. What Web capabilities can be used in a digital dashboard?
4. What is the advantage of using the Outlook View Control?
5. How do you reference an Outlook folder from an `href` link?

Exercises

1. Add the `SpreadsheetAndChart.htm` page from the Office Web Component chapter (Day 20) to the digital dashboard.

   The finished example, `spreadsheetandchart.htm`, is in the Finish folder.

2. Incorporate exercises from other presentation tier chapters (Days 16–20) into your digital dashboard. There is no correct answer here.

   There is no correct answer. This exercise lets you experiment with incorporating various new content into your dashboards.

21

WEEK 3

In Review

Congratulations on completing this book and gaining an
understanding of the Windows Distributed interNet
Applications (DNA) platform. Not only have you finished this
past week of learning the presentation tier, but you have also
completed your learning of both the data tier and the business
logic tier as well. At this point you should have a good feeling of how the different technologies participate in Windows
DNA and how you can use them in developing your applications.

Drilling down to the presentation tier this week, you learned
various ways to implement an interface for the user. You
began by looking at Visual Basic and how you could use it to
communicate with the business logic and data tiers. You
looked at the pros and cons of using DCOM, RDS, WinSock,
and Windows Internet components to access the application,
all of which can be implemented in a Visual Basic application. You also considered why you should or shouldn't create
a rich client with Visual Basic.

The next day you dug into ActiveX controls. You learned how
you could place these in your Visual Basic client application
as well as how to add them into a Web page. This makes them
ideal because they can be reused across different user interfaces. This also requires that, if you want to use ActiveX controls in a Web browser, the browser must support them.
Because ActiveX controls only work natively in Internet
Explorer, you might consider ActiveX controls only for
intranet applications.

The next part of the week moved into working with HTML
pages and Active Server Pages. You saw how DHTML and
JavaScript could be used to shift processing from the server to
the client and emulate some of the functionality that you

would see in a Visual Basic client application. This includes validation of data after it is entered, calculating fields based on user input, and other activities that implement business rules or processes.

Active Server Pages (ASPs) were looked at next. You learned about intrinsic object in ASPs including the Response, Request, and Server objects. You called components from your ASPs, processed information that was submitted to the user, and wrote back customized results to the user. HTML was zeroed in on next. The various standard HTML tags were looked at and explained. Cascading Style Sheets were introduced to show you how to separate style from content in your Web pages. Forms were covered and what ways you can have the user enter data. Also, frames were looked at, along with some advantages and disadvantages to using them. Frames are an easy way to give a standard look and feel to an existing Web site, but they can also cause the user to get lost if he accesses a page outside of the frame that was set up.

The Office 2000 Web components were also covered this week. These components offer a great way to enhance a user's experience:

- Spreadsheet component.   Captures the functionality of Excel in a Web browser.
- Chart component.   Delivers your data in a graphical format.
- PivotTable component.   Rotates, slices, rolls up, or expands information from an OLAP cube or a set of tabular data that is processed into a cube.
- Data Source component.   Contains no user interface. It accesses data that can then be delivered to other controls that use data as a PivotTable does.

Finally, you finished the week by looking at the Digital Dashboard. This technology enables you to customize Outlook 2000 and perform knowledge management. It lets you take personal and business information and place it into something that is pertinent to the user—not just items like tasks and appointments but also business related items like charts and spreadsheets, company financials, and industry news. By using Outlook 2000, you created your own dashboard and finished your introductions to Windows DNA.

Remember that the completion of this book marks both a time of completion, and also a time of embarking on a new way of creating scalable, flexible, high-performance applications. By completing these three weeks of work, you have built a foundation, which you can continue to build on. I would recommend that you now be selective in what you want to learn more about and continue to enhance your understanding of the different parts, keeping in mind how they all fit together as a whole. You might want to dig more into the SQL Server and stored procedures or perhaps learn more about doing transactions in MTS or maybe move onto COM+. Maybe you have current demands to look more into JavaScript and DHTML for an intranet application. No matter what challenges you have in front of you, look at how Windows DNA or a part of Windows DNA can be applied to find solutions. Continue to learn and good luck!

APPENDIX A

Answers to the Quiz and Exercise Questions

This appendix provides answers to the quiz and exercise sections at the end of each chapter.

Day 1

Quiz

1. What is the component model that Microsoft uses in Windows-based systems?

   Component Object Model.

2. What are the benefits of using COM?

   Language independence, self-defining interfaces, and global uniqueness.

3. What are the advantages and disadvantages of using a monolithic application?

Advantages:

Monolithic applications are wholly self-contained and you do not need to worry about sharing resources with other users. Therefore, they have more dedicated resources than a server-based application.

They are far less complex than client/server or multitiered applications in terms of resource and component management.

Disadvantages:

Monolithic applications do not know how to share data and resources with other users.

They are limited in scalability to the limits of a single computer.

To change any part of the application, the entire application must be rebuilt.

4. What are the advantages and disadvantages of using a client/server application?

Advantages:

Processing can be shared between the client and the server.

Data can be kept more secure by keeping it on the server and never sending it to the client's computer where it can be intercepted.

Server resources are frequently used, thus getting the most out of your information technology investment.

Disadvantages:

Client/server applications are limited in scalability.

Network availability is critical.

Network latency can affect performance.

5. Define an object.

An independent software component that contains the data (attributes) and behaviors (methods) that represent something within the problem/solution domain.

Day 2

Quiz

1. What are the presentation options available to a Windows DNA Application?

HTML, Script, DHTML, Component, and Windows native executable.

2. What are the scripting languages available in Windows DNA?

Out of the box you get JavaScript and VBScript. Other scripting languages such as PERL and REXX can be added through third-party add-ons.

A

3. What are the two types of components supported by Internet Explorer?

   ActiveX and Java.

4. What is the difference between ActiveX components and ActiveX controls?

   ActiveX controls have graphical user interface elements, whereas ActiveX components have no connection to the presentation space.

5. What are the two performance tools provided in Visual Studio 6 Enterprise Edition?

   Application Performance Explorer (APE) and the Visual Studio Analyzer.

Exercise

1. Run the Application Performance Explorer and try various application design scenarios. What kind of results did you get?

   There is no right answer to this exercise. The intent is to allow you to see how easy the APE is to use.

2. Launch Visual Basic and notice all the different types of applications the wizard can create for you. Try creating a standard EXE, an ActiveX DLL and a IIS application. How do they differ?

   The standard EXE will create a user form as its starting point. The ActiveX DLL creates a blank class module as its starting point, and the IIS application will create a Web Class as a starting point. Open the Web Class and notice that it is made up of an HTML template and custom Web items.

Day 3

Quiz

1. What are some of the tools and techniques you can use to gather and document requirements?

   One-on-one interviews and Joint Application Design (JAD) facilitated sessions can be used for gathering requirements. Use cases and sequence diagrams can be used for documenting requirements.

2. What tool does Microsoft provide to model your application?

   Microsoft Visual Modeler, which is a limited version of Rational's Rose software.

3. What are some of the benefits of using Microsoft Visual Modeler?

   Components are documented and modeled in a standard UML notation so that team members can understand them. Visual Modeler works with Microsoft development tools to generate and reverse-engineer source code.

4. What are the different relationships that can exist between data elements?

One-to-one, one-to-many, and many-to-many. Sometimes you will see a zero in the model, which means that the element is not required to have a relationship.

Exercise

1. The new high-tech businesses are asking their trading partners to all have Internet-based trading capabilities. They require the banks they deal with—Smalltown is one—to have the capability to process electronic funds transfers. Smalltown Bank has been given one year to enable these capabilities or lose the business. Put together a business case for this problem.

Given that Smalltown Bank has the capability to handle personal accounts, the application in this book, the requested Internet capabilities are an extension into the commercial side of the business. The business rules around the transfer limits will need to be increased. This adds a degree of risk. However, it would be an even greater risk to lose a commercial customer. Most of the components from personal banking can be reused so that the development effort should be substantially reduced.

Open the model with Visual Modeler and add objects in the data tier for Account, Transaction, and Spouse.

No specific answer.

Day 4

Quiz

1. What is the relationship between table and entity?

A table contains information about an entity. An entity can be a person, a thing, a place, or an event.

2. What is NULL?

NULL is a special value used to identify a missing value. You specify which columns can accept NULL values. Primary keys cannot contain NULLs.

3. What are other names for record and field?

Another name for record is row. Another name for field is column.

4. True/False. A primary key can only contain one column.

False. A primary key can contain many columns (in SQL Server, a primary key cannot exceed 256 bytes), although most tables have a primary key with a single column.

A

5. What's a foreign key?

A foreign key occurs when a table has a primary key from another table as one of its columns. This prevents the deletion of the primary key as long as the primary key is used as a foreign key. This is also ensures that the foreign key exists when data is inserted (or updated) in the table containing the foreign key.

6. What's the difference between DDL and DML?

DDL and DML are two subsets of the SQL language. DDL stands for Data Definition Language and consists of the statements used to create tables and indexes. DML stands for Data Manipulation Language and consists of the statements used to add (INSERT), update (UPDATE), retrieve (SELECT), and delete (DELETE) data.

7. What SQL statement do you use to retrieve data from a table?

To retrieve data from one or more tables, you use the SELECT statement.

8. What is an INNER JOIN?

An INNER JOIN is a way to retrieve data from two or more tables in a SELECT statement where the two columns specified in the join condition match. An INNER JOIN is often based on a foreign key relationship between the two tables.

9. What is an identity column, and what is it used for?

An identity column is a column that SQL Server maintains. This column contains a sequence of numbers starting with the seed. Each consecutive number is then equal to the previous number, plus the increment. The seed and increment of an identity column are specified when the table is created.

10. What happens when an INSERT statement does not specify the names of the columns?

If the INSERT statement does not specify the column names, then the value list must contain values for every column of the table, in the same order that the columns were specified when the table was created.

Exercises

1. Create an empty database for the SmallTownBank application. In the next exercise, you will populate this database with tables. In SQL Server, you use Enterprise Manager to manage databases. By default, you will find the shortcut in Programs, Microsoft SQL Server 7.

   Start the SQL Server 7 Enterprise Manager. Under Console Root, expand Microsoft SQL Server, SQL Server Group until you see the name of your server. Expand your server until you see the Databases, Data Transformation, Management, Security and Support Services folders.

Right-click Databases and select New Database. Enter **SmallTownBank** as the database name. You can keep the default settings for the File growth properties and the Transaction log settings. Click OK. SQL Server only takes a short while to create the database. You can see the newly created database in the databases folder.

2. Populate the database created in exercise 1 with the tables used by the SmallTownBank application. You will also add sample data to these tables so you can test the application as you build it. Use the VB Data View Window to create the following tables:

```
CREATE TABLE Customer
(
    CustomerKey INT IDENTITY (1, 1) NOT NULL ,
    FirstName CHAR(50) NOT NULL ,
    MiddleName CHAR(50) NULL ,
    LastName CHAR(50) NOT NULL ,
    SuffixName CHAR(5) NULL ,
    SocialSecurityNumber CHAR(9) NOT NULL ,
    Address1 CHAR(50) NOT NULL ,
    Address2 CHAR(50) NULL ,
    City CHAR(50) NOT NULL ,
    State CHAR(2) NOT NULL ,
    PostalCode CHAR(10) NOT NULL ,
    PhoneNumber CHAR(20) NULL ,
    EMailAddress CHAR(50) NULL ,
    UserID CHAR(20) NOT NULL ,
    SpouseID INT NULL
);

CREATE TABLE TransactionType
(
    TransactionTypeKey INT IDENTITY (1, 1) NOT NULL ,
    Description CHAR(50) NOT NULL
);

CREATE TABLE Account
(
    AccountKey INT IDENTITY (1, 1) NOT NULL ,
    AccountNumber CHAR(20) NOT NULL ,
    AccountTypeID INT NOT NULL ,
    CustomerID INT NOT NULL ,
    Balance MONEY NOT NULL
);

CREATE TABLE Spouse
(
    SpouseKey INT IDENTITY (1, 1) NOT NULL ,
    FirstName CHAR(50) NOT NULL ,
    MiddleName CHAR(50) NULL ,
```

```
    LastName CHAR(50) NULL ,
    SocialSecurityNumber CHAR(9) NULL
);

CREATE TABLE AccountTransaction
(
    TransactionKey INT IDENTITY (1, 1) NOT NULL ,
    AccountID INT NOT NULL ,
    CustomerID INT NOT NULL ,
    TransactionTypeID INT NOT NULL ,
    Amount MONEY NULL ,
    Description VARCHAR(50) NULL ,
    CheckNumber CHAR(10) NULL ,
    Payee CHAR(50) NULL ,
    DateEntered DATETIME NOT NULL
);
```

3. Create the relationships between the tables used by the SmallTownBank application. You will also add sample data to these tables so you can test the application as you build it. Use the VB Data View Window to create the relationships in Figure A.1.

FIGURE A.1

The relationships in the SmallTownBank application.

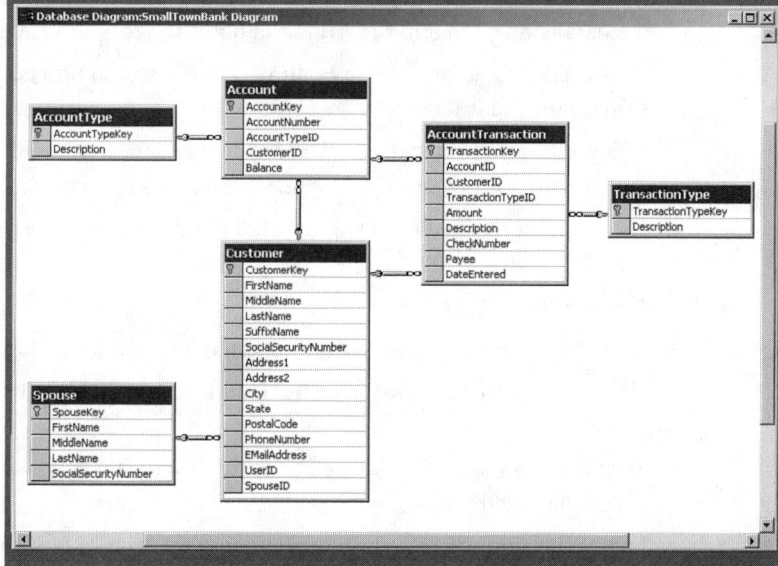

Then, you can add data to the tables. To avoid typing all the SQL statements, you can run a script found on the CD-ROM accompanying this book. You can use the SQL Query Analyzer (Programs, Microsoft SQL Server 7.0, Query Analyzer) to run the SQL statements. Make sure that the database selected in the DB combo box is the SmallTownBank database. Then select File, Open and locate the InitialData.sql file on the CD-ROM. Run this script. You can then run a few SELECT statements to verify that the data was entered in the tables.

Day 5

Quiz

1. What are the three types of data integrity?

   The three types of data integrity are entity or table integrity, domain or column integrity, and referential integrity.

2. True/False. A CHECK() constraint is checked after the triggers.

   False. Constraints are checked before the trigger. If the data violates the constraint, the data is rejected and the trigger is not invoked.

3. Which DML statements can be turned into a stored procedure with the help of the stored procedure wizard?

   Using the stored procedure wizard, you can create a stored procedure containing an INSERT, UPDATE, or DELETE statement against any table you select.

4. How do you retrieve the value of the identity column after you insert a row in a table?

   You use the @@IDENTITY keyword.

5. How do you pass a value by reference to a stored procedure?

   You use the OUT keyword after the parameter data type when creating the stored procedure.

6. True/False. In an UPDATE trigger, the modified values are stored in a logical table called "updated".

   False. The original rows are deleted from the trigger table and placed in the "deleted" table. Then the modified rows are added to both the trigger table and the "inserted" table.

A

7. How do you access a trigger from within a stored procedure?

You cannot directly access a trigger from within a stored procedure. Trigger is automatically called when you modify the data in the table it protects, so you can indirectly access a trigger by issuing an INSERT, DELETE, or UPDATE statement against the table.

8. True/False. A stored procedure can contain more than one SQL statement.

True. A stored procedure can contain any number of SQL statements.

9. How are stored procedures categorized?

Stored procedures are categorized into row returning and non-row returning procedures, depending on whether they contain a SELECT statement.

10. How do you check if a column has been modified in a trigger?

You use the IF UPDATE(*column*) statement.

Exercises

1. If you have Access, MSDE, or another database application, create a simple database and try to connect to it through ADO. Remember to create your DSN. Select some records out from it and display them on a form or debug window.

No specific answer.

2. In Visual Basic or Visual Interdev, create a function that returns a recordset, which contains the results of a query.

No specific answer.

3. Use the stored procedure wizard to create the following three stored procedures. You will need to modify the generated names and the parameters as explained previously.

Answer to Listing 1   First Stored Procedure

```
1: CREATE PROCEDURE sp_del_Account
2:     @AccountKey int
3: AS
4:     DELETE
5:     FROM
6:         Account
7:     WHERE
8:         AccountKey = @AccountKey
9: GO
```

Answer to Listing 2   Second Stored Procedure

```
CREATE PROCEDURE sp_upd_Account
    @AccountKey int,
    @AccountNumber char(20),
    @AccountTypeID int,
    @CustomerID int,
    @Balance money
AS
    UPDATE
        Account
    SET
        AccountNumber = @AccountNumber,
        AccountTypeID = @AccountTypeID,
        CustomerID = @CustomerID,
        Balance = @Balance
    WHERE
        AccountKey = @AccountKey
GO
```

Answer to Listing 3   Third Stored Procedure

```
CREATE PROCEDURE sp_ins_Account
    @AccountNumber char(20),
    @AccountTypeID int,
    @CustomerID int,
    @Balance money = NULL
AS
    SET NOCOUNT ON

    INSERT Account
        (
        AccountNumber,
        AccountTypeID,
        CustomerID,
        Balance
        )
    VALUES
        (
        @AccountNumber,
        @AccountTypeID,
        @CustomerID,
        @Balance
        )

    RETURN @@IDENTITY

    SET NOCOUNT OFF
GO
```

A

4. Use the script found on the CD to generate the remaining stored procedures. You can use the SQL Query Analyzer (Programs, Microsoft SQL Server 7.0, Query Analyzer) to run the SQL statements. Make sure that the database selected in the DB combo box is the SmallTownBank database. Then select File, Open and locate the `StoredProcedures.sql` file on the CD. Run this script. Make sure that all procedures were created. (You might have to `Refresh` the list first.)

Day 6

Quiz

1. True/False. Connection Strings always reference a DSN.

   False, you can have DSN-less connections.

2. Why would the RecordCount for a recordset always come back with '-1?'

   With ForwardOnly and ReadOnly recordsets, it will not return a recordcount.

3. What's the name of the default OLE DB Provider?

   MSDASQL.

4. What object and corresponding method you would use to update a record?

   `Command.Execute`.

5. What should you add to your command object when calling stored procedures and what methods do you use?

   Add parameters to the stored procedure using the `Append` method off the `Parameters` collection and the `CreateParameter` method on the `Command` object.

6. What are the two new objects with ADO 2.5?

   The `Record` and `Stream` objects.

Exercises

1. If you have Access, MSDE, or another database application; create simple database and try to connect to it through ADO. Remember to create your DSN. Select some records out from it and display them on a form or debug window.

   There are a variety of ways to implement this. I have chosen one way to do it, but there are at least half a dozen other ways, which would do the same thing.

```
Dim rst As ADODB.Recordset
Dim strConn
Dim cnn As ADODB.Connection
Set cnn = New ADODB.Connection
strConn = "DSN=DNA"
cmd.ActiveConnection = strConn
cmd.CommandText = "Select Name From Person"
cmd.CommandType = adCmdText
Set rst = cmd.Execute
If Not (rst.BOF and rst.EOF) Then
    Do While Not rst.BOF
        rst("Name")
        rst.MoveNext
    Loop
End If
rst.Close
Set rst = Nothing
cnn.Close
Set cnn = Nothing
```

Before writing this code, a database has already been created and a DSN setup in the control panel.

At the beginning of this listing the objects are declared and instantiated. Next, the ActiveConnection property is set. The SQL command is specified next, which is telling SQL to get all the names from the Person table. Executing the command returns a recordset. The recordset is looped through using a Do While loop until the end of the records. Finally, the objects are cleaned up.

2. In Visual Basic or Visual Interdev, create a function that returns a recordset, which contains the results of a query.

Answers may vary. A stored procedure call is not necessary. The following is done in VBScript for ASP.

```
Function GetPersonInfo(intPerson_ID)
'**********************************************************
'  11/11/99    JJM    Created
'  Purpose: Gets Person Information
'  Inputs: intPerson_ID
'**********************************************************
Set cmd = Server.CreateObject("ADODB.Command")
Set rs1 = Server.CreateObject("ADODB.Recordset")
cmd.CommandText = "spSel_Person"
cmd.CommandType = adCmdStoredProc
Set cmd.ActiveConnection = cnn
Set tmpParam = cmd.CreateParameter("@EmployeeID", adInteger,
cmd.Parameters.Append tmpParam
rst.Open cmd, , adOpenForwardOnly, adLockReadOnly
Set GetPersonInfo = rst
```

```
' Don't close or else the returned recordset will also be closed.
Set rst = Nothing
Set cmd.ActiveConnection = Nothing
Set cmd =Nothing
End Function
```

OUTPUT After the function declaration, which is standard in VB or Visual Interdev I put in a Function header. This is documentation to describe the function. Doing this consistently and at the time you create your functions and other pieces of code is relatively easy to do and makes you code much more understandable.

Objects are created and a stored procedure is set to be called. This is specified in the CommandText and CommandType. A parameter is set next and appended to the command object. Finally a recordset is opened.

The next and most important line sets the return value of the function to a Recordset object. By doing this, the function will return a recordset. After that you need to set the recordset and connection to Nothing and close the connection, but you do not want to close the recordset. The reason for this, is that the Recordset object and the recordset that the function are returning are the same recordset. Setting the recordset to Nothing gets rid of the object, but not the recordset it was pointing to. This is what you want so that when your function returns the recordset, it may be used to display the recordset information.

Day 7

Quiz

1. What does the acronym ACID stand for and what is it used for?

   ACID stands for Atomicity, Consistency, Isolation, and Durability. ACID is used to define the characteristics all transactions must satisfy to be considered a transaction.

2. How do you define an explicit, local transaction using Transact-SQL? How do you define an explicit, distributed transaction using Transact-SQL?

   Use the BEGIN TRANSACTION statement for local transactions and the BEGIN DISTRIBUTED TRANSACTION statement for distributed transactions.

3. What does the durability property of a transaction mean?

   The database must preserve the effects of all committed transactions as well as database consistency in the case of system or media failures. The effects of transactions must be permanent.

4. What are some of the ways you can improve the performance of your transactions?

To increase the performance of transactions, begin with a normalized database, keep transactions short, don't prompt for input during an open transaction, don't open a transaction while browsing data, and manipulate transaction isolation levels where possible.

5. What role does the MS DTC assume in distributed transactions?

MS DTC assumes the role of transaction manager, coordinating distributed transactions among applications, enlisted transaction managers, and resource managers.

Exercises

1. Using Transact-SQL, create a stored procedure that performs a distributed transaction to transfer funds between two accounts for the same customer, where each account resides in a different database.

1A. First, create an AccountType table in a database other than your DNA database. You can create the table by first generating a SQL script for the table using SQL Enterprise Manager. First, locate the AccountType table in the SQL Enterprise Manager, right-click the AccountType table, and select All tasks, Generate Scripts. See Figure A7.1.

FIGURE A7.1

Generate SQL scripts.

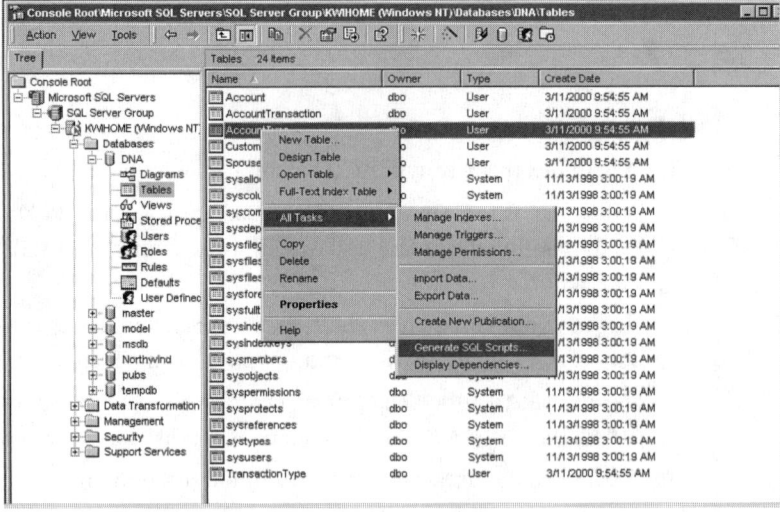

1B. The Generate SQL Scripts dialog box appears with the Account Type table selected. Click the OK button and name your script AccountType, as in Figure A7.2.

FIGURE A7.2

The Save Script dialog.

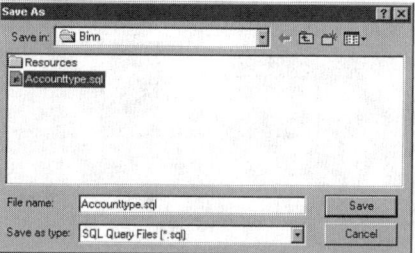

A

1C. Now to create the AccountType table in a different database, open the Query Analyzer, and select the Pubs database from the DB combo box. The Pubs database is a sample database installed with SQL Server. Next, select Open in the File menu and locate your AccountType script, as shown in Figure A7.3.

FIGURE A7.3

Open and run an AccountType script.

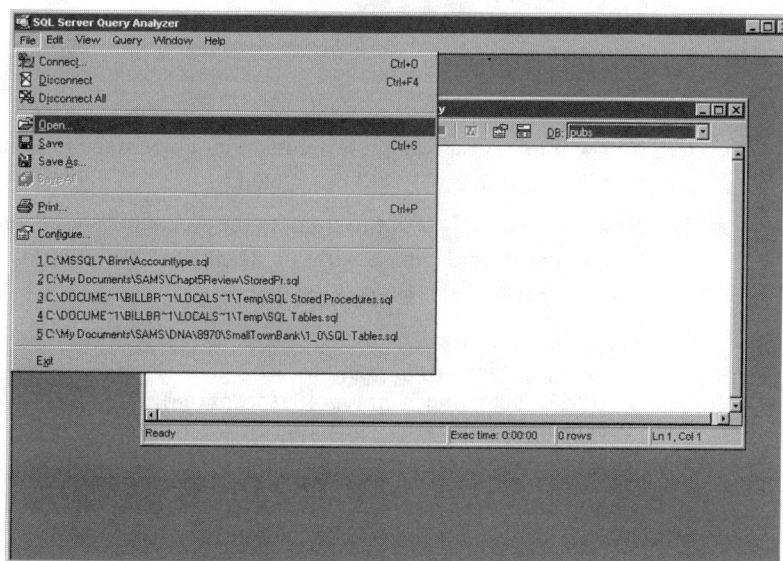

1D. Execute the script in Query Analyzer by clicking the green arrow, as shown in Figure A7.4.

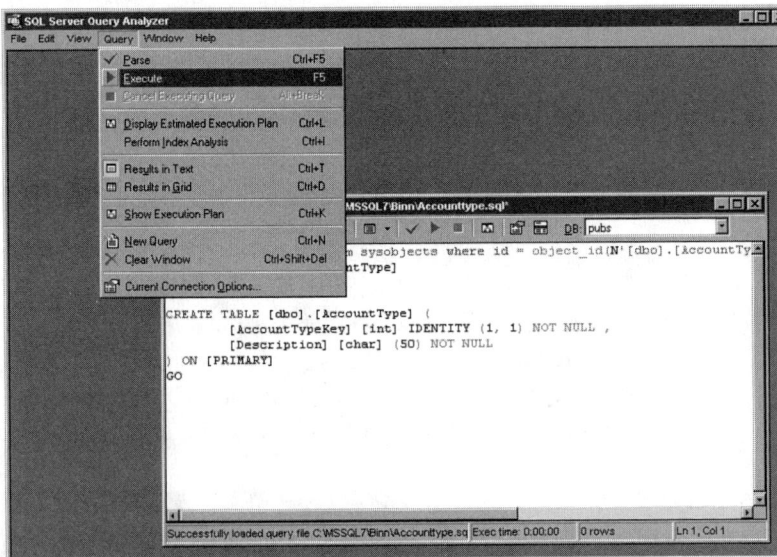

1E. You will receive a foreign key constraint error since all related tables are not present, but the table will still be created.

1F. Now create a SQL script to transfer the AccountType records from your DNA database to the Pubs database within a distributed transaction.

```
Create Procedure TransferAcctType
As
Begin
   BEGIN DISTRIBUTED TRAN
   INSERT pubs..AccountType(Description)
   SELECT Description FROM DNA..AccountType

   -- Remark out the Commit Transaction statement
   /* COMMIT TRAN */
End
```

1G. Execute this script. All rows from the DNA AccountType table will be transferred to the Pubs AccountType table in a distributed transaction, as shown in Figure A7.5.

FIGURE A7.5

Query output of the transfer.

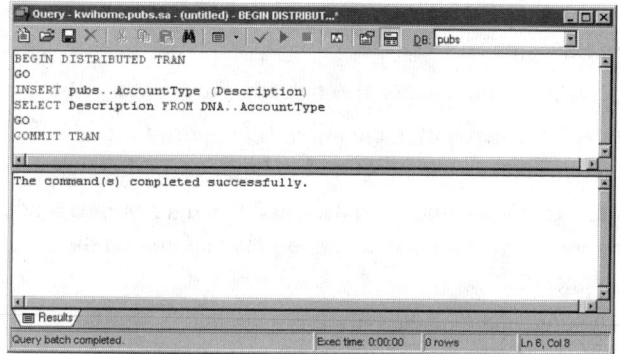

2. Create a batch of SQL Statements by altering your stored procedure created in exercise 1, so that the transaction is started, but does not end. Execute the batch of SQL statements using the Query Analyzer. Using MS DTC Admin Console, monitor your transaction. View the active transactions on the Transactions tab and statistics for all transactions on the Statistics tab. Try creating multiple transactions—some committed and some not—and view the output in the MS DTC Admin Console.

2A. Create a batch of SQL statements from the Stored Procedure created in exercise 1. Re-mark out any COMMIT or ROLLBACK transaction statements, and run this batch in several Query Analyzer windows. Open the MS DTC Admin Console as described in the "Managing Transactions with MS DTC" section. The key point here is to try things you've learned today and to view the results using the MS DTC Admin Console. This modified SQL code will get you started:

```
BEGIN DISTRIBUTED TRAN
Go
INSERT pubs..AccountType(Description)
SELECT Description FROM DNA..AccountType
Go
/* Remove this statement COMMIT TRAN */
```

Day 8

Quiz

1. What does COM stand for?

   COM stands for Component Object Model.

2. What two technologies were the immediate predecessors to COM.

   The two technologies that preceded COM were Dynamic Data Exchange (DDE) and Object Linking and Embedding (OLE).

3. True/False. COM components are stored in special operating system files with a .com extension.

   False. COM components are stored in files with a .dll, .exe, or .ocx extensions.

4. True/False. Microsoft application development tools such as Visual Basic, Visual C++, or Visual J++ are required to build a COM component.

   False. COM is a binary standard and is language independent. Any application development tools that can create files that uphold the binary standard can create components.

5. What is the name of the only interface that is absolutely required for every COM component?

   The IUnknown interface is the only required interface for a COM component.

6. Name the threading model(s) supported by Visual Basic.

   The single-threaded (STA) model is the only threading option supported currently supported by Visual Basic. Look for the next version of Visual Basic to support the multi-threading option.

7. True/False. MTS security uses the concept of roles, which requires coding changes to be made to your component.

   Okay, this question is a little bit of a trick question. MTS security does use the concept of roles, but does not require that you make coding changes to your component. You can use declarative security without making any coding changes.

8. Name the two methods used to implement programmatic security in an MTS component.

   The two methods used to implement programmatic security are IsSecurityEnabled and IsCallerInRole.

Exercises

1. After adding a component to MTS, you decide to implement both package and component level declarative security. After carefully adding the new role underneath both the Roles and the Role Membership folders, you next add your NT account to the new role under the users folder.

   You verify that your component is operating correctly, and then delete your NT account from the users folder. Although you expect access to your component to be denied, it operates correctly as before.

   What two factors could be causing security to be bypassed?

You should first, shut down the package containing your component and make sure that security is enabled for the package.

2. You are creating a method inside a MTS COM component that should only be used by clients in the role of an administrator. How would you create this method in the form of a Visual Basic function called AdminsOnly?

LISTING 8.2 Sample Code Implementing the AdminsOnly Function

```
 1: Public Function AdminsOnly() As Boolean
 2:
 3:     On Error Goto AdminsOnly_Error
 4:
 5:     Dim objContext As ObjectContext
 6:     Set objContext = GetObjectContext
 7:
 8:     If objContext.IsSecurityEnabled = False Then Goto AdminsOnly_Error
 9:     If objContext.IsCallerInRole("Administrator") = False Then Goto
        ➥AdminsOnly_Error
10:
11:     Logon = True
12:     Goto AdminsOnly_Exit
13:
14: AdminsOnly_Error:
15:
16:     Logon = False
17:
18: AdminsOnly_Exit:
19:
20:     Set objContext = Nothing
21:
22: End Function
```

Day 9

Quiz

1. When opening a new project, what kind of project do you want to select to create a COM component?

   ActiveX DLL.

2. What property procedure would you have if you wanted to make a property read-only?

   The Get property procedure, which reads back the value. The Let property procedure sets the value.

3. What are two advantages to using SourceSafe with project development?

There are many advantages, but two important ones are being able to check out files in a team environment, so that two people are not working on the same file at the same time, and being able to roll back to the prior checked version in copies of a file.

4. What keyword in the procedure declaration is required to make your component's procedures accessible to other applications?

Place the word Public at the start of the Sub or Function declaration.

Exercises

1. Create a simple component that has a method that squares a number. Call this component from a Standard EXE application.

Create a new ActiveX DLL. Set the project properties as described in the section, "Configuring Your Project." Call the project **Calculator** and call the class **Multiplication**. Add the following code to the class:

```
Public Function SquareX(intX As Integer) As Integer
    SquareX = intX * intX
End Function
```

This function takes an integer and returns its square.

Compile the DLL. Add a Standard EXE project. Make a reference to the component you just created in the project properties. Add a button to the form of the EXE. In the Click event add the following lines of code:

```
Dim objTemp as Calculator.Multiplication
Set objTemp = New Calculator.Multiplication
MsgBox objTemp.SquareX(4)
Set objTemp = Nothing
```

This calls the method of the class you just created and passes a 4 in for the integer. The return value is displayed in a message box. Run the form and click the button. It will display 16.

2. At this point, you need to update your existing project to include more of the functionality that you will have in the finished application. The accompanying CD-ROM contains the SmallTownBank project for tomorrow's lesson. Copy the project to your local hard drive and take a look at the additional methods that have been added. There is also an updated .mdl file to look at.

By looking at the files for tomorrow, you will have noticed a variety of changes. The SmallTownBank.mdl has had two other components added to it.

Day 10

Quiz

1. How many times will you call SetComplete and SetAbort while working with a transaction?

   You can call SetComplete as many times as you want, but after you have called SetAbort the transaction is rolled back. SetComplete enables MTS to recycle that component instance.

2. Where can you look to see what your components are doing?

   Look at the Transaction Monitor in MTS Explorer.

3. How can you create an object within a component to place in the same transaction as that component? For instance, Component A is running in a transaction. It calls Component B, which needs to run in the same transaction.

   You can use the CreateInstance method from the ObjectContext object. For example:

   ```
   ObjectContext.CreateInstance "SmallTownBank_Business.BankBusiness"
   ```

   The two other methods that you can use that will not operate within the same transaction are the Set command with the New operator and the CreateObject command.

4. Where do you set the transaction support for a component?

   In the class properties of the component in Visual Basic or in the component properties in MTS.

5. What are the different types of transactional support?

   "Requires a transaction," "Request a new transaction," "Supports transaction," and "Does not support transactions."

   These are a little different under Visual Basic with the MTSTransactionMode property. They correspond to "RequiresTransaction," "RequiresNewTransaction," "UsesTransaction," and "NoTransactions."

Exercise

1. Using the SmallTownBank components, change the types of transactions that the components support, specifically the BankData class. Look at the AccountTransaction table to see what effect that has.

   No specific answer.

Day 11

Quiz

1. What's the difference between ADODB and ADOR?

   ADOR is a lightweight version of ADODB. Unlike ADODB, it does not include the Connection object or Command object as well as other functionality.

2. What collection and method do you use to add additional columns to a recordset you are creating from scratch?

   The Fields collection and the Append method from the recordset object. An example of it is

   ```
   rst.Fields.Append "State", adChar, 2
   ```

3. What does the CursorLocation property need to be set to for a disconnected recordset?

   It would be set to adUseClient, as follows:

   ```
   rst.CursorLocation = adUseClient
   ```

4. What is the new object in ADO 2.5 that enables you to easily convert a recordset to an XML string?

   The Stream object.

5. What is the command that enables you to return a hierarchal recordset?

   The SHAPE command enables you to return hierarchal recordsets. It is part of ADO 2.x. Do not get it confused with being part of SQL.

Exercises

1. Create a Visual Basic group that has an ActiveX DLL project and a Standard EXE. In the DLL, add a method that calls the pubs database and retrieves all or part of a record. Have the form display the results in a textbox.

   The project is located on the CD-ROM that accompanies this book under \Day\11 and is called Ex1.vbg.

   In the form add a button and call it cmdGetRecord. Add a textbox and call it txtResults. The button will trigger an event to get the last name of the author.

   In the code window for the form, add the following code snippet:

   ```
   Private Sub cmdGetRecord_Click()
   Dim rst As ADOR.Recordset
   Dim objData As PubsData.Pubs
   Set objData = New PubsData.Pubs
   Set rst = objData.GetLastName("W-B33228M")
   ```

```
txtResults = ""
If Not (rst.BOF And rst.EOF) Then
    txtResults = rst(0) & vbCrLf
End If
rst.Close
Set rst = Nothing
Set objData = Nothing
End Sub
```

In the class window add the following code:

```
Public Function GetLastName(strAuthorNum As String) As ADODB.Recordset
Dim cnn As ADODB.Connection
Dim rst As ADODB.Recordset
Dim strSQL As String
Set cnn = New ADODB.Connection
cnn.ConnectionString = "Provider=SQLOLEDB;DRIVER=SQL
Server;SERVER=(local);DATABASE=pubs;UID=sa;PWD=;"
cnn.Open
strSQL = "SELECT au_lname FROM authors " & _
    "WHERE emp_id = '" & strAuthorNum & "'"
rst.Open strSQL, cnn, adOpenForwardOnly, adLockReadOnly
If Not (rst.BOF And rst.EOF) Then
    Set GetLastName = rst
Else
    Err.Raise vbObjectError + 1, "No records", "No records were returned."
End If
End Function
```

2. Modify the SmallTownBank components. If you look at the
SmallTownBank\11\Start, some changes have been made to the project. Many of
the functions that contained only a function declaration in both the
SmallTownBank_Data and the SmallTownBank_Business components have been
filled in with code. A comment has been added to the procedures designating the
code has been added for chapter 11. Also, there has been an error handler that has
been added to the SmallTownBank_Business component that can be called to easily
raise errors.

Your first task is to add in functions to handle all of the standard stored procedures
calls that will insert, update, delete and select all the records from the tables. The
code for these will be added to the BankData class of the SmallTownBank_Data
component and can be cut and pasted from Standard procedures for BankData
class.txt. This will also add in a function to use as a standard error handler and
also a function to replace GetConnectionString. Modify CreditAccount and
DebitAccount to use the error handler. The new GetConnectionString function
will get information from the registry.

Next, in the `DownloadAccountActivity` and `DownloadAccountBalance` procedures in the `BankBusiness` class add in an `If...Else` statement that checks the Integer parameter, `FileFormat`, on whether to return a recordset or an XML string. For now, you will just be returning a recordset. Therefore, you don't have to add any code for the XML case right now.

Finally, modify the procedures `Sel_AccountsByCustomerID` and `GetCustomer` in the `BankData` class to check whether records are returned. If there are no records returned, raise an error.

Check your changes with the project in `SmallTownBank\11\Finish`. You project should resemble the project in the Finish directory.

Day 12

Quiz

1. What are the key areas in which XML syntax is stricter than HTML?

   Case sensitive, always requires a closing tag, all attributes must be contained within quotes, elements must be contained within a single root element, and element must nest completely. These rules are collectively known as being "Well Formatted."

2. What is the purpose of eXtensible Styling Language (XSL)?

   XSL is best described as a programming language for XML. XSL is used to transform XML into another format. Typically this transformation is into HTML; however, you are not limited to strictly HTML, you can transform the XML into anything.

3. What are the ways you can present XML data?

   Cascading Style Sheet, XSL, and Tabular Data Binding on the client-side. On the server-side, you have full programmatic control to parse and present the XML data any way you want.

4. What are the differences between DTD and XML schemas?

   DTD is the data typing language that was used with SGML (the parent of HTML). DTD is a very powerful language that is used to define HTML. The problem with using DTD to define XML schemas is that it is an entirely different syntax than XML. XML Schemas, on the other hand, are written in XML, so they are easier for a person who knows XML to understand and develop.

A

5. What are the two versions of the Microsoft XML DOM, and when would you use each?

Rental single-threaded (Microsoft.XMLDOM) and Free multi-threading (Microsoft.XMLFreeThreadedDOM). The single-threaded version has better performance, but it can be a bottle neck if multiple clients need to use it. The free-threading version will provide better throughput in multi-user environments.

Exercises

1. Create an XML document using Notepad and then open it with Internet Explorer 5.0. Did it parse correctly? Now mangle the XML document and then open it again with IE 5.0. Notice the parser errors. Fix the document for the next exercise.

   Two files are included on the CD-ROM: bankstatement.xml and bankstatement_mangled.xml. You should see that the mangled version has no closing tag for the <MANGLED> tag.

2. In this exercise, create a Cascading Style Sheet to display your XML data. Add a reference to the style sheet in you XML document file. Now open the XML document in IE 5.0. Did it display the way you wanted?

   Two files that answer this exercise, bankstatement.css and bankstatement_css.xml, are included on the book's CD-ROM.

Day 13

Quiz

1. True/False. When COM+ deactivates an object, it does so on both the client and the server.

   False. When COM+ deactivates an object, it only does so on the server side. As far as the client is concerned, it still has a valid reference to the object.

2. True/False. The use of JIT is optional for components that do not require a transaction.

   True. However, it is mandatory for components that do require a transaction.

3. What is the best way to create a pooled object using Visual Basic 6.0?

   OK, this is a trick question. Objects that are pooled cannot be bound to a particular thread, as is the case with objects that make use of the Apartment threading model. Because the Visual Basic development environment can currently only create Apartment model components, you cannot create a pooled object using Visual Basic.

4. Name the four services that allow queued components to operate under COM+.

   The four services that make up COM+ queued components are

   - Recorder
   - Queue
   - Listener
   - Player

5. Events represent a programming model that is able to support the concept of late-bound events or method calls between a _____ and a _____, using COM+ event subsystem. Fill in the blanks.

   Events represent a programming model that is able to support the concept of late-bound events or method calls between a *publisher* and a *subscriber*, using COM+ event subsystem.

6. Using automatic transactions in COM+, when is a transaction considered to be started?

   A transaction is started when

   - A non-transactional client calls a component that requires a transaction or a new transaction.
   - A transactional client calls a component that requires a new transaction.

7. What is the name of the new COM+ threading model?

   The new threading model in COM+ introduces Neutral Apartments to simplify programming in multithreaded environments.

8. True/False. Constructor strings can be used to administratively define generic information (such as an ODBC DSN) that can be passed to an object at the time it is created.

   True. The capability to pass information defined administratively can reduce reliance on storing values in the registry or in an INI file.

Exercise

1. Create a role called Teller and assign that role to the Logon component that was configured for COM+ in today's lesson.

   In order to implement role-based security for the logon component, you must first create a role. Locate the SmallBank application in the left pane of the Component Services snap-in and double-click it. Next, click the Roles folder and then choose Action, New, Role from the toolbar. When the New Role dialog appears, enter "Teller" in the textbox and press the OK button.

A

Now that you have defined a role for the SmallBank application, you need to specify that the Teller role be required to access the logon component. To do this, locate the logon component (SmallTownBank_Logon.BankLogon) in the left-hand pane and double-click it. Now click the Role Membership folder and select Action, New, Role from the toolbar. When the Select Roles dialog appears, click Teller and press the OK button.

At this point, no one would be able to use the logon component because we have defined and assigned roles for the component, but not yet assigned any NT accounts or groups to the roles.

Locate the logon component (SmallTownBank_Logon.BankLogon) and double-click it to reveal the Roles folder. Double-click the Roles folder and also the Teller to reveal the Users folder. Click once on the Users folder, and select Action, New, User from the toolbar. When the Add Users and Groups to Role dialog appears, select Administrators (or any other appropriate account or group) and click the Add button. To add the local group to the role, press the OK button.

Day 14

Quiz

1. What capabilities does MSMQ give the developer?

   The capability to asynchronously process information which enables the queuing process continue with other tasks. Queues can add durability and fail-over capabilities so that in the event of a system failure data is not lost. It will either wait or flow to other systems and processes on a least-cost basis for service.

2. What are the five basic methods in MSMQ?

   Open, Listen, Read, Write, and Close. Other methods exist, however, these are the major ones.

3. What are the three layers in BizTalk?

   Application, BizTalk, and Data Communication. The application layer contains the XML-encoded information that is application specific. The BizTalk layer is the envelope and delivery information needed by the BizTalk server to deliver the application data. The data communication layer is relative to the transport mechanism, such as HTTP or MSMQ.

4. What are the protocols used by SOAP?

   HTTP is the transport protocol, and XML is the data-encoding format.

5. What is the new way that Visual Studio 7 will handle presentation tier elements?

Web forms is the way that all Visual Studio application will develop presentation elements. Web forms are a combination of DHTL forms and compiled executable code that will run at a server. By running the code at a server, the presentation richness can be varied based upon the client capabilities.

Exercise

1. This is all new technology that is changing and being enhanced as this book is being written. Go to the Microsoft web site and search on these technologies to see the latest information on these capabilities.

Tip: Microsoft keeps its developer-related information at http://msdn.microsoft.com. And more technical information can be found at http://www.microsoft.com/technet.

No specific answer.

Day 15

Quiz

1. What is the key benefit of using the WinSock control?

The WinSock control gives you a great deal of flexibility to implement and use any protocol that uses TCP/IP or UDP/IP as its network protocol.

2. What is the key disadvantage of using the WinSock control?

The major disadvantage of using the WinSock control is that you need to implement the protocol entirely when you are communicating. This can be very time-consuming. Of course, if you are communicating with your own server, then you can keep the protocol simple. However, when dealing with a well-defined protocol such as HTTP, extra processing is required to handle the addition and extraction of the protocol information.

3. How do the WinSock and WinInet control compare?

The WinInet control is a higher-level control that handles the management of the protocol information for the HTTP, HTTPS, FTP, and Gopher protocols. This means that you do not need to spend time implementing the protocol yourself.

4. What is the role of RDS in the Microsoft data architecture?

RDS allows two-tier client/server applications to be easily extended to a three-tier architecture by allowing the data recordset to be extended across the network so that data-enabled controls can use the remoted data to populate themselves.

A

5. In what situation would you most benefit from using DCOM?

You will get the most benefit from DCOM when you are using COM components within an entirely Microsoft environment. This scenario means that you are running your application on an intranet or some other internal network. DCOM support all network protocols, not just TCP/IP, like WinSock and WinInet.

Exercises

1. Create a secure connection to a Web server using the WinInet control.

By making a simple change to the protocol property, you are now communicating securely. The new protocol line would look like

```
MyInet.Protocol = icHTTPS
```

You can also add `UserID` and `Password` properties to the control.

2. Extend the WinSock with a custom server sample program to service a number of commands.

Determine the set of keywords that the server will understand, and then implement a select case statement to interpret the command and return the requested information.

Day 16

Quiz

1. What is the new type of Visual Basic project that you learned to create today?

ActiveX control project.

2. What is the extension of the file that your control is packaged in for distribution over the Internet?

It is a cabinet file, which has a `.CAB` extension.

3. What does Safe for Initialization mean?

This means that your control will do nothing harmful to the machine it runs on when the control starts up.

4. What does Safe for Scripting mean?

This means that your control does not have public methods, properties, or events that scripts can call, which could be harmful to the machine the control runs on. This includes not reading files as well as not writing or deleting files that can be specified through public functionality of the control.

5. What tag does the Package and Deployment Wizard create on an HTML page to display a control?

It uses the `<OBJECT>` tag to display the control.

6. How would you make a public ActiveX control property be read-only?

When creating the property procedures in the control's code window, you would only have a GET property procedure. Do not add a LET property procedure. This will allow a user to read the property value, but not write to it.

Exercises

1. Modify the LoadCustomer Transactions control to take in an optional long parameter. This will contain the CustomerKey and enable users to call the LoadCustomer method without first having to set the CustomerKey property. Test the control with the Harness project to make sure it works.

The following changes to Listing 16.1 will enable LoadCustomer to take an optional parameter.

Change line 1 to

```
Public Function LoadCustomer(lngCustomerID as Long) As Boolean
```

Change line 11 to

```
"Where A.CustomerID = " & lngCustomerID
```

This will cause the selection of customer accounts to be based on the lngCustomerID variable that is passed in, rather then on the module level variable. You could make additional changes to set the module level variable m_CustomerKey to the value of the parameter that is passed in and still leave m_CustomerKey as part of the SQL SELECT statement.

2. Create an ActiveX control that uses the Tree control, which is part of Microsoft Windows Common Controls 6.0 component. Add a public method called AddNode that enables you to add items to the tree. Add another public property called LabelEdit, which enables you to toggle the LabelEdit property of the Tree control back and forth. The LabelEdit property allows or disallows a user to manually edit the items in a tree. Create a harness program that calls this public method and property.

The solution to this exercise can be found in the Day 17 material (this control is used in tomorrow's chapter) on the CD-ROM accompanying this book. The AddNode method listing is

```
Public Sub AddNode(strParent, intRelation, strChild, strText)
If strParent = "" Then
    Call tvMenu.Nodes.Add(, intRelation, strChild, strText)
```

A

```
Else
    Call tvMenu.Nodes.Add(strParent, intRelation, strChild, strText)
End If
End Sub
```

This method takes in the parent node, relationship between the nodes, name of the child node, and the display text for the child node. If the parent node is an empty string, it places the node at the topmost level of the tree.

The LabelEdit property is simply a Let and a Get:

```
Public Property Let LabelEdit(ByVal vNewValue As Variant)
    tvMenu.LabelEdit = vNewValue
End Property
Public Property Get LabelEdit() As Variant
    LabelEdit = tvMenu.LabelEdit
End Property
```

It sets LabelEdit to the new value or sends it back. LabelEdit can be 0 or 1.

Day 17

Quiz

1. If you had a text box named txtStartDate on a form that was named frmMain, how could you read the value in JavaScript in order to validate the entry?

   StartDate = document.frmMain.txtStartDate.value;

2. What property could you set to cause the client browser to jump to another page?

   location.href = http://www.mcp.com;

   This would cause the browser to jump to the Macmillan Web site.

3. Given the following button

   ```
   <INPUT TYPE=BUTTON NAME=cmdTotal VALUE="Total Your Order">
   ```

   add an onclick event to it to call the function GetTotal.

   ```
   <INPUT TYPE=BUTTON NAME=cmdTotal VALUE="Total Your Order"
   ➥LANGUAGE=javascript onclick="GetTotal()">
   ```

   The LANGUAGE attribute specifies the language to use. Next the onclick event is set to the specified function, which is wrapped in quotes.

4. In Internet Explorer, how do you cause an event to stop bubbling up?

   event.cancelBubble = true;

   event is the current event. cancelBubble will then stop the event from continuing.

Exercises

1. Using client-side JavaScript, create a page that checks to make sure a number is between two values, 5 and 11. Display an alert box indicating whether the value is valid or not.

   The following code is one possible solution for this exercise.

```
<HTML><HEAD></HEAD>
<BODY>
<SCRIPT ID=clientEventHandlersJS LANGUAGE=javascript>
<!--
function cmdValidate_onclick() {
if (document.frmMain.AnyNumber.value > 5 &&
➥document.frmMain.AnyNumber.value <= 10)
        alert('The number you have entered is valid.');
    else
        alert('You have entered a number that is not valid.');
}
//-->
</SCRIPT>
<FORM ACTION="validate_client.asp" NAME="frmMain" METHOD="POST">
<P>Enter a number: <INPUT TYPE=TEXTBOX NAME=AnyNumber></P>
<INPUT TYPE=BUTTON NAME=cmdValidate VALUE="Validate Number"
➥LANGUAGE=javascript onclick="return cmdValidate_onclick()">
</FORM></BODY></HTML>
```

   An onclick event, cmdValidate_onclick, is associated with the button. When the button is clicked, it runs the event function. The function test the range of the number with an if...else statement. Based on the value, it displays one of two alert boxes.

2. In Day 16, you created an ActiveX control for you Visual Basic presentation layer. As you learned today these controls can also be used in browsers. Add a page with the appropriate scripting that will load and use the ActiveX Control from Day 16. To get started, you can use the code from the test harness application and convert that over to an HTML file.

   The solution is in customer_account.asp on the CD-ROM accompanying this book. The file is in the folder for today's material. If you add this along with the Account.CAB file from yesterday's material to a web, you will be able to mimic the functionality from yesterday's Visual Basic harness application. The page contents for customer_account.asp are shown below.

```
<HTML><HEAD>
<TITLE>Customer Account Information</TITLE>
<SCRIPT ID=clientEventHandlersJS LANGUAGE=javascript>
<!--
function cboCustomer_onchange() {
```

A

```
        if (cboCustomer.options[cboCustomer.selectedIndex].value > 0) {
            ctlTransactions.CustomerKey =
            ➥cboCustomer.options[cboCustomer.selectedIndex].value;
            ctlTransactions.LoadCustomer();
        }
    }
    function window_onload() {
        ctlTransactions.ServerName = "http://mycomputer"
        ctlTransactions.ConnectionString="Provider=SQLOLEDB;
        ➥DRIVER=SQL Server;SERVER=(local);
        ➥DATABASE=Bank_data;UID=sa;PWD=;"
    }
    //-->
    </SCRIPT>
    </HEAD>
    <BODY LANGUAGE=javascript onload="return window_onload()">
    <P>Select a customer:
    <%
    Dim objSMTData
    Dim rs
    Set objSMTData = Server.CreateObject("SmallTownBank_Data.BankData")
    Set rs = objSMTData.Sel_All_Customer
    ' Load the combo box with all of the SmallTownBank customers.
    Response.Write "<SELECT Name=""cboCustomer"" LANGUAGE=javascript
    ➥onchange=""return cboCustomer_onchange()"">"
    If Not (rs.BOF And rs.EOF) Then
        Do While Not rs.EOF
            Response.Write "<OPTION Value=""" & rs("CustomerKey") & """>"
            Response.Write Trim(rs("LastName")) & ", " & _
                Trim(rs("FirstName")) & " #" & _
                Trim(rs("SocialSecurityNumber")) & "</OPTION>" & vbcrlf
            rs.MoveNext
        Loop
    Else
        MsgBox "Listing customers failed."
    End If
    rs.Close
    Set rs = Nothing
    Set objSMTData = Nothing
    Response.Write "</SELECT>"
    %>
    <BR></P>
    <OBJECT classid="CLSID:21218C60-073E-11D4-BE55-00A02458DD9C"
        codebase="Account.CAB#version=1,0,0,0"
        id=ctlTransactions style="LEFT: 0px; TOP: 0px">
        <PARAM NAME="_ExtentX" VALUE="13494">
        <PARAM NAME="_ExtentY" VALUE="5345">
    </OBJECT>
    </BODY></HTML>
```

At the top of the page are two JavaScript functions. Skip these for right now to look a littler farther down. Almost right after the <BODY> tag is a "<%." Farther down the page is a "%>." Everything between these two tags is script that is executed on the server that you will learn more about on Day 18, "Active Server Pages." Suffice to say right now that the code you see here generates a combo box called cboCustomer with a list of all of the SmallTownBank customers. To do this, it uses the SmallTownBank_Data component, which you created earlier on Day 9, "Building COM Components in VB." After this server-side code segment, the <OBJECT> tag declares the ActiveX control that you created on Day 16.

Go back and look at the JavaScript functions now. The first function, cboCustomer_onchange, is triggered every time a selection from the cboCustomer combo box is made. This triggers the public method, LoadCustomer, after the CustomerKey property is set. This in turn causes the ActiveX control to get all of the customer's accounts and load them in the control's combo box. The second function, window_onload, is run when the page is first loaded. This sets two public properties on the control, ServerName and ConnectionString, to allow the control to use RDS to connect to the data store.

Day 18

Quiz

1. What would be the syntax to read a variable named txtCity from a page that could be either from a form or a querystring?

   ```
   Request("txtCity")
   ```

   Because it could come from either a form or querystring, don't specify the collection it is coming from. If you knew it was coming from one or the other, you can use

   ```
   Request.Form("txtCity")
   ```

   or

   ```
   Request.QueryString("txtCity")
   ```

2. What command would you use to cause IIS not to send content until the entire ASP was finished?

   ```
   Response.Buffer = True
   ```

   This command causes all content to stay buffered until the change is finished. It also gives you the ability to change headers or do a Response.Redirect even if you have already written information to the body of the page.

A

3. How do you instantiate an object in ASPS?

`Server.CreateObject`

You would pass in a string that would be the name of the component.

4. How do you require page transactions?

Right-click the ASP and select properties. From the properties dialog select Supports Transactions. Code will be added automatically to the top of the page.

5. What server variables contain the filename of the current ASP?

`PATH_INFO`, `PATH_TRANSLATED`, `SCRIPT_NAME`, and `URL` all contain the filename.

6. Using the `FileSystemObject` object, what command can you use to open a new file?

`Set objTS = objFSO.CreateTextFile(strFileName)`

Exercise

1. Up to this point, you have been placing logic on the client. You now can move that logic to run on the server and have it process the information.

Using the `SmallTownBank` application, take the code from Listing 18.12 and create a Web page that mimics the account transfer form that was made on Day 9. Experiment with the form that will take in account numbers and an amount to transfer; execute the server-side code, which moves the money around.

On the CD, you can find the file on `\\SmallTownBank\18`. It is called `transfer.asp`. You will have an opportunity tomorrow to learn more about the HTML tags involved. Try experimenting with this page. This will give you an opportunity to see how the components are working in an ASP. Here are a few things to try:

a. First try putting in valid data. Look at the AccountTransaction table and make sure the data has been inserted properly.

b. Try putting in an AccountID that doesn't exist for the account to transfer money to. Look at the AccountTransaction table. Was data entered?

c. Remove the SmallTownBank_Data component from MTS and try the transfer.asp page. Does it give an error or does the transaction still work? Place the component back into MTS when you are finished.

d. If you want to experiment more with transactional ASP's, you can also modify business.asp. Try removing the SetComplete and SetAbort calls. What happens now if you put in an invalid AccountID?

Day 20

Quiz

1. Where do you install the Web components from?

   The Microsoft Office Web Components ship with Microsoft Office 2000. One of the options in the Installer is to install the Office Web Components when you install Office 2000. They can also be installed from an application server, if you have the codebase parameter of the object set to point at the application server path. Remember that the client must have a Microsoft Office 2000 license in order to legally use the components.

2. What types of data sources can the PivotTable control use?

   PivotTables can use flat tabular data, prepared data cubes, or XML as data sources. Flat data is imported into the Data Source Component, which creates a runtime cube of the information. To be used, XML must contain the data field description metadata. You can get a properly formatted XML file by having an ADO recordset persist the data as XML for you. Other XML-enabled Microsoft data sources will also be able to provide all the metadata necessary to work.

3. Where can Office Web Components be hosted?

   The Office Web Components can be used in any container that can host ActiveX or COM components. Examples are Internet Explorer 4.01 or greater, FrontPage 99, Visual Basic 6, and Microsoft Office 2000.

4. What is the native format for Office Web Component data?

   Escaped XHTML is the native format. The parameter is `HTMLData`. It should be noted that Microsoft embeds a great deal of metadata in the XHTML data that is necessary for the controls to correctly work with the information. For this reason, it is best to not work directly with the XHTML data. Rather use the APIs and let the controls create the XHTML data.

5. How do you interact with the components?

   You interact with the components through the APIs using scripts. The components raise events to communicate its changes to your application. Your application can choose to act upon the event, or it can simply ignore it.

Exercises

1. Open the `SpreadsheetAndChart` HTML page and change the chart type to be `chChartTypeColumnStacked`. How did the graph change? Now try `chChartTypeArea`.

A

You should see that the graphs show the balance information differently. The `chChartTypeColumnStacked` displays vertical columns for each of the values. The `chChartTypeArea` displays the information as a line chart with the area below filled. Many chart types are available but not all of them all will give you the desired display, depending upon the value being rendered.

2. Open the `PivotTableBankStatement` HTML page and experiment with moving various columns onto the drop zones. How did the PivotTable change? Did you get any different insights into the data?

   You should be able to effect the way the information is reported by changing the grouping, column, and row fields.

Day 21

Quiz

1. What package installs the Outlook View Control?

   The Outlook View control is installed as part of the Digital Dashboard Starter Kit and the Team Folders Kit.

2. What is an information nugget?

   An information nugget is a DHTML division that enables content within a digital dashboard to be rolled up and expanded to allow for more information to be represented in a smaller space.

3. What Web capabilities can be used in a digital dashboard?

   Out of the box, most Web capabilities of Internet Explorer 5 can be used with the exception of framesets and iframes. If you need the capabilities of the full version of Internet Explorer, then you can have Outlook use that version with little additional performance penalty.

4. What is the advantage of using the Outlook View Control?

   The Outlook View Control enables you to access any folder and any view within Outlook. Additionally you can apply restrictions so that the content of the control is filtered by the restriction criteria.

5. How do you reference an Outlook folder from an `href` link?

   To point to an Outlook folder, use the `outlook:` prefix, for example, `href=" outlook://Personal Folders/<sub-folder>`.

Exercises

1. Add the SpreadsheetAndChart.htm page from the Office Web Component chapter (Day 20) to the digital dashboard.

   The finished example, spreadsheetandchart.htm, is in the Finish folder.

2. Incorporate exercises from other chapters into your digital dashboard.

   There is no correct answer. This exercise lets you experiment with incorporating various new content into your dashboards.

INDEX

Symbols

Other Related Titles

**Sams Teach Yourself
Active Server Pages 3.0
in 21 Days**
0-672-31863-6
*Scott Mitchell and
James Atkinson*
$39.99 US/$59.99 CAN

**Sams Teach Yourself
Web Publishing with
HTML 4 in 21 Days**
0-672-31345-6
Laura Lemay
$29.99 US/$42.95 CAN

Pure XML
0-672-31601-3
George Doss
$19.99 US/$29.95 CAN

**Sams Teach Yourself
SQL Server 7 in 21 Days**
0-672-31290-5
*Richard Waymire and
Rick Sawtell*
$39.99 US/$59.95 CAN

**Microsoft SQL Server 7
Programming Unleashed**
0-672-31293-X
*John Papa,
Paul Kimmel, et al.*
$24.99 US/$37.95 CAN

**Sams Teach Yourself
Transact-SQL in 21 Days**
0-672-31045-7
David Solomon
$35.00 US/$49.95 CAN

**Sams Teach Yourself
Visual Basic 6 in
21 Days**
0-672-31310-3
Greg Perry
$29.99 US/$42.95 CAN

**Sams Teach Yourself
SQL in 21 Days**
0-672-31674-9
*Ryan Stephens and
Ronald Plew*
$34.99 US/$52.95 CAN

**Sams Teach Yourself
ADO 2.5 in 21 Days**
0-672-31873-3
*Christophe Wille and
Christian Koller*
$39.99 US/$54.95 CAN

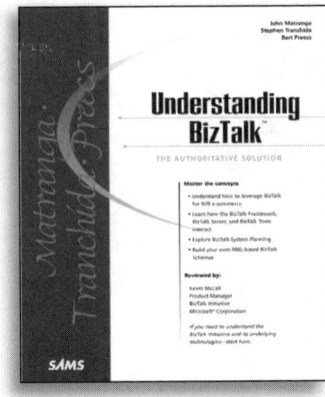

Understanding BizTalk
0-672-31787-7
*John Matranga,
Stephen Tranchida,
and Bart Preecs*
$29.99 US/$44.95 CAN

SAMS

www.samspublishing.com

All prices are subject to change.

Licensing Agreement

By opening this package, you are agreeing to be bound by the following agreement:

You may not copy or redistribute the entire CD-ROM as a whole. Copying and redistribution of individual software programs on the CD-ROM is governed by terms set by individual copyright holders.

This software is sold as-is, without warranty of any kind, either expressed or implied, including but not limited to the implied warranties of merchantability and fitness for a particular purpose. Neither the publisher nor its dealers or distributors assumes any liability for any alleged or actual damages arising from the use of this program. (Some states do not allow for the exclusion of implied warranties, so the exclusion may not apply to you.)

NOTE: This CD-ROM uses long and mixed-case filenames requiring the use of a protected-mode CD-ROM Driver.

What's on the CD-ROM

Key software products including CodeAssist 1.1, Spyworks 2.1, Visual Build 1.2 and XML Spy 3.0.

The CD-ROM includes

Sample e-commerce DNA application

DNA source code

Microsoft Windows DNA web resources

Installation Instructions

Windows 95, Windows 98, Windows NT 4, and Windows 2000

1. Insert the CD-ROM into your CD-ROM drive
2. From the Windows desktop, double-click on the "My Computer" icon.
3. Double-click on the icon representing your CD-ROM drive.
4. Double-click on the icon titled START.EXE to run the installation program.
5. Follow the onscreen instructions to finish the installation.

NOTE: If Windows 95, Windows 98, Windows NT 4.0 or Windows 2000 is installed on your computer, and you have the AutoPlay feature enabled, the setup.exe program starts automatically whenever you insert the disc into your CD-ROM drive.